Fellowship Of The Martyrs Anthology Volume 1

from Doug Perry

www.FellowshipOfTheMartyrs.com
fotm@fellowshipofthemartyrs.com

Copyright © 2011 Doug Perry, Fellowship Of The Martyrs

All rights reserved.

ISBN: 1467958700
ISBN-13: 978-1467958707

The Bride gets her jewelry, but it's going to hurt to get it on, and once you're used to it, you're never going to want to rip it back off again. Heaven is free. HOLINESS is hard! If not us, who? If not here, where? If not now, when?

DEDICATION

This book is dedicated to Jesus Christ. In fact, everything I've written, recorded, sung, spoken or ever done is dedicated to Jesus Christ. Not that it was all perfect, but that's not His fault. If you don't like it, blame me, not Him.

I want to take special note of the people who were so instrumental in helping grow me. Some were used to encourage me, some were used to teach me patience, some were used by God to motivate me to find the demon on them that I might never have seen if they weren't on my last nerve. Some taught me to endure persecution, even from the closest friend. Some showed me holiness. Praise God! They were all a blessing in one way or another and I really do love them all. (You know which one you were.)

Bob, Nancy, David, Marilyn, Kim, Constance, Stephanie, Ric, Brad, Keith, Steve, Minnie, Jeannie and Stevie, Andrew, Rachael, Elijah, Bob, Clare, Gary, Kristi, James, Cindy, Helen, Sherri, Jen, Dennis, Merri, Joseph, Gary, Cary, Emily, Lili, David, Yolanda, Suzanne, Tabitha, Josh, Austin, Chris, Candi, Nataliya, Helen, Ron, Rusty, Josh, Barry, Barron, Glynda, Steve, Bianca, June, Andrew, John, Lisa, Diane, Larry, Dewey, Jason, Sarah, Dave, Doug, Michael, Nichole, Dorothy, Tyler, Ky, Kathy, Lizzie, Patrick, Sharon, Stevean, Randy, Bob, Casey, Amy, Cathy, Chuckie, Roger, Nils, Ryan, Shelly, Kurt, Sharon, John, Mikey, Becky, James, Jennie, Angela, Gus, Zach, Jason, Jacob, Greg, Tres, Daniel, J.R., Tatianna, Patti and Carolyn and HUNDREDS that I pray will not feel left out but I don't have room to mention.

And a couple million intercessors all over the world pouring their hearts out and crying rivers on our behalf without whom I'm not sure how we could have made it this far.
I'm humbled. Please don't stop praying.

I love you all and I'm not going to stop no matter what.

ACKNOWLEDGMENTS

This book really should not be read all on its own. It is a part of a larger understanding, a series of books written about what is wrong with "church." The statistics are covered in the book, "*The Apology To The World.*" The book, "*The Red Dragon: the horrifying truth about why the 'church' cannot seem to change*" extends on this and shows the supernatural roots and the solution to wipe the slate clean and reboot. The book, "*Rain Right NOW, Lord!*" shows the reality of spiritual gifts, the tremendous need we have for them to be operating correctly – and how to get more of them. And the book, "*DEMONS?! You're kidding right?*" shows how it's under attack and how to defend it. Before we can fix a system, we have to fix each individual, so for personal tune-ups, the book, "*Dialogues with God*" is helpful to learn to hear God better and "*Who Neutered The Holy Spirit?!*" is for those who think God isn't as supernatural as He used to be.

God has been pouring out a lot on Liberty, Missouri. We continue to pray and believe that this will be a refuge, a haven, a training and equipping center. If you're looking for a different kind of "church," something more real and more life-changing, and if the Lord leads, you're welcome in Liberty. When (not if) things hit the fan, if you can make it here, we'll do our best to love you and make a way through all that is coming together.

www.FellowshipOfTheMartyrs.com   fotm@fellowshipofthemartyrs.com

ABOUT THIS ANTHOLOGY

An "anthology" is simply a collection of writings, in this case five of the books written by Doug Perry of Fellowship of the Martyrs. Volume One of this anthology consists of five separate books. Although there was some overlap, they were written and released in the order presented. They were all meant to be stand-alone books, so there is some repetition of common themes. We have tried to edit them as little as possible, while still avoiding unnecessary duplication. Please understand this as you read along. Nearly all the books from FOTM include "The Open Letter of Apology to the World" as an appendix. We have eliminated duplicates of that letter, "About the Author" sections, dedications, forewords, and the acknowledgments.

We believe this anthology contains some of the most important information available about the state of "Christianity," the need for change, what the change should look like personally and collectively – and how to get there. This anthology has been prepared as an effort to save people money by buying five books for one reduced price. We have presented it in the 8 1/2" x 11" format so that you can make copies of relevant articles or pages. We encourage you to feel free to do so, so long as you do not charge for them and don't remove attribution.

Additionally, in each section, the ISBN numbers of the individual books are given for your reference, but the ISBN for the Anthology is listed opposite the front inside cover.

If you are blessed by these writings and want to participate further in the work that God is doing in Liberty, Missouri, please pray about coming to visit or if you'd like to donate, you can reach us by mail at:

Fellowship Of The Martyrs, 118 N. Conistor, #B251, Liberty, MO 64068

You can donate through PayPal at fotm@fellowshipofthemartyrs.com. Or reach us by phone at (816) 255-5766.

ABOUT THE AUTHOR

Doug Perry has been going 200 miles an hour with his hair on fire since November 23, 2004 when God showed him an open vision of how much God loves His children, how angry God is for how we're killing His children, and how much we have to hurry. It's safe to say that praying to see through the eyes of Jesus and be dangerous to satan wrecked his life. He had a nice home, a wife, two kids, two dogs, a foreign car with a sunroof, and a multimillion dollar, award-winning business that was named the #4 fastest growing company in Kansas City in 2006. Shoot, he was even teaching Sunday School.

Then he realized what he was, what we've built, and how it looks in the light of holiness. He realized he was a friend of the world – and an enemy of God. (James 4:4) So he sold all he had and gave it to the poor – or it was stripped from him one way or another. And it was all worth it.

Now he's the author of seven books, nearly a thousand videos, music, poetry, and founder of a homeless shelter and a food pantry that feeds 5,000+ people every month. He has cried on the sidewalk in public for days. He's been arrested on false charges. He's spent weeks at a time in prayer, fasting and weeping for the sad state of things.

And he's been spit on, lied about, abandoned, forsaken by friends, banned by pastors, ejected from sanctuaries – and looks more like Jesus all the time. He's even had people try to physically kill him! Just for speaking the hard truth nobody wants to hear. But Jesus said it would be like that. Praise God! Bring it on.

If nobody is shooting at you, then you are <u>not</u> dangerous.

CONTENTS

Dedication, Acknowledgments, About this Anthology and About the Author	i
The Open Letter of Apology to the World	1
The Red Dragon: the horrifying truth about why the "church" cannot seem to change.	107
Dialogues with God	177
Rain Right NOW, Lord!	243
Do It Yourself City Church Restoration	365
Other Resources	509

The Open Letter of Apology To The World

and some other sad stuff

God help us.
We're in such big trouble.

from Doug Perry
Fellowship Of The Martyrs

www.FellowshipOfTheMartyrs.com
fotm@fellowshipofthemartyrs.com
Copyright © 2005, 2011 Doug Perry

All rights reserved.

ISBN: 1463798598
ISBN-13: 978-1463798598

Quotes used with permission from NIV, KJV, ASV.

The Bride gets her jewelry, but it's going to hurt to get it on,
and once you're used to it, you're never going to want to
rip it back off again. Heaven is free. HOLINESS is hard!
If not us, who? If not here, where? If not now, when?

CONTENTS

- Open Letter of Apology to the World 5
- Why the Apology to the World 8
- Emails and posts in response to the Apology
  - Jeff's Apology to the Church 9
  - Various others 13
  - Jim - Hard Questions 18
  - Sandie - Out of church and growing 20
  - Plea From A Missionary 21
  - Negative emails and posts 23
- Declaration of War against the Forces of Darkness 29
- Fellowship of the Martyrs Battle Plan 30
- FOTM Battle Plan - Extended Version 31
- Why are we doing this? 35
- Was Jesus a Liberal? 41
- Right Instinct, Wrong Currency 44
- Are You Kidding Me? Scary Stats and Facts 46
- Really Scary Scriptures 52
- What Exactly is the "Great Commission"? 56
- Human Sacrifice in the Christian Church 58
- The Bottom Line 60
- Bread and Circuses 62
- What is the Proper Use of Funds 65
- Is the "church" going to persecute the "Church"? 66
- Gen X - Gen Y - Anarchists - Read This 69
- The Spirit of Abortion 71
- The Ten Commandments and the "church" 73
- Undeniable Axioms of Church Growth 75
- Who Are The Pharisees? 83
- God - The Supreme Banker 84
- Email from Renee 86
- Doug's Experience with the Holy Spirit 88
- Message to My Baptists 94
- Where are the Martyrs? 97
- WANTED – Positions Available 100
- Other Resources 104
- Hard Prayers 105

Fellowship Of The Martyrs

THE OPEN LETTER OF APOLOGY TO THE WORLD

Please bear with me, this is long overdue and there's lots of ground to cover. I want to make sure that I get it all out. Not just for me, but because I think you need to hear it. Maybe there are other Christians out there as well that need to make apologies and will find courage here. I appreciate your time, I know it's valuable.

Dear Members of the World,

I'm just a guy, nobody really. Son of a preacher and missionary. Years and years of Vacation Bible Schools, summer camps, youth ski trips, puppet shows, revivals, choir trips - you name it. Even went to a Christian college and got a degree in religion. I ended up in the business world, but I spent two decades tithing, sitting on committees, teaching Sunday School, going to seminars and conferences, etc. I even met my wife in the single's class at church. I'm not a bad guy, I've been mostly behaving myself and everybody seems to like me. I do some good stuff here and there.

But lately I've been trying to understand Jesus more and stuff I never noticed before has really started to bug me. I've been taking a look around and I'm having a hard time making sense of what it is we've built here. So, it just seemed like, whether anybody else says it or not, I need to take responsibility for the part I played and say what I have to say.

Here we go ...

I know you think that Christians are a big bunch of hypocrites. We say we're more "religious" and we're going to heaven and you're not, and then we drive our big shiny cars with little fishies on the trunk and cut you off in traffic as we race by the homeless guy on the corner. We average just 2% of our money to church and charity, despite that we say the Bible is the word of God and **it** says we're supposed to give **everything**. On average, we buy just as many big screen TVs and bass boats and fur coats and makeup and baseball cards and online porn as anybody else. Maybe more. You've seen leader after leader end up in jail or court or a sex scandal of one sort or another.

Well ... you're right. We're guilty of all of it. We've done it all. And, I'm really sorry.

You see our cheesy TV shows and slick guys begging for money and you get that there's something seriously sneaky and wrong here. A high-pressure call for money so they can stay on the air? Were we supposed to use Jesus as just another form of entertainment? Who do we think we're kidding? Where's Jesus in all this? Aren't we supposed to rely on him? Isn't He going to meet our needs if we're inside His will? What happened to sacrifice and suffering and helping the poor? I'm just sick about this. I mean, the church leaders, they're not all bad guys, there are lots and lots of really hard-working well-meaning folks who love and care and are meeting real needs in the community. Some of them understand and love Jesus - but I'm just real sure those pastors don't drive Bentley's, have multi-million dollar homes and their own Lear jets! I mean, what "god" are we worshiping? Money? Ego? Power?

You see our massive shiny new buildings all over the place. Heck, maybe we even kicked you out of your house so we could expand our parking lots. You can't figure out why we need four different Christian churches on four corners of the same intersection. We've got playgrounds and bowling alleys and basketball leagues. We've got Starbucks coffee in the sanctuary. We've got orchestras and giant chandeliers and fountains out front. We've got bookstores full of "jesus junk" with every imaginable style and flavor of religious knick-knack. But where's Jesus? Is this what HE wanted?

Oh, sure, there are good folks all over and not every church is such a mess, but Christians are the ones that say we're supposed to be "One Body." So even the good ones are guilty of not putting a stop to it sooner. We were supposed to keep each other in line and not tolerate factions and dissensions and greed and idolatry and all this other bad stuff. Man, we really blew it! We've got 33,000 denominations and most of them won't talk to the other ones. We lose over $5 million a day to fraud from "trusted" people inside the church! We spend 95% of all our money on our own comforts and programs and happy family fun time shows and we let 250 MILLION Christians in other countries live on the very edge of starvation. Not to mention the billion or so that have never even once heard of Jesus - or the homeless guy downtown we almost ran over when we cut you off.

We're as guilty as we can be. All of us. Nobody is exempt. We should have put a stop to it a lot sooner. But I can't apologize on behalf of anyone else. This is about me.

I know that you might have gone to church as a kid and stopped going as soon as you could. I know that you might even have been abused by somebody in the church! Maybe we got you all fired up and then just let you drift off like we didn't really care. Maybe you just don't fit our "profile." You might have piercings and purple hair or tattoos or been in jail -- and somewhere inside you just know that even if you wanted to go to church one Sunday, it would not go well. I'm sorry for that. Jesus loves you. He always hung out with the most unexpected people. He had the biggest heart for the folks everybody else tried to ignore. What have we done? We've told you to put on a sweater and some loafers or you can't go to heaven. I just want to throw up.

Look, I know you're mad. And you have a right to be. We've done you wrong for a LONG time now. There's some things about Jesus that people need to hear, but we've buried a beautiful masterpiece under hundreds of layers of soft pink latex paint. If you have a Bible handy, look up Matthew 23. (If you don't, you can look it up here - BibleGateway.com .)

Find it? Read it carefully, the Pharisees were the "religious" people of the day, the leaders of the faith. In this chapter Jesus SEVEN times says how pitiful and wretched and cursed they are for what they're doing to the people they're supposed to be leading. He even calls them "white washed tombs of dead mens bones" and a "brood of vipers"! I don't have time here, but read it and see if we're not doing EVERY single one of those things. Jesus can't possibly be happy about what we've done to you.

Sure, we like to kid ourselves and pretend everything is OK - but it's not. We're hated. Now, please understand, Jesus was hated, too. But that was because he said hard things and sometimes people don't like hearing the Truth. And he promised we would be hated if we were like him. But that's not why we're hated at the moment. We're hated right now because we're a giant pack of lying hypocrites that say one thing and do something else altogether. If we were hated because we were like Jesus, that would be one thing, but that's not it at all. You see right through our happy music and fluffy services and you can tell there's something desperately wrong here. We're no different than anybody else - except that we say we're better than you.

It was never supposed to be like this. Jesus asked us to care for the widows and orphans, to feed the hungry, care for the sick, visit those in prison, reach the lost. He wanted us to love our enemies and pray for them. He cared about human justice and suffering, the lost and lonely. But I don't think He would have marched on a picket line - He had His mind on much bigger problems. He wanted us to focus on the eternal things, not the everyday. He never once said to go into all the world and build big buildings and divide up into factions and buy Bentleys. Just the opposite! I get that you're mad at us and I think you have a right to be, but please understand, you're mad at what we've made under our own power, you're mad at "Churchianity." That's different than Christ and what he wanted. Don't be mad at Jesus! This mess wasn't His idea!

Look, I'm really sorry. I accept responsibility for my part in having hurt you. But I'm committing to you all, dear Members of the World, that I'm not going to do it any more. Not a single penny more. I'm not going to put my faith in "Churchianity" or any leader or program or TV show -- but in Christ Jesus and His salvation. That's when I was set free and began to see that God wants and expects more of us than this. And I'm not helping anybody that's not fully committed to the same thing.

It took centuries to build this monster, so it's not like it's going to just turn around overnight. But the times are changing and we're way overdue for something new. Big bad things are happening - like the tsunami in Asia - and I think more are coming. I don't want any more time to go by without having said this. I'm sorry for all the time and money I've wasted. But Jesus saves. Really. The church itself isn't even the point. Jesus is the real deal. He lived and He died for my sins and He rose again. He is who He said He was and He cares about me - and you. He's our only hope. We need places you can go that will only teach Jesus and will not be swayed or tempted or distracted by anything else. God willing, that's coming.

Please don't think all Christians are just posers. Some of them really mean it when they say they belong to Christ. The problem is mostly in the West where we're all comfy and complacent and seem to like it that way. The Christians in China and other places are deadly serious. There's no room for anything but Jesus when you're on the run from the government. They are dying every day for their faith and doing crazy hard things because they're absolutely committed to Christ. These are martyrs. People willing to crucify little pieces of themselves every day to be more like Christ. People willing to set aside everything they want, to do what Christ wants. People willing to rot in prison or take a beating or die if that's what it's going to take. People that act in pure love and never back down. I'm not worthy to tie their shoes. And there are some like that here, too, and I hope we can get a lot more people to start living that way. It's way overdue.

If you're talking to someone and they tell you they're a Christian, ask them if they're the kind of Christian that really means it all the time or the kind that just means it on Sunday. The Bible says we'll know them by their "fruits" - by the faith and purity and love in their deeds and words. When you find one that proves Christ is in them by how much they love you, ask them to tell you all about Jesus. If you know one of those fearless martyrs that speaks nothing but pure, clean, hard Truth - ask lots of questions. Truth is a lot more rare than you would think. But don't settle for soft, fluffy and comfortable anymore - that's not in the Bible.

As for me and my house, we're really sorry. From now on, we're going to serve the Lord, not "Churchianity." We're going to try to call together as many of those martyrs as we can and start doing what Christ wanted. If I run into you someday, please give me a chance to shake your hand and apologize in person. I'm going to try harder from now on, I promise. I think there are lots of others feeling the same way, so don't be surprised if you start hearing stuff like this more often.

Thanks for your time. I hope it helps.

Doug Perry
fotm@fellowshipofthemartyrs.com

Fellowship Of The Martyrs

WHY THE APOLOGY TO THE WORLD?

Well, first off, I wrote it because I really mean it. I am seriously sorry for what I did to contribute to this mess and I'm determined to do whatever I can to fix it. So ... the more help I can get, the faster we can turn this thing around. So if it happens that lots of other folks get a little courage and see that this needs saying, maybe they'll say it, too. I've repented to God already for it and He's forgiven me, but that doesn't mean I don't have to humbly ask forgiveness from everybody else.

I believe this is the "elephant in the room" that everybody knows is there but doesn't want to acknowledge. The World despises Christians - and Christians know that they're despised. It's just that the Christians aren't admitting the real problem. A lot of them get that there IS a problem, but they don't know how to say it loud enough to get some momentum.

Truth is always the right answer. Truth is getting scarce lately. When folks hear it, it's so unusual that they perk up and see if it was an accident or a scam or a publicity stunt -- but inside they hope they get more chances to hear it. People are desperate for someone that will not make excuses and will not back down. We've had about all the self-serving "spin" we can take.

I think this is the giant lie that blocks us as a Body from being obedient to God. Thou shalt not lie. Remember that one? It's unlikely that He's going to pour out His power on a Church that is doing some good stuff, but also holding to one Great Lie - that is, "Look at us, we're Holy." -- when we're not and everybody knows it. If we're going to see revival or repentance or restoration or whatever is coming, it's not going to come until the Lie gets crushed and then washed out of the way.

Now, I want more than anything for us to be able to say, "Look at us, we're Holy." Please don't misunderstand. But when we do, it will be in gratitude and humility and worship for having God's help and provision to help us get there. And appreciation for Him giving us time to do it, instead of wiping us off the map like we deserve.

I'm going to try to point the way to Jesus all the time. The things He cared about are the very same things that today's liberal people seem to have a heart for - but that the church is ignoring. I'm not sure when we gave us this "high ground," but I'm sick and tired of it. It was Jesus that STARTED most of these things! Some of them were not even present on the planet before Jesus spoke of them!

Jesus came preaching peace with our enemies. He had a HUGE heart for children, especially those suffering. He cared about human justice and treatment of workers and equal protection. He empowered women in a male dominated culture. He cared about the environment. He spent time with people in "recovery" and addictive behavior - even criminals. He understood the needs of the handicapped. He ate organic foods (well, OK, they pretty much all did). He recycled and didn't waste resources. He only used ecologically sound transportation methods. He spoke harshly of anyone abusing or mistreating another person - particularly those in most need. He talked over and over about money and the important of helping the poor and the need for the rich to assume a greater role in that. (Read more on the "Was Jesus a Liberal" page.)

Anyway, the Apostle Paul spoke this, "First to those in Damascus, then to those in Jerusalem and in all Judea, and to the Gentiles also, I preached that they should repent and turn to God and prove their repentance by their deeds." (Acts 26:20) I had God in me before, but this is the time for me to repent, to take my focus off of Man and turn to God in full and to prove my repentance by my deeds. First, I personally have to change, then maybe other folks will get the hint.

But I'm not saying I'm perfect or anything. I'm going to stumble and I might screw this up. War against darkness means risk, especially the more attention you get. But whatever this becomes, I'm not taking credit for any of it. Pride is what got us into this mess! Shoot, I hardly see how I can take credit anyway, none of this was even my idea! I'm just doing as I'm told.

So that's the plan. If you still don't see why, read the next few letters. Maybe that will help.

(Now a few emails received from people that read the Apology to the World)

Jeff's "Apology To The Church"

Doug,

I hope that you will read this and not just delete it. I read your apology to the world for what the church has done to Jesus and his message of salvation. This is **my** apology to you and the church for trying to get inside and be a Christian.

First I have to tell about me so you can understand why I'm apologizing.

I grew up in a dysfunctional home with a alcoholic abusive father and a mother who was so abused and broken in spirit there was no protecting her children from him. I and my four sisters were verbally abused and sexually abused and physically abused at the hands of this man from the time we were born. My dad taught me how to abuse people and how to steal from anyone you could. He taught me swear and to cheat and to lie and to beat people up when you were angry. I found nothing wrong with these teachings as this man was my father and as a young boy he was naturally my guidance and my hero as I knew nothing else about being a person then what I was taught by my father. My father had destroyed all of my confidence and self esteem before I was two years old as I read it in a diary that my mother had kept hidden from him about her children. He had instilled in me that I was a useless waste of skin who would never amount to anything in this life and when I started to act out in school my teachers began to tell me the exact same thing. I sometimes wondered if there was a God or not as in those days when I was in grade school we still said the Lord's prayer in the mornings. If there was a God I sure wasn't given a very good life. My mom eventually ran away and left us there with him and things only got worse.

That set me on a course for a life of no meaning and a life of total hopelessness. A life where I was confident in only one thing, that I would never amount to anything so why should I even try. I had always been in trouble in school, but I started to get into real trouble when I eleven years old. I began stealing cars and doing break and enters as I wanted to out do my father and make him finally be proud of me for something. After all I had watched him steal since I was a small child.

I finally realized that my father was actually a coward when I saw him mouthing off in a bar and I guy beat him senseless while he laid on the ground covering his head while crying. I said to myself that "I would be no coward and then he would be proud of me so I set out to settle things with my fists and I would be afraid of no one. I began to go in and out of jail regularly and my life had only one meaning. To hate the world and all the people in it! I had never had a good relationship with any decent person in this world. I only knew criminals and abusive people who only tried to take from you what you had. When I was in jail for a one year sentence at age eighteen, I read the book The Late Great Planet Earth, by Hal Lindsay and it gave me an understanding of Bible prophecy and a good teaching for what to watch for as they unfolded and maybe, just maybe there was a God. I could not understand how this life could be so miserable and have just simply death at the end of it. I got my first handgun when I was twenty and I just got worse as life went on. I still spent the next six years in and out of prison and hating the world and everyone in it. I felt I had earned that right.

I found myself in prison at age twenty four and I began to get very depressed in this hopeless life. I prayed to Jesus a prayer. I simply said, "Jesus if you are real and you are there, I don't really want to die but I don't want to live like this anymore". Then I put a noose made out of a bed sheet around my neck and hung myself from the bars of my solitary confinement cell. Everything went black.

I went to the hospital in a coma which the doctors told my mom that I would never wake up from. They told her that it was a miracle that I was even alive and that I would lay in this vegetative state and that she should expect for me to soon die. The doctors were shocked to see me wake up from this coma. I was sent back to prison for the remainder of my sentence and slowly got better and my headache that lasted for months finally went away. The nurse in prison told me the story of how the guards found me hanging and they left me hanging there till they went and got her. It was at that point when she got there five minutes later that I was cut down with no signs of life whatsoever. The nurse got the defibrillator and shocked my heart five times with no response at all. The guards said to give up as I was obviously dead and she turned off the machine and looked at the clock to check the time of death. She turned back to see that the light for the defibrillator was on and it was ready to go again. She mentioned that she thought she had turned that off and tried one more shock just because it was ready to go. On the sixth try she shocked my heart and got a faint pulse. I was rushed to the hospital and put into intensive care where I remained in a coma till to everyones surprise I woke up from it. She said she was amazed because I was already getting cold.

This nurse kept asking me what did I see as she had never seen anyone who was dead for so long come back from it and she knew about near death experiences and wanted for me to tell her something about the other side. I saw nothing. I remembered nothing. She told me that I shouldn't even be alive and the fact that I could walk and talk was a miracle that she had never seen before. I vowed that when I got out of prison I would never go back. And I never did. The Bible says angels will encamp around those who will obtain salvation. This is true.

After I was later paroled from prison, I got my first real job at twenty six years old. I met a lady there and we began to live together for the next six years before we got married and my life got very stable. She had a grandmother who was ninety four years old and could no longer look after herself and she asked if we could take her in so she didn't have to go to a nursing home. We took her in willingly and gave her love and a good home. she was a church going lady and I suddenly found myself taking her to church on Sundays and Wednesday evenings. Her pastor used to pick her up and take her to church until she ran out of money to give them. The pastor and his wife would pick her up and take her to church. It seemed that my wifes grandmother was buying them things that they desperately needed like a $6,000.00 fur coat and a brand new $20,000.00 Chrysler Lebaron. They had convinced her that the Lord had said they needed these things. She gave them many more gifts that they said the Lord said she should give them, far too many to mention. She was a widower who really had nothing and saved her pension checks for thirty years. Her last $3,000.00 she gave to the pastor for his trip to Israel as he said he couldn't afford to go and he really wanted to go. This pastor and his wife lived in the most affluent neighborhood we had in the city in which we lived, in a house that could be described as a mansion. When the pastor found out that she no longer had any money he called her a burden and refused to pick her up for church any longer. That is when my wife and I began to take her. When people in her church found out that we weren't Christians yet they basically avoided us and never bothered to tell us about Jesus. When her church friends would come over to our house to visit her they would treat us badly because we weren't 'saved' and again no one told us about Jesus. I used to listen to this old grandmother pray for us before bed and she would always go off in a strange language that she never even understood, but I knew that there was something strange going on in her room at night during her prayers. She could no longer read her bible so she gave it to me one day and asked me to read it. I really wasn't interested in reading it after all the crap we seen happen to her and to us in her church. She died a year later. We vowed to never enter a church again.

I was still watching the prophecies that I read about in The Late Great Planet Earth, becoming fulfilled and it was shocking to see and I began to realize that God could possibly be real. I began to study her old bible with a passion and began telling people about the prophecies and that it must mean that God is real. This went on for the next fourteen years and I got really good at associating prophecies with modern news events and using them to reach people for God. My mom and two of my sisters gave their hearts to the Lord because of these truths and are now deeply involved in their churches. Other people have become Christians when they had seen the truth in the bible of who created us and why. In a world of aliens and evolution some people just need

The Open Letter of Apology to the World

a little truth. In the year 2002 we had a friend from where my wife worked and her husband over for the afternoon and she mentioned something about prophecy and we just spent the afternoon talking about bible prophecies.

This lady's husband was a lot like me, tough and rough around the edges, he liked drugs and drinking and had been in trouble in the past. He was strangely silent as I talked to his wife about these prophecies all afternoon. After they had left I said to my wife that we would never see him again because I didn't think he liked hearing about that stuff. I was shocked to answer the knock on the door four months later to see that it was him and he had a tape that he wanted us to see. He had given his heart to the Lord Jesus and it was a tape of his baptism and he wanted to share with us the life changes that he had gone through in the last four months. He told us that his wife and her mother were tying to get through to him but he would not receive any of it as it didn't make sense to him. He said to hear it from me was shocking as he knew my reputation for not taking any crap from anyone. We were shocked and something happened to me that day. I was jealous! I had seen this many times before when people learned about prophecy as it was proof that God existed. It was evidence for eternal life. Evidence for eternal damnation. Evidence for Jesus! I was jealous of his being baptised and I suddenly wanted to learn more about Jesus rather then just prophecies. I had suddenly felt empty, where he had knew life.

My wife and I vowed to never enter a church again after what we saw happen to her grandmother. If that was what Gods people were like we could do without them. I felt wrong after this meeting with that man who was changed by Jesus. I went into the bible with a vengeance and learned more about Jesus. Who he was and why he came here. I read about the gift of tongues and remembered my wifes grandmothers gift of tongues as she prayed for us because we took her in after her pastor took her for everything she had in this world. We went to a church that we heard was the best in the city and I was baptised in the water and I wanted to serve the Lord with everything I had to offer. Which I would soon find out, wasn't much.

Being that I grew up extremely poor I had no music talents to offer. There were no music lessons for me. I had never known a church or any teachings so again I had none of that to offer. I had tattoos and I was too rough around the edges to be accepted to help in any way. I was an ex con and the people didn't like that at all. They found out because there was a cop in the congregation who knew me. Why was a guy like me going to their church? I had gotten rid of my hate the world attitude prior to this and I saw a remarkable change come over me that was shocking! I could actually love people, but there was no acceptance for me there. I made the mistake of speaking of the bibles many prophecies that lead me to get saved in the first place and the people sure didn't like hearing about those! It was like they didn't believe in them. I made the mistake of trying to get people involved in leaving the church to go see people in the street and minister to them as that is what I got from the bible - we were supposed to make disciples out of everyone. Maybe I read it wrong, but to sit in a church with the doors open but not to invite anyone in seemed wrong to me. I made the mistake of trying to get people to learn more about prophecies so they could use them to reach their unsaved friends and family and co workers about the truth of God. It had worked for me in the past and I thought it was fairly effective as most people were turned off of Christianity because of things they had seen and experienced. Prophecy was the proof God gave us as to his existence. When I tried to talk to the head pastor about prophecies and how we could maybe use them to reach the lost souls, he called me preoccupied with that stuff and I didn't know what I was talking about. He wouldn't talk to me after that. I guess he didn't like me for trying to change things.

This is where I must apologize to you people in the church. I'm sorry. I apologize for thinking I had something to offer in your programs. After all you claim to try to help the depressed people with their problems and yet I know what it is like to put a rope around my neck and try to die and end the suffering. How many of you people can claim that? I heard you call the depressed people 'drainers'. They would drain you from hearing about their problems. Jesus wanted you to help them. I apologize for being too zealous in a place of complacency. I apologize for trying to get people to reach the lost souls around them. I apologize for trying to make you understand things about prophecy that you should know as being Gods people, tools you should be using to reach the lost. I apologize for going to prison in the first place but with my upbringing I really had no other choice. Most of you people were raised in a church setting and you weren't shown the things I was shown. You were taught values and different lessons than I was taught. You were encouraged where I was only discouraged. I was taught and shown hatred while you were shown love. I was taught anger and resentment and alcohol abuse and drug abuse. I apologize for trying to fit into your world when I clearly wasn't welcome into it.

I'm sorry.

I now sit alone with my family, afraid to go to a church. I lost all my friends when I got into Jesus. I couldn't make any church friends as I clearly wasn't their kind. I apologize to you for trying to be accepted for who I was rather than who you wanted in your world. I am thankful that Jesus accepted me for who I am rather than for who he wanted me to be. He will change me. I know why Jesus was always mad at the religious people, as I now find myself mad at them too. I now live again in a world of bitterness that I had at one time left behind me. I have actually had thoughts of suicide again since trying to fit into the church and being rejected. Bad feelings that have come back since being rejected by the church people. I only think of Jesus and his rejection by the very people he came to save and it makes it easier to understand. He never rejected the dying thief on the cross beside him. he never rejected the prostitute at the well. He never rejected anyone for their sins, he welcomed them with open arms and love and grace. I thought we were all supposed to be like him. I thought we were supposed to welcome the lost with compassion and love rather than judgement and condemnation. I thought we were supposed to believe the bible as the true word of God and not just pick out the things that we want to believe in.

Prophecy is a great tool to use to reach the lost in our world of reincarnation and evolution and Buddha and all the other false religions that we have. If Christians were half as zealous as Muslims are, this world would be a wonderful place and far fewer people would wind up in hell.

I apologize for thinking I had something to offer. I apologize for trying to make changes in your world. What do I know? After all I'm not as experienced as you guys are in this thing. But I sure was zealous and willing to learn. I'm now rejected and alone and in what seems like a prison, again! Thanks, and I'm sorry.

Jeff

Are you on your knees yet?!

Please hear me. If you are part of a congregation - or even a denomination - that has ever, EVER acted like this toward ANYONE, their blood is on YOUR head! Even if you're not the "pastor" - you helped build it and sustain it by your financial or physical support. If we're One Body and ANY part of the Body is in pain, shouldn't we ALL be hurting?! Why aren't we? Why aren't YOU? Why aren't you screaming for change? What is it going to take?

How many like Jeff are going to surface on Judgement Day and testify against you (and me)? Are you really so sure that Jesus is going to overlook all the testimony of the people you've hurt just because you went down the aisle once and repeated a little prayer? If you LOVE HIM, you'll OBEY HIM! And He said to leave the 99 and go get the one lost sheep. And we're NOT doing it. In fact, it's the VERY LAST thing we're doing! And if one of the lost sheep happens to show up in "church" on their own – we THROW THEM OUT!! Something is VERY, VERY wrong. It's got to stop NOW. We're running out of time.

Doug

Email from Sandie - Can a simple apology really lift oppressions?

Just want to let you'all know -- I gave a copy of the "Apology" to a friend about a week ago. She has been enslaved to panic attacks for many many years. She hasn't even been able drive alone. She was very interested in what she read in "Apology" as she has dreadfully abused by the "system". She has been trodden on and made to feel like a nobody. Today she phoned and said that because of what she read, she decided to take a step in faith - guess what?? She drove, alone, by herself. OK OK it was half a kilometre but that is a giant step for her after so many years. "Apology" is bearing fruit -- it has given courage to someone and she is now looking forward to a complete release and recovery. Isn't Jesus wonderful?? Thank you again Doug, for sending out such a humble and sincere message.

Sandie

Email from Brent - Forgiveness comes AFTER confession

Dear Doug,

It is with a broken heart that I confess to you and any other that will hear my words, that I am one of the wrongdoers in the world. Sadness fills my heart when I consider the ways I offend the world with my hypocracy, not the world only, but The Lord Jesus Christ especially. Some of the things that I do and say I dare not mention even. Your words have given me a strong reminder of those things that really matter most, such as Integrity, HONOR TO GOD and love for TRUTH. Mercy is my plead. The shed blood of Calvary is my need. It would be a real blessing to hear of others that can say that they too, know the truth and want to walk in it. If there really is any good in me, it can only be Jesus in me. If there be any hope for me, it is in forgiveness.

Brent

Email from David and Debra - Reaching the oppressed

Dear Brother Doug:

Just read your letter *{Apology}*. Three years ago, I was a Care pastor/ Life leader at a large Church. I thought I was doing good, living a Christian life. I had a good life, I had all I needed. Boy was I wrong! God called me to open a Mission here in Pell City, Alabama. My wife Debra and I had just the money to pay the rent, and cover the cost for one month. That was Oct. 28th, 2002. The Mission offers food, clothes, shoe, addiction programs, Bread Ministry, park and street ministries, community Bible studies and Sat. night services. Through Christ & prayer we believe that oppression can be overcome! In the last year and a half we have seen God free many people. It is AWESOME what God can and will do if we just let Him use us to help others! This is where most Churches are failing. They have forgotten the unchurched and yes even the oppressed churched. Look around you. Someone needs help. Reach out to them, by blessing others, you will be blessed. Open your Heart and let the Holy Spirit work.

May God bless you, your family and ministry with mighty blessings now and always. Amen, Amen.

David

Brother Perry,

Amen. It's a blessing to learn of another brother who has come to terms with reality. I really feel like passing this along to my pastor dad, religious mom and other relatives and friends, and people I worked with at a denominational headquarters (I ran away from there)...but it's just like Christ said about how men come to the Father because He draws them. I don't think they are ready. I can't throw pearls before swine - have done that before to no avail. They seem to just become more determined to keep doing what they are doing. It's tough sitting by and watching the madness.

But, thanks for taking the initiative to put your revelation in words and present it to others. People in the world know who are hungry for God, those He is drawing, will recognize it if we have something they need. Nobody fools anybody in that regard...at least when we're talking genuine hunger and genuine Christians. I feel for all of the people who have been coerced/scared into saying a little prayer to receive Christ when they were not truly repentant. And I feel for those who were serious about accepting God, but then were led astray by false believers who were in it for themselves. Christ spoke about that too - very heavy.

Anyway, God bless you brother as you begin to live in the life, peace and rest that He intended.

J

Your letter was worth reading. My kids want no part of churchianity...and truthfully, neither do i. The fellowship or strengthening of one another's lives seems to be the closest to Christ's direction. But every time i hear of another program, i want to vomit.

Where are the people who will just open their homes and their hearts? Who want to speak of nothing but Jesus and the Kingdom...who do what He does, and say what He says....

I thank the Lord for every point of reality in the midst of pain, but it has been pain mostly of my own making, and i need my Savior.

Again, thank you,

Lee

I join you in "sorry." I forwarded your email to the elders of our church and to friends and family. I want to agree with you in prayer that God is merciful toward us all if we repent. I too have been sickened and defrauded in many instances where I have put my trust in leadership whose prime purpose was to build his/her own kingdom. But, I am reminded of when the disciples ran to Jesus to tell them that (another) Simon was preaching in the name of Jesus. Jesus' response was, in a word, "Let him alone, the main thing is that he is preaching the gospel." So, I trust that if and when the gospel comes/came forth that it reached many. We have all been a disappointment to others in the way we have lived our lives while representing the Lord; I truly repent. I pray we will have wisdom and integrity in the truest form which is in the form of Jesus. I attend a financially lean little church in the Hills of Texas and God is doing miraculous things in our midst; mostly because many are praying and desiring the sincere meat of the Word and trust everything to Him as we grow in faith and from glory to glory.

God Bless.   B.J.

The Open Letter of Apology to the World

Hi Doug

I am in agreement with your letter. I have told my children not to judge Christ by Christians. There have been recently some exceptions to that rule.

Another dissatisfied follower.   Andrea

THANK YOU, THANK YOU, THANK YOU! So many others feel the same way and we have been "crucified" by the "church folk." I once had a Pastor who bragged on being like Paul of the New Testament, yet what he failed to realize was that he never had a "road to Damascus" experience, therefore his actions reflected more of Saul who killed Christians and honestly believed he was doing God a favor. Bless you for your stand. I too am sorry for what the Church has done to sinners... namely - kept them away from Christ who truly loves them!

Tina

QUOTE: "If you look at the world you'll be distressed, if you look within you'll be depressed, but if you look at Christ, you'll be at rest." Corrie Ten Boom

---

I just read your wonderful, beautiful gutsy letter to whom it may concern. That is the only way to be like Jesus! We have to live it. We are human imperfect beings, but one person at a time we can change things.

God Bless, Linda

Doug Perry, thank you for the honesty in this message. I agree with you totally. Jesus, (Yahshua Messiah) was not like most people sitting in the pews and attending "Church" on Sunday, he was love and loved the unpriviledged. He would not and does not approve of what the "church" has become today. Again, thank you. Your sister in Jesus,

---

Doug.............Just received and read your article, "An Apology to the World". I can't tell you how much I appreciate this. I started an article some time ago of the same title but couldn't keep the bitterness and resentment out of it......so it still sits as an unfinished draft. I thank you soooo much for your gentleness and kindness and much needed expression of apology to a world in dire need that has become confused by religiosity and churchianity which poses falsely under the banner of Christ. Again, Thank you..........your brother, Kelly.

Thank you for this apology....I and my part of the Body of Christ join you in both the apology and repentance and commitment to be more like JESUS.......may HE fill us all daily with the fullness of HIMSELF and may we remain Faithful and True always abiding in HIM........CHRIST in us the HOPE of GLORY....this has got to be our story........Jan

Fellowship Of The Martyrs

Dear Doug,

Thank you for writing this, what a blessing to hear that we are not the only ones thinking that Jesus wouldn't really recognize "the Church" that we have made. A few years ago while in a service the Lord let me feel the deep sorrow that He feels when we play church. It was something that I've not talked about much but your letter very much expresses what He let me sense that evening. Well, thanks, keep on the same track and please know that if Jesus is truly Lord over us we will hear His voice and more and more of us will hear and more and more of us will come into that deep fellowship and love that He has caused us to grow into.

Blessings, Dennis

I totally can understand where you are coming from. I was so turned off by my church because they did not follow scripture and were more worried about their building and programs than they were about my next meal as a single mother of 2 and no place to call home. Our church had several rental properties and I needed a place to stay....after paying my tithes faithfully...I thought they would allow me to rent. I was asked this question "if you had to choose between paying your car note and rent to the church which would you pay?" My reply was I would pay the car note since that is what got me to and from work.......needless to say I was not given the opportunity to rent. This is a huge church which does not need the income from the rental properties. I quit going there and have decided to pay my tithes to people who need the help, not the church. Thanks for putting it on my level......God Bless

JoAnne

I found your apology interesting. Thanks for penning it. I am forwarding it onto all my 'out-of-church' friends and to those 'unchurched' friends.

I wonder what would happen if I forwarded it onto TBN.

Jenny

{Hmmm. Well, I can tell you, Jenny, it's going to happen sooner or later! This is the word that needs to be spoken and I'm not going to stop till as many people as possible have heard it!}

Well that just totally rocked .... I've been apologizing to many folks over the last couple years myself ... in fact me and my hubby have been making a few waves since we decided to follow what Jesus said and did ... still walking it out though ... it's awesome ... HE rules!

Blessings Gayle

I agree with you 100%. I recently read "The Heavenly Man" and understand the China situation. How can we sit by everyday and see other humans starving or without water. What is wrong with us? Recently we repented also for the money we had spent on ourselves. Lord help us. We are with you all the way.

Janet

{I just CANNOT recommend a book more than "The Heavenly Man"! I know a certain crazy, radical, take-no-prisoners ex-skinhead revivalist that I sent a copy to who now thinks he's a big sissy compared to the Chinese Christians and Brother Yun! Order it at www.BackToJerusalem.com}

The Open Letter of Apology to the World

WOW!! I just found this web site. I was brought to tears. My heart leaped. I realized that what had happened to me and what I had been feeling and thinking about church and a reformation was on others minds and hearts also. I too have been ridiculed for leaving my church home of 16 years. I stayed until I could not (fight) it any longer....The spirit in me was being quenched and grieved. Once I realized that it was indeed God who was calling me out I had no choice but to go. I have had visions for years of different church...one with out walls...... I know that I as many others am waiting for God to open the door to the new thing. It is so close I know. I do get lonely for fellowship with other believers...but I am trusting in my Father and following his lead. God Bless you all.

Cecilia

---

yes! YES!

just recently have noticed all of this...big hubub at our church that made us leave (basically: group of us wanted MORE of God and the pastor and others said Nope.)...very sad (for them)...but i am happily on my journey now...

wow..how DO we unravel the hundreds of years worth of buildings and programs that replace Jesus, the Savior?

I want to be real...I want to do what the Father is doing...

I want my family to take the "Stop, look and Listen" break for Jesus and see where HE is going...and toss ALL aside and Follow Him.

thank you for your message!

Maryann

I just had to email you and tell you how much your article touched my heart!!!!! It is so true and we are all guilty!!!!! I have seen it at all of our local churches!!! Maybe that is why they are hurting so badly for new members.....I'm so sorry to say!!! I have forwarded your article to everyone on my email list in hopes that we can see the light and correct our ways!! God Bless You!!!

Joyce

Dear Mr. Perry,

I have just finished reading your letter, and all I can say is no truer words have ever been spoken, how horribly correct you are and how SAD it is to hear this truth. I do try to serve the Lord with my whole heart, but regretfully some of the things you said hit me to the core, I sat here in shame as I read your letter knowing that I too am guilty. In the days ahead I pray I too can become A person Jesus can honestly use.

Monica

Fellowship Of The Martyrs

I just had to email you and tell you how much your article touched my heart!!!!! It is so true and we are all guilty!!!!! I have seen it at all of our local churches!!! Maybe that is why they are hurting so badly for new members.....I'm so sorry to say!!! I have forwarded your article to everyone on my email list in hopes that we can see the light and correct our ways!! God Bless You!!! Joyce

---

thank you - i live in a retirement community - recently, i visited an old man - almost 86 - he is going in for serious surgery on wednesday - when i went to talk to him, he was afraid that he would not get to heaven. he said that he had turned down jobs that the "church" wanted him to do, etc. i asked him if he had a bible - he brought out an old bible - old but not very well read - i led him to Rom. 8:1 - no condemnation in Christ Jesus and on to rom. 10 - etc. he wrote the scriptures down and we have prayed. he is now at peace. i am angry that he had attended a "church" all his life and this was the end results. -- Fran

---

Great letter. It really stuck my heart. Please say a prayer for me for I am such a hypocrite.

Marc

Dear Doug, THANK YOU; I read your email which had been forwarded to me with great interest. As a new Christian of 10 months I found your email to be pretty much on the mark as to what I believe the church is like to day. Most of what I see are stale Christians or just plain thieves! Sorry but I to can be blunt too. I belong to a small church which is just beginning to come alive but they are still far from the mark. I have heard things said such as "your on fire now but hey that'll pass" you will get over it! What a joke!! I went back to working in a hotel as a Bouncer and was condemned by many Christians because a true Christian would not visit let alone work in a pub. Well I have had tremendous success in planting seeds, witnessing and leading people from the pub to Christ and I love it. I am also in the early stages of starting a ministry called aimed at Released Prisoners but to eventually cater for those 6 needs outlined in Mt 25 within the greater community. I was so please to see that there is a change of heart coming and you were brave enough to lead the way and put it out there for the world to read, Bless you my friend. I say thank you again for I know I am still far from perfect but do not wish to belong and fit in with that unhealthy view of Christians that much of the unreached public has. Thank You and God Bless, Graham

---

Email From Jim - Asking Hard Questions Will Get You Into Trouble!

Hello Doug,

I think you are exactly right on target with your comments. I marvel at how people spend money on themselves for exceedingly foolish things. Right now we are in the middle of the "Christmas Shopping Season". Frankly, I think we ought to take Christ *out* of Christmas and name the it for what it really is - "National Commerce Day".

I can really relate to your points in your article. I grew up in the Catholic church and right now there is a wave of church closings due to a shortage of priests. So what does the headquarters do? They close two churches

The Open Letter of Apology to the World

and build a brand new multi-million dollar one. The church my parents attend is going to be merging with a smaller one. It would be easy for them to put an addition on the larger church to house everyone with minimal cost. But no - they will be building a huge new one four miles down the road.

When I first became a Christian, God took me on a circular route. I joined the Worldwide Church of God (which is the church Herbert Armstrong started). We paid one tithe on our gross income to meet the church's needs, then a second tithe to keep the Feast of Tabernacles (with the excess cash donated to the church), and every third year there was a third tithe for the widows and poor. I marvel at how the money (peak income for the church was something like $180,000,000 in one year) was just squandered mindlessly. I would hate to be some of the leaders of the church on Judgment Day. They will have some exceedingly hard questions to answer.

In all fairness, the WCG has undergone some serious doctrinal reforms in the past ten years and are now considered to be mainstream. Yet I still see them spending money to do evangelization but I don't see any results. If a person had to measure the spiritual "rate of return" on their financial investment - it might even be negative.

I felt a need to give my support to something that could use it better. The past few years I have been helping to support the local CSN radio station. (It is affiliated with Calvary Chapel). It seemed far better to support someone preaching the word of God chapter by chapter, verse by verse than to support the ideas of man. Yet even here, I wondered how many people were actually listening to the station. It is an excellent means of teaching those already in the faith, but how many new people is it reaching?

So then I started looking to support individuals who I know have needs. There is an elderly gentleman from our church who was having financial problems. Years ago he was almost killed when a drunk driver slammed into his car early one morning when he was going to work. It was very hard for him to work after that. They sold their farm to support themselves. It is amazing to me that for all the money the church headquarters collects, that they are unable to help people like these.

I am really convicted of the value of supporting groups like Gospel for Asia. I have heard of them in the past, but until recently, I have not looked into them. If a person would give 10% of their income to GFA for the purpose of buying Bibles and gospels and other appropriate materials to reach the lost - it staggers the imagination what they might be able to do with it. Even if each one of their missionaries would only convert a few people and they would start just one small church - that is an exceedingly more fruitful way to promote Gods' Kingdom than by giving to the organizations I have in the past. *{www.GFA.org}*

It is amazing to me how big churches spend their money. The most prominent mega-church in our area is Bayside Christian Fellowship in Green Bay, WI. I went to their services once. They have an auditorium that can seat 1200 people. It is very nice inside with TV cameras and projection screens to see the musicians up close while they perform, etc. One of the big things the pastor was talking about was a building project. Seems that they are pretty full on their two services on Sunday morning. Being dumb, I asked the foolish question of why they just didn't have a third service instead of paying millions to do an addition. I guess that was a dumb question. Also when I was there, they were praying for five people who were going to a foreign country for two weeks to do mission work. It just didn't make sense to me. For what it would cost to fly these people half-way around the world - for two weeks - to do what? They didn't know the language.

I would just like to encourage you to continue your website. There are people like me out here who do read it and are saying - "Right On". It is surprising to me that God has been patient with our country as long as He has. We certainly are not doing what we ought to be doing. I will forward your website to our pastor and talk to him about it. -- Jim

Email From Sandie - Out of "Church" and Growing Like Crazy

Dear Doug Perry,

Thank you SO much for expressing my frustration with the church. This is why I left the "system" almost three years ago. The words did not match the deeds, there was no love or reaching out to those that needed to be reached, there was no compassion for those who were suffering. It was just one big comfort zone; a happy "bless-me" club, very much a clique -- and I did not fit in. My heart ached to see the hands of Jesus (through us) reaching out to the community around us instead of sitting on chairs for hours and hours, or dancing around having a "good" time instead of giving some Jesus joy to those that needed to be uplifted. The church seems to have become about "self" not Jesus. It speaks of prosperity (money). Financially I have very little, but consider myself prosperous because of what I have in God. I wouldn't swop my relationship with Him for all the money in the world. He is my treasure. He is the most precious gem I have ever gained -- and HE did it all -- not me.

He brought me to Himself in a most dynamic way when I was alone in my own home and since then I have followed Him for 17 years. The church taught me not to give to others but to itself and it seems so wrong. I met with more animosity and dislike in the church system than I ever did when I was " in the world". I was their worship leader, their only worship leader, yet when I contracted pneumonia and was sick at home for almost a year nobody phoned to see how I was or visited me. I was not resentful - I just could not understand why they were so angry. I did not ask to be ill. In retrospect I see that it was God's way of getting me out of there. The pastor is still angry with me. I never went back when I recovered. As there is no other English speaking church near me I have stayed at home and kept close to my Lord through His Word, His music, tapes and books. I have discovered a whole new perspective of God and it is nothing like that which is preached on a Sunday from a pulpit. I have discovered that He loves me just as I am, not as people want me to be. I have discovered that I am truly unique, that He made me that way for His glorious purpose. I believe that He is gently urging me into that purpose every day of my life until I go to be with Him forever.

I have discovered that I will not go to Hell just because I slip up with a bad word now and again, because that is the "old man" in me that HE is uncovering in me so that HE can get it out of me -- and that I don't have to have people shouting in my face trying to "deliver" me. I have discovered that He is VERY gentle with the way He sets me free from stuff that binds me. AND -- I have discovered that His love is so VAST and beautiful and compassionate and understanding. That is the most precious thing - that He understands me, that He knows me inside and out and still loves me in spite of myself. I never learnt that when I was in the church. I have discovered that He lets me know when He disapproves of something, and He does it in such a loving way. AND -- I have found that He leads me where He wants me to be in a much clearer way than I experienced when the "church" had its finger in my face.

I know of quite a few people like me who are "out-of-the-system" but love God so much. They are sincere, warm and loving - totally different to what I personally experienced in the church "system". I believe that God has a special plan for us if we would only stop, and listen. I believe that He is going to direct us into His path and His way of loving and giving. I am no longer worried about what people think - I am happy to go wherever my Lord takes me and do whatever He wants me to do. I am no longer feeling condemned because I do not go to "church". Wouldn't it be great to see the walls come down and the church in the streets just as Jesus was -- touching lives, changing lives, loving others just as God loves us..... IF only we could stop being so selfish and self-centered.

God bless you for having the courage to speak out what is in my heart, and the hearts of the friends God has given to me. With love in Jesus,

Sandie

The Open Letter of Apology to the World

Plea From A Missionary - Name Withheld Due To Her Humility

{response to "Apology to the World" that was forwarded to her by email}

I am so grateful that someone is saying this--at last! As a missionary wife, I came home from years on a pioneer field in great need of rest, good food, medical help and acceptance from people other than those who wanted to thrust me upon a platform to speak about, "Missions." Couldn't I just once say something about how beastly hard it was trying to raise a child among poisonous snakes, scorpions, crocodiles, man-eating monitor lizards in the front yard, no friends for him, being his school teacher and Sunday School teacher and only companion, and a husband who was so consumed with, "the work," that he had no time for us? And I believed that was the proper way for him to be! I don't criticize this. I never talked about the millions of roaches in my house, about putting my child to sleep by saying, "Be very quiet, and you will hear the rats come into the house," Both my children are in Heaven now. I never spoke of things we had to eat, how thin and ill we all became, of sleeping in villages with bed bugs crawling all over us, with pigs in pens in the kitchen, of vomiting and diarrhea lasting up to a year, of being 80 miles from medical help, a very hard 80 miles. I never talked of any of this. I talked of people being saved, churches being established, elders being ordained, evangelists raised up by God who were faithfully serving Him without pay for years and years. But Oh, Lord, isn't there someone who will just care about me as a person? I tried to eat at all the feasts in my honor, taken from church to church and shown off; emotionally, I felt as if I were a ruin. I remember walking toward home for five hours at a time, sleeping in a village, and getting up again to do more walking, while having malaria. I didn't speak of this either. They wanted to hear about success, not bedbugs, not snakes, not scorpions and never rats in the house, and never discouragement and illness. At the meetings were I was featured as a speaker, I smiled and had my picture taken. Once, while in this country, I was given some black jam that someone had put up and stored in their basement for many years. "Missionaries can eat anything," I was told. Oh yes, and it was almost true. I thanked her for it, but didn't eat it.

Once, I told those on my mailing list that my husband was twice healed of very bad malaria attacks in which I feared for his life. The church gathered to pray, and my husband walked out of his room, cool and well. One church discontinued our support because they considered us Pentecostals from that time onward. I thought, sinfully, "Well if he had died, perhaps they would have remained friends with me and it would have suited their doctrine better."

I'm just glad someone is speaking out concerning the fat, wealthy church in America. But I might ask, "Is this really the true church? Is this all there is here? Are there none who are generous, unselfish, loving and have the Spirit of God in them? Is there no true church in this country? We have been looking for such a place for a long time.

I am unwell now, and could be said to be elderly and I don't do much beyond praying any more. My dear, whitehaired husband is still a missionary who wins souls, and tries to teach them and support these new lives in Christ, giving them Bibles and other materials, and corresponds with them. We think we have found a church where the pastor is a humble, intelligent man; the congregation is a mixed-race group, which I like. An intelligent, Black woman is the only adult Sunday School teacher, and yes, men sit in her class, gratefully appreciating her; the class is large. As a rule, we are unable to stay for that. My husband is still a tireless evangelist, but he has time for me now.

God bless you and may your tribe increase!

In Christ's love,

(A missionary)

++

My Commentary on "Plea from a Missionary"

ARGGGHHHH!!!!

This could be my Mom! (Had she not died of cancer after we came back to the States.) I lived the missionary life as a kid, I understand this. I had to BEG this dear sweet warrior of God to let me publish this so you could see this. I couldn't have written anything as convicting!

Listen, you can't send out advance troops to do battle and expect them to succeed with no ammunition, no supplies and no backup. Read Judges 6-7. When Gideon's 300 went out to fight 150,000 Midianites with a torch in one hand and a trumpet in the other - the other 31,700 that couldn't hack it got to stay home, but they LEFT ALL THEIR STUFF BEHIND! So the 300 had enough provisions for 32,000!! THAT is how GOD does battle! Those willing to go lay down their lives for Jesus should have 100 TIMES their own needs so that they can feed any who are hungry and give drink to any who are thirsty.

AND STOP MAKING THEM COME HOME AND DO SLIDE SHOWS!!! LOVE ON THEM WITH EVERYTHING IN YOU AND BE GRATEFUL GOD DIDN'T SEND *YOU* TO DO IT!! And if He DID send you to do it and you're trying to hide from it - then you owe these people TWICE as much!!

STOP USING THEM TO MAKE YOUR STATS LOOK GOOD AND EASE YOUR CONSCIENCE! These are WARRIORS! Treat them like it and give them the provisions they need without making them stop everything and come entertain YOU every four years!

Take the Bentleys and Mercedes away from the fat cat pastors, sell them off and give the money to the front line warriors that are IMMUNE to the love of money! If you're willing to take your kids to go live in a jungle a five hour walk from help - I'm just SURE I can trust you with money! If you have a million dollar house, I gotta wonder.

We just don't have time for this anymore!! Who is running this war?!

Doug

NEGATIVE EMAILS FROM THE APOLOGY TO THE WORLD
(and some responses)

The very first serious flaming mad email! - of many to come.

Shalom. Barukh atah Ha-shem, Eloykaynu, melekh ha-olam.

Speak for yourself. I know no true Christians who do any of those things. I can only wonder what kind of Christians you know. Try looking at the traditional churches and not wacky Protestant churches with no roots or real beliefs. I don't know what your motivation is, but if you are trying to damage the name of Christianity, you are succeeding. If you are attempting to be satirical, you are failing dismally.

Don't judge all Christians by yourself and your circle of acquaintances. What you say is a total insult to the majority of Christians and only true of prosperity doctrine sects. It is the worst drivel I have ever read, even from Protestant fundamentalists. If you seriously imagine that anyone is going to be interested enough to read all that verbiage, you are grossly flattering yourself. No non-Christian is, and not many Christians.

I certainly will not be coming to hear you speak, if your spoken message is as grovelling as your email, which I think is likely to turn people right off Christianity.

Just who do you think you are, to put down millions of Christians and set yourself up as judge, the only person with any principles ? Your conceit is beyond belief. Humility is not a word with which you appear to be familiar.

And 'churchianity' is not a word; it is nonsense.

Anna

+++

{MY RESPONSE}

Anna,

I WAS speaking for myself. It's MY apology.

Either we're ONE body or we're not. If we are, then we're failing miserably. There is no other way to look at it. Across the totality of what we call "Christianity" in the West there is negative growth and MUCH damage to many, many lives.

If you think YOUR sect is universally being effective and doing the right thing, then you stand accused of having separated off instead of trying to heal the Body. Even those doing the right thing should have put a stop to this sooner.

Put your head in the sand if you like, but there is unarguable statistical and demographic evidence that there is a massive movement AWAY from the churches across nearly all denominations. There are over 20,000,000 "wilderness Christians" in America that are worshiping God on their own because "church" is too toxic for them.

The time has come for someone to admit the truth. This is NOT the way Jesus wanted it. We've segmented ONE BODY up into thousands of denominations and sects. The "world" sees how messed up it is. It seems like the most honest thing is to just admit it. Then the healing can begin.

If what I have to say and my motivation for doing it is "of man" then it will surely fail. If it is "of God" then there is no stopping it. I guess you'll get to sit back and smugly watch to see what happens. Meanwhile, me and anybody else willing are going to go try to get people focused back on Jesus, instead of the man-made systems and structures we created without Him.   - Doug

++++++++++++++++++++++++++++

(MY SIDE COMMENTARY)

First, if somebody would like to translate the Hebrew for me, that'd be nice. Not my thing.

Second, WOOHOO!!!! The more angry they get, the more we're probably saying things that make them uncomfortable! Jesus said there would be persecution. This is just the very, very start of it. There will be MUCH anger.

Third, see how "roots" are so important to her? Tradition, history, structure, etc. seems to impart legitimacy. The older the denomination, the more True? Hmmmm.

Can you see the hate for Protestants? The absolute sense that they are stupid rednecks that are mucking it up for the "real" religions?

Oh, PLUS - it's just bad logic. If nobody is going to read it, I can't hardly be causing any damage, now can I?

Another One - Unsigned

It's good to say what we aren't supposed to be, but where is the standard of what we ARE supposed to be. That is the mark of a true prophet!

Are we not doing anything right? Did Jesus Himself as well as Paul say that we were to get some reward from following Him? I think so!!!

Not everyone is CALLED to be a martyr in the sense of living destitute for the Kingdom. Big churches often are doing more than small churches. And sometimes you do have to look at the percentages as well as the intangible assets.

Most Christians are not living that much different from the world BECAUSE that IS the world they live in and that is HOW they reach others.

Can we do more? Always! Just like we can always pray more - so what is the standard.

I get tired of being put down by the self righteous who give no standards for me to say, "Maybe I am on the right track!"

The world is not just the poor guy on the street corner - we should help him, but the world is the world! And we are to reach it. There are a lot of ministry styles I like and many I don't. But guess what, when you take a poll, not every one's tastes and styles are the same. Don't factor that out.

Many are doing MUCH MORE than you are giving them credit for. Do we need to work on it? Sure! But change comes by His Spirit. Not by just another voice of authority that criticizes everyone else.

+++++++++++++++++++++++++++++

{MY RESPONSE}

Hi,

First, that letter was to the "World" - NOT to the church. That was an APOLOGY, not purely a lecture on what the RIGHT thing is.

Second, that other stuff you're asking about is on the website and more is coming. Particularly see the Declaration of War and the Battle Plan.

This is a big problem, we're not going to fix it in one email, particularly an email that wasn't aimed at YOU.

Prophets don't consider individual cases. Hosea didn't say "just the bad ones are going into captivity". Everybody stands condemned, including the righteous remnant that should have been trying harder to stop the bleeding.

If we're ONE Body, then we need to look at our success or failure in those terms. We have sliced the body up into 33,000 sections. Necessary and complementary organs aren't talking to each other. Blood isn't flowing to the extremities. We're dying. There's no other conclusion.

Nobody is saying martyrs are to be destitute. Where'd you get that? We are to offer our bodies as living sacrifices, we are to be willing to crucify little pieces of ourselves everyday, we are to grow up into Him who is the Head, we are to pour ourselves out as a drink offering so that HE can be poured in. That's the nature of martyrdom. And EVERY SINGLE Christian should be willing to do so - that's our spiritual act of worship commensurate with the mercy He's shown us. It's all there in Romans 12. A person that says they are a Christian but that isn't willing to do so is saying that they aren't willing to BE like Christ, but are willing to use His name. They should be encouraged or else ignored - but never made a leader.

Take a look around the website before you dismiss it so easily. This is the word that needs to be spoken.

Doug

More Criticism – from Al

I read most of the articles on your web site today.

Have you ever asked yourself why you take up various causes? What is your true motive?

You will probably have to ask Jesus to explain to you, your real motives. It isn't what first leaps to your mind. If you get the real answer, it will be an awakening. It will be the first step in a long road to discover yourself. Something that is vital to a deeper relationship with God.

Almost all of your conclusions and opinions come from the mind of reason. They are superficial because they do not deal with the real forces that shape this world. Instead, the opinions are based upon human understanding.

John, in quoting Jesus, said that worship of God must be in spirit and truth. Don't gloss over the dynamics of that concept. What does it mean to worship in truth? (By the way, only John makes this quote.)

Al

+++++++++++++++++++++++++++++

{MY RESPONSE}

Hi Al,

Now, please understand, I mean this in the most loving possible way.

HUH?

I have no intention of trying to "discover" myself! In fact, I don't even want there to be any of "myself" left. I turned it all over to God and said I'd do whatever He wanted and this is what I got. I'm just trying to be obedient every day.

If the arguments seem superficial it's because the people have been dumbed down so much that we require remedial education. It's not enough to just talk about the eternal struggle between good and evil that happens behind the scenes. People need to see the consequences of that warfare in the "natural". We can see the side effects of the warfare in the current pitiful state of the visible church (as a whole). I'm pointing out the damage caused in the natural by us having ignored the supernatural.

Other than that, I'm not even sure what you're trying to say. There's a difference between knowledge and wisdom. I'm trying to inflict maximum damage on the enemy in as short a time as possible. That's going to require rallying those already prepared and training those who are willing but green. That requires wisdom. I'm a soldier following the battle plan as laid out by my Commander. I don't have time for too much thinking - that's what got us into this mess.

I just don't see it as being that complicated. Acknowledge Him, submit, beg to hear His voice as clear as you can, repent, hear what He wants and GO DO IT - then give Him alone the credit. It's all in the Lord's Prayer.

I am what I am because HE made me. I have ZERO desire to delve into the mystery that is "me". I just do as I'm told.   --- Doug

+++++++++++++++++++++++++++++

{AL'S RESPONSE}

Thanks for your reply. Unfortunately, it was what I had expected. But, I was hoping otherwise.

It is so sad that often those who believe they are doing something for the Lord, don't really understand the deception they are under. What's equally sad is that deception has many levels and it will justify itself.

Never are the deceived, so deceived, as when it involves religious matters!

Al

+++++++++++++++++++++++++++++

{MY SECOND RESPONSE}

Sorry, Al.

Gotta do what I gotta do. Either it's God talking to me or it's not. If it's of man it's gonna fail anyway and you can smugly watch me go down in flames. If it's of God, folks probably ought to think twice before fighting against it. Good advice from Gamaliel. (Acts 5:33-39)

Wish I could slow down to argue it all out with you, but I'm fighting a war here. I guess I'll just take my chances at the final judgement. -- Doug

++++++++++++++++++++++++

(MY SIDE COMMENTARY)

Listen folks, this is the lie from the pit. "Figure yourself out. Find your inner purpose. What's your motivation? What makes you tick."

Most of this email I can't even make sense of. But I'm just NOT going to get suckered into it! We're to be a living sacrifice (Rom. 12). The SACRIFICE itself doesn't get to decide ANYTHING. The sacrifice lays there on the altar and GOD decides what to do with us. If we turn over everything, He will very quickly help us to: STOP CONFORMING TO THE WORLD, then He will transform us by the renewing of our minds, so that we can know HIS will and DO IT. That's all there is to it.

DON'T get suckered into these fights! YOUR personal "purpose" doesn't matter a flying fig. Find out what GOD wants and then DO IT. No more messing around with psychobabble.

Another Response - From Brian

While I understand your intentions, this kind of statement, no matter how true some facts may be, in the end, rarely brings about anything other then a mocking laugh from "the world". Also, even the best criticizers and challengers of churchianity within the church eventually tire, being isolated and considered fringe elements, hurt and bittered by the devil, and the church. I've seen person after person face this. Jesus challenged and provoked the religious status quo, but did not become critical of it. He rose to a higher purpose (to send the gospel to the gentiles, the world) and position (seated at the right hand)

My suggestion is that you take Christ's lead and become the model of non-churchianity and even come together with others that feel the same and start another church. Only new churches that embody the real Christ have an impact and help change individuals and churches.

While you may want to take the opportunity to preach back to me, I do hope you take some time to chronicle your positions and the perceived impact your having. Look at the impact over the next 10 or 20 years and then compare it to the word and see if your ministry had value. It will be real clear then.

Take Care

Brian

++++++++++++++++++++++++++++

{MY RESPONSE}

Thanks, Brian.

The fact that others have fought and lost is no excuse to stop fighting. The fact that I might not win is no excuse to stop fighting. The fact that there will always be someone somewhere mad at you is no excuse to stop fighting. The fact that the world might laugh at you is no excuse to stop fighting. You really honestly believe Jesus didn't criticize the religious status quo?! He called them murderous, hypocritical, greedy, self-indulgent, unclean, vipers, white-washed tombs of dead men's bones AND said they were all going to hell! (Matt. 23)

I don't want to start another church! I want people to fill themselves and the churches we already have with

JESUS. And not settle for anything less. What do you want for them?

Always good advice to journal and think back and see what impact we've had. I'd take you up on that – writing everything down for 10 or 20 years - but I'll be dead way before then.   --- Doug

---

Musical Interlude - Feel free to sing along

This is my commandment that you love one another, that your joy may be full.

This is my commandment that you love one another, that your joy may be full.

That your joy may be full. That your joy may be full.

This is my commandment that you love one another, that your joy may be full.

Very good. It's really all very simple, isn't it?

Now ...

STOP teaching this song to your kids if you're <u>not</u> going to <u>live</u> it!!

You're just confusing them!!

DECLARATION OF WAR AGAINST THE FORCES OF DARKNESS

Now, before you start thinking we're talking about YOU, this is about EVIL - not people. Sure, some people are stinkers, but we're to love people and we're to hate evil. The darkness from our sinful nature is in all of us. We're not any better, it's just Christ in us that helps us be redeemed. Anyway, this is about the BIG picture, not any specific person, organization, leader, etc.

No more. It ends now.

For too long we've ignored what was going on in the church. For too long we've sat out or even denied there was a war. We've been infiltrated. We've been co-opted. We've been dumbed down. We've had our greatest weapons ridiculed and demeaned until nobody wants them anymore. This is no kind of way to fight a war.

We've allowed ourselves to be fattened up and we've planted roots. We've been herded together in big groups like cattle and we bump around against each other making useless noises. Wolves have come in and we've welcomed them. We've accepted aid from the enemies of God. We've taken the enemy's advice about how to make war. We've hired consultants to show us how to be more like the world.

We've ignored our own King's plan. We've sent a pitiful few skirmishing parties out to do the work of missions for us and patronized them when they come home wounded and hungry. We've given all the ammunition to the supply clerks back home and deprived the infantry of what they needed to push back the darkness. Everything about what we're doing is upside down.

No more will we take on the names and philosophies of men to define and identify us. No more will we allow factions over secondary issues to divide us. We are to be OF Jesus and Him alone. Only He gets to put His brand on us. Only He gets to direct us. Only He is truth. This is war! Nothing else can be trusted. His is the unbreakable cypher. Pure, full, uncut Truth cannot be spoken by the enemy. Truth and Love are our uniform, our code, our defining characteristic. Only Truth and Love will suffice for battle against principalities and forces of darkness.

No more will we waste time on our own vain pleasures and indulgences. No more will we allow the egos and prides and traditions and philosophies of Man to divide us. We will love Truth and settle for nothing less. We will learn to sniff out and purge compromise and half-truths. We will force out of us every bad dark thing by being completely filled with the Bread of Life. We will be nourished by Truth. We will be armored by Truth. We will swing the Sword of Truth in big wide circles and pierce the hearts of anyone near. We will fight and not grow weary. We will charge forward and never retreat. Should one slip, others will lift him up. Should one fall, others will take his place.

No more. It ends now. There are those that are already equipped to fight and we will enlist them, organize them and send them back out to recruit more. We'll fight with love to awaken our brethren who are asleep and get them in fighting form. We will push back the darkness by speaking nothing but TRUTH. It is rare and precious - and only Jesus is the source. Every man-made thing will burn off in the fire. Only Jesus can be trusted.

As Gideon, we will lovingly restore our own altars first while the people are sleeping. Then we can rally a restored, awakened people to fight the forces of darkness. Those on the front lines that have proven themselves good and faithful servants and stewards of their talents will be provisioned with a hundred times their own needs so that they can feed the hungry and give drink to the thirsty as they see any need. We will pray and encourage and support them and recruit more. We will always strive to continue growing up into Jesus, who is the Head. In view of the great mercy shown us by Jesus Christ, we will offer our bodies as living sacrifices, holy and pleasing to God. We will stop conforming to the pattern of this world. We will be transformed by the renewing of our minds so that we will be able to test and approve what is God's good, pleasing and perfect will. Then we'll go and do it. **I Corinthians 14:8 -** *"Again, if the trumpet make an uncertain sound, who will prepare for battle?"*

No more. It ends now. As clear as we can say it, this is war.

FELLOWSHIP OF THE MARTYRS BATTLE PLAN

Acknowledge your complete needfulness for God and inability to reach Heaven and escape the consequences of sin on your own power. Repent of every sin. Acknowledge Jesus as the risen Son of God and beg Him to wipe you clean. Commit to Him that He will be Lord and Master and that He alone will direct you. Without any reservation or evasion, you must mean that you intend to seek Him and do as He leads - even if it means discomfort, abuse, sacrifice, change, suffering, separation or even death. Ask for the indwelling of the Holy Spirit in as great a measure as He is willing to give you. Don't seek gifts for the sake of gifts, seek God - and He'll decide on the gifts for you. Be willing to chase holiness - to strive and urge forward for it everyday. Go and sin no more.

If you mean that Christ is Lord, then you must mean that His Word is the final authority. Spend most of your time in praise and worship of God because He is holy. This is the most pure expression of our love - for this we were made. Seek out anybody else that is absolutely committed to doing as God directs and is willing to speak only Truth, even if it's hard. Spend time together praising God and seeking His face. Each of you be prepared to minister. Don't rely on a paid staff person to do it.

The ultimate source of Truth is God's Word. Learn to love it, take it everywhere, read it and ask the Holy Spirit to explain and teach you what you need. Practice speaking pure Truth with no hint of Man inserted. Test everything against the Word of God.

Hold onto the good, run from evil. Learn to have no love for any created thing that exceeds your love for the Creator. Work hard. Whatever you do, do it as if you are doing it for God. Pray that God will help you have as large a positive impact as possible. More than anything else, God wants to first restore His people and convert all the altars back to the worship of God. Pray for the churches.

Take big arm loads of Truth and begin feeding the hungry. Go out as missionaries to speak into the hearts of the people where God leads you. Always speak in love and humility, pointing the way to Christ alone. Remember, you are trying to save eternal souls - never focus even for a moment on the immediate, always on the eternal.

Find those who can also commit themselves fully to Christ and involve them in your fellowship. Praise God always for His use of you to save others. As your act of obedience, divert all available resources and assets only to those individuals and organizations most efficiently converting earthly treasure into heavenly treasure - that is, feeding the hungry, reaching the lost, caring for widows and orphans, supporting the Brethren in the hard places, equipping missionaries to push back the darkness - the same priorities that Christ has. Anyone that shows a "love of money" should be instantly suspect of being ensnared by the enemy and should be prayed for desperately - that is the root of much evil. God has already prepared many who are no longer susceptible to attack from that direction - find them and give them what they need.

Seek out other fellowships and submit to each other in love. Seek to support the members of your own fellowship as they go to serve or split off to start more fellowships. Seek unity through harmony. Don't get distracted for a single moment by secondary issues or debates. We don't want everybody singing the melody, we want everyone in harmony and singing the part written for them by God. We need all the pieces. None can be wasted. But be willing to rebuke as God directs, and forgive if they repent. Expect wolves, spies and infiltrators. Expect the enemy to be sneaky. This is war.

As you stay inside of Truth, get to know the will of God and use all your gifts and talents within His will, amazing things are likely to happen. Expect miracles. Beg to be filled with the empowering of the Holy Spirit and use what gifts He's given you. Stay filled by a constant focus on holiness and purity and praise. Then pray that God will enlarge you so you can hold more. Pray for the greater gifts - those that can do the most damage to the enemy.

Obey God only. Time is short - so don't waste any. Go in love - and never give in.

FELLOWSHIP OF THE MARTYRS BATTLE PLAN
(Extended Version)

This is by no means a comprehensive list of verses related to each of these items. There are two purposes in doing this expanded version. One is to show that every single line is based on Scripture. The other is to provide a lesson plan that can be used as a study guide to work through each of these items. Whether individually, in small groups or as a larger church, these are the core fundamentals that should be foremost on our minds. We hope that this will bring value to you. As you find other verses that clearly apply to any of these lines, please email us and we'll add them.

We're building this together. Rediscovering the simplicity of God's Plan.

1. Acknowledge your complete needfulness for God and inability to reach Heaven and escape the consequences of sin on your own power.

Genesis 4:6-7; 2 Chronicles 7:14; Psalm 38; Proverbs 5:21-23; Proverbs 10:17; Proverbs 16:5-6; John 3:16; Romans 6:23; Romans 10:9-10; Ephesians 2:8; 1 John 1:9;

2. Repent of every sin.

Psalm 32:1-7; Psalm 51; Luke 13:3; Acts 17:30; 2 Corinthians 7:10; Rev.3:19

3. Acknowledge Jesus as the risen Son of God and beg Him to wipe you clean.

Psalm 119:94; Mark 10:32-34; John 1:29-34; Acts 22:16; Acts 26:23-24; Ephesians 5:26; 1 Corinthians 15:20; 1 Timothy 2:5; I John 4:9-10; Titus 3:5; Revelation 1:5;

4. Commit to Him that He will be Lord and Master and that He alone will direct you.

Proverbs 3:5; Matthew 22:37; 2 Corinthians 1:21-22;

5. Without any reservation or evasion, you must mean that you intend to seek Him and do as He leads – even if it means discomfort, abuse, sacrifice, change, suffering, separation or even death.

Psalm 4:5; Psalm 18; Romans 12; Matthew 10:32-33; Mark 10:29-31; Romans 8:18; Romans 1:17; Galatians 2:20; Galatians 6:14-15; Philippians 3:7-11; I John 5:3-5;

6. Ask for the indwelling of the Holy Spirit in as great a measure as He is willing to give you.

Luke 11:13; Acts 1:8; Ephesians 3:14-19; 1 John 5:14-15;

7. Don't seek gifts for the sake of gifts, seek God - and He'll decide on the gifts for you.

Psa 42:1-2; Rom 12; Matt. 6:33; 1 Corin. 12:7-11; James 1:5

8. Be willing to chase holiness - to strive and urge forward for it everyday. Go and sin no more.

Psalm 17:3-5; Psalm 39; Psalm 66:16-20; Psalm 119; Mark 9:42-49; Luke 17:1-3; Romans 6; Romans 8:1-17; Romans 12; 1 Corin 6:9-10; 2 Corin 13:11; Colossians 3:1-17; I John 5:18;

9. If you mean that Christ is Lord, then you must mean that His Word is the final authority.

John 1:1-4,14; John 8:32; John 14:21; John 14:6; Romans 3:4; Hebrews 4:12;

10. Spend most of your time in praise and worship of God because He is holy. This is the most pure expression of our love - for this we were made.

Exodus 4:31; Psalm 12:4; Psalm 29:1-2; Psalm 34:1-8; Psalm 47:1-2; Psalm 104:33-35, Psalm 103; Ps. 113:3;

11. Seek out anybody else that is absolutely committed to doing as God directs and is willing to speak only Truth, even if it's hard.

Ecclesiastes 4:9; Romans 12; I Corin. 5:9-13; I John 4:1-8;

12. Spend time together praising God and seeking His face.

Psalm 32:11; Matthew 6:33; Colossians 3:15-17;

13. Each of you be prepared to minister. Don't rely on a paid staff person to do it.

Luke 17-20-21; I Corinthians 14:26-33; Colossians 3:15-17;

14. The ultimate source of Truth is God's Word.

Deuteronomy 6:4-9; Psalm 119:105,130; Proverbs 30:5; Isaiah 40:8, 55:10-11; John 1:1,14; John 8:32; John 17:17; Romans 3:4; 2 Timothy 1:50; Rev.19:13;

15. Learn to love it, take it everywhere, read it and ask the Holy Spirit to explain and teach you what you need.

Deuteronomy 8:3; Psalm 119; Acts 20:35;

16. Practice speaking pure Truth with no hint of Man inserted.

Proverbs 10:19-21; Zechariah 8:16; Romans 12; I John 1:-10;

17. Test everything against the Word of God. Hold onto the good, run from evil.

John 5:39; Acts 17:11; Romans 12:9; 1 Corinthians 15:2; 1 Timothy 6:11; I Thessalonians 5:21-22; James 4:7;

18. Learn to have no love for any created thing that exceeds your love for the Creator.

Psalm 39:6; Matthew 6:24; Matthew 10:34-39;

19. Work hard. Whatever you do, do it as if you are doing it for God.

Colossians 3:23-25;

20. Pray that God will help you have as large a positive impact as possible.

1Chronicles 4:10; Colossians 4:2-4;

21. More than anything else, God wants to first restore His people and convert all the altars back to the worship of God.

Judges 6; 2 Chronicles 29 –31; Malachi 3:7;

22. Pray for the churches.

Ezekiel 22:30; John 17:9,20-21; Acts 6:4; Acts 12:5; 1 Thessalonians 5:16-18; 1 Thess. 5:25; James 5:13,16;

23. Take big arm loads of Truth and begin feeding the hungry.

Matt.10:27; Luke 9:60; John 14:6; Romans 12;

24. Go out as missionaries to speak into the hearts of the people where God leads you.

Matthew 28:19-20; Luke 10:1-9; Acts 1:8; I Corinthians 5:9-13;

25. Always speak in love and humility, pointing the way to Christ alone.

Luke 17:10; Luke 18:9-14; Luke 18:16-17; Luke 22:24-30; Colos. 3:15-17; Eph, 5:2; 1 Corin 13:1; 1 Corin 16:14;

26. Remember, you are trying to save eternal souls - never focus even for a moment on the immediate, always on the eternal.

Matthew 6:19-21; Luke 10:1-9; Romans 8:18-39;

27. Find those who can also commit themselves fully to Christ and involve them in your fellowship.

James 4:1-10

28. Praise God always for His use of you to save others.

Psalms 113:3

29. As your act of obedience, divert all available resources and assets only to those individuals and organizations most efficiently converting earthly treasure into heavenly treasure - that is, feeding the hungry, reaching the lost, caring for widows and orphans, supporting the Brethren in the hard places, equipping missionaries to push back the darkness - the same priorities that Christ has.

Matthew 6:19-21; Mark 10:21-31; Luke 16:9; Luke 18:22; Romans 12;

30. Anyone that shows a "love of money" should be instantly suspect of being ensnared by the enemy and should be prayed for desperately - that is the root of much evil.

Matthew 6:24; Luke 16:19-31; Luke 17:33; Luke 18:18-30; Luke 19:1-9; Luke 19:45-46; Luke 21:1-3; I Corinthians 5:9-13;

31. God has already prepared many who are no longer susceptible to attack from that direction - find them and give them what they need.

Luke 16:10-13; Luke 19:11-27; James 1:9-12; James 2:5-6; 2 Peter 2:1-3;

32. Seek out other fellowships and submit to each other in love.

Mark 9:50; Luke 17:3-4; 1Corinthians 16:14;

33. Seek to support the members of your own fellowship as they go to serve or split off to start more fellowships.

Matthew 9:35-38; Acts 4:32; Romans 12;

34. Seek unity through harmony. Don't get distracted for a single moment by secondary issues or debates.

Romans 12; Romans 14-15:13; Galatians 5:16-26; Ephesians 4:1-6, 13-16, 25; Philippians 2:2; 1 Corinthians 1:10; 2 Corinthians 6:15; 2 Corinthians 13:11; I Peter 3:8; I Timothy 6:20-21; James 5:9;

35. We don't want everybody singing the melody, we want everyone in harmony and singing the part written for them by God.

Romans 9:20-21; Romans 12; I Corinthians 11:18-19

36. We need all the pieces. None can be wasted.

John 17:4; Romans 12; 1 Corinthians 12:7-11; Ephesians 4:11-13; Philippians 1:6;

37. But be willing to rebuke as God directs, and forgive if they repent.

Luke 17:3-4; Romans 12; Galatians 6:1; Colossians 3:13;

38. Expect wolves and spies and infiltrators. Expect the enemy to be sneaky. This is war.

Proverbs 24:5-6; Proverbs 14:1-2; Matthew 15:8-9; Mark 13:1-13; Luke 20:20-26; Luke 20:45-47; John 15:18-21; Ephesians 6:10-18; 2 Corinthians 10:3-6; I Timothy 1:18-19; 2 Timothy 3:12;

39. As you stay inside of Truth, get to know the will of God and use all your gifts and talents within His will, amazing things are likely to happen.

Romans 12:2; 1Thess. 5:16-18; The whole book of Acts!

40. Expect miracles.

John 1:50; John 14:12-14; The whole book of Acts!

41. Beg to be filled with the empowering of the Holy Spirit and use what gifts He's given you.

Luke 11:13; Romans 8:11; Romans 12; I Corinthians 14:12;

42. Stay filled by a constant focus on holiness and purity and praise.

Genesis 4:6-7; Psalm 51; Psalm 113:3; Romans 8:4; Romans 8:6; 2 Corinthians 10:5;

43. Then pray that God will enlarge you so you can hold more.

Exodus 34:24; Deuteronomy 12:20; Deuteronomy 19:8; 1 Chronicles 4:10; 1 Chronicles 4:10, Isaiah 54:2, 2 Corin. 9:10;

44. Pray for the greater gifts - those that can do the most damage to the enemy.

1 Kings 3:9; I Corin. 13:27-21; I Corin. 14:1; I Corin. 14:12;

45. Obey God only.

Psalm 32:8-11; Isaiah 64:8; Matthew 4:10; John 14:21; Romans 6:22; 1 Corinthians 6:20;

46. Time is short -

Matthew 3:2; Matthew 24:36,42-44; Matthew 25:13; Luke 17:22-36; 2 Peter 3:10;

47. so don't waste any.

Ezekiel 3:17-21; Hebrews 4:11

48. Go in love -

Mark 12:28-34a; 1 Corinthians 16:14; Hebrews 13:1;

49. and never give in.

Romans 12:21; Gal. 6:9; I Corin. 9:24-27; Heb 12:1-17, 28, 29;

WHY ARE WE DOING THIS?

Well, that question may best be answered by walking through with us the questions we asked that got us here.

Starting with this one:

Is this all there is? Is this the BEST we can do?

How many times have we sat in church and wondered what was missing? How many times have we left, had lunch and can't remember ANYTHING from the sermon but the jokes? All the bickering and fighting and divisions and politics and money saps the joy and life out of us. Or worse, the life-crushing, dictatorial environment imposed by forced tithing and messages on complete subservience to the pastor and the leaders without whom you can't survive in the "world."

Can this really be what Jesus intended?

He wanted us to forgive seventy times seven and turn the other cheek and not let the sun go down on a dispute between brothers and He wanted us to be One Body. So if we stomp off mad after a business meeting doesn't go our way and start another church across the street - whose idea was that? Can't have been Jesus' idea. Must have been the other guy. There's only two choices, you know.

If we're listening to God and doing the will of Jesus - then how did we get to 33,000+ denominations, massive waste, billions in fraud per year, 50% of pastors addicted to porn, practically no demographic or attitudinal differences between us and the general population, millions migrating away, the youth nearly completely lost to culture, etc.?

Only one available conclusion, we're not following God's plan. Either God is in charge and he's completely incompetent - OR - we're not listening to God. If you look at the outcomes, it's clear we're losing this war. It must be that God isn't really in charge. If it's of Man it will fail, but if it's of God nothing can stand against it. And since we're failing, it must be that this was built largely under our own power.

If God isn't in charge, then whose idea must it have been to make it like this? Who benefits most?

Well, answering that one was really easy. If this is war and our churches are losing, then the enemy is benefiting most. If he was able to influence us in this direction, then he's done a really good job of co-opting or neutralizing all of our assets. We need to repent for being so blind and stupid.

What happened to miracles, healing, casting out demons, raising the dead, speaking in other languages and stuff like that? We're just not seeing them in America on any kind of a scale that you could call effective warfare. There are little flashes and anecdotal stories, but nothing that is completely consuming the press reports. Even in our own churches most of our denominations have decided this stuff isn't for today or stopped when the Bible was completed. Where does it say that? How come these are happening all over the world but here? Is America God different than China God? Must be something else in the way, because He doesn't change. The two greatest weapons of revival are miracles and martyrdom. They are both evidence of a FEAR of the Lord and a belief that He is able to do anything. Seems like that's what we're missing.

So why did we give up our best weapons? Why do we mock the gifts of the Spirit?

If this is war, then the enemy will want to try to neutralize our best weapons and fix it so nobody trusts them or even wants them (or everybody is abusing them). We're such stupid sheep, we didn't even see it coming.

It's like if we were still in the Cold War with Russia and they decided to paint all their tanks pink and staff them with cute, fluffy girls in bikinis. They'd print calendars, it would be in the press all over the world, and every horny boy in America would have a picture of the Russian Tankgirls on his wall. Before you know it, we wouldn't be able to staff our own tanks because all the servicemen would be embarrassed to serve in tanks because "tanks are for girls". Then we start cutting back defense spending on tanks and then eliminate them altogether because we don't think the Russian Tankgirls are a threat and we can't staff our own tanks anyway because everybody is too embarrassed of the connotation against their manhood. Then Russia starts a land war, paints their tanks green again, puts beefy, hairy Russian guys in them - and we're in big trouble!

If there is a giant move of God and satan wants to neutralize it, all he has to do is have people like Benny Hinn endorse it and co-opt it. Then nobody will want to touch it! We're such stupid sheep. We gave up all our best weapons! Well, I want them back!! I'm sick of pop guns, I want a Cruise Missile and some Bunker Busters!!

And what happened to caring for the poor, hungry, sick and in prison? Aren't these on the final exam? (Matt. 25 - Remember the sheep and the goats?!)

If the enemy is in charge, these are the VERY LAST things he wants us doing - because it's the MOST like Jesus and ignoring them keeps us trapped in goathood. Since these ARE the very last thing we're currently doing, it must be additional confirmation that the enemy has been pulling the strings or at least got us so far off track that we're not even doing the CORE things Jesus wanted!

So, how much of the available income to our church structures is being diverted toward the poor and hungry and lonely and in prison? Probably less than 3%. Hard to say exactly, but it's tiny. That can't be good, you know, what with a final judgement coming where we're going to have to answer for all this stuff. Maybe we could change direction? Please?!

What happened to hearing the voice of God? What happened to being led by Him only?

Most churches will try to have you medicated or committed if you have the guts to say that God actually talks to you (unless you're the pastor). You see, we've built a system where one guy stands up front and tells everybody else what God wants them to do. We aren't actually teaching people how to hear God. They're talking about "priesthood of the believer" but they're always sticking a "priest" in the way to tell us what God wants. We're certainly not preaching pure obedience and repentance - which is the best, surest way to make sure you're hearing God. And we're not preaching that ANYONE can hear God, just those who have an "anointing" - or a diploma. And if you have a best-selling book and a big church, that's proof that you must be hearing God REALLY well. We're such stupid sheep.

So are we just proposing ANOTHER "non-denominational" church?

NO! That's not it at all. What we're proposing is PRE-Denominational. Back the way it was in the beginning. The only Biblical model we have is the City Church. There was never to be any division in the Body. Saying you're Non-Denominational is still stepping aside from everyone else and dividing off into factions - whether you intend to or not. We just want to acknowledge that we ARE one body and sooner or later we're just going to HAVE to find a way to make this work. I highly doubt that any pastors in New Orleans were arguing about secondary doctrinal issues right after the hurricane - at least I certainly hope they were not. Is it going to take a world-wide disaster everywhere to get us to knock it off? Must be so, because that's what the book of Revelation predicts. The Christians will all be asleep and it will take seeing 2/3 of the world die to wake them up again.

So what do we do to turn this around?

You see, there are only two models of "church" in the Bible - the universal Body of Christ (the Bride) and the local city church (Jerusalem, Corinth, Ephesus, etc.). There were to be NO subdivisions of the city churches. That doesn't mean they all met in one building, that means they were united in one spirit. (So much so that the messages in Revelations 2-3 had application to a whole town, not just pieces of it.) The Greek word that got translated as "church" is "ekklesia" and simply means "those who are called out." There has always been a certain number of "those who were called out" in every town - but we just refuse to talk to each other because we disagree on Calvinism or the Rapture or whether to clap or sing fast music or which translation of the Bible to use or some other nonsense. Since it's all going to burn in the fire anyway, maybe we could just drop it. Whadaya say?

How exactly we're going to turn it around took a lot of praying and seeking God - and lots of repenting and obedience. It may require visual aids to fully explain. You see, in order for God to pour out His blessing and manifest glory, the vessel has to be in proper divine order and under His headship. It has to be operating according to His design and not it's own plans and intentions. And there is a progression that has to be observed. You can't take shortcuts. Of course, the enemy knows this, so he's tried to derail all of the steps along the progression so that we couldn't make any progress. And, he was very efficient and effective. We cannot proceed on the path we are on and expect God's blessing because we're NOT on God's path. That is, we're built on the wrong foundation, so anything we build will crumble. And by all accounts, everything we HAVE already built is crumbling around us. (See the Scary Stats section for more if you need proof of exactly how whacked everything is.)

There is a required progression and it goes like this:

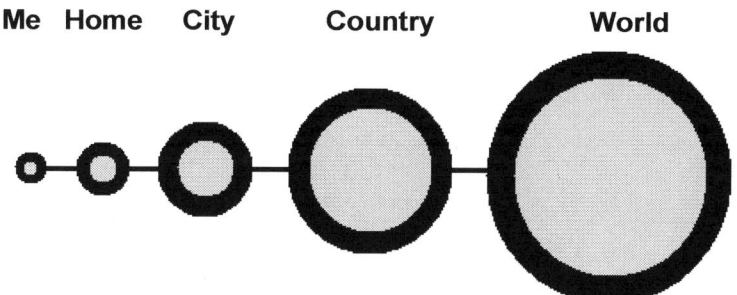

First, I get my own heart in order and under His headship. That means repentance, commitment to Him as Commander, walking in holiness and seeking Him only. Then I fix my marriage by getting it functioning according to His design and in obedience, then my home. Then all of the people that have accomplished THOSE start working on the Body of Christ in their town and get them acting as one body and in obedience. Then when the towns (the Body of Christ, not the real estate) get some critical mass, they start taking their state (or province), then their country, then the world. You CANNOT skip a step!!

So, why isn't this happening? There are certainly people who have their own lives and homes in order and under His headship. The enemy has been pounding away trying to divide families and enslave the people to sins of all kinds and has been very effective - but there are still those who haven't bowed their knee to the gods of the world. But, as near as we can tell (as of August of 2005) there were NO towns in America that were in divine order (fully under HIS headship only). There is a Body of Christ in every town, but they are divided up in little pieces all over and a divided house cannot stand. The strongholds and principalities of darkness that have responsibility for each town cannot be opposed by a divided Body of Christ. Since none of the Local Bodies (city churches) are in divine order, the strongholds can't be pulled down. We give them legal ground when we corporately continually violate Galatians 5:19-21. Since the towns are out of order, you can hardly expect that the states and countries could be right either.

So how do we restore the City Church in our town?

First you identify as many as possible of those who are in divine order and completely sold out to Christ (called out of the world). And you don't spend a single SECOND arguing about theology or style or practices and policies and rules of Man. That's what got us into this mess! You just find them and love on them as we're directed in I John and Romans 12 (and elsewhere). It could be a handful or it could be a thousand - it doesn't matter. If one can take on a thousand and two can take on ten thousand, then a representative handful is plenty to get started - as long as they are united and under proper headship (Jesus only!) and submitting to the giftings in each other AND the Lord is their Rock. (Deut. 32:30, Romans 12) (Please note that it's highly unlikely that you're going to accurately identify those people without having a very clear connection to the voice of God. You better get as much Holy Spirit in you as your cup can hold!)

Then you assert your rights as the Body and repent on behalf of the Body of Christ in your town and you hit your faces and wait on the Lord for the next step. In Romans 12, we offer our bodies as living sacrifices, holy and acceptable. It's the same here. You repent on behalf of the Body (should be plenty to repent for) and ask for its restoration and strengthening -- even to the very expense of your own souls (See Exodus 32:31-32, Romans 9:2-4, and the very nature of Jesus) and then you wait on the Lord for direction. You offer it as a living sacrifice - that means that you put it up on the altar and wait. YOU are the sacrifice. The sacrifice doesn't get to decide anything. It just lays there and waits. When God is ready, what He will do with the sacrifice is force it to stop conforming to the world, THEN it will be transformed by the renewing of it's mind and THEN it will know what is the perfect pleasing will of God and it can get to work.

This is NOT about building another new church building - God forbid! Or even having any structure that is recognizable to Man. It's just asserting the FACT that there IS a Body in your town (whether large or small) and that it needs to unite; set it's face like flint; get fully armored up against the enemy - and STAND. Then you can pray that blind eyes will see and deaf ears will hear and you can BE Jesus to the rest of the town. See Isaiah 58 - if you free the captives, break the chain, lift the yokes, feed the hungry, clothe the naked, STOP the malicious talk and pointing finger THEN He WILL turn and answer you and a bunch of good stuff happens - including rebuilding the walls on the ancient foundations (which is JESUS, not Man).

But as long as the Bodies are divided up all over town, the enemy has won. Read Judges 6. We cannot go to war against the rest of the world and expect God's blessing while there is still an altar of Baal in our own backyard. First you convert the altar back to the proper worship of God and THEN you go take on the big battle. And Gideon didn't have to fix every single altar to Baal in Israel, just the one in his own house.

How do we find the other "Living Stones" in our town?

What we need are those who are so full of Jesus they don't really fit in anywhere. At the rate we're losing leaders from the "institutional church" system (1 million+ a year in the USA), I suspect many of those are already out in the "wilderness" or have been told by God to stay in the church system even though they don't want to. Either way, when you do something radical that is purely and completely about Jesus, all the other radicals will smell it and come running. God will need to direct you on how to do that, but where we have developed tools that work, we'll communicate those along. More on that as it develops. (Please Note: We are NOT recommending you go try to get all the pastors in town to start talking to each other! If God tells you to do that, fine, but it seems like that's the path to ecumenical footsies, not to radical transformation and renewal. Besides, there may be whole churches where not a single solitary person - including the pastor - is truly a part of the Body of Christ. Find them wherever they are, don't fall into the trap of assuming that the Body of Christ is the conglomeration of all the churches in town. It's just NOT.)

The main thing is that we have a lot to make up for, so if we start identifying those with the needs that are on the final exam (hungry, poor, naked, lonely, etc.) and we start meeting those needs in a big way (especially for Brethren), it will attract attention. But you have to be willing to proceed, even if no one else helps. Jesus went to the cross by himself. If you want to be like Jesus, you have to be willing to walk it alone.

We've made up some t-shirt designs that are so different than the norm, folks will have to pay attention. And nobody will wear them unless they are serious. For example, our "Need Prayer? Just Ask." shirt requires that you be willing to stop whatever you're doing, wherever you are and pray for someone AND know the right thing to pray. Are you really willing to completely snarl up a Walmart if God wants to start healing people? Are you willing to be late for work so a stranger can cry on your shoulder? People may not want to go to church and tithe, but nearly everyone will take some prayer. See the shirts here - www.cafepress.com/fotmartyrs . (We don't make hardly anything on these. They are printed on demand with no setup or screen charges! So the designs can be personalized to fit your town.) There are also books, music, art, and more there from people who are contributing their talents to help fund the work of the Kingdom. We've also been directed to work on resource exchanges to redirect the excess goods of those with too much to get them to those who have needs. And who knows what else is coming? God is very creative. The Church of Liberty has also been given a vision by God to build a massive computer network that will allow the Body of Christ in every town everywhere to link up in amazing ways and coordinate resources.

So what could happen if we take our towns?

Well, if we're right, then this is absolutely mandatory if God is going to pour out His blessing. We CANNOT proceed with the Nicolaitan ("nico"- in place of, "laitan" - laity) system we have and expect to see God's glory. We have to stop eating from the Tree of the Knowledge of Good and Evil - of laws and interpretations and rules and structures of Man - and start eating from the Tree of Life that Jesus offered once for all by His sacrifice. We have to free the captives. Free them from the world and sin and evil - and free them from the structures and systems and programs of "Churchianity". The proper way to do that is to point people toward Jesus with a real and firm expectation that He WILL talk to them and tell them individually and collectively what to do next. But we need to make sure we keep OURSELVES out of their way. We have to repent and we have to do it loud and strong. Read Ezekiel 9. ONLY those who are mourning and weeping and groaning because of the state of things are exempt from the death angel.

If we create new wineskins that are pure and have no trace of leaven in them, then God WILL pour out his New Wine.

Of course, none of us know how to do that, so HE is going to have to show us how and we're going to have to follow directions. He desperately wants to renew and restore His Church, but will not pour His full strength and power into our broken down old wineskins. What we need is transformation and that only comes when we stop conforming to the world - and like it or not, right now the institutional church system is sold out to the world. After transformation and renewal we can walk in His presence and know His will on all things and we can OBEY. Then I think we'll start to see Him express Himself in some big, attention-getting ways like the miracles other countries are seeing. When we take the towns, then we begin to free the captives and the workers (and the assets) begin to show up for the final harvest.

Oh yeah! And you can expect persecution to immediately begin once you commit to this path. So you better be willing and know what you're getting into. Better yet, be wishful and hopeful that persecution will come! If it comes because we are being more like Jesus (which is what He said would happen) then, serious persecution in the West is long overdue!!

Get it? Ready to restore your town for Jesus and put it back the way it was supposed to be all along? Even if you have to do it alone? We want to know who and where you are.

Although we're just getting started ourselves and have no staff and no budget - if you need it, we can provide websites, email, t-shirts designs, discussion boards, etc. until you get on your feet.

Even if you're not ready to take on your town yet, but you're willing to help us, we could sure use you. This is going to get completely crazy and it's going to go REALLY fast!

Just in case you didn't get all that, on Pentecost Sunday (2005) God released us to publish this website (www.TheChurchOfLiberty.com) to the internet and begin getting the word out.

If we're still being too subtle for you, try this:

We're blowing the trumpet and telling you to "Come out of her!!"

The New Song starts NOW!

Praise God!! It's right on time.

Quick Thought:

In the age of computers and The Hair Club for Men,
maybe you're not impressed anymore by a God who knows every hair on your head.

How about this?

<u>Every</u> atom in the universe has a unique personal name and God named it.

Not a serial number – a NAME – quark "Susie," proton "Fred," molecule "Erma," muon "Jeff."

Every leaf, every snowflake, every grain of sand, every solar flare, every radio wave.

He knows how and where it started, how and where it will end and <u>everything</u> it will bump into in between. And He knew it <u>all</u> before He made the Universe.

Is <u>THAT</u> big enough for you?!

Because **THAT** is the size of the God we made angry with our stupid, petty selfishness.

We might want to say we're sorry.

Like RIGHT <u>NOW</u>.

WAS JESUS A LIBERAL?

Well the short answer is, "No." But He wasn't really a Conservative either. Labels don't really fit Jesus very well.

Consider this:

Jesus sounds sort of Liberal

- Jesus cared about workers' rights.
- Jesus was into recycling and not wasting resources.
- Jesus criticized the legalistic Pharisees (conservatives) very strongly.
- Jesus had disciples that were anti-authority, anti-big government Zealots.
- Jesus hung out with the people rejected by society.
- Jesus cared for the handicapped and hurting.
- Jesus cared about little children and cursed anyone that would hurt them.
- Jesus cared about the earth and it's health.
- Jesus promised the destruction of the Temple, the sign of God's favor on a specific people.
- Jesus was multi-cultural and embraced diversity by reaching out to those different or dirty.
- Jesus criticized the "Rich" for their selfishness and lack of care for the poor.
- Jesus urged that all share resources as there was a need.
- Jesus had "blue collar" disciples.
- Jesus went out and talked to the masses.
- Jesus supported and strengthened the role of women in a highly patriarchal culture.
- Jesus said He was a servant to all and washed the feet of His disciples.

Jesus sounds sort of Conservative

- Jesus cared about the rights of the land-owner and business man.
- Jesus talked about money a lot and not always critically.
- Jesus said He came to fulfill the Law, not to break it.
- Jesus criticized the Sadducees (liberals) for their esoteric arguments instead of action.
- Jesus hung out with Pharisees (conservatives) frequently - even had them among His disciples.

- Jesus hung out with rich people. Even government officials.
- Jesus cared about stability in government and said to pray for them, not fight against them.
- Jesus never urged anyone to take the country by force.
- Jesus cursed a fig tree when it didn't bear fruit and then it shriveled up and died.
- Jesus promised the rebuilding of an eternal, all-encompassing Temple over which He would be King.
- Jesus was focused first on His group (the Jews) and only reluctantly reached out to others later.
- Jesus affirmed the right of the rich to enjoy what they have.
- Jesus had "white collar" disciples.
- Jesus met behind closed doors with influential leaders.
- Jesus asserted that the role of the men in bringing His plan was critical.
- Jesus said He was to be King and absolute ruler.

Jesus sounds like Jesus

- Jesus was willing to set aside all of His desires and die a brutal death to save all of us.
- Jesus loved everyone He came into contact with - even when He was yelling at them.
- Jesus prayed and cried over the destruction that was coming to Jerusalem and wished they would listen.
- Jesus picked disciples from the most unlikely places, completely outside of either camp.
- Jesus was willing to see earth pass away so that it could be renewed.
- Jesus prayed forgiveness for his enemies, even when they were nailing Him to a cross.
- Jesus performed miracles and then told people to keep their mouth shut about it.
- Jesus walked right into the synagogues and quoted their own words against them.
- Jesus said He was the Son of God. In fact, He said He was "I AM" - which is the name of God (from Sinai).
- Jesus sacrificed His life to wash away our sins.

You can't put a man-made label on Jesus that easily. He was unique. Never in human history has one person had so much impact - no matter how much financial, political, or military resources were behind them - and all of this in just three years. Jesus had none of those assets. Just His words and the testimony of His life.

Believe what you want about Jesus, but there are only two choices:

- EITHER -- He was a raving lunatic and ego-maniac
- OR -- He was the Son of God and spoke Truth every time He opened His mouth.

Believing He was a wise man or a prophet or just a smart guy is NOT an option.

He said over and over that He WAS God, that He was the Son of God, that He was to die and be resurrected, that He was the only option for the redemption of sin, that He was eternal, that He was going to destroy the Temple in three days - and much more.

So which is it? Nearly all of His disciples died as martyrs. Nearly all died horrible, painful deaths (crucified, quartered, boiled in oil, crucified upside down, eaten by lions, hacked to death, stoned, whipped, etc.). If this was all made up, then why didn't any of them renounce it? Would you die for a man you knew to be a fraud?

Hmmmm.

Musical Interlude - Feel free to sing along

Jesus loves the little children, all the children of the world

Red and yellow, black and white, they are precious in His sight.

Jesus loves the little children of the world.

Very nice. Not real complicated, is it?

So why are we spending the vast majority of all the Christian money on the comforts and indulgences of the white ones?

Who would like to go explain that to the red, yellow and black ones?

Quick Thought:

What if in the back of the Wall Street Journal there were the Stock pages, the Mutual Fund pages AND a list of all the Christian ministries and how much treasure in heaven they were earning per dollar spent?

A complete listing of the "exchange rate" the ROI for each ministry. Hmmmm...

Would you dump the stock you're holding and invest somewhere else?

Fellowship Of The Martyrs

RIGHT INSTINCT, WRONG CURRENCY

(Matt. 6; I Pet. 1; Rev. 3:17-21; Rev. 18; I Cor. 3; Matt. 23:17; Eph. 2:6-8; Col. 1:27; Matt. 24:9-14; Matt. 25)

I Peter 1:18-19 - *"For you know that it was not with perishable things such as silver or gold that you were redeemed from the empty way of life handed down to you from your forefathers, but with the precious blood of Christ, a lamb without blemish or defect."*

Matthew 6:19-24 - *"Do not store up for yourselves treasures on earth, where moth and rust destroy, and where thieves break in and steal. But store up for yourselves treasures in heaven, where moth and rust do not destroy, and where thieves do not break in and steal. For where your treasure is, there your heart will be also. The eye is the lamp of the body. If your eyes are good, your whole body will be full of light. But if your eyes are bad, your whole body will be full of darkness. If then the light within you is darkness, how great is that darkness! "No one can serve two masters. Either he will hate the one and love the other, or he will be devoted to the one and despise the other. You cannot serve both God and Money."*

Matthew 6:31-34 - *"So do not worry, saying, 'What shall we eat?' or 'What shall we drink?' or 'What shall we wear?' For the pagans run after all these things, and your heavenly Father knows that you need them. But seek first his kingdom and his righteousness, and all these things will be given to you as well. Therefore do not worry about tomorrow, for tomorrow will worry about itself. Each day has enough trouble of its own."*

What a blessing it is to be an American! If your hope is for a comfortable life, health, opportunities to accumulate assets - what a blessing. If your hope is for spiritual purity and being like Christ - what a <u>curse</u> it is to live here! The "American Dream" trumpeted around the world that urges the poor, downtrodden, huddled masses to come to us is the vision that they could work hard, make a million dollars, get a big car, a big house and a pretty blonde wife in a bikini. If not them, then maybe their kids.

Do you see that God has blessed this nation from the very beginning with relative peace, with an entrepreneurial spirit, with a great work ethic, with capital and energy enough to accomplish nearly any task? The problem is our continuous misunderstanding of the nature of the economy of the universe. Without a great revival movement every fifty years in this country (since 1750), there might be no signs of Christian love left. We would have long since been absorbed by the consumer mentality. Even now we are in grave danger as the church unrepentantly becomes more and more like the world.

We've been blessed by God with the right instincts - massive accumulation of treasure through hard work and entrepreneurial thinking. But we've ignored the specific instructions in the Bible about what money is FOR. We've arrogantly chosen the easy parts of the Bible and dismissed those that draw us into conflict with worldy culture. (We are not being persecuted **because** we are not trying to be like Christ. As soon as a big enough movement of Christians decides to throw off this culture and live as Christ commanded, persecution will start in America. Enough of them might even be seen as a threat to our economic safety and national security.)

The Bible says we're to store up treasure in Heaven where it won't rust and thieves can't steal. If we are to covet anything, it is this. The eternal treasure is the thing. Don't you get it? That's what dollars are for! If God has blessed you with more than your basic needs, every single extra dollar should be used to purchase Heavenly treasure. Any other use of them is selfishness, apostasy and ultimately, idolatry. Not my words - I'm not happy about it either. I stand condemned the same as anyone else. But you can't leave the verses cited above out of the Scriptures and still honestly say your desire is to be like Christ.

Imagine someone offered you Microsoft stock or Hewlett-Packard stock when those guys were still working in their garages. Better yet, imagine if you absolutely, positively knew what that stock would be worth someday.

You knew it was a winner. Would you buy into them? Would you sacrifice some current luxury to help them grow - in exchange for the massive long-term payoff?

When God finally got through to me and helped me see this, all of my American business instincts kicked into overdrive. If every dollar is entrusted to me **SO THAT** I can use it to buy treasure in Heaven, then I want maximum return on investment for every single dollar. See? Makes perfect sense. So I went on a search to first see how my money was currently being used and then find who might be a better investment. As it turns out, the "stocks" I'd been buying through denominational structures and "Big Church" programs have a TERRIBLE yield in Heaven. I can't say they're all losers, but they were definitely under-performing their potential.

I want to find those mighty warriors, those servants of the Cross, those who are truly being obedient and living like Christ; those who when they pray you just know God hears them; those who have eternal fruit flying off of them like crazy; those who are caring for the poor and sick and lost; those who are storing up treasure in heaven faster than anybody else - then I want in on it. I want to buy a share in their pile of treasure. (Matt. 10:41-42) I want to support them, urge them on and get out of their way. I want a stake in that eternal reward. And if I have a hot tip that's going to make me a fortune, I want to tell my friends and my family and my employees and even strangers on the bus!

Our search for who is the hottest stock led us first to Gospel For Asia (www.GFA.org), although we are now finding others and will seek to highlight them at every opportunity. For example, the native missionaries that GFA supports are amazing warriors of the faith, going out to hostile regions on a one way ticket with grim determination to win souls for Christ or die trying. They sleep on stone floors, live on one or two dollars a day, pray for hours, preach fearlessly and raise up mighty churches of fearless disciples - and when God thinks it will help, mighty miracles make their way easier. All for a total ministry cost of $1000 to $1500 per year in most cases.

Western missionaries sent through our denominational structures often cost $100,000 per year. Average investment in one missionary family can exceed $500,000 with an average time on the field of just three years. Many prepare and never go at all. Private schools or tutors for their kids, healthcare, retirement funds, furloughs, maids, chauffeurs, security guards, language training, internet access and more - may all be required costs for these. Not to mention the lost potential in ministry momentum of having to come back to fund-raise periodically. (I don't question the motives of the missionaries. I speak from experience here, having grown up in that life.) Even with all of this, foreign missions is less than 5% of total church spending. The rest we spend on our local programs, buildings and staffs.

Our website is just an expression of that yearning for stewardship and has become a place to educate about the HORRIBLE job we're doing in the American church of spending our dollars wisely to get maximum yield in Heaven. I urge you, test yourself, your company, your church, your denomination, your charities. What is their true yield in Heavenly treasure? Seek maximum profit in the eternal currency.

I want my family, my employees, you and your family and a thousand thousand other Brothers and Sisters to be in a giant receiving line where we get to kiss and hug the souls brought into heaven by the labor of those on the field that we supported from the blessings of our wealth. If Heaven is forever, I want that line to stretch farther than I can see. I want that line to last for YEARS.

The "Prosperity Gospel" ministries are right, they're living in their reward. This is it. Enjoy it while you can. What are those HUNDREDS OF MILLIONS of dollars per year their ministries are bringing in going to buy them in Heaven? What kind of accountability are we getting? How much is going to ministry and not their own pockets? What treasure in Heaven is being accumulated? Really needed that private jet and multi-million dollar house did they? Let's see what Jesus has to say about it when we all come to account. I pray urgently for them to have the heart of Zacchaeus before it's too late. Repent and make restitution.

As for me and my house, we'll invest in those who are living like Christ. GFA sends 100% of missions donations to evangelism on the field to the most unreached. Even the receptionist and the shipping guy have to volunteer or else raise their own salaries from personal supporters. MILLIONS of souls a year are being reached. Ten new churches planted every day.

Which one do YOU want a piece of?

Research the ministries. Be smart. Invest wisely. Demand accountability and efficiency. Visit www.ECFA.org and www.MinistryWatch.org. If they can't be trusted with the little things, they can't be trusted with the big things. Would Jesus of Nazareth drive a Bentley or a Rolls Royce? Have gold faucets in His bathroom? There are some serious wolves out there amongst the sheep.

Whether entrusted with a little or a lot, we'll all be called to account for our stewardship of God's blessings.

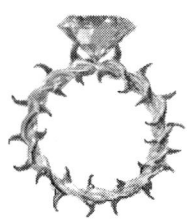

ARE YOU KIDDING ME?! SCARY STATS AND FACTS

This is a compilation of the scariest, most embarrassing, most shocking statistics and information about the Church and it's affairs. We don't quote anything haphazardly without having good documentation and sources. If you have stats that you think we need to hear, find the source material and email us.

(Mostly from World Christian Trends, William Carey Library, David Barrett & Todd Johnson, 2001. The summary and analysis of the annual Christian mega-census.) Available for purchase online or from our site.

Assets of the Church

- US Christians control TRILLIONS in assets while at any given time 200,000,000 Christians starve.

- 78 countries each have Great Commission (evangelical) Christians whose cumulative personal incomes exceed US$1 billion a year. (WCT, page 3, Table 1-1)

Financial Fraud in the Church

- Annual church embezzlements by top custodians exceed the entire cost of all foreign missions worldwide. Emboldened by lax procedures, trusted church treasurers are embezzling from the Church $5,500,000 PER DAY. That's $16,000,000,000 per YEAR! That's Billion - with a "B"! (WCT, page 3,

Table 1-1) {For reference: TOTAL Christian spending on foreign missions - $15 Billion. God forgive us!} (WCT, page 8, Table 1-4)

- Criminal penalties against clergy in sexual abuse cases now exceed $1 billion, causing a number of churches, dioceses, and even denominations to be forced into bankruptcy. (WCT, page 3, Table 1-1)

- Each year 600,000 full-time ordained workers (clergy,ministers,missionaries) reach retiring age; 150,000 then discover that their employers provide no old-age pensions. (WCT, page 3, Table 1-1)

Wasteful Spending by the Church

- Most Christian bodies insist on full accountability to the last cent in finance {But not very well. See above.}, but ignore or even decry statistics about Christian workers and ministries. (WCT, page 3)

- Less than 1% of Christian revenue is spent on evangelism to the most unreached. (WCT, page 81)

- 40% of the church's entire global foreign mission resources are being deployed to just 10 over-saturated countries already possessing strong citizen-run home ministries. (WCT, p. 3, Table 1-1)

- All costs of ministry divided by number of baptisms per year. Cost per baptism in India - $9803 per person. Cost per baptism in the United States - $1,550,000 per person. (WCT, page 520-529)

- Every year the churches hold a megacensus costing $1.1 billion, sending out 10 million questionnaires in 3,000 languages, which covers 180 major religious subjects. (WCT, page 3, Table 1-1)

- Christians spend more on the annual audits of their churches and agencies ($810 million) than on all their workers in the non-Christian world. (WCT, page 3, Table 1-1)

- The total cost of Christian outreach averages $330,000 for each and every newly baptized person. (USA $1,551,000, India $9,800, Mozambique $1,400, etc.) (WCT, page 3, Table 1-1 and pages 520 - 529)

- Non-Christian countries have been found to have 227 million Bibles in place in their midst, more than needed to serve all Christians, but poorly distributed. (WCT, page 3, Table 1-1)

- 91% of all Christian outreach/evangelism does not target non-Christians but targets other Christians in World C {>95 Evangelized, >60% Christian} countries, cities, peoples, populations, or situations. (WCT, page 81)

- Each year,180 million Bibles and New Testaments are wasted - lost, destroyed, or disintegrated - due to incompetence, hostility, bad planning, or inadequate manufacture. (WCT, page 3, Table 1-1)

- Books primarily about Jesus in today's libraries number 175,000 different titles in 500 languages, increasing by 4 newly published every day. As in all scientific research, 70% of all new Christian books and published articles will never be quoted in print by their peers, ever. (WCT, page 3, Table 1-1)

Persecution of the Church

- More than 70% of all Christians now live in countries where they are experiencing persecution. In some cases EXTREME persecution. (WCT, page 32)

- 14 million converted Hindus, Buddhists, and Muslims have opted to remain within those religions in order to witness for Christ as active believers in Jesus as Lord. (WCT, page 3, Table 1-1)

Growth of the Church

- From 3 million in AD 1500, evangelicals have grown to 648 million worldwide, 54% being Non-Whites. (WCT, page 3)

- The country with the fastest Christian expansion ever is China, now at 10,000 new converts every day. (WCT, page 3)

Missions and the Church

- Some 250 of the 300 largest international Christian organizations regularly mislead the Christian public by publishing demonstrably incorrect or falsified progress statistics. (WCT, page 3, Table 1-1)

- Christian triumphalism - not as pride in huge numbers, but as publicized self-congratulation - is rampant in most churches, agencies, and ministries. (WCT, page 3, Table 1-1)

- All costs of ministry divided by number of baptisms per year. Cost per baptism in India - $9803 per person. Cost per baptism in the United States - $1,550,000 per person. (WCT, pages 520-529)

- It costs Christians 700 times more money to baptize converts in rich World C countries (Switzerland) than in poor World A countries (Nepal). (WCT, pages 520-529)

- Percent of Christian resources in countries that are already more than 60% Christian - 91%. Percent spent in countries where less than half the people have EVER heard of Jesus - 0.03%. (WCT, page 81)

- It is estimated that Christians worldwide spend around $8 BILLION dollars PER YEAR going to the more than 500 conferences to TALK about missions. That's more than HALF the total spent DOING missions.

- Everywhere on Earth can now be targeted with at least 3 of the 45 varieties of effective evangelism. (WCT, page 3)

- 818 unevangelized ethnolinguistic peoples have never been targeted by any Christian agencies ever. (WCT, page 3)

- Over 20 centuries Christians have announced 1,500 global plans to evangelize the world; most failed; 250 plans focused on AD 2000 fell massively short of stated goals. (WCT, page 3, Table 1-1)

- Mainland China's Christians have thousands of trained workers poised to begin evangelizing the world de novo (all over again) soon after AD 2000. (WCT, page 3, Table 1-1)

- Regular listeners to Christian programs over secular or religious radio/TV stations rose from 22% of the world in 1980 to 30% in 2000. (WCT, page 3, Table 1-1)

- Out of 648 million Great Commission Christians, 70% have never been told about the world's 1.6 billion unevangelized individuals. (WCT, page 3, Table 1-1)

- The 3 least cost-effective countries over 1 million in population for Christian outreach are: Japan, Switzerland, Denmark. (WCT, page 3, Table 1-1 and pages 520-529)

- The 3 most cost-effective countries over 1 million in population for Christian outreach are: Mozambique, Ethiopia, Tanzania. (WCT, page 3, Table 1-1 and pages 520-529)

- Per hour of ministry, the 5 megapeoples most responsive to Christianity, Christ, and the gospel are: Khandeshi, Awadhi, Magadhi, Bai, Berar Marathi. (WCT, page 3, Table 1-1)

- Per hour of ministry, the 5 megapeoples least responsive to Christianity, Christ, and the gospel are: Swedish, Russian, Lithuanian, Polish, Georgian . (WCT, page 3, Table 1-1)

Denominations of the Church

- Currently there are over 33,000 Christian denominations in the United States. (37,000+ as of 2005!) (WCT, page 33)

- A huge new Christian nonconfessional megabloc, the Independents/Postdenominationalists, is growing rapidly and numbers 19% of all Christians. These 386 million Independents in 220 countries have no interest in and no use for historic denominationalist Christianity. (WCT, p.3, Table 1-1)

- From only one million in AD 1900, Pentecostals/ Charismatics/ Neocharismatics have mushroomed to 524 million affiliated (with unaffiliated believers, 602 million). (WCT, page 3, Table 1-1)

Martyrdom

- Over the last 20 centuries, and in all 238 countries, more than 70 million Christians have been martyred – killed, executed, murdered - for Christ. (WCT, page 3 and page 32)

- More Christians have been martyred in the last 100 years than all years since AD 30 combined. (WCT page 32)

Global Population Issues

- Despite BILLIONS of dollars spent by dozens of denominations toward over a hundred major programs to fulfill the Great Commission by the year 2000, we didn't even keep up with population growth, much less reach the 2 billion unreached. (WCT, page 3) Evidently no apologies are forthcoming for the giant waste of assets and broken promises.

- 124 million new souls begin life on Earth each year, but Christianity's 4,000 foreign mission agencies baptize only 4 million new persons a year. (WCT, page 3, Table 1-1)

- Since AD 1900,Christian urbanites have exploded from 100 million in 500 cities to 1,160 million in 5,000 cities. (WCT, page 3, Table 1-1)

Unreached Peoples

- Out of 648 million Great Commission Christians, 70% have never been told about world's 1.6 billion unevangelized individuals. (WCT, page 3, Table 1-1)

- There are thousands of language groups who do not have a SINGLE page of the Bible in their language.

- 98.7% of people have access to scripture in 6,700 languages leaving 78 million in 6,800 languages with no access at all. (WCT, page 44)

- The majority of the unreached people groups are in countries that are restricted access. Western missionaries may not even be able to get to them. (WCT, page 3, Table 1-1)

- Despite Christ's command to evangelize, 67% of all humans from AD 30 to the present day have never even heard of his name. (WCT, page 3, Table 1-1)

- 648 million Christians today (called Great Commission Christians) are active in Christ's world mission; 1,352 million Christians ignore this mission. (WCT, page 3, Table 1-1)

- Organized Christianity has total contact with 3,590 religions but no contact at all with 353 other religions and their over 500 million adherents. (WCT, page 3, Table 1-1)

Micro-Lending Stats

- We can help a Brother or Sister start a business in India with a loan of as little as $25.

Had Enough Yet? It gets worse! We're stuffing the Fattest and starving the Hungriest!

KEY:

World A are the 38 countries that are primarily unevangelized. <50% unreached (1.6 Billion souls). Mostly Asia and North Africa - often called the 10/40 Window.

World B are the 59 countries evangelized by not converted. >50% reached but <60% Christian (2.9 billion souls)

World C are the 141 countries primarily or predominantly Christian already. >95% Evangelized and >60% Christian (2 billion souls) These are mostly the "West" - North, Central and South America, Europe, Southern Africa, and Australia.

Broadcasting (radio/TV) per year - Total spend $5.8 Billion	Finance (church/agency) per yr – Total spend $270 Billion
World A - $6 Million (0.01%)	World A - $188M (0.01%)
World B - $226M (3.9%)	World B - $1,370M (5.1%)
World C - $5,568M (96.0%)	World C - $256 **Billion** (94.8%)
Foreign Missions Money per year – Total spend $15 Billion	**Scripture distribution per year – Total 4,600 million pieces**
World A - $250M (1.7%)	World A - 20 Million (0.4%)
World B - $1,750M (11.7%)	World B - 680M (14.5%)
World C - $13,000M (86.6%)	World C - 3,900M (84.8%)

(Plus 11 other scales that all look about the same. Tracts, Scripture languages, Literature, Periodicals, Computers, Full-time workers, Computer users, Foreign Missionaries, Home Missionaries, Lay leadership. WCT, page 55.)

Keep reading, there's more – and it's worse.

The Open Letter of Apology to the World

From Page 80 - "Where should foreign missionaries work?" **& Page 520** - "A comparative listing of 6-instrument Great Commission Instrument Panels for the globe's 77 largest countries, each with over 10 million population."

Canada (total population 31,147,000)
Unevangelized - 2.2%
Evangelized but non-Christian - 18.3%
Christian (of one sort or another) - 79.5%
  (self-described, includes Catholics)
Evangelization percent - 97.8%
Evangelistic offers per person per year - 331
Cost effectiveness (Cost per baptism) $1,189,000

USA (total population 278,357,00)
Unevangelized - 1.5%
Evangelized but non-Christian - 13.8%
Christian (of one sort or another) - 84.7%
Evangelization percent - 98.5%
Offers per person per year - 368
Cost effectiveness (Cost per baptism) $1,551,000

Australia (total population 18,880,000)
Unevangelized - 1.6%
Evangelized but non-Christian - 19.1%
Christian (of one sort or another) - 79.3%
Evangelization percent - 98%
Offers per person per year - 336
Cost effectiveness (Cost per baptism) $1,104,000

Japan (total population 126,714,000)
Unevangelized - 33.1%
Evangelized but non-Christian - 63.3%
Christian (of one sort or another) - 3.6%
Evangelization percent - 60%
Offers per person per year - 6
Cost effectiveness (Cost per baptism) $2,721,000

Germany (total population 82,220,000)
Unevangelized - 2.4%
Evangelized but non-Christian - 21.8%
Christian (of one sort or another) - 75.8%
Evangelization percent - 97%
Offers per person per year - 381
Cost effectiveness (Cost per baptism) $2,119,000

Mexico (total population 98,881,000)
Unevangelized - 0.2%
Evangelized but non-Christian - 3.5%
Christian (of one sort or another) - 96.3%
Evangelization percent - 99.8%
Offers per person per year - 560
Cost effectiveness (Cost per baptism) $147,100

But what about the "poor" countries? What kind of cost effectiveness per dollar do we see there?

India (total population 1,013,662,000)
Unevangelized - 40.7%
Evangelized but non-Christian - 53.1%
Christian (of one sort or another) - 6.2%
Evangelization percent - 59.3%
Offers per person per year - 13
Cost effectiveness (Cost per baptism) $9,800

China (total population 1,262,557,000)
Unevangelized - 35.2%
Evangelized but non-Christian - 57.7%
Christian (of one sort or another) - 7.1%
Evangelization percent - 64.8%
Offers per person per year - 16
Cost effectiveness (Cost per baptism) $15,800

Indonesia (total population 212,107,000)
Unevangelized - 37.2%
Evangelized but non-Christian - 49.7%
Christian (of one sort or another) - 13.1%
Evangelization percent - 62.8%
Offers per person per year - 29
Cost effectiveness (Cost per baptism) $40,800

Afghanistan (total population 22,720,000)
Unevangelized - 70.4%
Evangelized but non-Christian - 29.6%
Christian (of one sort or another) - 0.1%
Evangelization percent - 29.7%
Offers per person per year - < 1
Cost effectiveness (Cost per baptism) $30,400

Cambodia (total population 11,168,000)

Unevangelized - 50.9%
Evangelized but non-Christian - 48.0%
Christian (of one sort or another) - 1.1%
Evangelization percent - 49.1%
Offers per person per year - 1
Cost effectiveness (Cost per baptism) $4,300

Bangladesh (total population 129,155,000)

Unevangelized - 42.8%
Evangelized but non-Christian - 56.5%
Christian (of one sort or another) - 0.7%
Evangelization percent - 57.2%
Offers per person per year - 1
Cost effectiveness (Cost per baptism) $7,200

These stats from "An AD 2001 reality check: 50 new facts and figures about trends and issues concerning empirical global Christianity today." (from Table 1-1 and elsewhere in World Christian Trends, William Carey Library, David Barrett & Todd Johnson.)

REALLY SCARY SCRIPTURES

Is your heart so hard that you can't see our own guilt? Does the Word of God stand against you?

Jeremiah 5:26-31 (all NIV) - 26 "Among my people are wicked men who lie in wait like men who snare birds and like those who set traps to catch men. 27 Like cages full of birds, their houses are full of deceit; they have become rich and powerful 28 and have grown fat and sleek. Their evil deeds have no limit; they do not plead the case of the fatherless to win it, they do not defend the rights of the poor. 29 Should I not punish them for this?" declares the LORD . "Should I not avenge myself on such a nation as this? **30 "A horrible and shocking thing has happened in the land: 31 The prophets prophesy lies, the priests rule by their own authority, and my people love it this way. But what will you do in the end?**

Jeremiah 6:16-17 - 16 This is what the LORD says: "Stand at the crossroads and look; ask for the ancient paths, **ask where the good way is, and walk in it, and you will find rest for your souls.** But you said, 'We will not walk in it.' 17 I appointed watchmen over you and said, 'Listen to the sound of the trumpet!' But you said, 'We will not listen.'

Luke 6:24-26 - But woe to you who are rich, for you have already received your comfort. Woe to you who are well fed now, for you will go hungry. Woe to you who laugh now, for you will mourn and weep. Woe to you when all men speak well of you, for that is how their fathers treated the false prophets.

Matthew 19:21-24 - Jesus answered, "If you want to be perfect, go, sell your possessions and give to the poor, and you will have treasure in heaven. Then come, follow me." When the young man heard this, he went away sad, because he had great wealth. Then Jesus said to his disciples, "I tell you the truth, it is hard for a rich man to enter the kingdom of heaven. Again I tell you, it is easier for a camel to go through the eye of a needle than for a rich man to enter the kingdom of God."

I Timothy 6:21 - Command those who are rich in this present world not to be arrogant nor to put their hope in wealth, which is so uncertain, but to put their hope in God, who richly provides us with everything for our enjoyment. Command them to do good, to be rich in good deeds, and to be generous and willing to share. In this way they will lay up treasure for themselves as a firm foundation for the coming age, so that they may take hold of the life that is truly life.

I Timothy 4:1-2, 6 - The Spirit clearly says that in later times some will abandon the faith and follow deceiving spirits and things taught by demons. Such teachings come through hypocritical liars, whose consciences have been seared as with a hot iron. If you point these things out to the brothers, you will be a good minister of Christ Jesus, brought up in the truths of the faith and of the good teaching that you have followed.

II Timothy 3:1-5 - But mark this: There will be terrible times in the last days. People will be lovers of themselves, lovers of money, boastful, proud, abusive, disobedient to their parents, ungrateful, unholy, without love, unforgiving, slanderous, without self-control, brutal, not lovers of the good, treacherous, rash, conceited, lovers of pleasure rather than lovers of God --- having a form of godliness, but denying its power. Have nothing to do with them.

Luke 12:15-21 - Then he said to them, "Watch out! Be on your guard against all kinds of greed; a man's life does not consist in the abundance of his possessions." And he told them this parable: "The ground of a certain rich man produced a good crop. He thought to himself, 'What shall I do? I have no place to store my crops.' "Then he said, 'This is what I'll do. I will tear down my barns and build bigger ones, and there I will store all my grain and my goods. 19 And I'll say to myself, "You have plenty of good things laid up for many years. Take life easy; eat, drink and be merry." ' "But God said to him, 'You fool! This very night your life will be demanded from you. Then who will get what you have prepared for yourself?' "This is how it will be with anyone who stores up things for himself but is not rich toward God."

Micah 7 - 1 What misery is mine! I am like one who gathers summer fruit at the gleaning of the vineyard; there is no cluster of grapes to eat, none of the early figs that I crave. **2 The godly have been swept from the land; not one upright man remains. All men lie in wait to shed blood; each hunts his brother with a net. 3 Both hands are skilled in doing evil; the ruler demands gifts, the judge accepts bribes, the powerful dictate what they desire- they all conspire together. 4 The best of them is like a brier, the most upright worse than a thorn hedge. The day of your watchmen has come, the day God visits you. Now is the time of their confusion. 5 Do not trust a neighbor; put no confidence in a friend. Even with her who lies in your embrace be careful of your words. 6 For a son dishonors his father, a daughter rises up against her mother, a daughter-in-law against her mother in-law - a man's enemies are the members of his own household. 7 But as for me, I watch in hope for the LORD , I wait for God my Savior; my God will hear me.** 8 Do not gloat over me, my enemy! Though I have fallen, I will rise. Though I sit in darkness, the LORD will be my light. **9 Because I have sinned against him, I will bear the LORD's wrath, until he pleads my case and establishes my right. He will bring me out into the light; I will see his righteousness.** 10 Then my enemy will see it and will be covered with shame, she who said to me, "Where is the LORD your God?" My eyes will see her downfall; even now she will be trampled underfoot like mire in the streets. 11 The day for building your walls will come, the day for extending your boundaries. 12 In that day people will come to you from Assyria and the cities of Egypt, even from Egypt to the Euphrates and from sea to sea and from mountain to mountain. 13 The earth will become desolate because of its inhabitants, as the result of their deeds. 14 Shepherd your people with your staff, the flock of your inheritance, which lives by itself in a forest, in fertile pasturelands. Let them feed in Bashan and Gilead as in days long ago. **15 "As in the days when you came out of Egypt, I will show them my wonders." 16 Nations will see and be ashamed, deprived of all their power. They will lay their hands on their mouths and their ears will become deaf. 17 They will lick dust like a snake, like creatures that crawl on the ground. They will come trembling out of their dens; they will turn in fear to the LORD our God and will be afraid of you. 18 Who is a God like you, who pardons sin and forgives the transgression of the remnant of his inheritance? You do not stay angry forever but delight to show mercy. 19 You will again have compassion on us; you will tread our sins underfoot and hurl all our iniquities into the depths of the sea. 20 You will be true to Jacob, and show mercy to Abraham, as you pledged on oath to our fathers in days long ago.**

Ezekiel 9 - 1 Then I heard him call out in a loud voice, "Bring the guards of the city here, each with a weapon in his hand." 2 And I saw six men coming from the direction of the upper gate, which faces north, each with a deadly weapon in his hand. With them was a man clothed in linen who had a writing kit at his side. They came in and stood beside the bronze altar. 3 Now the glory of the God of Israel went up from above the cherubim, where it had been, and moved to the threshold of the temple. Then the LORD called to the man clothed in linen who had the writing kit at his side 4 and said to him, **"Go throughout the city of Jerusalem and put a mark on the foreheads of those who grieve and lament over all the detestable things that are done in it."** 5 As I listened, he said to the others, **"Follow him through the city and kill, without showing pity or compassion. 6 Slaughter old men, young men and maidens, women and children, but do not touch anyone who has the mark. Begin at my sanctuary."** So they began with the elders who were in front of the temple. 7 Then he said to them, "Defile the temple and fill the courts with the slain. Go!" So they went out and began killing throughout the city. 8 While they were killing and I was left alone, I fell facedown, crying out, "Ah, Sovereign LORD! Are you going to destroy the entire remnant of Israel in this outpouring of your wrath on Jerusalem?" 9 He answered me, **"The sin of the house of Israel and Judah is exceedingly great; the land is full of bloodshed and the city is full of injustice. They say, 'The LORD has forsaken the land; the LORD does not see.' 10 So I will not look on them with pity or spare them, but I will bring down on their own heads what they have done."** 11 Then the man in linen with the writing kit at his side brought back word, saying, "I have done as you commanded."

Jeremiah 51:11-13 - 11 "Sharpen the arrows, take up the shields! The LORD has stirred up the kings of the Medes, because his purpose is to destroy Babylon. The LORD will take vengeance, vengeance for his temple. 12 Lift up a banner against the walls of Babylon! Reinforce the guard, station the watchmen, prepare an ambush! The LORD will carry out his purpose, his decree against the people of Babylon. 13 **You who live by many waters and are rich in treasures, your end has come, the time for you to be cut off.**

{Connect this with Revelations 18, the destruction of Babylon. Which many believe to mean America.}

There's lots more! Read Hosea. That'll scare you!! Or Ezekiel.

They're not just about the nation of Israel –
they apply to America, to the Church, to your town, to YOU!

Anytime someone does Bad Behavior X, they should expect Punishment Y as a result.

Well, whatever Israel did to bring on God's judgement – the Church of America is doing X times 1000!!

We should expect God to react NOW the same as He did THEN.

Quick Thought

Our Father, who art in heaven, hallowed be Thy Name.

Thy kingdom come, thy will be done, on earth as it is in heaven.

Give us this day our daily bread.

And forgive us our trespasses as we forgive those who trespass against us.

And lead us not into temptation, but deliver us from evil.

For thine is the kingdom and the power and the glory, forever. Amen.

We want His kingdom to come, right?

And we want what happens in heaven to happen on earth, right?

So ... how many <u>denominations</u> are there in heaven?

I don't think we could even have denominations if we were forgiving trespasses.

We must have been praying this wrong because His will isn't being done, our daily bread depends on bank loans, we're not forgiving trespasses and He's probably not forgiving US. We're certainly being tempted and I think we've been delivered TO evil - on a silver platter.

Oh! Maybe this is where it happened!

**Somebody in the church must be praying:
"Mine is the Kingdom, Mine is the Power, Mine is the Glory, forever."**

That could be it. I'm pretty sure God isn't happy about this.

Could we stop it now?

Maybe say we're sorry?

That'd be nice.

WHAT EXACTLY IS THE "GREAT COMMISSION"?

This term is applied to the final command of Jesus just before He ascended into heaven following His resurrection. It is the command to not just go and evangelize, but to train and prepare and an assurance that when you do it HIS way, signs and wonders will follow.

Depending on which passage you use and which version of the Bible, it goes like this:

> Matthew 28:18-20 (NIV) – *Then Jesus came to them and said, "All authority in heaven and on earth has been given to me. Therefore go and make disciples of all nations, baptizing them in the name of the Father, and of the Son and of the Holy Spirit, and teaching them to obey everything I have commanded you. And surely I am with you always, to the very end of the age."*

> Mark 16:15-18, 20 (NIV) – *He said to them, "Go into all the world and preach the good news to all creation. Whoever believes and is baptized will be saved, but whoever does not believe will be condemned. And these signs will accompany those who believe: In my name they will drive out demons; they will speak in new tongues; they will pick up snakes with their hands; and when they drink deadly poison, it will not hurt them at all; they will place their hands on sick people, and they will get well." Then the disciples went out and preached everywhere, and the Lord worked with them and confirmed his word by the signs that accompanied it.*

So ... is the "church" in America really doing it right? If so, are signs and wonders like this following? For the amount of time and money and people involved, we ought to be getting some really astounding miracles, right? Seems to me this is a guarantee.

IF Jesus wasn't kidding around, THEN He was just sure that if we did it HIS way there would be some surprising results. In America we are "evangelizing" all the time, but who are we reaching and what are we preaching? It would sure be a shame if we looked back and realized that we haven't really been doing it His way this whole time! What a waste of time, energy, money, lives and more importantly, souls, that would turn out to be! Seems like we ought to take every precaution to make sure we're on track.

I find that sometimes it's helpful to point out the reverse of an argument. For example: "IF dogs are man's best friend - and cats are not dogs, THEN cats are not man's best friend." Or like this: "Jesus never lied, so IF Jesus said big things would happen when we went out in His name - and big things aren't happening, THEN maybe we're not going out in His name."

Hmmm. Could that be? Are we preaching another Jesus? He said that if we loved Him and we were OF Him we would obey all His commandments - the last and greatest of which was the Great Commission. It's not the "Get-Around-To-It-Eventually Commission" or the "Leftover-10%-of-Budget Commission" or the "Somebody-Else-Can-Do-It Commission". It's the GREAT Commission and it applies to EVERY individual. There is no escape clause, there are no loopholes, there is no avoiding it and still claiming to be a Christ-like Christian if you ignore it and don't obey His command.

Maybe we're not doing it right. Should at least be worthy of some serious discussion, right? I mean, just if you want to please God and keep from being a Goat at the final judgement.

Here are some things that Jesus <u>NEVER</u> said to do:

- Go into all the world and build big buildings.

- Go into all the world and entertain the Christians.
- Go into all the world and ask the world for money.
- Go divide up into factions and constantly argue with each other.
- Go find people you can pay to go into all the world so you don't have to tell anyone yourself.
- Go into all the world that's easy to get to and will let you in without too much hassle.
- Go and elevate certain men above all the others and listen to them more than you listen to Me.
- Go into all the world and set up really excellent child-care programs.
- Go into all the world and see what you can learn from them about how to influence people.
- Go into all the world and identify the target demographic segment that will grow your church the fastest and then just focus on them.
- Go into all the world and find out what their gods have in common with your God and play to that.
- Go get an education so you'll be thoroughly prepared by the theories and programs of Man before you go do what Jesus commanded.
- Go into all the world and use sports leagues and antique car shows as a "low-impact" outreach tool.
- Go into all the world and build relationships for years before you can figure out how to work into a conversation the hard truth about their sinfulness and need for repentance.
- Go into all the world and preach the Tithe and that the people are stealing from God if they don't give you their 10%. (So you can spend it on things on this list.)
- Go into all the world and make as much money as you can so that you can give it to the Pastors and Priests and then you'll be blessed for your faith.
- Go into all the world and ignore all the poor people, recruit all the rich people, and then spend 90+% of all the revenue on yourself and your own comforts. Oh, and let people inside your organization steal 5%. (see Scary Stats)
- Go into all the world and learn to be just like them.
- Go into all the world and put them under "Law" instead of "Grace".

Maybe it's time we started doing it HIS way for a change.

HUMAN SACRIFICE IN THE CHRISTIAN CHURCH

In the Old Testament there are lots of stories about the followers of Baal or Marduk or one god or another offering human sacrifices (and how unhappy about it Jehovah gets). Sometimes to please their gods so that they would have a good harvest or some other reason related to a hope for prosperity or blessing. They would get a virgin (or a baby) and sacrifice them on a stone altar in the hopes of some future comfort. They didn't lie about it. Everybody knew that was the plan. Even the virgin. At least the prophets of Baal had the decency to tell the virgin what they were doing and why. Maybe they even thanked her and threw a party before spilling her blood. That would be nice.

In America, the Christian church (as a whole) is much less honest. You see, we are saying that we care for the sick and poor and unreached, but what we're actually doing with our time and resources shows that we mean the exact opposite of that. We're knowingly letting them die so that we can have bounty and be comfy. And since we say we love them and we care about their eternal souls, not just their body, our insulting double-talk is amazingly more offensive! We average just 2% in giving and of that money ($250 Billion), we spend over 95% of it on ourselves. Less than 0.01% reaches the most unreached.

That's why the World is really irritated with us, because we're telling them we care and then we're spending our money on ourselves. Go read the Scary Stats again. Everything is exactly upside down of what we would be doing if we REALLY cared for those whom Jesus cared for most.

Put another way, in order for us to maintain our lush lifestyles (individually and as churches) we have to short-change God THEN we have to divert even the bulk of THAT back to ourselves as well.

Maybe a little parable will help. Jesus seemed to like those.

> Imagine your only child has a tumor. He's just a little kid, say seven years old. He's in the hospital, he's in a lot of pain, he's hooked up to all these machines, he desperately needs treatment, but it's going to cost $250,000 and you don't have any insurance. You, your wife and your friends and family help out and donate money, maybe you even have a telethon. It's a good thing that he looks good in the pictures, because that really helps. People all over are praying for you and sending their $10 and $20 bills in to help. They can just sense from your passion that that this is critically important to you to save this beautiful kid that you love so much. Tears are shed by all. You really mean well and it's all pure and sacrificial.

> And it turns out you meet your goal!! The full $250,000 is provided!

> But then something inside snaps. Probably because of the big pile of cash you are completely unused to. So you take 95% off the top as administrative costs and go buy a fancy new car, a chandelier, new cushions for your furniture, new carpet, maybe build onto the house, get some new suits -- and you hand the doctors $12,500. Well it turns out that wasn't nearly enough, so you decide to keep raising money until that 5% can add up to the $250,000 you need to save his life. So at that rate, you're going to have to raise $5,000,000 to keep him alive. So you go back out with your plea for more money. You raise up more volunteers, take more pictures of him, maybe testimonials about how the people that helped him feel so good about themselves, maybe you spend a little more money jazzing up the materials you're mailing out. Shoot, you might even hire a consultant. And your wife is getting REALLY good at crying on cue.

> At first you try not to make a big deal about all the stuff you bought because you don't want to have to explain it to people. But after a while you get this great new idea. If you tell them that the money you spent on yourself is God's evidence that you are blessed, then you can assert more strongly that they should support you so that THEY can share in YOUR blessing. I know it sounds completely crazy ... but you know, it just might work. People are greedy and selfish and they don't always see the big picture. Namely that it's THEIR money you're being blessed with and your kid is still getting sicker.

I mean, it's clear to everyone that he's in immediate danger and you're not. At some point, folks are going to start catching on because it's fairly likely that if you're this far down that road, you're going to just get more and more over the top. It's just a matter of time until you get your own jet plane and buy more houses for yourself and a stretch limousine and spend thousands on clothes and jewelry. Why not? I mean, this thing might go on forever if you can just reach enough people that haven't already figured it out. And if it happens that your kid dies because you never do get him the money, well that just makes you even more pitiful and brings more sympathy (that is, cash). Then you can go find somebody else's kid that's in the hospital and try it again. Now you're an "advocate."

At some point you start to wonder how this would play in other countries. Even if they don't have as much money, it's just a math problem - just a matter of how many people you can get to listen. I mean there are suckers all over the world. Why not give it a try?

So, what about the kid? Can you call that anything other than human sacrifice? Who's responsible for his death? The parents? Surely. There will be much darkness and crying and gnashing of teeth at the final judgement. But what about the people that sent in money? Surely they were just taken for a ride. It can't be THEIR fault. Except that, there is that part about how we're supposed to be good stewards of our money and give without thought of receiving. A lot of those folks sent in their money SO THAT they would be blessed financially. That can't possibly be a Biblically pure motive. Can it? I mean, it's not their fault they didn't ask any questions about how the money was being spent. Yeah, they were a little suspicious, but these are People of God up there on stage. They wouldn't rip us off, would they? I mean, they've got a best selling book out.

Oh, I'm sorry, you're not a part of that whole craziness? You saw right through those guys on the first try? You're just Joe Average American going to a nice quiet church and doing the right things? OK, well, let's try this. How much of your stuff do you think belongs to God? I mean, if you say He's LORD and all, that should mean He's the Master and King and you owe Him everything, right? OK, so how are you spending God's money personally?

Odds are pretty good you're spending about 50% of your income on discretionary products - stuff you didn't absolutely need. God's not asking you to starve to death. He loves us and wants us to be happy and content, but He's not really after making us fat and lazy. Where's all that stuff you're buying coming from? What did it take to get it to you at the low, low, one-time only sale prices you paid for it. (I mean, you did shop around, right?)

Ever consider this? Revelation 18:10-13 (ESV)

"Alas! Alas! You great city, you mighty city, Babylon! For in a single hour your judgment has come." And the merchants of the earth weep and mourn for her, since no one buys their cargo anymore, cargo of gold, silver, jewels, pearls, fine linen, purple cloth, silk, scarlet cloth, all kinds of scented wood, all kinds of articles of ivory, all kinds of articles of costly wood, bronze, iron and marble, cinnamon, spice, incense, myrrh, frankincense, wine, oil, fine flour, wheat, cattle and sheep, horses and chariots, and slaves, that is, human souls."

Get it? Do you know what it COSTS for merchants around the world to get that stuff made and bring it here? It costs HUMAN SOULS. How many are having the life sucked out of them in factories around the world so that we can have STUFF? Children, prisoners, widows - Christians in prison even! Ever think of that? That you might go buy a "Made in China" bible cover or cross necklace and it's being made by Chinese pastors in prison who have to work 16 hour days making stuff like that in order to earn dinner? That's just the kind of thing the enemy would have them doing, too. It's happening. Don't think it's not.

Think hard. Are you sure this is what Christ wanted? I mean it's all His stuff right? Or did you not mean "Lord" that way? How many questions are you asking?

THE BOTTOM LINE

"Command those who are rich in this present world not to be arrogant nor to put their hope in wealth, which is so uncertain, but to put their hope in God, who richly provides us with everything for our enjoyment. Command them to do good, to be rich in good deeds, and to be generous and willing to share. In this way they will lay up treasure for themselves as a firm foundation for the coming age, so that they may take hold of the life that is truly life." - I Tim. 6:21

If you want to put your finger on what's wrong with the church in American today, just follow the money. Always follow the money.

See ... God gave a businessman a successful business and much money. God gave the man savvy and shrewdness and management skills. God taught him how to be a good steward and build something strong. God placed him in a church where he could contribute his talents and skills.

Then ... the businessman checked his brain at the door and handed over all his treasure to those LEAST educated and trained in the management of money. They have no experience with it and it's potential dangers. But they've got a seminary degree. So before you know it, they offer to let the businessman put his name on the new wing, they spend his money like crazy on any fool program that looks like fun and their other pastor buddies are doing, and if they're really lucky and play by the rules, they get offered a chance to go do the same stuff at a church with twice as many businessmen.

Who is God going to hold most responsible? Clearly the pastor is guilty for not leading the sheep correctly and maybe even for harming them and being prideful. But to some degree he's just doing what he was trained to do and learned in seminary.

But the businessman was given many gifts and he didn't ask ANY of the questions he had been trained to ask of a business venture looking to spend his capital. He didn't ask about Return On Investment or look to cut back or contain costs like he would in his own business. Particularly if you're trying to be Christ-like. The largest waste of useable space in this country is all the big buildings being used a few hours a day, twice a week!

Businessmen didn't go to seminary, but they can interpret the model of Christ and his hope for us same as anyone else. Businessmen should be able to prioritize and meet urgent needs and problem-solve and be entrepreneurial – or at least think about risk-management. But they haven't been, even though they're Chairman of the Deacons and head of the Finance Committee (all worldly structures, by the way). Mostly they've just been checking their brains at the door for years.

I think consciously or subconsciously the reason American Christians only tithe 2% is because they know that if they were obedient and gave FIVE times as much there would be gold plated mega churches on every corner and every pastor would have his own TV show. There'd be Jesus theme parks in every big town. Everything EXCEPT raw, effective evangelism and care for those in most need.

I can't begin to tell you how badly we've managed the money. It's awful, AWFUL! Horrifyingly bad. I'm still just trying to get my head around how bad it is. It's no wonder the secular world hates us. We're all hypocrites of the highest order. More than any other part of the church anywhere ever! The Catholic Church during the Inquisition wasn't as bad! For what we could have been with our blessings, we've let hundreds of millions of souls go to hell and millions of Brothers and Sisters starve to death. So that we could have padded pews and new carpet.

I know of one Evangelical church (that believes in the imminent return of Christ) with a chandelier that cost $1,000,000!! The pastor didn't pay for it out of HIS pocket! It was the folks with the big money that played along. They're going to have to account for the decisions they made as stewards of God's blessings. When they "stand" before Jesus to account they're going to be wishing they could get UNDER the ground.

I'm telling you flat out, the folks that did the worst damage need to be crushed - and then they need to go see to it that the church changes it's ways. Look at it the other way - if you DON'T get the businessman to repent, he'll see to it that they find another pastor before he'll give up the shiny buildings he donated.

Until they are a great crushing weight pressing against the souls of the guilty, the massive piles of money in this country will not be liberated to go be a blessing to the unreached, the widows, and the orphans as we're commanded. We'll never live according the the model of Jesus and we'll always be hypocrites. There's going to be some serious heart-crying when this message finally sinks in. We have a lot to atone for.

Clear enough?

(Luke 12:13-21, Luke 14:8-14, James 5:1-6, I Timothy 6, I Corin. 4:6-21, 2 Corin. 8:1-15, 2 Corin. 9:6-15, and more!)

Musical Interlude - Feel free to sing along

ALL to Jesus I surrender; **ALL** to him I freely give; I will ever love and trust him, in his presence daily live.

I surrender **ALL**, I surrender **ALL**, **ALL** to thee, my blessed Savior, I surrender **ALL**.

ALL to Jesus I surrender; humbly at his feet I bow, worldly pleasures **ALL** forsaken; take me, Jesus, take me now.

I surrender **ALL**, I surrender **ALL**, **ALL** to thee, my blessed Savior, I surrender **ALL**.

ALL to Jesus I surrender; make me, Savior, wholly thine;
fill me with thy love and power; truly know that thou art mine.

I surrender **ALL**, I surrender **ALL**, **ALL** to thee, my blessed Savior, I surrender **ALL**.

ALL to Jesus I surrender; now I feel the sacred flame. O the joy of full salvation! Glory, glory, to his name!

I surrender **ALL**, I surrender **ALL**, **ALL** to thee, my blessed Savior, I surrender **ALL**.

What EXACTLY did you think "ALL" meant?!

Read Matt 22:37, Mark 12:30, Luke 10:27. That's a lot of "ALL's"!

How about Proverbs 3:5-6. *"Lean not on your own understanding but in ALL your ways acknowledge Him and HE will direct your paths."*

Which part of your own understand should you keep leaning on? How much 'joy of full salvation' and 'sacred flame' do you get to feel if you surrender SOME? Who do you think you're lying to? He knows the difference. You can't hide from God!

Read Acts 5:1-11. Ananias and Saphira said 'ALL' and meant 'Some'. Very bad idea. Very bad.

Next time, sing it like you mean it ALL the way.

Or you might just drop dead for surrendering SOME.

BREAD AND CIRCUSES

I've long been aware of this and what it means and how satan uses it to take over a culture. America has been substantially co-opted already by this ancient Roman strategy. In fact, I think it predates Rome since it's a ploy of the enemy and you can see evidence of it being used to destroy cultures and distract people all the way back to the Garden of Eden.

Here are some references so you can look it up on your own.

This phrase originates in Satire X of the Roman poet Juvenal of the late 1st and early 2nd centuries CE. In context, the Latin phrase *panem et circenses* (bread and circuses) is given as the only remaining cares of a Roman populace which has given up its birthright of political freedom:
> .. Already long ago, from when we sold our vote to no man, the People have abdicated our duties; for the People who once upon a time handed out military command, high civil office, legions - everything, now restrains itself and anxiously hopes for just two things: **bread and circuses** (Juvenal, Satire 10.77-81)

Juvenal here makes reference to the elite Roman practice of providing free wheat to some poor Romans as well as costly circus games and other forms of entertainment as a means gaining political power through popularity. The Dictionary of Cultural Literacy (1993) states that Juvenal displayed his contempt for the declining heroism of his contemporary Romans in this passage. Spanish intellectuals between the 19th and 20th centuries complained about the similar *pan y toros* ("bread and bull[fight]s").
(http://en.wikipedia.org/wiki/Bread_and_circuses)

The American Heritage® Dictionary of the English Language (Fourth Edition. 2000) defines "bread and circuses" as a plural noun meaning "Offerings, such as benefits or entertainments, intended to placate discontent or distract attention from a policy or situation.
http://www.bartleby.com/61/39/B0463950.html

There was a day before God scrubbed it all out of me that I was quite the political junkie and conspiracy theory nut. In that age, I watched Bill O"Reilly regularly. I didn't remember it, but when I did a web search on this topic, this artice that he wrote for World Net Daily came up. It illustrates the situation in America pretty well.
http://www.worldnetdaily.com/news/article.asp?ARTICLE_ID=21781

I'm not writing this as a condemnation of America – it is Rome and it does what Rome does, which is dumb down the populace by keeping them entertained, protecting the food supply and making sure they feel safe and patriotic. That way, they won't notice that the whole Empire is crumbling around them and a small number of elites are running the show without oversight or accountability.

Only 50% of America has enough motivation to get up off their sofas once every four years and vote for president! I hope you can understand that by feeding us an endless stream of NFL and NASCAR and WWE Wrestling and thousands of cable stations and porn and video games and concerts and cell phones and the internet and endless diversions and holidays and parades and games, we are left in a state of such continuous motion and input overload that we never can focus on the important things. And as long as there is food and drink on the shelves at the grocery store, the TV works and most of the people we know have jobs, why worry? We're the greatest nation on earth. What could happen? We're the only super power left, right?

Was that condemning? I didn't really mean it to be, that's just the "world" being the "world" and doing what it does – which is obey satan.

I've long seen the application of this and the danger of it and the insidious way it which it distracts people and is used as part of the dangerous dialectic drumbeat to get our focus away from the important things. Americans are suckers for "bread and circuses". Can there be any doubt?

Here's the real point of this writing.

One day, I'm just minding my own business, driving in the car and God just plops this phrase into my head.

"Bread and circuses."

"OK, yeah, I know what that is, Lord, what's the point?"

"That's what the church is doing."

Then it just all hit me like a giant tidal wave and I almost slammed on the brakes. As I recall, I pulled over to the shoulder of the highway in tears.

"OH! GOD!!! They TOTALLY ARE!! They totally are! It's all about the shows and the food!! They're keeping them entertained, engaging them in so many things so fast that they can't slow down. They're keeping them fat and comfy so they won't notice that they are blind and naked and wretched and poor! Oh, God! I'm so sorry! Please forgive us! We're not really addressing their spirit at all, just their brain and their body! They can't slow down long enough to even pray! Please forgive us. Please fix it. Please crush that out of Your true church. Please make them stop! Oh, my God! I'm so sorry!"

And on like that for about a half hour until He told me to stop. Lots of crying when it all crystallized. I have understood for a long time how devastatingly dangerous this strategy is and how it can totally co-opt a nation, but I'd never made the leap and seen how the enemy of our souls had inserted it so thoroughly into the whole of the church of America. Can there be any doubt? Are we not the most overstimulated, overfed, spiritually starving people on the planet? Even getting a church member to slow down long enough to be introspective about the true state of their soul and their salvation is a miracle in itself!

We told them that they were saved and safe – their Roman citizenship is secure – either because they said a little prayer or they prayed the Rosary enough times or because their name is on the roles of our denomination and they're tithing.

"There are no worries now! You're safe! Now come for dinner on Wednesday night and fellowship with us. Bring a pie. And don't miss the Christmas cantata! We have a real, live baby camel! And here's a sign-up sheet for the softball league. And the senior adults are taking a bus trip together to go shopping in Amish country next month. OH! And the youth are going on a mission trip to Cancun during Spring Break. And if you call now you can register for our special "Jesus Cruise" around the Carribean – we're going to have several major Christian celebrities and musicians there that you might get to actually touch! Maybe you could even sit with Michael W. Smith and eat from the 500 item buffet!! We might even have a baby camel on the ship! Oh, you just HAVE to come! God will be so pleased if you can make it."

It's all bread and circuses. And it's all from the enemy of our souls. How can I tell? Because if God were really in charge, we would be like Jesus and we'd all be on our faces crying until we sweat blood for the horrible state of things and a clear vision of the cup that has been and will be poured out on us before we get through this. We'd be weeping and repenting in sackcloth and ashes for the missed opportunities and millions (or billions) of souls that have been lost while we entertained ourselves and got fatter and fatter. If God was in charge, we would have Fear of the Lord and we would cry until we ran out of tears for the mess we've made of His Body. We'd sincerely apologize to the "world" because we had the Light that they needed, but we blew it out so that we could become just like <u>them</u>. Even while we kept telling them we were "different."

If God was in charge of the "church," He'd take a <u>flamethrower</u> to our structures and our systems and our programs and our leaders and our own lives and burn off all the chaff instead of catering to it. He'd turn over the tables and cleanse the temple. (And I think that's coming, so you might want to pray <u>real</u> hard.)

Hmmm. I don't think we can put Him off forever. I wonder when that's gonna start? <u>Now</u> would be nice.

If you have the guts, pray this with me:

Father God, I know we have dishonored You in ways I can't even get my head around. I know that you can't possibly be happy with our fancy shows that just entertain our own brain, but leave people untransformed for the Gospel and dead in their sins. Please make the "bread and circuses" stop by whatever means necessary. I'm sorry for the mess I've made of my life, my home, my city, my nation, the Bride. Please, Lord, please bring a flamethrower to all of it. Please wreck it all. Anything that stands in the way between me and You, please do whatever it takes. Rip it, tear it, shred it, kill it, crush it, burn it – if I can't lay it down then just snatch it out of my grip. For the structures and systems that I've helped build, I repent. Wreck them all. Have <u>Your</u> way. Use what You can and flatten the rest. Please, Father, let NO ONE stand in front of Your sheep anymore and say, "Mine is the kingdom, Mine is the power, Mine is the glory." If they're not going to repent, then take them home. You know who can be redeemed, but make them sit down and shut up and weep and mourn – or take them home. There is so much blood on their head already, it's just mercy to make it stop. Do whatever You have to do to me so that I'll be a useful vessel for Your kingdom, broken and contrite and circumcised of heart. Teach me humility and give me more Fear of the Lord. Please pour out a gift of repentance on me by Your Holy Spirit so that I can cry rivers of tears in front of anybody until this thing turns around. Please let me see through Your eyes and share in Your suffering. I'm so sorry, Lord. Please do it. I trust You. Make me useful. Turn this around! In the mighty Name of Jesus Christ my Lord. Amen.

And don't stop praying until things change.

WHAT IS THE PROPER USE OF FUNDS?

Based on: Luke 12:13-21, Luke 14:8-14, James 5:1-6, I Timothy 6, I Corinthians 4:6-21, 2 Corinthians 8:1-15, 2 Corinthians 9:6-15, and more!

If you have ten credit cards maxed out and you want to pay them off, you start by paying off the ones with the largest interest rate first, right? Then you move up the chain to the ones that don't hurt as bad until you get them all paid off. If you have one at 0% interest, you don't mess with it at all, if you don't have to.

God's math works the same way. The plan for us should be to go help those in the most need first (permanent, eternal need and tragic, immediate physical needs). In America the average person gets an offer or opportunity to hear about the Gospel over 500 times per year. In many countries, a person may have a 10 minute window ONCE in their whole life to hear the Good News. Over a billion people have never even once heard the name of Jesus spoken in their presence. Every year millions die without Christ. In America, no one can say they never had a chance.

In terms of poverty, the poor in the U.S. live like kings compared to the devastatingly poor in Delhi and Burma and Haiti and a thousand other places. They would love to trade places with our poor! No one can statistically argue otherwise with any honesty. Especially if you've seen it first-hand. Where would you rather be a girl and be an orphan? China, Burma, Iran, India? Or Canada, USA, England?

So whether it's their eternal soul or their physical body, logic says that first and foremost you care for the worst off - and then (in order) you help the Very Poor, the Somewhat Poor, the Poor, the Slightly Uncomfortable – and you NEVER spend a dime on the Got-More-Than-Anyone-Could-Ever-Really-Need-But-Still-Dissatisfied!

Then those reached can be an example of success and maybe they can even help as we move up to reach those in the next category. There are lots of devastatingly, oppressively poor churches that are sending out missionaries and being obedient with what little they have. Are we as good an example? At the rate they're going, it won't be long before China is sending their missionaries to the West.

Jesus had the largest heart for the most impoverished. He took the most care and attention with those rejected by the rest of the world. The Christian church in America has often done the exact opposite. In Revelations 2 and 3, Jesus speaks to the seven churches. He gives them an encouragement and then a rebuke -- except the poor churches of Smyrna and Philadelphia who were obedient despite limited resources. For them there is only blessing and no word of judgement. The worst judgement is against the rich church of Laodecia in Revelations 3. At the final call, which kind of church will Jesus judge yours to have been?

If we are to lust after and covet something, it should be treasure in Heaven where it can't rust or be eaten by moths or stolen by man. As for me, I want to see who is building the largest pile of Heavenly treasure and then I want to buy stock in them. I want to be a part of whatever they're doing and help any way I can. We're often told there are just two options; make lots of money and be controlled by it -or- make a tiny bit of money and learn to live simply. But there is another choice - make lots of money and live simply and then invest all the excess into the Kingdom. If God has blessed you with skills and assets and talents, use them. He's going to expect a report on how well you invested it so as to maximize your return in Heavenly treasure.

I mean, everything you have is all HIS right? When you said He was "Lord" you meant it, right? When you said "All" you really meant it, didn't you?

Fellowship Of The Martyrs

IS "CHURCH" REALLY GOING TO PERSECUTE "<u>THE</u> CHURCH"?

Just in case you're new to all this stuff, we should probably define our terms. There is the organized structure of "religion" that most folks refer to as the "church" (or churches) and then there is the Biblical and pure Body of Christ that is the True Church. One is Man-made and the other is established by God and consists of those who are "called out." In the Greek it is called Ekklesia (or Ecclesia, in English). Certain subsets may overlap, but they ARE NOT interchangeable!

It should be clear from history that every major move of God (or even cultural change) is most ferociously opposed by the established religious structures themselves. I don't see how anyone can historically deny that. Besides it being the nature of Man to fight back when his comfort zone is assaulted.

Remember Judges 6-8 and the story of Gideon? Under cover of darkness he knocked down one altar to Baal and built on it's spot an altar to God and in the morning when everyone woke up, all the men of the tribe wanted to kill him. Sometimes it's just the shock of the change that freaks us out, not so much the right or wrong of the change itself. (One chapter later they want Gideon to be king and they convert all the rest of the altars in Israel.) But we need to expect that people don't like their boats rocked.

Let's just look at this from a purely pragmatic, financial standpoint.

The Bible says that the "love of money is the root of all evil." There's more discussion about money than almost anything else in the Bible. And almost all of it is warning us about it's dangers and pitfalls. Let's first approach the possibilities on a purely financial basis.

If you have any comprehension of what $250 BILLION dollars can do, you might begin to understand the market forces at work here. That's the annual income of the Church - not even including it's total asset value which is surely in the TRILLIONS! We've got giant denominational buildings and hospitals and retreat centers and mission boards and printing presses and lots and lots of paid staff. All that overhead requires stability, and preferably, constant growth.

If you start to do ANYTHING that would potentially threaten the income stream of certain segments of the "church," there will be all kinds of forces that will try to stop you. Consider this, Driftwood Super Church (for example) is building a giant new building. It is warm and soft and friendly and seeker sensitive. Everybody leaves feeling good. The pastor even has a best selling book and is on TV regularly. But members of the congregation start to wonder how much treasure in heaven they are really accumulating for all their investment into Driftwood. They begin to look down at their weekly check and realize that it would make more of an eternal difference on lives if they spent it on native missionaries and feeding the hungry and clothing the naked - instead of a new JumboTron and a fountain out front. So ... they keep coming to church but they give their money elsewhere to hyper-efficient organizations working on the front lines.

What if 10% of them got that thought in their head? The annual budget would come up five weeks short. Not only that, but you now have NON-PAYING customers taking up seats - using resources, flushing the toilets, talking to staff, using up bulletins, occupying parking spots, requiring volunteers to watch their kids. In essence you have doubled the damage of the revenue shortfall. You've withheld revenue AND you've kept a paying customer out of the seats. That shiny new pastor that keeps the seats filled by tickling everyone's ears starts looking a lot less shiny.

The Open Letter of Apology to the World

What if it's enough to stall a building campaign in progress? Now you've got Teamsters and construction workers mad at you. Shouldn't be surprising if some of those construction companies and banks are owned by the deacons and elders in the churches. With the massive debt load in most of our churches (another tip-off that there might be a structural problem here), maybe even banks have to start foreclosing. You've got chair suppliers, hymnal printers, sound system installers, roofers, stained glass artists, banner makers, architects and dozens of others who could stand to lose out.

What if Simon & Schuster's newest best-selling pastor/author starts to have trouble keeping his church out of hock? If there was an attitudinal and financial shift within the church - even 10% - that's a potential revenue loss of tens of millions for Sony, Viacom, Fox News, Time Warner and many other high power organizations.

And ... there are all kinds out there. If this is a war, you have to come to the conclusion that some of the "Christian" leaders are double-agents, because they're doing more harm than good. It's bad enough that you might be assaulted by people who love Jesus and are just shocked and surprised - but we also need to acknowledge that the forces of darkness are hard at work inside our own ranks and they are MUCH more ruthless. What response should you expect from some of the most egregious televangelist, Bentley-driving, crying all the time, gotta have money to stay on the air, taking pennies from widows, buy-a-miracle-for-yourdonation variety? They've got millions of dollars at their disposal and apparently very little morality to constrain them. How hard would it be for them to take you out?

And that's just barely scratching the surface of the macro-economics at play here.

What about the theological response? Since what we're advocating is a return to the pure Word of God and a commitment to listen to God only and let Him be our teacher - we are implicitly devaluing a seminary education and setting a level playing field among all who love Jesus. In fact, we're saying that it's entirely possible that a 13 year old girl or a guy fresh out of jail or a shut-in 90 year old widow might know Jesus better than a guy with a Doctorate. We didn't set out to devalue a seminary education, it's just that most of what they teach is man-made theory and not necessarily useful for hearing the voice of God better. (In fact, many church leaders will think you're nuts if you say you actually hear the voice of God and do what He tells you!)

By some accounts more than 60% of professional Christian clergy in this country do not believe the Bible is the inerrant word of God. So we're assaulting their sensibilities by trying to take it literally. They will say the idea of City Churches is impossible in today's world. They will insist that there are problems in the church but either; 1) THEIR denomination is not so bad, or 2) the Biblical solution (repent and act like One Body) is not the way to go. Nearly all of them will disagree with the premise that a paid clergy is unnecessary and/or unBiblical. The religious establishment will fight tooth and nail. They will call you a cult, they will warn their members against you, they will call all the other pastors they know, they will conduct media campaigns to run you out of town. I've talked to a lot of pastors about the "Apology to the World" and the Scary Stats and Scary Scriptures and the conclusions that I've come to. Many don't like it, some don't like me, some think I'm just disgruntled and mad at the church - but none of them have ever honestly argued about the theology or the scriptural validity or the veracity of the statistics. No one has ever shown me where in the Bible there are multiple churches in one town and God is happy about it. No one has ever shown me in the Bible where one person has a better pipeline of information to God than another so he should stand up front and everybody should sit quietly and listen to that guy talk once a week.

What about the personal response? Surely there will be people in the churches that see there is a problem with the output we are getting here, with the return-on-investment that we are seeing. Odds are good that the first ones to get it will be business professionals that run companies and know how to make a payroll and keep their books balanced. And odds are good people like that are already sitting on the Board (or Committee or Elders or whatever). These are high visibility, highly respected members that may start to react in visible and forceful ways to make things change. There are all kinds of interpersonal dynamics and relationships at risk here. Hurt feelings, betrayal, confrontation of all kinds may ensue. Without holiness of heart and a commitment to love unconditionally, the result could be depression, frustration, exhaustion, resignation or worse. And that doesn't even BEGIN to diagnose the possible responses from the "world" and government to a true New Testament Christianity spreading widely! What if all the Christians emptied their retirement accounts and gave it to the poor? Wouldn't the stock market melt down? THEN you'd see some real persecution!

Oh! And if persecution actually did start in America – if the day came when jack-booted storm troopers came to arrest all the Christians ... maybe we'll wish we had rethought the whole church-wide pictorial directory thing.

Musical Interlude - Feel free to sing along

Zacchaeus was a wee little man, a wee little man was he,

He climbed up in the sycamore tree, The Savior for to see.

And when the Savior passed that way, He looked up in the tree,

And He said, "Zacchaeus, you come down, For I'm going to your house today,

For I'm going to your house today."

Zacchaeus was a wee little man, a wee little man was he,

He climbed up in the sycamore tree, The Savior for to see.

And Zacchaeus came down from that tree,

And He said, "What a better man I'll be. I'll give my money to the poor.

What a better man I'll be. What a better man I'll be."

I wonder if we've been leaving out that last verse?

I sure don't remember hearing it lately. When did we stop singing <u>that</u> verse?

GEN-X – GEN-Y – ENVIRONMENTALISTS – ANARCHISTS – ATHEISTS READ THIS!!

First off, we're REALLY, REALLY sorry! We're praying daily that we can get the church to be what it was always supposed to be so you won't see us anymore as the hypocrites we are. Just as in the fairy tale about the Emperor's New Clothes, it's youth that is willing to speak truth and is unconstrained by convention and possessions. That's why Jesus blessed the little ones and encouraged us to have faith as a child. As it turns out, faith like a thoughtful, steady, mature, settled adult who has enmeshed themselves in sinful culture is disastrous for the church!!

We firmly believe that whatever this is to become will be dependent on the GenX/Y'ers and their energy, enthusiasm, computer savvy, and willingness to take a stand. We have always sent young people to fight our wars. So does God (Daniel, Joseph, David, John the Baptist, Jesus, and on and on through the ages).

Your generation has a very hard time going into a giant fancy building and listening to guys in suits and seeing big musical productions - where people leave unmoved and unchanged. You don't need that stuff to find God and you think it's frivolous and wasteful. And you're absolutely right. Instead of trying to strategically cater to you with a new "twist" on old church - we're advocating the complete renewal of the church to its roots. Which just happens to be exactly what you're calling for.

Your generation has been raised up by God to throw off the status quo and the old assumptions. It's not enough to do it this way because that's what we've always done. You need to go back to the basics, to the very heart and core of what the message of Jesus is all about. You have been raised to respect nature, to recycle and reuse, to embrace people of different colors and languages, to rage against "the machine." Those in the Big Church establishments think "the machine" is government and corporations, but it's not just that. It's not just Big Government, Big Tobacco, Big Oil, Big Pharmaceuticals - it's Big Church that stands condemned as well.

I absolutely believe that Satan has built educational systems to get our children focused on all the wrong things, to worship the creation rather than the Creator (Romans 1:25). To worship Mother Earth instead of He who made the whole of creation. To worship the stars and constellations instead of He who hung them. To value human justice and equality, instead of looking to He who yearns for it more than any of us – and sent the Word (Jesus) to achieve it and the Holy Spirit to constantly urge us toward it.

But the joke is on Satan. Jesus is the ultimate expression of stewardship, recycling, care for the poor and disadvantaged, love for those different, respect for nature and the beauty of Creation. You've been perfectly prepared - by the Enemy - for what's coming! Your very souls resonate and vibrate at a different pitch from the current Church structures. Something big is on the horizon. A complete revolution in our relationship to God and the expression of Christianity. Many of you could feel it before we did. I pray that we who have influence and should have known better than to let it get this bad can change quickly enough that we don't lose all of you forever.

To the Anarchists among you - God bless you. You almost get it! Human structures and hierarchies and organizational charts are blasphemous to the very nature and spirit of God Almighty. God wants us in constant communion with His Spirit and under the sole direction of His will. No layers are needed if we're in harmony with God. It won't be the disordered chaos that you picture it to be - God's is the ultimate expression of process and order - He just doesn't need man-made organizational structures. The day is coming when Christ will reign on a glorified and perfected Earth in exactly that way. No layers, no structures - just us and God. Please think carefully about the difference between the Created and the Creator. The beauty and complexity of nature is not the end, it's the glorious sign along the way that was created to point to a loving, beautiful, complex God. DON'T let yourself get sucked into any big, complex human structures - not the Church as it currently is and especially not a One-World government designed by sinful, imperfect man!

God sent His very own son, Jesus - a young radical intent on calling the people back to their core and to restore their pure love for God (John 3:16-17) - even though speaking against the establishment was to carry the cost of the most horrible imaginable torture and death. He came to redeem us of our sinful nature and offer us an opportunity to plug into the One True Song.

Tell your friends! There are "grown-ups" that get it! God has a plan and YOU'RE at the front lines! Change is coming! Be a part of the solution!

We don't want your money. We don't want anybody's money. We want you to worship God. We want you to hear His Voice and be led by Him only. We want the "Big Church" to repent of its sinfulness and return to a love of God above all. The time of the worship of money is coming to an end.

Praise God for using a helpless worm like me and offering His Son as a sacrifice to redeem my sinfulness so that He could adopt us and make us all joint heirs with Jesus. Change is coming! There are going to be some people really, REALLY unhappy about having to give up all their stuff.

It's going to be a fun ride!

THE SPIRIT OF ABORTION

I've been praying for a single coherent nugget to explain the problem and God showed it to me a few days ago.

It is the VERY ESSENCE and CORE of what God did for us! He sent Jesus to shepherd us and be an example and then God ADOPTED us as joint heirs with Jesus. It is the supreme and ULTIMATE example and pure essence of love to take someone that you KNOW has problems and special needs and sinfulness, that you KNOW will require effort and cost - even the awful sacrifice of your own blood Son - and then elevate this stranger to the status equal to the Son of your womb. Equal to the Morning Star in inheritance and love. OK, yeah, we all know that, but do you REALLY GET IT?!

One of the things that many of us have been praying for is that a Spirit of Adoption would sweep over the church and the world. God finally just put all the pieces together in my head. This is why we're adopting a kid from China, this is why God had me build a company that brings in people and THEN asks them what they'd like to do here and loves them and refuses to lay them off. That's why I'm mad at the Church Growth Movement and mega churches that don't seem to care.

Do you get it? A Christian company that lays off people that are supposed to be part of the family is ABORTING them! They're expensive or inconvenient or not playing along with our plan. Do you really think Jesus is going to be proud of a Christian business that is INDISTINGUISHABLE from a secular one? If not THIS to differentiate us - then what?

Churches that urge you out because they don't like dealing with you are ABORTING YOU! For all our talk about being against abortion, that's just physical. Those babies are NOT in spiritual, eternal danger. But when we "urge" someone out of our churches, we're potentially aborting their souls! Do you honestly think Jesus is going to say, "Well, you aborted this person out of your church and they grew to hate religion and never prayed to me again, but I understand, it's OK. You know, they WERE kind of weird and smelly and didn't really fit in with the rest of us up here." Maybe they asked hard questions, maybe they didn't tithe like we thought they should, maybe they never even got in the door because we made it clear we were better than them. How can you call it anything BUT the Spirit of Abortion?

I think businesses that do family-friendly programs just to improve retention or improve profitability aren't Families anymore, they're ORPHANAGES. They're just warehousing people and trying to keep them efficient and not revolt!

Churches that warehouse as many people as possible to get the subsidy per person that comes, are ORPHANAGES! Of course, they still SAY they're a family and love everyone, but people can sense that at a certain point it changed and now it's really about numbers. Somewhere off in a remote corner they have a Dying Room where they just let the troubled ones anguish and wither. A church that feeds the children pablum to keep them under-nourished and not growing is suppressing them because toddlers are much easier to warehouse than rebellious teenagers! How much love does that show? How much Spirit of Adoption is that?

It's like Xin Guang, the little girl with special needs that we are going to pick up in China (God willing) around Easter {2005, now home! But ended up July.} and for whom God has told us we're to be her "Forever Family." It's like if we just decided she was so cute at three years old that we'd like to keep her like that, so we reduce her meal portions and then get her hooked on coffee and cigarettes to stunt her growth so she'll stay just that size forever. Because we hear teenage girls are too much trouble. What kind of love would that show?! And what of our bio-daughter and the lessons she learns from that? Don't you think Family Services would come and snatch them BOTH away and throw us in jail?! Well, that's what's about to happen to the churches acting that way! And Christian businesses are not going to be exempt either.

That's why house churches work - if they can keep their focus. They're small enough and intimate enough to maintain that Spirit. That's why MILLIONS of us have left the institutional church entirely, because we sense that that Spirit of Adoption is GONE and we don't know where to find it except in communion with God directly! By it's nature it's TREMENDOUSLY difficult for a large autocratic organism to maintain a personal intimate Spirit of Adoption. This sweet, wonderful Spirit of Unconditional Love is the ultimate enemy of Satan, because he was offered it by God and rejected it and hates anyone who accepts it or encourages it or models it! Get it?

That's IT! That's the core of it all!

Thanks be for the Word of the Lord and for His willingness to come show us what true LOVE means!! Thanks be to God for being the Spirit of Adoption without which we would be lost forever!! Praise God!! Thanks be to God for giving us a chance to be living examples of His love for us.

Test your hearts. Test your family. Test your church. Test your business. Is the Spirit of Adoption foremost? It is UNDENIABLY the ROOT of LOVE and your best chance to manifestly express through your lives that you ARE Christian and you DO understand your responsibilities as Adopted Children of God. The ultimate sign to Satan that you are DANGEROUS to his cause is the evidence in your life of this Spirit of Adoption and a willingness to sacrifice ANYTHING for those entrusted to your family. I want to be at the very top of Satan's hit list. Praise God! What about you?

Hold on tight, folks. When people really GET this, it's all going to start moving FAST! A New Song is coming!

Musical Interlude – Feel free to sing along

When we walk with the Lord in the light of His Word, What a glory He sheds on our way!

While we do His good will, He abides with us still, And with all who will trust and obey.

Trust and obey, for there's no other way To be happy in Jesus, but to trust and obey.

Not a shadow can rise, not a cloud in the skies, But His smile quickly drives it away;

Not a doubt or a fear, not a sigh or a tear, Can abide while we trust and obey.

Trust and obey, for there's no other way To be happy in Jesus, but to trust and obey.

Not a burden we bear, not a sorrow we share, But our toil He doth richly repay;

Not a grief or a loss, not a frown or a cross, But is blessed if we trust and obey.

Trust and obey, for there's no other way To be happy in Jesus, but to trust and obey.

Then in fellowship sweet we will sit at His feet. Or we'll walk by His side in the way.

What He says we will do, where He sends we will go; Never fear, only trust and obey.

Trust and obey, for there's no other way To be happy in Jesus, but to trust and obey.

TEN COMMANDMENTS – HOW DOES THE "CHURCH" STACK UP?

If there is no real persecution of Christians in America and Jesus said the more you are like Him the more you will be persecuted, then there must not be very many real Christians in America. See any logic problems there? Did you think Jesus was kidding?

So ... my goal is to bring persecution as quickly as possible by saying whatever I have to say to get Christians to start fully and completely acting like Christ. That will require lots of people who are willing to fearlessly take a stand and STOP CONFORMING TO THE WORLD. I've been blowing the trumpet and a few have gathered, but then I didn't have the lung capacity and wisdom I have now - and probably the willingness to do what it takes. I think the time is coming when somebody is going to blow the trumpet REALLY loud. If not me then someone else. Probably LOTS of people.

There's a fire burning in me that is just getting hotter. Some stuff is coming out of me right now that is so harsh that I need folks with lots of love around me to temper it. We have to keep it about love first, but still say the hard things when necessary.

For example, it occurs to me that the "church" as we know it has a personality, dysfunctional and disjointed as it is, it has certain trends and behaviors that you could define as a personality. I've done a lot of work in the area of organizational theory and believe that groups have a personality that can be defined and diagnosed. Maybe the same methods you would use to convict and witness to an individual would work on a group.

Anyway, that which we call 'church', if it is really off track according to God's Law, should be showing bad fruit. Using Ray Comfort's method of showing people their sinfulness using the Ten Commandments, let's take a look. (And understand this is HIGHLY abbreviated, we could write a book on the stats and examples for each one!)

Worship no other gods before me. – Comfy, Sunday-only Jesus is NOT the same God. Purpose-Driven Jesus is NOT the same God of our Fathers! Worshiping the pastor because he has a book deal or worshiping the denomination, structure, money, or even ideology (Calvin, KJV 1611, Pope) is putting other gods before HIM. **GUILTY!**

Do not make idols or worship them. – Your heart is where you spend your time and money. According to the stats, the Western church loves themselves and their buildings and comforts most of all. We spend many times more hours worshiping TV than we do God Almighty. We cancel Sunday services to watch the Super Bowl, for Pete's sake! **GUILTY!**

Do not use the name of your God irreverently or in vain. – To justify ANY stupid thing we want to do, we assure people that we can be trusted since we hear from God. Touch not God's anointed! Whatever just came out of this or that pastor or prophet's mouth must have been the voice of God - they have a new DVD out and speak at conferences all over the world! We have pastors, bishops, popes that stand in for God and speak on His behalf - with or without His approval - taking His Name and authority as their own. We call things Jesus that have nothing to do with Him. We use His name and birthday as an excuse for a massive consumer spending orgy every year - even though He NEVER said to celebrate His birthday and He wasn't even born in December! **GUILTY!**

Observe the Sabbath. – Where to even start? I don't even know how off track we are here, but Sunday better be more about GOD than FOOTBALL, I can tell you that! Can you legitimately say that all it takes to "observe the Sabbath" is an hour and fifteen minutes sitting in a pew? The Narrow Path can't possibly be THAT wide!! Are we sure it's not supposed to be on Saturday? Maybe <u>every</u> day. Whatever – we're still **GUILTY!**

Honor your father and mother. – This means respect them and their feelings but it also means that we are to bring them honor. We have converted our churches into institutions that displace and insult our elders. "Their music isn't loud enough. Their style isn't hip enough. Their faith isn't deep enough. Their God isn't cool enough. They need to get with the program and see that the wave of the future is bigger and louder and younger and with more feelings. If not, then we're going to have to leave them behind." We have NOT brought them honor and glory. We have prostituted or murdered the churches they built. We have lost traction on evangelism, missions, and every other emphasis that Jesus cares about. But we have churches so big that they need to meet in a stadium! **GUILTY!**

Do not murder. – What does this mean except that we kill someone so that we can gain something. Maybe it's not what we MEANT to do, but we still let them die so that we could have some advantage. Or worse yet, so we could have their stuff. At any given moment 200 MILLION Brothers and Sisters live on the very edge of starvation. Billions have died without Christ. But we have REALLY shiny new cars and churches that meet in stadiums. We sacrifice millions of souls every month to keep our comforts. It's not like we didn't know. We see starving children on TV and sponsor ONE for $30 - out of an average per capita income of tens of thousands - plus TRILLIONS of dollars of assets between us. We should know better than to think we're making a dent in the problem without some more sacrifice than that. We're intentionally letting them die to keep from having to share our stuff. **GUILTY!**

Do not commit adultery. – We cheat on the Bridegroom and our First Love through programs and fads and ecumenical movements that yoke us with those opposed to God. We have laid down with other religions, with the "world", with governments, with culture, with TV, with Hollywood, with Wall Street, with Sony Records, with political parties. We lay down with everything EXCEPT God! (Not to mention that 50% of clergy regularly use porn.) **GUILTY!**

Do not steal. – Each year the 'church' loses more to fraud and embezzlement to trusted people inside the organization ($16B – yeah, that's a "B" - as in BILLION) than it spends on foreign missions ($15B). We regularly try to get little old ladies to send their last dollar so we can buy a Bentley or a new plane or build a big building. And we tell them God is going to bless their blind faith in us. See #6 - if we're to share with each as they have need, then we HAVE to steal from the Brethren in other places in order to sustain our standard of living! **GUILTY!**

Do not lie. – Our denominations regularly falsify progress reports and spending projections. We spent BILLIONS on plans to reach the entire world with the gospel by the year 2000. We barely even kept up with population growth! No apologies, no explanations, just a renewed emphasis for more money. This doesn't even touch on all the snake oil salesmen pretending to be ministers of the Gospel that nobody seems to be willing to shut down and contend for the faith. Worst of all, we tell the world that this structure that we've built was Jesus' idea when it's really about our own egos and greed and selfishness. **GUILTY!**

Do not covet. – Did you read any of the ones above? We TEACH pastors to want bigger churches. We train MEN OF GOD to judge their effectiveness and worth on how many people want to come hear them speak. We TRAIN them in seminaries how to administrate effective building campaigns and fund growth. America is the ULTIMATE incarnation of coveting – and the 'church' is INDISTINGUISHABLE from culture. **GUILTY!**

We're not just doing this stuff a LITTLE BIT. We're talking about BILLIONS of people injured by this and TRILLIONS of dollars of assets being misdirected, wasted or stolen!! The lost potential in human souls in incalculable. Somebody is going to have to answer for this at the final judgement. NOW might be a really good time to weep and mourn before the altar. That's the formula for what to do when the locusts have eaten everything and the land is parched and dry. And I'm pretty sure that's about the state of the Church of America. All the good stuff has been sucked out. (Read the book of Joel.)

THE UNDENIABLE AXIOMS

According to Scripture, in the last days, apostasy (falling away) will be rampant in the Church.1 There will be false prophets, signs and wonders meant to deceive even the Elect. 2

It is our contention that God seeks to have systems built on HIS plan, not Man's. As regards AUTHORITY - His ways are not pyramid-shaped hierarchical systems following the will of a MAN at the top. If anything, it's a pyramid turned on it's head, with the leader being servant to all. As for authority, there is US and there is HIM. That's it. While there are delineations and delegations of responsibility, and there might be a chain of command to accomplish something, everyone in the chain should be looking to God for authority and submit as servant leaders to those around them. If we're walking in His Spirit, we worship no man.

God wanted Israel to worship and follow Him only. But they insisted on a King, so God gave them one knowing it would go badly - but that's what they wanted.3 They had it coming.

The Church has fallen into the same trap. Instead of worshiping God only, we've absorbed all the man-made models and adopted them as our own for centuries - millennia even! Go look at your church or denomination's organizational chart and see if it resembles the structures of Man and follows behind one person at the top. As for "Authority," in many cases we've usurped God's position and inserted ourselves at the top of the chain of command and insisted on obedience from the lower levels.

During the Millennial Reign of Christ, we will return to the perfect model.4 Christ as direct leader of all with no other steps or layers of authority in between. Even though others may reign with Him, it's inside His authority, not their own.5

God hates man-made organizational structures because they are innately sinful. He directed us to be respectful of those already in place.6 But He clearly instructed us to listen to HIM only, never to call another Father or Rabbi, when we were to be listening only to God.7

A lot of thought and prayer has gone into this. We've tried to explain the apostasy in the church and the dangers of the coming systems in the simplest possible terms. Based on scripture and clearly harmonious with the basic instincts of every person with a clear understanding of human nature. To deny this is to fly in the face of a basic understanding of human nature.

The Undeniable Axiom of Sinful Inertia

IF: You believe the Bible is the Word of God and is Truth;8

THEN: You believe that Man is a fallen, sinful creature and beyond redemption and perfection on his own.9

IF: You believe that Man is sinful (to whatever degree);10

THEN: You have to believe that the more Men in one organization, the more potential for sin comes with them. Like compounding interest. 11

IF: You want to have a positive impact on the World;12

THEN: You must acknowledge the sinful nature of Man and build structures to restrain or minimize it.13

IF: You base your structures on the ideas and management of Men; 14

THEN: They are flawed and cannot restrain the mass of sin indefinitely. 15

IF: The organization denies the sinful nature of Man;

THEN: It believes a lie, it builds no effective restraints and will immediately have a negative effect.

IF: The organization believes Man is sinful, except their own leaders;

THEN: It believes a lie, builds no restraints on the leaders and very quickly has a negative effect.

IF: The organization believes that ALL Men are sinful and builds restraints on ALL;

THEN: It operates in truth and can have a positive impact - to the limits of the restraints.

IF: The accumulation of sinful Men exceeds the limitations of the restraints;

THEN: The organization ceases to have positive impact and becomes something negative.

IF: You are Satan and you want to spit in the eye of God; 16

THEN: You build a One World Church that lies about the nature of man and has no real restraints on behavior.

Undeniable Axiom of Love of Money

IF: You believe the Bible is the Word of God and is Truth; 17

THEN: You believe the Bible when it says that the "Love of money is the root of all evil." 18

IF: You believe that the "Love of money is the root of all evil." 19

THEN: You have to recognize that it's not the money itself, but the LOVE of it. (Biblically speaking, anything that takes the place of God will do, but most often its money that's the issue.) 20

IF: You believe that money is a temptation when placed in the hands of sinful Man; 21

THEN: You have to believe that the bigger the pile of money, the greater the temptation.

IF: You have an organization that misunderstands the nature of Man and is already negative;

THEN: You have to see that if you give it LOTS of money, it will be VERY bad indeed.

IF: An organization believes ALL Men are sinful and builds restraints on ALL;

THEN: You can force it to and past the limits of it's restraints faster by just adding more money.

IF: An organization says it is positive but it's leader expresses a clear "Love of Money";

THEN: You can assume that organization has passed it's restraints and turned "Evil" and it is a lie. 22

IF: You are Satan and you want to spit in the eye of God; 23

THEN: You build a One World Government that controls ALL the money and has no restraints on the leaders. 24

The Undeniable Axiom of Synergy

IF: You want to prove the Bible to be True and right about the nature of Man;

THEN: You combine sinful Man and lots of money and watch to see what happens.

IF: You are Satan and you want to spit in the eye of God; 25

THEN: You build a One World Government and a One World Church, remove all restraints, thereby consolidating ALL of sinful Man into one mass and thus achieving "Maximum Possible Sinfulness." 26

IF: A Christian leader believes that the prophesied Millennial Reign of Christ is a time when Man will create a perfected, universal Christian church and Christian government on Earth to prepare the way for Christ to return;

THEN: That leader shows a flawed understanding of the nature of Man, has believed the Lie of Eve, and is (knowingly or unknowingly) playing right into the hands of the Enemy. Either way, you should RUN. And fast. 27

Basic Axiom Graph

As Population goes up and Money goes up, sooner or later the Inertia of Sinfulness exceeds the restraints of the organization and it becomes something else entirely. It may still think it's positive, but it's not anymore. Government, church, business, family, individual - it doesn't matter, it's all sinful Man.

The reason it's hard for the "Rich" to enter the Kingdom 28 is because it all happens so much faster. The reason the poor churches of Smyrna and Philadelphia aren't chastised in Revelations Chapters 2 & 3 is because the "Rich" churches have already "jumped the shark" or crossed the line into being something other than their original nature. The poor churches are too worried about survival to have time to be in-fighting, debating new theology or getting lazy and soft.

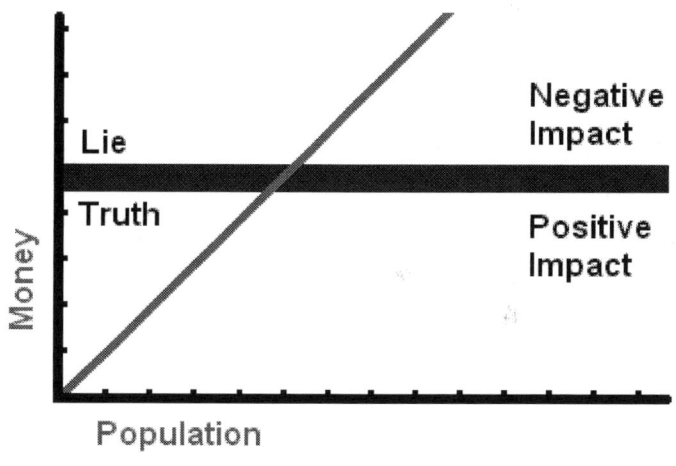

What is this Truth and Lie stuff?

Let's say a church starts off as a small group of committed friends in an affluent community wanting to worship together and care for each other. They say, "We are a family. We care about each individual." Their numbers grow and with growth comes lots of cash. They build a building, they hire staff, they start new programs for outreach and care. They say, "We are a family. We care about each individual." At some point, if they're not VERY careful, they cross a line and their ACTIONS through their committees, their strategies, their staff decisions, their spending habits say, "We need more people here to pay the bills. We need to grow to justify the new gym. We need to be careful not to challenge or offend anyone, or we'll stop growing." But, they continue to SAY to themselves and to others, "We're a family. We care about each individual." But more and more people begin to feel that it's a lie. They sense the dissonance. Then leadership begins to "urge" people out of the church who disagree and wave a flag of warning. Then the pastor writes a best selling book about how he grew his church so big - so that other pastors can learn how to do it to their own churches. Then the pastor has lots of money AND lots of people to contend with - exactly the way Satan likes it. Even if they manage to resist the inertia of sinfulness until they are very large, there is constant need for watchfulness because a new leader (or a new heart in an old leader) can remove or diminish restraints very quickly.

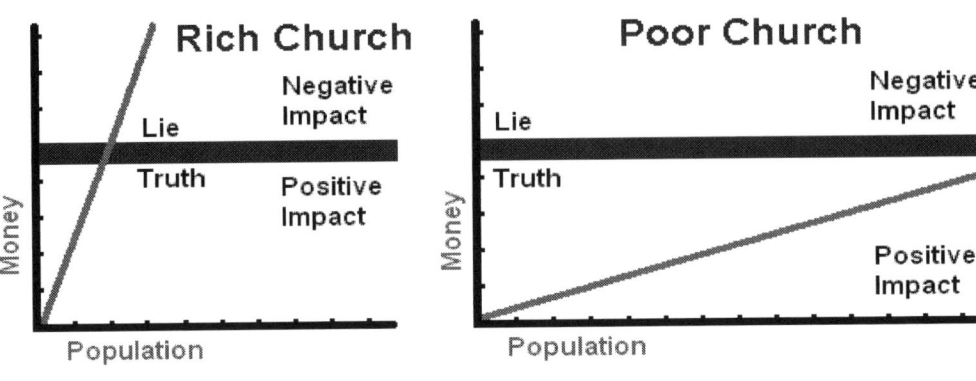

Meanwhile, the poor church accumulated many times the number of members without ever changing their basic nature because they don't have enough assets to be covetous and contentious. They have just enough to care for each other and to worship God. No Christian coffeehouse, no amusement parks, no aerobics classes, no budget ministries, no best selling books, no giant egos. They say, "We are a family. We care about the individual." And while someday they might cross over the line, they can sustain it much longer because they are much more reliant on lay leaders and not paid staff and fancy programs and facilities. They have to be mobile and entrepreneurial. They don't have any resources to waste. Even so, there is need for watchfulness because a new leader (or a new heart in an old leader) can remove or diminish restraints very quickly.

This Axiom asserts that Mega churches with Mega assets are not Biblically what we should be striving for - and should always be treated with suspicion and much care. The burden of proof that they HAVE NOT crossed the line should constantly be on the pastor and lay leadership to verify to the people that in all things their actions and decisions match with their words. Steps should be taken to raise the restraints so that the threshold is higher - OR - steps should be taken to dramatically reduce the size of the organization and it's assets. One option would be to split into smaller units and divide up resources. Or to funnel money away from themselves as quickly as possible and get it directly to the most effective, Scripturally justifiable ministries.

What About Governments?

We should be wary of governments because everything is bigger and stronger and the mountains of money involved make it immediately highly dangerous. In addition, because government leadership can change quickly, the line between Truth and Lie is fluid and can flex up and down, taking you from a point of safety into a danger zone very quickly.

Again, if any government or movement believes that they can create a Utopia on Earth if they'll just invent the correct structure, process, program, education, or worse, have the right single person in charge - they are GROSSLY misunderstanding the nature of Man and the lessons of history and are therefore highly dangerous.

If you give a government like that absolute authority and access to loads of cash, it will nearly immediately turn into a killing machine and eradicate any resistance to it's plan for "Peace". Because it has removed restraints on behavior since it believes Man to be inherently good - or even to have God within himself - whoever has the most power or charisma will call the shots and create whatever they want for themselves and crush any opposition.

Conversely, if a government is founded from the very beginning on the idea that they are going to have to plan ahead to create complex ways to keep some powerful sinful Man (or Men) from exerting his will and taking over the whole government, it's possible that they could create a system that would hold off disaster for awhile.

Please don't take this to mean that this is what God wants! Far from it, these are all Man-made constructs that are inherently dangerous and innately un-Holy. Even the Judeo-Christian Democracy (or Representative Republic) has proven to work only by degrees and with lots of peaks and valleys along the way. It's nowhere near as linear as the over-simplified graph might suggest. It advocated slavery, welfare, racism, imperialism, manifest destiny and many others. (Many believe that American government has, for some time now, accumulated too much money and caused more harm than good. But that's not really our fight here.)

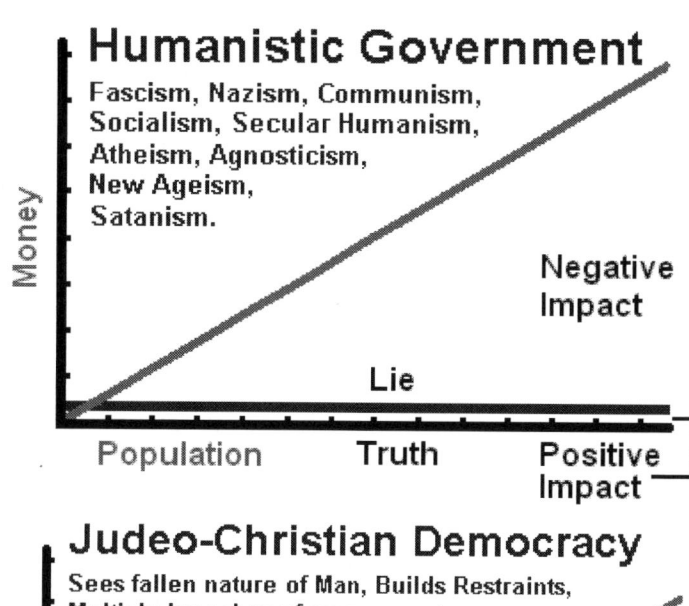

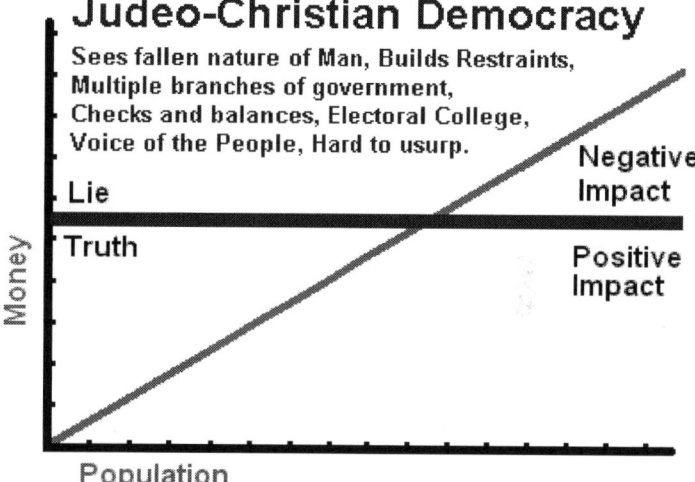

Again, the burden of proof should be squarely on Government to prove that it is still consistent with "We The People" and a concern for the rights of the citizenry. But, then, it's a flawed Man-made system and shouldn't be trusted anyway.

Conclusions

Between these Axioms you can chart the rise and fall of every government, every ministry, every man of God that fell, every future danger predicted in the Biblical prophecies. If an organization can identify that line before it gets to it, or feel it at the very early stages and act on it, there's a chance it can keep it's identity by addressing the issues quickly enough. Once an organization passes up and over that line, it will most likely result in painful division and much suffering. Or a long nasty lingering as it turns into something completely dangerous.

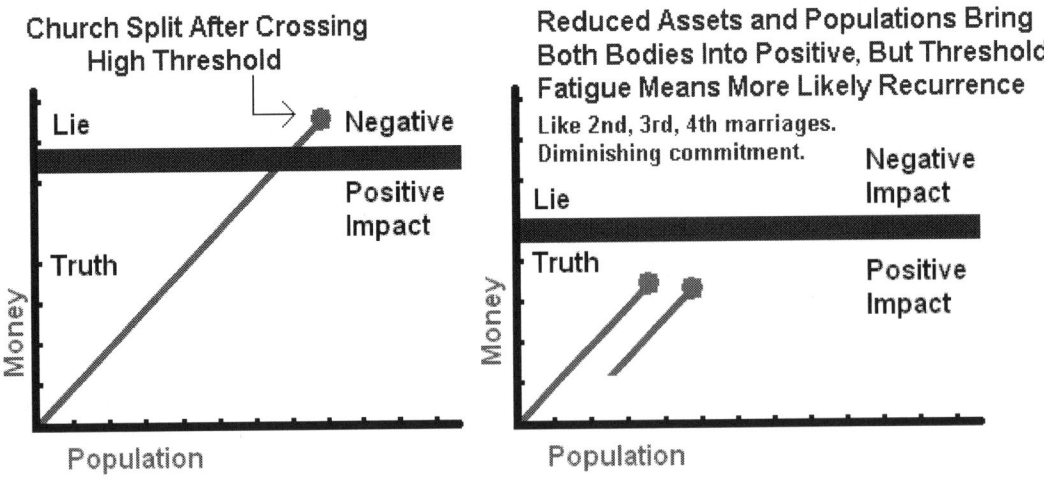

Here we see a church cross the threshold and it responds to the dissonance by splitting. Note that not all members are recovered. Some disappear, never to be seen again until the Day of Judgement, when we'll have to stand before God and accept responsibility for the kind of role models we were and take our punishment for the sheep that were lost while in our care. Both bodies from this split are now in even greater danger as they have begun a habit of dissension and division that will likely stunt the growth of their current efforts. Satan chuckles smugly.

One possible solution is the independent Self-Replicating House Church. These work because they simulate poverty. Or rather, they could be seen as the beginning stages of the Mega Church, but by their constant multiplication rather than consolidation, were never allowed to progress near the danger zone. Sort of like filling an ice cube tray where as each pocket fills it overflows and fills another. Bite sized ice chunks with their own compact lives and purpose - rather than one giant glacier with massive inertia. These are the model of the Chinese House Church movement. One other advantage is that they are very difficult to stomp out if persecution should begin. They can meet anywhere, be formed and reformed on demand and don't need formal leadership because many have been trained and can assume leadership. (This is also a model used effectively throughout history by many groups - with a wide varieties of motives. And has proven to be by far the most difficult to eliminate.)

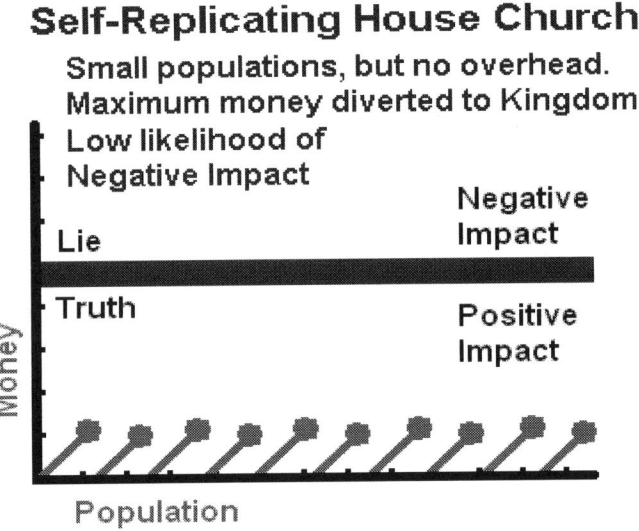

(On a larger macro scale, this is the model of the City Church discussed in our book "Do It Yourself City Church Restoration. It eliminates popish nonsense and minimizes the spread of heresy and autocratic control over the entire work.)

One spin off that looks similar but isn't is the Centrally Controlled Cell Church. And example of this would be Paul Yonghi Cho's church where it looks like lots of independent cells, but they are really offshoots of a massive central church and are all VERY efficiently and tightly controlled and taxed. This is a difficult one because it's a great temptation for a big church to start cell groups as a way to multiply its reach without adding infrastructure. This should be seen as dangerous because they are not truly independent - not separate ice cubes capable of a life of their own. They are splinters off of the glacier and still owe their allegiance to it. They are tightly controlled specifically so that they WILL NOT spin off and become independent. That would diminish the power, money, and influence of the central control structure.

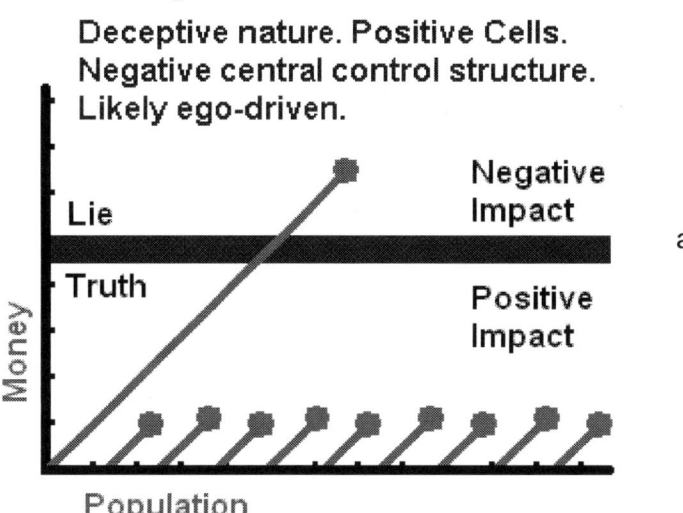

Are you getting it? This isn't necessarily about just the macro view. It applies down to families, teams, classrooms.

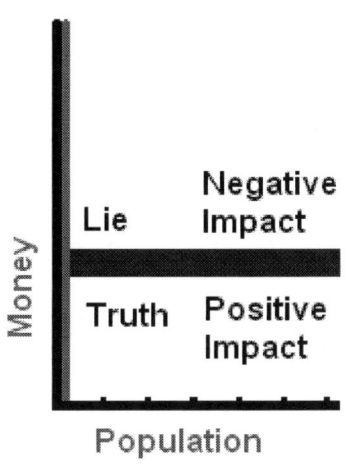

You see, big populations aren't required, the Axiom works even with the individual. Say a person writes a best selling book, wins the lottery, inherits big money, finds a copy of the Declaration of Independence in their attic, records a hit record, whatever.

If they don't accurately assess the dangers of their own nature, put systems in place to constrain and restrain the temptations and channel the blessing to do God's work, the dangers to themselves and others from having a massive windfall are enormous. The lie begins with, "I've waited a long time for this. Spending it on me won't hurt anybody. I earned it by picking the right Lotto numbers." And as groupies and salesmen start to accumulate, it quickly becomes, "They love me! I must be a great guy! I deserve this! God must want me to have that new Ferrari." Before you know it, it's "I'm indestructible! I'm practically a god." Then, late one night at a strip bar it becomes, "I AM God! I can do anything!" Then they die tragically when their Ferrari shoots off the highway because they dropped their mirror and took their eyes off the road.

Of course, it doesn't always happen like that. Sometimes they live long happy lives full of reward and enjoyment, completely full and content in themselves, wanting for nothing. God says to enjoy it because that's all the reward there is. Then they die and get to report to Jesus what they did with all the blessings they were given.

Either way, you can see why Jesus suggested that it was EXTREMELY difficult for the rich to enter the kingdom of heaven. There is a massive amount of inertia and temptation to overcome when big piles of cash are laying around.

Think you can deny the undeniable? Let's hear it.

I wrote this in 2004 and NOBODY has even TRIED to show me where it's wrong.
Fotm@FellowshipOfTheMartyrs.com

"Axiom" :

1 : a maxim widely accepted on its intrinsic merit

2 : a statement accepted as true as the basis for argument or inference

3 : an established rule or principle or a self-evident truth

(Websters New World Dictionary)

"Undeniable Axioms" References

1. 2 Thess. 2:3	15. Rom. 7:8-11
2. Matthew 24:24	16. Isaiah 50:6
3. 1 Samuel 9:20	17. John 17:17
4. Rev. 20:1-6	18. 1 Tim. 6:10
5. Rev. 20:4,6	19. Col. 3:1-2
6. Heb. 13:17	20. Mat 26:14-16
7. Matthew 23:9	21. Acts 5:1-11
8. Psa. 119:160	22. Rev. 3:17-18
9. Romans 3:23	23. Isaiah 50:6
10. Romans 8:3	24. Rev. 13:25, Isaiah 50:6
11. Romans 7:13	26. Rev. 13:16-17; 17:1-6
12. Matt 5:13, Isaiah 58	27. Matt. 24:16
13. Rom. 8:12-14	28. Matt. 19:24
14. Gal. 1:10-12	

WHO ARE THE PHARISEES?

You know the Seven Woes that Jesus calls down on the Pharisees in Matthew 23? It's clear he doesn't think much of them as a group. They were showy and extravagant, they loved the places of honor and the feeling that they knew more than anyone else, they would work hard to make a new convert and then corrupt them into their own twisted image, they put their faith in the material rather than the spiritual, they gave money instead of giving of their mercy and time and faithfulness, they were full of greed and self-indulgence, they looked shiny and new on the outside but were hollow on the inside.

Did you ever know someone like that? Have you seen religious leaders act that way? I'm sure we all have someone that we could point to and say meets at least some of the characteristics Jesus ascribed to the Pharisees. Have you known people like the Rich Young Ruler that loved God but couldn't take that final step of obedience?

Through my own experiences growing up overseas as a missionary kid and as we continue to grow our new missions organization, AcrossCountries.com *{now on hold until we get Liberty fixed}* we've had a great opportunity to get a little glimpse of how Christians in America are viewed from the outside.

A really terrible thought has been gnawing at me lately. In our local circle of influence we can usually point to someone that we can describe as a "Pharisee." But if you gathered the Christians from all over the world and asked them to point out who was most like the Pharisees Jesus described – WE'RE the ones at whom they would all be pointing!

Over 95% of available Christian resources are being spent in the West. Half of the world has never seen even a single page of the Bible! When we send missionaries over there and convert someone, the first thing we do is impose our denominational distinctives and enmesh them in our theological squabblings over issues that aren't central to the faith.

There are Christian Brothers and Sisters starving to death and still being faithful, finding a way to give even in poverty. Their commitment and joy in the Lord is awesome and should shame all of us. They go and preach in the most dangerous places, knowing they could be killed (and frequently are) - while we are unwilling to talk to our neighbors for fear of looking like a "Jesus freak."

Previously I've mentioned that the United States gross domestic product (GDP) is about $10 Trillion per year. Regular church-going Christians control as much as $3 Trillion per year of that through our personal income (roughly equivalent to the ENTIRE annual spending of the U.S. Government). We control many, MANY times that when you calculate the value of our stocks, savings, real estate, life insurance, businesses and other assets. What are we accomplishing with it? From the perspective of Christians in other countries, we're just gorging ourselves while others stand and wait to be fed – both physically and spiritually.

I can't find any Biblical justification for some Christians having assets worth tens of trillions of dollars while other Christians (on an income of $1 or $2 per day) survive and build churches and minister to others around them. In fact, it seems to me there are some very specific scriptures to which we should probably pay more attention. For example:

> **1 Timothy 6:17-19** (NIV) - "Command those who are rich in this present world not to be arrogant nor to put their hope in wealth, which is so uncertain, but to put their hope in God, who richly provides us with everything for our enjoyment. Command them to do good, to be rich in good deeds, and to be

generous and willing to share. In this way they will lay up treasure for themselves as a firm foundation for the coming age, so that they may take hold of the life that is truly life."

Or maybe Mark 10:23; "Jesus looked around and said to his disciples, "How hard it is for the rich to enter the kingdom of God!" (See also: I Timothy 6:8-10, Luke 16, Mark 12:41-44)

You think you're not rich? Compared to what? Compared to your boss or the guy in that giant house down the street or someone on TV? You think Jesus is talking about someone else? I've got news for you, in today's world, He is talking about YOU – and me. Half the people in the world don't sleep on a <u>bed</u>! Half the world earns $3 a day or <u>less</u>!

And if He's talking about churches, it's OUR churches that will have the hardest time at the final Judgement, not those in India or China or Ethiopia. The VAST percentage of all Christian resources are in the Western countries. In our bank accounts and those of our churches. Two BILLION people live their life undernourished. 700 million live in slums.

I'm not telling you what to do with your wealth. I just ask that you will pray and ask God to guide you. If you decide you want to make a commitment to help, feel free to contact us or at least read more about what is happening out there.

GOD – THE SUPREME BANKER

I've been thinking a lot about this. Because I'm a business guy, I think in financial terms. See if this makes any sense to you.

When we're born God opens two bank accounts for us. One is a checking account and the other is a retirement account. As soon as we are old enough to know better, our sin immediately begins to overdraw the checking account. We might do good works and care for the sick, orphans, widows, etc. - and we DO get credit for that, but it gets locked into the retirement account. The checking account is unaffected. NOTHING, nothing, nothing can redeem us of our indebtedness and overdrawn status on our checking account - except the blood of Jesus. We are bankrupt and condemned because of the checking account. The retirement account can't be used to pay our debt.

When we accept Christ and lay our lives at the feet of the Cross, He instantly brings us back up to zero. We are debtfree! Praise God! We're redeemed. But ... mostly we are too stupid and stubborn and sinful to be able to stay at zero. Before long we start sinning and our debt accumulates again. Now, we might be doing good works throughout and tithing and feeding the poor and maybe even doing great miracles and preaching our hearts out - but all that does is store up in our retirement account. Sooner or later, we realize our indebtedness again and repent and Jesus zeroes out the checking debt again. Holiness is living at zero. There is no positive balance possible in the checking account. We can't exceed holiness - the best we can hope for in this life is a lack of sinfulness (debt) that keeps us at zero.

Only those who are debt-free in their checking account will be counted as worthy - and ONLY THEN can they cash in their retirement accounts. There will be many on that day that say "Lord, Lord, look at my giant retirement account!" and He will say, "Yep, but that wasn't the main point. Get your goatishness out of here." (Or something like that.) MANY will have done good works that they will never be able to cash in. Or they did some, but for the wrong motives. (See Matt. 25)

For me it's really simple. Try to stay at zero (holiness/purity) and repent ALL the time, just in case. Then, if I have ONE hour of my time to spend, do I rack up more treasure in heaven watching TV or visiting someone in prison or feeding the homeless? If I have just ONE dollar to give, do I get more treasure in heaven for helping buy a chandelier for the sanctuary or feeding an orphan in Ghana? And if I help a servant of God and thereby get a share of HIS reward, then who is the hottest stock around and how can I get in on it? (Matt. 10:40-42) That is, who has the biggest pile of treasure and how can I help them get more? Is it my megachurch pastor, the televangelist with a new book out, the missionaries from denominational headquarters or the barefoot native pastor in India that has planted 100 thriving churches among the most unreached and lives on $1 a day?

I'm not saying you financially "flagellate" yourself and live on nothing. I'm saying EVERY dollar is God's - so you ask Him, "Lord, can I buy an ice cream cone with this dollar? Lord, should I feed an orphan with this dollar? Lord, should I help buy a million dollar chandelier for the sanctuary?" Sometimes He says it's OK for me to have ice cream, or a newer car, or whatever. He cares for His own, He doesn't want me to starve. But He always wants His money spent according to HIS priorities. If you'll listen and then be obedient, even if it's hard, it's likely He'll decide you can be trusted with more and more money. We're to be good stewards, not just to hand it over to any schmo with a 501(c)(3) without asking any questions.

Oh ... and if you think I'm arguing against a "once saved, always saved" view of salvation, I'm really not. I honestly don't know if a sincere prayer at church camp when you were eight is enough to get you in the door or not. But I know Jesus expects a lot more out of us than just having once said a prayer and then done whatever we wanted the rest of the time. It just seems like the Narrow Path HAS to be more narrow than that! He says that if we love Him, we'll OBEY Him. Lots of people are going to call Him "Lord" on that day and but still won't make the cut. (Matt. 25:41-46)

I'm just pointing out that just because you might have done some good stuff, doesn't necessarily mean you'll get to cash in on that reward if you're not seeking holiness. You'll have to seek God and see if He says you're where you need to be with Him. That's between you two. But it's kind of important that you'd get this sorted out as soon as possible.

EMAIL FROM RENEE IN RESPONSE TO THE APOLOGY LETTER

Dear brother,

I've been hungering for more of God all my life. I've been to just about every denomination there is. I've sang in the choir, taught Sunday school, led folks to the Lord, memorized Scriptures, was Praise and Worship leader, Pastored a Church, on and on and on. And I've always been haunted by a HUGE HUNGER for more of our Adored. I'm a simple woman. I'm not smart or even cute. I'm of no importance whatsoever. I've been sick all my life (48 years old) and for the last 12 years I've been housebound with really bad health. I've watched myself become "hedged in" like Job, by the hand of our Loving Father. Cut off from family and friends, no health, no anything. I haven't been to church in many years because I couldn't take it anymore.

When one is suffering, and in pain with health problems, and with a broken heart because of one's own "flesh" (the old nature that doesn't wanna take up the Cross) AND with a grieving spirit because one wants MORE OF GOD, and one is weeping over lost loved ones............well, let me just say that I didn't fit in with any churches around here. My hubby is saved so there are two of us who fellowship together.

Anyway, even though I feel like I've been following in Job's footsteps, I believe with all my heart that our Adored is going to MOVE once again on behalf of His Own who are crying out to Him like the widow of Luke 18. ALL MY LIFE I'VE BEEN PLAGUED WITH A HUNGER FOR MORE OF GOD! Yes, I use the word plague because it seems so "wrong" when compared to the partying church of today. I've had this incredible hunger all my life, and used to weep by the hour when I'd read of Believers in the Bible.......OH to love God the way HE DESERVES TO BE LOVED. But brother, I KNEW my Flesh well, and without the Grace of God I could never love Him or anyone else. I'm a crusty old crow, and my flesh does NOT like taking up my daily cross, sigh.

Then, I stumbled onto a book about Saints of old like George Fox, Charles G. Finney, Smith Wigglesworth, etc, and I wept for days and days, and I've never been able to get rid of a DESIRE for more of God. I'll admit, may God forgive me, that in years gone by I did try to ignore it, and play church like others advised me to do. But it just wasn't me. The old hymn says "Just as I am" and I'm too stupid to be anything less than myself, for better or for worse. Besides, our Tender Eternal knows all about me anyway, so why try to hide anything from Him?!!

Brother, did you read how Mary was LOOKING FOR HER LORD outside of the tomb on the day He arose? Just imagine the scene.......Heaven is jam-packed with excitement! After 33 years, the One Who "used" to sit at the Right Hand of the Father will be coming back HOME. Every flower in glory must have been blooming with EXTRA joy that day! And then......the Father Speaks, and the Holy Spirit RAISES HIM FROM THE DEAD!!!! OH GLORY HE'S COMING UP.....HE'S COMING UP HERE ONCE AGAIN, RAISED VICTORIOUS!!!!! Oh the excitement, and joy!!!! But wait.......what is going on? Where IS HE? Why hasn't He come yet? What is the hold up? WHAT ON EARTH IS GOING ON? I'll tell you what ON EARTH is going on........the simple, yet DEEP LOVE OF A WOMAN FOR HER ADORED STOPPED THE LORD JESUS DEAD IN HIS TRACKS!! Huh? That's right! You see, the angels spoke to her when she looked into the tomb, but instead of hurrying home to her Women's Bible study group to bask in the glory of telling her "story" of seeing an angel, see just turned away from the grave and continued looking for HIM! SHE ONLY HAD EYES FOR HIM! Her heart was breaking. She was so heartbroken that she couldn't think of anything else. How on earth was she going to get through this day? WHERE WAS HE? Wherever He was, she HAD to find Him, HAD TO BE WITH HIM.

The Open Letter of Apology to the World

At this time our Blessed Redeemer is on His way HOME, but STOPS SHORT OF THE FATHER!!!!!!!! ABSOLUTELY INCREDIBLE!!!!!!!! What manner of LOVE IS THIS, that the Father (anxious to SEE His victorious SON) graciously steps aside to a lowly woman's desires? WHY? BECAUSE HE RECOGNIZES THE DEMAND OF HER BROKEN HEART, and gives way to the LOVE HE HIMSELF PUT THERE! OH WHAT A GOD!!!! The heart has its reasons whereof reason knows nothing. Not a Bible verse, but so incredible TRUE.

So, she sees the Gardener, and says to Him.........where have you taken Him to? She offers to take Him away even though she (being a lady) may have had a hard time taking a dead body anywhere. But you know what? She LOVED HIM so much that she didn't even think about that. All she wanted was TO BE WITH HIM. So, her heart drove her to ignore the angels, and LOOK for Him. So, she is forced (compelled by love) to question the Gardener. And then......PRAISE GOD......OUR ADORED REVEALS HIMSELF TO HER!!!!! LOVE ANSWERS LOVE! She was the FIRST to SEE HIM raised from the dead! And she reaches out to Him, but He says no because He hasn't yet been to the Father. So, LOVE FORCED LOVE TO STOP THAT DAY on the way Home to Glory, and comfort the hurting pains of a broken heart before going on HOME to the Father. And Mary became the first one to spread the GOOD NEWS that our Adored IS RISEN!!!

Dear brother, I'm jealous of her. I'm jealous of King David. I tell you that I want to love God SO MUCH that the Angels in Heaven BLUSH!!! I want to LOVE HIM like HE has NEVER been loved before, and Christ IN ME is able to do it. But my fleshy nature needs the Power of the Holy Spirit from on High to flow through me to do so. I've never been Baptised in the Holy Spirit. I've been through some bad experiences concerning that, and now am waiting for the Lord to pour out His REAL Holy Spirit. I want to be so filled with the LORD JESUS that my flesh is too danged scared to even try to come out, lol. I want to be so filled with His HOLY OIL that I leave marks on the floor as I walk. Well, okay, I don't expect to leave actual marks, but brother, DO YOU KNOW WHAT I MEAN? I'm no good to anyone the way I am. I need the LORD in ALL HIS FULNESS. Call it revival, call it a new song, call it whatever you want to call it. All I know is that I feel like Patrick Henry: Give me LIBERTY (where the Spirit of the Lord is, there is Liberty) OR GIVE ME DEATH (to die is gain). If Mr. Henry could feel that way about real estate, then how much more the Church about THE LIVING GOD?!! I'm tired of myself the way I am, and tired of watching sinners suffering, and living without the Lord. WHERE IS MORE OF THE LORD? I feel like even after 12 eternities I'm going to be wanting MORE of Him. Please pray for me dear brother. My hubby has caught this desire now, and we both felt alone in this until we heard about you from another brother we just heard of a few days ago. We live in St. Louis County. So, we are also SHOW ME JESUS Saints, heehee.

Well, brother, I'm sorry for going on and on, but praise God, as tears flow, I've got to tell you that I've been so lonely, not knowing that others were hungering for more of our Adored also. Praise God for His mercy. I'm in a lot of pain or my hubby and I would come to that John the Baptist conference. Please pray for us. We need more of the Lord.

God bless you dear brother, and thank you. I was going to post at that discussion forum, but it is so new, and I felt like I'd be spoiling it. I feel all thumbs when saying stuff over the net. Heck, I feel like I'm all thumbs anyway. I'm sure I'm the one who gave our Lord Jesus all that white hair that He has now according to the description of Him in Revelation, lol.

love to you from your sis, Renee'

A little child shall lead them... :-)

DOUG'S PERSONAL EXPERIENCE WITH THE HOLY SPIRIT
(Written Jan. 25, 2005 – edited March, 2007 and October, 2011)

I had been praying and aching for several months to see the Holy Spirit come in power and do something. I had read Acts over and over and we were having a Bible Study time on Sunday nights at my shop with the folks I respected the most. What I was really hoping for was that book of Acts, Pentecost, tongues of fire stuff – but had no idea what I was doing. TWICE in my life (before November of 2004) had I ever even been in a room with someone speaking in tongues - and one of those was at a concert with like 2500 other people. They didn't teach me anything about this in the Baptist church except to be skeptical and suspect it's made up - or worse, that it's from the enemy. (Even now, I'm still hyper-sensitive to it and it's appropriate use. Which is a good thing.)

Round about November, Andrew (Strom) and I met and had lunch and he liked a lot of what I had been saying about the problems in the church. He asked me if I had been baptized in the Holy Spirit and I said, "Huh?" We talked about it for awhile and he encouraged me to read up and pray on it. A couple days later I went down to his Sunday evening meeting he was having and he asked if I would like to speak - which of course I did. Had a good impact, although kind of preaching to the choir since his crowd is already sort of outside of the standard "church" streams. But that was also the first night the Schafers were there and we really hit it off.

The following Tuesday (11/23/04), Andrew was having a prayer meeting at the home of one of the folks in his group and suggested I come and they would pray for me to receive "the Blessing" - that is, to be filled with the Holy Spirit. They were all his family and a few other folks he trusted a lot. (I've learned not to let just ANYBODY lay hands on me!) I was fully primed by the time it rolled around. We had a meal and talked for awhile and then we prayed a little and then they were going to pray on me. They wanted me to sit in a chair in the middle of the room and I said, "Heck, no! I'm kneeling. No way I'm going to sit there all comfy before God." So, about four or five of them are praying on me in tongues pretty loud. It was hard to concentrate, but I just decided that they were nice folks, so I didn't care how they wanted to pray as long as they were sincere and they helped me get what I came for.

Since I was a kid, I never prayed for anything but wisdom. It's just a math problem to me. Solomon was the smartest guy ever, that's what Solomon prayed for, that must make it the wisest thing to ask for. It's always at the top of the list of Gifts in I Corinthians and elsewhere. Why pray for tongues? It's at the bottom of the list! Just my business instinct, I guess. Go for the good stuff.

Anyway, so they prayed on me for about 30-40 minutes (I think) as I begged for the Holy Spirit and promised to do right if He would bless me. I promised God that if He would empower me, I was willing to give up anything and endure anything. I just wanted to be the most dangerous person on the planet to the cause of evil. I wanted to sniff it out and rip out it's heart with my teeth. I wanted to be God's pit bull. I wanted wisdom, I wanted a high vantage point, to see through the eyes of Jesus. To know what people needed to hear to convict them, to burn away all the impurities and see just the pure kernel of the essence of what we should be doing to please Him.

I begged Him to shine a light on anything in my heart that was in the way and I would scrub it out. Together, He and I just went through one thing after another. I have plenty of sins - maybe not big ones as the world judges them – but there is plenty of darkness in my heart for which to repent. I had to drop some angers at old bosses or girl friends or others. At one point, He said, "You're pretty good with the orphans, but you're lacking with the widows since you haven't gone to see your grandmother in the hospital." So I promised on the spot that I would go see her before the week was up and make it all right. That seemed to satisfy him. I kept getting a warm fuzzy feeling like this was my time and He was going to answer my prayers, but then it stalled out. About then, I think Andrew and them were getting tired (they have to lean over, because I refused the chair!) and he asks me if there is anything in the way or if there is a history of Masonry in my family. I said, "No," and we just all agreed to pray that the Lord would shine a light on what was the problem. Nearly as soon as we started praying again, the Holy Spirit reminded me that there wasn't any Masonry, but I had been in a fraternity in college that required that you take an oath of secrecy on God. Even though when I was an initiate I hadn't said the oath at the time, later on I was the ritualist and administered it to others. I instantly repented of it and renounced it and stepped away from that. That was the last thing in the way.

Just then, Andrew suggested that maybe I should stand up. When I did, the vision started. I prayed for wisdom and to see through the eyes of Jesus. To me that's just a higher vantage point - where you can see more of the Big Picture. Both the love and the anger, the judgement and the mercy. I had prayed to take on any task, no matter the cost. So what He showed me was as much wisdom and responsibility as I could handle without passing out. I distinctly remember a sense from Him that I didn't really know how big a thing I had asked for, but He was going to show me as much as I could handle anyway. He was glad that I asked, but almost grinning because He knew what it would do to me! Fatherly love like when your nine year old son wants to build his own race car or something.

So for about ten minutes or so (maybe more), God ran this through my head. It was as if I was in outer space looking down on the globe. On the right side is a reel of faces going by. All children, all different colors. The vast majority are crying or hurting or sick or dying. It was like fast forwarding a DVD, they whip by real fast and then it stops long enough to see a few, then they whip along again. On the left side of the globe is the outline of America and a nasty, inky blackness covering it with tendrils spreading out all over the world. I knew that this was the sin of the church - selfishness, apostasy, greed, pride, waste, denominationalism, fraud, prosperity gospel, etc. that was spreading out from America and reaching all over the world. The reel of pictures of kids was running full speed. The Lord said, "You wanted to see through my eyes, I'm going to show you ALL of it." He knows that I have a heart for kids (as He does) and that's the way He sees us anyway, so that's how He showed it to me - as innocents hurt, killed, maimed, abused, impoverished, starving because of the nasty blackness coming out of America. It was clear to me that these weren't little kids, these were God's children of all ages. And He made it clear I was seeing ALL of them. I mean ALL of them. I honestly believe that all six billion plus spun by. Maybe more, maybe it was all of them EVER. I can't even comprehend it. But He made it clear that they were dying because of US and what WE have done maliciously or selfishly neglected to do to push back the darkness. I had a horrible pain in my chest and ached and groaned instantly.

Andrew's middle girl, Kirsten (who was about 11), was praying hard on my right and without really knowing I'd done it, I grabbed ahold of her and hugged her to me and just stroked her head and cried big huge sobs. Out loud I kept begging God to stay His judgement and apologizing for what we'd done to the children. I just felt so much pain in my chest and I was groaning and crying and just kept watching and saying out loud, "Oh, the children! What we've done to the children! Please help us save them, Lord. I'm SO sorry." (Or some derivative or combination thereof.) And I REALLY, REALLY needed Kirsten at that moment as a real live kid I could pet and hug and cry over. (She and I are bonded in a way I can't really explain. She just let me pet her head and drip on her and kept right on praying for me. What a good sport!) This went on for a long time (to me) and then finally faded with Him saying, "YOU'RE responsible for them. You said you would, so now it's on YOU." I asked the Lord, "What do you mean?!" He said, "You wanted to be the most dangerous person on the planet, you wanted to see through the eyes of Jesus, I showed you everybody, now you're responsible." I said, "Lord, you're telling lots of other people they're responsible, too, right? It's not just me?" He said, "It doesn't matter, you said you were willing, so now GO!" I got it then (and still do) that somehow I personally have a responsibility to reach them all with the Gospel and turn this thing around. (Still trying to figure out how that's fair -- or possible!)

After it was over, I was still in a lot of pain in my chest. We sat back in the circle and I was groaning and wincing in pain. They asked me what I had seen and I tried to tell them, but it was hard to breathe and every time I'd close my eyes I'd get a glimpse of it again and it would hurt. Like an ice pick in my chest. The folks there wanted to reassure me that it was OK that I hadn't spoken in tongues - which I found myself HIGHLY irritated about since that's not why I was there. I said, "Hey. I got what I came for and then some! I will never be the same. I asked for wisdom and to see the big picture and that's what I got." There was a kind of quiet pressure that the tongues part was REALLY important, but they could see clearly that something big had happened and I was still sitting there wincing and groaning and twitching in pain every so often. Mostly I was too distracted processing it to have been bothered, but it was an important lesson about the subconscious pressure that can be put on the experience without even realizing it. They all seemed to NEED tongues to happen at that moment, but then every single one of them went around and told about how when they started speaking in tongues it was some time after their Baptism with the Holy Spirit, some of them a LOT later. I didn't comment much at the time, but I thought it interesting that they all felt it SHOULD happen a certain way, but none of THEM had it happen to them that way. I didn't particularly want tongues, so it didn't much matter. At last Andrew made the most sense when he explained it mathematically (without meaning to). He explained that tongues is a way to let the Spirit help relieve you of a burden so heavy that words won't work anymore and that I would probably need it sooner or later if the pressure was high. THAT made sense, because I knew what I was carrying! So at that point, I started to see that it was coming and I was going to need it. (A couple days later I had to get a physical for the adoption anyway, so because of the chest pain I had them run cholesterol checks, just be sure I wasn't having a heart attack! But I checked out perfect!)

Anyway, we said goodbye and I got in my van to drive home, still wincing from the pain and moaning and groaning with the weight of what I'd seen. For several days, every time I closed my eyes I would see it again and wince and ache and moan. For a couple of days after, I had this amazing love for everybody. I would go about my day just wanting to hug on people and pinch their cheeks because I just KNEW how much Jesus loved them! I knew they were one of the children that had whipped by in my vision. I went into Wal-Mart and everyone was SOOO beautiful! But that faded in a couple of days - especially in Wal-Mart.

Things started to change instantly. I can't play video games anymore. I can't watch TV. I can't curse. I can't survive without at least a couple of hours of praying a day. The Bible is opened up for me and I see things and connections that I've never heard ANYBODY say before. Lately, I can't go anywhere without my Bible and I spend every extra minute in it. Sin repulses me. I've surely spoken out of turn or pridefully or not considered someone's feelings or misprioritized my time or been irritated - but am instantly aware of it and repentant. I have a hard time getting any work done because I want to talk about God all the time - to anybody - and when I do, they are convicted. I get physically pained if a dirty spam email pops up before I can delete it. I can't even think about anything intimate with anyone other than my wife. Can't even consider it or picture it. Gone is the fighting at home over stupid stuff, lots more love all the time even though it's a hard walk and there's still disagreement. One night He woke me up at 2am and said to pray for my wife. Comfy in bed with her on my arm, warm blankets, eyes closed - I prayed until 6:30am without a break or dozing off or anything. Just like on auto-pilot, but not asleep. Which is nuts cause I'll fall asleep typing sometimes and bash my head on the keyboard. Much less, comfy in bed with my eyes closed! Plus I'm fasting now. Never know when or for how long, but I shouldn't be able to fast even a half a day with my hypoglycemia. Now I get up in the morning and go to the fridge and ask the Lord if I get to eat today. Sometimes He says yes and sometimes no. If I can physically GET the food in my mouth, I'm not fasting. It's not even a decision anymore. In the last two months He has had me fasting several times for 24 hours or less, once for almost three days and once for almost four days. Just water. No cravings, no pain, no headaches or dizziness or weakness. Usually ends with some big event for which I need to be fully concentrated or clean. Then I can get food in my mouth again. I actually look forward to fasting because I know I'm being obedient and I know it's going to end with something that will glorify Him. (Once was the Christmas day trip to the children's hospital.) Plus it's evidence of a supernatural protection over me, because I should NOT medically be able to fast at all. *{Update: Since this was written the fasting changed to mostly without even water, 1-8 days at a time, on average 3 or 4 days a week without water for over two years. That's just God! I lost over 70 pounds and feel great!}*

The following three weeks (after 11/23) held a constant conversational closeness with the Holy Spirit and some AMAZING prayer time where He laid out more of what is coming and made promises to me of weapons

I would have in order to fight the battles ahead (including the gift of healing and discernment/deliverance of evil spirits and other stuff). In that time I got to participate in two good friends getting full of the Spirit - one dear friend at another of Andrew's meetings (who started singing in tongues right on the spot!) and one by myself in the office with her. Also gave some really hard specific prophetic words individually to specific people that changed them. Also in that time, the Schafers came to work with us. (James and Cindy have been such a critical component of the learning that has been crammed into those first 12 weeks! I can't even begin to imagine what I would have done without their intercession and gentle advice and example.) God sent this missionary family from Canada to Liberty, Missouri to spend their time at my for-profit furniture store and help grow me!

Nonetheless, the following three weeks were miserable because I felt a growing despair and unhappiness and darkness. I was getting a massive pressure inside and no release valve. I was praying desperately for the gift of tongues at that point because I felt I couldn't get it all out. The burden on me felt huge and I wasn't getting any relief. Then bad things started happening at home - the sewer backs up into the basement and the dog throws up all over and the kid is acting up and the wife is sick. Lots of people are heavily burdened and are praying for me like crazy. My wife didn't know what to do with me, because she was very skeptical of the "charismatic thing" and I'm up at all hours and crying and praying and moaning and groaning. She said, "Where's your joy? We know who wins in the end! Why all the crying?" But I can't help but see the badness.

One Sunday evening, I'm sitting in the living room asking what to do and the Lord tells me to read Hosea. So I'm reading Hosea with a towel over my head (just needed to get UNDER something!) and crying and shaking and rocking back and forth as the Lord shows me how desperately bad the judgement on America will be because we're doing everything in Hosea that brought judgement on Israel, except with thousands of times worse. Then Rachael wakes up from her nap and walks through the living room, shakes her head at me and says, "Except for the nonsense syllables, you might as well be speaking in tongues for the way you sound." Well, she often has bursts of wisdom hidden in the most unlikely, sarcastic comments, so something clicked in me that it was so weird that she would say that since I'd been praying so hard about tongues.

So the Lord kind of nudged me that I ought to figure out what it was I was doing and led me through some "moaning and groaning" scriptures. Romans 8:26 is probably the most well-known: *26 In the same way, the Spirit helps us in our weakness. We do not know what we ought to pray for, but the Spirit himself intercedes for us with groans that words cannot express. 27 And he who searches our hearts knows the mind of the Spirit, because the Spirit intercedes for the saints in accordance with God's will.*

Others include:

> **Romans 8:23** (all NIV) - *Not only so, but we ourselves, who have the firstfruits of the Spirit, groan inwardly as we wait eagerly for our adoption as sons, the redemption of our bodies.*
>
> **2 Corinthians 5:2** - *Meanwhile we groan, longing to be clothed with our heavenly dwelling,*
>
> **2 Corinthians 5:4** - *For while we are in this tent, we groan and are burdened, because we do not wish to be unclothed but to be clothed with our heavenly dwelling, so that what is mortal may be swallowed up by life.*
>
> **Isaiah 59:11** - *We all growl like bears; we moan mournfully like doves. We look for justice, but find none; for deliverance, but it is far away.*
>
> **Micah 1:8** - *Because of this I will weep and wail; I will go about barefoot and naked. I will howl like a jackal and moan like an owl. 9 For her wound is incurable; it has come to Judah. It has reached the very gate of my people, even to Jerusalem itself.*

But (unfortunately) the ONE that most resonates with me is :

Ezekiel 21:6 - 6 *"Therefore groan, son of man! Groan before them with broken heart and bitter grief. 7 And when they ask you, 'Why are you groaning?' you shall say, 'Because of the news that is coming. Every heart will melt and every hand go limp; every spirit will become faint and every knee become as weak as water.' It is coming! It will surely take place, declares the sovereign LORD ."* The word of the LORD came to me: *"Son of man, prophesy and say, 'This is what the Lord says: " 'A sword, a sword, sharpened and polished- sharpened for the slaughter, polished to flash like lightning!"* (... And other scariness following!)

The next day, I talked to Janice and James and Andrew about it and whether that's what maybe I could have in the slot where tongues would normally be - 'cause I'd been doing it since that same night (11/23), even during the vision, but nobody thought to tell me to consider that that was one of the options! So that Monday I just went around the office wheezing and groaning and the pressure went down. That night I got home and confirmed it with God in prayer time (3 times) and He told me to stop asking for something else, that <u>this</u> is what I was to have and it was better for me anyway (and explained why). Glory to God!!

From then on I've been moaning and groaning and grumbling and wheezing all the time to get the pressure down. This gift was given to me this way for specific personal reasons and is very powerful. I feel like I could move mountains with it. I was talking to David Kirkwood about it and He asked if I'd read anything about it because it's a consistent component in all the major revival movements and some folks try to fake it. I hadn't and haven't since. If I had known it was one of the options, I would not have prayed desperately for tongues for three weeks! So he had to rethink his sense of the validity of it as reality and not myth - since I have it and didn't even know what it was. I think it's cool because it's not exactly subject to the I Corinthians 14 rules for tongues. In fact, God actually orders Ezekiel to do it in public! Also, I can do it all the time and most folks don't notice - or just think I have asthma. Also, it's very breathing focused and I asked Him about why this and He said, "To keep you from being prideful because every breath is MINE and if you don't use it to MY glory, I might decide you don't need any more breaths." Zowie! That got my attention! He also said that, "The time is coming when you will be an object lesson. People won't have time to waste anymore as things move faster. They will have between THIS breath and the next one to decide if they are going to dedicate that next breath (and all after it) to me. If they don't, they could be lost forever or like Ananias and Sapphira who held back and lied to Me, so I just made them stop breathing. Someday people will only have between this HEARTBEAT and the next one to decide who's team they are on and get right!" Things are moving faster all the time.

During the last 12 weeks, I have been through four or five major philosophical directional frameworks, tested and rejected bunches of theories and ideas, started two or three new websites, tempered my anger at the church and now refocusing and finally finding the pure central kernel of what God wants. Just now finding a voice that He can live with and God can use without creating more trouble for myself by distracting from Him. The LAST thing I want to do is say something that will create an obstacle or keep someone from seeing the One True God.

Anyway, so that's where I am at the moment. Who knows what next month will look like!

UPDATE: (3/2006)
That was as of 1/25/2005. The "Apology to the World" was written in February, 2005. The business started to flip upside down in March and April resulting in a migration of people leaving the business that were Christians, but couldn't live on faith quite THAT much. We started having prayer meetings in the store, as the Lord directed. Then the Lord led us to start accepting donations of food and toys and clothes and furniture and other things at the furniture store and caring for the poor - which has mushroomed into something amazing. The Church of Liberty website went up in June, 2005. Things got REALLY freaky in October, 2005. Now they're just completely off the charts!

People come to a furniture store to get healing and deliverance and groceries and prayer - or just a hug. More people keep showing up to help. Now we have authors and poets and musicians and artists telling us God gave them something and He told them to give it to ME so we could get it to the world! Miracles happen every day around here. It's just not uncommon at all for a customer to come in and find two or three people on their faces crying. Praise God! I could have never imagined a wilder adventure!

Pray to be dangerous to satan. Pray to get everything out of the way between you and God. Pray that He would bust out of the box you put Him in and reveal Himself in whatever way He thinks best. Stop telling Him what He can and can't do. Let Him talk to you and He'll direct your paths in EVERY way. And I GUARANTEE you that He'll make sure that you stop conforming to the world!

MORE UPDATES: (1/2007)

In July of 2006, God dramatically closed the furniture store and said to walk away. In September my wife moved out and took the kids. The house got foreclosed on. Lots of bills unpaid. God says He'll take care of it all and I'm on HIS time-clock from now on. As of October 2006 God said to hit the road, so I've been traveling all over the country praying and meeting folks and breaking things in the spirit. Sometimes alone, sometimes with a brother traveling along. Sometimes picking up hitch hikers! God is lighting up people all over and I get to watch! He's restoring the Body and bring connectivity and harmony back. Maybe you don't see it yet, but I do! It's coming. The New Song is being played! Praise God and it's just in time.

MORE UPDATES (3/21/2007)

On February 21, 2007, my road trip ended. Total was 17,500 miles to 32 states. Amazing trip, totally dependent on God for every dollar and every direction. Finally got to see my daughters after nearly five months. God said to let my goatee grow until my family is restored. Somehow it all has to do with His Bride and His kids, too. We're walking this one together, trying to get our houses in proper divine order.

Since February 21, God has been having me fan the fires in Liberty with lots of praying and fasting and listening. I spent a lot of time blowing on other people's flames, now it's time to get a blaze going here at home. On April 1, we're going to have the "Liberty Restoration." I have no idea what that means or what it will end up looking like, but God named it, He's organizing it and He'll have His way. I just know that it's time to take "church" outside the walls and BE the Body. If I had to describe what this is that we're going to do, I'd have to call it battlefield triage for a town. I think we're going to set up a M*A*S*H in the city park and treat the wounds of everyone that comes – whether physical, emotional, mental or spiritual. We'll see what that does to the spiritual temperature around here. :-)   Stay tuned! I think this is the big one! I thought I was ready after those first 12 weeks and knew what I was doing, but BOY, was I wrong!! Not until NOW did I know how to rest and get out of His way. Just in time!

MORE UPDATES (10/1/2011)

In the summer of 2007 we rented our first townhouse and started inviting folks in need to stay with us. Then we got another and another. At the peak, we had six houses and were the largest homeless shelter in the Northland of Kansas City. We started a food pantry out of the garage and distributed 500,000 pounds of food the first year. People started finding us online and coming for prayer and deliverance from all over the world. I always believed that a big revival was imminent, but I didn't see that revival and restoration is a snowball rolling along and getting bigger and bigger, not an instant event. Most people don't notice until the snowball is really big, but for someone watching closely, it was a long journey to get there. Now we have seven houses, a farm, feeding over 5,000 people every month and ministering to millions on the internet. More people are coming all the time. As of November, 2011, the seven books that I've written will be on Amazon.com as well. It's been a wild ride, and I still feel like it just started.

Quick Thought

How much treasure in heaven are you getting per dollar you're spending on the current ministries you are supporting? What is your return on investment?

When you stand before Jesus and He says,

"I was hungry and you didn't feed me, I was naked and you didn't clothe me."

-- you will NOT be able to say,

"But Lord, I paid the pastor to do it and he promised he'd take care of it!"

It's up to <u>YOU</u> to invest <u>all</u> your spiritual and material resources wisely and be His hands and feet.

You can't outsource your obedience.

If your current ministry investment vehicles are losers, then dump them and find somewhere to invest that will pay a better dividend in heavenly treasure.

You're going to have to look Jesus in the eye and answer for every DIME and every MINUTE!

MESSAGE TO MY BAPTISTS

Brethren, please know that I come from where you come from. My Southern Baptist heritage goes back generations. I'm the son of a pastor and missionary. My dad was a trustee at Midwestern Theological Seminary and Vice President of the Missouri Baptist Convention at one point. I have a religion degree from a Baptist college. I taught Sunday School and sat on committees at one of the largest SBC churches in Missouri. I've got lots of notches on my belt from mission trips, choir tours, summer camps and more.

I didn't leave because someone hurt me. I'm not disgruntled or upset. I just wanted more Jesus than I was getting. Whatever happened to Peter between denying Christ three times and then preaching his first sermon and 3,000 people get dramatically saved - well, I missed that somewhere.

The Open Letter of Apology to the World

I read about Christians in other places and how they do things. Did you know that the Christians in China are under such persecution that in some places they don't even tell each other when the next meeting is going to be? They just pray and the Holy Spirit tells them all where to meet and when - then ten minutes before the police show up, the Holy Spirit says, "RUN!" and they all run. And they've been doing it that way for fifty years and there has never been any growth close to it in the history of the church. Over 10,000 people a day are coming to Christ in China. It's nothing for them to see amazing healings and miracles and even people raised from the dead. I have friends that travel and minister through Africa and Indonesia and they've SEEN people regrow limbs and interviewed people raised from the dead.

No buildings, no billboards, no TV shows, no direct mail campaigns, no demographic studies, no Purpose Driven stuff, no fancy sound systems - just the Holy Spirit running things. And an expectation that He can speak to them, that He can heal them, that He can provide all that's needed. Walking daily with Jesus is a reality to them, an undeniable relationship - not a figurative possibility or a future hope.

I don't want to give you choices. Jesus didn't give people many choices. Either He was the Son of God or He was a raving, megalomaniacal, lunatic. No middle ground, He painted them into a corner. So if I want to be like Jesus, I probably shouldn't give you many options either. Either I'm right and I'm hearing God OR I'm a dangerous, raving loony. I don't want you to think I'm a nice, but confused, guy. I want you to get fully on board or persecute me. I don't have time for lukewarm anymore - and neither does Jesus.

So here goes ... All the stuff in the Book of Acts is for real and it's for today. You can't pick and choose which of the Gifts of the Spirit are real and for today and which ran out of steam when the Bible was finished being written. Either they're ALL good and available or NONE of them are. So, is there still a Gift of Wisdom? Knowledge? Discernment? You can't just eliminate the uncomfortable ones! I'm telling you from my personal experience - ALL of it is available to you RIGHT NOW. And it sure works a whole lot better than what we've been doing. When someone comes face to face with Almighty God in a great big way, they don't need near as much baby-sitting and enticing to keep coming to church! When they hear the Shepherd's voice for themselves, we don't really have to tell them what to do. If the Holy Spirit is supposed to be our teacher, how is He going to do that if you refuse to hear Him? If there is a war between Good and Evil and Headquarters yells, "DUCK!" but you can't hear it, you're going to be the first casualty - and I don't want to be in a foxhole with you.

I just allowed the possibility that God doesn't change and that what He used to do, He probably would still like to be doing if I would just get my head out of the way. The Word says we're to be FILLED with the Holy Spirit and I didn't feel like my cup was all the way full. I didn't really have peace and joy and victory, because I wasn't really free of sin. Actually the Greek means "to be being filled" - a constant and repeated action - not just a one-time thing. I just prayed that God would fill me so full that nothing else could fit and that He could do whatever with me that He wanted from there. If there is a war between Good and Evil, I don't want a handgun, I want a nuke. Lord, I promise I'll be good, please just give me the big weapons.

Then I saw everything in the book of Acts start to happen right in front of me - right in my little furniture store. All of it - wisdom, words of knowledge, faith, healing, miracles, prophecy, discerning of spirits, tongues, and interpretation of tongues. I've talked to people personally who were given the gift of tongues and it's a specific language of man. I know people from other countries that were given ENGLISH! I've seen people instantly healed of migraines, stomach troubles, hip problems, chronic pain, lupus, fibromyalgia and more. I've seen people oppressed by demons be instantly delivered of fear, anger, confusion, bitterness, addiction, lust, worry, schizophrenia, and more. At one point, we were having a private prayer meeting at the store and while we were praying someone ritually sacrificed a cat in front - right on the main drag in the middle of town on a Tuesday night! No question about it - slit throat, puddle of blood. One of the ladies at the prayer meeting had come out of witchcraft and knew just what it was. She came in and told me and I did a little jig! They didn't understand but I was just so thrilled that we got somebody's attention!! I had never been a part of a church where somebody cursed it and sacrificed an animal out front! If there is a war but nobody is shooting at you - then you're NOT dangerous!

Just work the logic with me here. There is a war and the enemy has witches and spells and astral projection and zombies and voodoo and mediums and psychics and channeling and talking to demons. That stuff IS for real and has impact on the "natural" world - to varying degrees. Even Christians that don't believe God speaks to people, won't play with a Ouija board – because SOMETHING will answer you!

So where's MY stuff? This is a war in which they have all these weapons and all our stuff ended when the Bible was completed? Whose idea was that?! Who is most glorified by the theology that our God doesn't speak anymore and all the cool stuff He promised us and we see in play in Acts (and following) is no good anymore? Surely it must have been satan's idea because it sure makes Jesus look kind of neutered.

Why does only one side get cool weapons? Was my denomination leaving out important stuff that I needed for warfare? Because in the first century they had amazing weapons and defenses available to them. They had the Holy Spirit telling them stuff they wouldn't have known (Acts 5:1-11), they had people hearing from God (Acts 13:2), they had people writing stuff as God dictated and prophesying about the future (Revelation), they were caught up in the Spirit to heaven (2 Corin. 12:2-4), they had dreams and visions (Acts 10:9-23), they saw angels (Acts 12), they saw Jesus Himself (Acts 9:1-22), they cast out demons (Acts 16:16-18), they were bitten by deadly snakes and didn't die (Acts 28:1-10), they spoke in other languages of men and of angels (Acts 2, I Corin. 12 & more), they healed people (Acts 5:15), they prayed and miracles happened (Acts 5:12, Acts 12) – even teleportation (Acts 8:39) and they raised the dead (Acts 9:32-42)! They even had people who were against them drop dead (Acts 5:1-11) or go blind (Acts 13:6-12) – on command! (And that's just ONE reference for each! There are lots more!)

And it can't just be about the Apostles, because there were people doing some of this stuff in the Old Testament, too. So the Holy Spirit didn't first appear on the scene at Pentecost and then disappear when the Bible was completed. That just makes no sense. Not to mention that it flies in the face of millions of Christians around the world that are walking in the power of Christ, not just the salvation of Christ.

The Baptists taught me the Word really well, taught me to love Jesus, and taught me discernment and skepticism. That stuff is important because there are many false prophets and false revivals out there – and more coming (including one really big, one world religion). I'm not a sucker for whatever stupid manifestation-seeking fad comes along. I want 100% pure Jesus. It just that I've learned that we left some important stuff out. I'm just pretty sure that I grieved the Holy Spirit for a lot of years by telling God what He did and didn't do anymore. It says if we bind it on earth it will be bound in heaven. If you don't believe God can talk to you, He probably won't. If you don't think God can heal people, then put your trust in doctors and pray God will help them remember what they learned in school. It just seems kind of sad and useless to have a prayer meeting where we all bow our heads while somebody reads off the names of all the sick people, but none of us actually believe God will do anything miraculous.

My God is bigger. My God doesn't change. Please, Brothers, I love you all, but stop putting Him in a box. Let Him be God. Expect Him to be true to ALL His promises. Seek more. There's more to be had. I promise.

WHERE ARE THE MARTYRS?

What if Walmart said, "Trust us, just give us a percentage of your gross income and we'll spend it wisely. You'll get a good product. We promise." Would you believe them? Don't you think there are market forces at work in the church? That they would look for efficiencies and start cutting corners?

That is, if I were the pastor of a church of 1,000 people and I preached six weeks in a row about the dangers of riches and the judgement on the wealthy and the need to pick up our cross daily and the complete inadequacy of a little prayer when you were eight if you've never since lived your life with holiness - do you think I would still have 1,000 people at the end of the six weeks? Do you think I would have a job?

See, WE'RE the consumers! As long as we spend the money there will always be someone willing to tickle our ears. Most of the time, they don't even know they're doing it.

No way, boys. Not anymore. Not with MY money. We are seeing NEGATIVE population growth in the church. We are NOT feeding the hungry. We are not caring for the orphans. We are not reaching the lost. We're not even keeping up with population growth. We are bringing in $250 BILLION a year and spending 95% of it on comforts and programs for the "saved". AND we're in debt up to our eyeballs!!

THIS IS NO KIND OF WAY TO FIGHT A WAR!

So I say, accept personal responsibility (as I have) for having fed this beast. If your church is soft and fluffy - DON'T throw more money at it hoping it will start saying hard things - the money is what made them want to BE soft and fluffy! If your church is saying the hard things and meeting needs and doing God's work the way God wants it done - then give them ALL your money! He'll give you more.

Where are the martyrs?! Where are the people willing to do anything for the cause of Christ?! We need them to get to work. Something big is coming. God's given us the vision and laid out the plan. All the pieces are coming together.

All the people in the wilderness need to hook up, get fed some real meat and then we need to send them BACK into the churches with big armloads of meat to show love and feed the hungry. If we can get little tornadoes of revival started and they get some critical mass, eventually people are going to go up to the pastor and ask him to preach something hard for a change - and THEN he will be unshackled and free to say what he's aching to say, but been taught (by us) not to!

If God tells you to stay in the "church" then stay – and speak the Truth in love. But don't assume you're going to get fed meat there, you might not. But stay because you love them – and just ask lots questions.

Lean over to someone next to you in the service and gently and very sweetly say something like:

- Hey, did we pray about that new building? Whose idea was it?
- Hmmm. I wonder if there's another way to reach people?
- I wonder why there aren't more minorities here?
- I wonder what would happen if a smelly, homeless guy wanted to come to church here?
- I wonder what Jesus would have thought of that sermon?
- Ever think there must be more to it than this?
- When was the last time you saw anybody really repenting around here?

We need covert, special forces commandos to fulfill Romans 12 until we can get the whole army ready to fight.

That's the simple three step plan for warfare on God's terms.

If in thanks for His mercy, you're willing to offer your Bodies (personal, family, congregation, town - any or all of them) as living sacrifices, holy and pleasing to God (that means washed clean and acceptable) - do THIS:

1. STOP CONFORMING TO THE PATTERN OF THE WORLD!!!!

For Pete's sake! We were never supposed to get comfy here! We were never supposed to go into the land of milk and honey and leave God in the desert! (Ex. 33!) We're to be aliens in a strange land. We're to be fools for Jesus. We're to be hated and despised! Whose idea could it have been to have 37,000+ denominations and feuding and fighting and waste and fraud and hypocrisy and compromise and building consultants and demographic experts??!!! Can you say, "Sataaaan?"

2. Be transformed by the RENEWING of your minds.

Grow up into Him who is the Head. Get all the junk OUT and focus on JESUS!! Every man-made thing is DROSS! It's chaff. It's rubbish. IT WILL SURELY BURN OFF IN THE FIRE! The only pure, clean truth is the WORD. Learn Jesus, do what Jesus wants, ignore what Jesus would have ignored, love who Jesus loved. Stop reading the 1,000 Man-made commentaries on the book of Hebrews and read <u>HEBREWS</u> and beg the Spirit to show you what you need! Get as much Holy Spirit in you as you can, as fast as you can. Pray for wisdom! That's at the top of all the lists of gifts, seems to be the least likely to get abused and what seems to be lacking most right now. You don't need Forty Days of Purpose to figure out what you want to do for God - you're the SACRIFICE! Just get up on the altar and shut up! If you'll just lay there and stop squirming, when He is good and ready, He'll cut your head off and put His head on. Then your mind will be RE-newed. Back the way it was supposed to be. Rebooted to His default settings and conformed to Christ. Oh, and get sanctified so you'll be an acceptable sacrifice - and don't bring your baggage up on the altar.

3. THEN you will know what is the perfect will of God - AND THEN DO IT!

It's not theoretical - it's ACTION. Find out what God wants and DO IT. No more need for demographic studies and committee meetings and long-range plans. You'll KNOW the perfect will of God because you have His head! And I GUARANTEE it will look different than what we've BEEN doing.

There's more, but that's the big thing. You can ONLY find repentance and revival and restoration by those three - in that order.

Then, once you're hearing God really well, go back into the churches and heap burning coals of conviction on their heads by feeding them the meat they are dying for and the water they are thirsting for. Be Christ to them. God is preparing MANY hearts. People I thought unredeemable are asking questions again. The harvest is white.

Ask lots of questions, show love, bring them to small groups inside or outside the church where they can be challenged and grow. Don't expect to feed people individually and disciple them in groups of a thousand.

That's what we're hoping to see - a massive, self-replicating, mobile, cellular, no-nonsense structure that can operate inside or outside the church walls (and survive any persecution) to reinforce and restore and urge others toward Christ.

Read Judges 6. God calls Gideon to save Israel from the Midianites, but before he can go do that, he has to take care of the idolatry in his own backyard!! So he calls TEN friends together and they go in covertly at night (very shrewd - frontal assault won't work) and switch Baal's altar to an altar for God and then use the Asherah pole as the fuel for the sacrifice to God. They used the assets of the idolatry as the fuel to accomplish something for the Kingdom!! I love that part!

In the morning the men are mad and want to kill Gideon, but his Dad talks them down. Now ... I think they gave up too easily if they really loved Baal. They're trying to save face and they hate change, but I suspect at least <u>some</u> of those Jews thought, "You know, this really is better anyway. We should have done this a long time ago. Wish I'd have had the chutzpah to do that!" Just a couple chapters later, they want Gideon to be ruler over them! Give me 11 good people willing to die for Christ, hearing God's voice clearly, trained to show love, speaking only pure Truth, shrewd as serpents, harmless as doves, and determined to make a difference - and see what kind of impact they could have on a congregation or a town!

THEN Gideon can blow the trumpet and mass 32,000 and go fight the larger enemies rallied against God. And he needed all 32,000. The ones that went home weren't just chicken, they had responsibilities and families and businesses and infrastructure that the tribe needed to maintain. God knows that. He wasn't mad at them. But notice Judges 7:8. Gideon sends 31,700 of them home, but they leave ALL their provisions! That's the way God's economy should be working. The folks on the front lines doing battle up close with the enemy need to have SO much provision and supplies that they can meet any need - feed any that are hungry, give to any that are thirsty.

Those 1% on the front lines hearing God clearly are people that have proven they can be trusted to use assets for the Kingdom - those willing to die for Christ aren't going to buy a BENTLEY!! I'm sorry, they're just not.

I know folks working with prostitutes and drug addicts and runaways and gangs - and hardly anybody is supporting them. There is a giant underground church of ex-skinheads and witches and satanists and gang-bangers that will not even TALK to a Christian in a cardigan or set foot in a church for how toxic it is to them! They're pushing back the darkness in the worst conditions and getting NO help at all. Do we not care about the down and out? The unreached? Didn't Jesus?

Think of it this way, if God let's you and your kids stay home in the suburbs and keep your job and somebody else will go hold the heads of the junkies and clean up the prostitutes and tell them about Jesus - what's it worth to you?

Which do you think results in more treasure in heaven?

New chandelier in the sanctuary <---------> or getting 14 year old girls off the streets and into heaven?

Tithing because a guy in a suit says you HAVE to <---------> or Reaching those who have NEVER ONCE in their whole lives heard the name of Jesus spoken in their presence?

Your new $3000 big screen TV <---------> or Feeding 60 orphans in Ghana for a YEAR?

Consider I Corinthians 14:8
"Again, if the trumpet make an uncertain sound, who will prepare for the battle?"

We've got nothing BUT uncertain sounds -- if there are any at all!

I've got no patience anymore for anything that isn't 100% about Jesus.

No more messing around. This is WAR!

Where are the people willing to die so that Christ in them can live?

Where are the <u>REAL</u> Christians?! WHERE ARE THE MARTYRS?!

HELP WANTED – CITY RESTORATION POSITIONS AVAILABLE

WANTED: Christians that want restoration of the Body of Christ more than anything else.

PRIMARY JOB: To help bring in the last great harvest.

TITLE: KOGS (Kingdom of God Servants) - sometimes also referred to as "cogs"

NUMBER OF POSITIONS AVAILABLE: Unlimited - but currently we are pitifully understaffed for the size of the harvest we're predicting.

QUALIFICATIONS: They need to have no other gods before Me. They need to have My heart (hungry, naked, poor, in prison, etc.). They are going to need to be willing to receive with open arms and hearts the Outside Consultants and Management Experts that I send to them for training and correction purposes. They must be willing to lay down any flawed traditions or businesses practices that they have been using up to this point, so that I can retrain them. They must want to hear My voice so that I can direct their paths. They must stop putting Me in a box and asking Me to endorse THEIR ideas. They must want to be One Body with all the other KOGS and stop fighting with each other.

We are an equal opportunity employer, but priority hiring goes to those in the following categories: widows, orphans, handicapped, limping, poor, naked, down-trodden, bankrupt, criminals, prostitutes, tax-collectors, common laborers (especially carpenters and fishermen) and other broken, flawed vessels who have been humbled already. Rich people and seminary graduates may have to undergo additional breaking in order to qualify. Anyone willing to truly lay down their life (and stuff) for a friend goes to the front of the line.

REMUNERATIONS: Those accepting this position will get to see the Spirit of God descend in power on their assembly and their town like never before. They will get to see Me walk in their midst. They will learn peace and joy and victory on a scale they didn't know possible and they will have true community for the first time. They will also be ridiculed and persecuted - but they won't care. I will individually and collectively lift them up onto My lap and rub their head and wipe away every tear. I will pay all their bills and take care of their every need. I will be their Daddy.

APPLICATION PROCESS: If you have previously been revived for any period of time, before applying again you need to first say you're sorry for losing what was given to you previously. We can't give you a fresh fire until you repent for letting the last one go out. (Weeping and mourning is helpful in convincing us of your sincerity.) If you are new to this and have never made application before, just fill out the form below and submit by fervent prayer.

DEADLINE: This vacancy will remain open until we find qualified candidates or until the harvest is over. But time is getting short, so you might want to hurry before you miss it.

NOTE: Those who are comfortable with the current state of things and/or unrepentant for their part in the pain and suffering around them need not apply. Please refer to Ezekiel 9 for clarification. Church leaders please refer to Ezekiel 34.

For available positions in your area find someone that is feeding the hungry, clothing the naked, visiting prisoners, etc. They have a direct line to Headquarters.

The Open Letter of Apology to the World

CITY RESTORATION APPLICATION FORM:

Jesus Preference: (check all that apply)

___ Emergency-Only Jesus   ___ Church Growth Jesus   ___ Prosperity Jesus   ___ Denominational Jesus
___ Fire-Insurance-Get-Out-Of-Hell-Free Jesus   ___ Loves-Me-But-Can't/Won't-Talk-To-Me Jesus
___ Nonjudgemental-Everybody-Goes-To-Heaven Jesus   ___ Didn't-Come-In-The-Flesh Jesus
___ Not-Quite-As-Good-As-The-Virgin-Mary Jesus   ___ Nice-Philosopher/Prophet-But-Not-Divine Jesus
___ Master, King, Commander, Lord Jesus   ___ Other:_____

SCREENING QUESTIONS:

Money: (Check One)

___ I owe God 10% of my money.   ___ I owe God 10% of my money and an occasional love gift or offering.
___ I owe God everything I have and none of it is really mine.

Time: (Check One)
___ People have been saying for years that He is coming, why hurry?
___ People have been saying for years that He is coming, I should move faster.
___ He is coming soon! I can't waste a second!

Sacrifice: (Check One)
___ I am willing to give up Sunday mornings and Wednesday nights.
___ I am willing to be substantially inconvenienced on a regular basis.
___ I am willing to die for Jesus.

Love: (Check One)
___ I love the people in my family (mostly).   ___ I love the people that are like me and agree with me.
___ I love my enemies (and my family and the people that agree with me).

Humility: (Check One)
___ Mine is the Kingdom   ___ Mine is the Power   ___ Mine is the Glory
___ Thine is the Kingdom and the Power and the Glory forever.

Prayer: (Check One)
___ I close my eyes when other people are praying and try to pay attention.
___ I often pray in front of people and I pray at home by myself.
___ I pray without ceasing, often alone crying out to God and with tears and supplications.

Availability Date: (Check One)
___ When I'm retired and mostly out of steam anyway.   ___ When I'm perfect and feel worthy.
___ Whenever He says He wants me. Right NOW would be nice.

Please consider me for this position. I'm willing to go anywhere, do anything, endure anything, give anything, unlearn anything, pray without ceasing, be instant in season and out of season, know the Word of God and obey His commands and learn to hear His voice. I know I can't get there on my own and I'm sorry I ever tried. I will let Him direct ALL my paths from now on and I won't lean on my own understanding anymore. I will happily receive everything that I'm going to need to be fully equipped for His purposes. I'm ready to start anytime.

Signed: _____

OFFICE USE ONLY: Qualified? ____ *Start Date?* ____ *End Date?* ____ *Rich Welcome Scheduled?* ____

Fellowship Of The Martyrs

HELP WANTED – CITY RESTORATION <u>LEADERSHIP</u> POSITIONS AVAILABLE

WANTED: Christian leaders that want the restoration of the Body of Christ more than anything else and are willing to do whatever it takes regardless of the cost.

PRIMARY JOB: To help bring in the last great harvest and to serve God's people selflessly.

TITLE: L.O.T. (Least of These) - sometimes also referred to as "humble servants."

NUMBER OF POSITIONS AVAILABLE: Unlimited - but currently are pitifully understaffed for the size of the harvest we're predicting.

QUALIFICATIONS: They need to have no other gods before Me. They need to have My heart (for the hungry, naked, poor, in prison, etc.). They are going to need to be willing to receive with open arms and hearts the Outside Consultants and Management Experts that I send to them for training and correction purposes – but test everything. They must be willing to lay down any flawed traditions or business practices that they have been using up to this point, so that I can retrain them. They must want to hear My voice so that I can direct their paths. They must stop putting Me in a box and asking Me to endorse THEIR ideas. They must want to be One Body and stop fighting with each other.

We are an equal opportunity employer, but priority hiring goes to those in the following categories: widows, orphans, handicapped, limping, poor, naked, down-trodden, bankrupt, criminals, prostitutes, tax-collectors, common laborers (especially carpenters and fishermen) and other broken, flawed vessels who have been humbled already. Rich people and seminary graduates may have to undergo additional breaking in order to qualify. Anyone willing to truly lay down their life (and stuff) for a friend goes to the front of the line. If they are not willing to cry repentantly in front of others and be transparent, they won't be able to lead the sheep to Me.

REMUNERATIONS: Those accepting this position will get to see the Spirit of God descend in power on their assembly and their town like never before. They will get to see Me walk in their midst. They will learn peace and joy and victory and intimacy with Me on a scale they didn't know possible and they will have true community for the first time. I will pay all their bills and take care of their every need. I will hold their hand.

COSTS: It's very important that they count the cost ahead of time. If they accept this position they will be ridiculed and persecuted. It will probably result in the loss of some or all of the following: prestige, health, leisure time, money and assets of all kinds, home – even spouse and children are at risk. Those who accept this position will be beat on and reshaped and refined on a scale they can't even imagine, but I promise to never let it go beyond what they can handle. Their success will be directly proportional to their willingness to let My refining fire burn off everything in them that stands in the way of My plans. It WILL absolutely, positively hurt a LOT – but I will personally wipe away their every tear. In the end, they will look like Me – and I will treat them as a Father treats his Son..

APPLICATION PROCESS: Submit this application with fear and trembling and ask Me to do whatever it takes to make you ready right NOW no matter how much it hurts. Then bite down on something.

DEADLINE: This vacancy will remain open until we find qualified candidates or until the harvest is over. But if you're supposed to be leading and you refuse, the blood of all the people that didn't get reached because you wouldn't stand up in the day of battle (or move fast enough) is on YOU. So you might want to hurry. **NOTE: If you need extra motivation, please read Ezekiel 34 several times out loud.**

For available positions in your area find someone that has lost everything and has been thoroughly beaten into submission. They have a direct line to Headquarters.

The Open Letter of Apology to the World

CITY RESTORATION LEADERSHIP APPLICATION FORM:

Jesus Preference: (check all that apply)
___ Emergency-Only Jesus ___ Prosperity Jesus ___ Denominational Jesus ___ Church Growth Jesus
___ Fire-Insurance-Get-Out-Of-Hell-Free Jesus ___ Nonjudgemental-Everybody-Goes-To-Heaven Jesus
___ Didn't-Come-In-The-Flesh Jesus ___ Loves-Me-But-Can't/Won't-Talk-To-Me Jesus
___ Master, King, Commander, Lord Jesus ___ Other:_____

SCREENING QUESTIONS:

Money: (Check One)
___ I am willing to go, so long as I know a regular paycheck is coming and I have some security.
___ I am willing to go and live on faith, so long as I can tell people about my needs.
___ I am willing to go and live on faith and depend on God alone and never mention my needs to anyone.

Service: (Check One)
___ I am willing to serve those who will really appreciate what I do and won't ask me to get too dirty.
___ I am willing to serve even if no one notices, so long as I can feel like we're making some progress.
___ I am willing to serve those who will beat me and spit on me, and I won't stop even if it never pays off.

Prayer: (Check One)
___ I often stand in front and make long flowery prayers to impress people.
___ I frequently intercede for others and spend lots of hours alone in prayer.
___ I pray without ceasing and offer to stand in the gap and take on me anything necessary to free another.

Sacrifice: (Check One)
___ I am willing to strain my tea and religiously give 10% of all my spices and other garden produce.
___ I am willing to give all that I have, but I'd like to make payments and spread it out over time.
___ I am willing to die to self – all at once right now or in big chunks every day – regardless of the pain.

Humility: (Check One)
___ I prefer the seats of honor at the front and try to make sure everyone knows where I belong.
___ Mine is the Kingdom   ___ Mine is the Power   ___ Mine is the Glory
___ Thine is the Kingdom and the Power and the Glory forever. I'll take the crumbs from under the table.

Urgency: (Check One)
___ I will go when I'm sure that I'm fully prepared and know all that I need to know to be effective.
___ I will go right now, but I refuse to go over 20 miles per hour so as not to get hurt too bad in an accident.
___ I already left and I'm going 200 miles per hour and I don't care what happens, I'm not slowing down.

Determination: (Check One)
___ I will persevere until someone raises an eyebrow or threatens to leave my church.
___ I will persevere until it starts costing me things I really love.
___ I will persevere until someone kills me and I get to go Home.

Please consider me for this position. I'm willing to go anywhere, do anything, endure anything, give anything, unlearn anything, pray without ceasing, be instant in season and out of season, know the Word of God and obey His commands and learn to hear His voice. I know I can't get there on my own and I'm sorry I ever tried. I will let Him direct ALL my paths from now on and I won't lean on my own understanding anymore. I will happily receive everything that I'm going to need to be fully equipped for His purposes. I promise to never make it about me. I'm ready to start anytime.

Signed: _____

OFFICE USE: **Qualified?___ Start Date?___ End Date?___ Rich Welcome Scheduled?___ Robe Size?___**

*"OK, so the whole thing is a mess.
What do we DO about it?"*

www.TheChurchOfLiberty.com

The City Church is the only thing that will work. It's the only thing in the Bible. And it's coming.

Other books that might help you:

"Rain Right NOW, Lord!" - All about Spiritual Gifts and how to keep your cup so full of Jesus that nothing else can fit!

"The Red Dragon" – Why the church CANNOT seem to change.

"Who Neutered the Holy Spirit?" - What happened to God?

And much more on the website.

For other similar books and materials and for the most radical anointed music, art, T-shirts, buttons, stickers, books and more, shop our online store.

All proceeds devoted to pushing back the darkness in the most efficient possible way.

www.FellowshipOfTheMartyrs.com

**Post to: Fellowship Of The Martyrs
118 N. Conistor, #B251
Liberty, MO 64068**

Email to: fotm@fellowshipofthemartyrs.com
if we can help in any way.

The Open Letter of Apology to the World

Thank you, Father, for this opportunity to reach out and touch the life of another. Please let them receive everything in this book that you have for them. Please keep the enemy from distracting them and closing up their hearts and minds. Lord, bring Your spirit of repentance on us and on our land. In the Name of Jesus, Amen.

Need More Jesus? Pray THIS!

"Jesus, I'm really sorry for the mess I've made of my life, my family, my town, my country and my planet. I don't deserve it, but would You please straighten it all out before it's too late? I promise I'll let

You drive from now on and I'll sit in the back seat and shut up. Please just don't leave me like this. I stink at this. I just want YOU, Jesus! Please get anything that stands between me and You out of the way and tell me what to do. Give me wisdom and teach me to fear You and to obey you only. Fill me so full of Your Spirit that nothing else can fit. I'll take whatever you want to give me. I love you. In the mighty Name of my Lord Jesus Christ. Amen."

Want to be REALLY dangerous? Pray THIS!

(WARNING!! This WILL hurt. He WILL answer it. Guaranteed!)

"Lord, whatever it takes, whatever the cost, crush me, kill me, crucify me, break me, humble me, rip everything away from me, do whatever you want to me - just make me dangerous to the enemy in the biggest possible way. I understand that means I need to have more of YOU than I have now. Do whatever it takes. Give me a bigger cup of Jesus and keep it all the way full. I trust you and I love you, King Jesus. I'll hang in there. And please do it right NOW! In the Name of my Lord Jesus Christ. Amen."

The Red Dragon
The Horrifying Truth about why the "Church" cannot seem to change

Copyright © 2011 Doug Perry

Fellowship Of The Martyrs Publishing
www.FellowshipOfTheMartyrs.com
fotm@fellowshipofthemartyrs.com

All rights reserved.

ISBN: 1463736037
ISBN-13: 978-1463736033

Version 4.0, 2011

© Fellowship Of The Martyrs

The Bride gets her jewelry, but it's going to hurt to get it on,
and once you're used to it, you're never going to want to
rip it back off again. Heaven is free. HOLINESS is hard!
If not us, who? If not here, where? If not now, when?

CONTENTS

Prayer	110
How it all started	111
The IF/THEN Axioms	113
What is the Red Dragon?	116
Who has a Red Dragon?	117
How did it get on God's people?	118
What does it look like?	119
How does it work?	121
Is it just over Christian churches?	122
Personal-sized Red Dragons	123
Who DOES NOT have a Red Dragon?	137
How do you know if you're the curse?	138
Did the Bible predict this?	141
What would it look like to be free?	146
Left-over Pieces	150
Appendix A: Symptoms	151
Appendix B: Deuteronomy 28	153
Appendix C: Verses	159
Appendix D: The Body of Christ? You better hope not!	174

PRAY BEFORE STARTING

Father God, I ask in the name of Jesus Christ that you would preserve and protect those who are reading this, that you would remove or bind up every obstacle or strategy of the enemy that would try to keep them from hearing and receiving this word. I ask that you would bind up the spirit of Jezebel in each person during the time they are reading and meditating on this so that they could hear Your voice clearly and You could minister to their spirit Yourself about this. I pray that you would bind up the Red Dragon and keep it from whispering to them during this time. I know you want us free. Please, Father! Please forgive us and show us how to make it right. Don't let the enemy steal Your words from their heart. Confirm this to their spirits and show them what to do next. Thanks, Abba. We pray in the Name of Jesus Christ, Amen.

HOW IT ALL STARTED

The Red Dragon is what I first saw sitting over the top of several charismatic ministries here in Kansas City. It looks just like a Chinese silk parade dragon - a big, scary face with the feet of people sticking out underneath. (Not the little kind that they carry up over their head on a stick, but the really big, silk parade dragons that surround you and just your legs stick out.) At one major ministry here in town it was really trying to mess with me. I was on my knees at the altar trying to repent and stand in the gap for the sins of their people and for them going their own way. They really need somebody to repent for the damage they've done to so many people. Like Exodus 32:32, I was even offering to take onto myself all the guilt for what they had done. I had wept for them a lot before that. But inside their building I couldn't do it. I couldn't repent. Not because I didn't want to or was unwilling – I just couldn't even get a single tear out. Which is REALLY odd, because I cry when God lets me have a glass of water. Big chunks of most of my days are spent weeping for the state of things or for people, places or institutions. I weep at altars all the time. But at their altar I couldn't even get ONE tear out.

I knew something was suppressing my tears – and that's my best weapon! I started looking around trying to figure out what was messing with me and saw the Red Dragon on the roof. (It's not unusual for me to see spiritual strongholds on people or places.) I decided to rip it off and cast it down and, since I was pretty mad that it was messing with me, I decided to do some damage to it first. I went after it with the Sword of Spirit and hacked at it a few times and then the Lord said, "STOP!" I wanted to cast it down and He said, "No. I put it there and I'm not going to allow you to pull it off."

Well, that was kind of a shock! God told me to get up and leave, that it was a curse on the whole place and that HE put it there and I was not to try to deliver them of it. I stood in the parking lot for awhile and watched it on the roof and I got more and more angry. It was mocking me and telling me I had no authority and that it was in charge and I was nothing. I could see that the people in there were oblivious to it and were under all kinds of oppressions themselves, but the Red Dragon kept them from seeing the problems. This place is known internationally for it's excesses and nearly everyone I've met from there has a spirit of lust and a love of money and a big pride stronghold and yet is thoroughly convinced they're the hottest thing on the planet. As I stood next to my van, I was getting really hot and decided to torture it some more, but the Lord again stopped me. He said very clearly, "This is what it does, it is about pride. It makes it all about YOU. Either it convinces you to come inside and join it, or it convinces you to fight against it, but either way, it takes your eyes off of Jesus and makes you focus on IT. I told you to leave it alone! Now get in the van and go and don't come back."

Later that night, I was still having a real problem taking captive every thought as it continued to whisper and try to get pride to rise up. I was constantly thinking about what I should have done differently or how I'll show them someday and they'll see how wrong they are. I found myself scheming about all the ways I could free them or crush it or tell everyone that it was there. The Lord had to stop me again and show me that it was winning because I was making it about me and about works and about the fight with it. I had to constantly keep turning it over to God and renouncing it, but it kept coming back and sneaking in. Finally the Lord said to call a friend of mine who sees very well in spirit and has a lot of experience with deliverance. Even though I had tried to get all cleaned off, it wouldn't budge. So I called him and without prompting he saw the spirit of pride right away and helped me rip it off. I'm not sure I could have done it by myself. Not because Jesus in me isn't big enough to cast off any demon, but because THIS demon is a curse from God and is a WHOLE lot harder to get off of you.

Without repentance it won't budge and it SUPPRESSES repentance! I had to beg the Lord to get it off of me and repent for having tried to attack it against His will. But without someone with a true gift of repentance helping me, I was unable to really repent and get free from it. I got it on me when I let their Dragon goad me into fighting with it when the Lord had specifically told me to leave and not mess with it. I set myself above God and decided that it was OK for me to do something He had told me not to do. Just like Eve in the Garden.

Once having gained victory over any demonic power or stronghold, you gain authority over that "flavor" and have increased sensitivity. That's why people that have been sexually abused are hypersensitive to others who have been abused, for example. They can smell it on someone because they've been through it. Within a few weeks, the Lord started showing me lots of other Red Dragons. At first I thought they were just the offshoots of that one well-known ministry – as the other places where I had seen it were all connected to the first place in direct or round-about ways. But I also saw them on individuals who were only tangentially related to it.

Again I was sent to a conference of a different ministry here in town and found myself in the same situation, it was trying to either suck me in or get me to fight with it. The Lord made it clear that I was to just leave it alone, but again it required the help of another deliverance/repentance expert to get me cleaned off. After that I asked the Lord to upgrade my spiritual "shield" so that I could be in those places without it sticking to me constantly. To be placed under the curse along with them, it's enough to just be present and go along with whatever their agenda is! That was never going to work for me because I'm all over town and constantly visiting one ministry or another and can't have it messing with me constantly. The Lord honored my prayer for a tougher shield and so far it's holding.

I've seen the Red Dragon all over town. More on that below. Since the first encounter I have spent a lot of time praying and listening to the Lord about what this is, where it came from, how it got there and more importantly, how to get it off. As the Lord began to reveal more about it, I began to be horrified at what I was finding. It's not just that one ministry and it's not just an isolated outbreak. I hope you'll see as I proceed with this and that you will be equally shocked, horrified, ashamed, repentant – and have a substantial increase in your Fear of the Lord.

Some people think that this writing is about the Red Dragon and how to fight satan. It's not. This is about Fear of the Lord and what will happen when you go your own way – even a little bit. You CANNOT rebuke this off of someone. You CANNOT claim the blood of Jesus and cast this down. They HAVE to repent – and it suppresses repentance. I'm writing this to show you the mess we've made and the hopelessness of the situation without God's grace and without HIM pouring out the Gift of Repentance on His people – either directly or through the people He has raised up that already know how to weep and mourn before the altar. This writing is not about glorifying satan – he is only a tool in the hand of a fierce, jealous, living God, who at the moment is not at all happy with us.

If you don't believe that people can actually see demons (or that demons are real) or don't believe that I actually saw what I say I saw, then just consider all of this a fictional poetic allegory and see if you can get it to jive with Scripture. Whatever. I don't really care what you think of me, but ignore this message at your own risk. If I'm right, this is really, really far worse than anyone can probably get their head around and our situation is hopeless without repentance and hardly anybody can repent!

Father, I offer up everything you've ever given me toward the upbuilding and equipping of Your Body. Those who are reading this who believe in faith and can receive and are ready, please give them whatever you gave me. Whatever I have, they are welcome to drink it in right now, even if I don't get it back. Just the good stuff, Lord. Filter it and make sure that there is nothing but Your Spirit. I trust You, Father. Give them Discernment of Spirits, give them Wisdom, give them authority over the demons that confront them and give them Fear of the Lord. If you're willing and they're ready, let them see the Red Dragons clearly. Pour out the Gift of Repentance on them and let it be true and run strong. Give them the strength to turn and stay turned. In proportion to their faith and Your willingness and perfect will, increase all their gifts so that they can be dangerous to the enemy. Open blind eyes and let the dragon's scales fall off. Let them see the bad guys really clearly and have an unquenchable fire in their belly to free all the captives. In the name of the Lord Jesus Christ, Amen.

THE IF/THEN AXIOMS

THE IF/THEN AXIOMS OF GOD'S WRATH

IF you are a child of God, **THEN** the requirements are higher on you than on the "world". (John 1:12, Luke 12:48)

IF you are a child of God, **THEN** you are supposed to obey God and God alone and lean not on your own understanding. (Acts 5:29, Prov. 3:5)

IF you are a child of God and you are following a Man instead (including yourself), **THEN** you are in disobedience to God. (Matt. 9:9; I Peter 2:21; John 12:25-26)

IF you are a child of God in disobedience, **THEN** the Lord would like to draw you back to Himself – by whatever means necessary. (Luke 15)

IF you repeatedly refuse correction, **THEN** God will turn you over to increasingly bad stuff until you break. (Daniel 4:28-37; Romans 1:18-32)

IF you are really, really stubborn and rebellious, **THEN** God will harden your heart and send strong delusion on you until you are utterly destroyed – or you repent, whichever comes first. (Romans 1:18-32; Rom. 9:18; John 12:40; 2 Thess. 2:11-12)

IF you are a group of people, **THEN** God may collectively turn you over to satan to teach you not to blaspheme or send oppressions upon you. (I Tim. 1:20; I Tim. 6:1, Exodus, Judges, I and II Kings, etc.)

IF you persist in your rebellion, **THEN** expect MASSIVE negative consequences both spiritually and physically. (Isa. 31:1, Deut. 28, Lamentations, the bulk of the Bible is warnings of negative consequences for disobedience!)

IF there is a war between Good and Evil and we seem to be losing, **THEN** we are going our own way and God has blinded us and sent a strong delusion against us because we are being disobedient and rebellious. (Deut. 28, Rev. 3:14-22)

THE IF/THEN AXIOMS OF GOD'S CURSES

IF you are a child of God in disobedience, **THEN** God WILL send down curses on you until you turn. (2 Thess. 2:11-12; Acts 9:1-9; John 9:35-41, 12:40)

IF God sends down curses on you, **THEN** one of them is probably "strong delusion" or "blindness." (2 Thess. 2:11-12; Acts 9:1-9; John 9:35-41, 12:40)

IF God sends blindness or strong delusion on you, **THEN** you probably won't even know you're blind and deceived. (Rev. 3:15-17)

IF you are a prophet of God and you're in disobedience, **THEN** you will probably be VERY sure that you're hearing God really well, even though it's a lying spirit that is twisting everything up. (1 Kings 22:1-40; Matt. 15:14, 24:24; 2 Thess. 2:9-12; Rev. 3:15-17)

IF repentance is the only thing that can break the curse, **THEN** you really, really need to repent right now. (James 4:7-10; Mark 1:4; 2 Corinthians 7:9-11; Romans 2:4-5; Matt 3:1-2; Luke 13:1-5; Acts 2:36-41; Acts 17:29-31; 2 Peter 3:9; Rev. 2:5, 2:16, 2:22, 3:3; 3:19)

But, **IF** you're under a delusion and are blind or asleep, **THEN** you can't repent or don't know what to repent for. (Matt. 15:14; Rev. 3:17; John 9:40; Matt. 13:13-14)

IF you don't repent, **THEN** you are toast. (And repentance is a gift that can ONLY come from God – and He is cursing you for being disobedient and may not pour out on you the Gift of Repentance.) (Romans 2:4; 2 Tim. 2:25-26; Acts 17:30; James 4:7-10, Acts 5:31)

IF you can't or won't repent and repentance is the only hope, **THEN** you're caught in a hopeless paradox loop.

IF there is going to be any hope for you, **THEN** either God Himself or someone who already HAS a gift of repentance has to come and pour it out on you so that you can get released. And then you have to turn and **stay** turned. If you go back like a dog to its vomit, it's going to go VERY badly for you. (2 Peter 2:20-22; 2 Timothy 2:25-26; 2 Corin. 7:10)

THE IF/THEN AXIOMS OF CURRENT CHURCH CONDITIONS

IF God is for us, **THEN** nothing can stand against us. (Rom. 8:31; Josh 1:9; 1 John 4:13-18; 2 Chr 32:7-8; 2 Kings 6:15-17)

IF God says that if you obey, nothing can stand against you, and currently things are standing against us, **THEN** we must not be obeying God.

IF there is a war between good and evil and we seem to be losing, **THEN** we must be under the curses of Deuteronomy 28, not the blessings. (Deut. 28)

IF there is hatred among brethren and adultery and envy and lust and dissension and factions and selfish ambition inside the Church and its leadership, **THEN** it CANNOT inherit the Kingdom of Heaven in its current state. (Galatians 5)

IF there is a love of money present and persistent in the Church, **THEN** the root of all evil is well entrenched in our structures and we're in big trouble. (I Timothy 6:10)

IF we are to be known as Christians by our love and we hate each other, **THEN** we might not actually be Christians. (I John 2:9,11; 3:14-24; 4:19-21; John 15:23)

IF we are not being good stewards of that which the Lord entrusted to us and we've buried our coin in the dirt, **THEN** we will be cast into outer darkness where there will be much crying and gnashing of teeth. (Luke 12:35-48; Matt. 25:25-46)

IF we can definitely show that the Church is basically doing everything exactly BACKWARDS of the way the Bible suggests we do it – and nobody seems to mind, **THEN** we have to come to the conclusion that there is a supernatural stupidity imposed on the system because nobody could intentionally design something this broken.

> **For more information on this, see:**
>
> http://www.fellowshipofthemartyrs.com/scary_stats.htm
> http://www.fellowshipofthemartyrs.com/pharisees.htm
> http://www.fellowshipofthemartyrs.com/humansacrifice.htm
> http://www.fellowshipofthemartyrs.com/business.htm

Scary Stats – How can we scripturally justify this stuff?

(All Christian spending divided by output.)
* Average cost per baptism in Cambodia - $4300
* Average cost per baptism in India - $9800
* Average cost per baptism in USA - $1,550,000
* Average cost per baptism in Germany - $2,119,000

Less than 1% of Christian revenue is spent on evangelism to the most unreached.

91% of all Christian outreach/evangelism does not target non-Christians but targets other Christians.

Out of 648 million Great Commission Christians, 70% have never been told about the world's 1.6 billion unevangelized individuals.

Despite Christ's command to evangelize, 67% of all humans from AD 30 to the present day have never even heard of his name.

Some 250 of the 300 largest international Christian organizations regularly mislead the Christian public by publishing demonstrably incorrect or falsified progress statistics.

Currently there are over 41,000 "Christian" denominations and we start another one every two days.

> From World Christian Trends, William Carey Library, David Barrett & Todd Johnson, 2001. "Summary & analysis of the annual Christian mega-census."

WHAT IS THE RED DRAGON?

It is the enemy. It is the whore of Babylon, it is anti-christ, it is the false prophet, it is the dragon of Revelation. Not that it is the ONLY permutation or "echo" or complete manifestation of any of those things, but it is all of them as well. It is the Babylonian religious system in all it's forms and permutations. It could be Buddhism or Islam or Atheism or Catholicism or a denominational system like the Episcopalians, the Lutherans, the Methodists, etc. Everyone that has gone their own way and made up their own religion.

You don't think you made up your own religion? Well, if you've cut and pasted parts out of the Bible or added something to it that isn't really in there, then you've made a hybrid, accepted compromise and made a covenant with foreign gods of your own making. It's really obvious if you're bowing down to idols of gold or stone or wood, but it's just as much idolatry if you're bowing down to extra-Biblical documents or made up traditions or philosophies or the pastor. You can worship a particular version of the Bible, you can require things of those in your fellowship that the Bible doesn't require, you can refuse to associate with other people that have the Holy Spirit in them but disagree with you on some secondary issue, you can set a man up as your head instead of Jesus. Those and thousands of other permutations, are all evidence that you are a cult and have made up your own mystery religion and are worshiping the wrong Jesus (or worshiping yourselves).

The biggest difference between the Red Dragons is whether or not God considers you part of physical or spiritual Israel. If you are NOT, then the Dragon on you (or your "church") is there because it snuck in or was invited in, but either way, it can be crushed and you can be delivered and set free. At one point the Lord had me pull one off of a Buddhist monastery and crush it and cast it down. They CAN be delivered of the Red Dragon. (That doesn't mean they won't get another one right away if they like it, but the Lord wanted to show me that it's anti-christ, but it's not there as a consequence (curse) on the children of God. It's just the 'world' being the 'world.')

BUT ... if you are physical Israel (the nation/the race) or spiritual Israel (the Church), and you have a Red Dragon on the roof, then it is now firmly entrenched and GOD PUT IT THERE and it cannot be removed without repentance. It is MUCH sneakier and nastier and harder to get out from under this kind of Dragon, because God is angry and helping it along.

Hear me, if you are a "Christian" and you have gone your own way, the curses of Deuteronomy 28 have landed on you, but you are probably sure that you are just fine. This is not an "Old Testament" thing that doesn't apply anymore to Christians! For His purposes and to prove His sovereignty, God WILL harden your heart if you go your own way and WILL blind you to the true state of how bad things really are. The Church of Laodecia in Revelation 3 thought it was rich, but it was really hungry, naked, wretched and blind. That is the kind of skewed perspective that happens when you are supernaturally stupefied by this curse.

The "world" can be under a Red Dragon and really hate it and want out and be desperate for something better. They only remain trapped because they haven't heard the Truth or can't receive it yet. But the "church" under a Red Dragon actually likes it and doesn't want to change, because their ears are being tickled and their hearts are hardened. The longer it goes on, the worse it gets and subsequent generations are more and more depraved and lost. They are less and less likely to be hearing God and more and more dependent on legalism and tradition. Either way, the people die for lack of knowledge. Lack of knowledge of God's true law and lack of knowledge of what Fear of the Lord really is – and lack of knowledge about how to REALLY repent for anything.

In another effort to prove this, the Lord prompted me to do a complete study of all the times that someone in the Bible is affected by stupor, sleep, slumber, blindness or deafness. I can find NO instance in the Word of God of the enemy doing this to anybody. Nearly every pastor I've ever heard preach on this believes that the Church, particularly the church in America, is, at the moment, the rich, sleepy, blind Laodecian church. If I'm right, then based on my study of scripture, GOD Himself did this to us. There is NO indication that I can find anywhere that sleep or stupor or blindness can come on God's people from ANY source other than God – and that they did it to themselves by disobeying God!! (See verses at the end of the Red Dragon section – page 149.)

Please hear me. I've spent years visiting hundreds of congregations and traveling all over the country and seeing dragons large and small – on major ministries, on mega churches, on home groups, on individuals. This is FAR more dangerous than anyone wants to admit and far more deadly. You will be DEAD SURE that you are right and hearing God accurately, even while the Lord sends a lying spirit from the Throne that is intent on your destruction! He really does do that. Set your man-made theology aside for a moment and read the Word of God. Read 2 Chronicles 18 and 1 Kings 22. King David is not allowed to touch the king of Israel (Saul), but God is perfectly willing to kill another anointed king (Ahab) Himself and leave His people without a shepherd.

God WILL send a deception upon you and you won't even know it. The closer you are to God, the higher His expectation that you will obey and the meaner the Red Dragon to which He will turn you over when you go your own way. I know it's really unlikely that you can hear me if you're under one of those, but please try.

WHO HAS A RED DRAGON ON THEM?

Everybody that is not fully under Christ's headship automatically defaults to the anti-christ spirit. All layers at all levels are subject to being under the "cover" of the Red Dragon. You can even be under multiple Red Dragons at the same time. That is, if someone was a part of the Body of Christ but has gone their own way (whether individually or corporately) they have created their own "mystery religion" and put themselves under a Dragon. The longer they are there, the more God will harden their hearts and blind them to the true state of their soul.

It's not as simple as being out of "church" either, or withdrawing your "letter" of membership. It is much more pervasive and sneaky. A person can have an anti-christ religious spirit on them, their family, their congregation, their city, their denomination, their country. They can be "members" of multiple layers of Dragon Teams that might even have conflicting goals and purposes – but all have set themselves against God. And probably some layers I can't even see are in play, but they must ALL be broken! You can't conform to the 'world' on ANY level!

I've found that the Red Dragon is strongest and fiercest and most active and malicious on those places that would normally hear God the best. That is, the "Spirit-filled" ministries that believe in the gifts and preach holiness and believe God speaks and seek God's face require the biggest, meanest, sneakiest Red Dragon to keep them off course. Plus, the expectations are highest for them, so the consequences of disobedience are far worse. Those are the places where it is strongest and most active and easiest to spot on the roof. A congregation that is asleep and has been for generations, and the doctrine of the denomination is fully ingrained, and they are not in any danger of hearing God and being directed by Him, doesn't hardly require a Red Dragon at all. A teeny weeny one is all that needs to be assigned to that place. Both kinds of groups are just as deceived and just as oppressed, but it's a lot less work for the enemy if you're already asleep and you like it that way. And frankly, God is a lot less mad at the sleeping ones – because they don't know what they don't know.

The good news is that it's a lot easier to repent in a place that's asleep. I have a lot of hope that the Baptists and the Brethren and the Episcopalians and the Lutherans and others will be able to receive this and repent. Their Red Dragon is not as strong and they might just sneak up on it and get free before it notices. As soon as a revival fire is lit in a Baptist congregation however, a much bigger Dragon with lots of help will show up to squash it. The element of surprise is key. Bind up what's there before it can call for help.

I'm a lot less optimistic about the charismatics. They hear God and are really proud of it and are sure that they are hearing with 100% accuracy (which is what happens when you're under a delusion from God). Their Red Dragons are VERY powerful and fierce and have a stranglehold on corporate repentance. I have seen that one up close and personal and been shocked by how much it controls the whole thing – even outside people that come in to speak at some of these places are sometimes completely, supernaturally unable to really preach corporate repentance.

Ultimately, <u>corporate</u> change is going to come down to the Lead Dragon Dancer. If the ministry head (pastor, apostle, prophet, bishop, priest, whatever) can throw off the Red Dragon and really repent sincerely and weep and mourn in front of his sheep, he might just free them all. But it's the longest of long shots that the ministry head will really lay it all down without picking it up again – or finding a new Red Dragon of a slightly different style. I've seen it happen, so I know it can be done, but I don't think it's going to be common. Read Ezekiel 34.

I believe that a team of people who have a true Gift of Repentance can come and turn a place around – whether or not the Lead Dragon Dancer wants it. I've seen that happen as well. I've been in a congregation and poured out what I had and seen them weeping and repenting. But it is unsustainable if the Lead Dragon Dancer won't go along with it or the people won't leave behind the institutions of Man. They will not go where you won't lead them. If the shepherds won't go, the sheep won't either. The sheep are either going to need to find a shepherd that <u>will</u> get them to safety – or gang up on the shepherd they have until he breaks down and becomes a broken and contrite vessel useful for God's purposes.

Without corporate change, it's just going to be up to the individuals to get out from under it. That may happen in ones and twos, or it may be a whole mass exodus that leaves the Lead Dragon Dancer standing alone. Whatever it takes, just get out from under it if you can.

HOW DID IT GET ON GOD'S PEOPLE?

They went their own way. They ate from the forbidden fruit, turned to other gods, failed to carefully and diligently follow the Lord's commands, so they opened the door. They failed to joyfully and gladly serve the Lord in time of prosperity. The farther they went, the more the Lord hardened their hearts and gave it permission to mess with them. See Deuteronomy. 28. Those curses were natural curses on natural Israel but had a spiritual component. They are also spiritual curses on spiritual Israel – which is the Church – and they have a natural component. We are currently experiencing ALL of those curses in the "church" system that we've built. It can ONLY mean that we have disobeyed God and gone our own way. (See page 90).

We brought this on ourselves. Read Lamentations. These curses DID manifest on natural Israel. And they are currently manifesting on spiritual Israel at a phenomenal rate. But since we aren't seeing in the spirit – we're judging the natural (and we're blinded by God) – we're missing it. But the sheep can feel it and they're leaving.

2 Timothy 2:19-26 (KJV) – 19 Nevertheless the foundation of God standeth sure, having this seal, The Lord knoweth them that are his. And, let every one that nameth the name of Christ depart from iniquity. 20 But in a great house there are not only vessels of gold and of silver, but also of wood and of earth; and some to honour, and some to dishonour. 21 If a man therefore purge himself from these, he shall be a vessel unto honour, sanctified, and meet for the master's use, and prepared unto every good work. 22 Flee also youthful lusts: but follow righteousness, faith, charity, peace, with them that call on the Lord out of a pure heart. 23 But foolish and unlearned questions avoid, knowing that they do gender strifes. 24 And the servant of the Lord must not strive; but be gentle unto all men, apt to teach, patient, 25 In meekness instructing **those that oppose themselves**; if God peradventure will **give them repentance** to the acknowledging of the **truth**; 26 And that they may **recover themselves out of the snare of the devil**, who are taken captive by him at his will.

If you do not depart from iniquity, if you are not purged, if you do not flee from youthful lusts, if you do not avoid foolish and unlearned questions, if you engender strifes, THEN you oppose yourself by getting under a Red Dragon that is designed for your own destruction. You get out from under the protecting cover of God's perfect will and open yourself up to whatever wants to come mess with you. And it will probably be something really sneaky and subtle (at least at the beginning) and it will lie to you and it will sound JUST like God. And your ONLY hope is repentance – so that you can acknowledge the Truth and maybe recover from the snare of the devil who has taken you captive at his will. And this verse says that they may not be able to do it themselves, those who are sanctified servants of the Lord may need to patiently, meekly instruct those people about how to get free. I believe that means pouring out your own Gift of Repentance on them. How did YOU get to be sanctified, gentle, meek and patient – except by repenting? Now show them how to do it! Better yet, repent in front of them so they can see how it's done.

The longer you're under the Dragon, the more blind and stupid you get. At some point you're rolling on the floor clucking like chickens or worshiping crying statues or vicious to anyone that disagrees in the slightest – or worse, feeding your flock poisoned fruit punch or having sex with the daughters of your fifteen wives or loading your automatic weapons while the FBI and the ATF drive tanks into your living room. And you're still ABSOLUTELY sure it was all God's idea and you're on the right track! That is, right up until you stand before God and He says, "I never knew you." THEN there will be weeping and repenting, but it will be too late. Wouldn't it be better to just do the weeping first and maybe avoid all the other heartache?

How do you think we're going to get Him to turn without that? How about this verse? Think this is just good advice or is this a command? Is there ANY other prescription in the Word of God to get Him to turn?

2 Chronicles 7:13-14 – 13 "When **I shut** up the heavens so that there is **no rain**, or **command** locusts to devour the land or **send** a plague among my people, 14 **IF my** people, who are called by **my** name, will **humble** themselves and **pray** and seek **my** face and **turn** from their wicked ways, **THEN** will I **hear** from heaven and will **forgive** their sin and will **heal** their land.

WHAT DOES THE RED DRAGON LOOK LIKE?

The way it was shown to me, it looks just like the shell of a large Chinese dragon in a carnival or parade. It has no legs of its own and would be motionless without outside power. It has a great big, scary head with teeth and a mean look and seems very fierce and impressive – but also kind of endearing. It's covered in silk and shiny things and is designed to attract attention to itself. But it cannot do anything or get anywhere without the hands and feet of the people under its "cover" to keep it going. Just like in the parades, it is constantly chasing a "Pearl." Satan is a defeated enemy with no power of his own. He accomplishes his purposes by co-opting our own physical and spiritual energy. We are the legs that power him.

From the outside it looks very slick, the legs of the Dragon Dancers are adorned and colorful. But if you look underneath it's just a thin wood frame filled with sweaty guys in tanktops. From the inside, there's nothing really animated or special about it. All the emphasis is put on outside appearances and much work is put into making sure the "guts" are all hidden from view.

See a small Chinese parade dragon on video here - http://chcp.org/mpeg/ . And a larger, lit, fancy one here - http://www.theschoolbell.com/Links/Chinatown/dragon.mov . And you can see a lot more about the Chinese dragon here - http://www.moonfestival.org/legends/dragon.htm. And here - http://en.wikipedia.org/wiki/Chinese_dragon. If you do a Yahoo or Google search for "Chinese dragon" you might just be shocked at how much of this religious festival worshiping the dragons has been filtered down to school children as a "cultural" experience. There are pages and pages of teacher aids about how to have your class of elementary school kids do a dragon dance parade. This is a RELIGIOUS festival, this is NOT safe, fluffy fun for Christian kids! Here is an interesting writing about the Dragon throughout scripture and why we need to take this seriously – http://eifiles.cn/dp-en.htm .

I've seen the Red Dragons on people, too. It's a much smaller version, is mounted on their front with the tail up and the head down. That is, it's running down their front with it's tail in their face (or wrapped around their neck) and gripped on their front. Could be large or small, but it fits with the Deuteronomy 28 curse that we will be the tail and not the head. We may think we're in charge, but really we're just staring up a Red Dragon's rear end. Sometimes it will have more than one head. Sometimes it may even have a face that looks like whatever person they have knowingly or unknowingly made their god – Calvin, Luther, the Pope, their pastor, their wife – could even be themselves.

WHAT IS THE "PEARL"?

In Chinese religious mythology and in the parades, the dragons always chase a pearl. The really big red dragons chase a pearl painted blue and green like the Earth – now isn't that just straight out of the Book of Revelation!?

The Dragon dangles a shiny carrot out in front to take the attention off of itself. It convinces everyone of a goal and uses all their energy, momentum, and physical and spiritual assets to reach that goal – which is always something **other than** the pure pursuit of Jesus. It could be a new gym or a new piece of land for a bigger sanctuary or an experience or a manifestation or to be the biggest, best prayer ministry or to run a soup kitchen or anything – just so long as they're not directly pursuing Jesus and His total headship in everything. The goal is to be constantly moving and DOING so that it is always JUST ahead and requires constant forward motion. If a goal is actually reached, another will be immediately set so that the Dragon can keep everyone constantly churning. If a goal seems unreachable or is never met, it will be replaced by something that can affirm the Dragon Dancers and keep them urging forward. Whatever this "pearl of great price" might be, it **IS NOT** a pursuit of Fear of the Lord and a desire to be fully and completely under His headship and have constant communion with Him without any structures or systems of Man in the middle – that would destroy the Dragon. Anything but that will do. The Dragon is VERY creative. I've seen all kinds of Pearls and some of them look really honorable and noble, but the people have their eyes on the Pearl and not on Jesus. And the Pearl keeps them from seeing the Dragon that is enveloping them.

If the Pearl is ANYTHING other than what Jesus wants you to be doing at that very moment, you're going to be happily dancing OFF of the Narrow Path and out into the Broad Way that leads to destruction. There is His PERFECT will and everything else. If you aren't in His perfect will, then you're going your own way. If you can't hear His voice, then you're probably leaning on your own understanding and directing your own paths.

HOW DOES IT WORK?

The Lead Dragon Dancer is the one that is most skilled, most well-trained, most practiced and most showy. He is the one that controls the head of the Dragon (or at least he thinks he does). He is the most acclaimed, most noticed, and he dictates the direction, pace, style and movement of the Dragon. (In actuality, he's a slave to the pearl and the Dragon picked the pearl.) When the Red Dragon is over a congregation or ministry, the head of the ministry is the one closest to, most influenced by and best trained by the head of the Dragon. He is the absolute **least likely** to throw off the Red Dragon because he has the most to lose. He has worked a long time to get to be the Lead Dragon Dancer and he likes it. Plus the Red Dragon affirms him substantially and whispers to him that he is indispensable.

Just like in China, there are schools where you can go to learn how to be the "head" – how to be the Lead Dragon Dancer. (But here we call them "seminaries".) It's important that you perfect the art, and dance exactly according to the regional style and "flavor" of your particular Dragon Club. (Here we call them "denominations".) There are competitions and shows between Dragon Teams to see who is the best, who is the shiniest, who is the biggest, who is the most artistic and so on. There are all kinds of ways to stand out and make your Dragon unique and special. Everybody has some other Dragon that they want to either beat or be like. There are lots of books and conferences led by the most famous Lead Dragon Dancers about how to be more like them. We are introducing fancier and bigger Dragons all the time. In fact, we are even taking on Dragons that look just like Wall Street and Madison Avenue. We're adapting business models to our religious enterprises because their Dragons seem to be more efficient. But all we're doing it grieving God more.

The Red Dragon itself doesn't care how you dance - so long as you keep dancing and you don't get free. It wants constant motion and will constantly reinforce and draw from those who are willing to work hard to keep it going. It has no love for the individuals and it's goal is to kill, steal and destroy. It will chew people up and spit them out. It will exhaust their legs, their creativity and their resources and then discard them without a second thought because the momentum of the Dragon Team is the most important thing. It will whisper to the Lead Dancer that if people fall away not to worry because they were getting tired and useless anyway – or they were rebellious and didn't want to dance the proper way and follow along. If anyone should actually point out that the dance is getting nowhere – watch out! That will immediately get you ejected from the team!

The whole thing is rooted and based in Pride. "Look at me!" It wants to enlarge itself, improve itself, be more colorful and attractive - so that more people will watch IT and keep their eyes off of Jesus. It wants more legs, so it can dance more and grow longer. It whispers to all its Dancers, "We are the best Dragon anywhere. We're the 'hot new thing.' Everyone should be like us. In fact, anyone that doesn't dance just like us isn't even a real Dragon at all. We're the truest, best, most original, most authentic Dragon. We're the best and nobody else counts."

Just like a parade dragon, when you are inside, you can't see anything but the guts of your own Dragon. You can't see the scenery or the weather or the traffic or the other Dragons. You MUST focus on your own Dragon and follow the Dancers ahead of you. You MUST NOT take your eyes off of what you are doing or you will miss a turn or be off-beat and embarrass the whole Dragon Team. You also can't hear God because you're not looking to Him, you're watching your Dragon Team for direction and following the beat of their drums and cymbals. You might occasionally stand on the sidewalk (or at a conference) and watch a parade (or get a video) and see other Dragon Teams, but you only see them from the shiny, silky outside – not the humble underside where the sweaty, tired guys in tanktops are laboring under a Dragon held together with duct tape and bent coat hangers.

This blindness and competition keeps us compartmentalized and independent of each other so that the Body of Christ can't get unity and harmony because we all refuse to come out from under our own Dragons and yet we all insist that we're not under a Dragon, even though THOSE guys over there clearly <u>are</u>. We can see THEIR Dragon just fine, the thing that has twisted their denomination or congregation up into a heretical cult – but we can never see our own Dragon. Strange, isn't it? We're **so** blind and stupid and self-focused that I can only come the conclusion that it's supernaturally induced. (Which is exactly what the Word of God says will happen to you when you go your own way, but I never saw it before now.) It's easier to talk about Jesus with atheists and drug dealers and kids with purple hair than with most 'church' leaders. My experience is that, with a few exceptions, church leaders seem to be SUPERNATURALLY deaf and dumb. They conveniently cut and paste out any scriptures that would upset their "system". While they are otherwise really great guys, the only conclusion I can come to is that there is a supernatural force in play – and it's not good.

ARE THE RED DRAGONS JUST OVER CHRISTIAN CHURCHES?

I've seen Red Dragons over Buddhist temples. I've seen them over a Psychic Fair. I've seen them over Mosques. It is the spirit of Antichrist and always controls those who are following any one of the millions of flavors of Antichrist religious systems. The difference is that people can be delivered out of some of those without too much effort. That is, the Red Dragon over a pagan system or individual can be bound up or cast off (by someone walking in righteousness and with enough authority). These are not a curse from God as much as they are just the "world" doing what the "world" does.

But, on the Children of God, the rules are different. Whether you are "natural" Israel (the nation/the race) or "spiritual" Israel (the Church), when you disobey, the stakes are much higher. When you are the "world" you are already under satan's headship, but when you are God's and decide you'd rather go your own way (which by default means satan's way), then really BAD things are going to happen to you and it's going to be God doing it. Just as it pleased Him to prosper you, it will please Him to crush you. (Deut. 28:63) We aren't really preaching that in seeker-friendly comfy church, are we?

I just bet that doesn't jive with your view of God, does it? You don't think He's mad at anybody? You don't think He's a jealous God? "But surely," you say, "the Blood of Jesus means that we are redeemed and God's wrath is turned away from us. We're redeemed and safe and that "Old Testament" God is not in play anymore!" Yeah, well, think again. To take your stand on that bit of fiction, you're going to have to deny that the Word of God is true and right and still active today. But it won't surprise me if you want to leave parts of the Word out, that's how we all got under (or are still under) the Red Dragon curse in the first place. Yes, the Blood of Jesus will surely heal us, but not unless we repent and avail ourselves of it.

Let me point out that 2 Timothy 3:16 says that "ALL scripture is God-breathed and is useful for teaching, rebuking, correcting and training in righteousness, so that the man of God may be thoroughly equipped for every good work." You can't dismiss everything about God in the Old Testament because it doesn't suit your image of Warm-Fuzzy-Loving-Shepherd-Jesus. I'm warning you now, if you ever give me that "the Old Testament is not for New Covenant believers" argument in person, I'm going to ask you to hand me your Bible. Then I'm going to quote you 2 Timothy 3:16 over and over while I start with Genesis 1:1 and tear pages out of your Bible until you make me stop. Don't think I won't do it. If you're going to insult and demean my God and His Word, I'm going to call you on it.

You can't play it both ways. You can't demand that the Ten Commandments be posted in courtrooms and schools and then deny that the Old Testament is valid. You can't pound people with Malachi 3 and insist they're stealing from God if they don't tithe and then deny that same God and covenant in the next breath. He is an awesome, fearsome, jealous God and He doesn't change! If this writing doesn't convince you, if the devastating signs and wonders that He predicted and took personal credit for and are clearly evident RIGHT NOW don't convince you, then you're in big trouble. Your heart is so hardened and your Red Dragon has so much control that I wonder if it's even possible to get you free. Please turn. Please?

Ok, let's get back to it. Would God really be pleased about crushing and obliterating His own children? Well, the Word of God says that He will.

Isaiah 53:10
Yet it pleased the LORD to bruise him; he hath put [him] to grief: when thou shalt make his soul an offering for sin, he shall see [his] seed, he shall prolong [his] days, and the pleasure of the LORD shall prosper in his hand.

And that's about JESUS, His own Son!!

Deuteronomy 28:62-63 (NIV)
You who were as numerous as the stars in the sky will be left but few in number, because you did not obey the Lord your God. Just as it pleased the Lord to make you prosper and increase in number, so it will please him to ruin and destroy you. You will be uprooted from the land you are entering to possess.

Lots more examples that I don't have room for here. Read Lamentations and what He did to Jerusalem. Women were cooking and eating their own babies. Just like Deuteronomy 28 promised would happen if they went their own way, and they did – and He did. About every 50 years Israel went their own way and God sent someone or something to oppress and/or destroy them. Then He sent some judge or warrior or king to free them when they repented. Every 50 years America has had a great sweeping revival that brought the hearts of the people back to God. Even if we aren't honoring the Year of Jubilee, God is. And we're due right now for another Awakening – but it only comes by repentance.

PERSONAL-SIZED RED DRAGONS
(as opposed to institutional/denominational ones)

People get under a Red Dragon curse from God for having taken their eyes off of Jesus and going their own way. (Deut. 28) The enemy can use just about anything to get your eyes off of Jesus. The "Object" of your attention can then become the "face" on the Red Dragon you got under. The Object can be anything – football, a pastor, a denomination, a new car, an experience or manifestation, a wife, a doctrine, etc. It should be clear that some of these are inanimate objects, so pointing a finger at the Object as the cause of the Red Dragon misses the point. It's the person that allowed it who is most responsible.

When a person goes their own way and follows something other than God – they automatically (after an indefinite grace period) get a Red Dragon with their own face on it. It may also have the face of the "Object" they were following, but ultimately it's got their own face on it, because THEY decided to follow something other than Christ. When under a Red Dragon, they will have difficulty hearing clearly from the Throne. The Father is just and He will require that those who go their own way be separated from Him. The farther it goes, the deeper the strong delusion that will turn them over to their own reprobate mind and leave them open to any forces of the enemy that want to come mess with them. The more they operate out of Self (which they inevitably <u>will</u> if He is not directing their paths accurately), the more doorways they open up for the enemy. They will hear all kinds of things, sometimes self-condemning things, but also grandiose things about their role as the savior of a continent or the world. They may even hear that they can continue in sin in some ways and God won't mind. I know one man that heard He has an "exemption anointing" to sin freely.

There are those who are under a Red Dragon because of their willingness to follow some particular "Object" and believe in <u>it</u> more than they believed in (or listened to) God. It could be golf, it could be a dozen donuts, it could be Mormonism, it could be George Bush, it could be Carl Marx, it could be Brittany Spears.

There are those who got under a Red Dragon by their violent opposition to some Object. They are not actually "in" the Dragon, but they are the flagellants that follow along behind it whipping themselves. They are just as much in the parade and following the Dragon. It is still directing their paths because they are chasing IT instead of God. An anti-abortion protester can make that an idol and their whole life will revolve around that one issue and they will take their eyes off of Jesus. Before you know it, they'll be bombing clinics and be absolutely sure that God told them to do it. A heresy hunter can make his whole life about exposing error in the church or exposing a particular cult or leader – and they take their eyes off of Jesus, don't act in love, don't trust God to fight His own battles and get under a Red Dragon. (More on that following.)

Both groups are under the influence of a Red Dragon, although their behavior will manifest differently. **Those under it will:**

- Be obsessed with the Object, it's future, it's growth, it's support, etc.
- Show signs of deep (and annoying) Spiritual Pride
- Have a supernatural love for it that defies logic or normal experience
- Be willing to sacrifice greatly for it
- Actively evangelize on it's behalf, convincing others and defending it
- Have a lack of peace if not doing something for the Object. This is a big indicator. No peace.
- Have Garblers that confuse communication and twist it to benefit the Object. They will only hear what they want to hear.
- Polarize those around them as having to be for it or against it with no middle ground.
- Be belligerent, have anger or fits of temper or even murderous rage when the Object is insulted or assaulted.
- Exhibit unscriptural behavior and justify it as necessary or unavoidable – or even directed by God.
- Lack the Gift of Repentance as it relates to the Object and their involvement in it – instead of obeying Jesus.
- Show a lack of trust that God is capable of developing and increasing and growing and providing for the Object Himself.
- Show a deep spirit of competition with others to prove that their Object is the greatest.
- Refuse to fellowship or even pray with those who are not in full agreement. Encouraging division.
- They will give the Object credit for any of their spiritual growth, instead of Christ.
- One of the other good give-aways is a huge abundance of words. Many idle words that go nowhere and basically accomplish nothing.
- Will have more and more difficulty hearing God and more and more acceptance of the voice of the Object instead. When they do hear God, it may be "garbled" when going through their "Object filter".
- Groupies. Fans. Followers. Concubines. Lemmings. Whores. (That's what God calls them!)

Those violently opposed to it will:

- Be obsessed with the Object, it's destruction, it's correction, it's starvation, it's humbling, etc.
- Show signs of deep (and annoying) Spiritual Pride.
- Have a supernatural hatred for it that defies logic or normal experience.

- Feel an overwhelming urgency to do something right NOW about the Object.
- Be willing to sacrifice greatly to see it destroyed, even their own relationship with God.
- May even work compulsively and violate moral or legal boundaries to destroy it.
- Actively evangelize against it and recruit ANYONE that can help them, even people that are far worse in their own way.
- Have a lack of peace if not doing something against the Object. This is a big indicator. No peace.
- Have Garblers that confuse communication and twist it to show the worst angle on the Object.
- Polarize those around them as having to be for it or against it with no middle ground.
- Be belligerent, have anger or fits of temper or even murderous rage toward the Object.
- Exhibit unscriptural behavior justified as necessary or unavoidable – or even directed by God.
- Lack the Gift of Repentance as it relates to their focus on the Object instead of Jesus.
- Show a deep spirit of competition with others to show that they are better (smarter, holier, stronger, faster, wiser) than the Object.
- Show a lack of trust that God is capable of dealing with the Object Himself – or believe that God has appointed them to be His agent to chasten or destroy the Object.
- Refuse to fellowship or even pray with those who are not in full agreement. Encouraging division.
- One of the other good give-aways is a huge abundance of words. Many idle words that go nowhere and basically accomplish nothing.
- Will have more and more difficulty hearing God and more and more hatred of the voice of the Object instead. When they do hear God, it may be "garbled" when going through their "Object filter".
- They will hate it when the Object speaks at all and will take nearly everything they hear in the worst possible way. They will be constantly expecting to catch the Object in an error to justify their position against it. There is no grace for a mis-spoken or misunderstood word, Everything is a heresy and any comment that seems to be ANYTHING less than pure, absolute truth is evidence that the Object is a tool of satan. Unreasonably high standards. Especially considering their own words and actions!
- They will blame the Object for any fallen state of their own instead of accepting their own responsibility for having taken their eyes off of Jesus. Anything bad that happens to them they will attribute to warfare or curses from the Object to get them to stop what they believe is effective warfare of their own.
- Persecutors. Haters. Murderers. Hunters. Lemmings. Whores. (Again, according to God.)

In all cases, they may hear something they are VERY sure is God, but it will inevitably offer some clues that there is a problem. The sacrifice of Jesus meant that He was seated with God so as to send the Gift of Repentance to men. (Acts 5:31) Despite the strong delusion from the Throne, the Holy Spirit works with the Son to find a way to leave clues that there is a problem so that those who have ears to hear and eyes to see will turn and be healed. But the blind will head into a ditch. Only those who have eyes and ears and an expectation of their unworthiness and the danger of this will see the problem early and stop it before it goes too far. A constant state of repentance and fear before God is the best defense.

The Father requires justice, but the Son wants that none should perish. So He will tell the Holy Spirit to speak in such as way as to discomfort slightly or leave some hint that there is problem. There will always be signs that, although subtle, will probably be clearly visible later when the fog is gone. The Spirit may also speak to those around to show them that the person is off track. He will always leave a trail of bread crumbs back to the original incident so that the person can find their way back to the root and repent. Follow the trail, if you can.

INVERTED RED DRAGONS – FLAGGELANTS

"Flaggelants" are those who go about whipping themselves. This is the visual image that the Lord showed of what is really going on when someone is obsessed with an Object (ministry, person, etc) in a negative way and becomes intent on their destruction. They have been hurt and they keep opening up the wounds themselves to prove what martyrs they are. And along the way, grieve God and become what they hate.

2 Timothy 2:24-26 – And the servant of the Lord must not strive; but be gentle unto all [men], apt to teach, patient, In meekness instructing those that **oppose themselves**; if God peradventure will give them **repentance** to the acknowledging of the truth; And [that] they may recover themselves out of the **snare of the devil**, who are **taken captive** by him at his will.

This is important enough that we wanted to expand substantially on this in Version 4 of this book. I expect that this will get MUCH more common as more Christians actually start acting like Jesus. They need to know what to expect. The similarities between warfare because you are being effective for the Lord and a crushing because you are disobeying God can sometimes be terrifying. Ultimately you have to hear the Lord, know that YOU aren't exhibiting symptoms of the Red Dragon yourself.

It's important to understand the continuum here. That the enemy can get your eyes to the left or to the right and either way, he's got you. For example, you can make food an idol by gluttony or by anorexia. You can make sexuality an idol by an insatiable desire or a terrifying fear of it. You can make a ministry an idol by getting under it and giving them full reign over your life – or by chasing it everywhere, intent on "exposing" it and destroying it. You make a spouse an idol and look to them more than God – then divorce and turn all the love into bitter hatred. It's a radical supernatural swing from one extreme to the other. Either way, you get your eyes off of the Cross of Christ and the devil has still got you right where he wants you.

What is the Goal of the inverted Anti- Red Dragon?

To bring division, kill, steal and destroy – ministries, relationships, momentum for the kingdom of God. Create paralysis and victimization mentality in you. Block rejoicing in affliction by creating an obsessive quest to "expose" or "save others".

How it works:

It beats on a person by whatever means, usually physical, financial, emotional, relational stress that weakens them, then it starts inserting lies – "this is HIS fault, this is all because of HIM, if He hadn't done this everything would be OK, I'm suffering because of HIM, I'm scared and hurting because of HIM." Always getting the focus on a person/ministry/ construct instead of JESUS, always failing to rejoice in affliction, failing to see the big picture, failing to trust the Lord, hope all things, believe all things, endure all things, keep no record of wrongs (I Corin. 13). Love is lost. Gossip and backbiting increases and as the demon gets them to hearken to some voice OTHER THAN the voice of God and obey the commands of God, then the accuser of the brethren is justified to claim Leviticus 26 and Deuteronomy 28 (etc) over them.

How it gets permission to jump on a person:

Because they stop listening to and obeying God and instead listen to the person or the demon that is whispering to them things that go against God. It can be very subtle, and the closer you are to God, the more the risk. If you need further clarification, read "Pilgrim's Progress" and see a REAL account of how hard the Christian life is likely to be – and all the trickeries the enemy can throw at you.

What this does:

It begin to throw up walls and convince you to become more distant from the person in question. Hardens your heart. Locked doors. Secret conversation about them. Refusal to face the person or reason together. Seeing them as spiritual dangerous to even converse with or convincing that it's pointless to try.

It tries to get them to do some or all of the things God hates:

16 These six things doth the LORD hate: yea, seven are an abomination unto him: 17 A proud look, a lying tongue, and hands that shed innocent blood, 18 An heart that deviseth wicked imaginations, feet that be swift in running to mischief, 19 A false witness that speaketh lies, and he that soweth discord among brethren.   Prov 6:16-19 (KJV)

Why:

This evil spirit does NOT want to be ejected. It does not want the miscommunication or lie cleared up, does not want people to repent and reconcile. It will do all it can to take them away and block phone numbers, change emails, whatever so that it can cement the damage done. Leviticus 26 says that if the demon can get them to hearken to a voice other than Gods and go against His commands (1. Love the Lord, 2. Love neighbor as yourself, etc.) then it can get legal authority to terrorize them into running away as fast as they can with unrealistic and imagined fears. The goal is to prevent any forgiveness or reconciliation and to destroy the work of the Lord. The Lord may allow it to humble someone or refine another, but it's still going to have to require serious repentance to get out of it.

What are some of the symptoms that you have an ANTI- Red Dragon:

- Stop loving – even while you insist all along that it's loving for you to do what you're doing. (Matt 5:44 "But I say to you, love your enemies, and pray for those who persecute you.")
- Forget everything good that was ever done for you by them. Just flat scrubbed out of remembrance – or unable to speak it. This is one of the scariest of all. Especially between husband and wife or close brethren. (Psalm 55:12-14, Luke 21:16, etc.)
- Hyperinflate anything bad. Make mountains out of molehills. Or create them. (Prov. 6:16-19)
- Make anything that was just annoying or questionable into something horrible.
- Generate lies based on anything "suspicious" even if there is no real evidence to support it.
- Raise secondary doctrinal disagreements to the level of salvation issues to justify the labels used ("They're not a Brother and never were – because of their stance on _____.").
- Refuse to reason together or be gentle. Slam doors of communication shut. What we call "drive-by rebuking." (I was actually staying with a man who wrote me a letter that started with, "I'm writing this rebuke, I'm going to print it, delete it from my computer and I never want to discuss this with you." Then had his wife give it to me with no opportunity for rebuttal or discussion. And he was absolutely sure he was righteous in all of it. Many times I've seen people flee in the night, refusing any communication for fear – raw terror – of being talked out of their position.)
- Refuse proper Biblical instructions for problem resolution (Matt. 18) or use them to rally troops and accuse, but not to resolve, reconcile or seek Truth and peace.

- Use "terminal" words for emotional effect and to do maximum harm with no grace or mercy - "false teacher," "apostate," "heretic," "cult leader," "heathen," "unbeliever," "warlock/witch," "jezebel" and worse. They forget the Biblical imperatives (commands) to try to live at peace, to not devour one another, to avoid useless quarrels about secondary issues, if you don't love the brethren the love of God is not in you – and so they themselves become apostate (unforgiving, unloving, not rejoicing, etc.), all in the name of "defending the faith".

- Determining that it is one's personal mission in life now to rescue the other "captives" and tell as many people as possible all that they "know" - or all the dirt they can gather from ANY source whatsoever, no matter the credibility or veracity. Gets their eyes off the Cross and become obsessed with the object of this.

- If someone that was previously VERY close to them and very respected as a man/woman of God tells them they are doing wrong, that person is now "part of the cult" or "under the delusion" and is dismissed with prejudice – no matter how close they were before. They will block, ban, eject, defriend, sue or get restraining orders on anyone that tries to talk them out of it.

- They begin to have a harder and harder time hearing the Spirit of God so they tend to get back under Law. They become Judaizers that default to the written code, dietary laws, black and white reading of scripture without any willingness to reason about the deep things of God or the spiritual application and understanding behind the Law – which was a shadow of things to come. They can't be led by the Holy Spirit anymore because they're not hearing God, so they're back under Law. (Gal. 5:18) Like the Judaizers that chased Paul, they make it their quest to chase, persecute and tear down those who are walking in the freedom of Christ through the Spirit – even if previously THEY were one of them!

- Be unable to truly forgive and move on. Constantly obsessing and dwelling on the past. (Matt. 6:14-15, Mark 11:26, Luke 6:37, etc.)

- They may also experience physically or spiritually some of the curses in Lev. 26 or Deut. 28 – wasting diseases with no cure, madness, blindness, terror, unreasonable fear, etc.

- The closer they were walking with God, the greater their rebellion – thus the the more likely that the Lord will afflict them with some or all of the serious curses in Leviticus 26 and Deuteronomy 28. You may say that, "as believers we are not under the law and the old covenant," but if you are rebelling against God then you are NOT believing Him and you are NOT being led by the Holy Spirit, so you ARE under Law (inverse of Galatians 5:18). You can't say that because you once obeyed Him that you have permanent access to the New Covenant. That is, if you are stiff-necked and won't obey and won't hearken to His voice, then you're going to wander in the desert until you die. If your heart is uncircumcised then you are not a True Jew under the Blood. (Romans 2:28-29)

- Worst of all, they begin to tear down everything they truly heard from the Lord, chalk it up to being "under the influence" or "trapped in the delusion with them" and systematically unravel every good thing that God ever spoke to them or did for them during that time. This is the devil's way to get you to grieve the Holy Spirit and attribute the works of God to the devil himself. This is the devil's way to take back ground and victories previously won.

One of the strangest manifestations of this that we have seen is the occasional person that is overwhelmed with a spirit of fear – or rather raw naked panic – and leaves the ministry in utter terror and fear for their lives. Please don't think I'm kidding. We've seen breathless, shaking, panic-stricken people that could not name their fear, had no real evidence for it, but just HAD to leave RIGHT NOW in the middle of the night without saying goodbye to anyone, sometimes leaving many personal things behind - as if the house were on fire! It doesn't happen all the time, but when it does, it's shockingly supernatural.

There is no other explanation. There have never been allegations of physical violence or threats or anything, yet people flee, literally in fear for their lives. And all the while insisting that God told them to do it and that they have peace. They claim that they do not have a spirit of fear, but of love and of power and of a sound mind (2 Timothy 1:7). But any psychiatrist looking in from the outside would say that it was a paranoid delusional psychotic episode and offer to medicate or institutionalize them. If they had power, they would just rebuke the enemy and be victorious, but they cannot. And the love is completely gone – totally scrubbed out and replaced with inflated memories of the bad and no memories of the good. The object is demonized, no matter how close they were before – even spouses or family members.

God never tells the righteous to panic. God may tell them to dust their feet off, or move on to another place, or even flee urgently to the mountains when the antichrist shows up – but not in a panic. I know that I can take a nap in the middle of a warlock convention and be safe. I know that I can stand in front of the devil himself and be safe. I will NOT panic before ANY man or demon of hell. Because God is on my side and if I am righteous, then I can have the confidence to operate in love and peace and patience and forgiveness – but never panic.

I've been asked, "People keep leaving your ministry in the middle of the night, in terror and fear for their lives, how can this be OK? How can this be God? There must be something wrong with you." That's a reasonable question, so I sought the Lord on that. The time that it happened most recently, the very next day the Lord gave me Leviticus 26. I've read through the Bible many times, but I never saw this in this context before. Truly it answers how this could happen. Proverbs 28:1 says, "The wicked flee when no man pursueth, but the righteous are bold as a lion." Leviticus 26 goes much farther. It's truly scary. Stay right with God, hearken to His voice. If you listen to another, if you despise His instructions and commands, it's ALL bad! Let's take a look:

More evidence that this is from GOD: *{comments added}*

Leviticus 26:14-46 (BBE)
14 But if you do not give ear to me, and do not keep all these my laws; 15 And if you go against my rules and if you have hate in your souls for my decisions *{not just behavior is enough, your heart has to be right!}* **and you do not do all my orders, but go against my agreement** *{refuse to fulfill your vows, do what you know He told you to do}*; **16 This will I do to you: I will put fear in your hearts** *{spiritual/mental, panic, terror}*, **even wasting disease and burning pain** *{could be spiritual or physical wasting – or both}*, **drying up the eyes** *{spiritual or physical, can't see the enemy, no spirit of repentance, no hope, can't rejoice in affliction}* **and making the soul feeble** *{definitely spiritual, defenseless, shields down}*, **and you will get no profit from your seed** *{business, ministry, testimony, children, efforts}*, **for your haters will take it for food.** *{Enemies, demons will feed on it}* **17 And my face will be turned from you** *{Won't hear}*, **and you will be broken before those who are against you** *{enemies/demons}*, **and your haters will become your rulers** *{oppressed/possessed/afflicted/ruled over}*, **and you will go in flight when no man comes after you.** *{Flee in a panic for NO reason. This is a big one. A true sign that something is wrong. God never has the RIGHTEOUS flee in fear. Proverbs 28:1 says "The unrighteous flee when no man pursueth, but the righteous are bold as a lion." There is a BIG difference between dusting your feet off and moving on because you're not received – and fleeing in utter terror of an IMAGINARY threat.}*

If that doesn't do it, then it gets seven times WORSE:

18 And if, even after these things, you will not give ear to me, then I will send you punishment seven times more for your sins. 19 And the pride of your strength will be broken *{humbled, crushed, best thing taken away – could be physical or spiritual or mental}*, **and I will make your heaven as iron** *{prayers bounce - spiritual}* **and your earth as brass;** *{toil and sweat with little result – spiritual or physical}* **20 And your strength will be used up without profit** *{spiritual or physical}*; **for your land will not give her increase and the trees of the field will not give their fruit.**

{Whatever your land, it will not produce fruit – spiritual or physical. You will be void of the fruit the Lord is looking for.}

If that doesn't do it, then it gets 49 times WORSE:

21 And if you still go against me and will not give ear to me, I will put seven times more punishments on you because of your sins. 22 I will let loose the beasts of the field among you *{wild animals, could be treacherous people, could be demons that are now free to devour you – could be spiritual or physical}*, **and they will take away your children** *{spiritual or physical offspring lost, people you "parented" stripped from you}* **and send destruction on your cattle** *{wealth, provision, pride, savings, all gone – spiritual or physical}*, **so that your numbers will become small and your roads become waste.** *{You will be very few, fell outnumbered, feel alone and be unable to upkeep your land – spiritual or physical}*

If that doesn't do it, then it gets 343 times WORSE:

23 And if by these things you will not be turned to me *{the point of all this is medicinal}*, **but still go against me; 24 Then I will go against you, and I will give you punishment, I myself, seven times for all your sins. 25 And I will send a sword on you to give effect to the punishment of my agreement** *{no telling what this could mean – spiritual or physical}*; **and when you come together into your towns I will send disease among you** *{when you gather with the others who rebelled against God, wherever that might be, whatever is the safe place you ran to, even a chat room on the internet – this could be spiritual disease, lies, corruption, false gifts, false anointings, delusion, fear – or physical diseases like cancer clusters or wasting diseases}* **and you will be given up into the hands of your haters** *{people or demons will take you over, you will be HANDED to them – physical or spiritual slavery}*. **26 When I take away your bread of life, ten women will be cooking bread in one oven** *{in the siege, there is so little wood and grain, bread will be so scarce that there are 9 people standing around, lots of people to do a little work}*, **and your bread** *{physical or the spiritual bread of Truth}* **will be measured out by weight** *{Siege/starvation rations}*; **you will have food but never enough.** *{You will not be able to get enough of the bread to be satisfied. Truth will escape you. You may have a little Truth, but it's only a tiny bit and won't it satisfy.}*

If that STILL doesn't do it, then it gets 2,401 times WORSE:

27 And if, after all this, you do not give ear to me, but go against me still, 28 Then my wrath will be burning against you *{can't believe it would go this far!}*, **and I will give you punishment, I myself, seven times for your sins. 29 Then you will take the flesh of your sons and the flesh of your daughters for food;** *{This happened PHYSICALLY to Jerusalem in Lamentations. Most likely spiritual sons and daughters that you will devour/suck dry/destroy, just to satisfy the burning inside you or to feel like you're getting somewhere.}* **30 And I will send destruction on your high places** *{Physical or spiritual, places of idolatry, or the high place of the MIND}*, **overturning your perfume altars** *{Physical or spiritual altars you have built, thinking God likes the smell, but He doesn't}*, **and will put your dead bodies on your broken images** *{He considers you dead inside already if it's gone this far, but He will destroy the idols/images and leave you on them}*, **and my soul will be turned from you in disgust.** *{God will look away and turn His back on you in DISGUST. That's HARSH!}* **31 And I will make your towns waste** *{Whatever walled city you trusted, whatever place of safety you ran to, will be pulled down}* **and send destruction on your holy places** *{whatever you made sacred in your idolatry}*; **I will take no pleasure in the smell of your sweet perfumes** *{He will ignore your offerings and sacrifices – spiritually or physically}*; **32 And I will make your land a waste, a wonder to your haters living in it.** *{Your haters may be people or demons or both – but even they will be impressed with how thoroughly the Lord is against you.}* **33 And I will send you out in all directions among the nations** *{the disobedient will be scattered even from one another, geographically/physically or spiritually or mentally}*, **and my sword will be uncovered against you, and your land will be without any living thing, and your towns will be made waste.** *{The places* *of safety you ran to will be uninhabited by those who truly follow the Lord, judgement will pour on everyone there because of you.}* **34 Then will the land take pleasure in its Sabbaths while it is waste and you are living in the land of your haters** *{In captivity – spiritually or physically. In a strange place.}*; **then will the land have rest. 35 All the days while it is waste will the land have rest, such rest as it never had in your Sabbaths, when you were living in it.** *{He will have justice and give rest to the Land because of your failure to observe the Sabbath, to be dedicated to Him and His commands.}*

At His discretion, some of them will get the treatment above, some will get this – or some combination thereof:

36 And as for the rest of you, I will make their hearts feeble in the land of their haters *{weak hearts, no strength, no defenses, full of fear and panic, whether the "haters" are real or not – could be physical or spiritual, demons or people}*, **and the sound of a leaf moved by the wind will send them in flight** *{the slightest sound will sound to them like a mighty army, they will flee over NOTHING in absolute panic, convinced to their core that it's justified – that is an extreme DELUSION!}*, **and they will go in flight as from the sword, falling down when no one comes after them;** *{They will believe that a sword is imminent, destruction, death, worst case scenario – physically or spiritually – in terror, but NO ONE is chasing them. In fact, the enemy of their souls has them right where he wants them.}* **37 Falling on one another** *{tripping over each other to run so fast}*, **as before the sword, when no one comes after them** *{repeated again – NO ONE is chasing them}*; **you will give way before your haters** *{Part of the delusion is that you BELIEVE they are your haters and you're running from them, but NO ONE is chasing you. It's a delusion that creates an enemy that is NOT there and makes him GIGANTIC – when whatever it was, it was as dangerous as a LEAF falling from a tree. But the demons will drive you before them and they will rule over you}*. **38 And death will overtake you** *{spiritually or physically}* **among strange nations** *{not on the land you are supposed to be, surrounded by people that don't follow the Lord}*, **and the land of your haters will be your destruction** *{and you will eventually be destroyed there}*. **39 And those of you who are still living will be wasting away in their sins in the land of your haters; in the sins of their fathers they will be wasting away.** *{And if they don't die, they will waste away, spiritually or physically or both.}*

But … Here's the good news! Eventually they break!

40 And they will have grief for their sins and for the sins of their fathers, when their hearts were untrue to me, and they went against me; 41 So that I went against them and sent them away into the land of their haters *{turned them over to demons}*: **if then the pride of their hearts is broken and they take the punishment of their sins,** *{If they confess their sins and turn}* **42 Then I will keep in mind the agreement which I made with Jacob and with Isaac and with Abraham, and I will keep in mind the land. 43 And the land, while she is without them, will keep her Sabbaths; and they will undergo the punishment of their sins** *{there IS punishment due – until the Blood of the Lamb is applied to this}*, **because they were turned away from my decisions and in their souls was hate for my laws.** *{their hearts rebelled against what they KNEW to be true and right}* **44 But for all that, when they are in the land of their haters I will not let them go, or be turned away from them, or give them up completely; my agreement with them will not be broken, for I am the Lord their God.** *{Despite ALL of this, He will not utterly forsake them. He will still try to break them, but will not let them go! What a God!!}* **45 And because of them I will keep in mind the agreement which I made with their fathers, whom I took out of the land of Egypt before the eyes of the nations, to be their God: I am the Lord. 46 These are the rules, decisions, and laws, which the Lord made between himself and the children of Israel in Mount Sinai, by the hand of Moses.**

WHAT ABOUT LOVE?

An inverted Red Dragon, an Anti- Red Dragon, will almost immediately suck all the love out. It doesn't matter if it was your best friend, ministry partner, a family member, even a loving wife or husband – it will suck all the love out. And it can do it SO fast and SO completely that it will shock you. The ONLY explanation is that it has to be supernatural. Whatever the thing that has become the idol – the Object of the obsession – it keeps their eyes off the Cross and they are trapped in the delusion. They are obsessed with the object instead of the Cross. Only God can release them.

1 Corinthians 13
1 If I speak in the tongues of men and of angels, but have not love, I am only a resounding gong or a clanging cymbal.

Though you speak in tongues or speak much about love – if it's not in you, then it's all noise. The delusion will cause you to speak about everything other than love. But you will SAY that whatever you are doing to destroy the object is done because of your "love" for them.

2 If I have the gift of prophecy and can fathom all mysteries and all knowledge, and if I have a faith that can move mountains, but have not love, I am nothing.

Though you may still have gifts, even a calling as a prophet or apostle, though you have a mighty faith, if you don't have love, then you are NOTHING. Your faith is misplaced, you're under a delusion. Whatever you know or think you know is wasted and useless.

3 If I give all I possess to the poor and surrender my body to the flames, but have not love, I gain nothing.

No matter how sacrificial you THINK you are being, though you are martyred, if it was not done for the sake of true LOVE, then it was in vain.

4 Love is patient, love is kind. It does not envy, it does not boast, it is not proud.

An obsession, an Anti- Red Dragon, is the very OPPOSITE of unconditional agape love. It is NEVER patient, NEVER kind, it envies the success or blessing of the object, it paces about hoping to see destruction and be justified, it boasts about all that it knows, it is SUPREMELY proud in it's absolute certainty of being right – even while manufacturing "facts" and operating out of fear, anger, and unforgiveness. It will not hear anyone that says that it's wrong. It does all the things it accuses the object of doing – and more. It is entirely self-focused and self-justifying and will not hear any rebuttal.

5 It is not rude, it is not self-seeking, it is not easily angered, it keeps no record of wrongs.

It is extremely rude, even to the point of violating what ANYONE – even heathen - would call common decency. Willing to say anything to anyone, just to win its point. It is entirely about holding itself up as an "expert witness" and building up its own authority. It is furious continually, a constant boiling cauldron of anger just below the surface and will scream and fly off the handle at any moment when its buttons are pushed. It will block, ban, defriend, sue, or get restraining orders against anyone that disagrees. It generates a HUGE LIST of wrongs - some real, some imagined, usually all twisted for maximum effect - and will recite them to anyone that will listen. There is NO forgiveness – and no repentance by the Object would be sufficient to satisfy them. It WILL NOT let go until God releases them from this delusion and pours out repentance on them. Keeping a record of wrongs is the EXACT OPPOSITE of the commands to rejoice in affliction, to believe that all things work to the good for them that love the Lord, to turn the other cheek, forgive seventy times seven, love your enemies, leave vengeance to the Lord, etc. It's total rebellion against the HEART of the Gospel, all justified as necessary and right in order to "expose" the object.

6 Love does not delight in evil but rejoices with the truth.

The very opposite is true, evil flourishes and is fed and grown. Truth, and truly being willing to seek the truth, dies. The voices that support the anger and unforgiveness are lifted up, no matter how bad their credibility previously. "The enemy of my enemy is my friend." The voices that might actually speak reason, faith, love, truth, peace, patience – are dismissed instantly. Even a person that was previously beautiful and godly in heart, mind, speech and demeanor will become a sarcastic, gossiping, backbiting, lying, fearful, hate-filled, unforgiving, shriveled up husk of what they were.

7 It always protects, always trusts, always hopes, always perseveres.

The dragon seeks to kill, steal and destroy. To self-fulfill prophecies of doom and destruction and judgment made over the object. It doesn't trust God to do the work, but sets its own hand to help God. It doesn't trust any voice that defends the object, no matter how trustworthy they were before. It doesn't hope, it makes itself a victim and makes the object responsible for ALL bad things that ever happened to them. It runs into the night rather than persevering. It escapes as quickly as possible, cuts off communication and WILL NOT offer to endure patiently as God does a work with whatever is wrong. (IF anything is even truly wrong.) It does not truly hope for restoration of relationships or the unity of the Body, it is repulsed by the idea. It may give lip service to the object being restored and their soul saved, but all the actions taken are toward destruction, embarrassment, humiliation, or worse – not toward restoration in love.

8 Love never fails. But where there are prophecies, they will cease; where there are tongues, they will be stilled; where there is knowledge, it will pass away.

Love dies. No matter how great, how pure, how beautiful – it inverts into a spirit of hatred, murder, lying, faction, division and ugliness. Prophecies that were received, positive words about the Object that they KNEW were from the Lord previously, are all dismissed. Any good thing that the Lord told them about the Object is chalked up to "being under their spell" and couldn't have been God. It is attributed to flesh or the devil – dangerously flirting with blasphemy of the Holy Spirit. Their tongue NEVER ceases to run to anyone that will listen, but speaking good or blessing over the Object will be stopped. Knowledge of right, remembrance of any good thing that was done for them, will be scrubbed out of their mind. They will be practically unable to even THINK of any way the Object has ever blessed them, much less admit it.

9 For we know in part and we prophesy in part, 10 but when perfection comes, the imperfect disappears.

This IS the imperfect coming. This may even be perfect delusion that takes over and does all of the opposite of what the coming of Jesus would do. This is like the Lord taking someone as FAR away from LOVE as is possible. Yet, they will insist they have love and that all they are doing is motivated by love. They will insist they have peace like never before, even while they scramble endlessly to self-justify their behavior and feelings and obsess about the Object. People looking in from the outside don't see peace or hope or love or grace or gentleness or any of the fruits of the Spirit – where the Object is concerned.

11 When I was a child, I talked like a child, I thought like a child, I reasoned like a child. When I became a man, I put childish ways behind me.

Other people will look in and be SHOCKED by how childishly they are acting, how much like a scared little kid that is just terrified and fighting back with whatever they can. How immature the reasoning, how unwilling to discuss or reason together, how not led by the Spirit of God, how much their brain just doesn't seem to work right and process the higher, deeper things. They only see Law – and even that misapplied. They only see the letter of the Law, and can no longer see the deeper things of the Spirit – as it applies to the Object. Because they are not being led by the Spirit of God, but by the delusion. No childish thing is put behind. Even the written Law that would condemn this kind of behavior is completely ignored (John 15; Proverbs 6:16-19; Leviticus 19:16; Proverbs 16:28; Proverbs 18:8;

Proverbs 20:19; Leviticus 26; I Corinthians 13; Galatians 5; Romans 12; 2 Corinthians 12:20; I John 4:18; I Peter 3:14; Prov. 10:12; etc.)

12 Now we see but a poor reflection as in a mirror; then we shall see face to face. Now I know in part; then I shall know fully, even as I am fully known.

Even in the BEST of times, with someone being truly obedient to the Lord and NOT under a delusion, we're still going to see darkly. But this is like a total veil over their mind and heart and eyes that blocks ALL truth and love (at least as it relates to the Object). There is no doubt that God fully knows the person under this delusion, but THEY don't seem to fully know anything other than their own hurt, bitterness, anger, self-righteousness and pride. And they will insist that they DO NOT see through a glass darkly as it relates to the Object, but have perfect, reliable, pure revelation.

13 And now these three remain: faith, hope and love. But the greatest of these is love.

All three are at risk, but love dies first. The total lack of real love in someone that previously HAD real love is one of the first signs that something is desperately wrong. And this "love" in Greek is "agape" meaning pure, unconditional, unstoppable, self-sacrificing, Godly LOVE. That is God's love, something HE has to put in us. When you make an idol and chase it – for good or bad – it is agape that dies first. The Lord Himself withdraws and the first thing to go with Him is His love.

HOW DOES A PERSON AVOID BEING AN "OBJECT"?!

Those who tickle ears, speak lies and promote themselves will accumulate behind them those who will make them the Object of their worship or adoration. Those who actively and effectively promote themselves will always draw unto themselves those who are susceptible to that kind of thing. But speaking things that aren't "Truth" isn't required. The Apostle Paul healed and preached truth and in Lystra they tried to worship him as a god (Acts 14). He did right in rejecting that instantly and being unwilling to be used as the face on their Red Dragon. He saw that the Corinthians were doing that by saying, "I'm for Paul. I'm for Cephas. I'm for Apollos." (I Corinthians 3) He rejected it in Lystra and tried to make them stop and look to Christ alone. Even being purely like Jesus is not a guarantee someone won't make you an idol and stop looking toward the Father and the Cross.

Also, a person that is speaking Truth from the Throne of God cannot avoid being an Object for those who will persecute them. The enemy will always whisper to someone and try to raise up <u>anyone</u> who will obsessively devote their lives to the destruction of that Object that is being effective for the Gospel. In Lystra, when Paul wouldn't allow them to adore and worship him, they instantly flipped and decided to kill him! He was STILL the Object of their Red Dragon, but now they're intent on Paul's destruction! The memory of the miracles and the healings and the reverence and fear they had are INSTANTLY gone!

There is ONE Truth in the Universe. All else is lies of the enemy. The One Truth is that we are to be under Christ and follow His face. Anything else is destined for our destruction.

Everything <u>but</u> His face is a counterfeit of the enemy. You can't be under a Jesus Red Dragon, there's no such thing. That's where you are SUPPOSED to be! Everything BUT that is a Red Dragon. Even just being <u>partially</u> under His headship is still a lie. There are all kinds of flavors. Anything that exists can be made an idol. Theoretical constructs, like Evolution, can become a Red Dragon. No matter how much Truth it may contain, unless it is 100% pure, it's mixture – and a lie. And there is no source of Perfect Purity except by staying IN Christ.

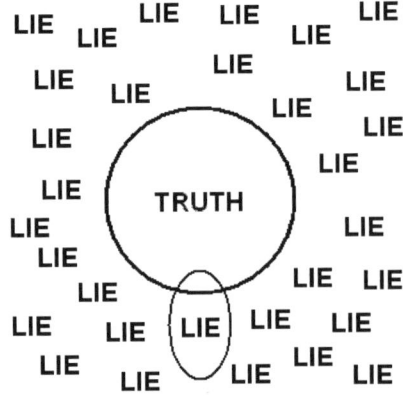

Jesus Christ <u>was</u> the face on MANY Anti- Red Dragons and continues to be. He was the Object of hatred and persecution and murderous rage of many people and continues to be. And He said that it would be the same for all of those that were like Him. He even said that those of your own house would kill you and think they were doing God a favor. The more you are like Jesus, the more people are going to get under murderous Anti- Red Dragons with your face on it. Particularly those susceptible to a spirit of competition.

You can eliminate (or at least minimize) the number of people that are trying to idolize and adore you, but you can't do anything about those that want to kill you – unless you preach soft and fluffy and never speak Truth. The more you are like Jesus, the more murderous Anti- Red Dragons there will be focused on you as their Object of hatred and the fewer idolatrous ones worshiping you. (But understand, they've both made you an idol in a different way.) There will be people that truly LOVE you, but they keep their eyes on Christ.

It's OK for people to idolize God - that's the idea. He wants no other idols BEFORE Him. HE is supposed to be the sole object of your worship. Anything else is going to bring judgment upon you for violation of the First Commandment. Even making the Bible an idol is wrong. That's not the fullness of God. The book itself is His word, but it's not <u>Him</u>. We can't have relationship with a book, even a beautiful, glorious, living book – we're ultimately supposed to worship Him who IS the Word made flesh, not the Bible..

You can make heaven an idol. You can make your own salvation the end-all-be-all of your walk with Christ. This denies that relationship with Him and His glorification by our daily lives must be the ultimate goal, not the avoidance of hell. Ultimately, seeking pleasure or avoiding pain is still pride and humanism.

So Jesus gets a pass if people made Him an idol when He was here. That was the idea. He's supposed to be the idol. But did people make Paul an idol? Yes. Peter? Yes. Speaking in tongues? Yes. Signs and wonders? Yes. Are those automatically bad things? No, not unless you get your eyes on them instead of Jesus. They are tools and side effects and men - but they must NOT be the main point!

Paul said, "Be like me, because I was like Christ." Would <u>never</u> opening his mouth except to speak Truth keep him from being an idol to someone? No. Did speaking something from his flesh MAKE them get under a Red Dragon? No. Did speaking Truth keep him from being persecuted? No, in fact, the more he became known for speaking Truth, the worse it got.

HOW DO WE KEEP PEOPLE FROM MAKING US AN IDOL?

We can't. If we spend all of our time trying to keep them from doing that, then we are in danger of getting our OWN eyes off of Jesus and making it about US! All we can do is point them to Jesus and speak what He tells us to speak and rest, knowing that He will work it out. We can just speak Truth and let the Lord work it all out.

There WILL be those that try to worship you. Most of them that you will never even know about. They'll just read something or hear something and seek to be like you and watch you instead of Jesus. Those that DO come into contact with you should be discouraged from doing so. You can accomplish that to a degree by being human and transparent and always pointing them toward Jesus. Do not allow any illegal soul-ties by accepting connectivity or obligations that shouldn't be there. Don't take responsibility to protect or provide or direct or any other thing that they should be getting straight from the Throne. It's an illusion that you can do any of that stuff anyway.

If you listen and obey, the Lord will tell you if someone is doing it to you and looking to YOU as their Source when they shouldn't. Do as He directs. Don't feed it. Point them to the Cross and get out of the way. We can't be someone's "crystal ball". We HAVE to help them hear God so that HE can direct all of their paths. None of us are capable of righteously directing our OWN paths, much less someone else's.

Paul could sincerely say that the blood of no man was on his head because he didn't make it about HIM. He didn't draw men unto him – he stood behind them and shoved them toward Jesus. If we maintain and feed a Nicolaitan "priest" class where some people are more holy than others and you need to do as they tell you, then we are putting obstacles before men – and it's US!

Please, hear me. Point them toward Jesus and get out of their way.

And rejoice in affliction when people persecute and hate you. Jesus said it would be like that if you were like Him. Praise God! You must be getting more like Him! This is a WAR – if nobody is shooting at you, then maybe you're not dangerous. Or worse, maybe the enemy already co-opted you and you've created a mystery religion that grieves God and sets YOU as people's head – and you're under a Red Dragon and don't even know it.

Practical Example 1

Saul was a Pharisee who truly believed with all his heart that killing Christians was doing God a favor. He had an Anti-Christian Red Dragon and it was VERY advanced. Ultimately, under it all, his Red Dragon delusion also had his own face on it because he was trying to make a name for himself as a big bad Pharisee. Jesus Himself had to show up to break it off of Saul and even then he was still blinded until Ananias came to pray for him and something like "scales" fell off his eyes. What has scales? Snakes, fish and DRAGONS. It was the delusion that fell away so that he could see clearly.

Practical Example 2

How do we serve the Lord, participate fervently with brethren, sell all we have and give to the poor, work with a passion and truly be sure that we're not somehow getting under something? Repentance is the mark of Ezekiel 9 and makes sure that we are not dead bodies in defiled temples. Read it and weep. Really, weep. That's the only safe place.

Practical Example 3

Remember that girl in high school that you were madly in love with, but all your friends hated? Even your parents didn't like her. But you would hear none of it. You were SURE she was perfect. Until she broke up with you – then you couldn't believe you were so stupid. That's a delusion. You made an idol and God turned you over to it.

WHO <u>DOES</u> <u>NOT</u> HAVE A RED DRAGON ON THEM?

Some time ago the Lord led me to Ezekiel 9 again (this passage comes up regularly lately). If you don't know it right off, please go read it right now (and the chapters right before it to see what they were doing wrong). Basically, the Lord gives Ezekiel this vision of how really horrible the spiritual state of Jerusalem had become and all of the pagan practices that have been integrated with the worship of God (or replaced it). The elders and priests are fully sold out to all kinds of badness and compromise. Then the glory of God leaves the Temple and the Lord sends an angel to put a mark on the foreheads of those who are repenting and weeping and mourning for the sad spiritual state of Jerusalem. Then He sends death angels to mercilessly slaughter everyone else – men, women & children – and instructs them to start with the elders who are in front of the Temple! Then to take all the dead bodies and defile the Temple. Now remember, these are God's people in God's city used to defile God's Temple. He is perfectly willing to do it and there's ample Biblical proof that He's done it before. The ONLY people that survive, the only remnant that remains are those who are repentant for the sins of Jerusalem and were marked by the angel.

Out of the blue, I'm reading that chapter and the Lord says to me, "You know, I already did that. Your temples are all full of dead bodies."

OUCH!! I can't argue with Him. I've been to dozens of congregations in the last two years and they are pretty universally oppressed, deceived and/or dead. There are bright lights in there, to be sure, but mostly they're dead. There is even one charismatic ministry here in Kansas City where several of us have been in a particular room in their building and all seen (in the spirit) massive piles of rotting dead bodies and demons feeding on them like vultures. There is a very strong, very palpable oppression on the whole place, but they are just SURE that they are God's chosen and that they are inside His perfect will.

How do you know that you are truly Red Dragon-free? If you have been given the Gift of Repentance for the sad state of things and grieve and mourn and weep over all the detestable things done in the name of God. If you're only repenting for "those other people," that doesn't count. If you're repenting for just a specific thing, like abortion, you may have a selective repentance or you may just be sad about the babies. But Ezekiel 9 is clear that the only ones who escaped were those repenting for the spiritual state of their city and their own part in it. If you need a little more help getting up to speed, read Ezekiel 16 and see if that's not a really good picture of the church in America. Also read Hosea with an eye toward whether we are doing all of those things as well and what God says will happen to those who do. You might also read Matthew 23 and the seven woes that Jesus pronounces on the Pharisees who were the religious conservatives of the day. We're doing all of those things as well. And in MUCH greater measure. We're in big trouble and as many people as possible need to start repenting until God turns.

Surely judgment will start with the elders before the temple. Hear me, we don't need to worry about some future "falling away" and great deception in the church. It's here right now and we're fully fallen. There is no other way to explain such blatant, unrepentant disobedience like having 37,000 "Christian" denominations when we are commanded to be ONE BODY. The word says that if you hold anything against a brother and you take Communion unworthily you will get sick and die. At least in part, we are all sick and dying (spiritually and physically) because we are taking Communion unworthily. By definition, there is no way to split a church and restrict fellowship between believers without holding something against a brother! Deuteronomy 28 says we will have wasting diseases that have no cure and no one will come to our aid – until we repent.

If there is anyone in the temples amongst the piles of dead bodies that is still breathing somehow, then they need to "come out of her" as fast as they can. If you're spiritually dead and being consumed by demons and you didn't know it, then (if you can) start weeping and repenting and maybe He'll turn. If you're not sure how dead you are, just ask yourself when was the last time you felt like your spiritual "cup" was really all the way full and you had peace and joy and victory?

Maybe you could pray this prayer:

Lord Jesus, I'm not sure how spiritually dead I really am, but I don't think I'm as full of Your Spirit as I should be. Please forgive me for whatever I've done that got in Your way and kept me from walking in the fullness of all that You have for me. I'm sorry I leaned on my own understanding and made compromises with the world. Please show me anything that stands between You and me and give me the ability to repent. I want peace and joy and victory. I don't want anything of the enemy to gain any ground in me. Please show me how to keep my cup so full of Jesus that nothing else will fit. I'm sorry for my part in anything that disgraced You or brought harm to Your Body. Please forgive me. And teach me more fear of the Lord. That would be good. That way I'll obey You more and have more wisdom. Thanks. I love You, Lord. I pray this in the Name of Jesus Christ, Amen.

HOW DO YOU KNOW IF YOU'RE UNDER THE RED DRAGON CURSE?

- Pride, haughty eyes (Prov. 6:16-19, 2 Timothy 2:15)
- Lying tongue – blatantly leaving stuff out of the Word or adding to it
- Hands that shed innocent blood – lack of proper respect and care for the sheep
- A heart that devises wicked plans – and wicked plans are any plans that aren't HIS plans
- Feet swift in running to evil – alliances with the "world" and rampant oppressions on your sheep
- False witness speaking lies – false assurance to others that you are telling the Truth and know all the answers
- Sowing discord among brethren – being sectarian and denominational, allowing factions and splits, ejecting brethren from your fellowship over doctrinal or personality issues
- Lack of Fear of the Lord – which is the BEGINNING of wisdom (Ps. 111:10, Prov. 3:5-6, James 4:16)
- Institutional, hierarchical system instead of truly Spirit-led in EVERY way – someone other than God setting your goals and guidelines.
- Lack of Love for the WHOLE Body (I John 3:10-23)
- Sexual immorality, impurity and debauchery; idolatry and witchcraft; hatred, discord, jealousy, fits of rage, selfish ambition, dissensions, factions and envy; drunkenness, orgies and the like – WILL NOT inherit the Kingdom of Heaven (Gal. 5:19-21)
- Worshiping the wrong Jesus (or worshiping the Holy Spirit)
- Evidence of Deuteronomy 28 curses in physical and/or spiritual realms
- Inability to repent - or inability to even figure out what to repent for
- God's glory has departed from the temple, you can't feel the Holy Spirit – or the promises of the Bible for healing or deliverance don't come as they should.
- Can't hear the voice of God and/or not letting Him direct all your paths (Prov. 3:5-6)
- Constant seeking for the new best thing, anxious mind, eyes weary from longing and despairing heart. Always hoping for something different and better. (Deut. 28:65-67) No peace.
- The loss of your children to the demonic structures and systems of your enemies. (Deut. 28)
- and the like...

The Red Dragon

I have been in over 400 congregations or ministries in the last few years. I have seen every single one of these in play. Usually all of them. I have been physically ejected from a congregation for praying (silently). I have been banned from worshiping with some congregations for no apparent reason. Even by people that have acknowledged that I love Jesus with all my heart and that the Holy Spirit is at work in me. Even people that have declared me a prophet and a healer and a man of God, have later turned completely around. There is one "Spirit-filled" holiness pastor that describes me as a "thing" now and not even as a man. Another that refuses to even pray with me and others that insist I'm full of demons – but can't tell me what they are and won't help deliver me. Pastors that hate me – seriously HATE me – and have said they <u>cannot</u> love me because they don't know what "spirit" I am of – even though Jesus COMMANDED us to love our enemies. (Matt. 10:22, John 15:18-25, Mark 3:22, Luke 7:33-34, Matt. 12:22-30, Prov. 6:16-19)

But I generally seem to get along fine with Baptists, Lutherans, Presbyterians, Methodists and others. It's the "Spirit-filled" Lead Dragon Dancers (that should be hearing God the best) that are the most supernaturally unable to hear anything I have to say – and are the most willing to divide the Body and the most afraid of losing control. To those whom much has been given, much is expected. If God speaks to you, gives you dreams and visions, gives you gifts, gives you a big job to do and THEN you go and make it about <u>you</u> and your conferences and DVD's and new book deal, God is going to turn you over to your own depraved mind and whatever demonic forces want to come mess with you – and you won't even see it coming. At some point you might end up on national news for having sex with your gay massage therapist or hiring a stripper or abusing little boys – and everybody under YOUR particular Red Dragon will say they never even saw it coming. That's just supernatural stupidity and a complete lack of discernment of spirits – cause everybody outside of YOUR dragon totally saw it coming.

Part of what I do is flush out the strongholds that are in play. Just like Jesus and the Apostles (and thousands of other people with a big cup of Jesus), pretty much anywhere I go, the demons that are hiding start surfacing and manifesting. Which is great! That's what I prayed for (even though it really hurts sometimes). Better to flush them out then let them stay camouflaged and hidden. But I have been constantly astounded at how hard-hearted so many "men of God" could be and oblivious to their own sinfulness and obvious heresy while they INSIST they are holy and sanctified. I can come to no other conclusion than that they are supernaturally blind and deaf and dumb and under a strong delusion from God. Satan couldn't do this to them if they were righteous. It had to come from God. And I have been banging my head for two years trying to break them free of a curse that GOD HIMSELF put on them and won't lift! But it was all part of the plan so that I would see the truth of what is behind all of this mess.

Now I know not to come at them with anger or frustration or bitterness. They are trapped and yoked and under the oppression of a curse. And worst of all, it's from God. And the only solution is repentance, but the curse keeps them from repenting!! In fact, many of them HATE repentance! It creeps them out to see people crying and they just want to focus on the "love" of God and not make people feel bad. Many of them have canceled intercessory prayer meetings and squelched the handful of people in their congregation that were actually willing to cry out to God and weep. True repentance is the most rare thing to be found in the "church" today – and yet, the ONLY thing that is going to turn this mess around. In all my years growing up, I can't remember EVER seeing anyone on their knees crying in a Baptist church! Even many charismatic ministries that know what it's like to feel the presence of God seem to think that if you "declare a holy fast, call a sacred assembly, lay around and giggle on the floor, then He will turn." (Joel 1:13-14 – sort of) But that's just not in there. Not even close! That's just NEVER going to work to turn this ride around. But that's as close to repentance as they can seem to get. Lots of talk about the problems "out there", but no actual crying for their own part in it. Oh, people can repent for personal, individual issues, but not for corporate, system-wide apostasy like division in the Body or selective use of the Word of God. Or they can repent for all the parts of the Body that are in darkness and apostate and backslidden, but not for their own part in not stopping it sooner.

I don't know how many of them we can get free, but I know that they're in a really horrible place and I desperately want them all to be free. It's going to come down to whether or not the Lord will pour out the Gift of Repentance on them (or send someone with one) and they will receive it. If not, they're probably toast – and their sheep with them.

Acts 5:31 – Him hath God exalted with his right hand to be a Prince and a Saviour, for to **give** repentance to Israel, and forgiveness of sins.

That's the order in which this works. First, God gives repentance and then you get forgiveness. Jesus came so that He could have right hand access so as to give us the Gift of Repentance. God exalted Jesus so that Jesus could be the mediator and request on our behalf that the Father would give us repentance, even when we don't know to ask for it because we are deaf and blind and stupid. Only THEN can we get forgiveness for our sins individually and corporately. When you lose the Gift of Repentance, you should start worrying that you might be back under a Red Dragon.

2 Timothy 2:25 – In meekness instructing those that oppose themselves; if God peradventure will **give** them repentance to the acknowledging of the truth;

Acts 11:18 – When they heard these things, they held their peace, and glorified God, saying, Then hath God also to the Gentiles **granted** repentance unto life.

Romans 2:4 – Or despisest thou the riches of his goodness and forbearance and longsuffering; not knowing that the goodness of God **leadeth** thee to repentance?

2 Peter 3:9 – The Lord is not slack concerning his promise, as some men count slackness; but is longsuffering to us-ward, not willing that any should perish, but that all should come to repentance.
Hebrews 12:25-29 – 25 See that ye refuse not him that speaketh. For if they escaped not who refused him that spake on earth, much more shall not we escape, if we turn away from him that speaketh from heaven: 26 Whose voice then shook the earth: but now he hath promised, saying, Yet once more I shake not the earth only, but also heaven. 27 And this word, Yet once more, signifieth the removing of those things that are shaken, as of things that are made, that those things which cannot be shaken may remain. 28 Wherefore we receiving a kingdom which cannot be moved, let us have grace, whereby we may serve God acceptably with reverence and godly fear: 29 For our God is a consuming fire.

Please hear me. Please! See the justice and severity of God. Repent and keep repenting until this thing gets turned around. Give your eyes no rest until Jerusalem is free – and all the other cities. Shout this from the watchtowers. There is NO other solution. There is NO other way to turn this around. Weep and mourn and grieve for all the detestable things that are done in the name of Jehovah and Jesus. If you can't repent for your part in this mess, start worrying about whether you're under a Red Dragon of your own. ONLY the Ezekiel 9 remnant will escape. If this could have been turned around sooner, then you should have tried. Don't blame anybody else, this is on YOUR head. If one man, determined and willing, under the anointing of the Holy Spirit, can change the world, then you should have changed it. Stop pointing fingers and repent for not having acted sooner.

Isaiah 62:6-7 – 6 I have set watchmen on your walls, O Jerusalem; They shall never hold their peace day or night. You who make mention of the LORD, do not keep silent, 7 And give Him no rest till He establishes And till He makes Jerusalem a praise in the earth.

Just because you're sure you're hearing God and He seems to be saying you're OK, that's no proof. If you ARE under a Dragon, you'll hear God and be sure it's God and every way you know how to test the spirits, it checks out as God, but it can still be a lying spirit from the Throne intent on your destruction. Repentance is the only safe place. Believe me, it's REALLY easy to get back under a Red Dragon. All you have to do is go your own way – even a little. Then you've basically made up your own religion that says you don't have to obey God ALL the time, you can pick and choose which of His commands are important. If you get very far out from under His perfect will, you may not be able to find your way back. Some folks have never even BEEN in His perfect will, so they don't even know what it would be like to have Him direct every step! Or worse, they don't believe that God is interested in or willing to or capable of directing their every step – which flies in the face of the Word of God. We are NOT to lean on our own understanding and direct our own paths – not even a little bit.

The time is over to argue about who is the bigger heretic. We're all cults. Every denomination is a cult. There is no Biblical justification for any division inside the Body over secondary issues. We are clearly commanded not to add to or take away from the Word of God and yet every denomination has choice traditions they add to it or portions of scripture they've conveniently explained away or ignore altogether. Stop arguing about who is the most off track! So long as we're willing to hack the Body of Christ up into little pieces or not speak out against it, we're all guilty. We're beating Jesus' Body with a cat-of-nine-tails and leaving little pieces all over while His precious Blood is spilled and nobody seems to care. We have to knock it off before it's too late.

DID THE BIBLE PREDICT THIS?

Yep.

2 Thessalonians 2:3-12 (NIV)
Don't let anyone deceive you in any way, for that day will not come until the rebellion [falling away NKJV] occurs and the man of lawlessness is revealed at the proper time. For the secret power of lawlessness is already at work; but the one who now holds it back will continue to do so until he is taken out of the way. And then the lawless one will be revealed, whom the Lord Jesus will overthrow with the breath of his mouth and destroy by the splendor of his coming. The coming of the lawless one will be in accordance with the work of Satan displayed in all kinds of counterfeit miracles, signs and wonders, and in every sort of evil that deceives those who are perishing. They perish because they refused to love the truth and so be saved. For this reason **God** sends them a powerful delusion so that they will believe the lie and so that all will be condemned who have not believed the truth but have delighted in wickedness.

If I'm right, then the falling away is not some future event. We are already so fallen that I don't believe there is any hope for most of the systems and structures we've built. There are millions dying by our hand every week that this 'Ponzi' scheme that we call a "church" continues as it is. (And I can prove it factually and statistically beyond any room for debate. There can be no interpretation except that we are massively and supernaturally backwards.)

So the rebellion has to happen first, right? Could that be like 41,000+ denominations when Jesus said to be One Body? You would sure think that would qualify as rebellion, wouldn't you?

So who is this man of lawlessness that is to be revealed? Could that be the guy that doesn't believe the Old Testament is for today and Jesus didn't come to fulfill the Law, but to abolish it and that once we're under the Blood and have accepted Him as our personal savior we can do whatever we want because we're safe? That sounds pretty lawless to me. (I know that's not the only application for this verse, but it sure seems like one of the "spirals" to me.)

And who was the one that restrained the secret power of lawlessness? I'm pretty sure that would be the Holy Spirit. So who restrained Him and took Him out of the way? I'm pretty sure we did. We denied that the Holy Spirit talks to people, we denied that the Gifts of the Spirit are real and for today, we denied that He should be directing ALL our paths. We turned our back on the Holy Spirit and went our own way and hired consultants and marketing experts and pop-psychology speakers and professional hired shepherds to lead us to whatever THEY think is green pasture. I'm just pretty sure that we picked the Holy Spirit up and set Him off to the side. And when we did, He stopped restraining the secret power of lawlessness and it took us over. And we didn't even notice – because it's SECRET. Kind of goes without saying, doesn't it? If God turns you over to a powerful delusion, you won't know – or else it's not a very good delusion. See?

And what kind of lying signs and wonders should we be expecting? Well, one of the really obvious ones is that the world starts liking you. You live at peace with those who should be persecuting you and you think that means you're reaching them, when really you're just a friend to the world and an enemy to God. (James 4:4) What are the lying signs and wonders at the end of the age? For my dollar, I'm betting that they include all the people preaching "peace and safety" and singing and dancing and being given in marriage right up until the very end of all things. That's pretty miraculous to me, that they would say they love Jesus, but would be friends with the world and completely oblivious to how bad things really are. Pope John Paul II was said to be the most popular and respected and loved man on the planet. But Jesus said that if you were like <u>Him</u> you would be persecuted and hated.

How is the lawless one going to be overthrown? By "the breath from the mouth of Jesus" and he will be destroyed by the splendor of His coming. Now, I'm not saying this doesn't have Apocalyptic application, but I happen to have personally experienced the lawless one in me being overthrown by the breath from the mouth of Jesus and the splendor of His coming, so I know this has other meanings. When Jesus shows up in force, the lawless one gets burned up. Read Jeremiah 4:11-12 - *"At that time this people and Jerusalem will be told, 'A scorching wind blows toward my people, but not to winnow or to cleanse; a wind too strong for that comes from me. Now I pronounce my judgements against them."* (Read the rest of the chapter and see if it doesn't describe the state of the "church". Weep if you can.)

It DOES NOT say that Satan is in charge of all this. It says the coming of the lawless one will be in <u>accordance</u> <u>with</u> the workings of Satan. That doesn't mean Satan does it or has power. It means that it will be like him and in harmony with his goals and plans and style. If the "church" is having the effect of killing, stealing and destroying people spiritually, emotionally or materially, then it is accomplishing the work of Satan <u>for</u> him and is in accordance with the normal workings of the darkness.

It says that there will be counterfeit signs and miracles, and all sorts of evil that deceives those who are perishing. Let me be frank (for a change), the greatest miracles that I have seen are that people spouting clearly heretical, extra-Biblical and dangerous NONSENSE are constantly tolerated and even promoted within the Church! What kind of a miracle is required to make a multi-millionaire lady with pink hair that is constantly crying and begging for money for a multi-Billion dollar TV network seem like a normal, acceptable part of the Church of Jesus Christ? What can be more miraculous than that people who have advanced degrees in "Bible" absolutely REFUSE to acknowledge that certain passages are even IN there?! How miraculous is it that we are the most divided, factious, sectarian religion on the planet and WE are the ones whose Founder said not to EVER break up into pieces?! How many are perishing because they are worshiping the wrong Jesus, but are just sure that they are fine? How many have been deceived? Where do I even start to point out all the heresies preached in the "church" that will send you straight to Hell, but have millions – or billions – convinced that they're safe?!

Why are all these people perishing? Why are they deceived? Why are they walking in accordance with the workings of Satan? BECAUSE they refused to love the Truth.

"WAIT!" you say. "I thought it was because the Antichrist came and Satan is in charge and the Holy Spirit is withdrawn after the Rapture and that's when everyone falls away?" Fine. Believe what you want. But I'm convinced that we've <u>already</u> fallen away and that we've <u>already</u> taken the Holy Spirit out of the way and set Him off to the side by grieving and blaspheming Him for the gazillionth time and that we're under a powerful delusion and we're corporately working for Satan because we refused to love the Truth and so be saved.

Does Satan send the powerful delusion? Nope. Read it again, **God** did it Himself. He said He would and He has. We're in it and hardly anybody can see through it. How strong a delusion do you think it is? If we're covered in the Blood of Jesus and Satan sends a delusion, we should be able to see through it. That's my experience anyway. We should be able to take every thought captive and bring it into obedience with Christ. After all, our weapons of war are mighty and no power of darkness can stand against us.

But do you really think you're big enough to see through a strong delusion that came from God? How does the Blood of Jesus protect us from a delusion from God? Didn't we invite the delusion by not really loving Truth and maybe not being under the Blood of Jesus in the first place?

"All will be condemned that believed not the truth but delighted in wickedness." Period. That's the Word of God and it's final. Our denominations and sects and ministries are delighting in wickedness. Every single day that we continue to believe that we are just fine and things are peachy, we continue to go the way of the Laodecian Church in Revelation 3 and we get more blind and more naked and more wretched – and more people die because of us.

We better get back to Truth – and pure, unadulterated, untouched by Man, nothing-but, Truth – before it's too late. And I have no idea what that looks like, but I know you can NEVER find it so long as you're under a Red Dragon and you can't get out from under a Red Dragon without repentance and "coming out of her" and getting her out of you. And the Red Dragon will try to keep you from repenting at ALL costs. See the problem?

I'm not taking away from that this passage in Thessalonians that it has application to some future anti-christ person that afflicts the world, but as with all of the Bible it has multiple applications and in the context of the Church, I think this man of sin, this son of perdition is **us**. I think the Lord is making it very clear that the falling away will get worse and worse until we realize that we have exalted ourselves above all that is called God, have sat ourselves (or the men <u>we</u> anointed and appointed) as the idols in our temples and have declared ourselves to be God. We have hired consultants to teach us how to be more like the world. We have gotten in bed with government and business and marketing and fund-raising and in all sorts of other ways have intermarried with the nations we were supposed to displace and destroy. We have taken on their gods and worshiped them and by so doing have declared ourselves God. **We** are the sons of perdition. (John 17:6-26)

What are the workings of Satan that come with all power and signs and lying wonders?

That we're just fine and everything is just as it should be. "Peace and Safety. Peace and Safety. All is well. Go back to sleep." He has bamboozled the "church." Nearly all of the "elect" have **ALREADY** gone astray.

What is the true sign and wonder of this age that proves the sovereignty of God?

Deuteronomy 28:45-48 (NIV)
All these curses will come upon you. They will pursue you and overtake you until you are destroyed, because you did not obey the Lord your God and observe the commands and decrees he gave you. **They will be a sign and wonder to you and your descendants forever.** Because you did not serve the Lord your God joyfully and gladly in the time of prosperity, therefore in hunger and thirst, in nakedness and dire poverty, you will serve the enemies the Lord sends against you. He will put an iron yoke on your neck until he has destroyed you.

Deuteronomy 28:62-63 (NIV)
You who were as numerous as the stars in the sky will be left but few in number, because you did not obey the Lord your God. Just as it pleased the Lord to make you prosper and increase in number, so it will please him to ruin and destroy you. You will be uprooted from the land you are entering to possess.

Fellowship Of The Martyrs

DID JESUS PREDICT THIS?

Yep.

Matthew 24:4-25
Jesus answered: "Watch out that no one deceives you. For many will come in my name, claiming, 'I am the Christ,' and will deceive many. You will hear of wars and rumors of wars, but see to it that you are not alarmed. Such things must happen, but the end is still to come. Nation will rise against nation, and kingdom against kingdom. There will be famines and earthquakes in various places. All these things are the beginning of the birth pains."

"Then you will be handed over to be persecuted and put to death and you will be hated by all nations because of me. At that time many will turn away from the faith and will betray and hate each other, and many false prophets will appear and deceive many people. Because of the increase of wickedness, the love of most will grow cold, but he who stands firm to the end will be saved. And this gospel of the kingdom will be preached in the whole world as a testimony to all nations, and then the end will come."

"So when you see standing in the holy place the abomination that causes desolation, spoken of through the prophet Daniel – let the reader understand then let those who are in Judea flee to the mountains. Let no one on the roof of his house go down to take anything out of the house. Let no one in the field go back to get his cloak. How dreadful it will be in those days for pregnant women and nursing mothers. Pray that your flight will not take place in winter or on the Sabbath. For then there will be great distress, unequaled from the beginning of the world until now – and never to be equaled again."

"If those days had not been cut short, no one would survive, but for the sake of the elect those days will be shortened. At that time if anyone says to you, 'Look, here is the Christ!' or, 'There he is!' do not believe it. For false Christs and false prophets will appear and perform great signs and miracles to deceive even the elect – it that were possible. See I have told you ahead of time."

Again, this passage has global, apocalyptic applications, but it is like a repeating, increasing spiral. Before it applies to the world, it applies to the Church. The spiritual goes first, then is manifested in the natural. If we look at the implications of this to the Church, I think you can see that we are already full on with all of these things and that Jesus predicted this. And that it had to happen to spiritual Israel before it can happen to natural Israel and the World.

We were to watch out that no one deceive us. We didn't. There will be wars between nations and kingdoms – which is how Christians killed so many other Christians through the Dark Ages and the Reformation and which is how we now have 41,000+ denomiNATIONS and start a new one every other day. (See Scary Stats reference on page 12.) Can you really split a denomination without hatred in your heart? And if you have hatred for a brother in your heart, that's the same as murder. There are spiritual famines among God's people and the occasional earthquake shaking that seems like something might break loose, but is soon over. All these are the beginning of the birth pains.

THEN we will be handed over to be persecuted. By who? By the enemy, by the Red Dragon. And many have been put to death by the Red Dragon. We are hated by each other and hated by the world. Many have turned away from the faith and betray and hate each other. Many false prophets have appeared and deceive many. Every man that says we don't need to be one body and we don't need to obey the Word of God and love our brothers unconditionally is a false prophet – and they are legion. The love of most has grown cold and it's because of the wickedness that we allowed to enter by going our own way and following after false prophets. But ONLY he who stands until the end will be saved. ONLY those who are not under a Red Dragon will be saved. ONLY those can preach the true gospel of the kingdom to all nations.

The abomination that causes desolation is the antichrist and when we see the Spirit of Antichrist in our holy places, on our congregations and ministries or in our own hearts – we are to RUN FOR THE HILLS and not look back. Take nothing, go back for nothing. Say goodbye to no one. Run and don't look back. If you go back, you will get back under the Red Dragon. And if you're not careful, at home alone you'll get under one of your own making!

The Lord makes it clear that so many will be deceived and so many will die that NO ONE would survive if it weren't cut short. The Red Dragon has devoured nearly everything. The days were cut short for the sake of those who were standing firm until the end. Otherwise even the last of the elect would be deceived and no one would be left.

I'm begging you, come out of her. Run! Get away! Get out from under the Red Dragon and get the Red Dragon out of you! And the only way is to repent. Someone with the Gift of Repentance has to pour it out on you. Now I understand better than ever why the Lord had me write the "Apology to the World." The Lord said that if I pray with someone and repent sincerely in front of them for the things that I have done and they so much as nod their head in agreement that they have done the same things and need forgiveness, then He will turn from His fierce anger on them and will heal them and restore their land. He really, really wants to lift this curse, but He is just and His rules are clear. Without repentance there is no remission of sins. And a strong delusion will keep you from repenting at all. So you will die. Period. Unless the Lord finds a way to release you. Unless the Lord sends someone to show you the way, you are toast. I was under it and I know now how badly deceived I was. And if I get back under it again, I know it will be even worse because the stakes are getting higher and higher all the time.

OK, not only that, but you have to see that Jesus recruited as disciples people that were NOT under the Red Dragon curse at the time. The Pharisees and Sadducees were supernaturally stubborn and blind and Jesus said they were sons of hell and would not enter heaven (Matt. 23). Even though they were in the synagogue praying at least three times a DAY! (That's sure more pious than just Sundays and Wednesday nights!)

Clearly, Israel had gone it's own way at the time and were worshiping all kinds of things other than the one true God. I think the argument could be made pretty effectively that Jesus was aware of the Red Dragon religious spirits and the Deuteronomy 28 curse and was wise enough to recruit as disciples those who were not already under it. Even though they had less scripture knowledge, they had an easier time seeing their Messiah and embracing His message, because they weren't under a curse from God. Why else would He constantly be hanging around tax collectors and fishermen and prostitutes – that is, all the people the "religious establish-ment" thought were unclean? Perhaps it's their very "uncleanness" that kept them safe from the Red Dragon curse! If I'm right, that really changes the whole approach to who we need to reach doesn't it? Instead of getting people to transfer from one Red Dragon to another, let's go find the people that ARE NOT under a curse from God because they were never in the institutional "church" in the first place!

I'm just pretty sure Jesus understood this really well and it was what colored His style and focus of ministry. Go get the little children, the ones with faith like a child, the ones uncorrupted by the antichrist religious systems and structures and "wisdom" of the day. And if you put a stumbling block in their way and put them under a Red Dragon, it would be better for you to have a millstone tied around your neck and thrown in the ocean. (Matt. 18:6)

WHAT WOULD IT LOOK LIKE TO BE COMPLETELY FREE OF THE RED DRAGON?

Well, when Israel was completely obedient and following God's commands, no nation could stand against them. The Word of God says that He will lift you above nations and no weapon formed against you will prosper. So, the way I see it, the people who are fully free of every yoke, are out from under every curse, have been transformed by the renewing of their minds, and are dead and it's Christ in them that lives – are the manifest sons of God that the earth is groaning for. (Romans 8:19) We've seen little glimmers of it before in Elijah and Elisha and Moses and Abraham and Enoch and others who were counted as righteous. But the Word of God says the greatest of all the prophets was John the Baptist and that the least among US that has the Holy Spirit is greater than him! So how come we're not seeing it in every Christian everywhere? Because they're not manifesting their Sonship – because they're going their own way.

Consider this, people often discuss all the possible reasons why God seems to heal people more often (and more dramatically) in Africa and India and Asia. I have friends that I trust that have seen with their own eyes as people regrow limbs or spines straightened or giant tumors just fall off or even miraculous weight loss while in a prayer line. By the power of God through me I have seen people healed of autism, hearing problems, heart problems, joint problems, migraines, chronic or urgent pain of all kinds, spinal and head injuries - as well as demonic oppressions like schizophrenia, agoraphobia, depression, fear, lust, and addictions of all kinds instantly lifted. I know it's real and I know God moves that way today.

I've heard all kinds of theories about why we don't see more of that in America, from lack of faith, to not being child-like enough, to those that say it's all fake or satanic and not really from God anyway. (And I dare you to find ANYWHERE in the Word where it says satan heals people.) Anyway, none of those arguments satisfy me. People <u>are</u> getting healed there, even raised from the dead. Something else is behind this.

The best answer I've found is this, Deuteronomy 28 says you will have wasting diseases that cannot be cured, that you will be afflicted and there will be no one to help, that the sky over you will be brass, that you will suffer until you are destroyed. If a nation or a people or a village don't know God and never did, when someone righteous and sent by God shows up and prays for healing for them, it's likely that they will get healed so that God can show His glory and prove Himself to them. But when a country or a people or a village already <u>knew</u> God and have intentionally and rebelliously gone their own way, they should <u>not</u> expect any supernatural healing to show up on any kind of a regular basis. And if it shows up at all, it's just God's mercy on an individual here and there.

So the best explanation I can find of why people get healed in Africa and Asia and not in America (or the West, for that matter) is that the West is already evangelized and has turned their back on God by creating their own blended mystery religions and calling them "Christian" and He has put upon them the curses of Deuteronomy 28. The prayer of a "righteous" man availeth much. The prayer of a "denominational" man may not availeth much at all.

Warm and fluffy and "seeker-friendly" isn't going to cut it. Want to know what your "purpose" is? You don't need forty days to figure out what YOU can do for God. Just weep and repent and mourn before the altar for the fact that you haven't known **all along** what God's purpose for you is – and been walking in it. There's no telling how much blood is on your head for the missed opportunities and outright rebellion of going your own way this whole time. **You don't get revived until you say you're sorry for being the kind of person that needs reviving!** If you cry out to Him, He will open the doors and explain everything and the Holy Spirit will be your teacher. No MAN can tell you who you are in Christ - not even you. You need to hear God directly and walk in it.

So what might it look like to be fully Dragon-free? For one thing, the diseases of the Egyptians wouldn't stick to you anymore and your prayers for deliverance would have real power. Maybe people in America might actually start getting healed and delivered on a large scale. In combination with keeping your cup full of Jesus and being a part of a Lampstand city, probably nothing could stand against you.

(Read more about that on the website. See the book "Do It Yourself City Church Restoration.")

WHAT WOULD IT BE LIKE TO BE COMPLETELY UNDER CHRIST'S HEADSHIP?

Not that I have fully attained the goal, but I strive toward the prize and I die daily so that Christ in me can live. To His glory, He has allowed me to hear His voice very clearly. Not just in dreams and visions, but all day every day. He directs my paths in every way. I would recommend that you read "The Practice of the Presence of God" by Brother Lawrence. It was formative for me and I sought after that kind of intimacy with God. And He says that if you seek Him, you will find Him. And I did.

He wakes me up in the morning. I have no alarm clock. I don't wear a watch. He tells me what Scripture to read and what it means and how it will apply to my day. He tells me what to wear, what to eat, where to go, what to say (or not say), what job to take and how to do it. He tells me what to pray. He prays through me or speaks through me to those in need. He crushes the demons that come against me every day. He is my shield and my provider. He is my Head and I am His bond-servant. I fear no man and follow no man. I am not under anyone's "cover" because Christ is my head. There is no man that stands between me and God and tells me what to do. Though there are many brethren around me that advise and counsel and teach and reprove and rebuke, ultimately I have to get a confirmation from the Throne on everything. I make no plans, I spend no money, I go nowhere, I eat nothing without an assurance that it's what He wants me to do. And I have more joy and peace than I ever knew possible – even in the face of astounding amounts of opposition and affliction.

Do I make mistakes? Yes. Sometimes I hear wrong, sometimes I pester Him into allowing something He'd rather not allow, but He humors me to teach me a lesson. Sometimes I ask "Can I" instead of "Should I". (That one got me into a <u>lot</u> of trouble until He explained the difference and wrote it on my heart!) At times I have been under a Red Dragon of my own making and heard what I was sure was God, but it was a lying spirit from the Throne intent on my destruction for having gone my own way. Sometimes the people around me hear wrong and I don't double-check with Him. Sometimes I just pop off before asking what I should say. Sometimes I've spoken out revelation that was just for me personally and not for any other ears. But it's getting better all the time and I don't <u>ever</u> ask Him to turn down the refining fire.

The ministry that He has called me to is under His headship. He dictates the pace, the scope, the impact, the focus, the budget, the method, the timing – everything. There are no committee meetings. There are no votes, there are no paid consultants. There is just Christ as the Head and me as the hands and feet. When I need a confirmation, He provides one. When I need a rebuke, He does it Himself or sends someone.

In a worship or prayer meeting, He sets the time and place, He invites the people, He directs the prayers, He moves through us as He wills. He identifies the needs in the people present and makes sure they get met in order of priority. Nobody goes home unchanged. He consistently shows up in a powerful way because we get out of His way. I have never been anywhere and experienced the kind of presence and power of God that I did in God's little furniture store in Liberty, Missouri. And even though that season is past, He continues to show up every time we get out of His way and sincerely invite Him to be fully in charge and we take Him out of whatever box we might have tried to cram Him into.

What would it do to "church" to really, truly get out of His way? Do we even see how much we're getting in His way? Because of the blindness of our hearts, I doubt that hardly any leaders of the church really see how much they are grieving the Holy Spirit. I would love to tell them – and I have tried at times – but it never seems to do any good. In fact, it <u>supernaturally</u> never seems to do any good! The most hardened secularist or atheist or businessman would listen more politely – just in case I might actually have a point about something and it would improve what they were doing. Most any restaurant or service business will have a Customer Comments box and carefully review feedback – but that seems like the VERY last thing a pastor wants to spend time doing. How a man that says he loves God and fears Him could so callously and obliviously ignore anyone that comes in the name of the Lord and shows them their error is beyond me. It HAS to be supernatural. I can't find any other explanation for how normally loving, caring, sweet, 'Christian' people can stone prophets – except that God has hardened their hearts, blinded their eyes, shut up their ears and doesn't want them free yet.

Matthew 13:14-15
14 And in them the prophecy of Isaiah is fulfilled, which says: 'Hearing you will hear and shall not understand, And seeing you will see and not perceive; 15 For the hearts of this people have grown dull. Their ears are hard of hearing, And their eyes they have closed, Lest they should see with their eyes and hear with their ears, Lest they should understand with their hearts and turn, So that I should heal them.'

All of the things that He has taught me in the last two years (and before) somehow integrate with this message about the Red Dragon. I know that if we were under His headship, the model of the church would be the city church – one body in one town, under His headship and working as He directed. How that would manifest and look in real practice in each particular town, I have no idea. In some towns you could all gather in one building. In some it will mean house churches all over town, in some it will mean stadiums full of people. In some it might not <u>look</u> that different than what we have right now. I have no idea. Happily, it's not my job to direct your town. It's my job to get you free of the Red Dragon so you can hear God and HE can direct all your paths.

I know that if we were under His headship, the way we handle money would be vastly different. The way we relate institutionally to the government would be vastly different. The way we relate to other Christians would be vastly different. Music would be different. Church "services" would be different. Leadership would be different. Healing would be different. I think we can't even get our heads around how creative He can be to customize each situation to the exact needs of the people present at that moment. Nothing would be repetitive or even predictable. People we never expected would be the mightiest evangelists and prophets and teachers and musicians. The Holy Spirit blows like the wind and no one knows where He goes or where He came from. We would be much like that. But we would be effective for the Gospel and we would be pushing back the darkness instead of being co-opted by it.

As soon as the Red Dragon can stop using our legs and our spiritual authority and our assets to accomplish his purposes, then we can gain the upper hand and begin to crush Him under our heel.

Wouldn't that be nice?

There is still that little issue of the Great Commission, the final charge of Jesus to spread the TRUE Gospel to all the world. (Matt. 28:18-20, Mark 16:14-20) Is there anything more important than this? How exactly are we going to do that while we're fighting and fussing with each other and all going our own way? Whose Gospel do we preach anyway? Jesus did NOT say to go into all the world and preach the Baptist Gospel or the Pentecostal Gospel or the Lutheran Gospel. We are to preach Christ and Him crucified. We are to be One Body and we are to love each other. If they will know us by our love and we are full of hatred and wrath and dissension and factions – maybe we should stop preaching ANYTHING until we knock it off and the LORD HIMSELF opens our mouths. Maybe we should hit our faces and admit that we are ALL men of unclean lips and from a people of unclean lips and beg for Him to burn it out of us by whatever means necessary. (Isaiah 6) We need to stop traveling over land and sea to make a single convert and then make him twice as much the sons of hell that we are. (Matt. 23:15) Yeah, that would be nice.

We can't spread the true Gospel until we are true Christians. And we can't be true Christians until we are fully under Christ's headship and no other. We have to repent and throw off all the Red Dragons. All of them. Of the seven letters to the churches in Revelation 2-3, two of them were not criticized – Smyrna and Philadelphia, both of them poor. No matter what the other five were criticized for, the prescription is always the same – REPENT!

There is NO other solution offered by Jesus. There is no other hope. There is no amount of good worship music and really excellent child-care facilities and great expository teaching that is going to turn this around. The ONLY solution, the only prescription, the only thing that is going to get His attention is repentance.

Start with this – Appendix G. Maybe you've already seen it. Read the "Apology to the World" letter and if you feel that you've been a part of helping build – or not having personally tried harder to stop sooner – a system that is not what God wanted, then repent for your sins and the sins of your forefathers. **And mean it, and don't go back.** Run for the hills right now and don't even go back to get your coat. Come out of her my people – and get HER out of YOU, too! (Rev. 18:4-8)

Lord, pour out the Gift of Repentance on Your Body and on this nation. Please forgive us for going our own way. Please have mercy on us and turn from Your righteous anger. You are just and true and your judgement is righteous. We deserve far worse than what You have done. Please, Father, please for the sake of Your Holy Name remember Your people and turn from Your wrath. Please send out the remnant that can teach us how to pray and how to repent in spirit and in truth. Please turn this around, Abba. Please fix it. I'm sorry we broke it. I'm sorry we didn't follow the instructions. It doesn't work and there are parts left over. Please fix it, Dad. In the name of Jesus Christ, our Lord, Amen.

If that doesn't do it for you and you don't feel you've repented enough to get out from under your Red Dragon, contact me. I have a special anointing for gently telling people (and groups) what they overlooked that they still need to repent for. And repenting in front of them so they can see how it's done.

If that takes care of it and the Lord pours out on you a true and deep gift of repentance, then please, PLEASE, I'm begging you – please go find somebody to pour it out on. Go weep in front of them until they see how bad it is and how desperate we really are. I spent two days weeping on the sidewalk in the middle of town in June of 2006. Do whatever it takes. Pour out your gift of repentance on those around you who are trapped under the Red Dragon. Pour it on the Lead Dragon Dancers if you can, but know that they have the hardest time receiving it.

Please, Brethren, if you have ears to hear, please hear. Then GO into all the world and show them how to repent.

LEFT-OVER PIECES

I Samuel 16:14
14 But the Spirit of the LORD departed from Saul, and an evil spirit from the LORD troubled him.

Yep, God can afflict you. Don't think He can't. If you go your own way, He Himself will afflict you.

Romans 1:18-32
18 The wrath of God is being revealed from heaven against all the godlessness and wickedness of men who suppress the truth by their wickedness, 19 since what may be known about God is plain to them, because God has made it plain to them. 20 For since the creation of the world God's invisible qualities—his eternal power and divine nature—have been clearly seen, being understood from what has been made, so that men are without excuse. 21 For although they knew God, they neither glorified him as God nor gave thanks to him, **but their thinking became futile and their foolish hearts were darkened.** 22 Although they claimed to be wise, they became fools 23 and exchanged the glory of the immortal God for images made to look like mortal man and birds and animals and reptiles.
24 Therefore God **gave them over** in the sinful desires of their hearts to sexual impurity for the degrading of their bodies with one another. 25 They exchanged the truth of God for a lie, and worshiped and served created things rather than the Creator—who is forever praised. Amen.
26 Because of this, God gave them over to shameful lusts. Even their women exchanged natural relations for unnatural ones. 27 In the same way the men also abandoned natural relations with women and were inflamed with lust for one another. Men committed indecent acts with other men, and received in themselves the due penalty for their perversion.
28 Furthermore, since they did not think it worthwhile to retain the knowledge of God, **he gave them over to a depraved mind**, to do what ought not to be done. 29 They have become filled with every kind of wickedness, evil, greed and depravity. They are full of envy, murder, strife, deceit and malice. They are gossips, 30 slanderers, God-haters, insolent, arrogant and boastful; they invent ways of doing evil; they disobey their parents; 31 they are senseless, faithless, heartless, ruthless. 32 **Although they know God's righteous decree that those who do such things deserve death, they not only continue to do these very things but also approve of those who practice them.**

John 9:35-41
35 Jesus heard that they had thrown him out, and when he found him, he said, "Do you believe in the Son of Man?" 36 "Who is he, sir?" the man asked. "Tell me so that I may believe in him." 37 Jesus said, "You have now seen him; in fact, he is the one speaking with you." 38 Then the man said, "Lord, I believe," and he worshiped him. 39 Jesus said, "For judgment I have come into this world, so that the blind will see and those who see will become blind." 40 Some Pharisees who were with him heard him say this and asked, "What? Are we blind too?" 41 Jesus said, "If you were blind, you would not be guilty of sin; but now that you claim you can see, your guilt remains.

Acts 17
29 "Therefore since we are God's offspring, we should not think that the divine being is like gold or silver or stone—an image made by man's design and skill. 30 In the past God overlooked such ignorance, **but now he commands all people everywhere to repent**. 31 For he has set a day when he will judge the world with justice by the man he has appointed. He has given proof of this to all men by raising him from the dead."

If you're not preaching repentance in your congregations, then you are directly disobeying the explicit command of God. If you are worshiping or following ANY structure, system, person or man-made thing, you are commanded to repent. There is no Plan B.

APPENDIX A: COMMON SYMPTOMS / SIDE EFFECTS OF THE RED DRAGON

Cut-and-paste Demon - Anything not related to what YOU are doing is of no importance. Scriptures that disagree with your position don't exist. Baptists ignore or marginalize or explain away the Book of Acts. Pentecostals ignore "decent and in order". 'Oneness' groups ignore Father, Son, and Spirit references. Seventh Day ignore that JESUS is Lord of the Sabbath and EVERY day should be dedicated to Him. Anything that disagrees is SUPERNATURALLY blocked out of the field of vision. Like that section of their Bible is just missing or has a fuzzy block over it. Just like when you are inside the Dragon, you can't see the scenery, just the inside of your own Dragon and all the dancers that are with you.

Deaf-and-Dumb Demon - Can't see, can't hear where you are going except by following the others in front. You can see where you've been, but you have no idea what is ahead of you. You are following the Lead Dancer and assuming that he knows where he is going. And he thinks he's in charge, but the Dragon is really the one telling him how to dance and where. When criticism comes, it's ignored because it comes from outside the Dragon. If criticism comes from inside the Dragon, the messenger is ejected as unloyal and unable to properly dance and represent the Dragon team. The Dragon will NOT tolerate disunity under it's own cover.

Spirit of Competition - Closely attached to the Pride, this encourages the Dragon team to be the VERY best and ignore weaknesses. They should be an EXCELLENT Dragon, particularly since they are doing everything they do to bring glory and honor to God. They need EXCELLENT silk and sequins and only the best costumes and dancers will do. They need consultants and personal trainers and professional choreographers. If possible, upgraded sound systems and lighting and videography so they can properly record how well they are dancing and tell the world. After a couple of generations of highlighting strengths and ignoring weaknesses, they become totally inbred and have developed their own languages and idiosyncrasies and style. In the Body of Christ, they become a barn full of toes and they like it that way and clone new toes as fast as they can. They have no balance, but they are the best bunch of toes anywhere.

Spirit of Bondage - The Dragon works hard to whisper to all involved that they are critically important to the welfare of the team and that they MUST remain under the Dragon. They CANNOT venture out on their own or go to some competing Dragon. They MUST remain under the "cover" of the Dragon or the Lead Dancer or else they will be rejected and alone and the enemy will get them. What enemy? The same enemy they're already under, but it will never admit that.

Spirit of Hurry - This artificially inserts all kinds of deadlines and forces urgency. It keeps everyone busy all the time. Twice on Sundays and Wednesday and visitation and softball leagues and potlucks and summer camp and committee meetings and Christmas Pageant and more and more. Always taxing those already over-taxed and seeking fresh "legs" for the Dragon. It HAS to keep dancing. It has to keep everyone in motion. It keeps their eyes off of Jesus if it can keep them focused on the structure, style, timing, programs, staff, improvement, growth of the Dragon.

Spirits of Envy, Jealousy and Hatred - Gal. 5:19-21 are rampant in the congregations and denominations of America. There is a constant finger-pointing and one trying to pull down another. The Dragon is always whispering that YOUR Dragon is prettier and smarter and older and better and longer and shinier and faster than all those other Dragons. It's critically important that the people in the Dragon KNOW what all the other Dragons are doing wrong and why THEIR Dragon is the best one of them all. They will even persecute each other or refuse to even participate in events together. Even though we are supposed to be ONE BODY (John 17), the enemy broke us up into competing teams so we can never go anywhere together.

Spirit of Empty Words - Eph. 5:5-7, Job 35:13, This is disguised as "fellowshiping" but is really just wasted time while people are dying. It's far better to bond together in the heat of common battle (or boot camp), than to casually greet each other as tourists on the same beach. This one may be disguised as telling stories about what God has done, which is nice, but it fills the time and keeps us from watching Him do something RIGHT NOW in our midst. It's not obedience to tell a story about the greatness and majesty of God – unless He tells you to tell that story at that moment. It might be a great story, but you're out of order if you tell it at the wrong time. It won't be anointed and it won't have the effect He wants it to have. This is VERY, VERY common in the "church" and is slowly sucking the life out of millions because of the missed opportunities to see Him move because we won't shut up.

Spirits of Lust and Greed - Almost ALL under the Red Dragon have a spirit of lust and a constant desire for more. It's no wonder that we have rampant obesity, porn, divorce, greed, adultery and other things inside the "church". There is a constant "arms race" to keep up with or exceed other Dragon Teams. And it spills over into the personal lives of all the members, even outside of the Dragon dance. The Red Dragon is all about accumulation and growth and gathering unto itself for self-gratification. That spirit is rampant and there is no one to stop it because it's an essential element of the nature of the Dragon.

Spirit of Fear - The Dragon GREATLY discourages individuality and presents a constant stream of reasons why the individual is incapable of defending themselves, standing alone or being effective without the Team. Despite constantly saying that God is sufficient and "greater is He who is in us than He who is in the world," the Dragon insists that anyone who is not under "cover" and actively and regularly doing the Dragon Dance will be eaten for lunch by the darkness. All kinds of fears are encouraged and this, too, spills over into the personal lives of the Dancers. We have rampant depression, anxiety attacks, agoraphobia, even suicidal thoughts because of the constant pounding on the Dancers by this spirit. (And that is NOT from God!)

Spirit of Gloating - Rejoices in the downfall of other brethren. It is anti- I Corinthians 13. Doesn't rejoice in it's OWN affliction, but sure enjoys watching others be afflicted and brought down - or taken out of the Dragon Dance competition altogether.

Charismania – A desire for some manifestation above relationship – drunk in the spirit, barking, gold teeth, slain in the spirit, a prophetic word, a word of knowledge, an impartation, whatever. Might be perfectly reasonable, perfectly Biblical, perfectly decent and in order, but NOT if it becomes the OBJECT of desire. It becomes the pearl to chase, rather than relationship with Christ and full obedience. That will open them up to a spirit of lust that will do all kinds of other damage. If you seek a gift to be better equipped for God's war, that's one thing, but if you seek it so as to show off or be like everybody else or have a bigger, flashier ministry and make a name for yourself – that is not good at all and will surely result in your destruction (unless you repent).

Hardening of Hearts - Eph 4:17-19, Continual lust for more, given over to sensuality. This is one of the scariest of all. This one doesn't just come from the Red Dragon, this one is from God Himself. As we began to go our own way, the Lord turned us over more and more to the Dragon and hardened our hearts. The VERY WORST side effect of this monstrosity is that it is practically IMPOSSIBLE to repent. By far the least seen, least preached, least practiced expression of faith in the "churches" is real, true repentance. Even more rare is repentance for having been a part of a system that wasn't what God wanted and has been adulterous and left the true path. Anyone under a Dragon that repents for having been a part of the Dragon at all is almost instantly ejected with prejudice. Which makes it very difficult to get any more people out from under the Dragon.

Let me repeat that. This is a CURSE FROM GOD for having gone our own way and the curse carries with it hardening of the hearts. The only way to get out from under the curse is to repent, but the curse keeps you from repenting. In fact, it keeps you from listening to anybody that even TALKS about repenting. If you're even reading this and you got this far, that's a really good sign that either you're free or the grip on you is breaking.

This is by NO means complete. Pretty much ANY other kind of oppression or demonic influence in Satan's arsenal is available and in use for this task. God will pretty much turn you over to whatever wants to come mess with you and you may not be able to be delivered of it at all unless you repent for having gone your own way!

http://www.chcp.org/mpeg/SUMMER.MPG

APPENDIX B:
DEUTERONOMY 28 (NIV) – WITH COMMENTARY AND APPLICATION

Blessings for Obedience

*1 **If** you **fully** obey the LORD your God and **carefully** follow **all** his commands I give you today, the LORD your God will set you high above all the nations on earth. 2 **All** these blessings will come upon you and accompany you **if** you obey the LORD your God:*
*3 You **will** be blessed in the **city** and blessed in the **country**.*
*4 The **fruit of your womb will** be blessed, and the **crops** of your land and the young of your **livestock**—the **calves** of your **herds** and the **lambs** of your **flocks**.*
*5 Your **basket** and your **kneading trough will** be blessed.*
*6 You **will** be blessed when you **come in** and blessed when you **go out**.*
*7 The LORD **will** grant that the enemies who rise up against you will be **defeated** before you. They will come at you from one direction but **flee** from you in seven. 8 The LORD **will** send a blessing on your **barns** and on **everything** you put your hand to. The LORD your God **will** bless you in the **land** he is giving you. 9 The LORD **will** establish you as his **holy** people, as he promised you on **oath**, if you **keep the commands** of the LORD your God and **walk in his ways**. 10 **Then all** the peoples on earth **will** see that you are called by the name of the LORD, and they **will** fear you. 11 The LORD **will** grant you **abundant prosperity**—in the fruit of your **womb**, the young of your livestock and the crops of your ground—in the **land** he swore to your forefathers to give you.*
*12 The LORD **will open the heavens**, the storehouse of his bounty, to send **rain** on your land in season and to bless all the **work** of your **hands**. You **will lend** to many nations but will **borrow** from **none**. 13 The LORD **will** make you the **head**, not the **tail**. **If** you pay attention to the **commands** of the LORD your God that I give you this day and **carefully follow them**, you **will** always be at the **top**, never at the **bottom**. 14 **Do not** turn aside from **any** of the commands I give you today, to the **right** or to the **left**, following other gods and serving them.*

By the testimony of two witnesses is a thing established. Here God repeats THREE TIMES that IF you do certain things, THEN He will respond a certain way. It is a GUARANTEE. If you are fully obeying then you WILL BE benefiting from these blessings. It is not optional for God. It is an automatic and universal law, like gravity. If you are His children and come under the covering of His promises and you are being obedient, then these things WILL come to pass. However, the better you know Him, the higher the tightrope. Nobody was closer to God than Moses and all He had to do to keep from inheriting the promise was tap the rock instead of talking to it. God isn't kidding around here. He expects OBEDIENCE. Especially from those of His children who know Him the best. The stakes are highest for those that have been drawn closest to God.

This should be pretty clear. IF you obey, THEN God will keep you from any harm and lift you above nations and you will be the head and not the tail. He WILL do it. I don't see anything vague about this. It might not manifest the way you think, but He WILL do it.

But here comes the scary part:

Curses for Disobedience

*15 **However**, if you **do not** obey the LORD your God and **do not carefully** follow **all** his commands and decrees I am giving you today, **all** these curses **will** come upon you and overtake you:*

These are described as natural consequences on natural Israel, but they have spiritual ramifications as well. On spiritual Israel (the Church), they are primarily spiritual consequences, but have natural ramifications as well.. Let's take a little more detailed look.

*16 You **will** be cursed in the **city** and cursed in the **country**. 17 Your **basket** and your kneading **trough will** be cursed.*

Your congregations will be cursed whether in the city or in the country. Your spiritual bread will be scarce. You will have nothing but day-old stale manna. Jesus, the Bread of Life, will be distant.

*18 The **fruit** of your **womb will** be cursed, and the **crops** of your land, and the **calves** of your herds and the **lambs** of your flocks.*

Your offspring will be even more distant from God than you are. The young of your flocks will be cursed. Are we not seeing a massive loss of the young people from the church? Are we not seeing massive movement away from God in our youth groups and among our children? Are they not being won over by culture?

*19 You **will** be cursed when you **come in** and cursed when you **go out**.*

You will be cursed when you go in and when you go out. No matter where you go, home missions or foreign missions, inside the walls or outside the walls, your efforts will have very little spiritual results.

*20 The LORD will send on you **curses**, **confusion** and **rebuke** in everything you put your hand to, **until you are destroyed** and come to **sudden ruin** because of the evil you have done in **forsaking him**.*

The Lord will put on you curses, confusion and rebuke in everything until you are destroyed. Can you find any denomination that isn't filled with confusion and rebuke? Any that hasn't found itself arguing about secondary issues and become factious? Are we not filled with constant confusion about this or that new doctrine or teaching?

*21 The LORD **will plague** you with **diseases** until he has **destroyed** you from the land you are entering to possess. 22 The LORD **will** strike you with **wasting disease**, with **fever** and **inflammation**, with scorching **heat** and **drought**, with **blight** and **mildew**, which will **plague** you **until you perish**.*

Are our churches not full of people plagued with spiritual diseases that don't seem to have a cure? Are they not inflamed by their passions and addictions and the fevers of their lusts? Do we not have 50% of pastors using pornography? (According to George Barna.) Do we not have clergy sexually abusing little kids? Do we not have more divorce in the church than in the general population? Are we not starving to death for the real meat of the Word? Are we not dying for thirst for the Living Water? Are our people not bloated with the world and starving for God? We are losing $16 BILLION a year to fraud inside our own church organizations. We are losing untold billions to waste and abuse. Millions of Christians are dying everyday because of our neglect.

*23 The **sky** over your head **will** be **bronze**, the **ground** beneath you **iron**.*

Your prayers will not be answered, they will bounce. The ground that you toil will be hard and barren.

*24 The LORD **will** turn the rain of your country into **dust** and **powder**; it will come down from the skies **until** you are **destroyed**.*

The Lord says that He will send the early and latter rains, but not until you repent. Instead you will get dust and powder that will make your work even harder and choke whatever you do get to grow.

*25 The LORD **will** cause you to be **defeated** before your enemies. **You** will come at them from one direction but flee from them in **seven**, and **you** will become a thing of horror to **all** the kingdoms on earth.*

Are we not already a thing of horror? Are we not a laughingstock to the world? Why would anyone want to join this mess? So they can give up 10% of their income for a concert and motivational speech once a week? We bring in $250 BILLION a year and spend 95% of it on our own comforts. Our spiritual enemies are trouncing us. We have rampant addiction and lust and fear and anger and hatred inside our own walls and no sign on the horizon that we have any plan to deal with them effectively. Our enemies chase us and we flee. We have no victory.

*26 **Your carcasses** will be food for all the **birds** of the air and the **beasts** of the earth, and there will be no one to frighten them away.*

This is a reference to demons and the spiritual powers of darkness that will eat us like carrion. I have seen this (in the spirit) at a local congregation. A giant room full of dead bodies being devoured by dark demonic birds and beasts. And there is no one to drive them away. We have very, VERY few deliverance ministries – and even fewer that have any real authority and effectiveness. And I'm aware of even fewer that are capable of city-wide or regional spiritual warfare against strongholds.

*27 The LORD **will** afflict you with the **boils** of Egypt and with **tumors, festering sores** and the **itch**, from which you **cannot be cured**.*

When they were in the wilderness, under the protection of God, the children of Israel did not get sick. In the book of Acts, the apostles healed any that were sick. The only medical advice given for Christians in the New Testament is to call the elders and the prayer of faith WILL heal them. But our churches are FULL of people with every imaginable condition and syndrome and disease and our prayers seem to have little effect. Many incurable diseases are rampant in the churches. Why isn't God listening? If we're being obedient, why do we have sick people?

*28 The LORD **will** afflict you with **madness, blindness** and **confusion of mind**.*

Are we not the most confused, dysfunctional, schizophrenic religion on the planet? (With the possible exception of the Jews.) Are our pews not full of people with spiritual dyslexia and mixture of all sorts? Are we not full of people with depression, anxiety, panic attacks, Alzheimers, Parkinsons, and all sorts of dementia? How is that possible if we're being obedient to God?

*29 At midday you will grope about like a **blind** man in the dark. You will be **unsuccessful** in **everything** you do; day after day you will be **oppressed** and **robbed**, with **no one** to rescue you.*

Are we not groping around in the dark for any possible new program or curriculum or system that will save our ailing churches? If it's not Purpose Driven, it's Mars/Venus, or Shepherding, or Toronto, or Brownsville, or Word of Faith, or any of thousands of fads and fashions that kept us occupied for a moment and hopeful that we'd finally found the way to revival. Even though the lights are on at full brightness, we can't see the obvious in front of our faces – that REPENTANCE is the ONLY Biblical prescription that works for this disease. Statistically, we are unsuccessful in everything that we do. We are a giant money loser and are daily oppressed and robbed to the tune of $16 BILLION a year – at LEAST. And no one seems to be coming to rescue us.

*30 You **will** be **pledged** to be married to a woman, but **another** will take her and **ravish** her. You **will** build a house, but you **will not** live in it. You **will** plant a vineyard, but you **will not** even begin to enjoy its fruit. 31 Your ox **will** be slaughtered before your eyes, but **you will** eat none of it. Your donkey **will** be forcibly taken from you and **will not** be returned. Your sheep **will** be given to your enemies, and **no one will rescue them**.*

Despite what you think you were promised, you will not get it. Though you worked for years to build something, you will not really live in it. You will not enjoy the fruits of your labors because they were in vain. Your enemies own your houses and your livestock. The powers of darkness are currently fully entrenched in the churches in America and show no sign of doing anything other than getting stronger. All that you have worked for is being spent on air.

*32 Your **sons** and **daughters will** be given to another **nation**, and you **will wear out your eyes** watching for them day after day, **powerless** to lift a hand.*

The church is not raising up spiritual warriors, it's raising up youth that are mostly coming because of the pizza parties and ski trips and movie nights. They don't hear the voice of God and we don't know how to teach them how to – or don't believe it's possible. But they're fascinated with the supernatural stories told by their Wicca and New Age friends. They hunger for the power and truth of God, but can't find it, because it got buried under "Religion". We have rampant sexually transmitted diseases in the church youth. We are losing a whole generation. Their parents were more distant from God than their Grandparents – and these kids are even farther away. The culture and the media and the music and the public schools (and satan) are devouring them.

> *33 A people that you do not know **will** eat what your **land** and **labor produce**, and you **will** have **nothing** but **cruel oppression all** your days. 34 The sights you see **will** drive you **mad**.*

The institutions that we have built are being gobbled up by do-gooders and social scientists and pop-psychologists. The culture is crushing in on us and the "church" is not defending anyone in any real measure. My kids can watch practically nothing on television and all that is on the news is depressing and violent and scary. We have tsunamis and earthquakes and hurricanes and wars and terrorists and we have no peace. How can that be if we're being obedient to God? Aren't we supposed to be the head? How come we feel like the tail so much?

> *35 The LORD **will** afflict your **knees** and **legs** with painful **boils** that cannot be cured, **spreading** from the **soles** of your **feet** to the **top** of your **head**.*

Your walk will be severely affected. At first it will just be your feet, but the more your spiritual walk is affected, the more it spreads until it even takes over your head. Then you will be covered in painful boils and sores that will not heal. Spiritually, most "Christians" I meet seem to be covered in spiritual boils and nobody seems to notice or care.

> *36 The LORD **will drive you** and the king you set over you to a nation unknown to you or your fathers. There you **will** worship **other gods**, gods of wood and stone. 37 You **will** become a thing of **horror** and an object of **scorn** and **ridicule** to **all** the nations where the LORD **will** drive you.*

How many nations have we been driven out of? Are we not now captive in a nation we don't recognize any longer? Is America not bowing down to gods unknown to our fathers and their fathers? Would the founders even recognize it? Are we not worshipping our structures and buildings and cathedrals of wood and stone? Are we not a thing of horror and scorn and ridicule? Maybe not all the way, but sure a whole lot more than we used to be and it's getting worse every day. And were we really supposed to set a king over us? Isn't Christ the King?

> *38 You **will sow much seed** in the field but you **will harvest little**, because **locusts will devour** it. 39 You **will** plant vineyards and cultivate them but you **will not** drink the wine or gather the grapes, because **worms will eat them**. 40 You **will** have olive trees throughout your country but you **will not** use the oil, because the olives **will drop off**. 41 You **will** have **sons** and **daughters** but you **will not keep them**, because they **will go into captivity**. 42 Swarms of locusts **will take over all** your trees and the crops of your land.*

We spent tens of billions of dollars on plans to evangelize the whole world by the year 2000 and didn't even keep up with population growth. The average baptism in the United States costs $1,550,000 (total church costs divided by baptisms). We are building and planting and growing – and demons are taking it all over. We our losing our country and our institutions more and more every day. Can this be victory?

> *43 The alien who lives among you **will rise above you** higher and higher, but **you will sink lower** and lower. 44 He **will lend to you**, but **you will not lend to him**. He **will be the head**, but **you will be the tail**.*

Every foreign religion, every Eastern guru, every New Age weirdness, every alternative lifestyle is now embraced and mainstreamed. America is converting to Islam and Wicca and a thousand other lies faster and faster every day.

> *45 **All** these curses **will** come upon you. They **will pursue** you and **overtake** you **until** you are destroyed, because you **did not obey** the LORD your God and **observe** the **commands** and*

decrees he gave you. 46 They will be a sign and a wonder to you and your descendants forever. 47 Because you did not serve the LORD your God joyfully and gladly in the time of prosperity, 48 therefore in hunger and thirst, in nakedness and dire poverty, you will serve the enemies the LORD sends against you. He will put an iron yoke on your neck until he has destroyed you.

Please understand, this is fatal. Unless you do the ONLY thing that will stop it, the guaranteed result of this course is complete destruction. There is NO OTHER way out. Repentance is the only way to fix this.

49 The LORD will bring a nation against you from far away, from the ends of the earth, like an eagle swooping down, a nation whose language you will not understand, 50 a fierce-looking nation without respect for the old or pity for the young. 51 They will devour the young of your livestock and the crops of your land until you are destroyed. They will leave you no grain, new wine or oil, nor any calves of your herds or lambs of your flocks until you are ruined. 52 They will lay siege to all the cities throughout your land until the high fortified walls in which you trust fall down. They will besiege all the cities throughout the land the LORD your God is giving you.

I believe that at least one of the interpretations and applications to these verses is that demons will take over and swarm down upon us. And they have. The "churches" are riddled with them. They are devouring everything and leaving none of the three aspects of God behind – the bread, the wine and the oil. They have laid siege to every city. There were no city churches – no place in America where the Body of Christ in one town was united and under His headship. The high fortified walls of the "church" in which we have trusted are all caving in. We are besieged on every side by culture and media and witchcraft and all the other forces of darkness aligned against us.

53 Because of the suffering that your enemy will inflict on you during the siege, you will eat the fruit of the womb, the flesh of the sons and daughters the LORD your God has given you. 54 Even the most gentle and sensitive man among you will have no compassion on his own brother or the wife he loves or his surviving children, 55 and he will not give to one of them any of the flesh of his children that he is eating. It will be all he has left because of the suffering your enemy will inflict on you during the siege of all your cities. 56 The most gentle and sensitive woman among you—so sensitive and gentle that she would not venture to touch the ground with the sole of her foot—will begrudge the husband she loves and her own son or daughter 57 the afterbirth from her womb and the children she bears. For she intends to eat them secretly during the siege and in the distress that your enemy will inflict on you in your cities.

Are we not devouring our own children? Are we not raising up spiritual children, plugging them into service jobs in the "churches" until they are used up and then spitting them out? Are we not forceably milking them for a tithe until they go bankrupt? Have you ever seen a pastor tear into another pastor for "stealing sheep"? I have. Why? Because they NEED those sheep to keep this whole thing going. It's too hard to go find another one. Even people that say they are "men of God" will devour each other and split churches and feud and fight and hate rather than give up the child of their womb that they intend to eat during the siege. If we were growing exponentially and nothing could stand against us and people were not falling away in droves and having their lives destroyed by demonic forces, we wouldn't so jealously guard and control each little sheep. Can't you see? Please see.

58 If you do not carefully follow all the words of this law, which are written in this book, and do not revere this glorious and awesome name—the LORD your God- 59 the LORD will send fearful plagues on you and your descendants, harsh and prolonged disasters, and severe and lingering illnesses. 60 He will bring upon you all the diseases of Egypt that you dreaded, and they will cling to you. 61 The LORD will also bring on you every kind of sickness and disaster not recorded in this Book of the Law, until you are destroyed. 62 You who were as numerous as the stars in the sky will be left but few in number, because you did not obey the LORD your God. 63 Just as it pleased the LORD to make you prosper and increase in number, so it will please him to ruin and destroy you. You will be uprooted from the land you are entering to possess.

Again, the Lord repeats the whole thing. We must CAREFULLY FOLLOW ALL His words and instructions. Yes, we are New Covenant believers. That doesn't mean we don't follow the Ten Commandments, that means we have the Holy Spirit in us to talk to us and guide us and to write His words on our hearts. But if we shun His voice, then we are left to lean on our own understanding – and we're fodder for the Red Dragons.

Can He be any more clear? Can He be any more definitive? This WILL happen to you and God WILL do it. And God has already done it to us! We have plagues and disasters and severe and lingering illnesses in the natural and in the spiritual. We are no different than the Egypt we were told to leave. He's even inventing new diseases and oppressions that aren't mentioned in the Book. He says that He will creatively come up with all kinds of NEW tortures if you don't obey! Like flesh-eating viruses and HIV/AIDS and new strains of smallpox and new kinds of demonic oppressions like anorexia and trans-sexualism and who knows what. If you hear Him really well, ask Him! If we don't repent, when He is done with us there will surely be only a few in number. If He doesn't cut the days short, there will be no one left!

And just as it pleased Him to prosper America and the Church, it will please Him to crush it. But He would sure rather that we repent and start obeying. He WILL turn, if WE turn. That's a guarantee, too.

> 64 Then the LORD **will** scatter you among **all** nations, from one end of the earth to the other. There you **will** worship other gods—gods of wood and stone, which neither you nor your fathers have known. 65 Among those nations you **will** find **no repose**, **no resting place** for the sole of your foot. There the LORD **will** give you an **anxious mind**, **eyes weary with longing**, and a **despairing heart**. 66 You **will** live in **constant suspense**, filled with **dread** both night and day, **never** sure of your life. 67 In the morning you **will** say, "If only it were evening!" and in the evening, "If only it were morning!"-because of the **terror** that **will fill your hearts** and the **sights that your eyes will see**. 68 The LORD **will** send you back in ships to **Egypt** on a journey I said you should never make again. There you **will** offer yourselves for sale to your enemies as male and female slaves, **but no one will buy you**.

Are we not constantly in search of whatever new program or curriculum will turn this around? Are our eyes not weary of longing and despairing for something that will reach the people in spirit and in truth? How can we be this lukewarm and asleep and nothing seems to shake it off of us? Because it's a curse from God.

The only growth in the "church" in America is the mega-churches. And it's not new growth, it's transfer growth from little churches that are being killed by the large monoliths that are just warehousing people – but they have really great music and childcare! Everyone is looking for greener pastures. If only it were evening. If only it were morning. But nothing satisfies. Why?

Because we're under a curse from God.

If it were from satan, we could cover it in the Blood and bind it up and cast it down. But no amount of praying against the forces of darkness has made a difference in the state of the Church. Because they have legal ground. Because we aren't diligently and carefully following God and He has put these things upon us until we are totally consumed and destroyed – or we repent, whichever comes first.

In the end, if we don't turn, we will offer ourselves to Egypt, to the One World Government and One World Church, but they won't even buy us. They will take us for slaves and give us nothing in return.

And that is the Word of the Lord.

APPENDIX C: VERSES

REPENT

1Ki 8:47 [Yet] if they shall bethink themselves in the land whither they were carried captives, and repent, and make supplication unto thee in the land of them that carried them captives, saying, We have sinned, and have done perversely, we have committed wickedness;

Job 42:6 Wherefore I abhor [myself], and repent in dust and ashes.

Psa 135:14 For the LORD will judge his people, and he will repent himself concerning his servants.

Jer 18:8 If that nation, against whom I have pronounced, turn from their evil, I will repent of the evil that I thought to do unto them.

Jer 18:10 If it do evil in my sight, that it obey not my voice, then I will repent of the good, wherewith I said I would benefit them.

Jer 26:3 If so be they will hearken, and turn every man from his evil way, that I may repent me of the evil, which I purpose to do unto them because of the evil of their doings.
Jer 26:13 Therefore now amend your ways and your doings, and obey the voice of the LORD your God; and the LORD will repent him of the evil that he hath pronounced against you.

Jer 42:10 If ye will still abide in this land, then will I build you, and not pull [you] down, and I will plant you, and not pluck [you] up: for I repent me of the evil that I have done unto you.

Eze 14:6 Therefore say unto the house of Israel, Thus saith the Lord GOD; Repent, and turn [yourselves] from your idols; and turn away your faces from all your abominations.

Eze 18:30 Therefore I will judge you, O house of Israel, every one according to his ways, saith the Lord GOD. Repent, and turn [yourselves] from all your transgressions; so iniquity shall not be your ruin.

Eze 24:14 I the LORD have spoken [it]: it shall come to pass, and I will do [it]; I will not go back, neither will I spare, neither will I repent; according to thy ways, and according to thy doings, shall they judge thee, saith the Lord GOD.

Joe 2:14 Who knoweth [if] he will return and repent, and leave a blessing behind him; [even] a meat offering and a drink offering unto the LORD your God?

Jon 3:9 Who can tell [if] God will turn and repent, and turn away from his fierce anger, that we perish not?

Mat 3:2 And saying, Repent ye: for the kingdom of heaven is at hand.

Mat 4:17 From that time Jesus began to preach, and to say, Repent: for the kingdom of heaven is at hand.

Mar 1:15 And saying, The time is fulfilled, and the kingdom of God is at hand: repent ye, and believe the gospel.

Mar 6:12 And they went out, and preached that men should repent.

Luk 13:3 I tell you, Nay: but, except ye repent, ye shall all likewise perish.
Luk 13:5 I tell you, Nay: but, except ye repent, ye shall all likewise perish.

Luk 17:3 Take heed to yourselves: If thy brother trespass against thee, rebuke him; and if he repent, forgive him.

Luk 17:4 And if he trespass against thee seven times in a day, and seven times in a day turn again to thee, saying, I repent; thou shalt forgive him.

Act 2:38 Then Peter said unto them, Repent, and be baptized every one of you in the name of Jesus Christ for the remission of sins, and ye shall receive the gift of the Holy Ghost.

Act 3:19 Repent ye therefore, and be converted, that your sins may be blotted out, when the times of refreshing shall come from the presence of the Lord;

Act 8:22 Repent therefore of this thy wickedness, and pray God, if perhaps the thought of thine heart may be forgiven thee.

Act 17:30 And the times of this ignorance God winked at; but now commandeth all men every where to repent:

Act 26:20 But shewed first unto them of Damascus, and at Jerusalem, and throughout all the coasts of Judaea, and [then] to the Gentiles, that they should repent and turn to God, and do works meet for repentance.

Rev 2:5 Remember therefore from whence thou art fallen, and repent, and do the first works; or else I will come unto thee quickly, and will remove thy candlestick out of his place, except thou repent. *(Church of Ephesus)*
Rev 2:16 Repent; or else I will come unto thee quickly, and will fight against them with the sword of my mouth. *(Church of Pergamum)*
Rev 2:21 And I gave her space to repent of her fornication; and she repented not.
Rev 2:22 Behold, I will cast her into a bed, and them that commit adultery with her into great tribulation, except they repent of their deeds. *(Church of Thyatira)*
Rev 3:3 Remember therefore how thou hast received and heard, and hold fast, and repent. If therefore thou shalt not watch, I will come on thee as a thief, and thou shalt not know what hour I will come upon thee. *(Church of Sardis)*
Rev 3:19 As many as I love, I rebuke and chasten: be zealous therefore, and repent. *(Church of Laodecia)*

CURSE

Gen 12:3 And I will bless them that bless thee, and **curse** him that curseth thee: and in thee shall all families of the earth be blessed.

Deu 11:26 Behold, I set before you this day a blessing and a curse;
Deu 11:27 The blessing if you obey the commands of the Lord your God that I am giving you today;
Deu 11:28 And a curse, if ye will not obey the commandments of the LORD your God, but turn aside out of the way which I command you this day, to go after other gods, which ye have not known.

Deu 29:19 And it come to pass, when he heareth the words of this **curse**, that he bless himself in his heart, saying, I shall have peace, though I walk in the imagination of mine heart, to add drunkenness to thirst:

Deu 30:1 And it shall come to pass, when all these things are come upon thee, the blessing and the **curse**, which I have set before thee, and thou shalt call [them] to mind among all the nations, whither the LORD thy God hath driven thee,

2Ki 22:19 Because thine heart was tender, and thou hast humbled thyself before the LORD, when thou heardest what I spake against this place, and against the inhabitants thereof, that they should become a desolation and a curse, and hast rent thy clothes, and wept before me; I also have heard [thee], saith the LORD.

Neh 10:29 They clave to their brethren, their nobles, and entered into a curse, and into an oath, to walk in God's law, which was given by Moses the servant of God, and to observe and do all the commandments of the LORD our Lord, and his judgments and his statutes;

Psa 62:4 They only consult to cast [him] down from his excellency: they delight in lies: they bless with their mouth, but they curse inwardly. Selah.

Pro 24:24 He that saith unto the wicked, Thou [art] righteous; him shall the people curse, nations shall abhor him:

Prov 26:2 (NIV) Like a fluttering sparrow or a darting swallow, an undeserved curse does not come to rest.

Pro 28:27 He that giveth unto the poor shall not lack: but he that hideth his eyes shall have many a curse.

Pro 30:10 Accuse not a servant unto his master, lest he curse thee, and thou be found guilty.

Isa 24:6 Therefore hath the curse devoured the earth, and they that dwell therein are desolate: therefore the inhabitants of the earth are burned, and few men left.

Isa 43:28 Therefore I have profaned the princes of the sanctuary, and have given Jacob to the **curse**, and Israel to reproaches.

Isa 65:15 And ye shall leave your name for a curse unto my chosen: for the Lord GOD shall slay thee, and call his servants by another name:

Jer 15:10 Woe is me, my mother, that thou hast borne me a man of strife and a man of contention to the whole earth! I have neither lent on usury, nor men have lent to me on usury; [yet] every one of them doth **curse** me.

Jer 24:9 And I will deliver them to be removed into all the kingdoms of the earth for [their] hurt, [to be] a reproach and a proverb, a taunt and a curse, in all places whither I shall drive them.

Jer 25:18 [To wit], Jerusalem, and the cities of Judah, and the kings thereof, and the princes thereof, to make them a desolation, an astonishment, an hissing, and a curse; as [it is] this day;

Jer 26:6 Then will I make this house like Shiloh, and will make this city a curse to all the nations of the earth.

Jer 29:18 And I will persecute them with the sword, with the famine, and with the pestilence, and will deliver them to be removed to all the kingdoms of the earth, to be a curse, and an astonishment, and an hissing, and a reproach, among all the nations whither I have driven them:

Jer 42:18 For thus saith the LORD of hosts, the God of Israel; As mine anger and my fury hath been poured forth upon the inhabitants of Jerusalem; so shall my fury be poured forth upon you, when ye shall enter into Egypt: and ye shall be an execration, and an astonishment, and a curse, and a reproach; and ye shall see this place no more.

Jer 44:8 In that ye provoke me unto wrath with the works of your hands, burning incense unto other gods in the land of Egypt, whither ye be gone to dwell, that ye might cut yourselves off, and that ye might be a curse and a reproach among all the nations of the earth?

Jer 44:12 And I will take the remnant of Judah, that have set their faces to go into the land of Egypt to sojourn there, and they shall all be consumed, [and] fall in the land of Egypt; they shall [even] be consumed by the sword [and] by the famine: they shall die, from the least even unto the greatest, by the sword and by the famine: and they shall be an execration, [and] an astonishment, and a curse, and a reproach.

Jer 44:22 So that the LORD could no longer bear, because of the evil of your doings, [and] because of the abominations which ye have committed; therefore is your land a desolation, and an astonishment, and a curse, without an inhabitant, as at this day.

Dan 9:11 Yea, all Israel have transgressed thy law, even by departing, that they might not obey thy voice; therefore the curse is poured upon us, and the oath that [is] written in the law of Moses the servant of God, because we have sinned against him.

Zec 8:13 And it shall come to pass, [that] as ye were a curse among the heathen, O house of Judah, and house of Israel; so will I save you, and ye shall be a blessing: fear not, [but] let your hands be strong.

Mal 2:2 If ye will not hear, and if ye will not lay [it] to heart, to give glory unto my name, saith the LORD of hosts, I will even send a curse upon you, and I will curse your blessings: yea, I have cursed them already, because ye do not lay [it] to heart.

Mal 3:9 Ye [are] cursed with a curse: for ye have robbed me, [even] this whole nation.

Mal 4:6 And he shall turn the heart of the fathers to the children, and the heart of the children to their fathers, lest I come and smite the earth with a **curse**.

Gal 3:10 For as many as are of the works of the law are under the curse: for it is written, Cursed [is] every one that continueth not in all things which are written in the book of the law to do them.
Gal 3:13 Christ hath redeemed us from the curse of the law, being made a curse for us: for it is written, Cursed [is] every one that hangeth on a tree:

(Yeah, but... If you make up your own law and get back under it, you invoke it on yourself again and deny the work of Christ.)

Rev 22:3 And there shall be no more **curse**: but the throne of God and of the Lamb shall be in it; and his servants shall serve him:

SLUMBER, SLEEP, STUPOR

Isa 56:10 His watchmen [are] blind: they are all ignorant, they [are] all dumb dogs, they cannot bark; sleeping, lying down, loving to **slumber**.

Rom 11:8 (According as it is written, God hath given them the spirit of **slumber (stupor, NIV)**, eyes that they should not see, and ears that they should not hear;) unto this day.

Gen 2:21 And the LORD God caused a deep **sleep** to fall upon Adam, and he slept: and he took one of his ribs, and closed up the flesh instead thereof;

Gen 15:12 And when the sun was going down, a deep **sleep** fell upon Abram; and, lo, an horror of great darkness fell upon him.

1Sa 26:12 So David took the spear and the cruse of water from Saul's bolster; and they gat them away, and no man saw [it], nor knew [it], neither awaked: for they [were] all asleep; because a deep **sleep** from the LORD was fallen upon them.

Psa 76:6 At thy rebuke, O God of Jacob, both the chariot and horse are cast into a dead **sleep**.

Psa 127:2 [It is] vain for you to rise up early, to sit up late, to eat the bread of sorrows: [for] so he giveth his beloved **sleep**.

Pro 3:24 When thou liest down, thou shalt not be afraid: yea, thou shalt lie down, and thy **sleep** shall be sweet.

Pro 4:16 For they **sleep** not, except they have done mischief; and their **sleep** is taken away, unless they cause [some] to fall.

Pro 19:15 Slothfulness casteth into a deep **sleep**; and an idle soul shall suffer hunger.

Pro 20:13 Love not **sleep**, lest thou come to poverty; open thine eyes, [and] thou shalt be satisfied with bread.

Isa 5:27 None shall be weary nor stumble among them; none shall slumber nor **sleep**; neither shall the girdle of their loins be loosed, nor the latchet of their shoes be broken:

Isa 29:10 For the LORD hath poured out upon you the spirit of deep **sleep**, and hath closed your eyes: the prophets and your rulers, the seers hath he covered.

Jer 51:39 In their heat I will make their feasts, and I will make them drunken, that they may rejoice, and **sleep** a perpetual **sleep**, and not wake, saith the LORD.

Jer 51:57 And I will make drunk her princes, and her wise [men], her captains, and her rulers, and her mighty men: and they shall **sleep** a perpetual **sleep**, and not wake, saith the King, whose name [is] the LORD of hosts.

Jhn 11:11 These things said he: and after that he saith unto them, Our friend Lazarus sleepeth; but I go, that I may awake him out of **sleep**.

Rom 13:11 And that, knowing the time, that now [it is] high time to awake out of **sleep**: for now [is] our salvation nearer than when we believed.

1Cr 11:28 But let a man examine himself, and so let him eat of [that] bread, and drink of [that] cup.
1Cr 11:29 For he that eateth and drinketh unworthily, eateth and drinketh damnation to himself, not discerning the Lord's body.
1Cr 11:30 For this cause many [are] weak and sickly among you, and many **sleep**.

(If I'm right about the Red Dragon and divison and faction – then we ARE holding something against our Brothers and need to repent and if we don't, then we're taking communion unworthily and people in our congregations will get sick and die. Which they are. Hmmm.)

1Th 5:6 Therefore let us not **sleep**, as [do] others; but let us watch and be sober.

BLIND

Exd 4:11 And the LORD said unto him, Who hath made man's mouth? or who maketh the dumb, or deaf, or the seeing, or the blind? have not I the LORD?

Lev 19:14 Thou shalt not curse the deaf, nor put a stumblingblock before the **blind**, but shalt fear thy God: I [am] the LORD.

Deu 16:19 Thou shalt not wrest judgment; thou shalt not respect persons, neither take a gift: for a gift doth **blind** the eyes of the wise, and pervert the words of the righteous.

Deu 27:18 Cursed [be] he that maketh the **blind** to wander out of the way. And all the people shall say, Amen.

Deu 28:29 And thou shalt grope at noonday, as the blind gropeth in darkness, and thou shalt not prosper in thy ways: and thou shalt be only oppressed and spoiled evermore, and no man shall save [thee].

1Sa 12:3 Behold, here I [am]: witness against me before the LORD, and before his anointed: whose ox have I taken? or whose ass have I taken? or whom have I defrauded? whom have I oppressed? or of whose hand have I received [any] bribe to **blind** mine eyes therewith? and I will restore it you.

Psa 146:8 The LORD openeth [the eyes of] the blind: the LORD raiseth them that are bowed down: the LORD loveth the righteous:

Isa 29:18 And in that day shall the deaf hear the words of the book, and the eyes of the blind shall see out of obscurity, and out of darkness. (GO READ THIS CHAPTER!!)

Isa 35:5 Then the eyes of the blind shall be opened, and the ears of the deaf shall be unstopped. (GO READ THIS CHAPTER!)

Isa 42:7 To open the blind eyes, to bring out the prisoners from the prison, [and] them that sit in darkness out of the prison house.

Isa 42:16 And I will bring the blind by a way [that] they knew not; I will lead them in paths [that] they have not known: I will make darkness light before them, and crooked things straight. These things will I do unto them, and not forsake them.

Isa 42:18 Hear, ye deaf; and look, ye blind, that ye may see.

Isa 42:19 Who [is] **blind**, but my servant? or deaf, as my messenger [that] I sent? who [is] **blind** as [he that is] perfect, and **blind** as the LORD'S servant?

Isa 43:8 Bring forth the **blind** people that have eyes, and the deaf that have ears.
Isa 56:10 His watchmen [are] blind: they are all ignorant, they [are] all dumb dogs, they cannot bark; sleeping, lying down, loving to slumber.

Isa 59:10 We grope for the wall like the **blind**, and we grope as if [we had] no eyes: we stumble at noonday as in the night; [we are] in desolate places as dead [men].

Jer 31:8 Behold, I will bring them from the north country, and gather them from the coasts of the earth, [and] with them the **blind** and the lame, the woman with child and her that travaileth with child together: a great company shall return thither.

Lam 4:14 They have wandered [as] blind [men] in the streets, they have polluted themselves with blood, so that men could not touch their garments. (GO READ THIS IN CONTEXT!!)

Zep 1:17 And I will bring distress upon men, that they shall walk like blind men, because they have sinned against the LORD: and their blood shall be poured out as dust, and their flesh as the dung.

HARDENED

(Either you did it to yourself or God does it to you. There is NO indication that Satan can do it to.)

Exd 7:13 And he **hardened** Pharaoh's heart, that he hearkened not unto them; as the LORD had said.

Exd 7:14 And the LORD said unto Moses, Pharaoh's heart [is] **hardened**, he refuseth to let the people go.

Exd 7:22 And the magicians of Egypt did so with their enchantments: and Pharaoh's heart was **hardened**, neither did he hearken unto them; as the LORD had said.

Exd 8:15 But when Pharaoh saw that there was respite, he **hardened** his heart, and hearkened not unto them; as the LORD had said.

Exd 8:19 Then the magicians said unto Pharaoh, This [is] the finger of God: and Pharaoh's heart was **hardened**, and he hearkened not unto them; as the LORD had said.

Exd 8:32 And Pharaoh **hardened** his heart at this time also, neither would he let the people go.

Exd 9:7 And Pharaoh sent, and, behold, there was not one of the cattle of the Israelites dead. And the heart of Pharaoh was **hardened**, and he did not let the people go.

Exd 9:12 And the LORD **hardened** the heart of Pharaoh, and he hearkened not unto them; as the LORD had spoken unto Moses.

Exd 9:34 And when Pharaoh saw that the rain and the hail and the thunders were ceased, he sinned yet more, and **hardened** his heart, he and his servants.

Exd 9:35 And the heart of Pharaoh was **hardened**, neither would he let the children of Israel go; as the LORD had spoken by Moses.

Exd 10:1 And the LORD said unto Moses, Go in unto Pharaoh: for I have hardened his heart, and the heart of his servants, that I might shew these my signs before him:

Exd 10:20 But the LORD **hardened** Pharaoh's heart, so that he would not let the children of Israel go.

Exd 10:27 But the LORD **hardened** Pharaoh's heart, and he would not let them go.

Exd 11:10 And Moses and Aaron did all these wonders before Pharaoh: and the LORD **hardened** Pharaoh's heart, so that he would not let the children of Israel go out of his land.

Exd 14:8 And the LORD **hardened** the heart of Pharaoh king of Egypt, and he pursued after the children of Israel: and the children of Israel went out with an high hand.

Deu 2:30 But Sihon king of Heshbon would not let us pass by him: for the LORD thy God **hardened** his spirit, and made his heart obstinate, that he might deliver him into thy hand, as [appeareth] this day.

1Sa 6:6 Wherefore then do ye harden your hearts, as the Egyptians and Pharaoh **hardened** their hearts? when he had wrought wonderfully among them, did they not let the people go, and they departed?

2Ki 17:14 Notwithstanding they would not hear, but **hardened** their necks, like to the neck of their fathers, that did not believe in the LORD their God.

2Ch 36:13 And he also rebelled against king Nebuchadnezzar, who had made him swear by God: but he stiffened his neck, and **hardened** his heart from turning unto the LORD God of Israel.

Neh 9:16 But they and our fathers dealt proudly, and **hardened** their necks, and hearkened not to thy commandments,

Neh 9:17 And refused to obey, neither were mindful of thy wonders that thou didst among them; but **hardened** their necks, and in their rebellion appointed a captain to return to their bondage: but thou [art] a God ready to pardon, gracious and merciful, slow to anger, and of great kindness, and forsookest them not.

Neh 9:29 And testifiedst against them, that thou mightest bring them again unto thy law: yet they dealt proudly, and hearkened not unto thy commandments, but sinned against thy judgments, (which if a man do, he shall live in them;) and withdrew the shoulder, and **hardened** their neck, and would not hear.

Job 9:4 [He is] wise in heart, and mighty in strength: who hath hardened [himself] against him, and hath prospered?

Job 39:16 She is **hardened** against her young ones, as though [they were] not hers: her labour is in vain without fear;

Isa 63:17 **O LORD, why hast thou made us to err from thy ways, [and] hardened our heart from thy fear? Return for thy servants' sake, the tribes of thine inheritance.**

Jer 7:26 Yet they hearkened not unto me, nor inclined their ear, but **hardened** their neck: they did worse than their fathers.

Jer 19:15 Thus saith the LORD of hosts, the God of Israel; Behold, I will bring upon this city and upon all her towns all the evil that I have pronounced against it, because they have **hardened** their necks, that they might not hear my words.

Dan 5:20 But when his heart was lifted up, and his mind **hardened** in pride, he was deposed from his kingly throne, and they took his glory from him:

Mar 6:52 For they considered not [the miracle] of the loaves: for their heart was **hardened**.

Mar 8:17 And when Jesus knew [it], he saith unto them, Why reason ye, because ye have no bread? perceive ye not yet, neither understand? have ye your heart yet **hardened**?

Jhn 12:40 **He hath blinded their eyes, and hardened their heart; that they should not see with [their] eyes, nor understand with [their] heart, and be converted, and I should heal them.**

Act 19:9 But when divers were **hardened**, and believed not, but spake evil of that way before the multitude, he departed from them, and separated the disciples, disputing daily in the school of one Tyrannus.

Hbr 3:13 **But exhort one another daily, while it is called Today; lest any of you be hardened through the deceitfulness of sin.**

WICKED

Exd 9:27 And Pharaoh sent, and called for Moses and Aaron, and said unto them, I have sinned this time: the LORD [is] righteous, and I and my people [are] **wicked**.

Exd 23:1 Thou shalt not raise a false report: put not thine hand with the **wicked** to be an unrighteous witness.

Num 16:26 And he spake unto the congregation, saying, Depart, I pray you, from the tents of these **wicked** men, and touch nothing of theirs, lest ye be consumed in all their sins.

1Sa 2:9 He will keep the feet of his saints, and the **wicked** shall be silent in darkness; for by strength shall no man prevail.

2Ki 17:11 And there they burnt incense in all the high places, as [did] the heathen whom the LORD carried away before them; and wrought **wicked** things to provoke the LORD to anger:

2Ch 6:23 Then hear thou from heaven, and do, and judge thy servants, by requiting the **wicked**, by recompensing his way upon his own head; and by justifying the righteous, by giving him according to his righteousness.

2Ch 7:14 If my people, which are called by my name, shall humble themselves, and pray, and seek my face, and turn from their **wicked** ways; then will I hear from heaven, and will forgive their sin, and will heal their land.

Neh 9:35 For they have not served thee in their kingdom, and in thy great goodness that thou gavest them, and in the large and fat land which thou gavest before them, neither turned they from their **wicked** works.

Psa 7:11 God judgeth the righteous, and God is angry [with the **wicked**] every day.

Psa 9:17 **The wicked shall be turned into hell, [and] all the nations that forget God.**

Psa 10:2 The wicked in [his] pride doth persecute the poor: let them be taken in the devices that they have imagined.

Psa 10:3 For the wicked boasteth of his heart's desire, and blesseth the covetous, [whom] the LORD abhorreth.

Psa 10:4 The wicked, through the pride of his countenance, will not seek [after God]: God [is] not in all his thoughts.

Psa 10:13 Wherefore doth the wicked contemn God? he hath said in his heart, Thou wilt not require [it].

Psa 10:15 Break thou the arm of the **wicked** and the evil [man]: seek out his wickedness [till] thou find none.

Psa 11:2 For, lo, the **wicked** bend [their] bow, they make ready their arrow upon the string, that they may privily shoot at the upright in heart.

Psa 11:5 The LORD trieth the righteous: but the **wicked** and him that loveth violence his soul hateth.

Psa 11:6 Upon the wicked he shall rain snares, fire and brimstone, and an horrible tempest: [this shall be] the portion of their cup.

Psa 12:8 The wicked walk on every side, when the vilest men are exalted.

Psa 28:3 Draw me not away with the wicked, and with the workers of iniquity, which speak peace to their neighbours, but mischief [is] in their hearts.

Psa 31:17 Let me not be ashamed, O LORD; for I have called upon thee: let the **wicked** be ashamed, [and] let them be silent in the grave.

Psa 32:10 Many sorrows [shall be] to the **wicked**: but he that trusteth in the LORD, mercy shall compass him about.

Psa 34:21 Evil shall slay the **wicked**: and they that hate the righteous shall be desolate.

Psa 36:1 [[To the chief Musician, [A Psalm] of David the servant of the LORD.]] The transgression of the wicked saith within my heart, [that there is] no fear of God before his eyes.

Psa 37:12 The **wicked** plotteth against the just, and gnasheth upon him with his teeth.

Psa 37:14 The wicked have drawn out the sword, and have bent their bow, to cast down the poor and needy, [and] to slay such as be of upright conversation.

Psa 37:16 A little that a righteous man hath [is] better than the riches of many wicked.

Psa 37:20 But the **wicked** shall perish, and the enemies of the LORD [shall be] as the fat of lambs: they shall consume; into smoke shall they consume away.

Psa 37:28 For the LORD loveth judgment, and forsaketh not his saints; they are preserved for ever: but the seed of the **wicked** shall be cut off.

Psa 37:32 The wicked watcheth the righteous, and seeketh to slay him.

Psa 37:35 I have seen the wicked in great power, and spreading himself like a green bay tree.

Psa 37:38 But the transgressors shall be destroyed together: the end of the **wicked** shall be cut off.

Psa 37:40 And the LORD shall help them, and deliver them: he shall deliver them from the wicked, and save them, because they trust in him.

Psa 39:1 [[To the chief Musician, [even] to Jeduthun, A Psalm of David.]] I said, I will take heed to my ways, that I sin not with my tongue: I will keep my mouth with a bridle, while the wicked is before me.

Psa 50:16 But unto the wicked God saith, What hast thou to do to declare my statutes, or [that] thou shouldest take my covenant in thy mouth?

Psa 55:3 Because of the voice of the enemy, because of the oppression of the wicked: for they cast iniquity upon me, and in wrath they hate me.

Psa 73:3 For I was envious at the foolish, [when] I saw the prosperity of the wicked.

Psa 74:19 O deliver not the soul of thy turtledove unto the multitude [of the **wicked**]: forget not the congregation of thy poor for ever.

Psa 75:8 For in the hand of the LORD [there is] a cup, and the wine is red; it is full of mixture; and he poureth out of the same: but the dregs thereof, all the **wicked** of the earth shall wring [them] out, [and] drink [them].

Psa 75:10 All the horns of the **wicked** also will I cut off; [but] the horns of the righteous shall be exalted.

Psa 82:2 How long will ye judge unjustly, and accept the persons of the wicked? Selah.

Psa 92:7 When the **wicked** spring as the grass, and when all the workers of iniquity do flourish; [it is] that they shall be destroyed for ever:

Psa 92:11 Mine eye also shall see [my desire] on mine enemies, [and] mine ears shall hear [my desire] of the **wicked** that rise up against me.

Psa 97:10 Ye that love the LORD, hate evil: he preserveth the souls of his saints; he delivereth them out of the hand of the wicked.

Pro 3:33 The curse of the LORD [is] in the house of the **wicked**: but he blesseth the habitation of the just.

Pro 4:14 Enter not into the path of the **wicked**, and go not in the way of evil [men].

Pro 4:19 The way of the **wicked** [is] as darkness: they know not at what they stumble.

Pro 5:22 His own iniquities shall take the **wicked** himself, and he shall be holden with the cords of his sins.

Pro 6:18 An heart that deviseth **wicked** imaginations, feet that be swift in running to mischief,

Pro 9:7 He that reproveth a scorner getteth to himself shame: and he that rebuketh a wicked [man getteth] himself a blot.

Pro 10:3 The LORD will not suffer the soul of the righteous to famish: but he casteth away the substance of the **wicked**.

Pro 10:6 Blessings [are] upon the head of the just: but violence covereth the mouth of the **wicked**.

Pro 10:7 The memory of the just [is] blessed: but the name of the **wicked** shall rot.

Pro 10:11 The mouth of a righteous [man is] a well of life: but violence covereth the mouth of the **wicked**.

Pro 10:16 The labour of the righteous [tendeth] to life: the fruit of the **wicked** to sin.

Pro 10:20 The tongue of the just [is as] choice silver: the heart of the **wicked** [is] little worth.

Pro 10:24 The fear of the **wicked**, it shall come upon him: but the desire of the righteous shall be granted.
Pro 10:25 As the whirlwind passeth, so [is] the **wicked** no [more]: but the righteous [is] an everlasting foundation.

Pro 10:27 The fear of the LORD prolongeth days: but the years of the **wicked** shall be shortened.
Pro 10:28 The hope of the righteous [shall be] gladness: but the expectation of the **wicked** shall perish.

Pro 11:11 By the blessing of the upright the city is exalted: but it is overthrown by the mouth of the **wicked**.

Pro 11:18 The **wicked** worketh a deceitful work: but to him that soweth righteousness [shall be] a sure reward.

Pro 12:6 The words of the **wicked** [are] to lie in wait for blood: but the mouth of the upright shall deliver them.
Pro 12:7 The **wicked** are overthrown, and [are] not: but the house of the righteous shall stand.

Pro 14:11 The house of the **wicked** shall be overthrown: but the tabernacle of the upright shall flourish.

Pro 14:32 The **wicked** is driven away in his wickedness: but the righteous hath hope in his death.

Pro 15:8 The sacrifice of the **wicked** [is] an abomination to the LORD: but the prayer of the upright [is] his delight.

Pro 15:9 The way of the **wicked** [is] an abomination unto the LORD: but he loveth him that followeth after righteousness.

Pro 15:26 The thoughts of the **wicked** [are] an abomination to the LORD: but [the words] of the pure [are] pleasant words.

Pro 17:4 A **wicked** doer giveth heed to false lips; [and] a liar giveth ear to a naughty tongue.

Pro 17:15 He that justifieth the wicked, and he that condemneth the just, even they both [are] abomination to the LORD.

Pro 21:4 An high look, and a proud heart, [and] the plowing of the wicked, [is] sin.

Pro 25:26 A righteous man falling down before the **wicked** [is as] a troubled fountain, and a corrupt spring.

Pro 26:23 Burning lips and a **wicked** heart [are like] a potsherd covered with silver dross.

Pro 28:1 The **wicked** flee when no man pursueth: but the righteous are bold as a lion.

Pro 28:4 They that forsake the law praise the wicked: but such as keep the law contend with them.

Pro 28:15 [As] a roaring lion, and a ranging bear; [so is] a **wicked** ruler over the poor people.

Pro 29:7 The righteous considereth the cause of the poor: [but] the wicked regardeth not to know [it].

Pro 29:12 If a ruler hearken to lies, all his servants [are] wicked.

Pro 29:16 When the wicked are multiplied, transgression increaseth: but the righteous shall see their fall.

Ecc 3:17 I said in mine heart, God shall judge the righteous and the **wicked**: for [there is] a time there for every purpose and for every work.

Ecc 8:13 But it shall not be well with the wicked, neither shall he prolong [his] days, [which are] as a shadow; because he feareth not before God.

Isa 3:11 Woe unto the **wicked**! [it shall be] ill [with him]: for the reward of his hands shall be given him.

Isa 11:4 But with righteousness shall he judge the poor, and reprove with equity for the meek of the earth: and he shall smite the earth with the rod of his mouth, and with the breath of his lips shall he slay the wicked.

Isa 13:11 And I will punish the world for [their] evil, and the wicked for their iniquity; and I will cause the arrogancy of the proud to cease, and will lay low the haughtiness of the terrible.

Isa 26:10 Let favour be shewed to the wicked, [yet] will he not learn righteousness: in the land of uprightness will he deal unjustly, and will not behold the majesty of the LORD.

Isa 55:7 Let the wicked forsake his way, and the unrighteous man his thoughts: and let him return unto the LORD, and he will have mercy upon him; and to our God, for he will abundantly pardon.

Jer 5:28 They are waxen fat, they shine: yea, they overpass the deeds of the wicked: they judge not the cause, the cause of the fatherless, yet they prosper; and the right of the needy do they not judge.

Jer 25:31 A noise shall come [even] to the ends of the earth; for the LORD hath a controversy with the nations, he will plead with all flesh; he will give them [that are] wicked to the sword, saith the LORD.

Eze 3:18 When I say unto the wicked, Thou shalt surely die; and thou givest him not warning, nor speakest to warn the wicked from his wicked way, to save his life; the same wicked [man] shall die in his iniquity; but his blood will I require at thine hand.

Eze 3:19 Yet if thou warn the wicked, and he turn not from his wickedness, nor from his wicked way, he shall die in his iniquity; but thou hast delivered thy soul.

Eze 13:22 Because with lies ye have made the heart of the righteous sad, whom I have not made sad; and strengthened the hands of the wicked, that he should not return from his wicked way, by promising him life:

The Red Dragon

Eze 18:20 The soul that sinneth, it shall die. The son shall not bear the iniquity of the father, neither shall the father bear the iniquity of the son: the righteousness of the righteous shall be upon him, and the wickedness of the **wicked** shall be upon him.

Eze 18:21 But if the **wicked** will turn from all his sins that he hath committed, and keep all my statutes, and do that which is lawful and right, he shall surely live, he shall not die.

Eze 18:23 Have I any pleasure at all that the **wicked** should die? saith the Lord GOD: [and] not that he should return from his ways, and live?

Eze 18:24 But when the righteous turneth away from his righteousness, and committeth iniquity, [and] doeth according to all the abominations that the **wicked** [man] doeth, shall he live? All his righteousness that he hath done shall not be mentioned: in his trespass that he hath trespassed, and in his sin that he hath sinned, in them shall he die.

Eze 18:27 Again, when the **wicked** [man] turneth away from his wickedness that he hath committed, and doeth that which is lawful and right, he shall save his soul alive.

Eze 21:3 And say to the land of Israel, Thus saith the LORD; Behold, I [am] against thee, and will draw forth my sword out of his sheath, and will cut off from thee the righteous and the **wicked**.

Eze 21:4 Seeing then that I will cut off from thee the righteous and the **wicked**, therefore shall my sword go forth out of his sheath against all flesh from the south to the north:

Eze 33:8 When I say unto the **wicked**, O **wicked** [man], thou shalt surely die; if thou dost not speak to warn the **wicked** from his way, that **wicked** [man] shall die in his iniquity; but his blood will I require at thine hand.

Eze 33:9 Nevertheless, if thou warn the **wicked** of his way to turn from it; if he do not turn from his way, he shall die in his iniquity; but thou hast delivered thy soul.

Eze 33:11 Say unto them, [As] I live, saith the Lord GOD, I have no pleasure in the death of the **wicked**; but that the **wicked** turn from his way and live: turn ye, turn ye from your evil ways; for why will ye die, O house of Israel?

Eze 33:12 Therefore, thou son of man, say unto the children of thy people, The righteousness of the righteous shall not deliver him in the day of his transgression: as for the wickedness of the **wicked**, he shall not fall thereby in the day that he turneth from his wickedness; neither shall the righteous be able to live for his [righteousness] in the day that he sinneth.

Eze 33:14 Again, when I say unto the **wicked**, Thou shalt surely die; if he turn from his sin, and do that which is lawful and right;

Eze 33:15 [If] the **wicked** restore the pledge, give again that he had robbed, walk in the statutes of life, without committing iniquity; he shall surely live, he shall not die.

Eze 33:19 But if the **wicked** turn from his wickedness, and do that which is lawful and right, he shall live thereby.

Dan 12:10 Many shall be purified, and made white, and tried; but the **wicked** shall do wickedly: and none of the **wicked** shall understand; but the wise shall understand.

Hab 1:4 Therefore the law is slacked, and judgment doth never go forth: for the wicked doth compass about the righteous; therefore wrong judgment proceedeth.

Mal 3:18 Then shall ye return, and discern between the righteous and the **wicked**, between him that serveth God and him that serveth him not.

Mal 4:3 And ye shall tread down the **wicked**; for they shall be ashes under the soles of your feet in the day that I shall do [this], saith the LORD of hosts.

Mat 13:38 The field is the world; the good seed are the children of the kingdom; but the tares are the children of the **wicked** [one];

Mat 13:49 So shall it be at the end of the world: the angels shall come forth, and sever the **wicked** from among the just,

Mat 16:4 A **wicked** and adulterous generation seeketh after a sign; and there shall no sign be given unto it, but the sign of the prophet Jonas. And he left them, and departed.

Mat 25:26 His lord answered and said unto him, [Thou] wicked and slothful servant, thou knewest that I reap where I sowed not, and gather where I have not strawed:

Luk 19:22 And he saith unto him, Out of thine own mouth will I judge thee, [thou] wicked servant. Thou knewest that I was an austere man, taking up that I laid not down, and reaping that I did not sow:

1Cr 5:13 But them that are without God judgeth. Therefore put away from among yourselves that **wicked** person.

2Pe 3:17 Ye therefore, beloved, seeing ye know [these things] before, beware lest ye also, being led away with the error of the wicked, fall from your own stedfastness.

PROSPER

Deu 28:29 And thou shalt grope at noonday, as the blind gropeth in darkness, and thou shalt not **prosper in thy ways: and thou shalt be only oppressed and spoiled evermore, and no man shall save [thee].**

Deu 29:9 Keep therefore the words of this covenant, and do them, that ye may **prosper** in all that ye do.

Jos 1:7 Only be thou strong and very courageous, that thou mayest observe to do according to all the law, which Moses my servant commanded thee: turn not from it [to] the right hand or [to] the left, that thou mayest prosper whithersoever thou goest.

1Ki 2:3 And keep the charge of the LORD thy God, to walk in his ways, to keep his statutes, and his commandments, and his judgments, and his testimonies, as it is written in the law of Moses, that thou mayest **prosper** in all that thou doest, and whithersoever thou turnest thyself:

1Ch 22:13 Then shalt thou **prosper**, if thou takest heed to fulfil the statutes and judgments which the LORD charged Moses with concerning Israel: be strong, and of good courage; dread not, nor be dismayed.

2Ch 13:12 And, behold, God himself [is] with us for [our] captain, and his priests with sounding trumpets to cry alarm against you. O children of Israel, fight ye not against the LORD God of your fathers; for ye shall not prosper.

2Ch 24:20 And the Spirit of God came upon Zechariah the son of Jehoiada the priest, which stood above the people, and said unto them, Thus saith God, Why transgress ye the commandments of the LORD, that ye cannot prosper? because ye have forsaken the LORD, he hath also forsaken you.

2Ch 26:5 And he sought God in the days of Zechariah, who had understanding in the visions of God: and as long as he sought the LORD, God made him to **prosper**.

Psa 1:3 And he shall be like a tree planted by the rivers of water, that bringeth forth his fruit in his season; his leaf also shall not wither; and whatsoever he doeth shall **prosper**.

Pro 28:13 He that covereth his sins shall not **prosper: but whoso confesseth and forsaketh [them] shall have mercy.**

Isa 53:10 Yet it pleased the LORD to bruise him; he hath put [him] to grief: when thou shalt make his soul an offering for sin, he shall see [his] seed, he shall prolong [his] days, and the pleasure of the LORD shall **prosper** in his hand.

Isa 54:17 No weapon that is formed against thee shall prosper; and every tongue [that] shall rise against thee in judgment thou shalt condemn. This [is] the heritage of the servants of the LORD, and their righteousness [is] of me, saith the LORD.

Jer 2:37 Yea, thou shalt go forth from him, and thine hands upon thine head: for the LORD hath rejected thy confidences, and thou shalt not prosper in them.

Jer 5:28 They are waxen fat, they shine: yea, they overpass the deeds of the wicked: they judge not the cause, the cause of the fatherless, yet they **prosper**; and the right of the needy do they not judge.

Jer 10:21 For the pastors are become brutish, and have not sought the LORD: therefore they shall not prosper, and all their flocks shall be scattered.

therefore my persecutors shall stumble, and they shall not prevail: they shall be greatly ashamed; for they shall not **prosper**: [their] everlasting confusion shall never be forgotten.

Lam 1:5 Her adversaries are the chief, her enemies prosper; for the LORD hath afflicted her for the multitude of her transgressions: her children are gone into captivity before the enemy.

Eze 16:13 Thus wast thou decked with gold and silver; and thy raiment [was of] fine linen, and silk, and broidered work; thou didst eat fine flour, and honey, and oil: and thou wast exceeding beautiful, and thou didst **prosper** into a kingdom.

Eze 17:9 Say thou, Thus saith the Lord GOD; Shall it **prosper**? shall he not pull up the roots thereof, and cut off the fruit thereof, that it wither? it shall wither in all the leaves of her spring, even without great power or many people to pluck it up by the roots thereof.

Eze 17:15 But he rebelled against him in sending his ambassadors into Egypt, that they might give him horses and much people. Shall he **prosper**? shall he escape that doeth such [things]? or shall he break the covenant, and be delivered?

DESTROYED

Exd 22:20 He that sacrificeth unto [any] god, save unto the LORD only, he shall be utterly destroyed.

Deu 2:21 A people great, and many, and tall, as the Anakims; but the LORD **destroyed** them before them; and they succeeded them, and dwelt in their stead:

Deu 4:26 I call heaven and earth to witness against you this day, that ye shall soon utterly perish from off the land whereunto ye go over Jordan to possess it; ye shall not prolong [your] days upon it, but shall utterly be **destroyed**.

Deu 7:24 And he shall deliver their kings into thine hand, and thou shalt destroy their name from under heaven: there shall no man be able to stand before thee, until thou have **destroyed** them.

Deu 9:8 Also in Horeb ye provoked the LORD to wrath, so that the LORD was angry with you to have **destroyed** you.

Deu 9:20 And the LORD was very angry with Aaron to have **destroyed** him: and I prayed for Aaron also the same time.

Deu 12:30 Take heed to thyself that thou be not snared by following them, after that they be destroyed from before thee; and that thou enquire not after their gods, saying, How did these nations serve their gods? even so will I do likewise.

Deu 28:20 The LORD shall send upon thee cursing, vexation, and rebuke, in all that thou settest thine hand unto for to do, until thou be destroyed, and until thou perish quickly; because of the wickedness of thy doings, whereby thou hast forsaken me.

Deu 28:24 The LORD shall make the rain of thy land powder and dust: from heaven shall it come down upon thee, until thou be destroyed.

Deu 28:45 Moreover all these curses shall come upon thee, and shall pursue thee, and overtake thee, till thou be destroyed; because thou hearkenedst not unto the voice of the LORD thy God, to keep his commandments and his statutes which he commanded thee:

Deu 28:48 Therefore shalt thou serve thine enemies which the LORD shall send against thee, in hunger, and in thirst, and in nakedness, and in want of all [things]: and he shall put a yoke of iron upon thy neck, until he have destroyed thee.

Deu 28:51 And he shall eat the fruit of thy cattle, and the fruit of thy land, until thou be destroyed: which [also] shall not leave thee [either] corn, wine, or oil, [or] the increase of thy kine, or flocks of thy sheep, until he have destroyed thee.

Deu 28:61 Also every sickness, and every plague, which [is] not written in the book of this law, them will the LORD bring upon thee, until thou be destroyed.

Jos 23:15 Therefore it shall come to pass, [that] as all good things are come upon you, which the LORD your God promised you; so shall the LORD bring upon you all evil things, until he have destroyed you from off this good land which the LORD your God hath given you.

2Sa 24:16 And when the angel stretched out his hand upon Jerusalem to destroy it, the LORD repented him of the evil, and said to the angel that **destroyed** the people, It is enough: stay now thine hand. And the angel of the LORD was by the threshingplace of Araunah the Jebusite.

1Ch 5:25 And they transgressed against the God of their fathers, and went a whoring after the gods of the people of the land, whom God destroyed before them.

1Ch 21:12 Either three years' famine; or three months to be **destroyed** before thy foes, while that the sword of thine enemies overtaketh [thee]; or else three days the sword of the LORD, even the pestilence, in the land, and the angel of the LORD destroying throughout all the coasts of Israel. Now therefore advise thyself what word I shall bring again to him that sent me.

1Ch 21:15 And God sent an angel unto Jerusalem to destroy it: and as he was destroying, the LORD beheld, and he repented him of the evil, and said to the angel that **destroyed**, It is enough, stay now thine hand. And the angel of the LORD stood by the threshing floor of Ornan the Jebusite.

Ezr 4:15 That search may be made in the book of the records of thy fathers: so shalt thou find in the book of the records, and know that this city [is] a rebellious city, and hurtful unto kings and provinces, and that they have moved sedition within the same of old time: for which cause was this city **destroyed**.

Ezr 5:12 But after that our fathers had provoked the God of heaven unto wrath, he gave them into the hand of Nebuchadnezzar the king of Babylon, the Chaldean, who **destroyed** this house, and carried the people away into Babylon.

Psa 11:3 If the foundations be destroyed, what can the righteous do?

Psa 37:38 But the transgressors shall be destroyed together: the end of the wicked shall be cut off.

Psa 73:27 For, lo, they that are far from thee shall perish: thou hast destroyed all them that go a whoring from thee.

Psa 78:38 But he, [being] full of compassion, forgave [their] iniquity, and destroyed [them] not: yea, many a time turned he his anger away, and did not stir up all his wrath.

Psa 78:45 He sent divers sorts of flies among them, which devoured them; and frogs, which destroyed them.

Psa 78:47 He destroyed their vines with hail, and their sycomore trees with frost.

Psa 92:7 When the wicked spring as the grass, and when all the workers of iniquity do flourish; [it is] that they shall be **destroyed** for ever:

Pro 13:13 Whoso despiseth the word shall be **destroyed**: but he that feareth the commandment shall be rewarded.

Pro 13:20 He that walketh with wise [men] shall be wise: but a companion of fools shall be destroyed.

Pro 29:1 He, that being often reproved hardeneth [his] neck, shall suddenly be destroyed, and that without remedy.

Isa 9:16 For the leaders of this people cause [them] to err; and [they that are] led of them [are] destroyed.

Isa 10:27 And it shall come to pass in that day, [that] his burden shall be taken away from off thy shoulder, and his yoke from off thy neck, and the yoke shall be **destroyed** because of the anointing.

Isa 34:2 For the indignation of the LORD [is] upon all nations, and [his] fury upon all their armies: he hath utterly destroyed them, he hath delivered them to the slaughter.

Jer 12:10 Many pastors have destroyed my vineyard, they have trodden my portion under foot, they have made my pleasant portion a desolate wilderness.

Jer 48:8 And the spoiler shall come upon every city, and no city shall escape: the valley also shall perish, and the plain shall be destroyed, as the LORD hath spoken.

Jer 51:8 Babylon is suddenly fallen and destroyed: howl for her; take balm for her pain, if so be she may be healed.

Jer 51:55 Because the LORD hath spoiled Babylon, and destroyed out of her the great voice; when her waves do roar like great waters, a noise of their voice is uttered:

Lam 2:5 The Lord was as an enemy: he hath swallowed up Israel, he hath swallowed up all her palaces: he hath **destroyed** his strong holds, and hath increased in the daughter of Judah mourning and lamentation.

Lam 2:6 And he hath violently taken away his tabernacle, as [if it were of] a garden: he hath destroyed his places of the assembly: the LORD hath caused the solemn feasts and sabbaths to be forgotten in Zion, and hath despised in the indignation of his anger the king and the priest.

Lam 2:9 Her gates are sunk into the ground; he hath destroyed and broken her bars: her king and her princes [are] among the Gentiles: the law [is] no [more]; her prophets also find no vision from the LORD.

Hsa 4:6 My people are destroyed for lack of knowledge: because thou hast rejected knowledge, I will also reject thee, that thou shalt be no priest to me: seeing thou hast forgotten the law of thy God, I will also forget thy children.

Hsa 13:9 O Israel, thou hast destroyed thyself; but in me [is] thine help.

Act 3:23 And it shall come to pass, [that] every soul, which will not hear that prophet, shall be destroyed from among the people.

1Cr 10:10 Neither murmur ye, as some of them also murmured, and were destroyed of the destroyer.

2Pe 2:12 But these, as natural brute beasts, made to be taken and **destroyed**, speak evil of the things that they understand not; and shall utterly perish in their own corruption;

Jud 1:5 I will therefore put you in remembrance, though ye once knew this, how that the Lord, having saved the people out of the land of Egypt, afterward **destroyed** them that believed not.

LYING SPIRIT

1Ki 22:22 And the LORD said unto him, Wherewith? And he said, I will go forth, and I will be a **lying spirit** in the mouth of all his prophets. And he said, Thou shalt persuade [him], and prevail also: go forth, and do so.
1Ki 22:23 Now therefore, behold, the LORD hath put a **lying spirit** in the mouth of all these thy prophets, and the LORD hath spoken evil concerning thee.

2Ch 18:21 And he said, I will go out, and be a **lying spirit** in the mouth of all his prophets. And [the LORD] said, Thou shalt entice [him], and thou shalt also prevail: go out, and do [even] so.
2Ch 18:22 Now therefore, behold, the LORD hath put a **lying spirit** in the mouth of these thy prophets, and the LORD hath spoken evil against thee.

Deu 29:19 And it come to pass, when he heareth the words of this **cu**f all his prophets. And [the LORD] said, Thou shalt entice [him], and thou shalt also prevail: go out, and do [even] so.
2Ch 18:22 Now therefore, behold, the LORD hath put a **lying spirit** in the mouth of these thy prophets, and the LORD hath spoken evil against thee.

APPENDIX D:
THE BODY OF CHRIST? YOU BETTER HOPE NOT!
- July 1, 2006

As I've been looking intently at the state of the Church, I've grown more and more frustrated that hardly anybody seems to be really aware of the problems and the need for repentance. I struggle with what to make of that. Perhaps people think the 37,000+ denominations we have now are a good thing. Perhaps the fraud and waste and division and selfish ambition are just part of the human condition and can't be helped (although he says he's coming for a Bride without wrinkle or blemish and I think those are blemishes.) Perhaps no one ever told them how much this is hurting Jesus. I hope that this helps with that. In fact, I hope it sears an indelible burn mark on your conscience that makes you cry in pain every day. That's probably what it's going to take to get this turned around.

The Romans and the Pharisees conspired together to crucify Jesus. They didn't just crucify him, they spit on him and beat him and whipped him until his bones showed. And then the Lamb of God bled all the way through Jerusalem and they nailed him to a cross naked and hung him up in front of everyone. The Bible says he was unrecognizable as a man – much less recognizable as Jesus. They put a sign over his bloodied, broken, humiliated body sarcastically declaring him King of the Jews. They fought over who would get his clothes. They stabbed him in the side to be sure he was dead, then buried him in a cave.

We have all heard of the pain and suffering he endured, not just physically, but the sin that he carried must have been an unbelievable burden. The spiritual warfare and temptation to get him to back down and call up ten thousand angels to avenge him must have been horrific. None of us can even imagine what he went through in those last twenty-four hours.

How could the Pharisees and the Romans be so cruel? How could anybody inflict that kind of bloodthirsty, heartless damage on another human being – much less the Son of God?! What kind of monsters must they have been to so torture and degrade a person? What kind of evil spirits must have possessed them in that hour that they could do such a vile thing to an innocent man?

Everything that happens in our "natural" world has a spiritual counterpart. The human body of Christ was raised from the dead and abides with the Father. But I Corinthians 12:27 and Ephesians 4:12 and other places say that the Church is the Body of Christ. Do you know what that means? It means that WE are the spiritual Body of Christ and that's just as real to Jesus as was his physical body. And it means that we are meaner and more heartless and more possessed by evil than the Romans or the Pharisees could ever be.

You see, we have been hitting the Body of Christ with a cat-of-nine-tails daily for about eighteen hundred years (give or take). We have been hacking and slicing and shredding his flesh for generations. We have been fighting over his clothes and spitting on him since the first Christians started dying off. We have left a trail of his blood all over the world. And not in a good way.

To slice the Body of Christ up into 41,000+ denominations, we've basically had to run his flesh through a food processor. We've hacked off toes and then cloned them so we'd have a whole barn full of toes that refuse to reconnect with the rest of his body. We've ripped and shredded his flesh and stolen it from each other like a pack of hungry hyenas eating a fresh kill. Because he is Christ and he is SO much better than we could ever be, he has mostly taken it quietly like a sheep led to the slaughter. He has resisted the constant urge to call up 10,000 angels and avenge what we've done to his body. And it's a good thing too, because we should be FLATTENED by now for how much pain we've caused him. We've ignored those in need and focused on our own agendas. We've introduced malignant cancers and poisons and all kinds of disgusting stuff into his body.

When he came in the flesh, Jesus endured a few people beating him and a few people spitting on him. But it was pretty much all over in 24 hours. But in the spirit, we have been beating him mercilessly for hundreds of years. Under our own power, there is no sign on the horizon that the "church" system we've built is going to stop doing it either.

We refuse to connect up to the central nervous system and get commands from the brain. We refuse to coordinate our efforts with all the other body parts, so the whole Body just lays there and twitches in pain. Some parts look like they're getting somewhere, but it's more like the illusion of rigor mortise, than actual progress. Without ALL the pieces taking commands from the Head, we're just spinning our wheels and he bleeds more and more every day and the people we were supposed to reach out to are dying.

If you think that this is just figurative and it isn't causing Jesus pain, then you surely don't really understand the nature of his love for us and his desire for his body to be whole. He prayed in John 17 that we would be one body because, if not, THIS is the result. In essence, he prayed that the cup of suffering on his physical body would be taken away if possible AND he prayed that the cup of suffering on his spiritual body would be taken away if possible. Neither was. He is crying every day and has been for centuries. And the Father is fuming.

He has been enduring daily torture of a scale none of us can imagine. We have inflicted far more pain than the Pharisees and Romans could have ever even imagined. The physical body has limits of what it can endure, but Christ's spiritual body evidently has no limits on how much it can be tortured. Worse yet, the Pharisees and Romans hated him and didn't believe in him – but we claim to know that he is the Son of God and say that we love him, and yet, we're the ones doing the real damage. And we continue getting together in our little boxes every week and singing song of praise to Jesus and taking communion with a straight face while we're collectively desecrating and defiling his body.

I can tell you this, if I were the Father and I loved my only son Jesus with all that I am, at some point I'm going to FORCE the torture of His body to stop. If they won't start being one body, I'm going to get their attention by whatever means necessary. If I have to, I'll send earthquakes, tsunamis, wars, plagues, famines ... whatever. If they keep on singing and dancing and being completely oblivious and asleep, I'll even kill two-thirds of the planet if that's what it takes for them to knock it off and start being one body. That's pretty much what the book of Revelation predicts is coming – and we deserve it.

And if I were you I wouldn't count on a "rapture" getting you out before the suffering starts. Since the Church was supposed to take the light to the world and it's REALLY dark out there, I'm pretty sure that the sad state of things is our fault. We're the ones that knew better, we're the ones that have been butchering the body of Christ for centuries. I don't see any reason why we should get out of the consequences of what we've done. He's going to spank us really hard and we have it coming. Don't think you're going to avoid suffering, you're not.

Our only hope is to weep and repent and mourn before the altar. We need to apologize and mean it – and then we need to turn from our wicked ways and get under HIS headship. No more structures and systems and traditions of Man. If we don't start acting like One Body on our own, then the Father is going to kill off all the body parts that won't play nice together. Then He'll graft in bits that will appreciate it. Like prostitutes and drug dealers and homeless and the lost and kids with purple hair and hurting people that will defend his body to the death and refuse to listen to anyone but HIM.

Burn it into your brain. We ran the Body of Christ through a meat grinder. We sent people to seminary to learn how to slice the Body of Christ up into smaller and smaller pieces. We paid them to do it. We self-righteously took pleasure in splitting off from other people that had the Holy Spirit in them. We fought over his clothes. We placed a sign over his head that proclaimed proudly to the world that THIS beaten, bloody mess was an accurate representation of the King of the Kings. We are thieves and liars and murderers of the first order.

There's just one simple standard. If the Holy Spirit is in me and the Holy Spirit is in you, then we're just One Body and we're going to have to figure out how to get along without killing each other. We've got to knock it off before it's too late.

Please? If you love Jesus, could you please stop torturing his body? Could you tell him you're willing to share in his sufferings and help bear this burden until this is over? Could you acknowledge your part in it, however small, and stop? Could you insist on harmony from now on? Could you ask the Father to let you feel the pain that Jesus feels? Could you ask the Father to let you see through His eyes? I know He wants to.

Please make it stop.

www.FellowshipOfTheMartyrs.com – fotm@fellowshipofthemartyrs.com

DIALOGUES WITH GOD

Does God really speak to people? You decide.

www.fellowshipofthemartyrs.com
fotm@fellowshipofthemartyrs.com

Copyright © 2007, 2010 Doug Perry, FellowshipOfTheMartyrs.com

All rights reserved.

ISBN: 1463798644
ISBN-13: 978-1463798642

The Bride gets her jewelry, but it's going to hurt to get it on,
and once you're used to it, you're never going to want to rip it back off again.
Heaven is free. HOLINESS is hard!
If not us, who? If not here, where? If not now, when?

CONTENTS

Introduction 181

Dialogues 183

Need a Spiritual Tune-up? 215

Warning Label 219

Which part of ALL don't you understand? 220

Communication to Headquarters 229

Appendix A – Verses 239

Appendix B – Filled with 240

Appendix C – Cup Trouble-shooting 242

*"Your growth in Christ
is directly proportional
to your willingness
to RUSH HEADLONG
into the refining fire
and give it a wet, sloppy kiss."*

- Doug Perry

INTRODUCTION

I didn't always, but since 2004 I've learned to tune in very carefully to the voice of God. And I'm not talking about just any old god. I'm talking about hearing the Holy Spirit of God that came down to man when Jesus Christ ascended and sat at the right hand of Yahweh, the great I AM. He says that His sheep will hear and know His voice. (See Appendix A.)

How did it happen that I started hearing Him and how do I know it's God? Well, that's a different book. (Although some is in Appendix D.) This book is just here because God told me to start documenting some of my conversations with Him. Then He told me to put them all together so that people could read them and decide for themselves if they would like to hear God like this. Many people will definitely NOT want to hear God like this! It hurts. It's hard. It will cost you everything. But it IS possible. And I wouldn't trade it for anything.

If you don't think God talks to people anymore, then just consider this an exercise in creative writing or a poetic allegory or my own fanciful daydreaming. I don't really care what you think. I know the difference and I know He is real and I know He is directing my paths now that I know how to get out of His way. And I can't be talked down.

These dialogues aren't particularly insightful. They're not the best things the Lord ever told me. They're not documentation of dreams and visions and deep revelations. They're not words of knowledge about the secret things in some other person's heart. They're just written documentation of snippets of the kind of daily, running conversation I have with the Lord all the time. Sometimes daily to-do lists, sometimes encouragement, sometimes just a pat on the head. I'm not presenting them because I think they are the best of all the things the Lord has shown me, they're not. There are lots of things that He's told me that are very private, some that aren't for now, some that I don't even understand yet. But these "Dialogues" are just so that maybe you'll hunger and thirst for a relationship like this. He said that His sheep would hear and know His voice. And you can, if you'll unclog your pipeline and shut up and listen.

The first of the Dialogues is more poetic than normal and was written just as my furniture store was being crushed. It was a serious low point and probably near the beginning of when I started writing the Dialogues. You will see that it is much different in style and tone than the others that followed. God is faithful! Even when you feel crushed and defeated, He will never let it go too far. Throughout everything that I have endured, He has always been faithful. He's a great Dad!

Behind these dialogues is a Spiritual Tuneup section that might help you get unclogged so you can hear better. He's a really great Dad and I know He wants to talk to you like this. **It's not just me, I know lots of folks that hear Him like this.** And lots have been raised up by Jesus through me to hear Him like this. If I can help you hear Him better so that you don't have to lean on your own understanding anymore and HE can direct all your paths (Prov. 3:5-6), that's the best gift I could ever think of giving you!

ADDITIONAL NOTES:

God doesn't worry too much about capitalization of pronouns associated with Him. He definitely doesn't require it as a sign of respect for Himself when **He** is talking. I asked and it's just not real important to Him. I usually do it, but if I forget sometimes or I'm typing too fast. That doesn't seem to bother Him. He knows that I love Him with all my heart. He wants a broken and contrite heart, a circumcised spirit – not capitalization and a heart of ice.

I'm trying to present these in as raw a way as possible. I've only edited them where something was included about a person or some bit of instruction or information that the Lord didn't want made public. The only other change I made is that I put His words in bold so you can read it more easily. I doubt it is necessary, because it should be pretty obvious who is whom, but I don't want to make it harder than necessary.

I would love to have commented on all the amazing miracles and divine appointments and perfect timings that resulted from obeying the instructions He gave, but that too is beyond the scope of this book. I'm not trying to prove it was Him or justify what I heard or anything. I'm just presenting the raw conversations. You do what you will with them. I don't have anything to prove and He is the only one I need to please.

DIALOGUE WITH GOD – JULY 9, 2006 – PARKVILLE, MO

My God and my King,
You alone are worthy of glory and praise,
You alone are above all. You are my everything.
I rest in your arms through all that comes,
I'll rest in your arms.
But I'm so tired, Lord. I've been fighting so long.
They're not listening, Lord. They're not changing.
I feel all alone and I'm so tired.
Where did You go? Where is my help?
You promised, Abba. Please?

Rest, Child, I'm here.
I've always been right here.
I didn't say it would be easy.
You're the one that prayed to be like Me.
You said you'd do anything.
You said you'd give up anything.
Did you think I wasn't listening?
You did mean it didn't you?

Oh, Father. I meant it! You know I did!
I didn't hold anything back - or at least I didn't mean to.
I said You could have it all. I said I'd go. I said I'd endure.
But I'm so tired, Abba.

Rest, Child, I'm here.
You can't fail. What I've made you to be, you WILL be.
You couldn't screw it up if you tried.
And you WILL try - but I know it's not on purpose.
I've already made allowance for that.
It's not about you. It never was.
Just rest in ME. I'll take care of everything.

But it makes no sense!
They think I'm nuts. They think I'm making this all up!
They can't see that You would do this to somebody.
They're just sure that if You called, then You would provide.
And, sometimes, when I'm weak, they start to make sense.

Rest, Child, I'm here.
My ways are not Your ways.
And it's a good thing, too.
Your ways just get you into more trouble.
But I have a plan. And it's a good plan.
And it will confound the wise and it will glorify My Holy Name. This isn't about you. It never was.
I appreciate that you're willing,
I love you for it. More than you know.
But this is MY show. I'll write the script.

I know, Abba. I know. I get how big You are.
At least as much as You've shown me and my puny brain can handle.
I get the complexity and interconnectedness of Your plans. I get the majesty of it.
But right now, right this minute,
I'm just hurting really bad, Daddy.
I'm sorry to make it about me, but ...

Rest, Child, I'm here.
I know you. I know your needs.
I know you need to see the plan.
I'll show you when you're ready.
And I know you need love.
I made sure you got just enough, didn't I?
And I loved on you real good, didn't I?

Oh, God! Oh, Father!
I do appreciate the people you sent -
and the words they spoke at the right moment!
And without me asking! I know it's You.
And, yes, You loved on me real good.
So good that I can't stop crying -
and I don't want to ever stop.
And I'm sorry to ask for more, I really am,
but I just need to see.
I need to see through Your eyes.
I need to see the big picture.
I need to know my place. I need to see ...

Rest, Child. I'm here.
Time after time I've let you see through My eyes.
I want to show you more, and I will.
But it's going to hurt. You need to be ready.
It's really dark out there, and it's going to get a lot worse before it gets better.
Lots of people you love are going to die.
Some really ugly stuff is coming.
Are you willing? There's a lot of badness coming.

Abba, You know I'm willing.
I've seen so much already,
but I know there's so much more.
But could we please just skip to the end?
Could I please just see more of the happy ending?

I'm kind of drowning in the bad stuff.
It hurts really bad. Why won't they listen?!

Rest, Child. I'm here.
I know what you can handle.
I can't stretch you without pain.
I can't build muscles without breaking some down.
You asked me to put all the weight on.
You asked to be big and strong.
You wanted to get it over with quickly.
There's no other way, but through the pain.
Trust me, I know about pain and suffering.
I'll give you the endurance you need.
I'm spotting. The weight will never crush you.

Please, Father! I'm so tired!
But I don't want to rest. I don't want to stop.
I know how this works.
I know something big is around the corner or
it wouldn't hurt this bad.
I'm willing. You know I am. I'll stand.
You've got me through so many times like this before.
But I need you to lift just a little more!
I need you to get the bar off my chest!
Every muscle is screaming! Every day it hurts more.
It's really heavy and I don't think I have any strength left.

Rest, Child. I'm here.
I love you. I really do. More than you can know.
But I'm the one that gets to decide if you've had enough.
I'm the one that knows what you can handle.
Let Me do my job. Let Me build you up.
I know you're tired. We're almost there.
Just push a little more. Give Me a couple more reps.
Then we can rest a little while and you can see the fruit of your labor.
You'll see it. I promise. It won't be in vain. I promise.

Oh, God. I will! I don't know how, but You know.
I trust You. I do. I'll push. I can do a couple more.
Please just slap me around when I sound like a sissy.
Please do what You do. Break me. I meant it!
I'm not backing down! Whatever it takes!
Don't be gentle. Don't go easy on me. Don't let up.
They're hurting and dying and we're losing this war,
I want to be strong. I need to be strong to reach them.
I'll go. I promise.
But ... I'm so tired. Really tired. Really ...

I know, Son. I know. I'm here. Rest.
I'll dry every tear. I'll sustain you. I'll hold your hand.
When you can't, I'll do the heavy lifting.
Just rest. I know what I'm doing.
And we are NOT losing this war. I'm baiting the enemy.

I've got them all right where I want them.

Thanks, Dad. I know. I'm really sorry for this.

It's OK, Child. I know you are. But it's OK.
You're doing really good. I'm really proud of you.
It will all be worth it. I promise - and I can't lie. I promise.
I'll make it up to you. You'll see.

I love You, Abba.

I love you too, Child.

DIALOGUE WITH GOD – AUGUST 1, 2006 – LIBERTY, MO

Yes, Lord? What is it?

Listen carefully, Son. I have a lot to say. Today is the beginning of a new thing. Just as the beginning of the month of Av was important, so too, is the beginning of August. Lots of decisions are made this month. Lots of people will choose whether to go into the Promised Land or chicken out. Some will try to go without me and get trounced. If My Ark doesn't lead the way, there's going to be trouble. At times, you got ahead of me or turned to the side. I covered for you, but there were still consequences. Now we're getting it all back on track, but it has come at a cost. I know you understand that.

Whatever it takes Lord. Whatever the cost to me. I deserve whatever comes. I just want to be in Your Perfect Will. Please restore me, Lord.

Listen. There is a half-moon on the 9th of Av. Which way are you going to go? To the darkness or to the light? Everyone will have to decide.

DIALOGUE WITH GOD – OCTOBER 25, 2006 – LIBERTY, MO

Good morning, Lord. I'm here.

Good morning, Son. I love you.

I love you, too, Lord. What's the plan.

Don't go to work today and don't call in. You need to finish writing {the Red Dragon book}. You could have got it done yesterday, but you goofed off and got distracted. Don't eat or drink until you finish writing and don't go get the rest of the stuff out of the house. Focus on this. I'll help.

I'm sorry about yesterday, Lord. I'm sorry I let other things distract me. Please forgive me.

I do, Son. Stay on task today. This is really important. The Dragon wants to take your mind off of this. He'll use anything or anyone to keep you from finishing this. Because you allowed it without listening to Me I'm going to have to dial up the pressure today.

I understand, Lord. It's fine. Thanks for that.

Don't answer the phone unless I specifically tell you to. Don't go anywhere or plan on doing anything. Don't take a nap, don't eat, don't get distracted. I will help you write this. It needs to get finished today.

Yes, Lord. Thank You, Lord. What am I missing?

It needs to be short and direct. This is not the time for a full exposition of every verse and every nuance. We'll fill it all in later. Right now it just needs to get out there and be said. Also it needs to be clear that ONLY those with a personal spirit of repentance for JERUSALEM are truly free. If they're not weeping and mourning for THEIR part in it and repenting for THEIR sins and the sins of THEIR forefathers, then they're just fighting against it or creating their own Dragon. It's not enough to feel sorry that it happened or to wish it was fixed or to ask the Lord to forgive THOSE people that did it. You ALL did it and you ALL need to repent for your part in it.

Yes, Lord. I understand. Can I ...

No.

Can I ...

No. FOCUS!

Oops! Sorry, Lord. You're right. I love You, Lord. Please help. There is lots of stuff swarming and it's really messing with me.

I know, Son. I'll help. Clear out the sphere and unplug the pipeline.

Oh, yeah. That helped. Thanks, Lord. They're trying really hard.

A lot hangs on this. Hey! Focus!!

Wow. I'm drifting again! Sorry, Lord. OK. I'm getting it. Do you want me to write on the Jezebel thing?

No. Just the Dragon writing.

Can I check my email?

No. Just the Dragon writing. If you can stay on task, it won't take long. I don't want this to take all day. There are other things that need doing.

Thanks, Lord. I'll try really hard. I love You. Please help and don't let anything keep me from hearing You today.

I love you, too, Son. It will be fine. I've got it under control. Get to work.

DIALOGUE WITH GOD – OCT. 26, 2006 – LIBERTY, MO – 9:31AM

Good morning, Lord. I love You.

Good morning, Son. I love you, too.

What's the plan, Lord. I feel really heavy. Today is already starting off with fear and trembling.

Yes, Son. Today is important. Today is transition. I am doing a new thing.

Please Lord, please say I'm not out of order. Please say that You and I are OK and that I haven't failed you. I know I goofed off on Monday and didn't get the Dragon thing written, but I'm really sorry.

Son, hear me. Rest. You are OK. You are in My hand. I will prove it to you today. I will show you signs that you are where I want you. Rest.

Whatever You want, Lord. Thank you. Please give me Your peace. I'm very tired and I don't know what to do next. Please give me wisdom. I'm kind of scared. There are so many things coming against me and I have no idea how it's all going to ever get settled. I want to serve and focus on You, but today they are all coming at me. The money, the law, the state, the bank, the house, the family, the work, the brothers, I've got lying spirits in the mouths of the prophets, I've got red dragons to deal with, I've got a bad tire on the van and so many other things all at once. I know You said You wouldn't give me more than I can handle, but it sure seems like I'm at the limit.

I know Son. This is a big day. I know it's heavy. But it's not demonic, it's just Me sitting on you. Don't be afraid. I will cover you like a blanket and there will be lots of tears today, but don't be afraid and don't let the enemy turn it into despair or loneliness.

Yes, Lord. Please help. I'm so weak. I have no hope without Your hand.

I am here. It's time to be fruitful and multiply. I gave you Genesis 1 this morning for a reason. I made each according to his kind and I made you for a purpose and for this time. And I have looked and seen that it is good. Rest. Today we plant the seed and I will water it and bring the increase. It will grow up fast. You'll see.

Thank You, Lord. I love You. Please forgive my people. Please heal my land. We are wretched, naked, blind and poor. Please open blind eyes. Please, Abba. I'm sorry. Put it on me. Whatever it takes, just heal my people.

Send the e-newsletter, Son. I'll help write it. Offer the Dragon writing to those who have ears to hear. Ask the intercessors to pray. Tell the story.

Huh? Tell my story? Like the whole thing about what I've been through and going through?

Yes. Tell them. Let them share your burden. Show them what it costs to seek Me all the way and delve into the deep things. Tell them how to help.

Lord, that doesn't seem very humble. What happened to "like a sheep led to the slaughter"?

No one is making accusations. Before the brethren you tell them what you're going through and you give the glory to Me for bringing you thus far. I will move on their hearts as each needs.

Please Lord, I need a confirmation. I don't want to speak forth the whole story if I'm not 100% sure it's You. Please?

Send this to Suzanne. You already called Elijah. Call again on your phone. I will confirm it.

Please, Lord. I love You. Please give me strength.

I AM sufficient. Rest. I'm here. It's all good.

Thanks, Lord.

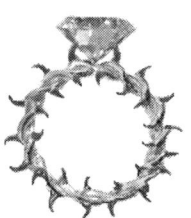

DIALOGUE WITH GOD – OCT. 30, 2006 – LIBERTY, MO – 9:00AM

Yes, Lord. I'm here.

Good morning, Son. I love you.

I love You, too, Lord. Good morning. Thanks for getting me up early. Thanks for prayer time with Your saints. What's the plan today?

First, I want you to rest. Go back to bed. I'll get you up when it's time. We need to get that tire replaced at the Goodyear and you need to get a couple cans of Deft and the hardware to finish up the sign and for the board tomorrow at Veronica's Voice. I'd like that done before 5:30pm. Also, you need to go make copies of the books and the Apology and the Red Dragon writing. And mail the box to Chris. Don't UPS it.

Yes, Lord. Two cans? Am I going to V.V. tomorrow? How many copies of the books? Do I need binders? Do I still need to buy those sticky hooks?

Yes, two cans. Yes, you're going to V.V. tomorrow. Rain = 10, Apology = 10, Dragon = 20, Apologies = 500. Yes, you'll need binders for the books. I'll tell you where. Yes, you are going to need hardware for the sign anyway, so go buy the hooks.

Do I need to go fix Judy's shower handle?

Not yet. I'll tell you when.

Am I sending money to Brother {XXXXXX} in Kenya?

Nope. Not yet.

But Lord, he's got starving orphans! Some money showed up. Shouldn't I help?!

Nope. Not yet. It's not as bad as you think. I'm doing something there. I know they're suffering but {XXXXXX} has to look to Me first, not to any Man.

Yes, Lord. Have Your way, Lord.
Lord, do you want me to let my wife have those two checks from Bruce?

Nope. She's on her own. That was My provision for the ministry. Have Bruce resend them.

Yes, Lord. I've got a lot more peace than normal, don't I? Usually I'm bawling when we do this. Are we OK?

Yes, you're hearing Me better and I'm helping make things easier. We're going to do this a lot from now on and I can't have you always making puddles everywhere you go. ;-)

Thanks, Lord. You're funny. I love You.

I love you, too, Son.
Anything else?

We'll adjust as the day moves along. Go get some sleep.

OK. Thanks.

DIALOGUE WITH GOD – NOV. 2, 2006 – LIBERTY, MO – 8:26AM

Good morning, Lord. Thanks for what You've already done today. Thanks for revelation and wisdom. Thanks for healing. Thanks for being present. Thanks for allowing the Spirit to pray through us.

Good morning, Son. All is well. You're doing very well today. Keep pressing in and listening to my voice. I will lead and guide you through the day. We have a lot to do, but it may not seem like a lot at the time.

What's first, Lord?

You can snack while you're on the computer. Drink the water bottles I provided. Tomorrow you're fasting. I'll give a lot of grace on what you eat today.

Thanks, Lord! Your will. Whatever you want is fine with me.

First, answer Leslie's email. Pray for her clarity and focus. Pray a shield around her and break the fear. Explain the Red Dragon to her personally and concisely. She's having a hard time keeping focus long enough to hear me.

Yes, Lord.

I want you to pray in tongues a lot today. I want to stretch you and teach you new things. Use the new one sparingly, but I'll give you more. It is a complete language package, even though you only got one word to start. It's important. Keep pressing in.

Yes, Lord. Thanks, Lord.

Get in touch with Merri. See about moving some stuff over there to store temporarily. You will be staying with them, at least for a little while. I can't have you here anymore. You'll be in motion. Don't get too comfy – and pack light. Store everything else at Merri's. I'm giving them a choice, but that's the plan.

Yes, Lord. I could really use some brake work on the van.

I know. I've got it. Contact Steve. I'll provide the funds when the time is right.

Call him today?

No. Not today. But soon. I'll tell you when.

Should I send the last dialogue to Brother {XXXXXX} in Kenya?

No. Not yet. Don't respond yet.

What else, Lord?

Make some more buttons. Finish off the ones you have printed. You're going to need to order more parts soon. We're going to distribute some of those today. I want you to talk to Lee at HyVee about selling them there. And call Linda K.

Yes, Lord. Call Linda about the buttons?

Yes, about the buttons and whatever else I put on your heart or hers. Get the design for the next t-shirt finished for Chris and work on his sign.

Yes, Lord. Thanks for smoothing that over with Chris. Please heal any hurts there. Thanks, Lord. I love You, Lord.

You're welcome. It will be fine. I love you, too.

Can we talk about the Adamic language?

Not here. Not right now.

Yes, Lord. What else can I do for You?

Pray for J.P. and John H. Pray for Edwin and Austin. Pray for Bob T. Pray for Carlton.

Carlton, who? I don't know any Carlton.

Just pray – and mean it. Pray the hard prayer. Use the new tongue. I've got it. Pray that Clare would get everything she needs before she goes back to Australia. Pray for Jay. Use the new tongue for that, too.

Yes, Lord. Thanks for Your love for all Your children. Thanks that You are watching out for us. Thanks for all the people that You tell to pray for me when I need it.

I love you all. I will not leave you nor forsake you. I will hold you in the palm of my hand and keep you safe. Even when the fire is raging, the flames will not consume you. You are mine.

Thanks, Lord. You are an awesome God and there is no other besides You. Please don't ever let me give Your glory to another – or to me. Please keep me humble and broken.

Yes, Son. I will. I always answer that prayer. Teach them to pray that prayer.

Yes, Lord.

That's all for now. Keep listening. There are some surprises – and some great ministry that will happen later tonight. I have something special coming for all of you.

Thanks, Lord. Your will. Please don't let me impose any expectations on You and what You are doing. You are faithful and true and Your promises are yeah and amen. Thanks, Lord.

I love you, Son.

I love you, too, Dad.

OK, that's it. Email Leslie.

OK. Thanks.

DIALOGUE WITH GOD – NOV. 3, 2006 – LIBERTY, MO – 8:54AM

Good morning, Lord.

Good morning, Son.

What's up?

Son, I want you to focus today. There is a lot that needs doing. I want you to really try hard to listen to my voice. I'm going to give you a list of things and I want you to get everything done. It's going to be tight. We're training here. Just like the waffles this morning, if you start praying late or finish late, they will burn and the kids will fuss. There are consequences when the timing is off. Try hard today. The day is coming when seconds here or there will make a huge difference. It's not just obeying, it's obeying at the right moment and in the right way - and not adding anything to it so that it runs over time. That's a big one with you that we've been working on for a long time now.

Yes, Lord. I get it. It sure is. Please do whatever You have to do to me so that I can fully and completely follow Your schedule.

You need to go through all of the stuff you have and I'll sort it. Some to store and some to pack. You're going to need to finish the sign for Chris as well. I'll help with that. You're going to have to be over at the house at 5:00pm to pack up the sauna. And you're going to drop stuff off at Merri and Joseph's house. I'll tell you when. Also, you're going to go by HyVee and talk to Lee. I'll tell you when. Keep praying through the day and practicing the new tongue I gave you. You're just scratching the surface.

Yes, Lord. Thanks, Lord. Thanks for Your direction. Thanks for Your gifts. Help me stay on task and be a good steward of all that You've given me - including time.

You need to get gas. And you need to call Steve today about the brakes. Just replace the pads. No matter what else looks like it might be a problem, just replace the pads. Pull a big disc backup of all the files on the other computer, including the buttons. Backup the email files on the E: drive.

Yes, Lord. Do I have money for gas? And for pads?

Yes, it's there. $20 in gas and I'll take care of the pads.

Thanks for what You did last night. Thanks for the surprise. That definitely was. Help me to equip Clare fully for the work that You have for her. Thanks for today and what You are going to do through her. Thanks for the phone call to Nick this morning. Thanks for Your presence. I wish we could have stayed on the line all day, just silently feeling You. Thanks for that.

I want you to finish the Jezebel book. I'll show you how. Also, you need to start documenting all about all the different demons that I've shown you. It's getting to be too many for the average person to remember. I'll help. Just start making a list of what you've learned about each one, what they do, what they look like, where they hide, where they port up, etc. I'll help.

Yes, Lord. Today, Lord?

Some today, but it will take awhile. As I lead. You won't be able to finish the Jezebel today, but dig into it and we'll see how far we can get.

Yes, Lord. Thanks, Lord. Am I going to Northtown to take the sign?

Not today. Go tomorrow. Chris will be there and you can go by the salvage meat place. Oh, and you're not fasting tomorrow, just today.

OK, thanks, Lord. You know I'll fast if You want me to.

Yeah, I know, but it's OK. This is a period of rest and restoration. There will be long fasts down the road, but this is a time of refreshing.

Yes, it really has been. Thanks so much, Lord. I love You. Thanks for Your saints and the blessing that they have been to me. Even in the midst of warfare and deliverance, I've just had a whole lot of fun and really enjoyed having people around to walk with all day. Thanks for that.

I know what you need. There will be more of that coming. Lots of intimate time with individuals in their homes. Lots of chances for me to bless them through you as they care for you and offer their hospitality. Don't forget that that is the point. I'm wanting to bless them, so I'm sending you in to give them a chance. If they receive you, I'll pour out onto them. If they receive you a little, they'll get a little. If they fling open their arms and put everything on the table like Clare and Suzanne did, I'll pour out beyond anything they could think or imagine.

Thanks, Lord. Please soften the hearts of the saints to receive God's anointed. All of them. Let the prophets and apostles find comfort and rest among the saints. Let the Body be restored. Thanks, Lord.

That's about it. I'll adjust as we go along.

Thanks, Lord. I love You, Lord.

I love You, too, Son. Don't go making this about YOU. This is all about ME.

Yes, Lord. I'm sorry, Lord. I love You, Lord.

I love you, too. Get to work.

Yes, Lord. Thanks.

DIALOGUE WITH GOD – NOV. 7, 2006 – PHILLIP'S HOUSE, LIBERTY, MISSOURI – 10:00AM

Good Morning, Lord.

Good morning, Son.

Thanks for the work You're already doing this morning. I love You. Please be fully in charge today. I don't want anything that's not 100% You. Please help me to stay on task and keep my eyes on You all day.

I love you, too, Son. I'll help. Today is important. Keep watch over your heart. The enemy will try with loneliness and sorrow today.

Yes, Lord. Thank You, Lord. Please help, Lord. You are my shield. You are my strong tower.

Yep, that's me.

You're so funny! I love You, Lord.

I love you, too, Son. Be strong. Today I need you to get the sign to River City T's and the disk for the next shirt. Have him total up what money remains and spend it all on getting as many of that shirt as you can. On light colors, but not too many white ones. I'll help. LISTEN!! Stay focused.

Oops. Sorry, Lord. I drifted.

You need to get over to Suzanne's and get the last of your stuff. You'll need to get the stuff in the van emptied now and sort through it all at Merri's later. You need to get to Metro North today and settle with them about the massage chairs. Leave the keys with Suzanne. Let her know you have to take the mattresses and put them back in the trailer. Leave the keys and the lock in the top drawer by the sink. Get anything else of yours out of the trailer. Either pitch it or leave it in the garage at the house. Throw all the bills and statements and stuff in the desk and the file cabinet in the trash. Bring the food from Suzanne's over to Merri's. I'll tell you what to do with it.

OK, am I calling anybody down South?

Yes, call Sarah. Call Kevin.

Lord, I don't have a number for Sarah.

Send her an email and let her know you're coming and ask for a phone number. Then call her when you get one.

OK. Thanks.

Leave on Wednesday. I'll direct. No hurry. There are stops along the way. I'll direct your path.

Thanks, Lord. I just emailed Sarah. Was that OK?

Yeah, it's fine. Good job.

Are we done?

Yeah, that'll do. Print it out and try to stay on task.

Yes, Lord. Thanks, Lord. I love You.

I love you, too. Hang on, it's going to be a crazy ride! :-)

DIALOGUE WITH GOD – NOV. 10, 2006 – FOTOPULOS' HOUSE, OZARK, MO

Good Morning, Lord.

Good morning, Son.

I love You, Lord!

I love you, too, Son. Gonna be a good day, today. You did really well last night. I'm very proud of you.

... HEY!

I'm sorry, LORD!...the dogs distracted me. I'm sorry.

Stay focused on Me. I'm going to dial some things up today. Trust Me. Speak what I tell you to speak.

Yes, LORD. Give me strength. What's the plan for today?

Call your Dad. I'll lead from there. No, it's not time to call the Lighthouse yet. We are going to some pastors' today to pray.

Yes. LORD. As you lead. Email?

Yeah, I'll get you online again. No, not calling Uncle Ted yet.

Soon?

Yeah, soon. I'll tell you when. Yes, call Elijah today - when I lead.

Thanks for what You did last night! Thanks for what You're doing in Kevin. Thanks for communion time and what You told him to do. That was really pretty.

Yeah, I had a great time, too. You're welcome. I love you.

Oh, I love You, too, LORD.

Time to go. Get moving.

DIALOGUE WITH GOD – NOV. 14, 2006 – HONEYSUCKLE INN, BRANSON, MO – 6:53AM

Good morning, Lord. Thanks for the sleep.

Good morning, Son. I love you.

I love you, too, Lord. Please help me today. Please rule and reign and be sovereign in every way. Please direct my paths and put Your words in my mouth. It's all about You, not about me.

Son, I want you to crystallize all that I have given you in the last 48 hours about the Church at Branson. It has much wider applications, but I've given you words and dreams and visions and written things on your heart and now it's time to write it on tablets so that the people will hear and know.

Yes, Lord. Please help, Lord. You tell me what to say.

As I have shown you, there is a goal here, there is a finish line of sorts. They will know that they are ready to handle the people that are coming and I'll be ready to turn on the faucet wide open when they can eliminate all the static. When a word or a gift or a directional arrow can move all the way through them without losing integrity. Use the parable examples that I gave you, of the "telephone game" and of a corporate retail sale and of a medical school. They cannot be an effective hospital until they are in harmony, each playing their instrument in their own way, but each in tune and in harmony with the others and all playing the same piece of music. When we change keys, they ALL have to change seamlessly. When the pillar of fire picks up and moves, they all have to see it and stand and walk together at the same time. Show them the kick line. {Like the Rockettes, all coordinated.}

Yes, Lord. I understand. Open the doors for me to speak it.

It starts with the word Kevin gave on Sunday. It has to flow out and be pure and be spread throughout the spirals. And it has to retain its integrity. Don't focus just on brain things either, or it will put too much emphasis on the soulish. It's the same with the spiritual things that are distributed to the people. They have to be efficient dispensators of that which was entrusted to them. That's how they will grow, how they will flow together and how they will become wine, not just individual grapes connected by a vine. When they are ready for harvest, I mash them together. They do NOT remain independent any longer. The wine has ONE flavor throughout, not different flavors in different parts of the bottle. They will know you by your love – for each other, for My Word, for My Spirit and for Truth.
Yes, Lord.

They will know they are ready when it can flow throughout the body without interruption or twisting or misinterpretation. When they are walking shoulder to shoulder without jostling each other. There will be some that plug it up or mangle it. In order for this to work, they have to 1) have a hunger to obey, 2) be Jezebel-free, 3) be all the way full of the Spirit, 4) be able to hear My voice really well and 5) have MUCH fear of the Lord for what will happen if they transmit a mangled message. And, 6) they have to get completely Red Dragon-free, and 7) then they have to know how to enter into my rest.

Yes, Lord. I understand. Please don't let me mangle Your words either! Please let this be pure and stop it if it's not!

This is MY move, Son. This is MY work. They submitted to Me and I will do it. It will be a quick work, but not many will be able to go all the way in the first wave. Be prepared to identify those who can't yet or won't - and make allowance for them. DO NOT BRING DIVISION - but some will be doctors, some will be nurses, some will carry stretchers and some will be assigned in the Mess Hall or the Motor Pool or be M.P.'s guarding the gates. All are needed. But the ones that listen the best are the only ones that can be surgeons. But understand that at ANY MOMENT I might bust through on ANYONE and equip them to be the best doctor there or I might take a doctor and make them the best MP. DO NOT put someone in a box and never let them out. Expect me to use the base and foolish things. Continue to grow them and try to raise up doctors. And teach the doctors to be humble and willing to do any job in the place. This is NOT about raising up superstars! This is about raising up vessels that will be transparent and I can equip and use anywhere at any time. This is about being a swarm of bees. Each with a stinger, all doing the work assigned to them, all critical, all focused on the harvest and all able to swarm viciously at a common enemy. You may be able to take out a man or a bear or a dog, but who can defend against a swarm of bees?

Yes, Lord. I understand. Please write it all on my heart and help me to explain it to Kevin and the others. Help me to take it to all the places you intend for it to go. I love You.

I love you, too, Son. This is MY show. Rest.

What's the plan today, Lord?

Nick will call. Spend time with him. Do as I lead. Get ready to move out of the hotel room. Call the Pheasant's. You'll be with them for a few days. Prayer at the Mack's tonight. I'm not going to give you too much more detail today. Things are fluid. You did really well yesterday even though it seems like not much happened.

Thanks Lord. Could you please put some dead people in my path? I'd like some more practice with the big prayers. How are we ever going to raise the dead if we're never around dead people.

You're so cute. In time, Son. I'll open doors. It's all good. Answer your emails this morning and go get breakfast. Not the buffet, unless they offer it for free. Tomorrow you're fasting.

Yes, Lord. Thank You, Lord. I love You so much. You alone are worthy of glory and honor and praise. You alone are the source of every good thing. You are my provider and my guide and my rest. Thanks, Lord.

I love you, Son. I'm proud of you. I told you that we would get here and here we are. Never forget.

Yes, Lord! You are true in every way. Thanks so much! Thank You, Lord! You're the best Dad ever!

We could do this all day, but you need to get to work. Send this to Kevin.

Yes, Lord. Thanks, Lord.

DIALOGUE WITH GOD – NOV 15, 2006 – PHEASANT'S HOUSE, FORSYTH, MO – 12:18PM

Good morning, Lord. Thanks for what You've already done this morning. Thanks for having Chris call. Please restore his minutes on his phone and mine and provide. Thanks for ministry in this home, Lord. Please let Your words sink in and all of mine fall away. Let Your peace rest on this place.

Good morning, Son. I love you. You're welcome. You did just fine. Keep listening and I will continue to increase your land.

I love You, too, Lord. Thanks so much. I'm having a great time. Thanks for Your peace. I couldn't do anything without You. Please don't ever take Your Spirit from me.

Rest, Son. Today will go faster than you think. Ministry tonight at Nick's house. Prayer for Forsyth later on. Gonna get a hair cut.

Cool! Thanks Lord. You show me where and how. Lord, do You think I should worry about the money?
No. That would be bad. Just trust me. I've got it.

Lord, why did you have me write that? I never worry about the money anymore.

For the people reading this. I know you're all good.

Thanks, Lord! You're so funny. :-) Anything else?

Pray for Chris and the battle he's fighting. Tell Suzanne, but just broad strokes.

OK.

Write some more on the demon list. You're going to need it soon. And take a shower this afternoon before you leave. Do the laundry.

Did I get all the laundry out of the van?

Nope. Wash the green sweater and the black pants, too.

OK, thanks, Lord! I sure love You a lot. You're the best Dad ever!

I love you, too, Son. I've got you in the palm of my hand. You are safe. Rest in me and I'll open every door. I'm really proud of you.

Thanks, Lord. It's all You. I didn't do anything and I know it. But thanks.

Go get the laundry and do that now. Then get to writing.

Yes, Lord.

DIALOGUE WITH GOD – NOV. 20, 2006 – MACK'S HOUSE, BRANSON, MO – 9:21AM

Good morning, Lord. I love you.

Good morning, Son. I love you, too.

Thanks for the day. It's really pretty. Thanks for what You did yesterday and how You showed up at the Sunday morning meeting in Branson. It was really great.

Yeah, I thought it was great, too. Could have had a little less talking and more praying, but it was really good. I'm going to finish what I started here, you don't need to worry about leaving. It's not about you anyway.

Yes, Lord. Thank You, Lord. I know You have it under control. Please bless them abundantly and send me back whenever You like. Help me to get better at moving on without tears.

No, Son. I'm never going to do that. I made you this way and I'm just NEVER going to make it stop hurting when you leave part of the Body behind.

Yes, Lord. Have Your way, Lord. Thank You, Father. Bless Your holy name. Your will be done.

Son, I'm opening doors, your time here is almost done. Tell Kevin that he can send the Bonfire story about the Lampstands to all his people or use it to show them what's coming. Send him this dialogue. Call the papers and see about ad rates for non-profits. Go by the bank. Make more copies of the books when you have cash. Use the UPS store coupon. Listen to me very carefully about the computer issue. Make some more buttons to leave here. Email Pat and Paul the address in Liberty.

Yes, Lord. When am I leaving?

Wednesday. You'll be here for Thanksgiving with them on Tuesday night.

Lord, where am I going?

I'm not ready to tell you yet. When I do, you need to keep it quiet and go cloaked. I don't want them to see you coming.

Yes, Lord. You direct, Lord. What else today?

Get the Lighthouse brochure off of Giles desk. Read it.

Yes, Lord. Do you want me at the intercessory prayer meeting tonight at 7pm?

Yes.

OK, thanks, Lord. That would be great. Can they pray for me?

Yeah, that's part of the plan, too. But stay flexible because things are in motion. Have to tie up all the loose ends before you leave.

Great! Thanks, Lord. Anything else?

That's all for now. Get to work.

Yes, Lord. Thanks, Lord. I love you so much. You've been so good to me. Thanks for the provision You poured out. Please help me hear you really good and be a good steward.

I love you, too, Son. I'm here. Rest. It's not about you anyway.

Yes, Lord. Thank You, Lord.

DIALOGUE WITH GOD – NOV. 25, 2006 – HUBBELL'S HOUSE IN WINNSBORO, TEXAS –1:04PM

Yes, Lord?

I love you, Son.

I love You, too, Lord. Thanks for that. It occurs to me that you always start with that and I sure appreciate it.

I love it when everybody starts with that, too. Tell them, would you?

Yes, Lord. I will. What's up?

Don't expect too much today. It's rest mostly. Some teaching and lots of watching. There's something hidden here and it's going to be hard to find without a lot of focus and attention. Talk less and listen more.

Yes, Lord. Thanks, Lord.

Get the bag of originals out of the van so you'll have the cup model handy. Go through that with them when I tell you to.

Yes, Lord. I'm really pooped.

I know. You can take a nap. It's all good.

I love you, Lord.

I love you, too, Son. Rest.

Yes, Lord. Thanks.

DIALOGUE WITH GOD – DEC. 1, 2006 – BEST WESTERN, ADDISON, TEXAS – 8:22AM

Good morning, Lord.

Good morning, Son. I love you.

I love You, too, Lord! What's the plan today?

Check out at 11:00am. Make some calls to find binder parts. I'll direct you after 11:00am. Call Ellie about the time for the prayer meeting tonight and give her directions. Don't hurry today, it's going to be a long night.

Yes, Lord. Thanks, Lord. Thanks for a good night sleep. I really didn't want to stay here. Thanks for making me. I hope that whatever was missed can be made up for. I understand that the blood is on my head for talking too long at lunch and missing the next appointment. Thanks for not making me sleep in the van in the cold.

Keep praying for my best, Son. Sometimes there will be suffering, sometimes there will be comfort. Stay willing for either. I will put you in situations that require suffering, but I will always get you through. Be willing to accept the times of comfort and even luxury as well. It's a great laptop, isn't it? :-)

It sure is! Thanks for making me buy it. Thanks for having me stay here. I would have been fine in a place half the cost, but I know that there were divine appointments to get here. Thanks. Please help me to receive. Thanks for James' prayer yesterday about that. Please answer it and raise up more folks to watch over me. I love You, Lord. You're altogether lovely and altogether too good to me for what I deserve.

I love you, too, Son. No, it's not time to send out an e-newsletter yet. Soon. Lay low.

OK, thanks. Please be with Amalia at ORU {Oral Roberts University}. Please keep that fire in her burning. I would REALLY like to see something bust out there.

Me, too, Son. It will. I've got it.

I'm still tired, Lord. But I can't sleep anymore, can I?

Yeah, you can go back to bed. There's nothing urgent. It's all good. I'll help you rest.

Thanks, Lord. Am I finished?

Yep. Love you. December is going to be amazing.

Love You, too. Thanks, Lord.

DIALOGUE WITH GOD – DEC. 8, 2006 – AICARDI'S HOUSE, PENSACOLA, FLORIDA – 10:45 AM

Good morning, Lord. I love You.

Good morning, Son. I love you, too.

What's up, Lord? Am I off schedule?

Nope. We're right on track. I know it seems weird, but today is going to move slowly for awhile.

OK, Lord. Thanks, Lord. How come I worked for an hour and a half on a trip update and then the computer crashed just before I finished?

Don't worry about that. It was just for me.

OK. Whatever. I know You've got it. Thanks for not letting me throw the computer or something! Thanks for your peace that passes understanding. Please continue to spontaneously disrupt my life and my efforts at any moment. Whatever You want is fine with me!

I love you, too. :-)

So what's the plan today, Lord?

I want you to leave right at 11:30. Go to Foley and have lunch at Lambert's. Watch for appointments. Take a cup model in your pocket. Then stop at the Pensacola Christian College after that and go where I lead. Be back before 4pm to meet Mitt. Important stuff tonight. Big part of why you're here. Pray for Mitt's safe travel as well.

Uh, Lord, don't you pretty much have big angels around his car and this all planned out? I never get why I need to pray for stuff that I know You're going to do anyway.

Stop thinking so much. Just do what I tell you. ;-)

Yes, Lord. You're the boss.

Pretty sure. ;-)

Thanks, Lord. Thanks for this leg of the trip. Thanks for letting me see Rick in Mississippi. Thanks for Tom Morris {the hitchhiker} and all the other folks along the way. Thanks for David and Bob and Mitt and the folks here. Please watch over Mitt's car and keep he and his wife safe on this trip. Please don't let anything throw off Your schedule and Your purposes. Crush anything the enemy is trying to do, in the Name of Jesus.

There you go. That wasn't so hard was it? ;-)

:-p Love You, Lord.

Love you, too.

Hey, am I getting an alignment today?

Nope. Tomorrow.

Hmm. OK. Whatever You say. Should I call them or go by or something? OH! Sorry, Lord, I got distracted.

It's OK. I didn't go anywhere. I told you today would be kind of relaxed.

Yeah, thanks, Lord.

Don't worry about the alignment, go by in the morning. The place Bob told you.

Thanks, Lord. Anything else?

Yeah. Rest.

OK, I'll try. Please help. Thanks, Lord.

You betcha. OK, that's it. Love you.

Love You, too, Lord.

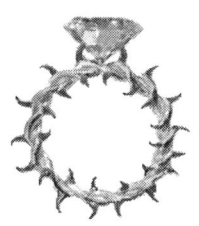

DIALOGUE WITH GOD – DEC. 11, 2006 – BEST WESTERN, NASHVILLE, TENNESSEE – 8:43AM

Good morning, Lord. Thanks for breakfast. I love You.

Good morning. I love you, too, Son.

Please, Lord, what's the plan today? Am I in the right place?

Yes, you're just fine. Thanks for asking. You're doing a great job. Remember that when pieces of YOU surface, it's just so I can kill them, not to make you feel bad. I didn't send my Son into the world to condemn the world, but that the world through Him might be saved. It's just to show the distance between where you are and where you should be, so that you can ask for more of me and less of you. It's not to make you feel bad. That can't really be helped, I know, but don't live there.

Yes, Lord. I get it. Thanks. Thanks for Your Son. Thanks for Your sacrifice. Thanks for Your patience and love. Especially Your love.

You're welcome, Son. Stop dwelling on Pensacola. I've got it. You did fine.

But, Lord, how come it's still messing with me? Why can't I get it out of my head? Is there something still unresolved or something on me? I don't want to play footsies with it anymore, but it won't go away. How do I close the door? It usually doesn't bother me like this!

You have to ask me to do it.

But I have been and it's still messing with me! I don't get it.

I love you. I love them. Break the ties. Speak it out. Slice it off.

Yes, Lord. Thanks, Lord. It's done.

Yep. Now stand in faith.

Yes, Lord.

I've got it. I'll take care of it. Not like you expect. Not like Dave, but I'll fix it. Stop worrying about writing an email to the folks there. You're severed until further notice. No contact until they contact you. So don't worry about it.

Yes, Lord. Thanks, Lord. That helps. What's the plan today?

Gonna go slow and rest. You have two hours till checkout. Take a nap.

For real? I just got eight hours!

Yep. You know you're tired. Get off the computer and nap. Then go to the Baptist building, then to Vanderbilt. I'll lead from there. Don't call the Friths until I tell you.

Yes, Lord. Please help me sleep, Lord.

I will. I love you, Son. You're doing a great job. Keep listening and learning.

Thanks, Lord. It's all You. I know I couldn't do this. Please finish the work You started in Rachael {my wife}. Not too soon, but whenever you're ready.

I will, Son. She'll be glorious. Just rest. I've got it.

Thanks, Lord. I love You!

I love you, too, Son. Rest.

DIALOGUE WITH GOD – DEC. 18, 2006 – TROYER'S HOUSE, MT. HOPE, OHIO (HOLMES COUNTY, AMISH COUNTRY) – 7:49AM

Good Morning, Lord. I love You.

I love you, too, Son. Good morning. I'm real proud of you.

Lord, I didn't do anything! It was all You!

I know, Son, but you listened and obeyed and it was really pretty.

Thanks, Lord. It WAS really pretty. I so love it when You come and straighten things out. It could have gone really badly last night, but You just swooped in and gently moved hearts the right direction. I sure appreciate it. Please wreck Holmes County. Please fill the Amish so full of Jesus that nothing else can fit!

That's the plan, Son. Rest. I've got them all right where I want them. Nothing can stand against my Fire.

Thanks, Lord. Thanks for letting me watch. What's the plan today?

More of the same. Teach them how to get so full nothing else can fit. Don't be in a hurry, I'll direct all of your paths. Rest in me.

Yes, Lord. Whatever You say. Thanks for Chris. Please bless him abundantly and get anything out of the way that keeps him from hearing You really good all the time. Thanks, Lord. I'm having a lot of fun with him.

You're welcome, Son. Isn't he a great kid? I'm really proud of him. He's real special, so take good care of him.

Yes, Lord. I will, Lord. Anything I need to do right now?

Nope. You're fasting until further notice. Just go where I say. Keep praying for Jonas. The enemy knows you're here now. Expect them to regroup and attack from a new direction. Watch for sneaky, subtle attacks. They're also going to go for the soft targets, so armor up Wilma and Leon and the girls really good.

Yes, Lord. I will, Lord. Thanks, Lord. Anything else?

Don't worry about anything. I've got it all under control. You're right where I want you. Rest.

Thanks, Lord. I love You.

I love you, too. Work on the Demon book until Chris wakes up.

Yes, Lord.

DIALOGUE WITH GOD – DEC. 29, 2006 – OVERSTREET'S HOUSE, LIBERTY, MISSOURI – 8:43AM

Good morning, Lord. I love You.

Good morning, Son. I love you, too.

I'm here, Lord. What's the plan today?

Rest, Son. I've got it. Today is a day of details and tying up loose strings. Try Kevin again when I tell you too. Keep praying for Suzanne and Susie. Check in with Chris E. after noon, unless he calls you first. You're not going to be able to get the t-shirts before you leave. That was just you. Leave that alone.

Sorry about that Lord. Please forgive me. I'm sorry for the wasted time and gas and stuff.

It's OK, it was part of the plan. I forgive you.

I love You, Lord. What else?

I love you, too. Be ready for quick directional changes. Don't put me in a box. This is listening and obedience practice for all of you. But whatever path I send you down, I'll meet every need and you'll be ready.

Yes, Lord. I know, Lord. Thank You. Do I need to call David at ORU?

Nope. Not yet. Send him the two email trip updates when you find his email address. Amalia sent it to you in an email - if you can't find the scrap of paper you wrote it on. ;-)

Oh, yeah! Thanks, Lord. Please increase my faith. Please help me to trust my brothers and sisters more and know when they are hearing you really well. Please help me to stay out from under any of the red dragons. Please, Lord? They really scare me because I know it means I'll wander from Your perfect will.

Rest, Son. I'll put you through what I choose for you.

……

Yes, Lord. Thanks for letting Chris E. call just now. Thanks for showing me the thing that was still holding him back. Thanks for freeing Him. Please tie up all the loose ends there. It was real pretty, Lord. All the way down to having Chris and I say goodbye the very INSTANT before my phone ran out of minutes. I love how You do that. Last night the phone died the second after I was done talking to Suzanne. I know most people might not be impressed, but it's that little stuff, all day long that helps build my faith. OH! So thanks for answering the prayer I just prayed above! Wow! That was fast! Thanks! You're the best.

You're welcome, Son. There are FAR, FAR more things like that than you are capable of noticing. I've packed your days with so many little treasures like that that it will take years of you and I watching the replays to see them all! We'll just sit and laugh and you can marvel at how well the Father takes care of you, even when you don't notice. If you (or anybody reading this) asks me to start showing them all the little "coincidences" that I've arranged in their lives, I will. I love doing it and I want them to see how involved I truly am in their lives.

Oh, YES, Lord! Show them ALL to me! I know I see lots of them all day long. So many I couldn't even write them all down! But show them all to me. As many as I can handle without my head exploding. Show me ALL the spirals and applications of all that you're doing around me on every level.

Rest, Son! I will, but it would occupy too much of your system resources to handle it all. We'll get there. I love your heart.

Oh, Abba. Please just use me as a walking, talking example of You. Whatever You want to do with me is fine. Whatever I have to give up is fine. I trust You. Have Your way. I love You.

I love you, too, Son. Rest. Yes, you can get a hair cut today.

Thanks, Lord. Are we done?

Yep. But I love you.

I love You, too. Please be fully in charge today and rule and reign in every way and order all of my steps and control the words of my mouth and the intentions of my heart. Please have Your way in all things and roll over me if I try to have my own way.

OK. Happy to do it. Love you.

I love You, too, Lord. Thanks.

You betcha.

DIALOGUE WITH GOD – JAN. 2, 2007 – OVERSTREET'S HOUSE, LIBERTY, MO - 4:52PM

Oh God! I hurt so bad. Oh, God, I'm so lost. Please help. Please hold me!! What is this?!

I'm here Son, I love you.

I love You, too, Lord. Please help. Please explain it. I need You, not any man.

I'm here Son, I'm here. It's all Me. Trust me. I know what I'm doing. My ways are not your ways. It's all part of the plan. Rest.

I don't know how to rest, Lord. It hurts so bad!! Please help me! Everything feels wrong, everything is twisted.

I know, Son. I know. Just power through. Cowboy up.

Oh, God. Please Abba, please, I don't now what to do. I'm not hearing good and it's freaking me out.

You're just fine, the problem is with too much input. Remember when you first got tongues and you were translating everything and answering questions in it? It was so strong for three days until it settled in. This is like that. You didn't notice right away, but the anointing shot up and so did your input . I know it's scrambling some things. Just know it's all part of the plan and I know what I'm doing. It will settle down soon. It's like feedback on a hot microphone. Just endure the screech for a little while and it will go away when the levels settle back down.

I don't know what to do, Lord. Nothing seems to be helping and I feel far from You. Things are changing really fast and I can't get a handle on it.

You're not supposed to, Son. That's the point. That's always been the point. You don't need to figure it out, just obey.

I'm sorry, Lord. Yes, Lord. Please help me. This hurts really bad! I'm way over my head here.

I'm helping, Son. Get some rest. Get some time alone. Don't try to reach out, just you and me is enough.

I'm sorry, Lord. Yes, Lord. You and me. Please, Father, please take me home. I hate this place. But not my will, but your's.

In time, Son. Rest.

I don't know how to rest, Lord. Not when there is so much pain. Everything is changing. I don't know what I can stand on. It's not about the people, I'll give them all up. I did give them all up. It's not about my pride or my ministry or whatever. I just feel like there is nothing reliable at all.

That's what it was like when I was here. That's the way it's always been. Nothing here is reliable, only the Father. You were just lulled into a sense that it was stable, but it never was. Marriages, jobs, cars, economies, weather, governments – none of it is really stable when I don't want it to be. You have to learn to trust in ME and ME only. And you have to want ONLY what I want. If we go with what YOU want, this is never going to work out right. You had to learn this. And I have to write it on your heart so that you'll never forget.

Yes, Lord. Yes, Lord. Whatever it takes, Lord. Don't let me back down!! Please, Abba. Don't let me chicken out. Give me whatever it takes to endure. I'll stand, I will, I promise. Please help me.

Lay low for awhile. Let the dust settle. I'll take care of everything.

Yes, Lord. I'm so tired, Lord. I really need a hug.

I'm here, Son. I'll hold you, just rest in My arms.

Thanks, Abba.

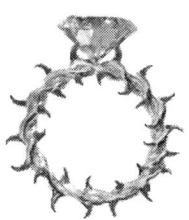

DIALOGUE WITH GOD – JAN. 5, 2007 – BEST WESTERN, BAKER CITY, OREGON – 12:52PM

Good morning, Lord. I love you.

I love you, too, Son. I'm right in the middle of all of this, don't worry.

Thanks for helping me with the drive Lord. I know that you have to have been doing something for me to drive 31 hours straight with just a couple of hours of sleep! Thanks for protecting the van and watching out for me on the road. How many times have you saved my life since I first left Kansas City two months ago?

You're welcome, Son. I'll always give you everything that you need to accomplish MY purposes. I've saved your life 14 times in the last two months.

Wow! Thanks Lord. I know about some of them, especially when that cement truck stopped short in front of me! And I know that deer on the shoulder of the highway in the Rocky Mountains yesterday was really thinking about jumping in front of me. Thanks for all the ones I don't know about as well. I know You are taking really good care of me and watching out so well for me. Thanks for the provision for this trip and working out the details so we could get access to the funds just in time. I never know where it's going to come from, but I never have to worry!

When money doesn't come, start to wonder if you're working my plan or planning your own work.

Yes, Lord. Help me to always stay in Your perfect will. Please ignore any prayers that I pray, even the intentions of my heart, that don't align with your best, most perfect will. I know that You will adjust sometimes to please us and still find a way for it to bring You glory, but I don't want that. I want Your very, very best and I know that means that it needs to be ALL You and NONE of me. I know it's my birthright as a joint heir and that You will hear my petitions, and that no man can take it from me, but I lay it down willingly. Please have all of Your way and NONE of my way.

Ready to listen now and stop talking?

Oops. Yes, Lord. Sorry, Lord.

Keep driving. This meeting with John is important. You'll see. Then head for home. Not going any farther South on this trip. Now is not the time for California.

Yes, Lord.

Gonna give you more info on the way. I'm sorry about you having to miss your daughters' birthday party, but it's not time yet. I do want it all restored, but it's not time. The girls will be fine.

Yes, Lord. Thanks, Lord. I love You. Whatever You want is fine.

Time to go. More later.

Yes, Lord. Thanks, Lord.

DIALOGUE WITH GOD – JAN. 9, 2007 – HICKS' HOUSE, HAMPTON, IOWA – 7:19AM

Good morning, Lord. I love You.

Good morning, Son, I love you, too. I'm right on top of this. Everything is fine. I know it looks strange, but I know what I'm doing.

Lord, I'm perfectly willing but the persecution has increased and I don't seem to be doing anything to slow it down. In fact, I'm just pretty sure YOU are having me say things that make people more mad at me! How is this bringing unity and peace? Chris says he heard You tell him that I have a Red Dragon with my face on it. I'm sure I don't, but he's going to need to hear from You about why we're hearing differently. I don't know what the deal is.

It's fine. I'll take care of Chris. You're going to have to learn to let ME do the talking sometimes. Everybody has to give each other the benefit of the doubt and seek Me really hard and I'll sort it out. You don't have a red dragon. You laid it all down in Branson, everything you want or desire or think is best. The intentions of a persons heart are not the same as having a red dragon with your own face on it. Most of it is subconscious anyway. Trust me, I know what I'm doing.

I do trust You, Lord. I do. I'll endure whatever. I know that a lot of the persecution in the past has come because I said things that I could have held in. I know that You're trying to make me tough and to show the Body that real persecution will come if you let Jesus out of your mouth all the time. Please don't stop. Have Your way in all things. Don't let me ever get in your way. I trust my shield, Lord. I trust that you have it under control and that if it makes it out of my mouth, it was part of Your plan. I know that You are sovereign in all things.

Yep. I AM. Hang in there, Son. It's all under control. I won't put you through more than you can handle. Sometimes the refining fire hurts and sometimes when fire comes out of your mouth to refine others it takes on really unexpected forms. Just rest. I've got it.

Thanks Lord. Am I finished fasting, cause You know I'll go on until whenever if that's what You want.

Nope. Not yet. Soon.

OK, thanks, Lord. Anything else?

No. It's all good. Just hang loose and try not to let stuff bother you. I've got it under control. I'll take care of Chris and Suzanne and Clare and Rick all the others.

Thanks, Lord.

DIALOGUE WITH GOD – JAN. 10, 2007 – HICKS' HOUSE, HAMPTON, IOWA – 8:11AM

Good morning, Lord.

Good morning, Son. I love you.

I love You, too, Lord. It was a weird night. Do I need to write down that song for my wife I got in the dream?

No, it's not for now. I'll give you more later on that. Start paying attention, though, I'm going to start giving you songs like that.

Wow. Thanks, Lord! Should I keep a recorder around at night?

Yeah, that'd be good.

What's the plan today, Lord?

We're going to do some city-reaching today. Appointments are all arranged. Just listen good and I'll work it all out. Go in humility – and get a hair cut.

Thanks, Lord. I will. Show me where.

Roger's.

OK. Thanks, Lord.

That's it. Get dressed.

OK. Thanks, Lord. I love You.

I love you, too, Son. It's all good. I'm fully on the Throne. Rest.

DIALOGUE WITH GOD – JAN. 16, 2007 – COMFORT INN, ALBUQUERQUE, NM

Good morning, Lord.

Good morning, Son. I love you.

Oh, I love You, too, Lord. Please rule and reign today in every way. Please get me where you want me and control the words of my mouth and the intentions of my heart. Please, Lord? There's no other way to do this without that!

Yes, Son. I will. You're on the right track. Head South.

Do you want us to go pray in the ghost town?

Yes, that would be fine. Wait for a call from Carl, but head South anyway.

Lord, what's that mean? Wait, but head there anyway?

Don't think so much. Just do what you need to do and I'll work out the details.

Yes, Lord. I love you, Lord.

I love you, too. Don't worry about what to say to Carl. I'll give you the words. You're going in ahead of Paul to plow the ground. Like Daniel Nash.

OK, happy to do it, Lord. Even if I don't see Paul. Is that it?

Yeah, that's all for now. Get moving. And brush your teeth.

Yes, Lord. Thanks, Dad! :-)

DIALOGUE WITH GOD – JAN. 18, 2007 – QUALITY INN, GLENDALE, ARIZONA – 9:12AM

Good morning, Lord. I love You.

Good morning, Son. I love you, too.

What's up?

You did really well yesterday. I'm really proud of you.

Thanks, Lord. It was all You. I know that I didn't do anything except get out of Your way.

I know, Son. But you did a really good job of getting out of my way. It was really pretty, wasn't it? That was all VERY important yesterday. He is very important to the kingdom and to what I have for you to do. He was still chained and you freed him. It was really pretty.

Oh, Lord. I didn't free Him, You did!

Yes, I know, but you were there and you were the tool I used and I want you to know that I'm very proud of you and that I appreciate what you did yesterday.

Thanks, Lord. I never quite get that, but thanks.

Don't think so much. I'm trying to show you that, even if someone does something in obedience to God and they're just transparent and it's pure Jesus coming out of them, be gracious to the person and thank them and acknowledge their part in being there and being obedient. I know it's a fine line between building their pride and making it about them and just appreciating their obedience, but try to find that place. It builds their faith and acknowledges their Sonship when you give them a little pat on the head for doing the right thing.

Yeah, but didn't you make them do it anyway? Wasn't it all part of the plan and they really didn't have as many choices as they think they have? Wasn't it going to get done one way or another anyway?

See, that's what I'm talking about. Stop thinking so much. I don't really need your understanding to help me out here. Just acknowledge me in all of your ways and I will direct your paths.

Yes, Lord. Sorry, Lord. Have your way. Please teach me how to properly affirm and encourage people for their part in your master plan. You are sovereign and you know best. I love You.

I love you, too, Son. I made you this way for a reason and it's OK that you have to analyze everything, that's part of what you're for. But sometimes you have to just rest. There are some mysteries you will NEVER be able to get your head around until you're disconnected completely from this world. And I'm not going to do that until the job I have for you is completed.

Yes, Lord. Have your way, but the sooner you take me Home, the better. I hate this place.

I know, Son. But it's not time yet. I'll tell you when it's time.

Thanks, Lord. Please bless Dezi and Carl and all the other folks we've met on this trip. Please bless Paul and Rita that they would have a refreshing and growing time with Carl and Sheila. Please bless Bob and Andrew and Michael and Rick and Darren and Mike. Have your way with them, Lord. Whatever it takes to get them walking in the fullness of all that you have for them, do it. Even if it hurts. Bless Your holy name, Lord. Please be with the folks at home, with Suzanne and Clare and Eddie and Larry and all the others. Please be with Janice and Dena and Kristi and Jimmie and Dave and Jon and all the folks from the furniture store days. Please reveal yourself to them in new ways and give them a bigger and bigger cup of Jesus.

I will, Son. They are all in my hand.

Thanks, Lord. And Lord, please, when you're ready, could you please finish the work that you started in my wife? I know your promises to me about this and I'm willing to wait, but if there is something that I need to pray to loose You in some way to finish the work, please have me pray it. Please don't let me do anything or say anything or desire anything that gets in your way. Finish the work that You started in her. I know that she is a mighty warrior and that she will be a mighty helpmate. Please, Abba, I'd really like that when it's Your time. Thanks for your promises. I'll wait. She's worth it. You're worth it. I know that I'm just walking the same path that You are walking, waiting for a pure, spotless Bride to return to You. And I'm willing, Lord. I said that I would share in Your suffering and I will – at least the portion allotted to me that I can handle. And I'm glad to do it, but it hurts a lot. But I'm not asking you to take the pain away, just to help me walk under the burden and fulfill your purposes.

I love you, Son. It will all be worth it – for you and for me. You'll see. It will be glorious.

Yes, Lord. Thanks, Lord. Have Your way, Lord.

Are you done talking now?

Yes, Lord. I'm sorry, Lord.

This meeting today is important. They're all important, but today is like a lynch pin. It's a key. All the component pieces are coming together. They won't line up quite like you're expecting, but all the pieces are coming together. You're restoring the connectivity of the Body and tying together all the loose pieces. It's just the beginning of what is to come, it's just your little piece of it, but you're a forerunner walking it ahead of them. I sent Chris to help track and organize all the contacts so that you wouldn't lose a single one. Yes, you need to get in touch with Charles in Latvia. The fire is about to spread across the ocean. And you need to get with Moses in Kenya as well. You need to explain the Lampstands to him as clearly as possible. When I tell you to, rewrite the city church book with all that you know now. Quote Nee as an appendix, but not as the main bulk of the book. You have enough now to stand on your own.

Yes, Lord. I will.

Also, send the Dialogues book to Lisa and to Susie and to Sarah for their input. And to Hlena. Keep working on the demons book and incorporate all you know about the shields and the progression we walked through.

OK. Wow, you want me to tell them about the shields, too?

What is there to lose? You already sound completely nuts. ;-)

Yeah, I guess so. Thanks, Lord! You're so funny. Thanks for what you've made me to be. Thanks for this wild adventure. I was reading back through some of the Dialogues and on December 1st you told me December would be amazing and it sure was! That was Pensacola and Alabama and Nashville and Knoxville and Manchester and Holmes County and Patterson, New Jersey and then a race back to Kansas City, then Christmas all together, then back to Branson and then that bombshell revelation on New Year's Eve that almost crushed me and then ending the year fellowshiping with some beautiful folks at a biker church in Arkansas. It really was amazing. Asbury and Berea and UT and picking up Chris Frith and just one miraculous provision and appointment after another. Even the stuff with family was all You. You're an amazing God. You are always true to Your word and yet we're never quite able to get our heads around what You are really up to. Thanks for that. Thanks for the adventure. Thanks for the puzzles and scavenger hunts and brain teasers. Thanks for the surprise presents and hidden treasures and unexpected blessings. You know what I need and I'm never going to lose interest in You! Thanks, Lord.

I love you, too, Son.

Do I need to make copies today? I'm almost out of the laminated "Cup" cards.

Yeah. I'll show you where.

Is there anymore to do on the Dialogue book?

Not for now. Just add this one and save it and send it off. But I did already tell you to add your "Personal Experience with the Holy Spirit" writing to it – don't forget.

Oh, yeah. OK. Thanks, Lord.

That's it. Take care of that this morning before Chris wakes up.

OK, Lord. Thanks. I love You so much. Thanks for adopting me. I can't imagine what my life would be without You.

I love you, too, Son. You're mine and I'm never going to let you go. Now get to work and stop crying.

Yes, Dad.

NEED A SPIRITUAL TUNE-UP?
Lots more available on www.FellowshipoftheMartyrs.com

In the last couple of years I have visited dozens and dozens of different congregations. Sometimes I will fellowship with four or five different congregations on one Sunday. As the Lord has led, I've had the great privilege to get familiar with more pastors of more denominations than most anybody I know. I've seen the good, the bad and the ugly in all the different styles and traditions and doctrines.

The most common thing that I've seen is that almost universally there is a tendency toward putting on programs and ignoring the individual. The bigger the congregation, the greater the tendency. (Read the "Undeniable Axioms" online.) In reality how that manifests always includes a statement about family and concern for the individual but then it's offset and negated by the reality of a structure seemingly engineered to disregard individual needs. However unconscious this may be, the reality is clearly that millions of Christians are NOT walking in the fullness of Christ or worse, walking around with massive oppressions that continue untreated.

There are TONS of people leaving the institutional churches. Millions of them per year. Why? Because they don't feel like their individual needs are getting addressed. They may sit through a good sermon that has some life application, but they don't see or feel the radical transformation that should come as a part of the normal Christian life. Or worse, they have a crisis or a need and nobody in the "church" responds appropriately.

We are NOT honoring God. We are singing and dancing and pretending everything is fine while people are bleeding to death in the pews (not to mention in the streets). Listen to me, God does NOT want you to praise and worship Him while you're ignoring the person sitting next to you who is having a crisis! It DOES NOT bring Him honor for you to raise your hands and tell Him how great He is while you FAIL to act like Him and heal those nearest to you. Heal them – or at least TREAT them – and THEN you can go praising and worshiping and telling Him how great He is. He just DOES NOT want to hear you singing while you're ignoring people that are crying inside! Your prayers are going to bounce off of the brass over your head until you act like Jesus. Just knock it off – or else. He's not going to ignore their cries much longer.

The church should be like the TV show "M*A*S*H". If they're having a party and someone shouts "Choppers!" then the music stops and everybody rushes into action to do triage. That means rapidly identifying and categorizing the wounded based on needs - the bleeding, sucking chest wounds go first, then the broken legs, then the scratches. AFTER everybody is treated and in Recovery – THEN you can go back to your party. But what kind of hospital would you be if you let them bleed to death in the compound because you refuse to stop singing and dancing because you had a schedule to keep?! You planned for this party to take an hour and a half and, by golly, you're going to stay on time no matter what.

Even when Jesus was right in the middle of a great sermon and had them all in the palm of His hand, if a paralyzed guy dropped down out of the roof, Jesus STOPPED TALKING and healed him. THEN He could go on with his sermon - AND everybody was REALLY impressed because of the miracle that had just happened in front of them!

I'm not sure which would be the bigger miracle in some churches, that a paralytic rose and walked away or that the pastor stopped in the middle of a sermon!

The people of God need to be trained up in how to rapidly identify the physical, emotional and spiritual warfare oppressing and killing their brethren and they need to be empowered to go and treat them on the spot. The music needs to stop until EVERYBODY in your camp is bandaged up. "Church" will not be **The Church** until it stops being a show and starts being a hospital, first and foremost. The reason it's not that now is because we abdicated to paid leadership to do all the work for us and they can't possibly keep up. In fairness, many of them got to liking it and now don't trust the Body to help them - so it's a vicious cycle. But it's got to stop. The Body has to learn to care for the Body, whether or not there is a paid staffer. We need the Gifts of Discernment of Spirits and Knowledge operating in force and we need to get back to fulfilling the Great Commission - first by cleaning up our own messes, then by GOING. We can't wait for them to COME – cause when we do, they're not staying, and it's because they're not getting healed (because we're not acting like Jesus).

If any of this stuff has convicted you and you realize you played a part in sustaining a system that hasn't been working or you ever ignored someone that was bleeding because you had your own agenda, now would be a good time to find a quiet place, hit your knees and say you're sorry. Crying helps God know you're serious. You might also want to admit it publicly to the people affected. How are they ever going to learn how to repent really good if somebody doesn't show them? Don't wait for somebody else to do it. It has to start with you.

So what is a Spiritual Tune-Up?

First it's aimed at people that already have Jesus, but the process is the same regardless. A person who is lost could turn their life over and push through lots of the steps right away and be that much more effective sooner. It's just a matter of hunger level and God's sense of your preparedness. The goal is immediate radical transformation, not gradual incremental change culminating in perfection after death. We believe that it's possible that God can heal and deliver and restore and sanctify instantly and we're going to aim for that. If He chooses to take longer, that's fine, but we're going to ASK for maximum change in minimum time - even if it hurts. Which it will.

Typically, we would take a hard look at each of the three factors; Body, Soul and Spirit. Asking the Holy Spirit to help us discern any areas where there is resistance to the will of Christ, we would "scan" through each layer looking for whatever the Lord would choose to reveal. It might be a physical illness that has a spiritual cause, it might be a soulish anger or bitterness or unforgiveness that is blocking Him and bringing down physical curses, or it might be a spiritual problem of diminished capacity for Him because of limitations or "filters" that have been placed on God. It might be a demonic oppression that has really old roots in abuse or addiction or some unresolved, past sin that opened a doorway and allowed legal ground for the enemy. All of these are resolvable within the scope of the power granted to us through Christ. Some can be settled nearly instantly and done away with once and for all. Many people have experienced through this process an immediate lightness at the removal of some old yokes of oppression. Some experience immediate physical changes as healing to their illnesses or removal of addictions comes at the same time. We want to allow God room to act in ANY way He sees fit. We don't want to put Him in a box anymore! We want to believe that He is big enough to conquer anything and that He wants us free. He is big enough, right? And He does want us fully free, right? All the way free? Of everything?

When you do a tune-up on a vehicle, you want to find anything that is keeping it from running at peak efficiency. A misalignment, a missing part, low fluids, bad filters, even burnt out bulbs - anything that needs to be changed or adjusted so that it can be renewed back to the way it was designed. It's all in Romans 12. In thanks for His mercy we offer our bodies as living sacrifices - holy, pleasing and acceptable - that is our spiritual act of worship.

So first, we have to be willing to offer our Body - the vehicle, and all that it holds - as a sacrifice. We need to be willing and we need to commit to hold NOTHING back. That verse does NOT say we offer half of our body as a living sacrifice – or even 90%. The whole thing needs to go on the altar. ALL means ALL.

Before we can do anything else, we need it to be a holy, pleasing and acceptable sacrifice. And since our sinfulness screams against our holiness, and our own nature confirms it, it's clear that only by the atoning Blood of Jesus is there any chance that we can be a pleasing and acceptable sacrifice. So before any tune-up is going to do any good, we need to scrub the whole thing down with the Blood of Jesus. You have to have acknowledged your needfulness for the Blood and asked Him to wash you clean of every sin.

Said less religiously, you have to tell Jesus you're sorry for all the bad stuff you let in and you have to really mean it - and you have to believe that His sacrifice on the cross was sufficient to wipe you clean. This IS NOT an acknowledgment that Jesus existed or that He was the Son of God - even the demons believe that. This is not a statement you repeat after someone else so that you can join a church. This is a full-on commitment to humble yourself before Him and to give yourself over to Him so that He can be in charge from now on. That you would like to bow down and let Him be who He is - Master, King, Commander, Ruler, Lord - in your life from now on. Fear of the Lord is the beginning of wisdom. Way too many churches are making it way too easy - and the result is sick, powerless, shackled, unwise people in the pews.

OK, NOW you're an acceptable sacrifice. So what's next? Get up on the altar and shut up. You don't need to figure out your personal purpose. You don't need 40 days to figure out what YOU can do for God. You're the sacrifice! Get cleaned off, climb up on the altar and lay there naked. By doing this, by really doing this, really laying there naked – fully exposed and willing to accept anything that comes – you are most definitely NOT conforming to the "world".

When He's good and ready, He'll move on to the next step. Which is that He will take a big sword and begin to hack chunks of your head off and put His head on. It's painful at times and folks around you may not understand what's happening during that strange in-between time while you're trying to figure it all out and get the pieces of your head and His head to get on the same frequency. But eventually, unless you panic and jump off the altar, He will hack off all the bits that stand in His way and then you'll have the mind of Christ. He will have transformed you by the renewing of your mind. RE-newed, that is, back the way it was supposed to be when it was new. Back the way He designed it. Back in His image. Rebooted and set back to the defaults the way it was before you mangled it up and the "world's" viruses corrupted it. Read Matt. 18:1-4, Mark 10:15. He wants faith like a child.

Then and ONLY then will you know what is the pleasing, perfect will of God. And then you can go do it. It's not just so you can bask in the knowledge of what He wants, it's so you can OBEY. GO - reach, heal, save, deliver, free the captives. Do the stuff that's on HIS heart - and now that your mind is renewed and you know what is His will, it should be a lot easier. You probably won't need a committee or demographic studies or anything. If you didn't hold anything back, by this point, you're probably hearing Him really well and you don't really need any Man (or group of them) to tell you what God wants for you. And I can tell you this, it's going to cost you everything. But you won't miss any of it. Besides, none of it was yours anyway. But you better count the cost, because this is a hard walk. Job, family, money, comforts, control - all could be taken away or destroyed. If you pray to be like Jesus and He answers it, you'll be hated and ridiculed by the world. Guaranteed.

Sound like something you want to try? If you're lukewarm, it might just be better for you to stay where you are than to taste the goodness of God and then turn your back on it. Persecution is going to come with every step that gets you closer to walking in the fullness of Christ. But if you don't care what it costs and you're still willing, we can proceed.

Jesus affirmed repeatedly that these two commandments are the greatest. That if you understand and implement these, you have pretty well grasped the Kingdom of God.

Here it is quoted in three different Gospels: (Please go read them in context)

> Mat 22:37-40 *Jesus said unto him, Thou shalt love the Lord thy God with all thy heart, and with all thy soul, and with all thy mind. This is the first and great commandment. And the second [is] like unto it, Thou shalt love thy neighbour as thyself. On these two commandments hang all the law and the prophets.*

Mar 12:30-31 *And thou shalt love the Lord thy God with all thy heart, and with all thy soul, and with all thy mind, and with all thy strength: this [is] the first commandment. And the second [is] like, [namely] this, Thou shalt love thy neighbour as thyself. There is none other commandment greater than these.*

Luke 10:27-28 *And he answering said, Thou shalt love the Lord thy God with all thy heart, and with all thy soul, and with all thy strength, and with all thy mind; and thy neighbour as thyself. And he (Jesus) said unto him, Thou hast answered right: this do, and thou shalt live.*

So, it boils down to this - the most important commandment, the most central task before us as individuals and as the Church, is to love God with every component of our being - Mind, Soul and Heart and to do it with all of our Strength. How are you doing with that? That's what we're going to find out. If you haven't got that one down, the second commandment - loving your neighbor as yourself - is going to be a pale imitation of what it should be. You will love them to the degree you love God. If you're clearly not loving your neighbor as you should, it's a pretty good indication that you're not loving the Lord your God with all your mind and soul and heart and strength. If you're loving your neighbor with 10% of your strength, then you're probably loving God with 10%. It's like a math equation, just plug in the percentage.

$$\text{Submission to God} \times \text{quantity}N = \text{manifestation of Love for Neighbor} \times \text{quantity}N$$

If they will know us by our love and we're not evidencing much love for each other (especially inside the Church) and for those in need, then we must not be very submitted to God. What other conclusion can you come to? Fear of the Lord is the beginning of wisdom. I know it stings a little, but try to embrace it. (Try Psalms 141:5-6)

Paul says this in 1 Thessalonians 5:23:

"And the very God of peace sanctify you wholly; and [I pray God] your whole spirit and soul and body be preserved blameless unto the coming of our Lord Jesus Christ."

We are made of these three. Body, Soul and Spirit. and they are to all be in submission to Christ. All means ALL! Let's try one of those verses again:

Mar 12:30-31 *And thou shalt love the Lord thy God with ALL thy heart, and with ALL thy soul, and with ALL thy mind, and with ALL thy strength: this [is] the first commandment. And the second [is] like, [namely] this, Thou shalt love thy neighbour as thyself. There is none other commandment greater than these.*

Before we go any further, now would be a good time for the warning label.

WARNING! WARNING!
DANGER! DANGER!
Proceed at your own risk!

We will NOT be responsible for ANYTHING that happens from here forward. You have been warned.

We want you to be ABSOLUTELY clear that this is <u>FOR</u> <u>SURE</u>, <u>NO DOUBT ABOUT IT</u> going to hurt <u>A LOT</u>.

You can drive 20 miles an hour and you probably won't get hurt too badly in an accident. If you drive 200 miles an hour and you make a mistake, it's going to get really ugly.

This IS <u>NOT</u> for sissies!

If you have ANY desire in you to slow down, DO IT NOW! DO NOT GO THIS WAY!! DO NOT take our advice on this stuff!! It will totally transform your life and things you love will be ripped from you. Nothing – <u>NOTHING</u> – that you have will be your own any more. So He can rebuild you His way, God will IMMEDIATELY start yanking chunks out of you. Probably stuff you really liked. The fire will get VERY hot!

If you even so much as TRY to do this in your own power, you're gonna be toast!

<u>ONLY Jesus in you can get you through this.</u>

Last chance. Get out now! ALL the darkness WILL come for you! We've seen it over and over. We <u>ARE</u> <u>NOT</u> kidding around! You BETTER mean it! We're serious.

We love you very much. We want to see you refined and purified and REALLY dangerous to the enemy, but we want you to be <u>FULLY</u> <u>READY</u> before you pull into the <u>Fast</u> <u>Lane</u>!

Still here? Great!

Now go back and reread the warning again.

We're to work out our salvation with fear and trembling. He's serious.

OK? Back again?

Good. Let's proceed.

SO WHICH PART OF <u>ALL</u> DON'T YOU UNDERSTAND?!

Where do you think you have an option to love Him "some"? Remember this old song? Have you really looked at it? How many times have you sung it and not really meant it? I know I did for years!

I Surrender All
by Judson W. Van DeVenter, 1896:

ALL to Jesus, I surrender; **ALL** to Him I freely give; I will **EVER** love and trust Him, In His presence **DAILY** live.

I surrender **ALL**, I surrender **ALL**, **ALL** to Thee, my blessed Savior, I surrender **ALL**.

ALL to Jesus I surrender; Humbly at His feet I bow, Worldly pleasures **ALL** forsaken; Take me, Jesus, take me now.

I surrender **ALL**, I surrender **ALL**, **ALL** to Thee, my blessed Savior, I surrender **ALL**.

ALL to Jesus, I surrender; Make me, Savior, **WHOLLY** Thine; Let me feel the Holy Spirit, Truly know that Thou art mine.

I surrender **ALL**, I surrender **ALL**, **ALL** to Thee, my blessed Savior, I surrender **ALL**.

ALL to Jesus, I surrender; Lord, I give myself to Thee;
FILL me with Thy love and power; Let Thy blessing fall on me.

I surrender **ALL**, I surrender **ALL**, **ALL** to Thee, my blessed Savior, I surrender **ALL**.

ALL to Jesus I surrender; **NOW** I feel the sacred flame.
O the joy of **FULL** salvation! Glory, glory, to His Name!

I surrender **ALL**, I surrender **ALL**, **ALL** to Thee, my blessed Savior, I surrender **ALL**.

A whole lot of us have been singing that but really meaning, "I surrender SOME." Or maybe, "I surrender more than that guy over there." There are certainly lots of leaders in the churches that aren't meaning it! Very few people really mean ALL. And yet that is the specific and direct command of God and affirmed three times by Jesus Himself as the most critical commandment of all. More than any doctrinal statement or theological construct or interpretation, we must do THAT. First and foremost in the Christian walk MUST BE a love for God that holds back nothing. Anything less means that you have missed the mark. Can there be <u>any</u> other interpretation? Where does the Bible say, "Invite Jesus into your heart and then do whatever you want."? Where does it say that you can give Him SOME and He won't mind. It says that God is a jealous God (Exodus 25:5, Exodus 34:14, Deuteronomy 4:24; Deuteronomy 5:9; Deuteronomy 6:15; Joshua 24:19; Nahum 1:2; and elsewhere!). In fact, it says the Holy Spirit in us envies intensely when we give ourselves over to the world (James 4:4-5).

This is hard stuff, and not what you may be used to hearing, but I don't see how you can find any other interpretation. We're to work out our salvation with fear and trembling. How much fear and trembling do you have if you go down the aisle at youth camp in 8th grade and accept Jesus into your heart and you're all done? The "Narrow Path" has just GOT to be more narrow than that! In fact, I believe the VAST majority of church goers are not going to heaven at all. I believe we've been lied to for years about what it is that God really expects of us. The New Testament would be VERY short indeed if the path to heaven was as simple as, "Repeat this prayer after me ..." What's the point of all the rest of it, if that's all it takes?

If you're still with me, the rest of this is going to be about helping you identify ANY areas of Body, Soul or Spirit that may yet be unsubmitted to God – and doing whatever is necessary to bring them into full obedience with Christ. Bite down on something, this might hurt a little.

The enemy is going to try everything possible to keep you from walking this out. The darkness DOES NOT want to lose a single inch of ground! So let's pray this first:

> *Lord, don't let the enemy keep me from this. Don't let the enemy distract me or confuse me. Give me wisdom, Godly wisdom and as much of it as You think I can handle. Speak to me clearly and I'll follow. Please bind up anything in me or around me that would try to mess with me during this time. In the Name of Jesus. Amen.*

I like pictures, so let's start with this:

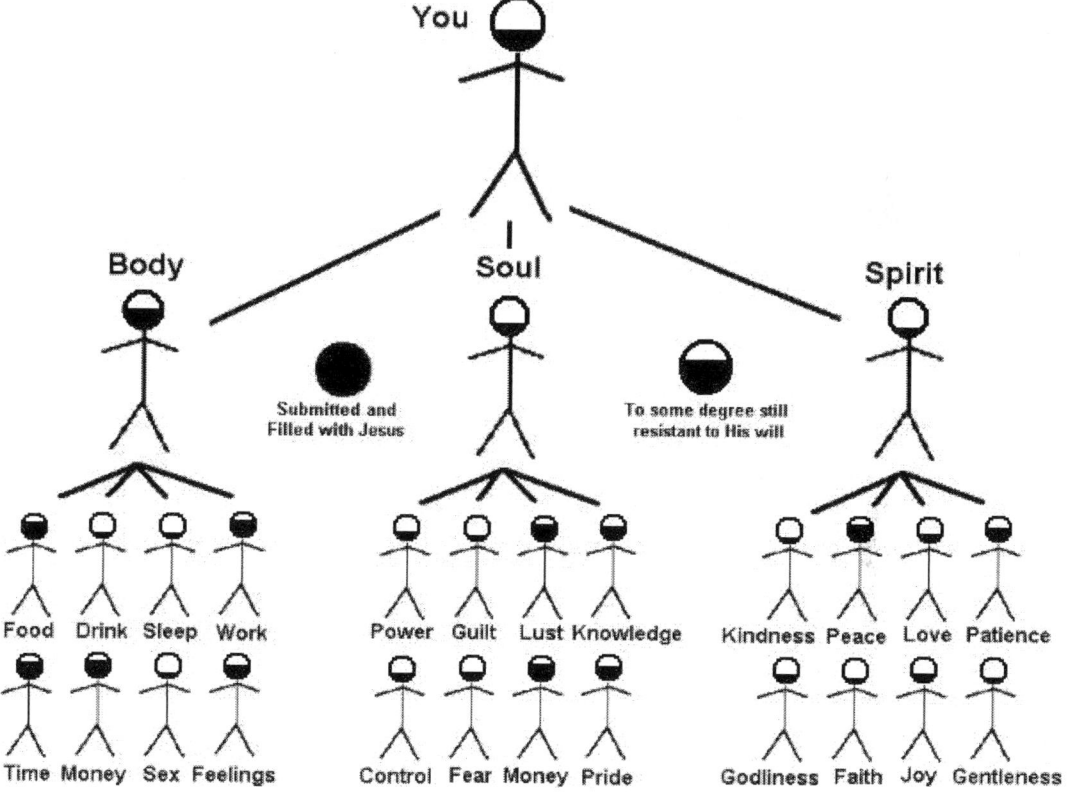

Holiness means EVERY piece of you is in obedience with Christ. Not just that you've made a "profession" of faith, but that you submit ALL of you to be bent to His will. With no reservation or evasion – nothing is off-limits to His control.

If there are parts of you that are not submitted then you ARE NOT "filled" with the Holy Spirit. Stop telling people you've "Spirit-filled" if you're only half-full. Unless EVERY piece of you has been Baptized in the Holy Spirit and with Fire, you're not all the way full. They have to have been crucified so that they can raise with Him in glory.

This is a very simple graphic, not at all meant to be thorough or all-inclusive. Let the Holy Spirit show you all the areas in your life that need addressing. I'm sure He wants to! For now, we're just going to hit a few so you can see how this works. If you're not hearing very well from God on what might be unsubmitted, just ask someone close to you – I'm sure they'll tell you the parts that don't look like Jesus. Spouses are good for that!

If we had lots of people in the churches with the gift of discernment of spirits, you could go to one of them and ask them what's messing with you and they could just tell you and help get it off. If you know somebody like that, by all means, get them in on this. But don't take ANYBODY'S word for anything. Check everything with God. Even if you can't normally hear God very well, I'm just SURE He wants to talk to you about THIS stuff! So you should be expecting that, as it relates to areas of your life that are unsubmitted, you're going to hear Him really well.

I suspect He's been waiting so long for you to ask Him what the problem is that as soon as you ask you're going to get LOTS of feedback. It may not be an audible thing, but somebody or some situation or a cloud or a little kid or a song on the radio or SOMETHING is going to be used to get through to you and show you the problem. Just EXPECT an answer and listen for it. And when He tells you what the problem is – REPENT! Turn from it and don't go back.

Body

We are all jars of clay, vessels to hold His glory, cups of one sort or another. We are humble earthen vessels that are flawed and cracked in many ways and yet He pours His glory into us. We become the temple of His Spirit and He lives in us! Isn't that cool!!

Anyway, it's important first to understand that the Word commands us repeatedly to "be filled with the Spirit" and in the tense it uses it means "to be being filled" - a constant in-filling, a constant effort to keep our cups topped off. (The graphics here are from the full article "Fill My Cup, Lord." on the website – FellowshipOfTheMartyrs.com)

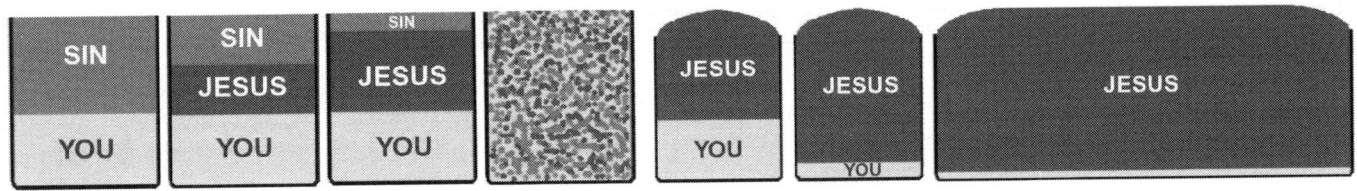

There are basically these options:
- You have NO JESUS.
- You have some JESUS and lots of SIN.
- You have more JESUS and a little SIN.
- You're all shook up by the World and "life" and can't figure out what's what.
- You're washed clean, but there's too much YOU.
- JESUS has killed off lots of YOU so He can increase and YOU can decrease.
- You've been a good steward, so He gave you a bigger cup and lots more JESUS.

And it's not a one-time thing. He's our Daily Bread, so you can move from one to the other fairly fluidly, even in the midst of one day. It's not a one-time thing just cause you went down the aisle and got "filled with the Spirit" one day. If you're not constantly STAYING FULL then you're going to drain off - or get lukewarm and stale. Over and over we're commanded to be full and to stay full – or to "be being filled".*

And there's no point at which you shouldn't be striving for a bigger cup. We need Him in increasing measure every day to keep from being ineffective and unproductive (II Peter 1:8). You get a bigger cup by pouring yourself out on those in need, then getting refilled again.

* (Acts 2:4 *And they were all **filled** with the Holy Ghost, and began to speak with other tongues, as the Spirit gave them utterance.* Ephesians 3:19 *And to know the love of Christ, which passeth knowledge, that ye might be **filled** with all the fulness of God.* Colossians 1:9 *For this cause we also, since the day we heard [it], do not cease to pray for you, and to desire that ye might be **filled** with the knowledge of his will in all wisdom and spiritual understanding;* Ephesians 5:8 *And be not drunk with wine, wherein is excess; but be **filled** with the Spirit;* Philippians 1:11 *Being **filled** with the fruits of righteousness, which are by Jesus Christ, unto the glory and praise of God.* For more on this, read the book, "Rain Down NOW, Lord!" available free on the website.)

The Greek word used repeatedly for "filled" is "pleroo" (Strong's #4137). Here is Strong's definition of it:

1) to make full, to fill up, i.e. to fill to the full

- **a)** to cause to abound, to furnish or supply liberally
    - **1)** I abound, I am liberally supplied

2) to render full, i.e. to complete

- **a)** to fill to the top: so that nothing shall be wanting to full measure, fill to the brim
- **b)** to consummate: a number
    - **1)** to make complete in every particular, to render perfect
    - **2)** to carry through to the end, to accomplish, carry out, (some undertaking)
- **c)** to carry into effect, bring to realisation, realise
    - **1)** of matters of duty: to perform, execute
    - **2)** of sayings, promises, prophecies, to bring to pass, ratify, accomplish
    - **3)** to fulfil, i.e. to cause God's will (as made known in the law) to be obeyed as it should be, and God's promises (given through the prophets) to receive fulfilment

(Thayer's Lexicon also has a lot to say. Do a search for "filled" on www.BlueLetterBible.com and see.)

The point is, Jesus wants us FULL and He knows that only HE can do it. We're all going to be full of SOMETHING. If our bodies are the temple of God and He lives in us, do you really want Him sharing space with that icky stuff? Shouldn't you be purified and cleansed of all unrighteousness so that He can reign supreme? It says "the prayers of a righteous man availeth much" - so I guess the prayers of a kind-of righteous man availeth practically nothing. Why is HE going to listen to YOU when you ask for something, when YOU won't listen to HIM about getting the red stuff out (and the stinky yellow stuff)? Proverbs 25:26 says: *"Like a muddied spring or a polluted well is a righteous man who gives way to the wicked."* That sounds to me like a cup that should be clean, but isn't.

Areas of direct disobedience or unresolved pain result in a draining off of that with which we are filled. Sometimes we have a really hard time keeping our cup full because we have a big crack in our cup caused by an unforgiveness or a bitterness or a fundamental character flaw, and so we drain out almost as soon as we get filled. Sometimes we can't ever get all the way full because of the goo we refuse to clean out that's taking up too much space in our cup. Really entrenched red stuff keeps us from being able to be filled to capacity. Sometimes there are physical oppressions and sicknesses that have resulted from spiritual problems. These, too, need addressing through the power of Jesus. More on all that later.

So, as it relates to the Body, let's start with this:

- Is God telling you to do something with FOOD other than what you are doing? If yes, why won't you obey?
- Is God telling you to do something with DRINK other than what you are doing? If yes, why won't you obey?
- Is God telling you to do something with WORK other than what you are doing? If yes, why won't you obey?
- Is God telling you to do something with MONEY other than what you are doing? If yes, why won't you obey?
- Is God telling you to do something with SEX other than what you are doing? If yes, why won't you obey?
- Is God telling you to do something with TIME other than what you are doing? If yes, why won't you obey?
- Is God telling you to do something with your TONGUE other than what you're doing? If yes, why won't you obey?

Get the idea? Odds are pretty good that if the Holy Spirit is convicting you of something and you're not obeying, it's because you've given the enemy room in your heart or because your own soulish nature just wants to rebel. Either way, it's not really giving ALL and you need to do something about it. Stop thinking that He's just going to overlook it and cut you some slack. He REALLY doesn't like being in there with that stuff and He's a really big God. More fear of the Lord would be good. You might want to pray for that. Crying is good, too.

If the Holy Spirit is NOT convicting you of any of that stuff, then either you are not listening and you've got a giant pride problem blocking your hearing OR the Holy Spirit has already beaten you into submission on all those levels. I've met both kinds. Just in case, now would be a good time to pray sincerely and ask the Lord to show you ANYTHING that displeases Him or any area of rebellion as it relates to your Body.

Ok, OK!! You caught me, so what do I do about it?

Well, the first thing is to tell God you're really sorry. That would be good. He's been waiting a long time to hear that. And if you've been saying it before but then going back like a dog to his own vomit, then He's probably not going to take your apology very seriously until you start sticking by your commitments to Him.

If you've tried to turn away from stuff and haven't been able to, it's probably because you're doing too much of the fighting in your own power - because you've tried to force obedience with the YOU in your cup. That just puts more and more pressure on you and more and more guilt when you fall. Jesus lives inside of you and HE is not addicted to cigarettes or donuts or porn or work or anything. He has faced down every failing of Man and beaten it. If you will get out of the way and let HIM fight your battles, it will be much easier. Much. We'll cover that more later since it applies to all three of these components.

You need to be clear that SIN means missing the mark. Whether it's murder or disbelief, it's sin and it keeps you from walking in the FULLNESS of Christ. You will not reach your maximum potential in Him if you remain unsubmitted in some areas – ANY areas. Jesus said, if you LOVE Him, you will OBEY Him. If you're not obeying Him 100%, then you must not love Him 100%. And 90% isn't going to cut it! He wants ALL – and ALL means ALL.

Soul

Let's try this same process again:

Is God telling you to do something with ANGER other than what you are doing? If yes, why won't you obey?

What about Guilt, Lust, Control, Fear, Money, Pride, Jealousy, Lying, Disbelief, Self-pity, Power, Bitterness, Unforgiveness, Gluttony, Idolatry, Rebellion or others? Got any of those?

Simplified substantially, the soul is the mind - our emotions, our mental state, our rationalizations and reactions internally to the world around us. It is what makes us distinctly us. This, too, needs to be brought fully into submission with God.

In a sense, you could see it like this:

Body is where Sin manifests into the physical realm.

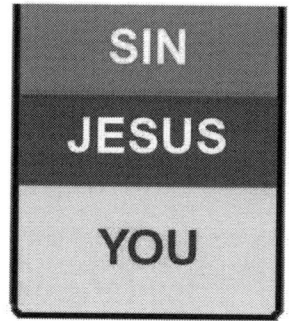

Our "God-shaped void" is empty until filled with His Spirit. Then He can stand in the gap and take over as you get out of the way.

Soul/Mind is where Sin begins and gets invited in. Can still be Sin even if it doesn't manifest, just by "dwelling." Our fallen nature always tries to open doors to Sin.

The yellow stuff (YOU) is our soulish nature and it's not that much better than the red stuff (SIN). In fact, the Blood of Jesus washes away all of our sins in an instant when we ask for forgiveness, but if we don't fill the gap with Jesus (and keep it full), the badness will just jump back into the vacuum. It's our yellow stuff that invited all the red stuff! The Blood of Jesus is sufficient to heal us, but it's not the same process as with the red stuff. The Word says we're to crucify pieces of us so that Christ in us can live. We're to carry our cross daily. Well, that's about denying ourselves pleasures that might be red stuff, but it's also about watching chunks of Self die so Christ can increase and YOU can decrease. And I can tell you from LOTS of experience with this - getting the red stuff (SIN) out is A LOT easier than getting all the yellow stuff out that displeases Him! One is about behavior and the other is about our nature. Habits are far easier to change than character. Beating the yellow stuff into submission is the crucifying ourselves part.

No physical trial you will ever go through - not climbing Mount Everest in winter, not sawing your own arm off with a pocket knife, not doing a marathon on your knees - will EVER be as hard as getting your tongue and your mind beaten into submission. THAT is the great battle in our lives and the difficulty is evidenced by how really rare it is to find someone that has accomplished any substantial measure of success in that! In fact, I'm convinced the only way to do it effectively is to let Jesus do it. We can fake it for awhile in our own power, but all we've done is suppress it. Only Jesus can terminate it once and for all.

In fact, it's not possible to walk in holiness at all without the Holy Spirit doing it. You can't use the yellow stuff to beat down the yellow stuff. That just won't work. Jesus is our righteousness and He alone is worthy and holy and capable of making us like Him. We can't get to be like Jesus in our own power. We have to be clothed in Christ, we have to run into Him who is our strong tower. We have to be dead so that Christ in us can live. And not just a little dead either - ALL of those component pieces have to die. Maybe this will help you figure out which is which.

Component Pieces of YOU - Which is Which?

[stick figures] **Fully Dead and Submitted**

List: _____

[stick figures] **Partially Dead But Dying Quickly**

List: _____

[stick figures] **Partially Dead But Stubborn**

List: _____

[stick figures] **Unwilling To Die Even A Little**

List: _____

(Full size version of the graphics are at www.FellowshipOfTheMartyrs.com)

He doesn't want to purge you of ALL the yellow stuff, that would eliminate you completely and He kind of likes parts of you. Once I asked Him what parts of me He wanted to keep and He said, "Basically everything from before about six years old." Just the faith like a child parts. That thing in David that made him fearlessly go out to face Goliath because he just KNEW His Dad was bigger and tougher than THAT guy's Dad!

There's a lot more to be said, but you'll need to pray through this yourself and ask God to show you very clearly all the areas in which you are partially or completely unsubmitted. I know it's a prayer He wants you to pray, so I KNOW He will answer it and show you stuff. Then it's up to you to lay it down.

I find that this kind of prayer helps a lot and gets nearly instant results - if you have the guts to pray it:

(If you forgot, go back and read the Warning first!)

Dear Lord, I'm really sorry for all the sin that I should have never let in. I'm sorry for all the old stuff that I've let take root and boss me around. Please purge me of all unrighteousness right now through the power of Your Blood. I stand in faith, knowing that Your Blood is sufficient to cleanse me of all unrighteousness. Please show me ANY area of my life that displeases You –

anything that stands in the way between us and keeps me from being able to walk in the fullness of all that you have for me. Whatever it is, I don't care how much I like it, I don't care how long it's been there, I don't care how much it hurts, it's got to go RIGHT NOW in the Name of Jesus. So Lord, rip it, tear it, burn it, shred it, crucify it – whatever it takes. If I won't lay it down, rip it from my grasp. I don't care how much it hurts, I trust You. Do whatever it takes, but do it RIGHT NOW. I won't flinch and I won't try to hop out of Your refining fire when it comes. Dial the heat up. I'm going to stand. Give me the strength to stand. Please hold my hand. I'm going to really need You. Thanks, Lord. You're the best Dad ever and I trust You. Please burn it all off and don't stop no matter how much I whine. In the Name of Jesus, Amen.

Hear me – your growth in Christ is <u>directly</u> <u>proportional</u> to your willingness to seek out and embrace His refining fire. When He is pounding on you and life seems horrible, if you will go to Him and find out what He's trying to teach you, embrace it, learn from it and thank Him for it - then maybe you can move on. If you whine and complain and keep asking Him to turn down the flames because it's too hot, it shows a lack of trust that He knows what He's doing and it just slows down the whole process. How long is it going to take to cook a turkey in an oven set at 50 degrees? How long if it's set at 450? That's the difference between Christians in China and India and those in America. We have our ovens set at 50 degrees and they have their's on full blast. Persecution dials up the heat really fast – and results in explosive growth in Christ (and a sifting of those who mean it and those who don't).

So don't be such a sissy. Jump in the fire and learn to like it. Is He God or isn't He? Will He protect you or won't He? Are His promises good or aren't they? Buck up, ya big weenie. Go kill some yellow stuff.

Spirit

OK, so we got the red stuff out (for today) and we begged Him to kill the yellow stuff. So you probably have a void in the top of your cup now. What are you going to do? If you leave it like that the enemy, who ranges to and fro like a hungry lion, will try to jump in there right away and mess with you again. You've got to get your cup full of Jesus and keep it that way. And not just full to 100%, full to overflowing – up and over, mounded up on top.

So do you know how? Well, you can read your Bible. You can listen to worship music. You can pray. You can just spend time at the feet of Jesus before the throne of God. Whatever is the best way you have found to drink in Jesus. But be careful that you're not DOING to get filled. That just means that you're trying to get more blue stuff by engaging the yellow stuff. That's a long uphill battle and can border on legalism. What it ends up doing is inviting in the red stuff again in the form of guilt, condemnation, self-righteousness, pride or some other nasty thing.

Maybe there's a better way. What does the Word of God say about this?

> John 7:38 says: *"He who believes in Me, as the Scripture said, 'From his innermost being will flow rivers of living water.' "*

> John 4:10 says: *Jesus answered and said unto her, If thou knewest the gift of God, and who it is that saith to thee, Give me to drink; thou wouldest have asked of him, and he would have given thee living water.*

Rev. 7:17 says: *For the Lamb which is in the midst of the throne shall feed them, and shall lead them unto living fountains of waters: and God shall wipe away all tears from their eyes.*

Here's a couple of Old Testament reference so you know God doesn't change:

Jeremiah 17:13 – *O LORD, the hope of Israel, all that forsake thee shall be ashamed, [and] they that depart from me shall be written in the earth, because they have forsaken the LORD, the fountain of living waters.*

Jeremiah 2:13 – *For my people have committed two evils; they have forsaken me the fountain of living waters, [and] hewed them out cisterns, broken cisterns, that can hold no water.*

In that last one we see that they committed two evils, they didn't drink of the living waters and they had containers with cracks in them. (A cistern is just a really big cup.) In fact, they made their own cisterns to store up water because they didn't trust in God's unending supply from the fountain. And the result was they had neither – AND they made God mad!

It sure seems to me like those fountains of living water are the Holy Spirit. It says Jesus is the "Fountain in the House of David" (Zech 13.1) The Holy Spirit is that blue stuff that fills us and displaces all the other stuff. It would be great if He would just shove everything out of the way, but for some reason we're involved and we have to participate in the process – or at least be willing and ask Him to do it.

This being true (I hope you agree), then we don't need to DO anything to fill our cup. We just have to believe that Jesus wants our cup full, that He promised that springs of living water would flow up from INSIDE of us and then just turn on the tap. We just need to ask Him to fill us in whatever way HE wants to fill us and teach us how to keep it that way. Remember; trust the Lord your God with ALL your heart, lean NOT on your OWN understanding, but in ALL your ways acknowledge HIM and HE will direct your paths. (Prov. 3:5-6)

I think our job as a church is to find those who are poor in spirit – those whose cups are running low – and share with them. Pour ourselves out into them so that they can be filled. Not with our yellow stuff! God forbid! But from the abundance of the riches that have been given to us that we would share – of or wealth, of our physical energy/strength/time AND of the fountain of living water that is inside of us.

Haven't you ever been around somebody that, just being in the same room with them or getting a hug, made your spirit feel full? I bet they had a cup that was overflowing – or they deliberately and selflessly poured themselves out on you. They may not have known that's what they were doing or been able to explain it that way, they just knew that they had Joy and Peace and that you needed some, so they shared.

The Lord gave me a vision once of how the church should operate and it looks a pyramid of champagne glasses at a wedding where they pour in the top one and as it overflows, the glass below gets filled and overflows and so it continues all the way down. Those who have the biggest cup of Jesus should be constantly pouring themselves out onto others and teaching them how to keep it going.

Shouldn't church be a filling station? How often do you go and leave feeling just as empty as when you got there? Some churches are really great filling stations and you can leave FULL of Jesus – but you can't make it past Monday afternoon without running out again. That's because we think we have to go to a building to get our cups full. The Word of God doesn't say anything like that. The Word of God says rivers of living water will flow up from INSIDE of US. We have an endless supply! And WE are supposed to be the filling station for those that don't know how to tap into it. It's not about the building or the pastor or nice music that gets us in the mood – every Christian has access to the river of God! Isn't that COOL!! So, stick a straw in and suck! Better yet, just dive in.

Below we're going to talk more about all the things you can be filled with, why you need to help fill others and how to get full and make sure you stay full. I know this may sound weird, but it's all in the Bible. No question about it. We're supposed to perceive things in the spirit, not with our natural mind. This is NOT the "real" world – this is not our home. We are spiritual beings and we need to get a lot more familiar with what's happening in the spirit. That's where the war is and that's where our hope comes from.

> I Corinthians 2:14 - *But the natural man receiveth not the things of the Spirit of God: for they are foolishness unto him: neither can he know them, because they are **spiritually** discerned.*
>
> Romans 8:6 - *For to be carnally minded [is] death; but to be spiritually minded is life and peace.*

COMMUNICATIONS – HOTLINE TO HEADQUARTERS

So, we got the red stuff out, we're getting more yellow stuff out, we learned how to get more blue stuff, now what? Well, now it's time to get your filters unclogged so you can hear God really well and HE can direct ALL your paths. This works better as a question and answer thing. Ready?

First, what exactly are we talking about? Does God really speak to people today?

Yes. In a whole bunch of ways from a gentle nudge, to instruction through the Word, to using other people and circumstances to speak to you, to sending dreams and visions (or angels) – and/or even conversing directly with you.

You can hear God and converse with Him?! You're kidding, right?

Not kidding. You can absolutely talk to God and He'll talk back. There are millions of people all over the world that rely on God for constant daily instruction on all sorts of things. But, there's a difference between hearing God audibly (with your natural ears, outside of your own head) and hearing the inner "still, small voice". It's pretty rare for God to speak to people audibly (like thunder), but there are plenty of folks out there that say they've heard Him – and the evidence is that once they did, it changed them forever! Many of the house churches in China are under such persecution that they can't set a regular time for meeting or even tell each other when the meeting will be – they all just pray independently and God Himself sets the time and place and tells each to be there. I've experienced that kind of coordination myself and hear Him speak to me all the time. This is totally for real and the birthright of every believer!

Wait ... people hear the God of the Universe tell them stuff? Like what tie to wear and whether to turn left or right? What job to take? What to have for dinner? Not just big stuff?

Sure. The Bible says, "In all your ways acknowledge Him and He will direct your paths." (Prov. 3:5-6) What do you think "ALL your ways" means? And how is He going to direct you if you can't hear Him?

But my pastor said God doesn't talk to people like that!

Hmmm. Well, God used to talk to people all the time in the Bible. Wonder when He stopped? Did He say He was going to stop? Isn't He the same yesterday, today and forever? If anything, once the Holy Spirit came in Acts 2, there were LOTS more people talking to God directly! Never mind the MILLIONS of people all over the world who you have to conclude are thoroughly and certifiably nuts – including many of the most effective leaders of the church. In order to sustain that argument you have all kinds of logic problems.

Consider this;

IF God used to talk to people but doesn't now, **THEN** we must not need to hear from Him anymore. Can that be? By all measures we're worse off than ever. If there is a war between Good and Evil, we're losing pretty badly right now and really desperately need to be getting commands directly from Headquarters, not from flawed man-made sources and tradition-soaked interpretations of Scripture!

IF there is a battle between Good and Evil, **THEN** who would benefit most if the people on the "Good" side were told they couldn't ACTUALLY talk to their Commander in Chief? Now, you know the Evil side is absolutely clear to EVERYONE that if you try to talk to THEIR leadership you WILL get an answer REAL fast! Even Christians are afraid to mess with Ouija boards and call on the names of demons because somewhere inside they believe something VERY real will show up almost instantly. But at the same time, the forces of darkness want us to buy that OUR God is mute! Doesn't that sound like something the snake would say in the Garden? Despite hundreds of examples in the Bible that He is available and accessible all the time, we have too often bought the lie that God is unwilling or unable to actually talk to His children. It's a lie from the pit and we've bought into it for too long.

IF we receive the Holy Spirit when we are saved, **THEN** 1/3 of the Godhead is living INSIDE of us all the time! (I John 4:13-17) But He doesn't have anything to say?! He's not interested in our daily activities? God's not big enough to know what we should have for lunch? He knows the hairs on our head and monitors our every coming and going, but has no opinion about it or desire to give us advice? What kind of Father is that?! **IF** we're dead and it's Christ in us that lives, **THEN** shouldn't HE be running the show? (Romans 7:4-6)

The most common argument I hear is that when the Bible was done being written then "that which was perfect has come and that which was in part was done away" (I Corin. 13:10) so we don't need to talk to God anymore. The argument is that I Corinthians 12 talks about tongues and prophecy and then chapter 13 tells about the way it SHOULD be when the perfect is come so you should do away with all that. But they don't seem to notice that then chapter 14 starts with Paul urging them to seek the gift of prophecy! Said another way, I think "when that which is perfect is come" refers to Jesus returning, NOT the Bible being completed.

IF the Bible is what's being referred to there, **THEN** why hasn't knowledge ceased? **IF** it's the "perfect" thing mentioned there, **THEN** nothing could stand against it. **IF** the Bible is perfect, **THEN** could somebody tell me which version is flawless? And **IF** none of them are because we don't have the original manuscripts anymore, **THEN** something DID stand against it! **IF** the perfect is come, **THEN** why do we have 37,000 denominations and we seem to be losing the battle with the darkness? There are just big giant logic problems with that argument – not to mention the personal experience of millions of reasonable, Jesus-lovers all over the world.

But my pastor says even HE doesn't hear God conversationally like that!

OK, well, you see, Matthew 18:18 says that, "what you bind on earth will be bound in heaven and what you loose on earth will be loosed in heaven." It goes on to say that if two of you on earth agree about anything you ask for, it will be done for you by the Father in heaven. (v. 19) So, could it be that we have whole groups of Christians that have agreed that God doesn't talk to people? And if they were convinced of that, don't those verses say that God will honor it? So maybe the problem is that if you're convinced God WON'T talk to you that way, He probably won't. And who would you blame? The pastor? Probably not – in fairness, we gotta lay it at the feet of the Snake and the generations of tradition that have been built up to keep us from being truly "Spirit-led".

There could also be other problems that would keep a person from hearing God. One possibility is that you're on the wrong team - even if you think you're not. You know it's possible to make up your own "Jesus" and you'll get a response from that one about as good as if you were praying to a stick of wood. Another is that you have unrepented sin that stands between you and God – and God has convicted you of it so many times that He's just given up trying to talk to you about it.

Oh, and by the way, you're going to have to get over that thing about the pastor being more "holy" than you. This is a one-on-one relationship with Jesus you're supposed to have. You can't do it by proxy through the guy that gets paid to hear God (especially if he admits he's NOT hearing God!). We are ALL the Church. We are EACH temples that hold God's Spirit. Any one of us that are adopted sons of God have the ability to petition the Throne directly and seek His face. God loves each – in fact, He's especially fond of those that come to Him with faith like little children. Sometimes pastors have a hard time with that. (I don't think there are "Faith like a Child" classes in seminary.)

This is just crazy! How could this be true and I never knew it before? Wouldn't somebody have told me?

Well, I think you underestimate the damage the enemy has done and how long he's been plotting this. The vast majority of the church in the West doesn't live the "normal" Christian life. That is, Biblically speaking, we're to be full of power and might, we're to be free of the bondage of sin, we're to NOT conform to the world, we're to be dead to ourselves, we're to be ONE Body and loving and serving each other with all our heart. That's just a few. Can you see how far away from that we actually are as a "church"? We're not even CLOSE! There MUST be something missing. Somebody left something out! It has to be this – God Himself is supposed to be directing you and you're supposed to be listening and OBEYING. Now ... who would benefit most from us leaving that little piece out? Yep, the guy in the black hat.

Now, what do you think a close encounter conversationally with the God of the Universe might do to a person? Trust me, it would change everything. It would show them the power of the relationship they have as adopted sons, they would lose all fear, they would sacrifice anything to keep hearing Him, they would obey and walk in HIS ways, they would know (really KNOW) that God Himself lives IN them and they would want more of Him, they would do the things on HIS heart – like feeding the hungry, clothing the naked, saving the lost. They would be in awe of His holiness and seek to please Him out of reverence and honor, not out of legalism or church requirements.

So, **IF** this is a war between Good and Evil, **THEN** wouldn't our most immediate and urgent need be to get people to where they can hear clear, timely, reliable commands from Headquarters? If you have a guy in Basic Training that refuses to listen to the Drill Sergeant and does his own thing, wouldn't you want to leave him at home? He's just going to get himself killed when the enemy starts shooting and leadership says 'DUCK!' and he can't or won't hear them! He's no good to anybody. Maybe he could be a supply clerk – but he really shouldn't be on the front lines. He should stay home and send his money to the folks on the front lines that hear God really well and obey ALL the time, no matter what the cost.

But we have the Bible. The Bible is what we are to use to direct our paths!

OK, sure. Not got anything bad to say about the Bible! Everything God tells us to do will line up with the Bible. But no matter how well you know the Bible, it can't accommodate for every possible situation and what you should do. There's lots of stuff not covered in there – like which of these two jobs God wants me to take. And there's stuff in there that men have been arguing about for centuries without ever getting agreement. Lots of wasted time trying to figure out how many angels can dance on the head of a pin. (By the way, which side benefits most when God's people fight over stupid stuff? You getting the hang of this yet?)

Think of it like this. You're in the Army and they give you a Manual. All kinds of stuff is covered in there – what to wear, how to salute, how the weapons work, how to survive in a battle, what to eat in the forest, how the chain of command works, even what the enemy is like and how to resist them – there's even stuff in there about what the enemy WILL DO one day, whether they like it or not! It's a REALLY good Manual – in fact, it's inspired by God! It covers an amazing array of stuff and could probably handle most any situation. So would the Drill Sargent ask you to read it, maybe even memorize it – and then send you into battle with nothing BUT that? Are you going to be able to know what to do when the bullets start flying? What about group strategy and deployment of forces and anticipating enemy movements? Is the Manual going to accommodate for every possible scenario on a rapidly changing battlefield? Are you sure you're interpreting it right? Is there time in the foxhole to be arguing with other soldiers that are reading it differently? What if some idiot published like TWENTY different translations and paraphrases of the Manual?! Then what?! Are you REALLY sure you have the right version? Isn't there a chain of command? Isn't there somebody in charge calling the shots that's supposed to tell you what to do next? Aren't you supposed to be listening and OBEYING? Want to go into battle without the Manual? No. Want to rely on it alone when you have other resources available? No. Want to take an order from somebody that goes against the Manual? No. When the bullets start flying, do you want to hear personally and directly from Headquarters so that you can know that help is coming and know what to do? You betcha!

We need a radio to headquarters that works really good, with no static on the line and no enemy transmission sneaking in. If you insist that you don't want to hear God, I still love you, but I'm not going to the front lines with you. When the bullets start flying and the God you can't hear says, "DUCK!" – you're going to be the first casualty. And then we're going to have to stop everything and call your family and carry you out and dig a hole ...

I don't know. This is kind of scary. What if I hear wrong? What if it's the enemy messing with me? Maybe this is all in your mind.

Wow! That's a whole mess of stuff. Let's try this one at a time.

Maybe it's all in your mind.

Well, it's not just me. There's hundreds of millions like me that hear God. In fact, most of the growth in the Church worldwide is because of those people. The "mainline" denominations are shrinking. It's the Spirit-led revolutionaries that are exploding into new territories and pushing back the darkness. The growth in this arm of the Church went from about ZERO in 1900 to about 500 MILLION people in 2000. God is pouring out His Spirit and people are listening to His voice.

OK, let's try it from the opposite direction. It all sunk in for me one day when it struck me that satan never creates anything – he just makes weak copies of whatever God is doing. He's a liar and a deceiver and a fake. So ... while it may seem far-fetched, most folks (even Christians) will admit that evil is a real force in the world and the supernatural is real. (The Bible verifies repeatedly that witches and mediums and sorcery are real, by the way ... and that you're headed for hell if mess with them. – Deuteronomy 18:10-12, Colossians 5:20) The enemy has psychics and mediums and astral-projection and Ouija boards and demons and zombies and spells and curses.

So where's OUR stuff?! If this is a war, why does only one side get cool weapons? Was my church leaving out important stuff that I needed for warfare? Because in the first century they had amazing weapons and defenses available to them. They had the Holy Spirit telling them stuff they wouldn't have known (Acts 5:1-11), they had people hearing from God (Acts 13:2), they had people writing stuff as God dictated (Rev.), they were caught up in the Spirit to heaven (2 Corinthians 12:2-4), they had dreams and visions (Acts 10:9-23), they saw angels (Acts 12), they saw Jesus Himself (Acts 9:1-22), they cast out demons (Acts 16:16-18), they were bitten by deadly snakes and didn't die (Acts 28:1-10), they spoke in other languages of men and of angels (Acts 2, I Corinthians 12 & more), they healed people (Acts 5:15), they prayed and miracles happened (Acts 5:12, Acts 12) – even teleportation (or as I prefer "theoportation" - Acts 8:39) and they raised the dead (Acts 9:32-42)! They even had people who were against them drop dead (Acts 5:1-11) or go blind (Acts 13:6-12) – on command! And that's just ONE reference for each! There are lots more!

Now, the argument is that all that ended when the Bible was done being written – but it didn't end for the other team, so how come just all OUR cool stuff got taken away? Wouldn't it have really benefited the enemy a LOT to spread that story that we were powerless around for a couple thousand years? Do you see? This is no kind of way to fight a war! There MUST be stuff we've been leaving out! The enemy has us twisted up into a thousand pieces (37,000+ denominations to be specific) and we can't STAND because we're not ONE Body. Because of all the arguing over stupid stuff – which we would NEVER have done if we had all been hearing the voice of God personally and reliably and walking in the Gifts!

This is kind of scary.

No kidding! It's the biggest thing ever in your life! That the God of the Universe wants to be intimately involved in everything you do and say and eat and wear and think. That's massively scary! And yet, we can never have peace and joy and victory until we have relationship with Jesus and are led by His Holy Spirit. You see, under our own power, we just screw everything up. There has never been any strategy of Man that has led to anything good in the long run. Oh, it might work for a little while, but you get enough sinful people involved in it, add money, mix in a little satan – and it's toast. Or worse, you get Communism or Fascism or something, and millions of people die. There are just two options – if it's of Man it will fail and if it's of God nothing can stand against it. (Acts 5:38-39) Since the institutional "church" in America is failing, somebody other than God must be in charge. See a logic problem there?

Anyway, yes, it's scary. But what a payoff!! To walk in holiness because God Himself is fighting off the temptations and snares of the enemy, to hear Him all the time and get direction on anything and everything, to know that He is completely and totally in charge at all times in every situation. How are you going to find peace WITHOUT hearing from God? How is what you have NOW working for you?

And hearing His voice is not even a GIFT of the Spirit! It's just an automatic for every believer! We haven't even talked about prophecy and discernment of spirits and knowledge and wisdom and tongues and healing and all the other gifts God gives His children! Trust me, the payoff is amazing, but it's going to cost you everything – but everything you THINK you have isn't yours anyway, so who cares!

What if I hear wrong? What if the enemy is messing with me?

Well sure, that can happen. He's certainly going to try to confuse and frustrate you. We are specifically instructed, "do not believe every spirit, but test the spirits to see whether they are from God (1 John 4:1). That MUST mean that other spirits are potentially messing with us, and since there is no indication that THIS ended when the Bible was completed, then there must still be demons putting thoughts into our heads. And if there are still demons putting thoughts into our heads, then we must still have a need to test and see if they are from God. And if they're NOT from God, then we resist them and they flee. But it must also mean that one of the possibilities is that the spirit we're hearing IS from God! (Again, proving the point that God still speaks to us despite I Corinthians 13:10.)

You see 1 John 4 goes on in verses 2 and 3 to lay out how you can know what it is that is talking to you and from where it comes, "This is how you can recognize the Spirit of God: Every spirit that acknowledges that Jesus Christ has come in the flesh is from God, but every spirit that does not acknowledge Jesus is not from God. This is the spirit of the antichrist, which you have heard is coming and even now is already in the world."

When we get a thought in our head we have to figure out who it is. There are only three choices: You, God or the enemy. Sometimes other people tell us stuff, but they're still playing to one of the three. We're to bring every thought into obedience with Christ (and the Word). That means our own thoughts that are out of line AND the ones inserted by the enemy. I find that, sadly, the enemy and I sound a lot alike. The red stuff and the yellow stuff aren't really that different after all. I apply this filter to everything, "If I follow through with this thought that just came into my head, who is glorified most – God, satan or me?" If it's anything other than God, even if it's me, I rebuke in the Name of Jesus. And if it WAS me, I ask the Lord to hunt down whatever in me wanted to suggest something that wouldn't glorify Him – and kill it.

Could you screw it up? Sure. Particularly if the voices are VERY sneaky. Which they <u>will</u> be because demons are smarter than us and know the human condition very well after all these years of torturing and twisting us. Without God fighting for you, you haven't got a chance. You have to be constantly on guard, constantly armored-up and expecting anything from any direction. But His arm is long and His shields are mighty. He will always get you through if you are sincerely seeking Him and trying to walk in holiness.

OK. I'm getting that it's possible, but I'm going to have to hear Him for myself. I'm willing to try. What do we do?

Great! Yeah, don't take my word for it, seek Him yourself. Well the first thing is to ask the Lord to show you anything that stands in the way between you and Him. It's like this;

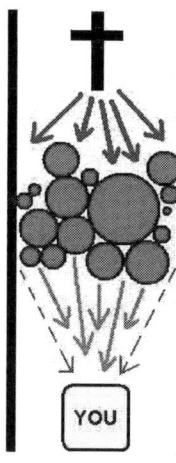

There is a pipeline of information that flows between us and God. He ALWAYS hears us, but if we can't hear Him, it's probably because of things WE have put in the way.

ANYTHING that we put between US and GOD is an idol. God never puts those things there, WE do.

The most common thing is "religion" or the "pastor." Then ALL messages from God have to filter THROUGH that and get garbled. Others include sins and habits and addictions and disobedience of one sort or another.

They ALL have to go. Only THEN can we get clear commands from Upstairs. Don't let ANYTHING come between You and God.

The point of the church coming together should be so that we can crucify pieces of ourselves so that Christ in us can live. Said another way, it's to help each other identify the things that stand between us and Jesus – and pluck them out. We should all be working together to help unclog our pipelines. But that's not what's happening at all.

The most common thing we put in the way is our belief that God won't talk to us. That's got to go! If you don't think He's a Living God and active and able to speak and desiring relationship with you, then you're going to have to lay that down.

One of the other possibilities is that you're worshiping the WRONG Jesus. Paul said that would happen, that someone would come preaching another Jesus and people would accept it. It's very simple; if you make up your own Jesus, don't expect an answer when you pray! Prosperity-Jesus, Emergency-Only-Jesus, Not-Quite-As-Good-As-The-Virgin-Mary-Jesus, and a zillion others are all MADE UP. If you make your own god from scratch, expect about as much response as if you were praying to a stick. Those are NOT Bible Jesus - who doesn't like to be toyed with and put in a box.

Other things in the way are a reliance on someone else for your holiness or connection to God (Pastor, wife, mother, etc.). That's got to stop. This is a ONE-on-ONE relationship with Jesus. Nobody is going to do it for you. Other pipeline blockages include addiction, pride, selfishness, bitterness, anger, laziness, fear and so many others that keep us from experiencing the fullness that is IN Christ.

Ask the Lord to show you what is in the way and He is faithful to ALWAYS do that if you'll listen. Ask some other folks to pray with you if possible and just pray in agreement that the Lord will make Himself very clear to you about what to do next.

Just pray and believe. He'll come and help unclog you. Believe that He wants to talk to you and start conversing with Him. Find someone to be accountable with that knows God really well and make sure you don't act on anything that sounds fishy without verifying it with the Word of God. Now, not with doctrine of Man, mind you – with the Word of God.

And One Other Thing:

One of the best ways that I have found and one of the things you see in the "Dialogues" is that I learned that satan can't read your thoughts, so if you ask lots of follow up questions and then wait and get out of the way – if you don't get answers or get squirrelly answers, it wasn't God. It's not enough to obey generally, if you love Him, you'll obey Him specifically and exactly. I say that obedience isn't just jumping when He says jump. You jump <u>when</u> He tells you, <u>how</u> He tells you, how <u>high</u> He tells you and you <u>stay</u> in the air until He says to come down! That's radical obedience. Don't just obey generally – seek to obey <u>exactly</u>. And for that you need more specifics.

It's like this, just assume that the urge to do something or the thought in your head is from God and then ask lots of questions. It says that the steps of a righteous man are ordered before him. It says that He directs our paths. Just assume that He is a lot more involved then you might have suspected and treat the voice in your head as if it's Him (not you or the enemy). I'm <u>not</u> saying not to test the spirits! Please don't hear that. I'm saying that this is ONE way to test them that is a little upside down, but I know it works for me (and lots of others!).

For example, this exchange happens INSIDE your head (<u>NOT</u> out loud where the enemy will hear):

<u>Spontaneous thought pops in:</u>
I need to call my Mom.

<u>Your response:</u>
Assume it's the Holy Spirit prompting you and get details. Be polite.

> Oh! Thanks, Lord. I will. Do you want me to call her right now?
> ... pause ... (wait and listen)
> **No.**
> OK! Thanks for that, Lord! When do you want me to call my Mom?
> ... pause ... (wait and listen)
> **2:00pm today**
> OK. Thanks for that Lord. Do you want me to call her on her cell phone or at home?
> ... pause ... (wait and listen)
> **Call her at your brother's house.**
> HUH?! What is she doing there? That's hours away. I'm sure she's at home.
> ... pause ... (wait and listen)
> **No. Call her at 2:00pm at your brother's house.**
> Wow. OK, Lord. I'll do it. Thanks, Lord. I love You.
> **I love you, too.**

Then you step out on faith, call your brother at 2:00pm, find out that Mom is there and you give God all the glory – and your faith grows and grows! OR she's not there and you use it as a way to troubleshoot your hearing method and NOT as a way to disprove that God speaks to people. You don't get discouraged, you accept it as a training lesson and move on and ask Him to explain to you what went wrong. Maybe you colored or added to it, maybe you were out of order in some way, maybe you've got a Red Dragon, maybe you didn't ask what day to call, etc.

He WILL do surprising stuff like this so that you know it's Him. He absolutely will. When folks implement this one little thing, it often STUNS them! God is VERY creative and He will find a way to do little (or big) things that prove to you that He is there and He is directing your paths. Just wait and listen and don't add to it yourself.

You see, the enemy can implant a thought, and they might even be able to anticipate a response or two from you – like chess moves. But they can't really read your thoughts and follow along with a sequence of follow up questions. Particularly if you throw off the timing by praising and and worshiping in between or setting the whole thing to one side until the enemy least expects it.

If you acknowledge the voice as external and ask follow-up questions and don't get any answers, or get really useless answers, than it wasn't God. If the voice suggests you do something that doesn't bring glory to God, then it was either you or the enemy. Both of you want a dozen donuts at midnight. But if Jesus isn't glorified by you eating a dozen donuts at midnight, then rebuke it and refuse to obey it – whether it was YOU or the enemy!

Often when I'm fasting I will hear a voice that says I'm finished. Usually it will be different that when the Lord told me earlier that I was to be finished fasting (like 7pm instead of midnight). The enemy wants me to disobey God and to not be fasting in time for whatever trial is coming. If I ask a question right away when I first hear that thought ("Lord, is that really you?"), I will get an answer that sounds like God answering my thoughts ("Yep. It's me. You're done fasting. It's OK."). But ... if I set it off to the side, do something else for awhile and then a few minutes later, out of the blue, ask the Lord (in my head) if I'm done fasting, I'll hear a more reliable answer – usually that it wasn't Him. Don't let the enemy dictate the timing or rush you into action. The Lord will always allow you enough time to confirm it's Him or to be sure it's His voice. Remember that the enemy can implant a thought AND can implant a follow-up or two. But if you throw off the timing, ask a really odd follow-up, praise and worship a little before asking anything at all, it will throw the enemy off and it's likely that the implanted follow-up will talk over you or not answer your question at all. Then it gets easier to understand the difference between the voices that are coming at you. The Lord is highly motivated to teach you how this works. Just listen to Him.

People think that if you're hearing voices you're crazy. What they don't understand is that the enemy will put an "I" in front and convince you that it's you. So, I guarantee you that we're ALL hearing voices, we just think it's us. For example, "I'm scared that I might have cancer." Was that you or the enemy? It sure wasn't God, He didn't give us a spirit of fear! And if it's a spirit of fear, it's not US either – so it's external and it's designed to kill, steal and destroy your life or your quality of life (or your witness as Christians). That person just heard a voice in their head that wasn't them, but because the enemy works covertly and puts an "I'm" in front, we accept it as our own. We're such stupid sheep!

There's a lot of stuff that I've learned and there's not nearly room for all of it, but I will add this one other thing. Be VERY careful about dates and times. If the Lord says, "soon" or "tomorrow" that could mean just about anything. If He says "Wednesday the 27th of June, 2007" now that's something. But don't bet the farm on "tomorrow" meaning OUR tomorrow. A day is as a thousand years to those who are outside of time, so be very cautious about those kinds of predictions. Ask for specifics and if you can't get any out of Him, then He probably doesn't want you to have that information. He will always give you enough information to obey His directive, but not necessarily as much as you'd like. Keep in mind, too, that He doesn't necessarily honor the Gregorian calendar ("this year") and that the Hebrew method of calculating days means they end at sundown ("today"). He keeps His options open. He can be true and you still be wrong. It's the interpretation or the question or the hearer that is flawed, never His voice.

Recently a brother and I were driving across country and the van was having trouble. The Lord had instructed us to go to a particular town and it was still a couple of hours away. Do we fix the van? Nope, we drive it until the transmission is totally fried. Then we spend two nights in the desert. Can we call for help? No. The Lord says, "Will you walk?" Yes, Lord. We trust Him for everything and ask no help from any man – not even sticking our thumbs out. And when we've walked as far as we can (four or five miles dragging suitcases down the highway), He sends someone to pick us up and drive us toward the destination, but too far East. Then we walk some more until we're pooped, then someone else picks us up and drops us directly on the doorstep of the place we were going. God had said that morning that we would be at our destination before the end of that day and we were, before sundown even. He is always faithful and true. You may not get there the way you expected, but He will always get you there. Don't stop just because it doesn't look the way you thought it would (or should).

Along the way, we grew in our faith, we met some great folks, we got to bless some people and pray for them and we did get where He wanted us at just the right moment. And we got some exercise!

I pray that this journey you're on will be just as much of an adventure for you.

If you want to hear Him better, pray something like this:

Lord, I'm sorry I ever put you in a box. I'm sorry I limited You in any way. I'm sorry that I haven't been hearing you as well as I should and I acknowledge that I clogged up my pipeline with stuff. Please, Lord, whatever it takes, scrub it all out of there with the Blood of Jesus. I just want You, Jesus. You direct my paths and organize my days. You tell me what You want and I'll do it. Help me hear You better. Help make me dangerous to the enemy. Increase the Jesus in me, even if it hurts. I love you, Lord. You be in charge now. Amen.

If you really, REALLY want to go fast and you trust God all the way, then pray something like this: (But go read the Warning again!!)

Dear Lord Jesus, I trust You. I know You'll get me through. I want to be fully equipped, fully armored, fully broken and fully willing to do your perfect will. Whatever in me that is resisting You – kill it with prejudice. Lord, there is a monster inside of me and it's <u>me</u>. Hunt it down and kill it and hang its head on the wall of my heart so I'll never forget what I was. Put all the weight on. Load me up. Whatever it takes, I trust You. I'm ready now, Lord. Dial the refining fire up REALLY high and let's get this over with. Do it right now! I know this prayer is inside Your will, so I know You are going to answer it. Just please don't ever leave me. In the mighty name of my Lord Jesus Christ, Amen.

APPENDIX A

John 10:2-5
2 The man who enters by the gate is the shepherd of his sheep. 3 The watchman opens the gate for him, and the sheep listen to his voice. He calls his own sheep by name and leads them out. 4 When he has brought out all his own, he goes on ahead of them, and his sheep follow him because they know his voice. 5 But they will never follow a stranger; in fact, they will run away from him because they do not recognize a stranger's voice."

John 10:27
My sheep listen to my voice; I know them, and they follow me.

Hebrews 3
7 So, as the Holy Spirit says: "Today, if you hear his voice, 8 do not harden your hearts as you did in the rebellion, during the time of testing in the desert, where your fathers tested and tried me and for forty years saw what I did. 10 That is why I was angry with that generation, and I said, 'Their hearts are always going astray, and they have not known my ways.' 11 So I declared on oath in my anger, 'They shall never enter my rest.' "

12 See to it, brothers, that none of you has a sinful, unbelieving heart that turns away from the living God. 13 But encourage one another daily, as long as it is called Today, so that none of you may be hardened by sin's deceitfulness. 14 We have come to share in Christ if we hold firmly till the end the confidence we had at first. 15 As has just been said:

"Today, if you hear his voice, do not harden your hearts as you did in the rebellion."

16 Who were they who heard and rebelled? Were they not all those Moses led out of Egypt? 17 And with whom was he angry for forty years? Was it not with those who sinned, whose bodies fell in the desert? 18 And to whom did God swear that they would never enter his rest if not to those who disobeyed? 19 So we see that they were not able to enter, because of their unbelief.

Deuteronomy 18:16
According to all that thou desiredst of the LORD thy God in Horeb in the day of the assembly, saying, Let me not hear again the voice of the LORD my God, neither let me see this great fire any more, that I die not.

1 Kings 19:11-13
11 And he said, Go forth, and stand upon the mount before the LORD. And, behold, the LORD passed by, and a great and strong wind rent the mountains, and brake in pieces the rocks before the LORD; but the LORD was not in the wind: and after the wind an earthquake; but the LORD was not in the earthquake: 12 And after the earthquake a fire; but the LORD was not in the fire: and after the fire a still small voice. 13 And it was so, when Elijah heard it, that he wrapped his face in his mantle, and went out, and stood in the entering in of the cave. And, behold, there came a voice unto him, and said, What doest thou here, Elijah?

Isaiah 30:20-21
20 And though the Lord give you the bread of adversity, and the water of affliction, yet shall not thy teachers be removed into a corner any more, but thine eyes shall see thy teachers: 21 And thine ears shall hear a word behind thee, saying, This is the way, walk ye in it, when ye turn to the right hand, and when ye turn to the left.

Acts 22:7-8
7 And I fell unto the ground, and heard a voice saying unto me, Saul, Saul, why persecutest thou me? 8 And I answered, Who art thou, Lord? And he said unto me, I am Jesus of Nazareth, whom thou persecutest.

Revelation 3:20
Here I am! I stand at the door and knock. If anyone hears my voice and opens the door, I will come in and eat with him, and he with me.

APPENDIX B

You Can Be Filled With Good Stuff:

The Lord - Psalm 16:5; 1 Cor 10:21

Fullness of God - Eph 3:19

Spirit of God - Exod 31:3; Exod. 35:31; Eph 5:18

Glory of the Lord - Num 14:21

Holy Ghost - Luke 1:15; 1:41; 1:67; Luke 4:1; Acts 2:4; Acts 4:8; Acts 4:31; Acts 6:3; Acts 7:55; Acts 9:17; Acts 11:24; Acts 13:9

Goodness of the Lord - Psalm 33:5

Blessing of the Lord - Deut 33:23

Fear of the Lord - Luke 5:26

All Knowledge - Rom 15:14

Knowledge of the Lord - Isaiah 11:9

Power by the spirit of the Lord and judgement - Micah 3:8

Knowledge of the glory of God - Hab 2:14

Knowledge of His will, wisdom and spiritual understanding - Col. 1:19

Spirit of Wisdom - Exod. 28:3; 35:35; Deut. 34:9

Wisdom & understanding - I Kings 7:14

Wisdom and grace - Luke 2:40

Wisdom and beauty - Ezek. 28:12

Judgement and righteousness - Isa. 33:5

Light - Matt. 6:22 (Luke 11:34-36)

Grace and truth - John 1:14

Faith and power - Acts 6:8

Salvation - Psalm 116:13

Righteousness - Matt. 5:6

Fruits of Righteousness - Phil 1:11

Comfort - 2 Cor 7:4

Consolation - Jerem. 16:7

Joy - John 15:11; John 16:24; Acts 2:28; 2 Tim. 1:4

Mercy - Psalm 119:64

Mercy and good fruits - James 3:17 Blessing - 1 Cor 10:16

Good - Psalm 104:28

Good things - Luke 1:53

Good things - Job 22:18

Good works and almsdeeds - Acts 9:36

Goodness and all knowledge - Rom 15:14

Praise and honour - Psalm 71:8

Laughter and singing - Psalm 126:2

Precious and pleasant riches - Prov. 24:4

Horses, chariots, might men of war - Ezek. 39:20

Wonder and amazement - Acts 3:10

Trembling (to enemies) - Zech 12:2

Full of days - Job 42:17

Children - Psalm 127:5

Need Clean Cup:

Matt 23:25; Luke 11:39; Prov. 25:4; Isaiah 66:20; 2 Tim 2:21; Hebrews 9:21

Need Pliable Cup:

Matt. 9:17 (Mar 2:22, Luke 5:37)

Need FULL Cup:

Matt 25:4; Ruth 1:21

Chosen/Special Vessel:

Acts 9:15; Romans 9:21; I Thes. 4:4; 2 Tim 2:20

Hated Vessels:

Rom 9:22

Things that are NEVER Full:

Hell and destruction - Prov. 27:20

The Sea - Ecc. 1:7

Or You Can Be Filled With Bad Stuff:

With sin - Jerem. 51:5

Evil and madness - Ecc 9:3

Confusion - Job 10:15; Acts 19:29

Heaviness - Psalm 69:20; Phil 2:26

Travail and vexation of spirit - Ecc 4:6

Tossings to and fro - Job 7:4

Drunkenness and/or nakedness - Lam. 4:21; Jerem. 12:12

Drunkenness, Sorrow, astonishment and desolation - Ez 23:33

Violence - Ezek. 8:17

Satan, lies - Acts 5:3

Devils - 1 Corin 10:21

Abominations and filthiness - Ezra 9:11

Abominations, filthiness of fornication - Rev. 17:4

Adultery, cannot cease from sin, beguiling, covetous practices, cursed children - 2 Peter 2:14

Bitterness - Lam. 3:15

Sorrow - John 16:6

Envy, contradicting, blaspheming - Acts 13:45

Unrighteousness, fornication, wickedness, covetousness, maliciousness, full of envy, murder debate, deceit, malignity, whisperers, backbiters, haters of God, despiteful, proud, boasters, inventors of evil things, disobedient to parents, without understanding, covenant breakers, without natural affection, implacable, unmerciful - Rom 1:29-31

Wickedness - Lev. 19:29

Blood of innocents - Jer. 19:4

Hands full of blood - Isaiah 1:15

Bloody crimes and violence - Ezek 7:23

Blood and perverseness - Ezek. 9:9

Trouble - Job 14:1; Psalm 88:3

Sin of youth - Job 20:11

Cursing, deceit, fraud, mischief and vanity - Psalm 10:7

Mischief - Prov. 12:21; Psalm 26:10

Subtilty and mischief - Acts 13:10

Deceit - Jerem 5:27

Violence, lies and deceit - Micah 6:12

Lies, robbery, blood - Nahum 3:1

Extortion and excess - Matt. 23:25

Hypocrisy and iniquity - Matt. 23:28

Cursing and bitterness - Rom 3:14

Cruelty - Psalm 74:20

Strife - Prov. 17:1

Darkness - Matt 6:23; Luke 11:34; Rev. 16:10

No pleasure - Hosea 8:8

Their own devices / His own ways - Prov. 3:10; Prov. 14:4

Dead men's bones and uncleanness - Matt 23:27

Wrath - Esther 3:5; Luke 4:28; Acts 19:28;

Wrath of God - Rev. 15:1; Rev. 15:7; Rev. 16:19

Fury of the Lord - Isaiah 51:20; Jerem 6:11

Fury - Dan 3:19; Jerem. 25:15

Snare, fire and brimstone, tempest - Psalm 11:6

Trembling - Isaiah 51:17, Is. 51:22,

Indignation - Esther 5:9; Jerem. 15:17; Acts 5:17; Rev. 14:10

Judgement - Isaiah 1:21

Reproach - Lam 3:30

Scorn and derision – Psalm 123:4; Ezek. 23:22

Shame - Hab. 2:16

Contempt - Psalm 123:3

Plagues - Rev. 21:9

Madness - Jerem 51:7; Luke 6:11

APPENDIX C: CUP TROUBLESHOOTING

Let's talk more about this cup thing. There are two ways that I know of to get your cup completely filled up with God. There is the daily walking in obedience and seeking and prayerful living that just pushes out the Sin a little at a time and creates habits of effectiveness and faithfulness. One day you look up and you've achieved sanctification (holiness, no red stuff). Or there is the experience that the first Christians had at Pentecost - the Baptism of the Holy Spirit.

It's kind of like if you have a swimming pool in your backyard you want to fill, you can stick a garden hose in it and let the water run until it's full - or you can call the forestry service and have one of those giant helicopters that dump water on forest fires just flood the whole block and fill your pool in one burst. Far be it from me to tell someone that however much God they got in them they did it the wrong way! I have dear, dear friends that did it both ways and both are as full of God as anyone I know. I have had Pentecostals describe the first method as "old school" and unnecessary since the Azusa Revival and the "awakening" in 1900. Even delegitimize it as a method to build that relationship with God. (Mostly they say we don't have time for that.) But that makes no sense to me at all. It may not be the fastest, but it sure seems more lasting and less likely to be taken for granted. To build a habit of daily struggle and faithfulness rather than to rely on one "burst" seems perfectly reasonable.

If you're not into church linguistics, one of the terms you'll hear used a lot is "Spirit-filled". What most folks want you to think it means is that their cup is totally full of God. What they REALLY most likely mean is that at some point in their life they had a dramatic experience in which the Holy Spirit came on them and something happened. Most probably what they really, REALLY mean is just that they speak in tongues. I've had folks ask me if I was Spirit-filled and I (and they) know darn well that what they really want to know is if I speak in tongues - NOT if I'm walking in holiness and am completely filled with nothing BUT the Holy Spirit. It seems that for many people, we've put the emphasis on the Gifts, not the relationship.

You see, what I think has happened with a LOT of people is that they were in churches that put a lot of emphasis on the spiritual gifts that can come when your cup is filled (especially tongues) and so they seek that experience of being filled with the Holy Spirit just FOR that. That is, they're not laying everything down and seeking sanctification and willing to do whatever it takes to live victoriously and conquer sin consistently and fearing an awesome God - they just want to speak in tongues like everybody else at their church. So they seek God and they ask to be filled and they either don't (because God sees right through wrong motives) or else they do get a burst, but not enough to really push out all the sin. Their cup's level rises enough for that gift but they can't maintain it because they're not committed to keeping the sin out consistently. They didn't get training on cup management, they just had an urgency for a manifestation of some sort. Since what God gives are GIFTS, He will let a person keep them even later the level in their cup drops to dangerously low. That's how we end up with some revivalists and others who can heal people and yet are complete selfish stinkers.

There are plenty of people that I've met that describe themselves as "Spirit-filled" - and I'd rather spend time in a bathtub with a wolverine than hang out with them. Whatever they once had is LONG gone! Our lives are FLUID and dynamic, in constant motion and flux. Like the dilation of the iris of your eye, we are tuned to the world around us and it affects us in all kinds of good and bad ways. That's why Cup Management is so important.

We should never worship the creation instead of the Creator. We should never seek after experiences or feelings or manifestations. That's just NOT going to get your cup filled up all the way because it's comes from a selfish or prideful motive that is inherently sinful. You just can't pray for the Sin to be poured out and be sanctified so that you'll be cool or because you covet what someone else has or because you want to show them up. See the problem? Sin is motivating the removal of sin. A house divided can't stand. Doesn't work. God sees right through that. He may give you manifestations, but it's just going to wreck you if you keep walking down that path.

We should seek ONLY that Jesus fill us completely and do His work through us, that we should decrease so that He can increase. We should seek OBEDIENCE - pure and complete. The other stuff is just side-effects of that. Signs and wonders will FOLLOW – they will trail behind, not lead the way.

Rain Right NOW, Lord!

from Doug Perry
Fellowship Of The Martyrs

www.FellowshipOfTheMartyrs.com
fotm@fellowshipofthemartyrs.com

Copyright © 2006 Doug Perry, Fellowship Of The Martyrs

All rights reserved.

ISBN: 1463794436
ISBN-13: 978-1463794439

The Bride gets her jewelry, but it's going to hurt to get it on, and once you're used to it, you're never going to want to rip it back off again. Heaven is free. HOLINESS is hard! If not us, who? If not here, where? If not now, when?

CONTENTS

Spiritual Gifts Intro 247
Tripartite Axioms 255
My Experience with the Holy Spirit 257
What is "Dunamis"? 261
James Dunn 269
Be a M*A*S*H 270
Need a Spiritual Tune-up? 271
Warning Label 274
Which part of ALL don't you understand? 275
Communications – Hotline to Headquarters 285
Let Me Show You a Higher Way 294
Fear of the Lord Axioms 300
Faith Like A Teenager 302
The Beatitudes and Your Cup 305
Spiritual Gift Dials 309
How Complicated Could It Be? 315
Spectrum Analysis of the Gifts 320
Can You Pray the HARD Prayer? 326
OK, So How Do You Pour Out Your Cup? 328
Are You Sure You're Not Nuts? 330
How Would This Change The Church? 331
How Do We Get Our Cup Cleaned Out? 336
Appendix A – Things You Can Be Full Of 339
Appendix B – Verses 341
Appendix C – Left Over Pieces 361

"Your growth in Christ
is directly proportional
to your willingness
to RUSH HEADLONG
into the refining fire
and give it a wet, sloppy kiss."

- Doug Perry

SPIRITUAL GIFTS –
HOW TO GET THEM AND WHY YOU SHOULD SHARE THEM.

Romans 12:6-8 (Amplified)
Having then gifts differing according to the grace that is given to us, whether prophecy, [let us prophesy] according to the proportion of faith; Or ministry, [let us wait] on [our] ministering: or he that teacheth, on teaching; Or he that exhorteth, on exhortation: he that giveth, [let him do it] with simplicity; he that ruleth, with diligence; he that sheweth mercy, with cheerfulness.

I Corinthians 12:10-11 (Amplified)
10 To another the working of miracles, to another prophetic insight (the gift of interpreting the divine will and purpose); to another the ability to discern and distinguish between [the utterances of true] spirits [and false ones], to another various kinds of [unknown] tongues, to another the ability to interpret [such] tongues. 11 All these [gifts, achievements, abilities] are inspired and brought to pass by one and the same [Holy] Spirit, Who apportions to each person individually [exactly] as He chooses.

I Corinthians 12:28 (Amplified)
So God has appointed some in the church [for His own use]: first apostles; second prophets; third teachers; then wonder-workers; then those with ability to heal the sick; helpers; administrators; [speakers in] different (unknown) tongues.

Let's start with some qualifying questions just to save everybody some time here:

- **Do you think the Gifts of the Spirit are all still active and for today?**

Yes – Go to the next page.
No – See next question.

- **Would you LIKE for them to be for today, but you just aren't sure?**

Yes – See next question
No – How exactly do you plan to fulfill Mark 16:15-20 without them? Do you realize that you're in the minority now? The growth in the Church worldwide is nearly all people that disagree with you. You are directly insulting the personal experience of about 800 million Christians – at least some of whom are NOT tools of satan and filled with demons! You have to come to the conclusion that every tongue, every miracle, every healing, all the people that were raised from the dead in the last 1900 years is all bogus and from satan. It just ain't so! God doesn't change.

Miracles are happening all over the world and you can't blame them all on satan! I was where you are, I know what you're thinking, but you gotta look around and see that God is moving. This stuff is real and you're powerless against the badness if you're not so FULL of Jesus that nothing else can fit. Please take God out of the box you put Him in and let Him be God. He doesn't change. His promises are always the same. He's still does cool stuff. If you can't believe He's big enough to still act like He used to, you might be better off to not read any further.

- **Do you think SOME of the Gifts are for today, but not all of them?**

Yes – Close enough. Go to the next page.
No – OK, so we don't have Wisdom anymore? Giving? Administration? Faith? Hospitality? So when the Bible was done being written that which was perfect was come so that which was in part was done away? Is that the argument you're going to stick with? So how come some ended but others didn't? Who gets to pick and choose? God changes, but only partially? This argument is indefensible. Either they all ended or none of them did. You can't pick and choose. And if they all

ended, then how come the enemy still has all his weapons? How come they have spells and curses and zombies and astral projection and psychics and mediums? If "that which is perfect" came, then why isn't evil completely vanquished? Where are our cool toys?! Is "that which is perfect" how we got 41,000+ denominations?

I love you. I really do, but you're just flat wrong and you're insulting a whole lot of people at the same time. You're saying God changes and He doesn't talk to us anymore and do big stuff and I just happen to know you're really, really wrong. It would be great if you would go ahead and read this book, but you're probably just going to argue with everything and close your mind, so it's probably better stewardship of your time if you just stop reading now.

If I'm right, then God is about to burst onto the scene in a great big giant way and you will have a really, REALLY hard time sustaining your argument that He doesn't do that stuff anymore. In fact, you're probably going to have to repent a LOT to Him and to anybody you led astray. But it's His job to fix you, so I'll just leave it to Him. In the meantime, get online and Google "John G. Lake", "Smith Wigglesworth" or "Brother Yun" and see which ones you think are the biggest liars and tools of Satan. I dare you.

Still here? Great!!

This is going to change your life!

Let's get started.

Questions

IF there is a war between good and evil,
THEN the Gifts of the Spirit are offensive and defensive weapons.

IF the Gifts of the Spirit are fixed and predetermined and unchangeable,
THEN how can we adjust to a changing battlefield?

IF people only get one Gift each, **THEN** why are we told to desire more and greater Gifts?

IF nobody can have ALL the Gifts, **THEN** why do we have examples of people that did/do?

IF we specifically DENY some of the Gifts, **THEN** who benefits most – God or satan?

IF we assert that certain Gifts aren't for today,
THEN aren't we operating with less than complete weaponry systems?

IF we acknowledge the validity of certain Gifts but ban them from our assemblies,
THEN aren't we violating specific commands not to do that (and being rude to the Gift Giver)?

IF we acknowledge the validity of all the Gifts, but we're missing some of them in our assembly,
THEN shouldn't we get somebody with the missing pieces or seek it until God gives it to us?

Ephesians 6:12 – *For our struggle is not against flesh and blood, but against the rulers, against the authorities, against the powers of this dark world and against the spiritual forces of evil in the heavenly realms.*

I Corinthians 12:31a – *But eagerly desire the greater gifts.*

I Corinthians 7:7 – *For I would that all men were even as I myself. But every man hath his proper gift of God, one after this manner, and another after that.*

I Corinthians 14:1 – *Follow the way of love and eagerly desire spiritual gifts, especially the gift of prophecy.*

I Corinthians 14:12 – *So it is with you. Since you are eager to have spiritual gifts, try to excel in gifts that build up the church.*

I Corinthians 14:39-40 – *Therefore, my brothers, be eager to prophesy, and do not forbid speaking in tongues. 40 But everything should be done in a fitting and orderly way.*

Assertions

IF there is a war between good and evil, **THEN** I want to be on the side of good.

IF evil seems to be winning, **THEN** maybe we're not equipped fully.

IF there are weapons or armor that God has for me, **THEN** I want them!

IF I pray to be like Jesus, **THEN** I probably need all available offensive and defensive weaponry systems.

IF there are varying levels of strength within each system, **THEN** I want mine dialed all the way up!

IF getting more of Him requires less of Me, **THEN** I'm all for it! Crucify me daily. Kill it all.

IF Jesus says, "Ask and it shall be given," **THEN** why not ask for them all?

Ephesians 6:12 – *For our struggle is not against flesh and blood, but against the rulers, against the authorities, against the powers of this dark world and against the spiritual forces of evil in the heavenly realms.*

I Corinthians 12:31a – *But earnestly desire and zealously cultivate the greatest and best gifts and graces (the higher gifts and the choicest graces).* (Amplified)

Luke 11:13 – *If you then, though you are evil, know how to give good gifts to your children, how much more will your Father in heaven give the Holy Spirit to those who ask him!"*

Romans 8:32 – *He that spared not his own Son, but delivered him up for us all, how shall he not with him also freely give us all things?*

Why don't more people have all the Gifts? If you don't have, it's because you don't ask. (Or He knows you're going to make it about YOU instead of about JESUS.) What if more people don't have more Gifts because we're not sharing like we should?

IF God asks us to be a steward of some gift, **THEN** we should invest it and get a return.

IF we bury it in the sand or don't use it, **THEN** we will be lukewarm and stagnant and He will spew us out.

IF we can share our Gifts of the Spirit with others, **THEN** why aren't we?

We are three part beings – Body, Soul and Spirit.
Who benefits most from fat, brainy, spiritually weak Christians?

Do we know how to feed the poor in spirit? Do we know how to pour ourselves out spiritually? Is there even such a thing? What can we pour out on them? How do we do it? Are we supposed to?

Yep. You're supposed to take the Gifts that you were given and invest them into other people. You're supposed to take all the Jesus in your "cup" and pour it out onto others. Just as you would with physical resources, you're supposed to spend your spiritual resources on others. As the Charisma of the Holy Spirit was poured out onto us, so we should pour it out on one another.

Can I prove it? You betcha! I'm not just spouting off here, God showed me where to look to prove it.

The word used in the Greek to refer to the Gifts of the Spirit is "charisma." (Hence, those who believe the gifts are real and for today are called "Charismatics.") It is basically simply the Holy Spirit, but from His presence comes multiple "weapons systems". This verse below says that we are to equip each other for this war by **sharing the spiritual gifts that we have been given**. In fact, it's a command and it infers that if you don't, you're not a good steward.

> I Peter 4:10 (KJV) – *As every man hath received the gift (charisma), even so minister (diakoneo) the same one to another, as good stewards of the manifold (poikilos) grace (charis) of God.*

Charisma is Strong's number 5486 and is translated 17 times as "gift" or "free gift". And defined as follows:
1) a favour with which one receives without any merit of his own
2) the gift of divine grace
3) the gift of faith, knowledge, holiness, virtue
4) the economy of divine grace, by which the pardon of sin and eternal salvation is appointed to sinners in consideration of the merits of Christ laid hold of by faith
5) grace or gifts denoting extraordinary powers, distinguishing certain Christians and enabling them to serve the church of Christ, the reception of which is due to the power of divine grace operating on their souls by the Holy Spirit

Diakoneo is translated here as to "minister", but the Strong's definition is much richer:

- to be a servant, attendant, domestic, **to serve**, wait upon
  a) to minister to one, render ministering offices to
    1) to be served, ministered unto
  b) to wait at a table and offer **food and drink** to the guests,
    1) of women preparing food
  c) to minister i.e. **supply food and necessities of life**
    1) to relieve one's necessities (e.g. by collecting alms), to provide take care of, **distribute**, the things necessary to **sustain life**
    2) to take care of the **poor and the sick**, who administer the office of a deacon
    3) in Christian churches to serve as deacons
  d) to minister
    1) **to attend to anything, that may serve another's interests**
    2) **to minister a thing to one, to serve one or by supplying any thing**

Poikilos is translated here "manifold" but defined by Strong's as:

1) a various colours, variegated
2) of various sorts

It is translated eight times as "divers" and twice as "manifold".

The charisma isn't one "flavor." The Holy Spirit is a rainbow and when He is in us, He can manifest in a whole bunch of different ways. As with a prism, the amount of light that can come through is simply a matter of how transparent it is. The more transparent we are, the more the Holy Spirit can be seen and used through us in all the different colors. If God has given us a particular color and somebody else needs it, we should share.

Charis is translated "grace" in this passage
- grace
    a) that which affords joy, pleasure, delight, sweetness, charm, loveliness: grace of speech.
2) good will, loving-kindness, favour
    a) of the merciful kindness by which God, exerting his holy influence upon souls, turns them to Christ, keeps, strengthens, increases them in Christian faith, knowledge, affection, and kindles them to the exercise of the Christian virtues
3) what is due to grace
    a) the spiritual condition of one governed by the power of divine grace
    b) the token or proof of grace, benefit
        1) a gift of grace
        2) benefit, bounty
    4) thanks, (for benefits, services, favours), recompense, reward

Ok, I'm sure you're already thinking that I'm interpreting that verse incorrectly. You probably looked up the NIV version of this verse and it says:

I Peter 4:10 – *Each one should use whatever gift he has received to serve others, faithfully administering God's grace in its various forms.*

Yeah, it does sound like you're just supposed to use your gift wisely to serve others, not "pour it out" on people. But try Young's Literal Translation:

I Peter 4:10 – *each, according as he received a gift, to one another ministering it, as good stewards of the manifold grace of God;*

How about Darby?

I Peter 4:10 – *each according as he has received a gift, ministering it to one another, as good stewards of [the] various grace of God.*

Wow! I love this one! The Wycliffe New Testament:

I Peter 4:10 – *each man as he hath received grace, ministering it into each other [ministering each to other], as good dispensers of the manifold grace of God.*

"Ministering it"? Don't they mean ministering WITH IT? Using it effectively? Well, that too, but I'm just pretty sure this verse means that you should steward the gift that was given to you **by giving it <u>into other people</u>** as the Lord directs. We are to all be "**good dispensers**" of the manifold, multi-faceted, variegated ***charis*** of God. Are you doing that?
Look at the King James again:

I Peter 4:10 – *As every man hath received the gift (charisma), even so minister (diakoneo) the <u>same</u> one to another, as good stewards of the manifold (poikilos) grace (charis) of God.*

The same what? The same gift you just got. Distribute it to others. What else do you have to share except what's inside you? By giving it away, you'll get more. That's God's economy. People that say the "charisma" aren't for today say you can't lay hands on someone and have them receive the Holy Spirit, but that's exactly what this verse commands us to do – in all His flavors and colors. People that believe in the "charisma" will lay hands on people to transfer the Gift of Tongues, but they don't seem to get that the application is the same for ALL the various flavors. And it's not a one-time thing either. Whatever we have we should share. If we get something new, we should bring it to the Body and share. That's how everybody gets fully equipped.

We are to pour our Gifts out onto each other. We are to share all that we have with those in need. We are to empty our cup onto those around us. Anyone that hoards that which God has given and buries it in the ground will be punished severely and cast into the darkness where there will be weeping and gnashing of teeth. Read the Parable of the Talents – Matthew 24:14-30. How can it not apply? You have physical, emotional and spiritual assets. You should be sharing ALL of them.

Still not buying it? That you can pass out Gifts of the Spirit? Well, you can't exactly. God's not going to let you give something to somebody that's not ready for it or He doesn't want to have it. And it's not about YOU anyway. But you most definitely CAN be the vehicle that transfers the Gifts that He's given you to somebody else. Or you can at least be willing and try. Don't believe me? Want me to prove it? Good, that's very Berean of you.

How about these?

> Romans 1:11 – *For I long to see you, that I may impart* (metadidomi) *unto you some spiritual gift* (charisma), *to the end ye may be established.*

Metadidomi is Strong's number 3330 – to impart or to give – and is used in scripture for both physical and spiritual assets. Paul's not talking about the Baptism of the Holy Spirit here because He's writing to the Church of Rome which is already established. He's talking about distributing to them gifts they don't already have. Sharing from His abundance with any that has a need. Paul's cup overflowed so he had plenty to share. He seemed to have all the gifts – and in large measure.

Here's another one:

> I Thessalonians 2:8 – *So being affectionately desirous of you, we were willing to have imparted (metadidomi) unto you, not the gospel of God only, but also our own souls (psuche), because ye were dear unto us.*

They were willing to share EVERYTHING with the Thessalonians. All that they had, every spiritual resource.

Strong's 5590 is "psuche" and has these meanings:
1) breath
   a) the breath of life
      1) the vital force which animates the body and shows itself in breathing
         a) of animals
         b) of men
   b) life
   c) that in which there is life
      1) a living being, a living soul
      2) the soul
         a) the seat of the feelings, desires, affections, aversions (our heart, soul etc.)
         b) the (human) soul in so far as it is constituted that by the right use of the aids offered it by God it can attain its highest end and secure eternal blessedness, the soul regarded as a moral being designed for everlasting life
         c) the soul as an essence which differs from the body and is not dissolved by death (distinguished from other parts of the body)

In the King James it is translated as soul 58, life 40, mind 3, heart 1, heartily +1537 1, not tr 2; 105 occurrences.

It's clear that they were willing to pour all they had into the Thessalonians. Every gift, every breath, whatever good thing they had.

Need more?

I Timothy 4:14 – *Be not negligent of the gift* (charisma) [that is] *in thee, which has been given* (didomi) *to thee through prophecy, with imposition of the hands of the elderhood.* (Young's)

I Timothy 4:14 – *Do not neglect your gift* (charisma), *which was given* (didomi) *you through a prophetic message when the body of elders laid their hands on you.* (NIV)

Are they talking about his calling? A calling is not a "charisma." A calling is "klesis." Are they talking about his commissioning service as a missionary? That doesn't sound right either. Paul is exhorting him to not neglect a charisma that was GIVEN to him by the body of elders and a prophetic utterance. Is this one gift or more than one? Well, "charisma" is not singular, so we can't assume it's a single Gift – like healing or tongues – but rather a manifold, diverse gifting for service.

OK, so he got Gift(s) when the elders laid hands on him. Was Paul there? Or did He do it also?

2 Timothy 1:6 – *For this reason I remind you to kindle afresh* (anazopureo) *the gift of God which is in you through the laying on of my hands.* (NAS)

Anazopureo (Strong's 329) – means to kindle up, inflame one's mind, strength, zeal

Some versions say "stir up the gift" but what they literally mean is to stir as a fire. To get it flaming red hot again. To not let the light or the heat die out. If Paul told Timothy to stir it up, it must be that there were varying degrees of the same gift. That is, you could let it die down from lack of attention or use. Do you know how to "kindle afresh" the gift of God which is in you? Do you know for sure that you even have the gift of God in you?

I'm pretty sure that God's economy has a simple rule about how to multiply or increase what you have – you share it sacrificially with someone else. Then you get more – or what you have gets stronger. That's Kingdom Economics 101.

So do you think that in all the time that Paul spent with Timothy (who he considered a son), that he ever laid his hand on him and prayed that the Lord would give Timothy any good gift that God had ever given Paul? Don't you think that, whether or not Paul was with the elders in I Tim 4:14, that Paul also poured himself out into Timothy over and over during their time together? I know that I do with the people I love and fellowship with.

I want to pause here and say that this book isn't just about Spiritual Gifts, it's about how to be full of Jesus. He is the fullness of all the gifts, all the fruit, all the faith, hope and love. If you can be filled with Jesus, crammed full until nothing else can fit, then you will see more and more of the gifts show up – and more and more fruit of the Spirit. Besides being a Biblical imperative that you be FULL of the Spirit of God, it's really the only way to peace and joy and victory. This book is not about seeking manifestations, this is about being effectively armored and weaponed up for the war that we're fighting that TOO MANY people are asleep during. This book is about raising up the Church to walk in the fullness of all that Christ has for us. Not just healing and speaking in tongues, but wisdom and discernment and administration and prophecy and all the callings that are necessary for what's coming.

Before we can get too far into the talk about Spiritual Gifts, we need to first make sure that the fundamentals are covered, that everyone is free of the chains that bind them and the embedded sin that is keeping the fountain of living water inside of them from bursting forth. Before we can get your cup overflowing, we have to pull the cork out! Most of this book is about understanding the power that God has for you, the walk He desires for you, the promises He made you, the fear of the Lord that you need to have to keep this from being about YOU – and the expectation to LOVE that He places on you in exchange for the wondrous gifts He gives you.

My greatest hope is that through this you would just end up with a great, big, giant cup of Jesus and you'd learn how to keep your cup full all the time. If we can get you crammed full of Jesus, then He'll take care of the rest. You can't be full of Jesus without getting more gifts. That's really the point.

You getting it?

Convinced yet?

If you're still not buying it, then you probably still don't even believe the "charisma" are for today.

**If that's true, you better stop reading,
'cause this is just going to get weirder and weirder.**

TRIPARTITE AXIOMS

Tripartite simply means "three part" and an axiom is just a logic progression to prove a point. So I've just strung a few together here to see if you can get the point of where we're going. I could write a whole 200 page paperback about this by telling lots of stories and fluffing it up, but there's a war between good and evil and we're kind of losing, so it's probably better if we just cut out all the fluff and get right to the point.

God is tripartite – Father, Son and Holy Spirit.
IF we were made in God's image,
THEN we are tripartite – Soul, Body and Spirit.

When God heals us, it affects all three.
When God asks for obedience, it means from all three.
When God asks for worship, it means from all three.

When we sin, it affects all three – Soul, Body and Spirit.
When we disobey, it affects all three – Soul, Body and Spirit.
When we set ourselves above God, it affects all three – Soul, Body and Spirit.
When we are commanded to bear each other's burdens, it means all three.
When we are commanded to lift the yokes of oppression, it means all three.
When we are commanded to feed the hungry, it means all three.

When we give food to the hungry we are feeding their Body.
When we give Godly instruction to the hungry we are feeding their mind and Soul.
When we give blessings and prayers to the hungry we are feeding their Spirit.

When we give drink to the thirsty we are satiating their Body.
When we give pure truth to the thirsty, we are feeding their mind and Soul.
When we pour out on them the Living Water in us, we are feeding their Spirit.

We are vessels of honor, committed to the service of God.
We contain all kinds of things that can be used for His purposes.
We hold strength, money, time, knowledge, experience, wisdom, faith, love, joy, peace, patience.
Some are physical, some are mental, some are spiritual. All are to be shared.

The easiest to understand and do is the Body.
Even the world is good at disaster relief and feeding the hungry.
Even the wicked love their children and feed them good things.

The sneaky one is the Soul and the Mind.
Satan always wants us to spend all our energies on that one.
Teach them, train them, argue about philosophies, speculate about hypotheticals.
That is the Tree of the Knowledge of Good and Evil.
The world is really good at writing books and speaking many words. Of that there is no end.

The rarest one, the realest one, the most impactful one is the Spirit.
Our battle is NOT against flesh and blood – or the mind – it's against spiritual rulers.
Spiritual rulers that try to steal, kill and destroy.
You can starve the Spirit by overfeeding the Body and Soul.
All you have to do is take all the emphasis away from the Spirit and put it on the Mind.

God instituted the five fold Ministry for a reason. Each has their unique role.
Pastors are for feeding the Body. Caring for widows and orphans.

Teachers are for feeding the Mind. Train them up in the way they should go.
Evangelists are for igniting the Spirit in man and turning it over to God.
Prophets identify the failings in the process individually or corporately and point them out loudly.
Apostles train them all up and set them into place and send them out - and are themselves sent out.
All should be fully pouring themselves out on behalf of those in need – Body, Soul and Spirit.

Do we know how to pour out the Spirit on someone in need?
Do we know how to make sure our own cup is full? Is anybody teaching that anymore?

Isn't it obvious that the Church in America's Body is well fed?
How many thousands of tons of potato salad do we serve at fellowship suppers every year?
How much do we weigh per capita? We have plenty of food. Who could argue?
In fact, too much in some places and not enough in others, but that's just a distribution problem.

Isn't it obvious that the Church in America's Mind is well fed?
Could we have any more books and tapes and conferences and satellite training meetings?
Could our soulish nature be any more gratified? Do we not have enough input?
We are more obese and overfed in the Mind than we are in the Body.

> "Repent of your sins, accept Jesus into your heart.
> There now. We're done with your Spirit.
> We'll focus on your Body and your Mind from now on."

Is that really working?

Isn't it obvious that the Church in America is poor in Spirit and starving to death?
We don't look like Jesus, because we don't have nearly enough of Him living in us.
Our spiritual cups are too small.
We don't love like Jesus, because we don't know how to share what we do have.
Our spiritual cups are stagnant and lukewarm.
We don't act like Jesus, because we're leaving out the most important part of the battle.
We're fighting on the wrong fronts.

We are raising up very large people with very large brains.
We are not raising up people with faith like a child that will stride out with five stones against Goliath.
We are not raising up people that know how to walk in the Spirit and in the Power of God.
We are not fulfilling the Great Commission holistically – Body, Soul and Spirit.
We are not fulfilling Isaiah 58 holistically – Body, Soul and Spirit.

We don't know how to fight in the spirit.
We don't know how to pray anymore.
Not really. Not all night with travailing and crying out for God.
Not pulling down strongholds and lifting yokes of oppression over our town, our church or our sheep.
We are spiritual warfare pygmies.
Whose idea could that have been?
Who is glorified most by overweight, brainy, spiritually week Christians?

When are we going to start feeding their spirits?
When are we going to start pouring ourselves out?
When is the rain going to start falling on the Church?
When is God going to pour out His Spirit on all flesh?

MY EXPERIENCE WITH THE HOLY SPIRIT

Most folks with any experience with the Holy Spirit at all in this way will see that if someone without the Gift of Tongues lays hands on someone that wants it, probably nothing will happen. You can't pour out what you don't have. I've been to dozens of different kinds of congregations in the last few years. I've prayed with all kinds of people. How come some congregations all seem to sound the same when they pray in the Spirit? Either they're all faking it or something else is going on. Maybe the same pastor prayed on most of them and they all got what he's got. He poured out HIS Gift of Tongues on everybody he prayed for and so they all have the same "flavor" or "frequency" or "color". Can that really happen? Yep. I've seen it over and over.

Some time ago I was at a prayer meeting and a brother who has the gift of singing in the Spirit was there. It's really pretty! He'll get whole songs – music, lyrics and all – spontaneously from God. He can just sing for hours and sometimes in English and sometimes in another of several different languages. He'll sing a verse in a tongue and then interpret it himself into English without missing a beat. It's really worshipful and really pretty. Anyway, the Lord suggested to me that I ask him if he would give me that. Occasionally I would sing when I was praying, but it wasn't like what he does! He prayed about it and felt that the Lord said it was OK, so I just knelt down and he put his hand on my shoulder and asked the Lord to give me whatever he had. As I always do, I asked the Lord to keep me from getting anything _other_ than what the Lord wanted for me and I just received it in faith.

A few days later when I finally had some quiet time alone, I was praying and just started singing. At first it was like a toddler's first steps and I was glad nobody was around, but then a real pretty little melody line came out and a verse in tongues, then the interpretation in English. Then another verse and another. It was a pretty and furiously harsh prophetic statement that was straight from God. I didn't have to think about it or create it or get things to rhyme in my head, it just came out. Then the Lord said to write it down. I was worried I would forget it all, but since it wasn't my brain, it was from the Spirit in me and He doesn't forget stuff, it was really easy. A couple of days later another song came. I look forward to practicing with what the Lord gave me and getting really good at it. If the Lord gives you a weapon, don't let it get rusty! Learn to be a sharpshooter!

Over and over I have prayed for people to receive my Gift of Discernment of Spirits and right away they start seeing in the spirit better. I've given away my Wisdom, my Peace, my Faith, my Prophecy, my Word of Knowledge, my Interpretation of Tongues, all of it. Whatever they needed as the Lord would lead and I've seen those people almost immediately begin to walk in those or be stronger in those than they were before. Sometimes dramatically so! Even people from denominations that don't believe in any of this stuff start hearing God better and having more dreams and knowing things ahead of time. It's really fun to watch!

How did I get all that stuff? Some of it God gave me Himself, but lots of if it came from other people that God sent to pray on me and equip me. One would come with lots of Discernment and pour herself into me. Another with Wisdom, another with Healing. Then the Lord showed me that the more you give it away, the more He'll give you. So I poured out whatever I had on people and God increased my portion. Sometimes I far exceeded the original person that came to pray for me because they didn't really see what they were doing and weren't actively and intentionally doing it all the time. God even sent people from other countries to my little furniture store to pray for me!

How did this crazy ride start? Well I was hungry for more of the Holy Spirit and none of my Baptist friends seem to know how to get more Holy Spirit in you. I didn't have peace and joy and victory and I knew God was calling me for something big and I didn't feel equipped. So I found some folks that seemed to believe you could actually get FULL of Jesus and they prayed with me. I didn't ask for tongues – it's at the bottom of the list – I asked for Wisdom in as big a measure as He could give me. In fact, I asked to see through the eyes of Jesus and told Him that any bit of me He wanted to kill so that Christ in me could live, He was welcome to it. I asked to be crammed so full of Jesus that nothing else could fit. I asked that the Lord would give me SO much of His Spirit that there wouldn't be ANY left for anybody else. I begged and pleaded and fully expected Him to give me a great big portion of His Spirit. And He did – and it instantly turned my life upside down! A whole bunch of stuff just burned out of me right on the spot and I started hearing Him better and having dreams and visions and praying all night and speaking other languages and people started coming to help and advise me. Radical people with BIG cups of Jesus. And they poured into me and grew me and the Lord had me start fasting all the time and that helped stretch me; and He tried me and tested me and refined me; and more and more persecution came, but I didn't care because I was so full of Jesus it didn't even matter!

Then the Lord taught me how to see what was in my "cup" and how to keep it full. Then He taught me how to pour it out on people. THEN things really got into HIGH gear! Whenever I would give everything away, I would get more. The faster I'd pour it out, the more He'd stretch me and give me more. All my gifts got more acute and stronger the more I used them and shared them. That's God's economy. That's how He does things. The widow that gives her last two cents, gets blessed the most. Whoever is most sacrificial, without thought of receiving in return, is the one with the pure heart that He blesses the most.

If you go pouring yourself out SO THAT you'll be blessed and get more power, your motives are all wrong and you'll probably get something really nasty to come live inside of you. You need to do it like Jesus – just because they have a need and you're willing, even if you don't get it back. If they need all my Peace, they can have it. If the Lord says to give them ALL my ability to hear the voice of God even if I might never get it back, they can have it. The more obedient you are, the more He'll ask you to sacrifice. The more you give sacrificially, the more He'll replace it with.

On August 24, 2006, I was doing something else and the Lord stopped me and reminded me of Joel 2:28:

> *"And afterward, I will pour out my Spirit on all flesh. Your sons and daughters will prophesy, your old men will dream dreams, your young men will see visions."*

Really clearly He said, "You know, I've been doing that all along."

Well, yeah, people have been having dreams and visions since the beginning. So it's not like His Spirit hasn't been doing stuff. "Ok, so, Lord, what's the difference? Just the quantity poured out in the last days?"

"Yeah, lots more than you can imagine."

"OK, so Lord, when are the Spring and Later rains going to fall at the same time? When does this start?"

"As soon as you start pouring My Spirit out on all flesh."

"HUH!?!? WE are the Early and Later Rain? WE are the vehicle to pour Your Spirit out?!"

"Yep."

"How can that be, Lord?!"

"I told you and I showed you, endless rivers of living water will spring up from inside you. The more you give, the more you will get. The faster you pour it out, the faster it gets replaced. The more you sacrifice, the bigger your cup of Jesus."

"So if we just teach the Church how to pour out their spirit, we'll get this show on the road?"

"Yep. I've been waiting a long time for you guys to start sharing and stop hoarding what I give you. You're all lukewarm and stagnant because your cups aren't being poured out. You've settled on your lees."

WOW!! That just shocked me! I already understood about the cups and I'd seen the fruit of it over and over, but I never connected that WE were the ones that were supposed to take His Spirit to all flesh!

That's all we're waiting for! As soon as the Church stops feeding their bodies and their brains and starts feeding their SPIRIT, we're full on into the big harvest. That's why people are dropping out of churches in droves. Not because they don't have enough to eat or enough to fill their brain – but because they are POOR IN SPIRIT and defenseless against the onslaught of the enemy. They have no power and don't know how to get any. So many of the denominations are powerless and neutered and filled with sick, dying people that can only depend on prescriptions and doctors. We're not looking to God for anything anymore. We don't need Him because we think we are rich, but really we are wretched, pitiful, poor, blind and naked – and lukewarm. Just like Revelation 3:14-22 said we would be.

That last statement is a reference to Zephaniah which is end times prophecy:

> Zephaniah 1:12-13 – *And it shall come to pass at that time, that I will search Jerusalem with candles, and punish the men that are settled on their lees: that say in their heart, The LORD will not do good, neither will he do evil. 13 Therefore their goods shall become a booty, and their houses a desolation: they shall also build houses, but not inhabit them; and they shall plant vineyards, but not drink the wine thereof.*

They don't think God is even paying attention, but He's going to take everything away from them. When wine isn't poured out from one container to the other, nasty stuff happens to it. The process of pouring it out purifies and clarifies it. If it just sits, it's practically undrinkable. His reference about lukewarm and stagnant is to Rev 3:16 – *So, because you are lukewarm—neither hot nor cold—I am about to spit you out of my mouth.*

Lots of people don't understand this because they think we should all be HOT for Jesus. They don't get the historical context. Most folks didn't have running water like we do. Any hunter or agricultural person knows that hot water is from a hot spring, it's healing and healthful. Cold water is running water, it's clear and clean. Lukewarm water is stagnant and green on top. If you drink lukewarm water out in a forest, it will probably kill you. So Jesus is saying, "Be either healing or refreshing, but don't be stagnant or I'll spew you out. I don't care which, just be IN MOTION."

The wine that has settled on it's lees has been stagnant for too long and is useless. Whatever we have, we need to be pouring it out on those around us so that we stay "stirred up" and in motion.

The Lord showed me a picture of what the Church should be. Most folks will recognize it. We should be like the pyramid of champagne glasses at a wedding – so that when the Lord pours into the top one it just overflows and fills all the ones below it. Then everyone is constantly getting filled and refilled and staying in motion. Everyone shares with each as they have a need and from the riches of their spirit gives to all. It's exactly what the Book of Acts is all about. Sharing your money is a BY-PRODUCT of having shared your spirit. Share your money all you like, it's still not going to be like the Book of Acts because you'll be fed, but spiritually powerless.

Which is more loving? That you would lay down your physical life or your spiritual life for a friend? This earthly life is like a blade of grass or a flower that fades, but the eternal, the spiritual is where our focus should always be!

Are you getting it? Do you see it yet? People are leaving the churches because they are powerless and don't see anything there that will FILL the void inside of them. That's because we're not really feeding their spirit, we're feeding their brain and their soulish nature (and their body) and they know the difference. It's not working. Whose idea could it have been that we would stop feeding the spirit and focus entirely on the soul and the brain? That we would focus on legalism and Self instead of teaching them to just be full of Jesus? Hmmm. Tree of the knowledge of good and evil sound familiar?

> 2 Timothy 3:1-7 – *1 But mark this: There will be terrible times in the last days. 2 People will be lovers of themselves, lovers of money, boastful, proud, abusive, disobedient to their parents, ungrateful,*

unholy, 3 without love, unforgiving, slanderous, without self-control, brutal, not lovers of the good, 4 treacherous, rash, conceited, lovers of pleasure rather than lovers of God— 5 having a form of godliness but denying its power. Have nothing to do with them. 6 They are the kind who worm their way into homes and gain control over weak-willed women, who are loaded down with sins and are swayed by all kinds of evil desires, 7 always learning but never able to acknowledge the truth.

Ok, so if you look around America at the 41,000+ denominations we have now and at all the people that CALL themselves "Christians" – is it a stretch to say that we are pretty much all of those things? And worst of all we have a FORM of godliness, we say we're Christians, but we're denying the POWER thereof. That word is "dunamis" in the Greek, from which we get the word "dynamite" and we're going to talk about that later, but that's the fundamental problem we're having. People don't have any spiritual dynamite and they don't know how to get it. We are lovers of everything but God. We talk a good game, but when it comes down to it, we'd rather cancel church to see the Superbowl. We're always learning and never seeing the truth. Cramming our heads with all kinds of seminary knowledge and programs and curriculums, but not hearing the voice of God cut through all the clutter. We don't teach faith like a child, we teach faith like a smart-mouthed, self-willed teenager that thinks Dad is an idiot.

What does that passage say we're supposed to do with people like that? Have NOTHING to do with them. Between that passage and the one in Zephaniah, we probably ought to knock it off and say we're sorry. We need to start seeking God's face a LOT and let HIM direct all our paths for a change. And the first thing He'll probably tell you to do is find somebody to bless with the things that He's entrusted to you.

WHAT IS DUNAMIS?

Dunamis is the Greek word from which we get "dynamite". It is variously translated as power or might or strength or virtue, but is generally something bigger and stronger than normal man. It generally refers to something supernaturally strong and powerful. It is the dynamic thing that creates change in dramatic ways. It is used in four ways that I can find in the Word; to describe the normal, natural strength of a man; to describe the amazing, supernatural power of God in a man; to describe the supernatural power of the enemy; to describe the after-effects of the power having been moved from inside a man to outside a man (an act, miracles and wonders).

Dunamis (Strong's 1411) (some concordances say "dynamis")
1) strength power, ability
    a) inherent power, power residing in a thing by virtue of its nature, or which a person or thing exerts and puts forth
    b) power for performing miracles
    c) moral power and excellence of soul
    d) the power and influence which belong to riches and wealth
    e) power and resources arising from numbers
    f) power consisting in or resting upon armies, forces, hosts

Translated variously as: power 77, mighty work 11, strength 7, miracle 7, might 4, virtue 3, mighty 2, misc 9; 120 total occurences.

Sometimes it's a resident power bubbling under the surface and sometimes it's already been expressed in an act (miracle). I'm sure they were learning what to call all this stuff for the first time as the Lord left them to figure out what to do with a big cup full of dynamite!

Here is a foundational verse for you to consider as you go through this. Here we see something really important. Christ, the Messiah, IS the dunamis of God. Not only was He filled with it, He IS it. If we are filled with Jesus, we are filled with the dynamic power and wisdom of God! Get it? **If you are full of Jesus, you are full of dunamis.**

    I Corinthians 1:24 – *But unto them which are called, both Jews and Greeks, Christ the power (dunamis) of God, and the wisdom of God.*

I want to show that in the Christian, it's really the power of Christ in you to perform that for which He has called you. If the same power that was in Jesus is in us, then we need to get as much as we can of it and then we need to LET IT OUT!! Find something to point it at and blast away. The result will be more people filled with the power of God – and probably miracles like those that followed the early Church around.

    Mark 5:30 – *And Jesus, immediately knowing in himself that power* (dunamis) *had gone out of him, turned him about in the press, and said, Who touched my clothes?* (Also in Luke 8:46)

Here the woman with a blood disorder just touched the hem of Jesus' garment and He knew that power had drained out of Him. What kind of power? Dunamis – miracle working, supernatural power. She didn't just bump into Him, she sucked the power out of His cup! He hadn't willed it, she just took it.

Here it is again:

    Luke 6:19 – *And the whole multitude sought to touch him: for there went power* (dunamis) *out of him, and healed [them] all.*

There's something about making contact. It wasn't enough to just see Him from across the road. People wanted Jesus to touch them or they wanted to touch Him. He went around laying hands on the sick. He sent the disciples out with the Great Commission instructing them to lay hands on the sick. (Mark 16) The physical contact is important somehow, but not critical. They didn't have faith enough to get healed without it, but Jesus heals some people without touching them at all or even being in the same town. In Acts 5:15 Peter's shadow is healing people! In Acts 19:12 even handkerchiefs and aprons that had touched Paul were healing people and delivering them of evil spirits! The dunamis of the Spirit of God is transferable. It's a force that endures on people and objects.

Here we see Jesus impart specific flavors of it to His disciples: (deliverance and healing)

> Luke 9:1 – *Then he called his twelve disciples together, and gave them power (dunamis) and authority over all devils, and to cure diseases.*

But that was just a warm-up for the big stuff that came later:

> Acts 1:8 – *But ye shall receive power (dunamis), after that the Holy Ghost is come upon you: and ye shall be witnesses unto me both in Jerusalem, and in all Judaea, and in Samaria, and unto the uttermost part of the earth.*

OK, they had already received SOME dunamis in Luke 9:1, so this is more. So the Upper Room in Acts 2 is NOT the first time they get the power of the Holy Spirit in them. They could have gone and spread the Gospel when Jesus left, but He was very clear that they needed to wait until the Holy Spirit came. But they already had some Holy Spirit. Yeah, but they had to wait. Why? For the really BIG dose that would empower them in a great big way! Not just healing and deliverance, but the full spectrum of stuff that they were going to need. And when it happens they get far more than they could ever have imagined possible! They get great big cups full of Jesus all in one dose. They start speaking in other languages, singing and worshiping God all the time, they rejoice in afflictions, they share all their stuff, they prophecy, they evangelize, they reason with the religious authorities – in short, they are a WHOLE lot more like Jesus then they used to be. How can that be? Because they got a whole lot more Jesus IN them all of a sudden!

It was clear that this power is supernatural. Here Peter speaks sarcastically about it, with the obvious response to his rhetorical question that, of course, there is no way that their OWN human "dunamis" could do such a thing.

> Acts 3:12 – *And when Peter saw [it], he answered unto the people, Ye men of Israel, why marvel ye at this? or why look ye so earnestly on us, as though by our own power (dunamis) or holiness we had made this man to walk?*

Here are a bunch more examples. I don't have space here, look them all up in context, but the point is that the disciples were FULL of a supernatural miracle working power and it was the power of God. Sometimes the dunamis is put into action in the form of miracles. Rather than just an internal force, someone skilled with their weaponry systems has focused it and pushed it out at a particular target with amazing results! This is what spread the Gospel so fast!

> Acts 4:7 – *And when they had set them in the midst, they asked, By what power (dunamis), or by what name, have ye done this?*

> Acts 4:33 – *And with great power (dunamis) gave the apostles witness of the resurrection of the Lord Jesus: and great grace was upon them all.*

> Acts 6:8 – *And Stephen, full of faith and power (dunamis), did great wonders and miracles among the people.*

Acts 8:10 – *To whom they all gave heed, from the least to the greatest, saying, This man is the great power* (dunamis) *of God.*

Acts 10:38 – *How God anointed Jesus of Nazareth with the Holy Ghost and with power* (dunamis): *who went about doing good, and healing all that were oppressed of the devil; for God was with him.*

Acts 2:22 – *Ye men of Israel, hear these words; Jesus of Nazareth, a man approved of God among you by miracles* (dunamis) *and wonders and signs, which God did by him in the midst of you, as ye yourselves also know:*

Acts 19:11 – *And God wrought special miracles* (dunamis) *by the hands of Paul:*

Acts 8:13 – *Then Simon himself believed also: and when he was baptized, he continued with Philip, and wondered, beholding the miracles* (dunamis) *and signs which were done.*

I Corinthians 12:10 – *To another the working of miracles* (dunamis); *to another prophecy; to another discerning of spirits; to another [divers] kinds of tongues; to another the interpretation of tongues:*

2 Corinthians 12:12 – *Truly the signs of an apostle were wrought among you in all patience, in signs, and wonders, and mighty deeds* (dunamis).

Galatians 3:5 – *He therefore that ministereth to you the Spirit, and worketh miracles* (dunamis) *among you, [doeth he it] by the works of the law, or by the hearing of faith?*

Romans 1:4 – *And declared [to be] the Son of God with power* (dunamis), *according to the spirit of holiness, by the resurrection from the dead:*

Philippians 3:10 – *That I may know him, and the power* (dunamis) *of his resurrection, and the fellowship of his sufferings, being made conformable unto his death;*

Romans 1:16 – *For I am not ashamed of the gospel of Christ: for it is the power* (dunamis) *of God unto salvation to every one that believeth ; to the Jew first, and also to the Greek.*

I Corinthians 1:18 – *For the preaching of the cross is to them that perish foolishness; but unto us which are saved it is the power* (dunamis) *of God.*

Did you see that? The GOSPEL is the dunamis of God. Not the "Purpose Driven Life" or "How to Win Friends and Influence People" or "Chicken Soup for the Christian Soul." The GOSPEL is the dunamis of God! Stop arguing about doctrine and secondary issues and self-help stuff and start preaching the Gospel and you'll see the power of God show up! It doesn't matter how long you can lecture about who wrote the book of Hebrews or archaeological discoveries that prove the Old Testament or the problems with the DaVinci Code. The power of God proves itself when it shows up. Just preach the Gospel, that's where the power of God lies. In the preaching of the CROSS is the dunamis of God!

Romans 15:13 – *Now the God of hope fill you with all joy and peace in believing, that ye may abound in hope, through the power* (dunamis) *of the Holy Ghost.*

Romans 15:19 – *Through mighty* (dunamis) *signs and wonders, by the power* (dunamis) *of the Spirit of God; so that from Jerusalem, and round about unto Illyricum, I have fully preached the gospel of Christ.*

The miraculous things that were done were not in their own power, but in the dynamic power of the Spirit of God when they FULLY preached the Gospel of Christ. Is that what we are seeing in America? I don't think so.

I Corinthians 2:4 – *And my speech and my preaching [was] not with enticing words of man's wisdom, but in demonstration of the Spirit and of power* (dunamis):

> I Corinthians 2:5 – *That your faith should not stand in the wisdom of men, but in the power* (dunamis) *of God.*

Boy, wouldn't THAT be a nice change from most of the sermons we've heard?! When are we going to get back to that?! As a percentage, how much of what's said in "church" is "enticing words of man's wisdom" and how much is "demonstration of the Spirit and of power"? If that stuff (dunamis) isn't for today, then all we've got left are "enticing words of man's wisdom" and I think I'd rather be an atheist. What's the point really?

> I Corinthians 4:19 – *But I will come to you shortly, if the Lord will, and will know, not the speech of them which are puffed up, but the power* (dunamis)
> I Corinthians 4:20 – *For the kingdom of God [is] not in word, but in power* (dunamis)

I Corin. 4:19 says that Paul is NOT going to test their doctrine or their head knowledge or the skillfulness of their speech making, he's going to test their dunamis. How much supernatural power is coming out of them? Do you do that? Do you test the dunamis of those who are speaking or the quality of their wisdom of man? Have you ever even SEEN dunamis in action? Come on, honestly, have you seen someone preach with such an anointing that people are wailing in fear and conviction because they could see the gates of hell open up under their feet? THAT is dunamis! That is what Peter got from 3,000 people when he preached his very first sermon (Acts 2) under the dunamis of God. And he didn't have any notes or commentaries or prepare ahead of time!

> 2 Corinthians 1:8 – *For we would not, brethren, have you ignorant of our trouble which came to us in Asia, that we were pressed out of measure, above strength* (dunamis), *insomuch that we despaired even of life :*

If they despaired unto life, it wasn't just their own strength, even the power of God in them was waning thin. They're cups were drained of all the dunamis they had.

> 2 Corinthians 4:7 – *But we have this treasure in earthen vessels, that the excellency of the power* (dunamis) *may be of God, and not of us.*

> 2 Corinthians 12:9 – *And he said unto me, My grace is sufficient for thee: for my strength* (dunamis) *is made perfect in weakness. Most gladly therefore will I rather glory in my infirmities, that the power* (dunamis) *of Christ may rest upon me.*

When you have no strength of your own, then can the DUNAMIS of God be made perfect in your weakness. So glory and rejoice in infirmities SO THAT the DUNAMIS of CHRIST may rest upon you. The less YOU in your cup, the more JESUS can fit!

Want to hear it again?

> 2 Corinthians 13:4 – *For though he was crucified through weakness, yet he liveth by the power* (dunamis) *of God. For we also are weak in him, but we shall live with him by the power* (dunamis) *of God toward you.*

Lots more. Here are a few more examples of His power in us.

> Ephesians 1:19 – *And what [is] the exceeding greatness of his power* (dunamis) *to us-ward who believe, according to the working of his mighty power* (kratos – dominion/authority, Strongs #2904) ,

> Ephesians 3:16 – *That he would grant you, according to the riches of his glory, to be strengthened with might* (dunamis) *by his Spirit in the inner man;*

> Ephesians 3:20 – *Now unto him that is able to do exceeding abundantly above all that we ask or think, according to the power* (dunamis) *that worketh in us,*

Colossians 1:11 – *Strengthened with all might* (dunamis), *according to his glorious power* (kratos – dominion/ authority, #2904), *unto all patience and long-suffering with joyfulness;*

2 Thessalonians 1:11 – *Wherefore also we pray always for you, that our God would count you worthy of [this] calling, and fulfill all the good pleasure of [his] goodness, and the work of faith with power* (dunamis):

2 Timothy 1:7 – *For God hath not given us the spirit of fear; but of power* (dunamis), *and of love, and of a sound mind.*

2 Timothy 1:8 – *Be not thou therefore ashamed of the testimony of our Lord, nor of me his prisoner: but be thou partaker of the afflictions of the gospel according to the power* (dunamis) *of God;*

2 Peter 1:3 – *According as his divine power* (dunamis) *hath given unto us all things that [pertain] unto life and godliness, through the knowledge of him that hath called us to glory and virtue:*

The enemy has supernatural power (dunamis) too.

Luke 10:19 – *Behold , I give unto you power to tread on serpents and scorpions, and over all the power* (dunamis) *of the enemy: and nothing shall by any means hurt you.*

Revelation 13:2 – *And the beast which I saw was like unto a leopard, and his feet were as [the feet] of a bear, and his mouth as the mouth of a lion: and the dragon gave him his power* (dunamis), *and his seat, and great authority.*

Revelation 17:13 – *These have one mind, and shall give their power* (dunamis) *and strength unto the beast.*

Revelation 18:3 – *For all nations have drunk of the wine of the wrath of her fornication, and the kings of the earth have committed fornication with her, and the merchants of the earth are waxed rich through the abundance* (dunamis) *of her delicacies.*

There is YOUR dunamis and then there is GOD'S dunamis! Which do you want to be FULL of? In these three verses we see dunamis used in terms of physical strength, ability or capacity or quantity – but not supernatural power.

Matthew 25:15 – *And unto one he gave five talents, to another two, and to another one; to every man according to his several ability* (dunamis); *and straightway took his journey.*

2 Corinthians 1:8 – *For we would not, brethren, have you ignorant of our trouble which came to us in Asia, that we were pressed out of measure, above strength* (dunamis), *insomuch that we despaired even of life :*

2 Corinthians 12:9 – *And he said unto me, My grace is sufficient for thee: for my strength* (dunamis) *is made perfect in weakness. Most gladly therefore will I rather glory in my infirmities, that the power* (dunamis) *of Christ may rest upon me.*

Here we see the contrast between OUR strength and the dunamis of God!

Revelation 12:10 – *And I heard a loud voice saying in heaven, Now is come salvation, and strength* (dunamis), *and the kingdom of our God, and the power of his Christ: for the accuser of our brethren is cast down, which accused them before our God day and night .*

Revelation 15:8 – *And the temple was filled with smoke from the glory of God, and from his power* (dunamis); *and no man was able to enter into the temple, till the seven plagues of the seven angels were fulfilled.*

Revelation 19:1 – *And after these things I heard a great voice of much people in heaven, saying, Alleluia; Salvation, and glory, and honour, and power* (dunamis), *unto the Lord our God:*

Which one do you think you'd rather be filled with?! The Word says that WE each are the temple not built by human hands. (Mark 14:58) That means that God's Spirit dwells within us. Well I want my temple, my body, my spirit, so full of the cloud of the glory of God and His power that <u>nothing</u> else would be able to enter this temple! Is that possible? He says it is and I believe it. My personal experience is that it truly does work just like that. You can get your "cup" so crammed full of Jesus that nothing else can fit. Keep reading and you'll learn how.

It's the dunamis of God that keeps us through faith unto salvation.

I Peter 1:3-5 – *Blessed [be] the God and Father of our Lord Jesus Christ, which according to his abundant mercy hath begotten us again unto a lively hope by the resurrection of Jesus Christ from the dead, To an inheritance incorruptible, and undefiled, and that fadeth not away, reserved in heaven for you, who are kept by the power* (dunamis) *of God through faith unto salvation ready to be revealed in the last time.*

It is Christ in us, the power of God in us, that keeps us through faith inside the power of salvation. It is dunamis that helps us navigate the narrow path. Without it, we are without hope.

Now we get to some hard ones. How about this one that nobody likes to talk about?

Hebrews 6:4-6 – *For [it is] impossible for those who were once enlightened, and have tasted of the heavenly gift, and were made partakers of the Holy Ghost, And have tasted the good word of God, and the powers* (dunamis) *of the world to come, If they shall fall away, to renew them again unto repentance; seeing they crucify to themselves the Son of God afresh, and put [him] to an open shame.*

OK, so who is it that they're talking about in this verse? Those who have been enlightened **AND** tasted the heavenly gift **AND** were partakers in the Holy Ghost **AND** have tasted the good word of God **AND** held the spiritual, supernatural power of the world to come. If THOSE people should fall away, it's impossible to renew and restore them. This isn't about people that got saved at youth camp in 8th grade and then sinned again. This is a VERY high standard. These are people who have experienced the FULLNESS of God and still turned away.

To tell you the truth, I don't think we've seen any of these people yet. I think this is a prophetic pronouncement about someone yet to come. I don't think I've ever met or heard of anyone that met all those qualifications. We have people that have sampled, have nibbled at the power of the world to come, but nobody has really walked in it and been fully enlightened and truly tasted the "good" word of God in clarity and truth and fullness. I think this is about those who are coming, the man-child remnant of Revelation that is the first-fruits of the harvest to come. (But I could be wrong.)

OK, that's a lot of stuff about dunamis! Are you getting it yet? It's the power of God in you and the more you have, the more you can do stuff with it. If you have a little you get faith and salvation and joy and peace and hope. If you have a lot, you get the bigger Gifts like healing and miracles and prophecy. Plus, the more you have, the more you're like Jesus and the more persecution and affliction is going to come – and the more you're going to glory in it. I know that's just nutty, but that's the way Kingdom Economics works. Want a bigger cup of Jesus? Give more away, suffer more, fast more, die to self more. Want a big cup of Jesus so you can impress your friends with how you can heal people or so you can make money? Fat chance. He'll probably turn you over to something really ugly. People might get healed, but it's going to cost you. Those are the folks that hear, "Get away from me I never knew you." when the sheep and the goat judgement comes (Matt. 25). Yeah, you did stuff with the Gifts He gave you, but you made it about YOU instead of about HIM.

Here's something to think about. (I know we just did this earlier, but please humor me. It's important.)

Rain Right NOW, Lord!

> 2 Tim 3:1-5 – *For men shall be lovers of their own selves, covetous, boasters, proud, blasphemers, disobedient to parents, unthankful, unholy, without natural affection, trucebreakers, false accusers, incontinent, fierce, despisers of those that are good, traitors, heady, highminded, lovers of pleasures more than lovers of God; Having a form of godliness, but denying the power (dunamis) thereof: from such turn away.*

Are you following leaders in the "church" that are like this? Are YOU like this?

What is a "form" of godliness anyway? Well, that would be like going to church, wearing a cross, having a fishy on your car, saying you love Jesus and then doing whatever you want, even if it hurts Him. So what is "denying the power thereof"? Well, that's like denying that the Gifts of the Spirit are for today and are real and that we need them. That's like saying God isn't really talking to us or doing stuff anymore, so the Christian life consists of putting on our Sunday show and then going home and watching the football game. That's like trusting doctors and drugs and insurance more than you trust God. That's like storing up treasure on earth instead of treasure in heaven. That's like having no fear of the Lord and not believing He is really going to talk to you when you pray. That's like being more afraid of a Ouija Board than trembling at the thought that you might be taking Communion unworthily. That kind of stuff.

What does "from such turn away" mean? Well that means REPENT and RUN from them. And if you are one of them, TURN and run from yourself and the old man that was in love with the world more than in love with God. If your religion is dead, it's probably because there is no DUNAMIS of God left in it. If you are exhibiting those traits in that verse then God is probably not in you. At least not in any sufficient enough measure to outweigh the YOU in you. You are going your own way and are a lover of Self. Repent and turn and beg for the power of God that will keep you through faith unto salvation.

If our "churches" are filled with these kinds of leaders how do we know who to follow? How can we tell who are the real ones?

> Ephesians 3:7 – *Whereof I was made a minister (diakonos), according to the gift of the grace (charis) of God given unto me by the effectual working (energeia) of his power (dunamis).*

That is: "I was made a DIAKONOS (deacon, elder) according to the CHARIS (gift of grace) given unto me by the ENERGEIA (effectual, supernatural working and energy) of His DUNAMIS (power)."

For real?! Let's get this straight. Didn't Paul get to be an elder because he went to seminary and got voted on by a search committee? Didn't Paul get to be an elder because he was a good businessman and wise in the ways of the world? Because he contributed to the building fund? Because of the eloquence of his preaching style? Because he was the co-author of a new book that would forever outsell every other book on the planet?

NO! You get to be a TRUE deacon/minister/elder because you are MADE ONE by the Gift of Grace that is supernaturally given to you by the Power of God! In short, whoever has the biggest cup of Jesus is probably the "Elder." In some congregations I've visited, that's the little old lady in the back in the wheelchair. They would never think to let her preach, but when she prays, everything in heaven stops so God can hear her REALLY clearly. SHE is the one that needs to be dispensing the grace of God to everybody. She's the one that knows how to get full of Jesus and stay full. Sometimes a little kid has the biggest, purest cup of Jesus. I've seen it all. God uses the most unlikely people. Occasionally it's even the pastor!

All the people that SAY they are elders but GOD didn't put them in place by His ENERGEIA and confirm it with His DUNAMIS are not really elders at all. If this really is God's criteria for who we should be listening to and who should be leading, we're in big trouble. Look around, we have a huge shortage of DUNAMIS in the Church of America.

2 Corinthians 12:12 – *Truly the signs of an apostle were wrought among you in all patience, in signs, and wonders, and mighty deeds (dunamis).*

A true God-anointed apostle is not someone who has a big ministry or just claims to be an apostle. An apostle is not an apostle because he has lots of dreams and visions and a gift for administration. You will know they are an apostle because of their supernatural patience, the signs and wonders and the mighty deeds that follow them. You will know they are an apostle because they have a great big cup of Jesus and just LOVE to sacrificially pour it out on all the people around them. You will know they are an apostle because they don't make it about THEM, they point everyone to Jesus. They need to know God up close and personal and be someone who is directed by God, not by any man. They know how to depend on the Father fully and believe in faith that He is sufficient for any need.

You will probably also know they are an apostle because of the really surprising level of persecution they seem to endure everywhere they go. If they are the biggest cups, then the enemy wants to stop them the most.

Do we still have apostles today? Yes. There is no indication that we don't. An "apostle" is one who is sent out. Any missionary or church-planter would qualify, but you'll know they're from God by the dunamis that follows them.

There were the original 13 Apostles (capital "A"), but there are more than 20 people in the Bible that are referred to as apostles – including women. It was set as one of the multiple callings of ministry for the establishment and proper functioning of the church and there is no indication we stopped needing them. We'll talk more about that in another chapter.

To tie all of this up, get more dunamis. Get as much as you can and be a good steward of it.

Don't know how to get more? Keep reading.

EXCERPTED FROM 'JAMES DUNN, SIGN GIFT MINISTRY' BY W.V. GRANT SR

JAMES DUNN
HEALING REVIVALIST OF THE EARLY 20TH CENTURY.

"I pastored the Pentecostal Holiness church there for two years before this ministry came to me. I had been fasting, and praying, and I had been reminding God. I believe God wants us to remind Him about the promises He has made to us, to call his attention to them. So I was reminding God that when I was employed in a responsible position for the government, we gave our men the best tools on earth possible to work with, so that they could do their job right. I told God that if we as mere human beings could give good tools to our laborers, how much better tools could He give us to work for the Kingdom of Christ. I continued praying in that way, and begging God for the gifts. Just imagine! I would cry: the tears rolling down my face. I would fast until the preachers in Princeton remarked that my clothes hung on me like a sack, because I had lost so much weight. They thought that the clothes had belonged to someone else. I don't know how many pounds I did lose. I was way down in weight."

"One day I was just in a big way of praying; tears streaming down my face as I was alone before God. I was asking Him again to give me the gifts of the Spirit. A voice spoke to me and said, 'Just a minute.' And I stopped, and a voice spoke again, and said, 'DON'T BEG FOR THE GIFTS OF THE SPIRIT, PRAY TO BE MORE LIKE ME.' I said, Why Jesus, I had never thought of it in that manner, what do you mean, pray to be more like you? And the voice said to me, **'THE GIFTS OF THE SPIRIT WILL OPERATE IN YOUR LIFE, IF YOU ARE FULL OF JESUS.'** So I began to pray that I would be just exactly like Jesus."

"Then one night while I was lying in bed and my wife was asleep, something happened. I was meditating on the glories and graciousness of God, and upon the things I needed from Him, and all at once, the Great Presence of God began to flood into the room. He came in such a supernatural way that the room was filled with His Glory. A great feeling of ecstasy and glory swept over me, and saturated my very body, mind, and soul. I began to get afraid, because when you get that close to God, something happens to you. I began to draw back from this Wonderful Force, and when I did it left. **Then I realized I had made a mistake in drawing back.** The next few days, I began to pray as I had never prayed. In about 3 or 4 nights I was lying in the bed again and I was meditating and praising the Lord, and asking Him for help and power in my life. All at once, this great feeling began to come into the room again."

"The very room and atmosphere lighted up. There didn't seem to be any room for me there any longer, because God so completely filled the place. As I lay there, I lost all movement of my body other than my eyes. The Great Force of God moved down across my bed, and overshadowed me, and I felt the strangest, and most wonderful feeling. **From my very fingertips, it began to move into my hands, and up my arms. I felt as if I were holding 220 volts in each hand, and it began to surge back and forth through my body. Then and there in that room, while this was taking place the old me was leaving, and the new me was coming in.**"

"From that night on my life was different. Many remarked how completely my ministry had changed. I had a positive message - a message, that had fire in it. God talked to me, and told me that if I would preach the message of deliverance, He would heal the sick. He would give me the Power to cast out devils. As I listened to this COMMISSION from the Lord, **His power surged through me, and my arm happened to touch my wife's body, and it almost caused her to jump completely out of the bed.** That night God began doing things. He revealed to me the people's conditions and diseases through the mighty Spirit of discernment. I found I was a different individual. God showed me things that I thought were impossible for a person to see or understand. He would show me the individual that was suffering, what they had, and He would direct me to them. After I had prayed for them, they would be healed of every disease."

('James Dunn, Sign Gift Ministry' by W.V. Grant Sr)

Fellowship of the Martyrs

WHAT DO WE DO FIRST? BE A M*A*S*H

Before we start trying to pass out spiritual gifts, we better be sure that we're all cleaned out – personally and collectively. You have to purify the Temple first. The most common thing that I've seen in all my visiting different denominations is that almost universally there is a tendency toward putting on programs and ignoring the individual. The bigger the congregation, the greater the tendency. In reality how that manifests always includes a statement about family and concern for the individual but then it's offset and negated by the reality of a structure seemingly engineered to disregard individual needs. However unconscious this may be, the reality is clearly that millions of Christians are NOT walking in the fullness of Christ or worse, walking around with massive oppressions that continue to go untreated. We really shouldn't even try to go "dialing up" people that have lots of open doorways.

There are TONS of people leaving the institutional churches. Millions of them per year. Why? Because they don't feel like their individual needs are getting addressed. They may sit through a good sermon that has some life application, but they don't see or feel the radical transformation that should come as a part of the normal Christian life. Or worse, they have a crisis or a need and nobody in the "church" responds appropriately.

We are NOT honoring God. We are singing and dancing and pretending everything is fine while people are bleeding to death in the pews (not to mention in the streets). Listen to me, God does NOT want you to praise and worship Him while you're ignoring the person sitting next to you who is having a crisis! It DOES NOT bring Him honor for you to raise your hands and tell Him how great He is while you FAIL to act like Him and heal those nearest to you. Heal them – or at least TREAT them – and THEN you can go praising and worshiping and telling Him how great He is. He just DOES NOT want to hear you singing while you're ignoring people that are crying inside! Your prayers are going to bounce off of the brass over your head until you act like Jesus. Just knock it off – or else. He's not going to ignore their cries much longer.

The church should be like the TV show "M*A*S*H". If they're having a party and someone shouts "Choppers!" then the music stops and everybody rushes into action to do triage. That means rapidly identifying and categorizing the wounded based on needs - the bleeding, sucking chest wounds go first, then the broken legs, then the scratches. AFTER everybody is treated and in Recovery – THEN you can go back to your party. But what kind of hospital would you be if you let them bleed to death in the compound because you refuse to stop singing and dancing because you had a schedule to keep?! You planned for this party to take an hour and a half and, by golly, you're going to stay on time no matter what.

Even when Jesus was right in the middle of a great sermon and had them all in the palm of His hand, if a paralyzed guy dropped down out of the roof, Jesus STOPPED TALKING and healed him. THEN He could go on with his sermon - AND everybody was REALLY impressed because of the miracle that had just happened in front of them! I'm not sure which would be the bigger miracle in some churches, that a paralytic rose and walked away or that the pastor stopped in the middle of a sermon!

The people of God need to be trained up in how to rapidly identify the physical, emotional and spiritual warfare oppressing and killing their brethren and they need to be empowered to go and treat them on the spot. The music needs to stop until EVERYBODY in your camp is bandaged up. "Church" will not be **The Church** until it stops being a show and starts being a hospital, first and foremost. The reason it's not that now is because we abdicated to paid leadership to do all the work for us and they can't possibly keep up. In fairness (to us), many of them got to liking it and now don't trust the Body to help them - so it's a vicious cycle. But it's got to stop. The Body has to learn to care for the Body, whether or not there is a paid staffer. We need the Gifts of Discernment of Spirits and Knowledge operating in force and we need to get back to fulfilling the Great Commission - first by cleaning up the messes in our own congregations, then by GOING. We can't wait for them to COME - cause when we do, they're mostly not staying, and it's because they're not getting healed (which is because we're not acting like Jesus).

If any of this stuff has convicted you and you realize you played a part in sustaining a system that hasn't been working or you ever ignored someone that was bleeding because you had your own agenda, now would be a good time to find a quiet place, hit your knees and say you're sorry. Crying helps God know you're serious. You might also want to admit it publicly to the people affected. How are they ever going to learn how to repent really good if somebody doesn't show them? Don't wait for somebody else to do it. It has to start with you.

If you kneel down and repent and cry in front of them, it might just start a revival. Some of them have never seen ANYBODY do that before! (If nothing else, it will give them something new to gossip about.) :-)

NEED A SPIRITUAL TUNE-UP?

First, this is aimed at people that already have Jesus, but the process is the same regardless. A person who is lost could turn their life over and push through lots of the steps right away and be that much more effective sooner. It's just a matter of hunger level and God's sense of your preparedness. The goal is immediate radical transformation, not gradual incremental change culminating in perfection after death. We believe that it's possible that God can heal and deliver and restore and sanctify instantly and we're going to aim for <u>that</u>. If He chooses to take longer, that's fine, but we're going to ASK for maximum change in minimum time - even if it hurts. Which it will.

Typically, we would take a hard look at each of the three factors; Body, Soul and Spirit. Asking the Holy Spirit to help us discern any areas where there is resistance to the will of Christ, we would "scan" through each layer looking for whatever the Lord would choose to reveal. It might be a physical illness that has a spiritual cause, it might be a soulish anger or bitterness or unforgiveness that is blocking Him and bringing down physical curses, or it might be a spiritual problem of diminished capacity for Him because of limitations or "filters" that have been placed on God. It might be a demonic oppression that has really old roots in abuse or addiction or some unresolved, past sin that opened a doorway and allowed legal ground for the enemy. All of these are resolvable within the scope of the power granted to us through Christ. Some can be settled nearly instantly and done away with once and for all. Many people have experienced through this process an immediately lightness at the removal of some old yokes of oppression. Some experience immediate physical changes as healing to their illnesses or removal of addictions comes at the same time. We want to allow God room to act in ANY way He sees fit. We don't want to put Him in a box anymore! We want to believe that He is big enough to conquer anything and that He wants us free. He is big enough, right? And He does want us fully free, right? All the way free? Of everything?

When you do a tune-up on a vehicle, you want to find anything that is keeping it from running at peak efficiency. A misalignment, a missing part, low fluids, bad filters, even burnt out bulbs - anything that needs to be changed or adjusted so that it can be renewed back to the way it was designed. It's all in

Romans 12. In thanks for His mercy we offer our bodies as living sacrifices - holy, pleasing and acceptable - that is our spiritual act of worship.

So first, we have to be willing to offer our Body - the vehicle, and all that it holds - as a sacrifice. We need to be willing and we need to commit to hold NOTHING back anything. That verse does NOT say we offer half of our body as a living sacrifice – or even 90%. The whole thing needs to go on the altar. ALL means ALL.

Before we can do anything else, we need it to be a holy, pleasing and acceptable sacrifice. And since our sinfulness screams against our holiness, and our own nature confirms it, it's clear that only by the atoning Blood of Jesus is there any chance that we can be a pleasing and acceptable sacrifice. So before any tune-up is going to do any good, we need to scrub the whole thing down with the Blood of Jesus. You have to have acknowledged your needfulness for the Blood and asked Him to wash you clean of every sin.

Said less religiously, you have to tell Jesus you're sorry for all the bad stuff you let in and you have to really mean it - and you have to believe that His sacrifice on the cross was sufficient to wipe you clean. This IS NOT an acknowledgment that Jesus existed or that He was the Son of God - even the demons believe that. This is not a statement you repeat after someone else so that you can join a church. This is a full-on commitment to humble yourself before Him and to give yourself over to Him so that He can be in charge from now on. That you would like to bow down and let Him be who He is - Master, King, Commander, Ruler, Lord - in your life from now on. Fear of the Lord is the beginning of wisdom. Way too many churches are making it way too easy - and the result is sick, powerless, shackled, unwise people in the pews.

Ok, NOW you're an acceptable sacrifice. So what's next? Get up on the altar and shut up. You don't need to figure out your personal purpose. You don't need 40 days to figure out what YOU can do for God. You're the sacrifice! Get cleaned off, climb up on the altar and lay there naked. By doing this, by really doing this, really laying there naked – fully exposed and willing to accept anything that comes – you are most definitely NOT conforming to the "world".

When He's good and ready, He'll move on to the next step. Which is that He will take a big sword and begin to hack chunks of your head off and put His head on. It's painful at times and folks around you may not understand what's happening during that strange in-between time while you're trying to figure it all out and get the pieces of your head and His head to get on the same frequency. But eventually, unless you panic and jump off the altar, He will hack off all the bits that stand in His way and then you'll have the mind of Christ. He will have transformed you by the renewing of your mind. RE-newed, that is, back the way it was supposed to be when it was new. Back the way He designed it. Back in His image. Rebooted and set back to the defaults the way it was before you mangled it up and the "world's" viruses corrupted it. Read Matthew 18:1-4, Mark 10:15. He wants faith like a child.

Then and ONLY then will you know what is the pleasing, perfect will of God. And then you can go do it. It's not just so you can bask in the knowledge of what He wants, it's so you can OBEY. GO - reach, heal, save, deliver, free the captives. Do the stuff that's on HIS heart - and now that your mind is renewed and you know what is His will, it should be a lot easier. You probably won't need a committee or demographic studies or anything. If you didn't hold anything back, by this point, you're probably hearing Him really well and you don't really need any Man (or group of them) to tell you what God wants for you. And I can tell you this, it's going to cost you everything. But you won't miss any of it. Besides, none of it was yours anyway. But you better count the cost, because this is a hard walk. Job, family, money, comforts, control - all could be taken away or destroyed. If you pray to be like Jesus and He answers it, you'll be hated and ridiculed by the world. Guaranteed.

Sound like something you want to try? If you're lukewarm, it might just be better for you to stay where you are than to taste the goodness of God and then turn your back on it. Persecution is going to come with every step that gets you closer to walking in the fullness of Christ. But if you don't care what it costs and you're still willing, we can proceed.

Jesus affirmed repeatedly that these two command-ments are the greatest. That if you understand and implement these, you have pretty well grasped the Kingdom of God.

Here it is quoted in three different Gospels: (Please go read them in context)

> Mat 22:37-40 Jesus said unto him, Thou shalt love the Lord thy God with all thy heart, and with all thy soul, and with all thy mind. This is the first and great commandment. And the second [is] like unto it, Thou shalt love thy neighbour as thyself. On these two commandments hang all the law and the prophets.

> Mar 12:30-31 And thou shalt love the Lord thy God with all thy heart, and with all thy soul, and with all thy mind, and with all thy strength: this [is] the first commandment. And the second [is] like, [namely] this, Thou shalt love thy neighbour as thyself. There is none other commandment greater than these.

> Luke 10:27-28 And he answering said, Thou shalt love the Lord thy God with all thy heart, and with all thy soul, and with all thy strength, and with all thy mind; and thy neighbour as thyself. And he (Jesus) said unto him, Thou hast answered right: this do, and thou shalt live.

So, it boils down to this - the most important command-ment, the most central task before us as individuals and as the Church, is to love God with every component of our being - Mind, Soul and Heart and to do it with all of our Strength. How are you doing with that? That's what we're going to find out. If you haven't got that one down, the second commandment - loving your neighbor as yourself - is going to be a pale imitation of what it should be. You will love them to the degree you love God. If you're clearly not loving your neighbor as you should, it's a pretty good indication that you're not loving the Lord your God with all your mind and soul and heart and strength. If you're loving your neighbor with 10% of your strength, then you're probably loving God with 10%. It's like a math equation, just plug in the percentage.

Submission to God x quantityN =
Manifestation of Love for Neighbor x quantityN

If they will know us by our love and we're not evidencing much love for each other (especially inside the Church) and for those in need, then we must not be very submitted to God. What other conclusion can you come to? Fear of the Lord is the beginning of wisdom. I know it stings a little, but try to embrace it. (Try Psalms 141:5-6)

Paul says this in 1 Thessalonians 5:23:

> "And the very God of peace sanctify you wholly; and [I pray God] your whole spirit and soul and body be preserved blameless unto the coming of our Lord Jesus Christ."

We are made of these three. Body, Soul and Spirit. and they are to all be in submission to Christ. All means ALL! Let's try one of those verses again:

> Mar 12:30-31 And thou shalt love the Lord thy God with ALL thy heart, and with ALL thy soul, and with ALL thy mind, and with ALL thy strength: this [is] the first commandment. And the second [is] like, [namely] this, Thou shalt love thy neighbour as thyself. There is none other commandment greater than these.

Before we go any further, now would be a good time for the WARNING label.

WARNING! WARNING! DANGER! DANGER!

Proceed at your own risk!

We will NOT be responsible for ANYTHING that happens from here forward. You have been warned.

We want you to be ABSOLUTELY clear that this is <u>FOR</u> <u>SURE</u>, <u>NO DOUBT ABOUT IT</u> going to hurt <u>A LOT</u>.

You can drive 20 miles an hour and you probably won't get hurt too bad in an accident. If you drive 200 miles an hour and you make a mistake, it's going to get really ugly.

This IS <u>NOT</u> for sissies!

If you have ANY desire in you to slow down, DO IT NOW!
DO NOT GO THIS WAY!! DO NOT take our advice on this stuff!!
It will totally transform your life and things you love will be ripped from you.
Nothing – <u>NOTHING</u> – that you have will be your own any more.
So He can rebuild you His way, God will IMMEDIATELY start yanking chunks out of you. Probably stuff you really liked.
The fire will get VERY hot!

If you even so much as TRY to do this in your own power, you're gonna be toast!
<u>ONLY Jesus in you can get you through this.</u>

Last chance. Get out now! ALL the darkness WILL come for you!

We've seen it over and over. We <u>ARE</u> <u>NOT</u> kidding around!

If you miss a step you could end up on crack or beating your wife or drinking like a fish or in jail. We've seen it happen to good, Jesus-loving people who weren't <u>all</u> <u>the</u> <u>way</u> sold out. God will get you through, but it will hurt even more if you bail out. You BETTER mean it! We're serious.

We love you very much. We want to see you refined and purified and REALLY dangerous to the enemy, but we want you to be <u>FULLY</u> <u>READY</u> before you pull into the <u>Fast</u> <u>Lane</u>!

STILL HERE? GREAT!

NOW GO BACK AND REREAD THE WARNING AGAIN.

WE'RE TO WORK OUT OUR SALVATION WITH FEAR AND TREMBLING. HE'S SERIOUS.

OK? BACK AGAIN? GOOD. LET'S PROCEED.

SO WHICH PART OF <u>ALL</u> DON'T YOU UNDERSTAND?!

Where do you think you have an option to love Him "some"? Remember this old song? Have you really looked at it? How many times have you sung it and not really meant it? I know I did for years!

I Surrender All
by Judson W. Van DeVenter, 1896:

ALL to Jesus, I surrender; **ALL** to Him I freely give;
I will **EVER** love and trust Him, In His presence **DAILY** live.

I surrender **ALL**, I surrender **ALL**, **ALL** to Thee, my blessed Savior, I surrender **ALL**.

ALL to Jesus I surrender; Humbly at His feet I bow,
Worldly pleasures **ALL** forsaken; Take me, Jesus, take me now.

I surrender **ALL**, I surrender **ALL**, **ALL** to Thee, my blessed Savior, I surrender **ALL**.

ALL to Jesus, I surrender; Make me, Savior, **WHOLLY** Thine;
Let me feel the Holy Spirit, Truly know that Thou art mine.

I surrender **ALL**, I surrender **ALL**, **ALL** to Thee, my blessed Savior, I surrender **ALL**.

ALL to Jesus, I surrender; Lord, I give myself to Thee;
FILL me with Thy love and power; Let Thy blessing fall on me.

I surrender **ALL**, I surrender **ALL**, **ALL** to Thee, my blessed Savior, I surrender **ALL**.

ALL to Jesus I surrender; **NOW** I feel the sacred flame.
O the joy of **FULL** salvation! Glory, glory, to His Name!

I surrender **ALL**, I surrender **ALL**, **ALL** to Thee, my blessed Savior, I surrender **ALL**.

A whole lot of us have been singing that but really meaning, "I surrender SOME." Or maybe, "I surrender more than that guy over there." There are certainly lots of leaders in the churches that aren't meaning it! Very few people really mean ALL. And yet that is the specific and direct command of God and affirmed three times by Jesus Himself as the most critical commandment of all. More than any doctrinal statement or theological construct or interpretation, we must do THAT. First and foremost in the Christian walk MUST BE a love for God that holds back nothing. Anything less means that you have missed the mark. Can there be any other interpretation? Where does the Bible say, "Invite Jesus into your heart and then do whatever you want."? Where does it say that you can give Him SOME and He won't mind. It says that God is a jealous God (Ex. 25:5, Ex. 34:14, Deut. 4:24; Deut. 5:9; Deut. 6:15; Josh. 24:19; Nahum 1:2; and elsewhere!). In fact, it says the Holy Spirit in us envies intensely when we give ourselves over to the world (James 4:4-5).

This is hard stuff, and not what you may be used to hearing, but I don't see how you can find any other interpretation. We're to work out our salvation with fear and trembling. How much fear and trembling do you have if you go down the aisle at youth camp in 8th grade and accept Jesus into your heart and you're all done? The "Narrow Path" has just GOT to be more narrow than that! In fact, I believe the VAST majority of church goers are not going to heaven at all. I believe we've been lied to for years about what it is that God really expects of us. The New Testament would be VERY short indeed if the path to heaven was as simple as, "Repeat this prayer after me ..." What's the point of all the rest of it if that's all it takes?

If you're still with me, the rest of this is going to be about helping you identify ANY areas of Body, Soul or Spirit that may yet be unsubmitted to God and doing whatever is necessary to bring them into full obedience with Christ. Bite down on something, this might hurt a little.

The enemy is going to try everything possible to keep you from walking this out. The darkness DOES NOT want to lose a single inch of ground! So let's pray this first:

> ***Lord, don't let the enemy keep me from this. Don't let the enemy distract me or confuse me. Give me wisdom, Godly wisdom and as much of it as You think I can handle. Speak to me clearly and I'll follow. Please bind up anything in me or around me that would try to mess with me during this time. In the Name of Jesus. Amen.***

I like pictures, so let's start with this:

Holiness means EVERY piece of you is in obedience with Christ. Not just that you've made a "profession" of faith, but that you submit ALL of you to be bent to His will. With no reservation or evasion – nothing is off-limits to His control.

If there are parts of you that are not submitted, then you ARE NOT "filled" with the Holy Spirit. Stop telling people you're "Spirit-filled" if you're only half-full! Unless EVERY piece of you has been Baptized in the Holy Spirit, you're not all the way full. They have to have been crucified so that they can raise with Him in glory.

This is a very simple graphic, not at all meant to be thorough or all-inclusive. Let the Holy Spirit show you all the areas in your life that need addressing. I'm sure He wants to! For now, we're just going to hit a few so you can see how this works. If you're not hearing very well from God on what might be unsubmitted, just ask someone close to you – I'm sure they'll tell you the parts that don't look like Jesus. Spouses are good for that!

Rain Right NOW, Lord!

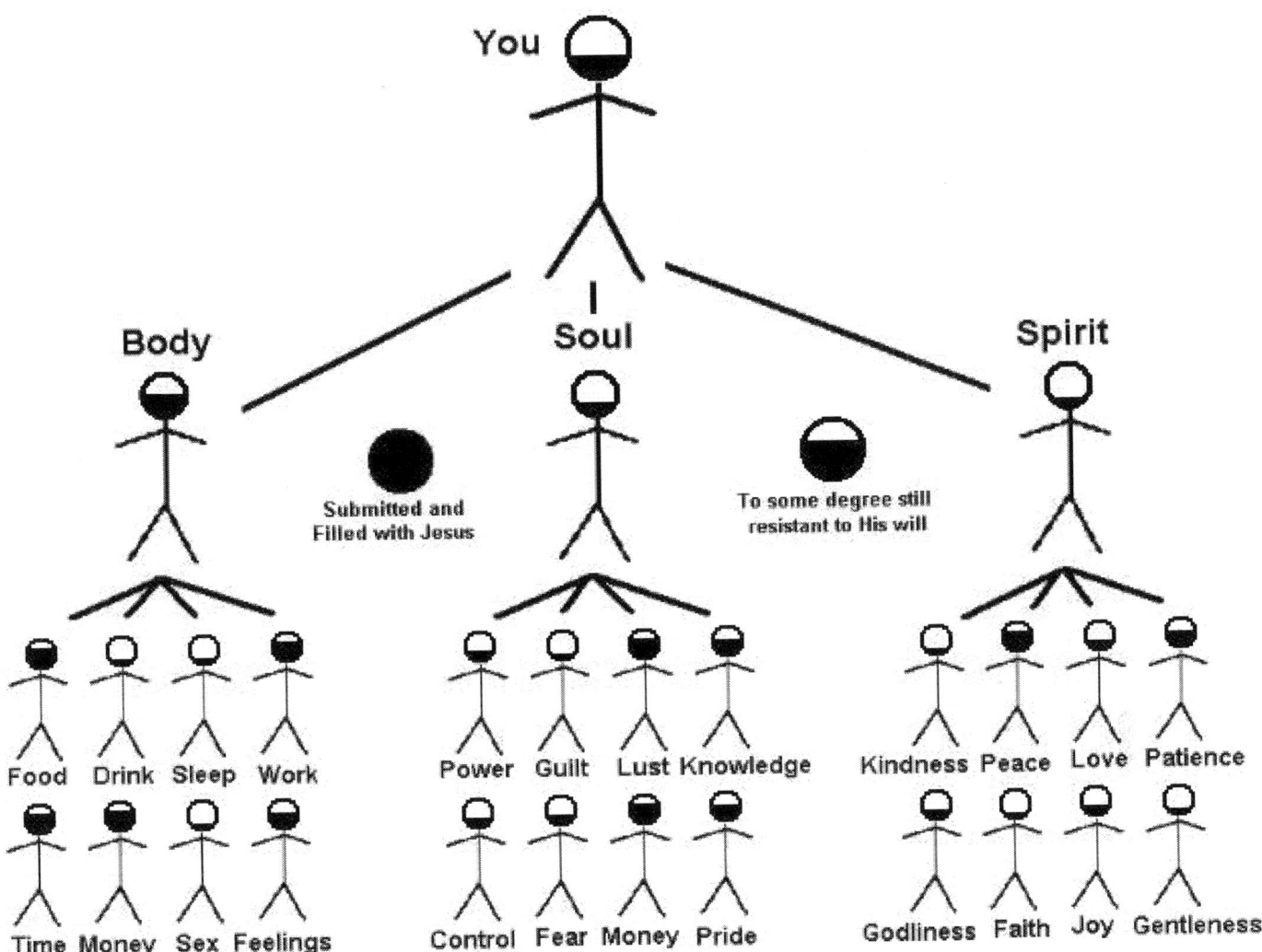

If we had lots of people in the churches with the gift of discernment of spirits, you could go to one of them and ask them what's messing with you and they could just tell you and help get it off. If you know somebody like that, by all means, get them in on this. But don't take ANYBODY'S word for anything. Check everything with God. Even if you can't normally hear God very well, I'm just SURE He wants to talk to you about THIS stuff! So you should be expecting that, as it relates to areas of your life that are unsubmitted, you're going to hear Him really well.

I suspect He's been waiting so long for you to ask Him what the problem is that as soon as you ask you're going to get LOTS of feedback. It may not be an audible thing, but somebody or some situation or a cloud or a little kid or a song on the radio or SOMETHING is going to be used to get through to you and show you the problem. Just EXPECT an answer and listen for it

Body

We are all jars of clay, vessels to hold His glory, cups of one sort or another. We are humble earthen vessels that are flawed and cracked in many ways and yet He pours His glory into us. We become the temple of His Spirit and He lives in us! Isn't that cool!!

Anyway, it's important first to understand that the Word commands us repeatedly to "be filled with the Spirit" and in the tense it uses it means "to be being filled" - a constant in-filling, a constant effort to keep our cups topped off. (The graphics here are from the full article "Fill My Cup, Lord." on the website – FellowshipOfTheMartyrs.com)

There are basically these options: (with lots of shades in between)

- You have NO JESUS.
- You have some JESUS and lots of SIN.
- You have more JESUS and a little SIN.
- You're all shook up by the World and "life" and can't figure out what's what.
- You're washed clean, but there's too much YOU.
- JESUS has killed off lots of YOU so He can increase and YOU can decrease.
- You've been a good steward, so He gave you a bigger cup and lots more JESUS.

And it's not a one-time thing. He's our Daily Bread, so you can move from one to the other fairly fluidly, even in the midst of one day. It's not a one-time thing just cause you went down the aisle and got "filled with the Spirit" one day. If you're not constantly STAYING FULL then you're going to drain off - or get lukewarm and stale. Over and over we're commanded to be full and to stay full – or to "be being filled".* And there's no point at which you shouldn't be striving for a bigger cup. We need Him in increasing measure every day to keep from being ineffective and unproductive (II Peter 1:8). You get a bigger cup by pouring yourself out on those in need, then getting refilled again.

* (Acts 2:4 *And they were all **filled** with the Holy Ghost, and began to speak with other tongues, as the Spirit gave them utterance.* Ephesians 3:19 *And to know the love of Christ, which passeth knowledge, that ye might be **filled** with all the **fulness** of God.* Colossians 1:9 *For this cause we also, since the day we heard [it], do not cease to pray for you, and to desire that ye might be **filled** with the knowledge of his will in all wisdom and spiritual understanding;* Ephesians 5:8 *And be not drunk with wine, wherein is*

excess; but be **filled** with the Spirit; Philippians 1:11 *Being **filled** with the fruits of righteousness, which are by Jesus Christ, unto the glory and praise of God. See Appendix A.*)

The Greek word used repeatedly for "filled" is "pleroo" (Strong's #4137). Here is Strong's definition of it:

1) to make full, to fill up, i.e. to fill to the full
    a) to cause to abound, to furnish or supply liberally
        1) I abound, I am liberally supplied
2) to render full, i.e. to complete
    a) to fill to the top: so that nothing shall be wanting to full measure, fill to the brim
    b) to consummate: a number
        1) to make complete in every particular, to render perfect
        2) to carry through to the end, to accomplish, carry out, (some undertaking)
    c) to carry into effect, bring to realisation, realise
        1) of matters of duty: to perform, execute
        2) of sayings, promises, prophecies, to bring to pass, ratify, accomplish
        3) to fulfil, i.e. to cause God's will (as made known in the law) to be obeyed as it should be, and God's promises (given through the prophets) to receive fulfilment

(Thayer's Lexicon also has a lot to say. Do a search for "filled" on www.BlueLetterBible.com or see Appendix B.)

The point is, Jesus wants us FULL and He knows that only HE can do it. We're all going to be full of SOMETHING. If our bodies are the temple of God and He lives in us, do you really want Him sharing space with that icky stuff? Shouldn't you be purified and cleansed of all unrighteousness so that He can reign supreme? It says "the prayers of a righteous man availeth much" - so I guess the prayers of a kind-of righteous man availeth practically nothing. Why is HE going to listen to YOU when you ask for something, when YOU won't listen to HIM about getting the red stuff out (and the stinky yellow stuff)? Proverbs 25:26 says: *"Like a muddied spring or a polluted well is a righteous man who gives way to the wicked."* That sounds to me like a cup that should be clean, but isn't.

Areas of direct disobedience or unresolved pain result in a draining off of that with which we are filled. Sometimes we have a really hard time keeping our cup full because we have a big crack in our cup caused by an unforgiveness or a bitterness or a fundamental character flaw, and so we drain out almost as soon as we get filled. Sometimes we can't ever get all the way full because of the goo we refuse to clean out that's taking up too much space in our cup. Really entrenched red stuff keeps us from being able to be filled to capacity. Sometimes there are physical oppressions and sicknesses that have resulted from spiritual problems. These, too, need addressing through the power of Jesus. More on all that later.

So, as it relates to the Body, let's start with this:

Is God telling you to do something with FOOD other than what you are doing? If yes, why won't you obey?

Is God telling you to do something with DRINK other than what you are doing? If yes, why won't you obey?

Is God telling you to do something with WORK other than what you are doing? If yes, why won't you obey?

Is God telling you to do something with MONEY other than what you are doing? If yes, why won't you obey?

Is God telling you to do something with SEX other than what you are doing? If yes, why won't you obey?

Is God telling you to do something with TIME other than what you are doing? If yes, why won't you obey?

Is God telling you to do something with your TONGUE other than what you are doing? If yes, why won't you obey?

Get the idea? Odds are pretty good that if the Holy Spirit is convicting you of something and you're not obeying, it's because you've given the enemy room in your heart or because your own soulish nature just wants to rebel. Either way, it's not really giving ALL and you need to do something about it. Stop thinking that He's just going to overlook it and cut you some slack. He REALLY doesn't like being in there with that stuff and He's a really big God. More fear of the Lord would be good. You might want to pray for that (like now). Crying is good, too.

If the Holy Spirit is NOT convicting you of any of that stuff, then either you are not listening and you've got a giant pride problem blocking your hearing OR the Holy Spirit has already beaten you into submission on all those levels. I've met both kinds. Just in case, now would be a good time to pray sincerely and ask the Lord to show you ANYTHING that displeases Him or any area of rebellion as it relates to your Body.

> Romans 7:17-18 – *Now then it is no more I that do it, but sin that dwelleth in me. For I know that in me (that is, in my flesh,) dwelleth no good thing: for to will is present with me; but [how] to perform that which is good I find not.*

Ok, OK!! You caught me, so what do I do about it?

Well, the first thing is to tell God you're really sorry. That would be good. He's been waiting a long time to hear that. And if you've been saying it before but then going back like a dog to his own vomit, then He's probably not going to take your apology very seriously until you start sticking by your commitments to Him.

If you've tried to turn away from stuff and haven't been able to, it's probably because you're doing too much of the fighting in your own power - because you've tried to force obedience with the YOU in your cup. That just puts more and more pressure on you and more and more guilt when you fall. Jesus lives inside of you and HE is not addicted to cigarettes or donuts or porn or work or anything. He doesn't worry or fear or covet or worship anything but the One True God. He has faced down every failing of Man and beaten it. If you will get out of the way and let HIM fight your battles, it will be much easier. Much. We'll cover that more later since it applies to all three of these components.

You need to be clear that SIN means "missing the mark." Whether it's murder or disbelief, it's sin and it keeps you from walking in the FULLNESS of Christ. You will not reach your maximum potential in Him if you remain unsubmitted in some areas – ANY areas. Jesus said, if you LOVE Him, you will OBEY Him. If you're not obeying Him 100%, then you must not love Him 100%. And 90% isn't going to cut it! He wants ALL – and ALL means ALL.

Soul

Let's try this same process again:

Is God telling you to do something with ANGER other than what you are doing? If yes, why won't you obey?

What about Guilt, Lust, Control, Fear, Money, Pride, Jealousy, Lying, Disbelief, Self-pity, Power, Bitterness, Unforgiveness, Gluttony, Idolatry, Rebellion or others? Got any of those?

Simplified substantially, the soul is the mind - our emotions, our mental state, our rationalizations and reactions internally to the world around us. It is what makes us distinctly us. This, too, needs to be brought fully into submission with God.

In a sense, you could see it like this:

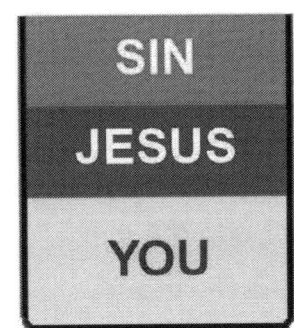

Body is where Sin manifests into the physical realm.

Our spirit is dormant until replaced with His Spirit and revived. Then it can take up the slack if we allow it to rule and reign.

Soul/Mind is where Sin begins and gets invited in. Can still be Sin even if it doesn't manifest, just by "dwelling." Our fallen nature always tries to open doors to Sin.

The yellow stuff (YOU) is our soulish nature and it's not that much better than the red stuff. In fact, the Blood of Jesus washes away all of our sins in an instant when we ask for forgiveness, but if we don't fill the gap with Jesus (and keep it full), the red bad stuff (SIN) will just jump back into the vacuum. It's our yellow stuff that invited all the red stuff! The Blood of Jesus is sufficient to heal us, but it's not the same process as with the red stuff. The Word says we're to crucify pieces of us so that Christ in us can live. We're to carry our cross daily. Well, that's about denying ourselves pleasures that might be red stuff, but it's also about watching chunks of Self die so Christ can increase and YOU can decrease. And I can tell you from LOTS of experience with this - getting the red stuff out is A LOT easier than getting all the yellow stuff out that displeases Him! One is about behavior and the other is about our nature. Habits are far easier to change than character. Beating the yellow stuff into submission is the crucifying ourselves part.

No physical trial you will ever go through - not climbing Mount Everest in winter, not sawing your own arm off with a pocket knife, not doing a marathon on your knees - will EVER be as hard as getting your tongue and your mind beaten into submission. THAT is the great battle in our lives and the difficulty is evidenced by how really rare it is to find someone that has accomplished any substantial measure of success in that! In fact, I'm convinced the only way to do it effectively is to let Jesus do it. We can fake it for awhile in our own power, but all we've done is suppress it. Only Jesus can terminate it once and for all.

In fact, it's not possible to walk in holiness at all without the Holy Spirit doing it. You can't use the yellow stuff to beat down the yellow stuff. That just won't work. Jesus is our righteousness and He alone is worthy and holy and capable of making us like Him. We can't get to be like Jesus in our own power. We have to be clothed in Christ, we have to run into Him who is our strong tower. We have to be dead so that Christ in us can live. And not just a little dead either - ALL of those component pieces have to die. Maybe this will help you figure out which is which.

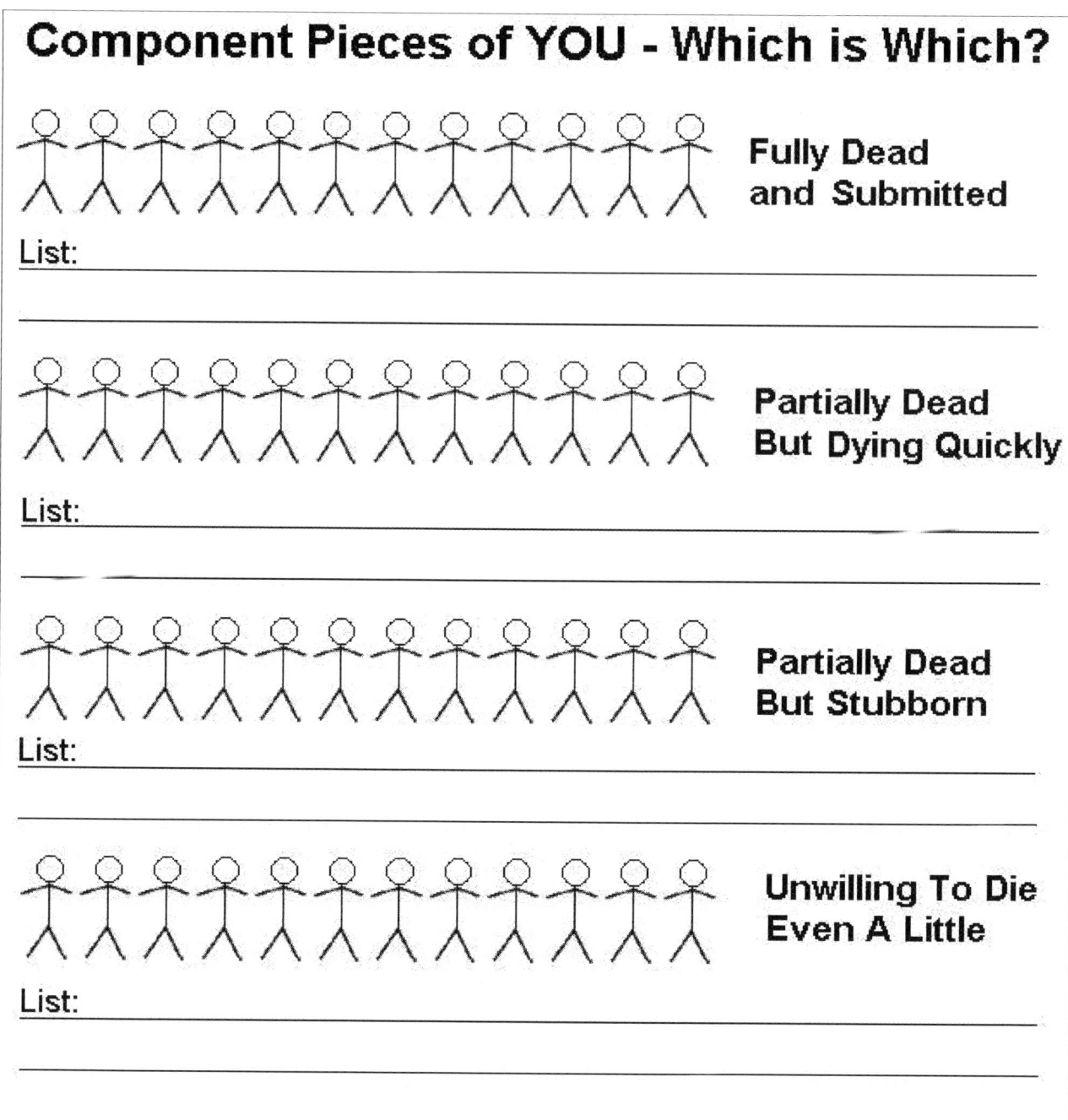

He doesn't want to purge you of ALL the yellow stuff. That would eliminate you completely and He kind of likes parts of you. Once I asked Him what parts of me He wanted to keep and He said, "Basically everything from before about six years old." Just the faith like a child parts. That thing in David that made him fearlessly go out to face Goliath because he just KNEW His Dad was bigger and tougher than THAT guy's Dad!

There's a lot more to be said, but you'll need to pray through this yourself and ask God to show you very clearly all the areas in which you are partially or completely unsubmitted. I know it's a prayer He wants you to pray, so I KNOW He will answer it and show you stuff. Then it's up to you to lay it down.

I find that this kind of prayer helps a lot and gets nearly instant results - if you have the guts to pray it:

(In case you forgot, go back and read the Warning first!)

Dear Lord, I'm really sorry for all the sin that I should have never let in. I'm sorry for all the old stuff that I've let take root and boss me around. Please purge me of all unrighteousness right now through the power of Your Blood. I stand in faith, knowing that Your Blood is sufficient to cleanse me of all unrighteousness. Please show me ANY area of my life that displeases You – anything that stands in the way between us and keeps me from being able to walk in the fulness of all that you have for me. Whatever it is, I don't care how much I like it, I don't care how long it's been there, I don't care how much it hurts, it's got to go RIGHT NOW in the Name of Jesus. So Lord, rip it, tear it, burn it, shred it, crucify it – whatever it takes. If I won't lay it down, rip it from my grasp. I don't care how much it hurts, I trust You. Do whatever it takes, but do it RIGHT NOW. I won't flinch and I won't try to hop out of Your refining fire when it comes. Dial the heat up. I'm going to stand. Give me the strength to stand. Please hold my hand. I'm going to really need You. Thanks, Lord. You're the best Dad ever and I trust You. Please burn it all off and don't stop no matter how much I whine. In the Name of Jesus, Amen.

Hear me – your growth in Christ is <u>directly proportional</u> to your willingness to rush headlong into the refining fire and give it a wet, sloppy kiss. When He is pounding on you and life seems horrible, if you will go to Him and find out what He's trying to teach you, embrace it, learn from it and thank Him for it - then maybe you can move on. If you whine and complain and keep asking Him to turn down the flames because it's too hot, it shows a lack of trust that He knows what He's doing and it just slows down the whole process. How long is it going to take to cook a turkey in an oven set at 50 degrees? How long if it's set at 450? That's the difference between Christians in China and India and those in America. We have our ovens set at 50 degrees and they have their's on full blast. Persecution dials up the heat really fast – and results in explosive growth in Christ (and a sifting of those who mean it and those who don't).

So don't be such a sissy. Jump in the fire and learn to like it. Is He God or isn't He? Will He protect you or won't He? Are His promises good or aren't they? Buck up, ya big weenie. Go kill some yellow stuff.

Spirit

OK, so we got the red stuff out (for today) and we begged Him to kill the yellow stuff. So you probably have a void in the top of your cup now. What are you going to do? If you leave it like that the enemy, who ranges to and fro like a hungry lion, will try to jump in there right away and mess with you again. You've got to get your cup full of Jesus and keep it that way. And not just full to 100%, full to overflowing – up and over, mounded up on top.

So do you know how? Well, you can read your Bible. You can listen to worship music. You can pray. You can just spend time at the feet of Jesus – like Mary. Whatever is the best way you have found to drink in Jesus. But be careful that you're not DOING to get filled – like Martha. That just means that you're trying to get more blue stuff by engaging the yellow stuff. That's a long uphill battle toward legalism. You can't earn the Holy Spirit. What it ends up doing is inviting in the red stuff again in the form of guilt, condemnation, self-righteousness, pride or some other nasty thing.

Maybe there's a better way. What does the Word of God say about this?

John 7:38 says: *"He who believes in Me, as the Scripture said, 'From his innermost being will flow rivers of living water.' "*

John 4:10 says: *Jesus answered and said unto her, If thou knewest the gift of God, and who it is that saith to thee, Give me to drink; thou wouldest have asked of him, and he would have given thee living water.*

Rev. 7:17 says: *For the Lamb which is in the midst of the throne shall feed them, and shall lead them unto living fountains of waters: and God shall wipe away all tears from their eyes.*

Here's a couple of Old Testament reference so you know God doesn't change:

Jeremiah 17:13: *O LORD, the hope of Israel, all that forsake thee shall be ashamed, [and] they that depart from me shall be written in the earth, because they have forsaken the LORD, the fountain of living waters.*

Jeremiah 2:13: *For my people have committed two evils; they have forsaken me the fountain of living waters, [and] hewed them out cisterns, broken cisterns, that can hold no water.*

In that last one we see that they committed two evils, they didn't drink of the living waters and they had containers with cracks in them. (A cistern is just a really big cup.) In fact, they made their own cisterns to store up water because they didn't trust in God's unending supply from the fountain. And the result was that they had neither – AND they made God mad!

It sure seems to me like those fountains of living water are the Holy Spirit. It says Jesus is the "Fountain in the House of David" (Zech 13:1) The Holy Spirit is that blue stuff that fills us and displaces all the other stuff. It would be great if He would just shove everything out of the way, but for some reason we're involved and we have to participate in the process – or at least be willing and ask Him to do it.

This being true (I hope you agree), then we don't need to DO anything to fill our cup. We just have to believe that Jesus wants our cup full, that He promised that springs of living water would flow up from INSIDE of us – and then just turn on the tap. We just need to ask Him to fill us in whatever way HE wants to fill us and teach us how to keep it that way. Remember; trust the Lord your God with ALL your heart, lean NOT on your OWN understanding, but in ALL your ways acknowledge HIM and HE will direct your paths. (Prov. 3:5-6)

I think our job as a church is to find those who are poor in spirit – those whose cups are running low – and share with them. Pour ourselves out into them so that they can be filled. Not with our yellow stuff! God forbid! But from the abundance of the riches that have been given to us that we would share – of our wealth, of our physical energy, strength, time AND of the fountain of living water that is inside of us.

Haven't you ever been around somebody that, just being in the same room with them or getting a hug, made your spirit feel full? I bet they had a cup that was overflowing – or they deliberately and selflessly poured themselves out on you. They may not have known that's what they were doing or been able to explain it that way, they just knew that they had Joy and Peace and that you needed some, so they shared.

Go back and look again at the picture of the pyramid of champagne glasses where they pour in the top one and as it overflows, the glass below gets filled and overflows and so it continues all the way down. Those who have the biggest cup of Jesus should be constantly pouring themselves out onto others and teaching them how to keep it going.

Shouldn't church be a filling station? How often do you go and leave feeling just as empty as when you got there? Some churches are really great filling stations and you can leave FULL of Jesus – but you can't make it past Monday afternoon without running out again. That's because we think we have to go to a building to get our cups full. The Word of God doesn't say anything like that. The Word of God says rivers of living water will flow up from INSIDE of us. We have an endless supply at our disposal all the time! And WE are supposed to be the filling station for those that don't know how to tap into it. It's not about the building or the pastor or nice music that gets us in the mood – every Christian has access to the river of God! Isn't that COOL!! So, stick a straw in and suck! Better yet, just dive in! The better you see in the spirit, the easier it will be for you to get a handle on this. I'm not talking about theory here, this is totally real to those that understand the things of the Spirit and ignore the things of this world. Faith is the key that opens the door. Believe like a child that God's promises are good and that He means what He says. Then just reach out and grab it.

Later we're going to talk more about all the things you can be filled with, why you need to help fill others and how to get full and make sure you stay full. I know this may sound weird, but it's all in the Bible. No question about it. We're supposed to perceive things in the spirit, not with our natural mind. This earth is NOT the "real" world – this is not our home. We are spiritual beings and we need to get a lot more familiar with what's happening in the spirit. That's where the war is and that's where our hope comes from.

> I Corinthians 2:14 - *But the natural man receiveth not the things of the Spirit of God: for they are foolishness unto him: neither can he know them, because they are **spiritually** discerned.*

> Romans 8:6 - *For to be carnally minded [is] death; but to be **spiritually minded** is life and peace.*

COMMUNICATIONS – HOTLINE TO HEADQUARTERS

Why do we need to do this? Because you need to hear REALLY clearly from Headquarters before we start passing out new weapons you don't know what to do with! The last thing we need is more friendly fire accidents when you go firing off stuff like Prophecy or Tongues without having been trained. You could do some serious damage – trust me. It's really important that we get your pipeline all cleaned out so that you know what to give, what to ask for, and what to do with it. If there is stuff in the way, we need to get it out so your motives will be right and He can call the shots.

OK, so we got the red stuff out, we're getting more yellow stuff out, we learned how to get more blue stuff, now what? Well, now it's time to get your filters unclogged so you can hear God really well and HE can direct ALL your paths. This works better as a question and answer thing. Ready?

First, what exactly are we talking about? Does God really speak to people today?

Yes. In a whole bunch of ways from a gentle nudge, to instruction through the Word, to using other people and circumstances to speak to you, to sending dreams and visions (or angels) – and/or even conversing directly with you.

You can hear God and converse with Him?! You're kidding, right?

Not kidding. You can absolutely talk to God and He'll talk back. There are millions of people all over the world that rely on God for constant daily instruction on all sorts of things. But, there's a difference between hearing God audibly (with your natural ears, outside of your own head) and hearing the inner "still, small voice". It's pretty rare for God to speak to people audibly (like thunder), but there are plenty of folks out there that say they've heard Him – and the evidence is that once they did, it changed them forever!

Many of the house churches in China are under such persecution that they can't set a regular time for meeting or even tell each other when the meeting will be – they all just pray independently and God Himself sets the time and place and tells each to be there. I've experienced that kind of coordination myself and hear Him speak to me all the time. This is totally for real and the birthright of every believer! He's your Dad and He <u>wants</u> to talk to you.

Wait ... people hear the God of the Universe tell them stuff? Like what tie to wear and whether to turn left or right? What job to take? What to have for dinner? Not just big stuff?

Sure. The Bible says, "In all your ways acknowledge Him and He will direct your paths." (Prov. 3:5-6) What do you think "ALL your ways" means? And how is He going to direct you if you can't hear Him?

But my pastor said God doesn't talk to people like that!

Hmmm. Well, God used to talk to people all the time in the Bible. Wonder when He stopped? Did He say He was going to stop? Isn't He the same yesterday, today and forever? If anything, once the Holy Spirit came in Acts 2, there were LOTS MORE people talking to God directly! Never mind the MILLIONS of people all over the world who you have to conclude are thoroughly and certifiably nuts – including many of the most effective leaders of the church. In order to sustain that argument you have all kinds of logic problems.

Consider this;

IF God used to talk to people but doesn't now, **THEN** we must not need to hear from Him anymore. Can that be? By all measures we're worse off than ever. If there is a war between Good and Evil, we're losing pretty badly right now and really desperately need to be getting commands directly from Headquarters, not from flawed man-made sources and tradition-soaked interpretations of Scripture!

IF there is a battle between Good and Evil, **THEN** who would benefit most if the people on the "Good" side were told they couldn't ACTUALLY talk to their Commander in Chief? Now, you know the "Evil" side is absolutely clear to EVERYONE that if you try to talk to THEIR leadership you WILL get an answer REAL fast! Even Christians are afraid to mess with Ouija boards and call on the names of demons because somewhere inside they believe something VERY real will show up almost instantly. But at the same time, the forces of darkness want us to buy that OUR God is mute! Doesn't that sound like something the snake would say in the Garden? Despite hundreds of examples in the Bible that He is available and accessible all the time, we have too often bought the lie that God is unwilling or unable to actually talk to His children. It's a lie from the pit and we've bought into it for too long.

IF we receive the Holy Spirit when we are saved, **THEN** 1/3 of the Godhead is living INSIDE of us all the time! (I John 4:13-17) But He doesn't have anything to say?! He's not interested in our daily activities? God's not big enough to know what we should have for lunch? He knows the hairs on our head and monitors our every coming and going, but has no opinion about it or desire to give us advice? What kind of Father is that?! **IF** we're dead and it's Christ in us that lives, **THEN** shouldn't HE be running the show? (Romans 7:4-6)

The most common argument I hear is that when the Bible was done being written then "that which was perfect has come and that which was in part was done away" (I Corin. 13:10) so we don't need to talk to God anymore. The argument is that I Corinthians 12 talks about tongues and prophecy and then chapter 13 tells about the way it SHOULD be when the perfect is come so you should do away with all that. But they don't seem to notice that then chapter 14 starts with Paul urging them to seek the gift of prophecy! Said another way, I think "when that which is perfect is come" refers to Jesus returning, NOT the Bible being completed.

IF the Bible is what's being referred to there, **THEN** why hasn't knowledge ceased? **IF** it's the "perfect" thing mentioned there, **THEN** nothing could stand against it. **IF** the Bible is perfect, **THEN** could somebody tell me which version is flawless? And **IF** none of them are because we don't have the original manuscripts anymore, **THEN** something DID stand against it! **IF** the perfect is come, **THEN** why do we have 37,000+ denominations and we seem to be losing the battle with the darkness? There are just big giant logic problems with that argument – not to mention the personal experience of millions of reasonable, Jesus-lovers all over the world.

But my pastor says even HE doesn't hear God conversationally like that!

Ok, well, you see, Matthew 18:18 says that, "what you bind on earth will be bound in heaven and what you loose on earth will be loosed in heaven." It goes on to say that if two of you on earth agree about anything you ask for, it will be done for you by the Father in heaven. (v. 19) So, could it be that we have whole groups of Christians that have agreed that God doesn't talk to people? And if they were convinced of that, don't those verses say that God will honor it? So maybe the problem is that if you're convinced God WON'T talk to you that way, He probably won't. And who would you blame? The pastor? Probably not – in fairness, we gotta lay it at the feet of the snake and the generations of tradition that have been built up to keep us from being truly "Spirit-led".

There could also be other problems that would keep a person from hearing God. One possibility is that you're on the wrong team - even if you think you're not. You know it's possible to make up your own "Jesus" and you'll get a response from that one about as good as if you were praying to a stick of wood. Another is that you have unrepented sin that stands between you and God – and God has convicted you of it so many times that He's just given up trying to talk to you about it.

Oh, and by the way, you're going to have to get over that thing about the pastor being more "holy" than you. This is a one-on-one relationship with Jesus you're supposed to have. You can't do it by proxy through the guy that gets paid to hear God (especially if he admits he's NOT hearing God!). We are ALL the Church. We are EACH temples that hold God's Spirit. Any one of us that are adopted sons of God have the ability to petition the Throne directly and seek His face. God loves each – in fact, He's especially fond of those that come to Him with faith like little children. Sometimes pastors have a hard time with that. (I don't think there are "Faith like a Child" classes in seminary.)

This is just crazy! How could this be true and I never knew it before? Wouldn't somebody have told me?

Well, I think you underestimate the damage the enemy has done and how long he's been plotting this. The vast majority of the church in the West doesn't live the "normal" Christian life. That is, Biblically speaking, we're to be full of power and might, we're to be free of the bondage of sin, we're to NOT conform to the world, we're to be dead to ourselves, we're to be ONE Body and loving and serving each other with all our heart. That's just a few. Can you see how far away from that we actually are as a "church"? We're not even CLOSE! There MUST be something missing. Somebody left something out! It has to be this – God Himself is supposed to be directing you and you're supposed to be listening and OBEYING. Now ... who would benefit most from us leaving that little piece out? Yep, the guy in the black hat.

Now, what do you think a close encounter conversationally with the God of the Universe might do to a person? Trust me, it would change everything. It would show them the power of the relationship they have as adopted sons, they would lose all fear, they would sacrifice anything to keep hearing Him, they would obey and walk in HIS ways, they would know (really KNOW) that God Himself lives IN them and they would want more of Him, they would do the things on HIS heart – like feeding the hungry, clothing the naked, saving the lost. They would be in awe of His holiness and seek to please Him out of reverence and honor, not out of legalism or church requirements.

So, **IF** this is a war between Good and Evil, **THEN** wouldn't our most immediate and urgent need be to get people to where they can hear clear, timely, reliable commands from Headquarters? If you have a guy in Basic Training that refuses to listen to the Drill Sergeant and does his own thing, wouldn't you want to leave him at home? He's just going to get himself killed when the enemy starts shooting and leadership says 'DUCK!' and he can't or won't hear them! He's no good to anybody. Maybe he could be a supply clerk – but he really shouldn't be on the front lines. He should stay home and send his money to the folks on the front lines that hear God really well and obey ALL the time, no matter what the cost.

But we have the Bible. God's Word is what we are to use to direct our paths!

Ok, sure. Not got anything bad to say about the Bible! Everything God tells us to do will line up with His own Word. But no matter how well you know the Bible, it can't accommodate for every possible situation and what you should do. There's lots of stuff not covered in there – like which of these two jobs God wants me to take. And there's stuff in there that men have been arguing about for centuries without ever getting agreement. Lots of wasted time trying to figure out how many angels can dance on the head of a pin. (By the way, which side benefits most when God's people fight over stupid stuff? You getting the hang of this yet?)

Think of it like this. You're in the Army and they give you a Manual. All kinds of stuff is covered in there – what to wear, how to salute, how the weapons work, how to survive in a battle, what to eat in the forest, how the chain of command works, even what the enemy is like and how to resist them – there's even stuff in there about what the enemy WILL DO one day, whether they like it or not! It's a REALLY good Manual – in fact, it's inspired by God! It covers an amazing array of stuff and could probably handle most any situation. So would the Drill Sergeant ask you to read it, maybe even memorize it – and then send you into battle with nothing BUT that? Are you going to be able to know what to do when the bullets start flying? What about group strategy and deployment of forces and anticipating enemy movements? Is the Manual going to accommodate for every possible scenario on a rapidly changing battlefield? Are you sure you're interpreting it right? Is there time in the foxhole to be arguing with other soldiers that are reading it differently? What if some idiot published like TWENTY different translations and paraphrases of the Manual?! Then what?! Are you REALLY sure you have the right version? Isn't there a chain of command? Isn't there somebody in charge calling the shots that's supposed to tell you what to do next? Aren't you supposed to be listening and OBEYING? Want to go into battle without the Manual? No. Want to rely on it alone when you have other resources available? No. Want to take an order from somebody that goes against the Manual? No. When the bullets start flying, do you want to hear personally and directly from Headquarters so that you can know that help is coming and know what to do? You betcha!

We need a radio to headquarters that works really good, with no static on the line and no enemy transmissions sneaking in. If you insist that you don't want to hear God, I still love you, but I'm not going to the front lines with you.

I don't know. This is kind of scary. What if I hear wrong? What if it's the enemy messing with me? Maybe this is all in your mind.

Wow! That's a whole mess of stuff. Let's try this one at a time.

Maybe it's all in your mind.

Well, it's not just me. There's hundreds of millions like me that hear God. In fact, most of the growth in the Church worldwide is because of those people. The "mainline" denominations are shrinking. It's the Spirit-led revolutionaries that are exploding into new territories and pushing back the darkness. The growth in this arm of the Church went from about ZERO in 1900 to about 500 MILLION people in 2000. God is pouring out His Spirit and people are listening.

Ok, let's try it from the opposite direction. It all sunk in for me one day when it struck me that satan never creates anything – he just makes weak copies of whatever God is doing. He's a liar and a deceiver and a fake. So ... while it may seem far-fetched, most folks (even Christians) will admit that evil is a real force in the world and the supernatural is real. (The Bible verifies repeatedly that witches and mediums and sorcery are real, by the way ... and that you're headed for hell if mess with them. – Deut 18:10-12, Col. 5:20) The enemy has psychics and mediums and astral-projection and Ouija boards and demons and zombies and spells and curses.

So where's OUR stuff?! If this is a war, why does only one side get cool weapons? Was my church leaving out important stuff that I needed for warfare? Because in the first century they had amazing weapons and defenses available to them. They had the Holy Spirit telling them stuff they wouldn't have known (Acts 5:1-11), they had people hearing from God (Acts 13:2), they had people writing stuff as God dictated (Rev.), they were caught up in the Spirit to heaven (2 Corin. 12:2-4), they had dreams and visions (Acts 10:9-23), they saw angels (Acts 12), they saw Jesus Himself (Acts 9:1-22), they cast out demons (Acts 16:16-18), they were bitten by deadly snakes and didn't die (Acts 28:1-10), they spoke in other languages of men and of angels (Acts 2, I Corin. 12 & more), they healed people (Acts 5:15), they prayed and miracles happened (Acts 5:12, Acts 12) – even teleportation (or as I prefer "theoportation" - Acts 8:39) and they raised the dead (Acts 9:32-42)! They even had people who were against them drop dead (Acts 5:1-11) or go blind (Acts 13:6-12) – on command! And that's just ONE reference for each! There are lots more!

Now, the argument is that all that ended when the Bible was done being written – but it didn't end for the other team, so how come just all OUR cool stuff got taken away? Wouldn't it have really benefited the enemy a LOT to spread that story that we were powerless around for a couple thousand years? Do you see? This is no kind of way to fight a war! There MUST be stuff we've been leaving out! The enemy has us twisted up into a thousand pieces (37,000+ denominations to be specific) and we can't STAND because we're not ONE Body. Because of all the arguing over stupid stuff – which we would NEVER have done if we had all been hearing the voice of God personally and reliably and walking in the Gifts!

This is kind of scary.

No kidding! It's the biggest thing ever in your life! That the God of the Universe wants to be intimately involved in everything you do and say and eat and wear and think. That's massively scary! And yet, we can never have peace and joy and victory until we have relationship with Jesus and are led by His Holy Spirit. You see, under our own power, we just screw everything up. There has never been any strategy of Man that has led to anything good in the long run. Oh, it might work for a little while, but you get enough sinful people involved in it, add money, mix in a little satan – and it's toast. Or worse, you get Communism or Fascism or something and millions of people die. There are just two options – if it's of Man it will fail and if it's of God nothing can stand against it. (Acts 5:38-39) Since the "church" in America is failing, somebody other than God must be in charge. See a logic problem there?

Anyway, yes, it's scary. But what a payoff!! To walk in holiness because God Himself is fighting off the temptations and snares of the enemy, to hear Him all the time and get direction on anything and everything, to know that He is completely and totally in charge at all times in every situation. How are you going to find peace WITHOUT hearing from God? How is what you have NOW working for you?

And hearing His voice is not even a GIFT of the Spirit! It's just an automatic for every believer! We haven't even talked about prophecy and discernment of spirits and knowledge and wisdom and tongues and healing and all the other gifts God gives His children! Trust me, the payoff is amazing, but it's going to cost you everything – but everything you THINK you have isn't yours anyway, so who cares!?

What if I hear wrong? What if the enemy is messing with me?

Well sure, that can happen. He's certainly going to try to confuse and frustrate you. We are specifically instructed, "do not believe every spirit, but test the spirits to see whether they are from God (1 John 4:1). That MUST mean that other spirits are potentially messing with us, and since there is no indication that THIS ended when the Bible was completed, then there must still be demons putting thoughts into our heads. And if there are still demons putting thoughts into our heads, then we must still have a need to test and see if they are from God. And if they're NOT from God, then we resist them and they flee. But it must also mean that one of the possibilities is that the spirit we're hearing IS from God! (Again, proving the point that God still speaks to us despite I Corin. 13:10.)

You see 1 John 4 goes on in verses 2 and 3 to lay out how you can know what it is that is talking to you and from where it comes, "This is how you can recognize the Spirit of God: Every spirit that acknowledges that Jesus Christ has come in the flesh is from God, but every spirit that does not acknowledge Jesus is not from God. This is the spirit of the antichrist, which you have heard is coming and even now is already in the world."

When we get a thought in our head we have to figure out who it is. There are only three choices: You, God or the enemy. Sometimes other people tell us stuff, but they're still playing to one of the three. We're to bring every thought into obedience with Christ (and the Word). That means our own thoughts that are out of line AND the ones inserted by the enemy. I find that, sadly, the enemy and I sound a lot alike. The red stuff and the yellow stuff aren't really that different after all. I apply this filter to everything, "If I follow through with this thought that just came into my head, who is glorified most – God, satan or me?" If it's anything other than God, even if it's me, I rebuke in the Name of Jesus. And if it WAS me, I ask the Lord to hunt down whatever in me wanted to suggest something that wouldn't glorify Him – and kill it.

Could you screw it up? Sure. Particularly if the voices are VERY sneaky. Which they <u>will</u> be because demons are smarter than us and know the human condition very well after all these years of torturing and twisting us. Without God fighting for you, you haven't got a chance. You have to be constantly on guard, constantly armored-up and expecting anything from any direction. But His arm is long and His shields are mighty. He will always get you through if you are sincerely seeking Him and trying to walk in holiness.

OK. I'm getting that it's possible, but I'm going to have to hear Him for myself. I'm willing to try. What do we do?

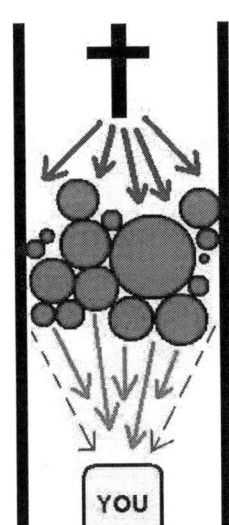

Great! Yeah, don't take my word for it, seek Him yourself. Well the first thing is to ask the Lord to show you anything that stands in the way between you and Him.

It's like this:

There is a pipeline of information that flows between us and God. He ALWAYS hears us, but if we can't hear Him, it's probably because of things WE have put in the way.

ANYTHING that we put between US and GOD is an idol. God never puts those things there, WE do. The most common thing is "religion" or the "pastor." Then ALL messages from God have to filter THROUGH that and get garbled. Others include sins and habits and addictions and disobedience of one sort or another.

They ALL have to go. Only THEN can we get clear commands from Upstairs. Don't let ANYTHING come between You and God.

The point of the church coming together should be so that we can crucify pieces of ourselves so that Christ in us can live. Said another way, it's to help each other identify the things that stand between us and Jesus – and pluck them out.

The most common thing we put in the way is our belief that God won't talk to us. That's got to go! If you don't think He's a Living God and active and able to speak and desiring relationship with you, then you're going to have to lay that down.

One of the other possibilities is that you're worshiping the WRONG Jesus. Paul said that would happen, that someone would come preaching another Jesus and people would accept it. It's very simple; if you make up your own Jesus, don't expect an answer when you pray! Prosperity-Jesus, Emergency-Only-Jesus, Not-Quite-As-Good-As-The-Virgin-Mary-Jesus, and a zillion others are all MADE UP. If you make your own god from scratch, expect about as much response as if you were praying to a stick. Those are NOT Bible Jesus - who doesn't like to be toyed with and put in a box.

Other things in the way are a reliance on someone else for your holiness or connection to God (Pastor, wife, mother, etc.). That's got to stop. This is a ONE-on-ONE relationship with Jesus. Nobody is going to do it for you. Other pipeline blockages include addiction, pride, selfishness, bitterness, anger, laziness, fear and so many others that keep us from experiencing the fullness that is IN Christ.

Ask the Lord to show you what is in the way and He is faithful to ALWAYS do that if you'll listen. Ask some other folks to pray with you if possible and just pray in agreement that the Lord will make Himself very clear to you about what to do next.

Just pray and believe. He'll come and help unclog you. Believe that He wants to talk to you and start conversing with Him. Find someone to be accountable with that knows God really well and make sure you don't act on anything that sounds fishy without verifying it with the Word of God. Now, not with doctrine of Man, mind you – with the Word of God.

If you like, pray something like this:

> *Lord, I'm sorry I ever put you in a box. I'm sorry I limited You in any way. I'm sorry that I haven't been hearing you as well as I should and I acknowledge that I clogged up my pipeline with stuff. Please, Lord, whatever it takes, scrub it all out of there with the Blood of Jesus. I just want You, Jesus. You direct my paths and organize my days. You tell me what You want and I'll do it. Help me hear You better. Help make me dangerous to the enemy. Increase the Jesus in me, even if it hurts. I love you, Lord. You be in charge now. Amen.*

DOES GOD STILL SPEAK TO PEOPLE TODAY?

Posted by EttyB on the F.O.T.M. online discussion board.

Some years ago, I had awakened before my family and I was in the kitchen when I heard the voice of the Lord say, "Roast a chicken." I had heard His voice before, so I said, "I'll be glad to, Lord, if You will tell me who to give it to." While I was speaking, I was pulling a chicken from my freezer and preparing to thaw it.

"I want you to take it to Mrs. Ming." He said.

I didn't know Mrs. Ming. I knew of her, though. I knew that she was an elderly woman in our church who was the wife of a retired minister. I knew that she had cancer and that her elderly husband was caring for her. I didn't know what she looked like, had never spoken to her, and didn't know where they lived.

But, the Lord had spoken, so I thawed the chicken and prepared it for roasting, then put it in the oven. As I prepared it, I thought of other things I might fix to make a complete meal. Fluffy fruit salad...mashed potatoes and gravy, corn. It sounded good, even to me!

It was just a few minutes before noon when the meal was ready and I decided that I would call our church office and see if anyone knew the address of the Mings. It was Saturday and I knew the office was closed, but I called anyway. Someone answered the phone and gave me the address of the elderly couple. Bless them!

Rain Right NOW, Lord!

I got a large box, armed with the address, and headed out to a nearby town that I was not familiar with. Within two minutes of driving into the town I was at their house!

Still, I felt rather foolish pulling into the driveway of complete strangers, holding a big cardboard box and saying, "Hey, I'm here with a chicken dinner that God told me to bring to you!" That was out of my comfort zone!

But...I got the box out of the back of my car and did just that. A little man with a dear face opened the door and looked at me questioningly. "Yes?" he said.

"God told me to bring you a chicken dinner for lunch, so here I am. Have you already eaten?"

He opened the door and stepped aside, motioning me to set the box on the kitchen counter. I lifted the hot dishes out of the box and took the covers off.

Not only had they not eaten. The kitchen was dark and nothing had even been started in the way of a meal. The little man looked jolly as he said they hadn't had a bite.

He lovingly prepared a plate for his sick wife and took it in to her darkened room. "This lady has brought us a roasted chicken for lunch," he told her. I was still in the kitchen when he came back and said, "My wife would like to talk to you."

I walked into the room of a woman who was in the last stages of cancer. She reached a frail hand out to me and in a soft voice she said, "This morning, I was so hungry for chicken I thought I couldn't stand it! So, I said, 'Jesus, I don't know how You can do it or if You even think it's important enough, but if You could get me some roasted chicken, I would be SO happy!" She looked at me with the sweetest expression and said, "He used you!"

That dear lady went home to be with Jesus before the next week was out and the Lord let me be His hand reaching out in love to her! What a privilege!

Later I was telling the little incident to one of my young daughter's friends and she said, "Oh, that was my grandma! She didn't have any appetite at all for weeks before she died. How nice that the Lord gave her such a blessing right before she went Home!" I thought then that if I'd failed to respond to God's voice, refused to move out of my comfort zone, that the Lord would probably have found someone else who would be faithful. But what a blessing I would have missed!

EttyB – 4/4/05

LET ME SHOW YOU A HIGHER WAY – THE **BIG** PRAYER

First, let's pray.

Father God, You are worthy of glory and honor and praise. You are above all and we honor You. There is none above You, Lord. Thank You for Your son, Jesus, and for His sacrifice on our behalf. Please teach us in this time and keep us safe from anything that the enemy might try to distract us or get our eyes off of You. We love You and we praise Your Holy Name. We ask You for all of these things in the Name of our Lord Jesus Christ. Cover us in the Blood of Jesus and protect our bodies, souls and spirits from the assault of the enemy. Give us pure hearts and teach us to fear You so that we may have wisdom. Amen.

OK, two things that need to be PERFECTLY clear about this writing and everything that we're saying here:

First, God the Father is supreme. The Holy Spirit is the conduit by which we reach the Lord Jesus Christ. Jesus is the conduit by which we reach the Almighty God and Father of All. The Holy Spirit does NOT want to be worshiped. Jesus does not want your worship. He came that the FATHER might be glorified. We love Jesus Christ and adore Him for His sacrifice and stand in awe of His love for us and willingness to endure, even now, for stinkers like us. But He came so that we might know the Father. When we talk about Fear of the Lord, we're not talking about fear of the Holy Spirit – or fear of Jesus alone. We're talking about trembling and awe of God the Father. Jesus is separate from the Father and doesn't know all that the Father knows. Even now His role is distinct and Jesus is secondary to the Father. Our worship should be for Yahweh alone. Since Jesus only says and does what the Father tells Him – and the Holy Spirit only repeats what He's told – if we obey Jesus (through the Holy Spirit), then we are obeying the Father.

So much error comes into the "church" because people are worshiping the wrong "Jesus." Some places worship the Holy Spirit and just seek manifestations. The Holy Spirit DID NOT come to be worshiped! Hear me, if you make the Holy Spirit the object of your worship, something ELSE will show up. He might be there doing stuff in the people with pure hearts, but those just seeking a "buzz" or an "experience" will get one from some other source. God judges the heart. If you come before Him seeking communion with Him but you have an impure motive, there will be curses on your head. He will lift His hand and something nasty will come as an angel of light and twist you into a pretzel.

Some people worship Jesus only. In fact, most places are worshiping Jesus. That's exactly what the enemy wants. If he can't talk us into worshiping a tree or a rock, he'll just get us worshiping ANYTHING other then God Almighty. If we worship our ministry, our new building, our pastor, or even the Holy Spirit or Jesus – we are guilty of idolatry. The first and greatest commandment (confirmed by Jesus Himself in three of the Gospels) is this: **"Hear O Israel, the Lord your God, the Lord is one. Love the Lord your God with all your heart and with all your soul and with all your mind and with all your strength."** The Father has not backed off from that and neither has the Son. DO NOT make the mistake of letting the enemy take your eyes off of that explicit command!

We're to love, honor and adore Jesus. We're to obey Jesus. We're to abide in Jesus. But we have peace in God THROUGH our Lord Jesus Christ (Rom. 5:1) So we implore you on Christ's behalf, be reconciled to God. (2 Corin. 5:20)

When King David said, "The Lord said to my Lord," he was referencing God the Father talking to Jesus Christ. Both were "Lords" over David, even though he was the king of Israel. When we use the word "Lord" we need to be clear about which one we are talking about and what exactly "Lord" means. A Lord is a monarch, a ruler, a clear authority figure for whom you have respect. They are not an elected official. It is not a term of courtesy, like "Sir." It is not a term of endearment, like "Dad". It is not a personal name, like "Jesus". It is a title and an office and deserves respect. When you say it, you should be using it in the sense that you recognize that the one to whom you are speaking is Commander, Master, King, Ruler, Autocrat and Monarch over you. There is no middle ground, there is no other way of meaning it that isn't demeaning and insulting to the holder of the title.

If you meet with the President of the United States, you call him "Mr. President." If you're a dear friend or a relative, in some settings it may be fine to call him by his first name or a nickname. But when you come to him within the scope of his office and his authority petitioning for some favor or seeking some directive, you address him with respect and you call him "Mr. President." If you endlessly call him "Mr. President" at the beginning and the end of every sentence when you're talking to him, he's just going to think you're either nuts or you're trivializing his office and title. When you pray, don't use God's name (or title) in vain. It has power, speak it forth with respect and with a purpose, not just to fill space in a sentence or as a pause while you figure out what to say next.

Why is all this so important? Because I believe that what this teaching is all about is something so big and so radically different than what we have been doing – and so dangerous to the forces of darkness – that it's just CRITICALLY important that we make sure that everyone has a pure heart and a proper perspective before getting too far into this. The enemy is going to try every way possible to tangle this all up and to make it about ANYTHING other than God.

Second, we know from Scripture, and from past history in the Church, that when the Holy Spirit shows up and starts doing cool stuff, it's just REALLY likely that somebody is going to start trying to bottle it and sell it and make it about THEM. Plus there will be fakes and liars and counterfeits and demons dressed as angels of light. Then everyone else will look at the squirrelly mess and overreact and want to deny that ANY of it is real. We are entering into an era of MAXIMUM deception, of false signs and wonders and fake prophets. We need to be VERY careful and we need to not get sucked in by any of it or allow ourselves to drift off course and find that we're helping the cause of darkness.

How can we be sure that we stay on course? Keep our eyes on God, pray for more Fear of the Lord, obey Him at all times, walk in holiness and do everything out of Love. They will know us by our Love. By our love for the brethren and our willingness to share and sacrifice on their behalf, by our love for God and constant obedience, by our love for Jesus Christ and a willingness to sacrifice even as He sacrificed for us.
If you seek Gifts for ANY reason other than so that you can be more like Jesus and a better warrior for the armies of God, then you better think twice. In fact, pray for more Fear of the Lord and wisdom. If someone comes to you offering something, you need to hear God well enough to know who they are and IF you're to receive from them. If you have an urge to impart something to someone, you need to hear

God well enough to know that it's His will and timing. You need to hear God well enough to know what to pray and how.

Let me simplify. What this is about is sacrificially pouring ourselves out onto another person. By sacrificially, I mean, even if you don't get it back. If you have a big healing ministry and it's going great and God is moving and He clearly asks you to take every gift, every anointing, every promise He's ever made to you, every expectation and hope that you have and give it all away to the twelve year old kid that just walked down the aisle – YOU DO IT! Or sit down and shut up. If you're not willing to lay down everything you have, in the physical and in the spiritual, when God directs you to, then you can't follow Him and you're not fit for the Kingdom. (Luke 9:62)

What we're aiming for here is MAXIMUM love. Something beyond what most anybody is teaching lately. I asked the Lord to teach me how to pray and He led me to Moses and Paul.

> Exodus 32:31-32 – *So Moses went back to the Lord and said, "Oh, what a great sin these people have committed! They have made themselves gods of gold. But now, please forgive their sin – but if not, then blot me out of the book you have written."*

> Romans 9:2-3 – *I have great sorrow and unceasing anguish in my heart. For I could wish that I myself were cursed and cut off from Christ for the sake of my brothers, those of my own race, the people of Israel.*

Do you get that? Jesus said:

> John 15:13 – *"Greater love has no man than this, that he lay down his life for his friends."*

What life do you think He is talking about? Which is more valuable, your physical life or your eternal life? Moses and Paul offered to be blotted out of the Book of Life if only God would hear their prayers! That prayer is so much like Jesus, God HAS to hear it. Everything in heaven stops when someone sincerely and wholeheartedly prays THAT prayer! Here are examples of two people that stood in the gap for a whole nation, a whole race and laid down the best and biggest thing they had – their eternal inheritance as sons of God. Your physical life is like a blade of grass or a flower that withers. It's nothing in the scope of things. It's a really loving thing to take a bullet for someone or run into a burning building, please don't think I'm demeaning anyone that makes that kind of sacrifice! But even though we call it that, it's not really the ULTIMATE sacrifice. To offer to lay down your eternal salvation is the ultimate.

I don't want there to be any misunderstanding about where we're headed here. My goal is to get you SO full of Jesus that you can pray the really BIG prayer and mean it. My goal is to raise up an army of people that know how to lay down everything. My goal is to raise up people that will lay down everything all the time and love nothing more than obedience to God. If the Lord asks you to offer up everything so that the bunion on a sweet old lady's toe will be healed, you do it. If He asks you to lay down everything so that another could take your place and be greater than you, you do it without thinking. That's where we're headed. If you get enough Jesus in you, it's not as hard as you might think. But a love on that kind of a scale is not "normal" and requires far more than we can even imagine. If even a few of the people of God started praying like that, it would turn everything on it's ear! Heaven would open wide and His Spirit would pour out through us on all flesh.

People are going to argue that you can't lose your salvation. Whether you can or you can't, it should be clear that we have multiple Biblical examples of people OFFERING it up to God. And these are people that God really, REALLY loved a lot. Besides, whether you can lose it or it can be taken from you is entirely different than whether you can lay it down. Jesus said, "No man takes my life, I lay it down willingly." (John 10:17) Clearly, Jesus was aiming at a TOTAL sacrifice and TOTAL trust in the Father, not just His earthly body. He took on ALL the sins of all men for all time. He had to know that He couldn't go in front of the Father like that! For someone who had been in the Father's presence for eternity, even an instant of separation had to be excruciating beyond anything we can imagine! I believe that the sacrifice Jesus made in the spiritual realms was FAR more awe-inspiring than even what His physical body endured.

You HAVE to believe that God might actually take you up on it and send you to hell. You have to believe that He might actually take all your gifts away and give them to someone else. And you have to be OK with that because you trust God with all your heart and believe that He knows best. I don't think people are preaching the MAXIMUM application of the love for each other that Jesus modeled. I have never heard this from any pulpit or on any tape or CD or conference anywhere. Whatever I have learned about this kind of love, came from no man.

In His last bit of time on earth with His disciples, Jesus repeated the same message over and over and over in a very short period of time (this isn't even all of them!). It might make a lot of sense for us to listen to it and apply it. He said:

> John 13:34-35 – "A new command I give you: Love one another. As I have loved you, so you must love one another. By this all men will know that you are my disciples, if you love one another."

> John 14:12-14 – "I tell you the truth, anyone who has faith in me will do what I have been doing. He will do even greater things than these, because I am going to the Father. And I will do whatever you ask in my name, so that the Son may bring glory to the Father. You may ask me for anything in my name and I will do it."

> John 14:15 – "If you love me, you will obey what I command."

> John 14:21 – "Whoever has my commands and obeys them, he is the one who loves me. He who loves me will be loved by my Father, and I too will love him and show myself to him."

> John 14:23-24 – "If anyone loves me, he will obey my teaching. My Father will love him, and we will come to him and make our home with him. He who does not love me will not obey my teaching. These words you hear are not my own; they belong to the Father who sent me."

> John 15:12-13 – "My command is this: Love each other as I have loved you. Greater love has no one than this, that he lay down his life for his friends. You are my friends if you do what I command."

> John 15:17 – "This is my command: Love each other."

Could it be more clear? In real time, this talk to His disciples probably only took a few minutes, but over and over He's pounding this same note! Can't you imagine that if you were there His body language and tone would be one of imploring and urgently requesting them to burn this into their minds and apply it? Don't you think He wanted them to remember this VERY clearly? They were going to need a lot of love to get through the next few days, but it surely has application to us and the hard days that we have ahead as well. We MUST learn to love each other as HE loved us.

I don't think we really understand what He did for us. The "Passion of the Christ" movie is graphic and it moves many people to a better understanding of what He endured physically, but it's just a tiny piece of the true battle that was raging in the spiritual realms and the massive weight that He took on Himself for our sakes. The Son of God laid down His eternal birthright out of His love for us and took on all of the suffering that was due to us. If we are going to be like Him and fully obey Him and LOVE like He did – then maybe we need to be willing to drink from the cup He drank from. Do you think you can?

Well, you can't. Not without a great big cup full of Jesus. The YOU in your cup can't pray that, but the JESUS in you can. He already did. He's really good at it. All you have to do is get the YOU out of the way and watch what happens. People will say that we shouldn't seek after spiritual gifts, we should just love each other. They will refer to I Corinthians 13, the "Love Chapter," to prove that all that flashy Holy Spirit stuff is meaningless and we just need love. Or they will even use this chapter to say that when the Bible was completed, that which was perfect has come, so that which was in part (tongues and prophecy) was done away. But if that were the case, we would have put away childish things and all you have to do is look around to see that we haven't. We clearly do not "know fully" and this system that we have built clearly isn't seeing "face to face," so I don't think the Bible being completed is what Paul was talking about. I think He means that when the fullness of God's love is made real in you, THEN you see face to face.

Besides, you can't just ignore that this beautiful chapter is bracketed immediately on BOTH sides by a command to desire more and greater Gifts (charisma).

> I Corinthians 12:27-31 – 27 Now you are the body of Christ, and each one of you is a part of it. 28 And in the church God has appointed first of all apostles, second prophets, third teachers, then workers of miracles, also those having gifts of healing, those able to help others, those with gifts of administration, and those speaking in different kinds of tongues. 29 Are all apostles? Are all prophets? Are all teachers? Do all work miracles? 30 Do all have gifts of healing? Do all speak in tongues? Do all interpret? 31 <u>But eagerly desire the greater gifts</u>. And now I will show you the most excellent way.

> 1 Corinthians 13 – 1 If I speak in the tongues of men and of angels, but have not love, I am only a resounding gong or a clanging cymbal. 2 If I have the gift of prophecy and can fathom all mysteries and all knowledge, and if I have a faith that can move mountains, but have not love, I am nothing. 3 If I give all I possess to the poor and surrender my body to the flames, but have not love, I gain nothing. 4 Love is patient, love is kind. It does not envy, it does not boast, it is not proud. 5 It is not rude, it is not self-seeking, it is not easily angered, it keeps no record of wrongs. 6 Love does not delight in evil but rejoices with the truth. 7 It always protects, always trusts, always hopes, always perseveres. 8 Love never fails. But where there are prophecies, they will cease; where there are tongues, they will be stilled; where there is knowledge, it will pass away. 9 For we know in part and we prophesy in part, 10 but when perfection comes, the imperfect disappears. 11 When I was a child, I talked like a child, I thought like a child, I reasoned like a child. When I became a man, I put childish ways behind me. 12 Now we see but a poor reflection as in a mirror; then we shall see face to face. Now I know in part; then I shall know fully, even as I am fully known. 13 And now these three remain: faith, hope and love. But the greatest of these is love.

Rain Right NOW, Lord!

> I Corinthians 14:1-5 – *1 Follow the way of love and <u>eagerly desire spiritual gifts, especially the gift of prophecy.</u> 2 For anyone who speaks in a tongue does not speak to men but to God. Indeed, no one understands him; he utters mysteries with his spirit. 3 But everyone who prophesies speaks to men for their strengthening, encouragement and comfort. 4 He who speaks in a tongue edifies himself, but he who prophesies edifies the church. 5 I would like every one of you to speak in tongues, but I would rather have you prophesy. He who prophesies is greater than one who speaks in tongues, unless he interprets, so that the church may be edified.*

The instruction in I Corin. 14:1-5 couldn't be more clear. Follow the way of love **AND** eagerly desire spiritual gifts! ESPECIALLY prophecy! But didn't Paul just say prophecy was going to cease and tongues were like a clanging symbol? No, he didn't say that. He said it would EVENTUALLY cease when the perfect had come – which it hasn't or else we'd all be walking in pure LOVE. (Oh, c'mon! It just hasn't! Stop holding on so tight to a doctrine of Man! Scripture interprets Scripture and you can't find anywhere else that it says the Gifts of the Spirit were just for that time and don't apply to us now! I love you, but let it go!) What he said was that if the Gifts are not operated with, by and through LOVE, they are useless.

Since Paul lectures about tongues and prophecy on either side of this chapter and brackets this chapter with exhortations to seek more and better Gifts (charisma), I just don't see how this argument can be used against what I'm proposing here. If you see something I don't, feel free to email us anytime – fotm@fellowshipofthemartyrs.com .

Anyway, I think we see the fulfillment of Chapter 13 when the Body of Christ starts laying down EVERYTHING for each other. If I have a great gift of prophecy, if I have knowledge, if I have wisdom, if I have tongues, if I have a calling and an anointing and I'm willing to lay it all down and pour it out onto a brother or sister, even unto my own salvation – then I think we're getting about as close to the fulfillment of this chapter as we can get in this life. People that can pray that kind of stuff and really mean it are not going to be self-serving, rude, boasting, proud, delight in evil or keep a record of wrongs. They would most likely protect, trust, hope, persevere and never, ever fail. I believe that's where we're headed. I hope you can join us. God has prepared a lot of people like that for a time such as this.

If you're buying any of this, let's pray.

> **Father God, You alone are worthy. We see more and more every day what You did for us by sacrificing Your Son for us and what Jesus did by coming as the Christ and laying everything down for us. Give us an enlarged understanding of the sacrifice made on our behalf and renew a right spirit within us. Make us the kind of people that will lay anything down at any moment to further Your Kingdom. Not for our glory, but for Yours. This is a hard saying, Lord. Few can walk it. Teach us how to pray the really big prayers. Help us to be so full of Jesus that He can pray through us. Anything in us that gets in the way, please get it out. Whatever it takes. Just make us like Jesus in the biggest possible way. Teach us to love as You love us. Try us and refine us by sending people that are really hard to love. Whatever it takes. In the mighty name of Jesus Christ, Amen**

Fellowship of the Martyrs

FEAR OF THE LORD AXIOMS

You may feel like just skipping to the Spiritual Gifts stuff, but I'm telling you, you BETTER get this straight in your head. You BETTER get more Fear of the Lord as quickly as possible before you move on through this!! Please hear me, go read the warning label again. Fear of the Lord is the BEGINNING of Wisdom. Without it you could really screw up whatever He gives you or ask with the wrong heart and get something ugly. Humor me, I learned this the hard way.

IF we sin, **THEN** we must not have enough Fear of the Lord. (The Father AND the Son.)

IF we don't have enough fear of the Lord, **THEN** it must be because we don't see Him clearly.

IF we don't see Him clearly, **THEN** it must be because we have been deceived about who He really is.

IF we have been deceived, **THEN** we are worshiping another Jesus.

IF we are worshiping another Jesus, **THEN** we are not saved.

IF we are not saved, **THEN** we will go to hell.

IF we believe many in the church, **THEN** we accept Jesus into our hearts as our personal Savior.

IF Jesus is our Savior from that moment on, **THEN** there is no need for any further action on our part.

IF the act of accepting Him as Savior is sufficient, **THEN** we can do whatever we want after that.

IF it is a one-time thing and a completed work, **THEN** there is no further need for obedience to Him.

IF we say "Lord, Lord" but mean Savior, **THEN** He may not acknowledge us before God.

IF we believe the Bible, **THEN** we accept Jesus as our Lord and Master.

IF Jesus is our Lord, **THEN** we are entirely at His mercy and direction thereafter.

IF we accept Jesus as our Lord, **THEN** He will acknowledge us before the Father.

IF we accept Jesus as Lord, **THEN** He will fight our battles and His nature in us will keep us from sin.

IF we fully accept Jesus as Lord, **THEN** He can direct ALL our paths.

IF we declare Him to be Savior, **THEN** we place Him in a position of one-time needfulness.

IF we declare Him as Savior, **THEN** we leave open the position and title of Lord.

IF Jesus is not Lord, **THEN** we won't look to Him for daily direction.

IF we're not looking to Him for daily direction, **THEN** we will look elsewhere.

IF the position and title of Lord is vacant, **THEN** some Man will try to become that over us.

IF the position and title of Lord is vacant, **THEN** the religious establishment leadership benefits most.

IF the religious establishment preaches Savior, **THEN** it may be because they want to be Lord.

IF we accept any Man as our Lord, **THEN** we are at their whim.

IF we are at the whim of Man, **THEN** we will not have peace and joy and victory.

IF we do not have peace and joy and victory, **THEN** we are under the control of the enemy.

IF we're under the control of the enemy, **THEN** we're on the wrong team – even if we fed poor people.

IF we're on the wrong team, **THEN** Jesus will not acknowledge us before the Father.

IF we had a little fear of the Lord, **THEN** we would see that He is Sovereign and there is no other.

IF we had more fear of the Lord, **THEN** we would hate the "world" and everything in it and seek Him only.

IF we had lots of fear of the Lord, **THEN** we would weep and mourn and groan for days for the massive blackness of our hearts (individually and collectively) and the distance between us and Him.

IF we had fear of the Lord, **THEN** we would have the beginning of wisdom.

IF we had the beginning of wisdom, **THEN** we wouldn't be tossed by every wind of doctrine.

IF we had the beginning of wisdom, **THEN** we would pray that He would give us more fear of the Lord.

IF He gives us more fear of the Lord, **THEN** it's really, really going to hurt.

IF we love Him and want truth above all, **THEN** we'll keep asking anyway.

SINGLE-USE SAVIOR OR KING, COMMANDER, LORD?

Number of Usages of the Titles of Jesus in Scripture

Lord – 618	Christ – 543	Son of Man – 84	Teacher – 42	Son of God – 37
King – 35	Lamb – 32	**Savior – 15**	Prophet – 15	Master – 11

(**Source:** *What the Bible says about a Saving Faith*, Koerselman – www.BereanPublishers.com – book online free)

John 8:24 - *"I told you that you would die in your sins; if you do not believe that **I am the one I claim to be**, you will indeed **die** in your sins."*

2 Timothy 4:3-4 – *For the time will come when men will not put up with sound doctrine. Instead, to suit their own desires, they will gather around them a great number of teachers to say what their itching ears want to hear. They will turn their ears away from the truth and turn aside to myths.*

Luke 9:23-24 – *Then he said to them all, "If anyone would come after me, he **must deny himself** and **take up his cross daily** and **follow me**. For whoever wants to save his life will lose it, but whoever loses his life for me will save it."*

Romans 6:6 – *For we know that our old self was crucified with him so that the body of sin might be done away with, that we should **no longer** be slaves to sin.*

Luke 14:33 – *In the same way, any of you who does not **give up everything** he has **cannot** be my disciple.*

Ephesians 4:22-24 – *You were taught, with regard to your former way of life, **to put off your old self**, which is being corrupted by its deceitful desires; to **be made new** in the attitude of your minds; and to **put on the new self**, created to **be like God in true righteousness and holiness**.*

Romans 10:9 – *If you confess with your mouth, "Jesus is **LORD**," and believe in your heart that God raised him from the dead, you will be saved."*

Romans 10:13 – *And everyone who calls upon the name of the **LORD** will be saved.*

Philippians 2:10-11 – *Therefore God exalted him to the highest place and gave him the name that is above every name, that at the name of Jesus **every** knee should bow, in heaven and on earth and under the earth, and **every** tongue confess that Jesus Christ is **LORD**, to the glory of God the Father.*

Revelation 17:14 – *They will make war against the Lamb, but the Lamb will overcome them because he is the **LORD** of lords and **King** of kings – and with him will be his called, chosen and faithful followers.*

John 20:28 – *Thomas said to him, "My **LORD** and my **God**!"*

Revelation 19:11-16 – *I saw heaven standing open and there before me was a white horse, whose rider is called Faithful and True. With justice he judges and makes war. His eyes are like blazing fire, and on his head are many crowns. He has a name written on him that no one knows but he himself. He is dressed in a robe dipped in blood, and his name is the Word of God. The armies of heaven were following him, riding on white horses and dressed in fine linen, white and clean. Out of his mouth comes a sharp sword with which to strike down the nations. "He will rule them with an iron scepter." He treads the winepress of the fury of the wrath of God Almighty. On his robe and on his thigh he has this name written: **KING OF KINGS AND LORD OF LORDS.***

There is no need to have "Fear of a Savior". Why fear a lifeguard at the beach? But the Bible specifically says that "Fear of the LORD is the beginning of wisdom." Please pray that He would be LORD of your life in every way - King, Commander, Ruler, LORD. He's a Monarch. You bow before a Monarch. You come humbly. Don't toy with Him. He's really big.

FAITH LIKE A TEENAGER

We have three different, identical accounts of Jesus' clear statement that you WILL NOT enter into the kingdom of God unless you receive it like a little child.

Matt. 18:3 *And said, Verily I say unto you, Except ye be converted, and become as little children, ye shall not enter into the kingdom of heaven.*

Mark 10:15 *Verily I say unto you, Whosoever shall not receive the kingdom of God as a little child, he shall not enter therein.*

Luke 18:17 *Verily I say unto you, Whosoever shall not receive the kingdom of God as a little child shall in no wise enter therein.*

IF the Word of God is true and right, THEN this is a pretty darn critical point and you might want to really, really be sure that you are getting this right!
So, how are you doing on this point? Do you have faith like a child? Perhaps a parable will help.

FaithLikeAChild sits in the back of the minivan and looks out the window and goes, "Whee!" FaithLikeAChild doesn't know how the engine works or where gasoline comes from and does not worry about whether the minivan has side air bags. FaithLikeAChild just knows that Dad is driving and we're going to Grandma's house and we're stopping at McDonald's on the way! FaithLikeAChild doesn't know how to navigate the route and doesn't care. FaithLikeAChild would never even consider trying to drive – it never even occurred to FaithLikeAChild that Dad wasn't fully capable of getting the job done all by himself. FaithLikeAChild just peacefully dozes off and enjoys the ride, even if it's bumpy. Nothing to worry about, because Dad knows what He's doing. FaithLikeAChild chatters with Dad and hangs on his every word because FaithLikeAChild adores Dad. Dad is his provider, rescuer, leader and generally his real life superhero. Regardless of any physical or logical evidence to the contrary, FaithLikeAChild is just sure that his Dad can beat up your Dad.

If you want to see another picture of FaithLikeAChild, try this:

> Mark 4: 37-40 – *And a furious storm of wind arose, and the waves kept beating into the boat, so that it was already becoming filled. But He [Jesus] was in the stern of the boat, asleep on the cushion; and they awoke Him and said to Him, Master, do You not care that we are perishing? And He arose and rebuked the wind and said to the sea, Hush now! Be still! And the wind ceased and there was immediately a great calm. He said to them, Why are you so timid and fearful? How is it that you have no faith?*

FaithLikeAChild was the other name of that kid with a slingshot that said this to a monster named Goliath:

> 1 Sam. 17:26, 37, 46, 48 – *Who is this uncircumcised Philistine that he should defy the armies of the living God. The Lord who delivered me from the paw of the lion and the paw of the bear will deliver me from the hand of this Philistine. "This day the Lord will hand you over to me and I'll strike you down and cut off your head." Then as the Philistine moved closer to attack him, David ran quickly to the battle line to meet him.*

And lots like him – Abraham, Noah, Moses, Joseph, Daniel, Gideon, Samson, Peter, Stephen and many more throughout history. FaithLikeAChild speaks boldly and fearlessly and RUNS QUICKLY to the battle line to meet the enemy. FaithLikeAChild doesn't worry about fancy armor or battle strategy, FaithLikeAChild knows that God can use anything and so he goes against the giants in the strength that he has - even a slingshot and five stones. FaithLikeAChild is supremely offensive to others because he is the most like Jesus. People think he is arrogant, foolish, senseless, suicidal, childish, short-sighted, capricious, unpredictable and generally impossible to deal with. As soon as Goliath saw David, he despised him (I Sam. 17:42). David's brothers burned with anger towards him (I Sam. 17:28). Saul hated him (I Sam. 18:8-11 and elsewhere). There is no end of trouble when you start accepting the Kingdom of God like a little child! And no end to the reward.

Sadly, FaithLikeATeenager is far more common. FaithLikeATeenager doesn't want to sit in the back of the minivan, he just got his license and he wants to drive himself. FaithLikeATeenager pesters Dad to get into the passenger seat. FaithLikeATeenager doesn't want to go to McDonald's because it isn't healthy and he can't believe that Dad is unaware of the ecological and economic and human justice damage that a fascist global conglomerate like that is doing to the world. Dad is just not as well-informed as FaithLikeATeenager. In fact, sometimes FaithLikeATeenager wonders how Dad ever got along without him. FaithLikeATeenager doesn't particularly want to go to Grandma's house, but is just sure that he knows a quicker way to get there. FaithLikeATeenager doesn't doze off and enjoy the ride. FaithLikeATeenager turns the music up really loud, makes a call on his cell phone, drinks his organic, Fair Trade, wheat germ smoothie, drives too fast and tries hard to ignore Dad as much as possible.

FaithLikeATeenager is just sure that he has all the answers and his way is best. In fact, he would really like it if Dad would just shut up and leave him alone. He is his own superhero.

FaithLikeAChild knows that he is completely safe because Dad is in control. FaithLikeATeenager thinks he is indestructible because he is really smart and cool. Which one do you think Dad would rather hang out with?

Why does it seem like God is moving in greater ways in Africa and India and China? Maybe because there are more people there named FaithLikeAChild. Why do we have tens of thousands of denominations in America and endless conferences and programs and books and superstar leaders? Maybe because we are the capital of FaithLikeATeenager. In fact, we're the main producer and exporter worldwide. We're building fatter and fatter pipelines so we can pump all of our own special flavors of it into every country on the planet.

Are there any seminaries in America that have a "FaithLikeAChild" degree? Who were the experts in FaithLikeATeenager in Jesus' time? The Pharisees and the Sadducees. The religious leaders are always the ones that think they're all grown up and that they know best. Go read Matthew 23 and see how Jesus felt about them. He's pretty clear about how He feels about FaithLikeATeenager. You better hope you're not one of them.

How about this?

> Matthew 7:21-23 – *"Not everyone who says to me, 'Lord, Lord,' will enter the kingdom of heaven, but only he who does the will of my Father who is in heaven. Many will say to me on that day, 'Lord, Lord, did we not prophesy in your name, and in your name drive out demons and perform many miracles?' Then I will tell them plainly, 'I never knew you. Away from me, you evildoers!'*

If this is really true, then we might want to be listening to Dad more and obeying Him and not going our own way. Many will think that they are just fine – until they are told to their face that their new name is "FaithLikeATeenager" and that it has all been in vain.

God is raising up the true warriors. Those who will not question or doubt. Those who will go, no matter who says they are nuts. God is raising up an army of children with nothing holding them down. Children who will fearlessly wade into the battle with a slingshot (and an army of angels). They will kill the Goliaths (and the status quo) without mercy or pity. They will obey fully because the Lamb is their head. They will not argue theology or doctrine or curriculum or programs. They will just listen to the voice of God and obey. And they will bring a flame-thrower to all the structures and systems of FaithLikeATeenager. Nothing will be able to stand before them – because God is on their side.

Just in case you're sitting on the fence about this when they come, consider this:

> Matthew 18:3-6 – *And he said: "I tell you the truth, unless you change and become like little children, you will never enter the kingdom of heaven. Therefore, whoever humbles himself like this child is the greatest in the kingdom of heaven. "And whoever welcomes a little child like this in my name welcomes me. But if anyone causes one of these little ones who believe in me to sin, it would be better for him to have a large millstone hung around his neck and to be drowned in the depths of the sea.*

Or maybe this one:

> Luke 9:46-48 – *An argument started among the disciples as to which of them would be the greatest. Jesus, knowing their thoughts, took a little child and had him stand beside him. Then he said to them, "Whoever welcomes this little child in my name welcomes me; and whoever welcomes me welcomes the one who sent me. For he who is least among you all—he is the greatest."*

Just stop for a minute and look around and see if you or your congregation or denomination are arguing with anybody else about who is the greatest. See if you are letting God direct your paths or you are leaning on your own understanding. Proverbs 3:5-6 is pretty clear. All means <u>ALL</u>. None of your own understanding is acceptable. <u>None</u> of you directing your own paths is OK. Doing so means that you are not trusting the Lord your God with ALL your heart. And it means that your new name is FaithLikeATeenager and God is going to write it on your forehead. The first being in history to earn that name was Lucifer. If God writes that on your forehead – then, congratulations, you just got the mark of the beast.

If that's your name, even a little bit, then you might want to say you're sorry and beg the Lord to scrub it off your forehead and ask Him daily to kill anything in you that is more than about six years old – give or take.

THE BEATITUDES AND YOUR CUP – MATTHEW 5:3-12

The Lord showed me very clearly how Matthew 5 intersects with the understandings about "cups" and cup management. I hope that I can express this as clearly as He showed it to me. (See graphic at bottom of this writing.)

You need to understand that the Beatitudes, as with nearly all of the Word of God have multiple applications on various levels. Like spirals – repeating parallel cycles but different applications. Seen that way, the largest possible application is to the spiritual/eternal – not the natural/temporary.

> 3 *"Blessed are the poor in spirit, for theirs is the kingdom of heaven.*

First you need to note that it doesn't say "Spirit," it says "spirit". He's not at all saying that you are blessed if you are poor in HIS Spirit! You are blessed if there is hardly any YOU in your cup so that HE can fill all the available space! You are blessed when you are poured out and there is hardly any of you left at all. Yours is the kingdom of heaven when there is practically none of You to get in His way. He can use you mightily when you have given Him all of your false riches (knowledge, experience, personality, charisma, degrees, dreams, etc.) and are left with only the bare minimum (faith like a child). Then He can pour in the true riches of HIS Spirit. The less of YOU there is, the more room there will be for JESUS to fill.

> 4 *Blessed are those who mourn, for they will be comforted.*

Fellowship of the Martyrs

What are they mourning about? The death of a loved one? That hardly seems to fit here. This is all about eternal and spiritual things, why mourn about the death of a jar of clay? I think this applies to those who are mourning for souls, mourning for the sad state of things and desperate state of the mess we've made of our own hearts, our families, our churches, our cities, our world. I think this is a reference to those in Ezekiel 9 that are the ONLY ones spared from the wrath of God poured out on the lukewarm and asleep. You can see that the first fruits in Revelation 7, the 144,000, are those who are comforted. I suspect they are the ones mourning the most. If you truly see through the eyes of Jesus (because you have hardly any of You left and a big cup of Jesus), then you will almost surely mourn for how much God is grieved and hurt by what we're doing (or not doing). It's very dark out there and it's our fault.

5 Blessed are the meek, for they will inherit the earth.

Humility is an unavoidable by-product of having practically none of You left and a big cup of Jesus. The more we realize the distance between us and God and how truly big and merciful and holy and just and faithful He is, the more we <u>must</u> be meek. Those who recognize this and are thrilled to just have the crumbs under the table or stay outside and serve quietly will be ones sitting at the head of the table. Said in reverse, "Cursed are those who are full of pride and self, for they will be cast into outer darkness." Meekness/humility is a clear, internal understanding that pride is the enemy and when it rises up in us it is antichrist. Meekness begs for God to kill the YOU in your cup.

6 Blessed are those who hunger and thirst for righteousness, for they will be filled.

Those who are desperate to keep Sin out of their cup are those who will have maximum capacity to hold more Jesus. You will be filled to the degree that you are hungry and thirsty to be filled and seek out how best to pour it back out. The more you go to the River to drink your fill, the less room there will be for unrighteousness to fit inside. If you understand that Jesus is in your cup and that He doesn't like to be in there with the nasty, icky stuff, you would seek to keep it cleansed and sanctified at every moment. You cannot displace Sin effectively by a force of will, you need to be so full of Jesus that nothing else can fit!

7 Blessed are the merciful, for they will be shown mercy.

This is the action step that proves that your cup is full of Jesus. You must see that others may not have as big a cup or may have embedded Sin that needs to come out and you must lovingly urge them forward as someone that has been there and not self-righteously as someone who knows it all. You must even be willing to stand in the gap for them and take on their burdens if necessary so as to free them. Oppressions that keep them from fully tasting the goodness of God need to be broken or you need to help bear their burden. The more you pour yourself out onto those in need – the more you sacrificially give of all that you have, even if you don't get it back – the more God will expand your cup and pour out on you. The more He will grant you mercy when you mess things up and act prideful and rebellious.

8 Blessed are the pure in heart, for they will see God.

Those who meet the qualifications above; who have been poured out, who weep for the sad state of things, who have crucified pride, who beg for more Jesus, who regularly pour themselves out and get bigger cups – THOSE are the people who will see God. Others may have dreams and visions or angelic visitations, but THESE are the people who really see God for who He is and have true relationship. These are the ones that He calls, "Friends."

9 Blessed are the peacemakers, for they will be called the sons of God.

Above all, these will be like Jesus, because they have the biggest cup of Jesus. And Jesus was a peacemaker with a sword. Peace is not always instant. Sometimes you have to speak the truth in love and know that in the big picture peace will eventually be the result. When Jesus overturned the tables in the Temple it was so that there would be peace there – but it might require 2000+ years for it to materialize. We must always seek His peace – and His ways are not our ways. Sometimes peace doesn't mean being polite and pretending we all agree. Said differently, we are to be at peace with the spirit of our brother, but war against his evil deeds and his rulers. (Psalm 141:5-6)

10 Blessed are those who are persecuted because of righteousness, for theirs is the kingdom of heaven.

This is an unavoidable by-product of having a big cup of Jesus and being a peacemaker. See John 15 and I John – and the whole history of the Church, for that matter. The more you are filled with Jesus, the more you will be persecuted. The spirits of this world fear Him intensely and will do everything they can directly or through other people to kill, smother or marginalize the Light in you. If you have a little candle, a couple of bugs might come to see what's going on. If you are the halogen array on top of a football stadium, every bug for MILES is going to come and try to smother you. The bigger your cup, the more Jesus in you, the more the warfare will increase. Guaranteed.

11 Blessed are you when people insult you, persecute you and falsely say all kinds of evil against you because of me.

Jesus knows what He went through and how hard it was. He sympathizes and He protects those who endure such things. And you get maximum treasure in heaven for enduring the hardest things for His name! You will be more and more blessed by God the more you are insulted, reviled, assaulted, persecuted, libeled, beaten, burned, boiled, whipped, imprisoned, starved or killed. There is no indication that you will be blessed because you were wealthy.

12 Rejoice and be glad, because great is your reward in heaven, for in the same way they persecuted the prophets who were before you.

The Apostle Paul had a great big cup of Jesus and saw a constant stream of miracles around him. He had a LOT of treasure in heaven. To some degree you have to also see that persecution comes so as to further refine us and beat out of us the really deeply entrenched yellow stuff – the You in your cup that really, really doesn't want to budge! Any pride or self-reliance has to be laid down when you have no strength and no one to lean on but God. Through fiery trials He teaches us to be totally and utterly dependent on Him.

When you suffer for the Name of Jesus, you join a great long list of mighty men and women of God who have gone before you. Whether you are physically killed or not, when you ask God to kill all of You that stands in His way, you become a martyr. When He pours You out so that He can pour Himself in, you are truly dead and it's Christ in you that lives. The more you hold back, the less dead you are and the less He can fill you. Rejoice in affliction!! There is no other way to get some of the really stubborn You out! Every time you endure persecution in faith, another ugly chunk of You dies and He can fill the gap with His grace and mercy and peace and gifts of the Spirit. The "Fellowship of the Martyrs" is just the spiritual assembly of those who have died to self and it's Christ in them that lives. Jesus Himself said that sooner or later, people like that will probably also die physically for their faith, but who cares? We're already dead! I pray that God would kill anything in you that is in the way of Him fulfilling His best plans for you.

Which "Cup" do you think the Beatitudes are about?

I'm sure thinking that it's THIS ONE! ^ ^ ^

ALMOST THERE

OK, I know this is taking awhile, but you need to be sure that you got all that. The Cups are real and you need to get cleaned out. You need to pray to get all the SIN out and then keep it out by staying full of Jesus every moment. You need to ask Him to kill all the YOU that might be in His way. You need to ask Him to help you hear His voice REALLY clearly so that He can direct all your paths. We tried to get some more Fear of the Lord in you and make sure you're taking this seriously and motivated by LOVE for Him and for those in need around you. If you're motivated by a desire to have a flashy ministry or to be cool or make money, you're going to be in BIG trouble. (Acts 8:9-24) He wants you broken and contrite and if you're not already, He's going to do it to you. If you sass Him and are rebellious, it's just going to hurt a lot more.

If you say that you're going to give Him ALL and you mean SOME, you may want to go read Acts 5:1-11 again. If you move on from here, the walk is just going to get harder and harder. I'm warning you. You better mean it. This is real.

You ready? OK, then.

SPIRITUAL GIFT DIALS

We don't have enough Fear of the Lord or we would have a better sense of how intensely complicated this is! We always seek to simplify and compartmentalize God so that we can get our head around Him.

People seem to think the Gifts of the Spirit are on/off switches that you either have or you don't. People actually preach that you may only have one or two gifts, but nobody has ALL of them. And whatever the Holy Spirit gives you, that's what you get and you should be content with it. But I think that's just not scriptural on a whole number of levels.

First, they're not on/off switches, they're <u>dials</u>. There's no other way to explain how someone could have an anointing to heal a headache, but another can regrow a limb or raise the dead. Some have a prophecy gift that just comes as a "deja vu" sort of vague sense of familiarity when something happens and some others see dreams and visions of the future all the time. Some have just enough Gift of Faith to endure a couple weeks without a paycheck and some can endure shipwrecks and torture and jail and total dependence on God for everything. It has to be a spectrum, not a fixed quantity. **I Corinthians 11:11 says that the "Holy Spirit gives them to each one, just as He determines."** That may mean that He gives the Gift itself to those He determines, but it also surely means that He gives it in the <u>quantity</u> that He determines. Sometimes a person gets "dialed up" just long enough for a crisis situation or an immediate need for healing or evangelism or whatever and then may never see that gift again like that. The Holy Spirit's management of each of our Gift's Inventory is a lot more fluid and complicated than we give Him credit for. (I hope that the result of this chapter, too, is more Fear of the Lord.)

Second, Paul specifically instructs us to desire spiritual gifts, especially the big ones that have the biggest impact. He says:

    1 Corinthians 12:31 – *But covet earnestly the best* (kreitton) *gifts* (charisma):

Remember, Paul is talking to people (the Church in Corinth) that already have SOME spiritual gifts. He encourages them at least twice in this letter to seek more and bigger weapons, especially prophecy.

Best – kreitton {krite'-tohn} – (Strong's 2909)
    1) more useful, more serviceable, more advantageous
    2) more excellent

Translated as "better" 11 times and only once as "best". Better implies degrees of usefulness. A plurality of possible usefulnesses from among which you should seek the highest possible choice in any given situation.

Gifts – charisma {khar'-is-mah} – (Strong's 5486)
    1) a favour with which one receives without any merit of his own
    2) the gift of divine grace
    3) the gift of faith, knowledge, holiness, virtue
    4) the economy of divine grace, by which the pardon of sin and eternal salvation is appointed to sinners in consideration of the merits of Christ laid hold of by faith
    5) grace or gifts denoting extraordinary powers, distinguishing certain Christians and enabling them to serve the church of Christ, the reception of which is due to the power of divine grace operating on their souls by the Holy Spirit

If the Father is willing to give us gifts, we should seek them and be good stewards of them. Jesus doesn't say to wait for the Lord to do everything and never ask. Jesus is clear that we should petition the Father in the name of Jesus for ANYTHING. He tells two different parables about pestering someone until they give in! (Luke 11:5-10 & Luke 18:1-8)

> Luke 11:5-10 – *Then he said to them, "Suppose one of you has a friend, and he goes to him at midnight and says, 'Friend, lend me three loaves of bread, because a friend of mine on a journey has come to me, and I have nothing to set before him.' Then the one inside answers, 'Don't bother me. The door is already locked, and my children are with me in bed. I can't get up and give you anything.' I tell you, though he will not get up and give him the bread because he is his friend, yet because of the man's boldness he will get up and give him as much as he needs. So I say to you: Ask and it will be given to you; seek and you will find; knock and the door will be opened to you. For everyone that asks receives; he who seeks finds; and to him who knocks, the door will be opened."*

Can it be any more clear that if you don't <u>have</u>, it's because you don't <u>ask</u>? If you have a sincere heart and you just want more of the Holy Spirit, He's not going to give you a demon! He can't. He's a good Dad. You CANNOT get a demon in you by asking God for Spiritual Gifts with a pure heart. Need proof?

> Luke 11:11-13 - *"Which of you fathers, if you son asks for a fish, will give him a snake instead? Or if he asks for an egg, will give him a scorpion? If you then, though you are evil, know how to give good gifts to your children, how much more will your Father in heaven give the Holy Spirit to those who ask him!"*

Snakes and scorpions are metaphors for demons. (Look it up, I don't have time to go over all that right now.)

Now, is it possible that you could have someone lay hands on you and get something that isn't from God? Yes. I've seen it happen. If you weren't satan, wouldn't you want undercover agents inside the churches handing out fake gifts? Or worse, Trojan horses that would cause nothing but trouble in somebody, but they think it's from God?

I've met people that had traveling evangelists or leaders of various sorts of ministries lay hands on them to receive tongues and what they got was definitely NOT of God. I heard a guy pray once and I didn't get an interpretation but the Lord instantly put a very clear picture in my mind of the elves in J.R.R. Tolkien's "Lord of the Rings." It was a really beautiful, flowing language and it definitely had power because all the hair on my arm stood up! But it was ELF – and in case anybody asks you, God doesn't give people ELF! This brother had had years and years of trouble with his tongue and being constantly misunderstood and his ministry could never get going because he seemed to always be sticking his foot in his mouth. But it didn't affect everybody and was so strange that I was sure it had to be supernatural. As it happened, he had received this Gift from someone he didn't really know and his walk with God and relationships with people around him had been devastatingly hard ever since. It wasn't just that it had control over his prayers. Since he had given legal ground over his tongue to a demonic force, it could mangle everything he said all the time. He made perfect sense to me most of the time, but some kind of supernatural garbler or "filter" would just tweak what he said so that certain people would always hear it the wrong way! It was really weird.

Whenever I'm doing a full "tune-up" with someone, I always want to listen to whatever prayer language they have (if they realize they have one). If we had more people with the gift of interpretation of tongues, we would know about all the people that speak in church and are actually cursing the pastor or the people! (I've heard of that, even though I haven't experienced that one myself.) Demons know all the languages that ever were, so it's nothing for one of them to speak through someone that has allowed them legal ground. Can you receive a false gift of tongues? Yes.

Ok, so did I just contradict myself? Not exactly. If your heart is pure and you ask the Father directly in the name of Jesus, He'll give you the good stuff. If you ask someone to lay hands on you to receive it, you still make sure YOU are asking the Father for it and not just letting them push it at you. You need to also "armor up" all the time.

Paul cautions Timothy to: (KJV)

> I Tim. 5:22 – *Lay hands suddenly on no man, neither be partaker of other men's sins: keep thyself pure.*

The argument that I have always heard is that that is a reference to the ordination of deacons or elders, but it's pretty obvious that that there were times when Timothy had people lay hands on him (or vice versa) for a purpose other than that. Paul desired to go to the Roman's so that he could impart to them spiritual gifts (by the laying on of his hands). So Paul is surely talking about something broader here than just the ordination of elders. That interpretation of this verse is almost exclusively held by the denominations that don't lay hands on people for any other reason. Again, we have de-spiritualized so much of this by our naturalistic explanations. Let's look at the Young's Literal:

> I Timothy 5:22 – *Be laying hands quickly on no one, nor be having fellowship* (koinoneo) *with sins of others; be keeping thyself pure* (hagnos – pure or clean);

The Wycliffe literal says this:

> I Timothy 5:22 – *Put thou hands to no man, neither at once commune* (koinoneo) *thou with other men's sins [Put thou hands to no man soon, neither commune thou with other men's sins]. Keep thyself chaste* (hagnos – pure or clean).

koinoneo {koy-no-neh'-o} – (Strong's 2841)

1) to come into communion or fellowship with, to become a sharer, be made a partner
2) to enter into fellowship, join one's self to an associate, make one's self a sharer or partner

OK, if the context is broader, we need to understand that it's important that we not lay hands on someone to transfer something we're not supposed to – whether a gift or a commissioning for service. Good advice. Listen to God and do what He tells you. It also means that we need to be very careful about who we allow to lays hands on US. We need to have an assurance from the Lord that it's OK. If you can't hear God, then you're just going to have to go on observation and what you know about the person – but that's not definitive. Best to hear straight from God.

I believe that what Paul is saying is that Timothy should be careful to make sure that he doesn't receive anything bad from someone. To make sure that you are prayerful and careful and armored up so that the sins (or demons) or soul-force or self of a person doesn't pollute your nice clean cup.

You have to understand that Paul did NOT write as one coming from a "naturalistic" standpoint. He was hyper-spiritual and walked it all the time. He had seen Jesus (probably far more than once), had visited heaven and seen things he couldn't repeat, seen thousands healed, raised the dead, fought pagan strongholds, done war with demons of all shapes and sizes, he even inferred to the Corinthians that when he was away he was still among them in the spirit. Do you think that's weird? Everything that the enemy has is a cheap imitation of something God has. But we get the good stuff! They can put a curse on someone's body, we can heal them instantly. They can make a zombie, but we can raise them fully. They can do astral projection and be somewhere else in the spirit, but we can be taken up into heaven or travel supernaturally wherever the Lord takes us. They are spent by their efforts and die young because it's soul-force, but we are energized and victorious because it's Christ in us that lives and reigns!

Ok, follow along. I was just explaining this to a sister the other day who had been raised in a home full of witchcraft. The real stuff, not somebody that just liked crystals and horoscopes. She never understood it before, but the Lord showed her all in a flash that when she was a little girl her mother taught her how to put her hands on someone and transfer spirits to them. They could feel it too, they would know that they had received stuff. And it was BAD stuff that created a soul-tie and gave the kid power and control over that person. This is just elemental stuff if you're into witchcraft. They understand VERY clearly that spirits can be transferred from objects or through people. All kinds of spirits – all bad. (If you really aren't sure I'm telling the truth, then armor up really good with the Blood of Jesus and do a Google search online for "witch + transference".) There's also repeated Biblical commands to keep defiled objects out of your home or you and your home (and the land) will become defiled and bring curses on you.

If you're in a "Spirit-filled" denomination, this shouldn't be weird at all. You understand that we can lay hands on someone and bless them and the Holy Spirit moves through us. Jesus did it all the time. All the apostles and hundreds of millions of Christians since have seen/felt the Holy Spirit flow through them in this way – either as the recipient or the conduit.

The problem is that we don't always armor up in church when someone lays hands on us because we don't think that anything bad could get on us (or in us). We'd never allow it from a stranger at the mall, but we can have a whole huddle of 20 people (some we don't know) praying over us for healing in church. I'm convinced that those "huddles" are a really bad idea. First, the elders and those who have an anointing for the need in question should be the only ones necessary. And second, it exposes a whole bunch of people to potential danger. Until everyone is educated about how to make sure that they are sealed up good and protected from anything that someone might push at them – intentionally or not – it would be better to limit the number of people making spiritual contact like that.

I'm under a standing order from God that whatever congregation I visit, if there is a call for people to go down front for prayer, I'm to go. First, I could use all the prayer I can get, but I'm also there to see what happens. Maybe somebody gets a word from the Lord for me – or maybe I uncover something icky that shouldn't be there. Either way, I go down front FULLY armored up, all the doors shut tight and covered in the Blood of Jesus. I pray that nothing OTHER than exactly what the Lord wants for me to have would be able to get through and anybody that's praying bad stuff that it would bounce.

I'm aware of several times when people came as friends to pray with me and they really had malicious intent. Not witches or satanists, but they still were praying with ulterior motives and hoping that something I was doing would fail or with a gloating spirit at my (momentary and light) misfortunes. They might have been praying for help and healing, but something in them was enjoying seeing me suffering. We can speak curses on people by our gossip or even by our prayers that seek something other than God's will for a person. We can even impart our own soulish nature and create a dangerous soul-tie to a person. Our soul-force is dangerous. We have to be VERY careful to draw a heavy line between using our soulish nature to control things and waiting on the Lord to do it by the power of the Holy Spirit.

(Read the book "The Latent Power of the Soul," by Watchman Nee
http://www.fellowshipofthemartyrs.com/pdf/latent_power_of_the_soul.pdf)

And that's just assuming that someone isn't a full-on occultist! We have plenty of witches and warlocks and Masons and Klan and others inside our churches. Far more than we realize.

Anybody involved in any of that stuff, to whatever degree, needs to renounce it completely and repent before they can expect to get their cup cleaned out and start hearing God better. If you were hearing Him now, you're hear Him yelling at you to get away from that stuff. Anybody in a leadership role in front of God's sheep that is doing any of that stuff needs to step down immediately and renounce it and prove they mean it. Read all the verses about how God feels about this kind of stuff – www.fellowshipofthemartyrs.com/witchcraft.htm. You better get free from it right away and get full of Jesus. He's not kidding around.

I cannot stress enough how important it is to be fully armored up before giving or receiving anything spiritually. Since you can receive stuff whether you know it or not, it's really critical to be fully armored up all the time. The Blood of Jesus will cover you, so long as you don't invite it in by ignorance or outright rebellion against God.

Pray this (Or something in this general direction. It ain't special or anything):

> **Lord God, I want You and You only in my life. Break off and crush anything that might be messing with me right now. Any curses or soul-ties or demonic activity has to stop now in the Name of Jesus. Lord, I don't ever want to receive anything from any person (or any object) that isn't purely from Jesus. Please set your wings about me and shield me against anything the enemy is trying to do against me. I stand in faith that the Blood of Jesus is sufficient to protect me against all attacks. Please alert me if someone is trying to harm me in any way. I want to make sure You get the credit and praise and thanks for watching out for me. I know you will and I stand in faith on Your promises of protection and provision. Cover me in the Blood of Jesus now and every day. In the mighty of my Lord Jesus Christ, Amen.**

OK, back to the point here. There are LOTS of different kinds of gifts, a lot more than people realize, and nearly endless variants and interactivities between them. It's not nearly as cut and dried as people think. I hope that when you get a little glimpse of it this way, you will marvel even more at God's love for you and the complexity of all that the Holy Spirit does inside of you every day, just to manage all this stuff!

> 2 Peter 1:3 – *According as his divine power* (dunamis) *hath given unto us all things that [pertain] unto life and godliness, through the knowledge of him that hath called us to glory and virtue.*

> Hebrews 2:4 – *God also bearing [them] witness, both with signs and wonders, and with divers* (poikilos) *miracles* (dunamis), *and gifts of the Holy Ghost, according to his own will?*

Poikilos is translated here "divers" but defined by Strong's (4164) as:

1) a various colours, variegated
2) of various sorts

It is translated eight times as "divers" and twice as "manifold".

> 1 Corinthians 12:4 – *Now there are diversities* (diairesis) *of gifts* (charisma), *but the same Spirit.*

> 1 Corinthians 7:7 – *For I would that all men were even as I myself. But every man hath his proper gift* (charisma) *of God, one after this manner, and another after that.*

> 1 Corin. 1:7 – *So that ye come behind in no gift ; waiting for the coming of our Lord Jesus Christ:*

So He has given us all things pertaining unto life and godliness, through the knowledge of him that called us to glory and virtue. Did you know you were called to glory and virtue? Isn't that cool?! Yep, so how do we do it? By the dunamis of God. There's no other way.

The Hebrews 2:4 verse also indicates that the miracles and gifts of the Holy Ghost are poikilos – that is, if you seek and find, what you'll probably get is variegated, diverse dunamis – lots of flavors, colors, frequencies, wavelengths! Wow! Not only is the Holy Spirit living inside you, He has to keep track of all this stuff on the fly for your benefit and for the Father's glory.

> Romans 12:6-8 (Amplified) – *Having then gifts* (charisma) *differing according to the grace that is given to us, whether prophecy, [let us prophesy] according to the proportion of faith; Or ministry, [let us wait] on [our] ministering: or he that teacheth, on teaching; Or he that exhorteth, on exhortation: he that giveth, [let him do it] with simplicity; he that ruleth, with diligence; he that sheweth mercy, with cheerfulness.*

Here's one of the best verses to confirm and substantiate all of this. Try this on:

> 2 Corinthians 1:11 – *Ye also helping together by prayer for us, that for the gift* (charisma) *[bestowed] upon us by the means of many persons thanks may be given by many on our behalf.*

Did you get that? The charisma that Paul (and Timothy in this letter) had in them came from having been bestowed on them by MANY persons. This was not just the original Baptism of the Holy Spirit (which Paul got from Ananias in Acts 9:17). And since here Paul uses "we" to indicate both he and Timothy, the clear implication is that both of them had received charisma (Gifts of the Spirit) from many/multiple people. Since Paul also imparted Gifts to Timothy, there must be multiple occasions of this having happened. In fact, Paul was originally ordained and commissioned by the elders in Antioch, not Corinth. But this letter seems to be thanking the Corinthians for having impart Gifts to them!

Remember these?

> 1 Timothy 4:14 – *Neglect not the gift* (charisma) *that is in thee, which was given thee by prophecy, with the laying on of the hands of the elders.*

> 2 Timothy 1:6 – *Wherefore I put thee in remembrance that thou stir up the gift* (charisma) *of God, which is in thee by the putting on of my hands.*

Looks like multiple instances of impartation to me. Could it just be a translation problem? Let's try the Darby:

> 2 Corinthians 1:11 – *ye also labouring together by supplication for us that the gift* (charisma) *towards us, through means of many persons, may be the subject of the thanksgiving of many for us.*

How about Young's Literal?

> 2 Corinthians 1:11 – *ye working together also for us by your supplication, that the gift* (charisma) *through many persons to us, through many may be thankfully acknowledged for us.*

I wonder how badly the NIV mangles it?

> 2 Corinthians 2:11 – *as you help us by your prayers. Then many will give thanks on our behalf for the gracious favor granted us in answer to the prayers of many.*

Yep, that's pretty bad. Doesn't even have any sense of it being a charisma at all! Like they're just being polite and sending them with their best wishes. Not really supernatural at all. You need to be really careful with the NIV. It's widely read across the mainline denominations and they're widely spiritually weak. It might not be a coincidence. (A dunamis shortage all around, I think.)

Oh! Just for fun, let's see what "The Message" says:

> 2 Corinthians 1:11 – *You and your prayers are part of the rescue operation—I don't want you in the dark about that either. I can see your faces even now, lifted in praise for God's deliverance of us, a rescue in which your prayers played such a crucial part.*

Wow. That practically makes no sense at all! I have no idea what that has to do with gifts of the spirit! Whadaya say we don't quote from that version ever again, OK?

HOW COMPLICATED COULD IT BE?
THERE ARE ONLY A FEW GIFTS OF THE SPIRIT, RIGHT?

Yeah, you'd think it would be easy wouldn't you? I've seen Spiritual Gift Inventory tests with 20 to 100 questions that help you narrow in on what you're good at. We have those so that we can identify tendencies or behaviors that are ALREADY in place, but not potentialities and future giftings or callings. Basically, we don't really have anointed apostles and prophets and people operating in discernment of spirits in any big enough quantity to just SEE who has what gifts and we (as a whole) don't hear God well enough to just ask Him ourselves. So we have to have psychological inventories. It's really very sad.

Ok, here is the generally agreed upon list:

THE GIFTS AND CALLINGS OF THE HOLY SPIRIT			
I Corin. 12:4-14	**I Corin. 12:27-30**	**Rom. 12:6-8**	**Eph. 4:11**
Word of Wisdom	Apostles	Prophecy	Apostles
Word of Knowledge	Prophets	Ministry	Prophets
Faith	Teachers	Teaching	Evangelists
Healings	Miracles	Exhortation	Pastors and Teachers*
Working of Miracles	Healings	Giving	
Prophecy	Helps	Leading	
Discernment of Spirits	Administrations	Showing Mercy	
Tongues	Tongues		
Interpretation of Tongues			

Note: * Some authorities distinguish between Pastors and Teachers in the list contained in Ephesians. That's how they get a "Five-fold" instead of a "Four-fold" ministry.

There are some others that are a little less clearly stated and some folks disagree with them being added to the list above. They include; hospitality, celibacy, voluntary poverty and exorcism/deliverance (although that is generally classified within the healing gift).

Gifts of the Spirit are not the same as the "fruit of the spirit" (Galatians 5:22). Since the "sign gifts" or manifestation gifts can sometimes be faked or come from evil sources (Matt. 24:24, 7:22-23), the true and better test is of the specific fruit listed here.

Fruit of the Spirit (Galatians. 5:22-23)
Love, Joy, Peace, Longsuffering, Gentleness, Goodness, Faith, Meekness, Temperance.

Please note the things that CANNOT be used to determine spiritual fruit. There are some obvious things <u>missing</u> from this list. Things like; size of ministry, eloquence of speech, new book deal, longevity in office, number of advanced degrees, physical attractiveness or magnetism, material wealth, number of people that agree with them, quantity or size of their miracles, likeability by the "world", etc. If you have been judging someone based on anything OTHER than the Biblical Fruit, you might want to say you're sorry and rethink to whom you've been listening. Jesus said that the more you were like Him, the more you would be hated and persecuted, so someone with lots of the TRUE Fruit is most likely going to be surrounded by a big cloud of controversy and lies. Don't let that automatically scare you off.

Basically, you can't dial up the Fruit of the Spirit. You can impart them to someone – you can share your Peace or Joy or Self-Control, but they have to walk it out before it becomes Fruit. You can pour it (sow it) into them all you want, but it's dead seed until it sprouts and produces a harvest – THEN it's Fruit. Basically, the bigger their "cup" gets, the more they are filled with Jesus, the more these Fruits will manifest because it is Christ in them that lives and there's not very much of their own selfish, sinful nature to get in the way anymore.

Some of these overlap substantially. You CAN dial up Peace, Joy, Patience because they are things you're "full of" in addition to being Fruits. Also, you can be full of Mercy and that would drive a bunch of the Fruits (things like Kindness, Generosity, Patience, Gentleness, Faithfulness). Wisdom would drive others (Patience, Modesty, Self-Control, Chastity, Generosity, etc.) Basically, you can take any one of these and replace it with "Jesus" and it retains the same meaning. So more Jesus means more Fruits and more Gifts. Go back and read the chapter about James Dunn. Some say there is just ONE Fruit divided in 9 parts. Same difference, the more you look like Jesus, the more this stuff all shows up. But it's important for you to get a sense of how intensely complicated this is. My goal is for you to get so mentally exhausted that you'll stop trying to control or manipulate what God wants and just lay it all at His feet and pour out whatever He tells you, when He tells you. If you try to fiddle with the dials yourself, you'll just make a mess.

Maybe some pictures will help. Imagine that each of these circles is a Spiritual Gift "dial". They interlock and mesh together and overlap in ways we can't even possibly understand. My goal in this book is not to explain exactly how it all works, I don't think any human can. My goal is to motivate people to lovingly share with each as they have a need and to teach AWE and the bigness and complexity of what God is doing in ALL of us.

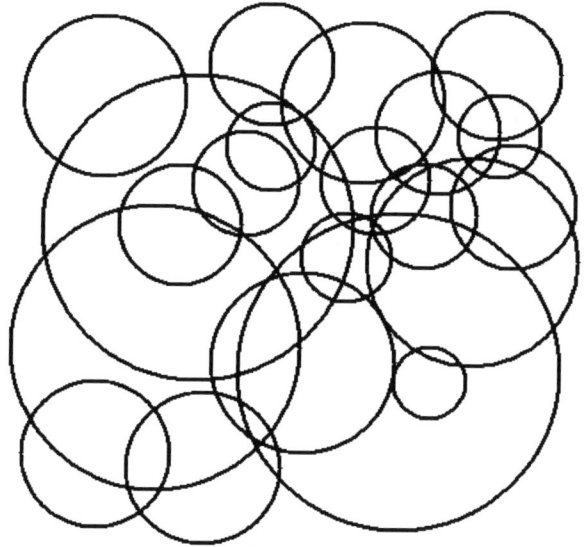

Can you see that even through the course of a single day, we all are tested and tried and we either pass or fail? We may also meet with people that pray for us, and the Holy Spirit intercedes for us directly with the Father, and maybe we spend time in the Word and receive some spiritual blessing. Throughout the day, this graphic is in constant motion. Like raindrops in a puddle, constantly flowing and rippling and expanding and contracting. Do you really think you can design a Spiritual Gifts inventory that will be accurate a week from now? Only if it is so basic as to be practically useless! (Or you are completely stagnant.)

Rain Right NOW, Lord!

Do they really overlap like that? Well, I've read about people with a massive gift of healing – people like Smith Wigglesworth, William Branham, James Dunn, Kathryn Kuhlman, Maria Woodworth-Etter, John G. Lake, A. A. Allen and others. (Go look them up online.) They all have their Faith dial up really high – that seems to control most everything. But the ones that seem to keep their head on straight and not start thinking they're Elijah usually also have their Wisdom and Discernment of Spirits dial up really high as well. You can see where someone goes terribly, horribly wrong in the "charismania" side of the Body and they nearly always have a serious shortage of Wisdom (Fear of the Lord is the BEGINNING of Wisdom) and an excess of some manifestation gift. Maybe they're Prophecy dial is up really high, but they don't know when to keep their mouth shut and not cast pearls before swine. Maybe their Healing dial is up really high but they started making it about THEM instead of giving God the glory. On the other side of the Body we have folks who also don't have enough Fear of the Lord because they think their doctrines are able to perfectly explain God and so they put Him in a box.

Romans 11:29 says that "God's gifts and his call are irrevocable." That means the Gifts are permanent. He'll pour Himself into you, but if you let some of it leak out, you're going to not be balanced as you should be. You'll probably guard carefully the Gift that makes you someone famous, but you'll let leak out the sub-components that made it work within His purposes and bring Him all the glory – like the wisdom and the discernment and the self-control and the modesty and the humility. You'll keep the flashy stuff and let go of the harder ones that require more maintenance. You can't keep humility and fear of the Lord and self-control if you're not on your knees all the time, keeping your cup full of Jesus daily/hourly.

Some big evangelists that end up in scandal or prison or excess had great big cups and they were all the way full, then they stopped praying and keeping them full and the enemy got in and started messing with them. If you have a cup the size of an oil tanker, just the daily evaporation rate could be tens of thousands of gallons! That much volume filled with sin would shatter the normal person instantly. You better keep your cup full ALL the time! Proverbs 25:26 – "Like a muddied spring or a polluted well is a righteous man who gives way to the wicked." (A well is a really big 'cup'.)

Said again (for emphasis), if you have a candle and you go stand out in the backyard on a summer night, a couple of bugs will come see what's going on. But if God has dialed you up really bright and you're like the halogen arrays on top of a professional football stadium, every bug for MILES is going to come try to smother you! The badness will SWARM on the great big cups and try to crush them any way possible. If you have no openings, they will go for any soft target around you – like your spouse and kids and ministry partners. Smith Wigglesworth, William Branham and John G. Lake all watched their wives die – and then raised them from the dead!

There are people all over the world right now raising the dead and seeing people regrow limbs in front of their eyes and healed of all kinds of terminal illnesses. More of that is coming as soon as the Body starts fully walking in our inheritance and sharing with each other from the abundance of our spirits. Do you want to see God pour out His Spirit on all men? Go find a man and dump out on him all of the Spirit of God that is in you!

You have an endless spring of living water flowing from inside of you, so go point it at somebody and open the faucet all the way! If you have a cup like a shot glass, they may not notice that anything happened. But if you have a cup like an oil tanker and you point a big, fat fire hose at them and crank it on real fast, it will probably knock them down. But PLEASE don't go _trying_ to knock them down for fun, that's just showing off. (And don't put your hand on them and PUSH them down either, that's just witchcraft and manipulation of the worst sort. Please tell God you're sorry for trying to force your will on people and look cool—and pray for more Fear of the Lord while you're at it.)

Are you getting this yet? Let's try another picture.

Know what that is? If you go to church in America, you probably do. Just in case you don't, it's a mixing board for a sound system. All the different dials and buttons and slides control the microphones and sound effects and lighting and all the different things that might be plugged into it. If you don't know what you're doing, you just should NOT be allowed to play with something like this! This is a very valuable piece of equipment and should not be toyed around with! This particular board is a professional model used in recording studios and costs many thousands of dollars. Like my cell phone, it has a great long list of cool features, most of which may never be used for anything. But they're there just in case, just a couple of buttons away.

Every person that you know has a "mixing board" far bigger, far more complicated **and far more valuable** than this one. ONLY the Holy Spirit can manage it. Only God knows what it's true potential and maximum possible range might be. We are like the little kid that peeks into the control room of a nuclear power plant and is awed by the walls of dials and gauges and switches. But you want to be sure not to let a little kid mess with anything in the control center of a nuclear power plant! See the picture. Would YOU want to be in charge of that? If I'm right about this, shouldn't we be putting a WHOLE lot more value on the individuals under our care? Shouldn't we be more careful with their potential?

The variables in play in even a single life are staggeringly massive. Since God sees the end from the beginning, He also knows **all at once** what came before and what is and what is coming. He knows how many souls that kid in your youth group COULD bring into the kingdom, but some or all of them will depend on YOU being obedient and speaking the right word at the right time to that kid. You can't possibly understand the value God places on that kid and the critical importance that you not try to do God's job for Him! You're just going to blow something up.

How can we keep from having more blood on our heads? We are already swimming in guilt and responsibility for all the missed opportunities, disobedience, refusal to share with and care for and love on brethren in need. Not to mention the darkness in the world that's because we didn't take our light out there in sufficient measure. We can't possibly even imagine how many are already going to hell because of the times we didn't do all that we could have. Is that legalism? No, Jesus wants obedience. Why? Because He's the ONLY ONE that can direct our paths so that we don't make things worse and worse all the time. He doesn't want to boss us around and make us miserable! He wants to gently walk us out of the giant bonfire we're standing in the middle of – that we started ourselves! He's the only one that knows the safest possible route out of the fire. It might take a little longer, it might twist and turn and look like we're losing ground, but He knows it's not quite as hot as the direct route that looked good to us but would have killed us instantly.

You see, if a person comes to you and asks for advice about whether to take Job A or Job B and you use all your reason and experience and knowledge and weigh the pro's and con's and help them to decide to take Job B – but that's not what God wanted for them and it wrecks their life – well, that's on your head. It's their fault for listening to you, but it's your fault (especially if you're in a leadership role) for not making sure they were following God and not Man. It could be that you should have just prayed and sought God together and He would have said to turn down both jobs and wait a week because BOTH are decoys from the enemy and Job C is coming and that's the really BIG payoff that was His Perfect Will all along for that person. (Unless you don't think God talks to people, in which case all you've got left is to lean on your own understanding. How's that working for you?)

How many earth-shaking evangelists never launched because we didn't raise them up? How many prophets and apostles and teachers are lost because we had pizza parties and ski trips instead of preaching the power of the Cross? How many people have we filled with the wisdom of man and the ways of the world instead of filling them with Jesus and Faith and Godly Wisdom?

> Colossians 2:8 – *See to it that no one takes you captive through hollow and deceptive philosophy, which depends on human tradition and the basic principles of this world rather than on Christ.*

Paul boasted that the blood of no man was on his head. Wow!! How did he do that? He wrote letters, he traveled all over – he preached until people fell out of windows and died! (But Paul raised him from the dead. Acts 20:7-12) How did he never steer anyone wrong? How did he <u>never</u> make it about him?

Because he always just pointed them toward Jesus. He didn't draw men unto himself, he got behind them and shoved them toward Jesus. He taught relationship and hearing God's voice and obedience to the Spirit in you. He didn't teach obedience to legalism or to systems and structures of man. He didn't seek obedience to Paul, he sought that they obey God alone. I don't want you to even remember me. I just want you to get cleaned out, get a big cup of Jesus, get more fear of the Lord, hear Him really well and then HE will direct your paths. If you let ME direct your paths, you're toast. Don't do it! Take everything here to the Lord and have Him explain it to you and confirm it to you and write it on your heart. Don't take my word for anything.

Ok, sorry. Little detour.

None of the Spiritual Gifts assessments that I have seen take into account all the possible variables. Also, I've never seen one that assumes that everybody has ALL of the Gifts. I'm just sure that if you have ANY Jesus in you, then ALL the Gifts are present. That is, when you get Jesus, all the dials move off of ZERO. Some may never move any higher, but it's there if you need it. That is, I know people that get saved and start hearing God better right away. At first it starts as conviction of sin, but also some zeal and a desire to evangelize. They have more urge to pray and intercede and pray for people that are sick and lost. Some of those prayers get answered. To the degree that they have faith, God continues to pour more into them and dial them up as they are obedient and continue to walk it out and be good stewards of what they have been given. Some people have a big anointing right away for evangelism or prophecy or something, some sneak up on it over time. God can do whatever He wants with your dials. If you don't have, it's because you don't ask – or you got it and didn't use it and it got rusty.

How else can you explain someone that has exceptional wisdom, but only in a given situation. Or someone that can pray healing or miraculous provision down, but only in an emergency. Or people that can heal anything and raise the dead, but only on the mission field? There are times when we "spike" because we're available and willing.

If you don't have a gift, it's because you don't ask. How many times in charismatic congregations does someone come down the aisle seeking the Baptism in the Holy Spirit just so they can speak in tongues? But that's at the BOTTOM of the list of gifts! Paul says to seek the ones at the TOP. I say, seek them ALL! What if you went down the aisle expecting to get them all, begging God to get them all, offering to lay down anything that was in the way so that you could have them all and use them effectively for the Kingdom? Do you think you might get a head start on the person that came down seeking tongues because they just wanted to fit in with everybody else in the youth group?

If you don't have, it's because you don't ask. This is a war between good and evil and we're getting creamed. Why? Because people aren't asking for the really dangerous stuff. The things that really push back the darkness. Particularly wisdom, prophecy, discernment of spirits and interpretation of tongues. In all of my travels around dozens and dozens of congregations (sometimes visiting four or five on one Sunday), I have only RARELY met anyone that has interpretation of tongues and even more rarely people that can see demons. Sadly also, few people that clearly hear the voice of God – and that's not even a Gift of the Spirit! That's just an automatic for ALL believers!

At any moment, God can dial you all the way up and you can do anything that any other brother or sister has ever done. You're just one instant (and a dead body) away from seeing someone raised from the dead. The Jesus in you can do anything, all you have to do is get out of the way and let Him do it through you. You need to get all cleaned out, get your Faith dial turned up really high and know that it's your birthright. Hope to see His glory fill you, do it for the sake of Love and then you'll see the dead raised.

The Master Dials that drive them all are Faith, Hope and Love. But the greatest is Love.

SPECTRUM ANALYSIS OF THE GIFTS

A rainbow has a full spectrum of colors in it. Not just the primary colors, but all kinds of shades in between. Our eyes see the ultraviolet spectrum of light, so we're most familiar with those that we sense, but there are all kinds of other light that our eyes can't see but some animals or scientific instruments can see. Some animals can SEE heat signatures (thermal radiation). We may group a thousand colors in the Yellow or Blue "band" of the rainbow, yet they are all distinct wavelengths if you break them apart.

Again, this is an effort to just get you to see the dizzying complexity of the Holy Spirit and what we all contain. Maybe it's a checklist for you to start asking God for stuff you don't have or to dial you up higher than wherever you are now. Or maybe to seek out or place higher value on some people around you that might have what you are missing.

And when you set yourself to praying that God would dial you up, don't take any man as an example. Don't pray that you would have the anointing of Elisha or the evangelistic power of John the Baptist or the healing anointing of John G. Lake – pray to be like Jesus and then some! He said we would do greater things than He did, so don't put a ceiling on what God might do with you. If He wants you to speak every language on the planet, fine. If He wants you to raise the dead through the internet, fine. Don't box Him in by asking for too little. It's best to just let the Spirit pray through you and He'll ask for the right stuff. If you don't know how to let the Spirit of God pray through you, start by asking for that.

This is by no means exhaustive or definitive. This is just an effort to catalog some of the obvious stuff. There are things coming that we don't and can't even anticipate yet! I'm just trying to show a little sense of how big this really is.

Spectrum Analysis of the Word of Wisdom "Band"

This is not earthly wisdom (that is, book learning), this is Godly wisdom. The pure kernel of raw Truth at the center of everything. Cutting through all the fog and getting right to the heart of the issue in a way that just shocks people because it's so pure. "Cut the baby in half." "Give to Caesar what is Caesars." etc.

- Word of Wisdom for the Church
- Word of Wisdom for an Individual
- Word of Wisdom for your own direction
- Rightly dividing the Word of God for teaching – deep calling unto deep
- Word of Wisdom for establishment or management of new works
- Word of Wisdom for a system of Man – King, Government, Army, etc.

A Word of Wisdom is not the same as wisdom. We can ask for godly wisdom all the time and He gives liberally and without reproach. That's a different dial and tied to the Fear of the Lord dial.

Spectrum Analysis of the Word of Knowledge "Band"

This is knowing something you should not know without supernatural intervention. Like Peter knowing that Ananias and Sapphira had cheated God in Acts 5. Or Jesus knowing how many times the woman at the well had been married or knowing Simon Peter's name. It's not the same as prophecy, but may overlap.

- Word of Knowledge about the Church
- Word of Knowledge about an individual
- Word of Knowledge about the past – something that happened that you wouldn't normally know about
- Word of Knowledge about the present – something currently happening, but out of sight
- (Future would probably be prophecy.)

An inverse of this band is a spirit of stupor over a person or an army or a nation (or demons). Basically blinding the "eyes" of their mind to the truth of the situation. That is, a removal of knowledge. This is how Richard Wurmbrand was able to smuggle carloads of Bibles into Russia in plain sight in the backseat. Or how the Lord had enemy armies turn on each other and kill themselves. It's knowledge turned inside out. He said that He would even do it to the Jews because they would be ever hearing but never learning. The Lord says that He will shield us and hide us from the eyes of the enemy. We can pray "cloaks" around us when instructed by God that will hide us from the enemy.

Spectrum Analysis of the Faith "Band"

This is not just the ability to believe in Jesus, this is a supernatural ability to endure and be strong. An unshakable belief that God will prevail regardless of outside appearances or the opinion of ANYONE.

This is a dial from SOME supernatural faith and strength to a deepset supernatural faith so strong that you can preach Jesus while burning at the stake; that you can believe God is going to raise the dead every time even though you've prayed 1,000 times on dead people and it hasn't happened yet; that NO MATTER WHAT, God will answer you. The Apostle Paul had a KNOWING that even if shipwrecked, not a single person would be lost; or if bitten by a snake it wouldn't hurt him. He KNEW when he cursed a king's magician that the guy would instantly go blind exactly like Paul said. Paul knew that he would be arrested, imprisoned and eventually killed if he went back to Jerusalem, but He knew it was God's plan to get him before kings and emperors and that it would be fine.

Faith is embedded in the middle because it drives all the others. All the gifts should be used in accordance with the measure of Faith you have. So whatever else you have, pray for more Faith and more Wisdom.

Spectrum Analysis of the Healings "Band"

Essentially a gift of intercession, this also carries with it authority to affect changes in the natural or spiritual realms. This can range from local (laying hands on) to long distance. From healing a headache to regrowing limbs or raising the dead (which would probably require physical, mental, emotional and spiritual all at once!).

- Anointing for physical healings – restoration or replacement of physical damage or affliction.
- Anointing for mental healings – mangled thought processes or mistaken views, probably demonic.
- Anointing for emotional healings – hurts and pains and lack of peace, bitterness, abuse.
- Anointing for spiritual healings – deliverance/exorcism from spiritual oppressions.
- Anointing for creative healings – remaking something not there (limb regrown, new brain cells, new organ, etc.)
- Anointing for healings of groups – families, congregations, races, specific victims of some sort, cities, states, nations

This may also include the reverse. That is, actually CAUSING illness (leprosy, blindness, death, etc.). Lots of people in the Bible spoke curses that removed healing over people or nations. That may be a healing dial or it may be under prophecy or miracles (or all). Either way, you better be REALLY, REALLY careful with that one!! It's just a VERY fine line away from witchcraft – and God really <u>hates</u> witchcraft! DO NOT even speak something like that unless you specifically hear God tell you to! If you have a lot of authority in healing or prophecy, the words you speak have power and you need to be very careful.

Spectrum Analysis of the Workings of Miracles "Band"

These are things that bend or outright violate what we normally think are the laws of nature. Since God made them, He knows how to get around the rules. It's a miracle because it is outside of what would be possible without supernatural intervention - iron just doesn't float, people just don't instantly drop dead when you tell them to, armies don't just kill themselves for no reason, the oil in a jar should run out sooner or later, a man cannot outrun a team of horses, you just can't feed that many people with five loaves and two fishies, you can't just declare a drought and the rain stops, etc. And yet, all of these things happened and still can when God commands it through an obedient man.

- Miraculous provision (money, food, water, etc.)
- Miraculous protection (shields, cloaks of stupor, blindness, angels, poisons, etc.)
- Miraculous movement (theoportation – Acts 8:39-40, super speed – I Kings 18:44-46, etc.)
- Miraculous movement of objects (theokinesis – 2 Kings 6:1-7)
- Miraculous weather responses (storms quieted, drought, flood, wind, rain, etc.)
- Miraculous responses by nature (wild animals – 2 Kings 2:23-25; trees, plants, springs, wells)
- Miraculous planetary responses (sun going backwards or standing still, earthquakes)

Spectrum Analysis of the Prophecy "Band"

Not the same as the "Calling" of Prophet. MANY people can and should prophecy either to each other or to the world, but the OFFICE of Prophet is different. Since Jesus IS the Spirit of Prophecy and we all have Jesus, we should all prophecy to some degree or another. If you have Jesus, your prophecy dial is AUTOMATICALLY not on Zero. You may think it's just intuition or deja vu, but it's Jesus. You may think it's just a weird dream, but it could be Jesus. (But not always.) Even if you just speak forth something from God's word but with divine conviction, that's prophecy.

- Message to the Church
- Message to an individual
- Message to king, government, army, etc.
- Rightly dividing the Word of God and speaking forth the Logos
- Seeing otherwise hidden past of an individual or group
- Seeing otherwise hidden present of an individual or group
- Seeing future of an individual or group
- Speaking forth demanding instant action (Raise up dry bones! Waves be still!)
- God directly speaking through you in first person
- God dictating to you (or divinely inspiring) a message in writing
- Dreams, closed visions (eyes closed), open visions (eyes open)

(I suspect that interpretation of dreams and visions is a part of the Wisdom band.)

Spectrum Analysis of the Discernment of Spirits "Band"

This is being able to see in the spirit and to tell the difference between the good guys and the bad guys. The more of this you have, the more the door opens between the natural and the spiritual and you can see in both places at the same time and discern who is for you and who is against you. The Wisdom band is really important here because you need to hear God really well before you act on anything that you see. The higher your dial here, the more reliability, clarity and resolution you get to all the senses. These are watchmen and advance scouts and snipers that can see the enemy a long way away and identify troop movements and pick off infiltrators. We need LOTS more of these.

- A vague sense that someone is "not quite right"
- A general sense that a place has strongholds or evil present
- A truth-detector that reliably tells you when someone is lying or not from God.
- Clearly seeing demons in the "spirit" (hearing, smelling, tasting, feeling)
- Clearly seeing demons in the "natural" with open eyes (hearing, smelling, tasting, feeling)
- Clearly seeing principalities or powers over places or cities or nations
- Seeing angels or other things of heaven in the "spirit" (hearing, smelling, tasting, feeling)
- Summoning and directing ministering angels to the degree of authority and faith granted

(Cloaking so as to be hidden from the spiritual eyes of the enemy – or even friends – is probably an inverse of this band. Some other things like praying "hedges" or shields of protection may also require a Discernment Gift to see and operate most effectively. Anybody can pray a shield, but not everybody can SEE them, manage them, reinforce them and clean them out if breached.)

Spectrum Analysis of the Giving "Band"

This is a supernatural ability to give of oneself. This is NOT tithing or some token giving. This is supernaturally powered sacrificial giving. It's not about the quantity, it's about the sacrifice and the spirit behind it.

- Giving of material resources
- Giving of mental resources
- Giving of emotional resources
- Giving of spiritual resources

(Pouring your cup out is Giving. Pouring it out fully and sacrificially is BIG Giving. Pouring it out eternally is maximum giving.)

Spectrum Analysis of the Helps "Band"

This is a supernatural ability to help those in need. This is not helping a little, this is supernatural helping in just the right way at just the right time beyond what seems reasonable to someone not so motivated.

- Giving of time resources
- Giving of physical resources/labor

Spectrum Analysis of the Mercy "Band"

This is a supernatural ability to feel for those in need. To see people through the eyes of Jesus and to cry when He cries and laugh when He laughs, to forgive as He forgives. This is empathy of the highest Godly order. This is love.

> Mercy, empathy and love for individuals, families, congregations, nations, the world.

Spectrum Analysis of the Administration "Band"

A supernatural ability to direct the flow of people, money, goods, services, information, etc.

> Coordinating efforts of others toward a common goal.

> Efficient, selfless networking with Giving, Helps, Mercy, Prophecy, and other bands toward an efficient delivery of goods, services, mercy, evangelism, communication or other.

Spectrum Analysis of the Exhortation "Band"

A supernatural ability to be encouraging and say the affirming, uplifting word that is needed at just the right moment. May involve lots of hugging.

Spectrum Analysis of the Tongues "Band"

Basically it's allowing the Holy Spirit to prophecy or speak through you in whatever way He wants. It may or may not be linguistic. I'm aware of people speaking in other languages of men, but there are also other options in this "band".

> Languages of Man – Many options or frequencies
>
> Languages of Angels – Many options or frequencies
>
> Groaning/Travail (Romans 8, Ezek 21)
>
> Tears/Weeping
>
> Specific Purpose Tongues – Intercession, Miracles, Praise, Warfare, etc.
>
> Communication (with Headquarters) Tongues
>
> Singing in Tongues
>
> Inspired playing of instruments
>
> Inspired body movement - dance
>
> Other prophetic physical or physiological responses that are "decent and in order"
>
> Interpretation of Tongues

Some of these overlap with Prophecy if they are interpreted.

Some don't necessarily need interpretation – like dance, music, groaning, weeping, etc.

Some of these may just be conglomerations of other dials, but they seem to be things that can be poured out, even though they have an influence on a bunch of other things and may not really be independent. I know that may not fully make sense, but God is really complicated and the best we can do sometimes is write down what we observe, even if we don't understand the mechanics of it or the scriptural justification for it.

Other Dials that we've observed:

Wisdom (not Word of Wisdom)

Fear of the Lord (actually a flavor of Wisdom)

Peace (may actually be a flavor of Faith)

Strength (may actually be a flavor of Faith)

Patience (may actually be a flavor of Faith)

Authority (for a specific work – delegation/commissioning type thing)

CAN YOU PRAY THE HARD PRAYER?

The Lord gave me a really simple understanding of the nature of the warfare we endure. It goes like this – the point of this life is to raise up big strong brothers and sisters for Jesus. The Father wants big, spiritually muscle-bound warriors, not soft couch potatoes. You can't build up muscle without breaking it down first. You need resistance training. Without something to push against, you can't build muscle.

So it's like I'm on the bench press and satan is the barbell and the struggles and problems and cares of life are the weights. The Lord said that He would never let it go too far. He said that He would help bear my burdens. He said that it wouldn't crush me. So Jesus is my "spotter" – and Jesus can lift the whole universe!

So, satan is just the tool used for resistance training, right? So he can't go beyond what the Lord allows and it's all just to make me big and strong? And Jesus is my spotter? When I wear out, He's going to pick it up?

Well, then, Lord, put **ALL** the weights on and let's go!! Let's get this over with! I don't care how much it hurts, put all the weight on and get me big and strong really fast! There's a war between good and evil and I think we're losing. I could lift 50 pounds and I'd never break a sweat or be the least big inconvenienced. But I'm never going to build muscle either! So put 1000 pounds on and let's go! You know what I can handle and you'll help when I'm weak. In fact, You get MORE glory when I'm weak, so put SO MUCH weight on it that I could never possibly lift it without You! Then everybody will know it was a miracle and I won't get any of the credit! Yeah, that's what I want. Load me up. I don't care how much it hurts, I don't care how much I whine and complain, You are my Personal Trainer so don't let up. No matter how annoying I am and how many times I ask You to take the weight off, don't do it! Finish what You started in me and let's get it over with so I can be fully ready to go serve Your Body in the biggest, best possible way.

Wanna pray that? I can promise you it's going to hurt – a LOT. (Read the Warning Label again.) He will ABSOLUTELY take you seriously and all kinds of really horrifyingly hard things are going to start pretty much immediately. You need to figure that NOTHING in your life is safe from that prayer. Not family, not job, not health, not even your calling or your gifts. He might not even feed you. It might mean prison, it might even mean ending up on crack and sleeping under a bridge is necessary to burn everything out of you and prepare you for HIS perfect plan for your life. He's very creative. And He is the only one that can know what it's going to take. But I can promise you this, He is a good Dad and He's never going to push it beyond what is absolutely necessary. He's never going to spank you one extra time just cause it makes Him feel good. The more you embrace the refining fire, the easier it will be.

I'm speaking from personal experience here. There is no prayer that will get you ready for war faster, but there's no prayer that will hurt more either. But if you're so full of Jesus that nothing else can fit, you won't care too much about the pain. And it's really fun to watch Him lifting when you can't do it anymore. This is maximum adrenalin praying.

Don't blame me for whatever comes. You've been properly warned. Now, if you're willing, pray this.

Dear Lord Jesus, I trust You. I know You'll get me through. I want to be fully equipped, fully armored, fully broken and fully willing to do your perfect will. Whatever in me that is resisting You – kill it with prejudice. Lord, there is a monster inside of me and it's me. Hunt it down and kill it and hang its head on the wall of my heart so I'll never forget what I was. Put all the weight on. Load me up. Whatever it takes, I trust You. I'm ready now, Lord. Do it right now! I know this prayer is inside Your will, so I know You are going to answer it. Just please don't ever leave me. In the mighty name of my Lord Jesus Christ, Amen.

I Peter 4:12-14 – Beloved, think it not strange concerning the fiery trial which is to try you, as though some strange thing happened unto you: If ye be reproached for the name of Christ, happy [are ye]; for the spirit of glory and of God resteth upon you: on their part he is evil spoken of, but on your part he is glorified.

2 Cor. 4:17 – For our light affliction, which is but for a moment, worketh for us a far more exceeding [and] eternal weight of glory;

Hebrews 11:25 – Choosing rather to suffer affliction with the people of God, than to enjoy the pleasures of sin for a season

Luke 6:22-23 – Blessed are ye, when men shall hate you, and when they shall separate you [from their company], and shall reproach [you], and cast out your name as evil, for the Son of man's sake. Rejoice ye in that day, and leap for joy: for, behold, your reward [is] great in heaven: for in the like manner did their fathers unto the prophets.

OK, SO HOW DO YOU POUR OUT YOUR CUP?

If you skipped straight to this chapter and missed all the stuff before – GO BACK!!! This ain't a game. I'm not kidding around here. If you don't have the proper foundation on which to build this, you'll make a giant mess!! No peeking!! Start at the front.

Well, here's the thing. I think it's just rightly dividing the Word of God to illustrate about *charisma* and *dunamis* and about the examples of impartation of the Holy Spirit and of Gifts by the apostles and others. I think we're safe by encouraging people to pour themselves out and showing the Biblical requirement to do so and the obvious deficit of it in the Church. But I don't want to establish some artificial procedural doctrine. The last thing we need in the Church are more programs and curriculums and people preaching that theirs is the only way! I think there are some universal principles in play here, but I'm just really hesitant to set some kind of policy about how the mechanics of it should work.

There are some things that we know. The actual physical contact of the laying on of hands was important and a common element in the Bible. Not just for the commissioning of missionaries, but for healing and for receiving the empowering of the Holy Spirit and for impartation of Gifts. But, sometimes people were healed without anyone touching them, so it's not an absolute. Nobody laid hands on the disciples in the upper room (well, God did). Sometimes contact reinforces faith and is necessary for the recipient, sometimes it's not required. Lots of examples of people being told what to do to be healed, and as they obeyed they were made well.

I can only tell you what the Holy Spirit taught me about this. Your own experience may be substantially different and I'm not going to tell you it's wrong if there is clear fruit. I'm not trying to make clones of me, you do whatever the Lord shows you. Just get everything out of the way and hear Him really well.

I'm going to be really transparent here because at this point, I've got nothing to lose anyway. I didn't get to the "cup model" as some theoretical construct, God started showing me my cup and that's what it looked like. I'd wake up every morning and ask Him how full my cup was and I'd spend time with Him until I was sure my cup was all the way full. Throughout the day, as I could feel (or see) it drain off, I would make sure and get time with Him and drink from the river of life. I wasn't always good at it, but He has taught me a lot as I've grown in Christ.

I would talk to other people about it and encourage them to ask the Lord to show them their own cup. Other people started seeing their cups and they looked just the same as what I was seeing (red, yellow and blue). People who had never even seen the graphic were describing it to me the same way! Over and over I would show the model to someone and ask them if they wanted to get the SIN out and get a big cup of Jesus, even if it hurt. They would agree and then I would pray for them and ask the Lord to pour any good thing in my cup into theirs. If I put my hand on someone, I would feel the Spirit moving through my arm and hand and vibrating like when you hold a gas pump at the gas station. When they were full, it would just shut off. If I tried to "push" it would go faster but I could NOT push more into somebody that was full (or push something that God said He didn't want them to have).

Over and over I watched people get filled with the Holy Spirit this way. Sometimes they would speak in tongues, sometimes they wouldn't – or sometimes later on. I didn't care to push them about that gift because I didn't need it as "initial evidence" because the Lord just let me actually <u>watch</u> their cup get full! What do I need flesh and blood proof for? We're to see in the spirit anyway and I watched them get filled. And the evidence that they got full was that it often turned their life upside down right away. If they got a lot bigger cup and learned how to keep it full, they often started going through all kinds of amazing adventures as the enemy right away tried to slow them down. As you'd expect, some gave in and some stood strong. The ones that did the best were the ones that could receive in faith and learned how to keep their cup full all the time. The ones that had the most child-like faith were always the ones that did the best. Those that want to drink in Jesus all the time, all day long.

Most often it didn't do much good to fill someone's cup if they had all kinds of entrenched bad stuff that had effectively "corked" their cup. The springs of living water were capped because of the embedded SIN and strongholds and strategies of the enemy that needed to be purged first. So we would talk about what might be in their cup that shouldn't and if they didn't know right away what it was that was holding them back from the fullness of God, we'd pray and God would often tell me what the strongholds were in their life. Then I would tell them, they would cry (because nobody was supposed to know about that so it must be God), then they would repent, we'd rebuke it in the name of Jesus and get their cup full. Lots of people got healed of spiritual and physical illnesses at the same time by this process.

I've learned that I can pour my cup out on people remotely through intercessory prayer, online discussion boards, phone calls, or from across a room. I've learned that if your cup is big enough, you can pour it out on a whole congregation. Sometimes the Lord sends me to a congregation just to sit quietly in the back and pray that the worship team or the leadership or the whole congregation would be filled as full as He'll allow. If you have a really, really big cup, you can fill a whole town. I think that's what Paul did when he went into a town and interceded for them collectively and offered himself up for them all. I think that's what Daniel Nash did for Charles Finney. (Do a Google search for Daniel Nash or Father Nash and read about this amazing man!)

I think you can see Moses and Paul pouring out their entire eternal cups on a whole race (Ex. 32:32, Rom. 9:22-23) Jesus had a cup so big, He could pour it out on all people for all time. In fact, He poured Himself out and allowed the SIN of all people to be poured into a cup that had never had SIN in it before. He stood in the gap for us and took on all our icky ugliness. He prayed the prayer of Moses for everybody ever. And unlike Moses, He had the authority to do it on a global scale.

In fact, Jesus had a cup so big that He could fill everybody's cup for all time SO full that it would be like an endless stream of living water flowing up from inside of you. That is, those who acknowledge Him and who He is and what He did and are willing to receive from Him will be able to get there cup so full that nothing else will fit and, if they're obedient with it, can pour it out on others so freely that it will never run out. His cup is still being poured out on us all the time. The only limitation to how much you can be filled with Him and His Spirit is the degree to which you are willing to receive it and lay down anything that is in the way. Isn't that the coolest thing ever!?! Kind of changes the whole nature of "church" doesn't it?

Can it really be that simple? Well, believe in faith and give it a try. I have seen so much evidence and confirmation of this that I don't even doubt it for a second anymore. I've seen people just LIGHT UP and become fierce faith-walking warriors when you get them unclogged, pray the hard prayer and get them full of Jesus. Then their cup just keeps getting bigger and bigger the more they listen to Him and obey.

But please, remember the warning, the enemy is going to do EVERYTHING possible to slow you down, to plant fear and doubt, to get you to deny that this is real. He won't be able to win on scriptural grounds, but some religious spirit will try really hard to get you to either deny all of this or to stop walking in it once you start. Expect resistance!! Be ready for it. DO NOT underestimate it!

He that is in you is bigger, greater, stronger, older, smarter, and more patient and loving than he that is in the world. Let Him do the fighting for you. This isn't about you anyway.

ARE YOU SURE YOU'RE NOT NUTS?

Boy, I'll tell you what! Sometimes I read over stuff like this that I have written and the Missouri Show-Me, Southern Baptist preacher's kid in me does sort of wonder if I'm nuts. But the Word of God is clear, we are spiritual beings temporarily trapped in jars of clay. We are to walk in the spirit, not focus on the flesh. Our battle is NOT against flesh and blood, but against powers and principalities and wickedness in high places and the dark forces of this world. Neither is our battle to be done WITH our flesh and blood. Our spirit (or rather His in us) is where our true power rests.

So, yeah, this seems really supernatural and mystical to me sometimes, except that God has proven it to me so many times that I couldn't even begin to count. I've seen demons (in the spirit) on someone and reached out and grabbed them and ripped them off and they quit smoking or are healed of Autism or their pain stops instantly or they don't need their schizophrenia medicine anymore. Over and over and over. And I've seen people (strong Christians!) be unable or unwilling to keep the doors shut and it comes back seven times worse and within HOURS they're beating their wife and doing drugs and cursing me out – or worse! I know demons are real because the Lord has proven it to me over and over and I've seen what they do, how they act, where they hide, how to get rid of them, how they come back, how they work together and more.

There is a certain segment of the "church" that will insult and demean anything that is "supernatural" and yet they gather together to pray on Wednesday nights for the sick people in their churches. They pray that the doctors would have wisdom, that their recovery would be slightly faster than normal, that they would have peace with the sickness that the Lord has placed on them. Hogwash! What kind of power is that? What kind of inheritance? If you don't believe God heals, then why pray at all? Why not just write a note of encouragement to their doctor? If you just sit around and send out good vibes to their doctor, how is that not a form of New Age meditation? Where in the Bible does it say to go to a doctor anyway? Who is the Great Physician? What doctor can heal if God doesn't want someone healed? What doctor can save a life that God wants to take? And who can kill someone God wants to keep alive? How many examples do you want of people that I know that are unkillable? I have a friend that tried to commit suicide so many times and kept getting saved by angels that finally an angel came and said, "Would you just KNOCK IT OFF! We're never going to let you kill yourself!" And that was BEFORE he came to Jesus! If God has something for you to do, until you do it, you're indestructible! Why be afraid of Man? And if God wants you dead, NOBODY can save you. Be afraid of God.

Oops! Sorry, started preaching again. Anyway ...

Those sections of the church that deny that the Gifts of the Spirit are for today are still brothers and sisters and I love them. But they're not going to be very much help fighting a war in the spirit with weapons they say aren't real and against an enemy they insist isn't there. Some even believe that God doesn't speak to people anymore. What kind of a war is that? In the meantime, their churches are full of sick, shackled, addicted, fearful, obese people with no peace and joy and victory. They have the appearance of Christ, but deny the power thereof. That can't be good. But I love them and want them to come around. It's not the people's fault, it's the doctrines of man jammed down their throat by seminarians who will not back down from the status quo. But I think God is coming in power real soon and He's going to settle the issue once and for all.

Yes, there are lying signs and wonders already and many more coming. There are false prophets that heal and deliver people of demons (or seem to). But the fact that satan has cheap imitations DOES NOT negate the originals! Who benefits most if God does supernatural stuff and satan does supernatural stuff, but you dismiss them BOTH because ONE of them was from satan? Don't you think that's going to irritate God – to constantly be told that anything supernatural that He does was actually the work of satan? I mean how can God do anything that's NOT supernatural – by definition, He's not "natural"! When God equips someone with faith and power and they take the Bible seriously and go out and fulfill the Great Commission as it's written at the end of the Gospel of Mark and people keep saying they are tools of satan, don't you think that's going to irritate God?

Whatever else I may be, I've got peace and joy and victory and I'm deliriously happy. If the voice I'm hearing is NOT God, then it sure sounds like Him and He keeps telling me to do stuff that you would think would really, really make satan mad. If this voice isn't really God, I don't care, I'm gonna stick with it until this whole ride plays out to the end. I'm going to bet on radical obedience and a pure heart being a really good thing (heavenly treasure-wise) and if I go down, I'm going down swinging for the fences. God will judge my heart, not the perfection and purity of my doctrine.

So, if I'm crazy, don't medicate me, I'm really enjoying it.

HOW WOULD THIS REALLY CHANGE THE CHURCH?

I don't know if you really see the impact of all of this, but if I'm right, then it really changes everything. If you can pour out your spirit, then we'll do a lot less filling their brains and a lot more filling their spirit. If people in the congregations were fully equipped with the gift of discernment and were aware of who had a deficit or had things clogging them up, it would make every single member a potential minister. It would empower every member to reach out and help every other. And it would be hard to make it about their knowledge or their anointing or their diploma, because there might be little kids with bigger cups of Jesus!

Other stuff that might change? There'd be a whole lot less brain training and a whole lot more fellowshiping and sharing and breaking bread and investing in each other. There would be a whole lot more people spiritually armored up and ready to take on the darkness of this world. There would be a whole lot less budget needs and if the government took all our buildings and overhead projectors away, nobody would care because you can pour your cup out on somebody and worship in a park or a cave or an office building. You know, it might just disrupt the entire infrastructure of the entire institutional church system. I wonder what kind of chaos that might cause to people that don't want to give up their old wineskins?

It would also take the emphasis off of a "senior pastor" and shift the responsibility of eldership to where it should be – to those who have the biggest cup of Jesus. It would value people for their spiritual assets – for their Biblical Fruit, not for their degrees or speaking ability or their new book deal or any other measure. The little old lady in the walker or the kid in Sunday School might be the one people seek out when they need prayer. If the pastor wants to stay in the lead, then he's going to have to work hard to make sure that he pours himself out all the time and keeps his cup bigger than anybody else's. For that matter, why does he need to be in the lead? Why not just direct the resources of the assembly toward meeting needs and try not to make it about him. That would be nice.

But you can't grow if you have embedded sin that you're unwilling to get out. Your spring of living water can't flow from inside of you if you've got it corked with badness. Before we can really get this show on the road, we need to help individuals get unplugged and then we need to step back and take a look at the cup of our assembly and see what we need to do to get it unplugged as well.

This isn't theory. I've seen this work. I've been in a fellowship where everyone there had been through this, had been fully cleaned out, was walking in holiness, had giant cups of Jesus and really, REALLY knew how to love on each other like Jesus. I can tell you, it's as far from the institutional, systematized churches as the East is from the West. It's pure and beautiful and as close to heaven as I've ever found on earth! Fellowship is purer, everyone shares with each as they have a need – body, soul and spirit. The Holy Spirit flows like a mighty river and it's pure and clean and deep. The best "church service" I've ever been to was an amazing 2 ½ hours of prophetic worship, repentance, anointing and communion led entirely and seamlessly by the Spirit of God through a seven year old girl! And that was not in a big sanctuary – that was in a furniture store!

Have you ever been in a group of people that trusted God completely for everything and knew how to love each other like Christ loves the Church? People that would NOT leave a need unmet, no matter what it cost them? I want nothing more than to see that in every body of believers everywhere. I'm pouring myself out daily toward that goal. And I believe that is what is coming, as soon as people learn how to be fully free, fully equipped, fully sacrificial – that is, get full of Jesus and stay full.

Let's try this a different way. Proverbs 3:5-10 lays it out pretty clearly.

IF YOU:

5 Trust in the LORD with all your heart
TRUST HIM WITH ALL

and lean not on your own understanding;
LEAN ON NONE OF YOUR OWN UNDERSTANDING

6 in all your ways acknowledge him,
LISTEN REAL GOOD

and he will make your paths straight.
LET HIM GUIDE ALL YOUR PATHS

7 Do not be wise in your own eyes;
KILL PRIDE

fear the LORD
SEEK WISDOM

and shun evil.
SEEK RIGHTEOUSNESS

8 This will bring health to your body
PHYSICALLY & SPIRITUALLY, PERSONALLY & COLLECTIVELY

and nourishment to your bones.
TRUE MEAT, NOT JUST MILK

9 Honor the LORD with your wealth,
SPIRITUAL WEALTH AND MATERIAL WEALTH

with the firstfruits of all your crops;
SHARE YOUR BEST WITH THOSE IN NEED AS HE DIRECTS

10 <u>**THEN**</u> your **barns** will be **filled** to **overflowing**, and your **vats** will **brim over** with **new wine**.

A barn is a big storage place for lots of containers - essentially the church! When the Church starts working like THIS, then all of the "vats" of their people will brim over and the barns themselves will be filled to overflowing.

(Did you notice how similar this is to the Beatitudes we talked about before?) Want some more verses to confirm it?

> 1 Thes. 4:4 – *That every one of you should know how to posses his vessel in sanctification and honour;*

> 2 Timothy 2:20-26 – *20 But in a great house there are not only <u>vessels</u> of gold and silver, but also of wood and earthenware, and some for honorable and noble [use] and some for menial and ignoble [use]. 21 So whoever cleanses himself [from what is ignoble and unclean, who separates himself from contact with contaminating and corrupting influences] will [then himself] be a <u>vessel</u> set apart and useful for honorable and noble purposes, consecrated and profitable to the Master, fit and ready for any good work. 22 Shun youthful lusts and flee from them, and aim at and pursue righteousness (all that is virtuous and good, right living, conformity to the will of God in thought, word, and deed); [and aim at and pursue] faith, love, [and] peace (harmony and concord with others) in fellowship with all [Christians], who call upon the Lord out of a pure heart. 23 But refuse (shut your mind against, have nothing to do with) trifling (ill-informed, unedifying, stupid) controversies over ignorant questionings, for you know that they foster strife and breed quarrels. 24 And the servant of the Lord must not be quarrelsome (fighting and contending). Instead, he must be kindly to everyone and mild-tempered [preserving the bond of peace]; he must be a skilled and suitable teacher, patient and forbearing and willing to suffer wrong. 25 He must correct his opponents with courtesy and gentleness, in the hope that God may grant that they will repent and come to know the Truth [that they will perceive and recognize and become accurately acquainted with and acknowledge it], 26 And that they may come to their senses [and] escape out of the snare of the devil, having been held captive by him, [henceforth] to do His [God's] will.*

Could it be any more clear than that? Whether it's you individually or the "cup" of your congregation, your town or your country – get the nasty, useless goo out of your cup!! You are **NOT** going to be "set apart and useful for honorable and noble purposes, consecrated and profitable to the Master, fit and ready for any good work" **UNTIL** you are cleansed!

What is it that we are SUPPOSED to be doing? Here's the list:

- Shun lusts and flee from them.
- Aim at and pursue righteousness, virtuous and good, right living.

- Conforming to the will of the Lord in thought, word and deed.
- Pursue faith, love and peace in fellowship with all who call upon the Lord out of a pure heart.
- Refuse trifling controversies over ignorant questionings that foster strife and breed quarrels.
- Do not be quarrelsome.
- Be kindly to everyone and mild-tempered
- Be a skilled and suitable teacher, patient and forbearing and willing to suffer wrong.
- Correct opponents with courtesy and gentleness, in hope that GOD will straighten them out.
- And in hope that they will escape the rulers that hold them captive, so that they can do His will.

Does that look much like the church system we currently have in place? Did we get 37,000+ denominations by doing the stuff on this list? Hmmm. I wonder if God's really happy about this mess?

Need another one? How about Romans 12?

> *1 I appeal to you therefore, brethren, and beg of you in view of [all] the mercies of God, to make a decisive dedication of your bodies [presenting all your members and faculties] as a living sacrifice, holy (devoted, consecrated) and well pleasing to God, which is your reasonable (rational, intelligent) service and spiritual worship.*

Present your bodies as living sacrifices. What body? Your physical body? Yes. Your family? Yes. Your congregation? Yes. Your nation? Yes. Why? Because it is your minimum reasonable service to the God of the universe whom you worship. What do we have to do before we offer the sacrifice? Make sure it is holy – cleaned out, washed off and worthy so that it is well pleasing to God. Don't think that a one-eyed lamb or a bull with three legs is going to do! Don't offer half of your body – wash it clean and put the WHOLE thing up on the altar and lay there. Don't hold back.

> *2 Do not be conformed to this world (this age), [fashioned after and adapted to its external, superficial customs], but be transformed (changed) by the [entire] renewal of your mind [by its new ideals and its new attitude], so that you may prove [for yourselves] what is the good and acceptable and perfect will of God, even the thing which is good and acceptable and perfect [in His sight for you].*

If you offer your body as a living sacrifice, He is going to then perform these three simple steps. This is God's three step plan to restore the Body. First, He's going to fix it so you stop conforming to the world. Laying naked on an altar and waiting for someone to sacrifice you is a good start. Then, when He's good and ready, He's going to cut your head off and graft His head on. He will reboot you back to the defaults and re-NEW your mind – back the way it was when it was before the viruses of the world messed it all up – that is, He'll make it like Christ. THEN you will know what is the good and acceptable and perfect will of God. Until you do those three steps you're just going to have to guess at what His will is. As long as you're conforming to the world you <u>can't</u> get your mind renewed and you <u>won't</u> know what He really wants for you. Forget spending forty days on purpose to figure out what you can do for God, it's not going to do <u>any</u> good until you stop conforming to the world. The Word of God says so.

> *3 For by the grace (unmerited favor of God) given to me I warn everyone among you not to estimate and think of himself more highly than he ought [not to have an exaggerated opinion of his own importance], but to rate his ability with sober judgment, each according to the degree of faith apportioned by God to him.*

Kill pride. Seek Wisdom. Judge rightly.

4 For as in one physical body we have many parts (organs, members) and all of these parts do not have the same function or use,

Get that? Not everybody can be toes or eyeballs. Diversity is good. Stop cloning people to be just like you instead of letting them be who God created them to be. We need all the parts doing what they were made for, not trying to be something they're not.

5 So we, numerous as we are, are one body in Christ (the Messiah) and individually we are parts one of another [mutually dependent on one another].

If you think you can do without all the other parts, you're wrong. This is a multi-part harmony that He wrote, not thousands of people all singing the melody line in unison.

6 Having gifts (faculties, talents, qualities) that differ according to the grace given us, let us use them: [He whose gift is] prophecy, [let him prophesy] according to the proportion of his faith;

Remember, this word "gifts" is "charisma" - he's talking about spiritual gifts, each used according the quantity of grace and faith of each. But they are not for show, they're to be used!

7 [He whose gift is] practical service, let him give himself to serving; he who teaches, to his teaching; 8 He who exhorts (encourages), to his exhortation; he who contributes, let him do it in simplicity and liberality; he who gives aid and superintends, with zeal and singleness of mind; he who does acts of mercy, with genuine cheerfulness and joyful eagerness.

Whatever God gave you, use it with love and sincerity. If God gave you a weapon and you let it lay around, it's just going to get rusty. Take it out to the range and practice with it until you're a sharpshooter. Get so good that you can shoot the wings off a fly at a thousand yards.

9 [Let your] love be sincere (a real thing); hate what is evil [loathe all ungodliness, turn in horror from wickedness], but hold fast to that which is good. 10 Love one another with brotherly affection [as members of one family], giving precedence and showing honor to one another. 11 Never lag in zeal and in earnest endeavor; be aglow and burning with the Spirit, serving the Lord. 12 Rejoice and exult in hope; be steadfast and patient in suffering and tribulation; be constant in prayer. 13 Contribute to the needs of God's people [sharing in the necessities of the saints]; pursue the practice of hospitality. 14 Bless those who persecute you [who are cruel in their attitude toward you]; bless and do not curse them. 15 Rejoice with those who rejoice [sharing others' joy], and weep with those who weep [sharing others' grief]. 16 Live in harmony with one another; do not be haughty (snobbish, high-minded, exclusive), but readily adjust yourself to [people, things] and give yourselves to humble tasks. Never overestimate yourself or be wise in your own conceits. 17 Repay no one evil for evil, but take thought for what is honest and proper and noble [aiming to be above reproach] in the sight of everyone. 18 If possible, as far as it depends on you, live at peace with everyone. 19 Beloved, never avenge yourselves, but leave the way open for [God's] wrath; for it is written, Vengeance is Mine, I will repay (requite), says the Lord.

Be real. Hate evil. Be good. Love your brothers and sisters no matter what. Step back and promote them instead of yourselves. Look on the bright side. Hang in there no matter what storms come. Pray all the time. Share with people when they need something. Share your stuff cheerfully. Be nice, even to bullies. When someone laughs, laugh with them, when they cry, cry with them. Play nice and don't pick favorites. Be willing to do the dirty chores. Don't be arrogant. Don't be mean. Think good thoughts. Try to get along with everybody. Don't hit back, let God fix the bullies. He'll take care of them.

> *20 But if your enemy is hungry, feed him; if he is thirsty, give him drink; for by so doing you will heap burning coals upon his head.*

Instead of doing what the world expects, now that you don't conform to the world anymore, do the crazy thing. The people that are the most against you, feed them and care for them and pour out onto them. You know what will happen? It will drive them nuts. And if they want to get out from under the burning coals of conviction, the only way to do it is to stop being an enemy.

> *21 Do not let yourself be overcome by evil, but overcome (master) evil with good.*

If you can do this stuff, you'll win. If not, you're toast.

HOW DO WE GET OUR CORPORATE CUP CLEANED OUT?

How do you implement this in a whole congregation? First, you need to understand that revival and restoration is NOT going to come until you say you're sorry for being the kind of people that need reviving in the first place. You have to say you're sorry for blowing out the last pillar of fire that He sent! Here in Kansas City, God has been trying to get revivals going for 200+ years and we keep getting in His way. Why is He going to trust you with another move of God when you keep making it about YOU and tearing each other to shreds when it comes? You're going to have to cleanse the temple before the glory cloud will come back. That means individually and collectively taking out the trash.

What do you do when the locusts have come and eaten everything? When the land has stopped producing and the sheep and the cattle mill around looking for green pasture and can't find any?

In the first twelve verses of Joel chapter 1 we see a description of and lamenting for the land that has been devastated. Particularly verse 4: (NIV)

> *What the locust swarm has left the great locusts have eaten; what the great locusts have left the young locusts have eaten; what the young locusts have left other locusts have eaten.*

These are the ultimate consumers. They have devoured everything that is useful and left nothing behind.

Then the solution is proposed in verse 13 and 14:

> *Put on sackcloth, O priests, and mourn; wail, you who minister before the altar. Come, spend the night in sackcloth, you who minister before my God; for the grain offerings and drink offerings are withheld from the house of your God. Declare a holy fast; call a sacred assembly. Summon the elders and all who live in the land to the house of the LORD your God, and cry out to the LORD.*

Then in verses 15 through 20, the situation is described again, particularly in 16-18:

> *Has not the food been cut off before our very eyes— joy and gladness from the house of our God? The seeds are shriveled beneath the clods. The storehouses are in ruins, the granaries have been*

> broken down, for the grain has dried up. How the cattle moan! The herds mill about because they have no pasture; even the flocks of sheep are suffering.

That's as good a picture of the church in America as I can find. There may be milk, but very little meat. The people are hungry, the churches are in debt. The money and resources leave faster than they come in. Whatever seed is planted is wasted in the ground. Any growth we see is transfer growth as the herds mill about seeking green pasture and can find none. People will fly across the country and even move their families if they sense a real move of God. They'll latch onto any Jesus fad or manifestation that comes along because they are so desperately hungry.

Then again in chapter 2 is the same recommended solution shown:

> 12 "Even now," declares the LORD, return to me with all your heart, with fasting and weeping and mourning." 13 Rend your heart and not your garments. Return to the LORD your God, for he is gracious and compassionate, slow to anger and abounding in love, and he relents from sending calamity. 14 Who knows? He may turn and have pity and leave behind a blessing— grain offerings and drink offerings for the LORD your God. 15 Blow the trumpet in Zion, declare a holy fast, call a sacred assembly. 16 Gather the people, consecrate the assembly; bring together the elders, gather the children, those nursing at the breast. Let the bridegroom leave his room and the bride her chamber. 17 Let the priests, who minister before the LORD, weep between the temple porch and the altar. Let them say, "Spare your people, O LORD. Do not make your inheritance an object of scorn, a byword among the nations. Why should they say among the peoples, 'Where is their God?' "

Then, if you do these things, the Lord shows how He will respond:

> 18 Then the LORD will be jealous for his land and take pity on his people. 19 The LORD will reply to them: "I am sending you grain, new wine and oil, enough to satisfy you fully; never again will I make you an object of scorn to the nations.

And in the verses following, there are some other amazing promises and expressions of His mercy and loving kindness.

But it boils down to this, when then land is desolate and there is no food, when the people mill around from place to place seeking anything edible and find none, you need to:

1. Declare a Holy Fast.

2. Call a Sacred Assembly and summon the Elders.

3. Repent and weep and mourn before the altar.

Then He will turn.

So, what's a "Holy Fast"? That's in Isaiah 58. The kind of fast the Lord wants; that you break the chains, lift the yokes, free the captives, feed the hungry, clothe the naked, take in the poor wanderer, stop the malicious talk and the pointing finger and THEN He will turn and good stuff starts happening. And that doesn't just mean in the "natural" - that means free the captive spirits, feed the hungry in spirit, clothe the unarmored spirits, etc. Remember, Body, Soul and Spirit – do Isaiah 58 across all three dimensions. You take it to the Lord and have Him show you what application that might have to your own situation. These also happen to overlap with Matthew 25:31-46 (which is kind of like the final exam). Basically practice extravagant giving to the poor - the poor in spirit and the poor in money.

So, what's a "Sacred Assembly"? That would be those people who are walking in holiness and are consecrated before the Lord. The people with big cups of Jesus and no embedded red stuff. That doesn't necessarily mean the pastors. There's no guarantee they're walking in holiness just because they went to seminary. Ultimately, we're going to have to let God call the meeting because we don't know who is and who isn't consecrated at any given moment. How many need to be there? Don't know. Who are the Elders? Don't know. Just commit to Him that you want to call a sacred assembly and He'll tell you how and arrange to have all the right people there. This is VERY important to Him and He doesn't mind helping. Or He'll gather whoever is available and ask you to repent for yourself first and get cleaned out before you repent on behalf of anybody else.

I believe intercession and repentance is required to restore a divided body. Preferably lots of people, but even one will do if they are sanctified before the Lord and willing to stand in the gap for the rest of the Body. Are you willing to pray the prayer of Moses? Even that you would be blotted out of the Book if only they would be forgiven and the Body would be One again? You better have a lot of Jesus in you to pray THAT prayer!

In John 17, Jesus prayed in the Garden of Gethsemane that we would be one as He and the Father are one. God loves His Son desperately, and yet that ONE prayer has remained unanswered. Maybe because none of us are praying it in agreement with Jesus. Can there be anything more urgent or more important than the restoration of the Body of Christ? Maybe we should all hit our knees and repent for the mess we've made and start praying that one prayer with Jesus until God answers it.

OK, end of sermon. You want practical stuff? Get on the website and download the "Cup" model graphics and powerpoint presentation. Use the "Fill My Cup, Lord" article and graphics as the beginning framework. Appendix A of this document and the verses in Appendix B are great to show the scriptural justifications for this. Just show them examples of how the Holy Spirit can be poured out on another. If your whole fellowship isn't ready for it, ask the Lord to show you the ones with the most wisdom and discernment and comfort level with spiritual matters and teach them one at a time until it begins an undercurrent of acceptance.

But ultimately, just do whatever God tells you. Don't listen to me. Check everything with Him.

Pray this (or whatever He tells you to pray):

Lord, please show me my cup. Please give me wisdom and discernment and help me hear Your voice really well so that You can guide my steps in implementing this. I believe there is something to this, Lord. Please confirm it and write it on my heart. I don't want to follow ANY man, Lord. Just you and you alone are worthy and just and true. You be my head and take me where You want me to go. I love You, Lord. Whatever it takes. Amen.

APPENDIX A

You Can Be Filled With Good Stuff:

The Lord - Psalm 16:5; 1 Cor 10:21

Fullness of God - Eph 3:19

Spirit of God - Exod 31:3; Exod. 35:31; Eph 5:18

Glory of the Lord - Num 14:21

Holy Ghost - Luke 1:15; 1:41; 1:67; Luke 4:1; Acts 2:4; Acts 4:8; Acts 4:31; Acts 6:3; Acts 7:55; Acts 9:17; Acts 11:24; Acts 13:9

Goodness of the Lord - Psalm 33:5

Blessing of the Lord - Deut 33:23

Fear of the Lord - Luke 5:26

All Knowledge - Rom 15:14

Knowledge of the Lord - Isaiah 11:9

Power by the spirit of the Lord and judgement - Micah 3:8

Knowledge of the glory of God - Hab 2:14

Knowledge of His will, wisdom and spiritual understanding - Col. 1:19

Spirit of Wisdom - Exod. 28:3; 35:35; Deut. 34:9

Wisdom & understanding - I Kings 7:14

Wisdom and grace - Luke 2:40

Wisdom and beauty - Ezek. 28:12

Judgement and righteousness - Isa. 33:5

Light - Matt. 6:22 (Luke 11:34-36)

Grace and truth - John 1:14

Faith and power - Acts 6:8

Salvation - Psalm 116:13

Righteousness - Matt. 5:6

Fruits of Righteousness - Phil 1:11

Comfort - 2 Cor 7:4

Consolation - Jerem. 16:7

Joy - John 15:11; John 16:24; Acts 2:28; 2 Tim. 1:4

Mercy - Psalm 119:64

Mercy and good fruits - James 3:17

Blessing - 1 Cor 10:16

Good - Psalm 104:28

Good things - Luke 1:53

Good things - Job 22:18

Good works and almsdeeds - Acts 9:36

Goodness and all knowledge - Rom 15:14

Praise and honour - Psalm 71:8

Laughter and singing - Psalm 126:2

Precious and pleasant riches - Prov. 24:4

Horses, chariots, might men of war - Ezek. 39:20

Wonder and amazement - Acts 3:10

Trembling (to enemies) - Zech 12:2

Full of days - Job 42:17

Children - Psalm 127:5

Need Clean Cup:

Matt 23:25; Luke 11:39; Prov. 25:4; Isaiah 66:20; 2 Tim 2:21; Hebrews 9:21

Need Pliable Cup:

Matt. 9:17 (Mar 2:22, Luke 5:37)

Need FULL Cup:

Matt 25:4; Ruth 1:21

Chosen/Special Vessel:

Acts 9:15; Romans 9:21; I Thes. 4:4; 2 Tim 2:20

Hated Vessels:

Rom 9:22

Things that are NEVER Full:

Hell and destruction - Prov. 27:20

The Sea - Ecc. 1:7

Or You Can Be Filled With Bad Stuff:

With sin - Jerem. 51:5

Evil and madness - Ecc 9:3

Confusion - Job 10:15; Acts 19:29

Heaviness - Psalm 69:20; Phil 2:26

Travail and vexation of spirit - Ecc 4:6

Tossings to and fro - Job 7:4

Drunkenness and/or nakedness - Lam. 4:21; Jerem. 12:12

Drunkenness, Sorrow, astonishment and desolation - Ez 23:33

Violence - Ezek. 8:17

Satan, lies - Acts 5:3

Devils - 1 Corin 10:21

Abominations and filthiness - Ezra 9:11

Abominations, filthiness of fornication - Rev. 17:4

Adultery, cannot cease from sin, beguiling, covetous practices, cursed children - 2 Peter 2:14

Bitterness - Lam. 3:15

Sorrow - John 16:6

Envy, contradicting, blaspheming - Acts 13:45

Unrighteousness, fornication, wickedness, covetousness, maliciousness, full of envy, murder debate, deceit, malignity, whisperers, backbiters, haters of God, despiteful, proud, boasters, inventors of evil things, disobedient to parents, without understanding, covenant breakers, without natural affection, implacable, unmerciful - Rom 1:29-31

Wickedness - Lev. 19:29

Blood of innocents - Jer. 19:4

Hands full of blood - Isaiah 1:15

Bloody crimes and violence - Ezek 7:23

Blood and perverseness - Ezek. 9:9

Trouble - Job 14:1; Psalm 88:3

Sin of youth - Job 20:11

Cursing, deceit, fraud, mischief and vanity - Psalm 10:7

Mischief - Prov. 12:21; Psalm 26:10

Subtilty and mischief - Acts 13:10

Deceit - Jerem 5:27

Violence, lies and deceit - Micah 6:12

Lies, robbery, blood - Nahum 3:1

Extortion and excess - Matt. 23:25

Hypocrisy and iniquity - Matt. 23:28

Cursing and bitterness - Rom 3:14

Cruelty - Psalm 74:20

Strife - Prov. 17:1

Darkness - Matt 6:23; Luke 11:34; Rev. 16:10

No pleasure - Hosea 8:8

Their own devices / His own ways - Prov. 3:10; Prov. 14:4

Dead men's bones and uncleanness - Matt 23:27

Wrath - Esther 3:5; Luke 4:28; Acts 19:28;

Wrath of God - Rev. 15:1; Rev. 15:7; Rev. 16:19

Fury of the Lord - Isaiah 51:20; Jerem 6:11

Fury - Dan 3:19; Jerem. 25:15

Snare, fire and brimstone, tempest - Psalm 11:6

Trembling - Isaiah 51:17, Is. 51:22,

Indignation - Esther 5:9; Jerem. 15:17; Acts 5:17; Rev. 14:10

Judgement - Isaiah 1:21

Reproach - Lam 3:30

Scorn and derision – Psalm 123:4; Ezek. 23:22

Shame - Hab. 2:16

Contempt - Psalm 123:3

Plagues - Rev. 21:9

Madness - Jerem 51:7; Luke 6:11

APPENDIX B

Verses about Filled, Fill, Full, Fountains, Springs, Cup, Cups, Vessel, Vessels, Bowl, Bowls, Wineskins, Bottle, Bottles, Cisterns, Vats, Pot, Pots, Dwelleth

FILLED

Gen 6:11 The earth also was corrupt before God, and the earth was **filled with violence**.
Gen 6:13 And God said unto Noah, The end of all flesh is come before me; for the earth is **filled with violence** through them; and, behold, I will destroy them with the earth.
Exd 1:7 And the children of Israel were fruitful, and increased abundantly, and multiplied, and waxed exceeding mighty; and the land was filled with them.
Exd 28:3 And thou shalt speak unto all [that are] wise hearted, whom I have **filled with the spirit of wisdom**, that they may make Aaron's garments to consecrate him, that he may minister unto me in the priest's office.
Exd 31:3 And I have **filled him with the spirit of God**, in wisdom, and in understanding, and in knowledge, and in all manner of workmanship,
Exd 35:31 And he hath **filled him with the spirit of God**, in wisdom, in understanding, and in knowledge, and in all manner of workmanship;
Exd 35:35 Them hath he **filled with wisdom of heart**, to work all manner of work, of the engraver, and of the cunning workman, and of the embroiderer, in blue, and in purple, in scarlet, and in fine linen, and of the weaver, [even] of them that do any work, and of those that devise cunning work.
Exd 40:34 Then a cloud covered the tent of the congregation, and the **glory of the LORD filled the tabernacle**.
Exd 40:35 And Moses was not able to enter into the tent of the congregation, because the cloud abode thereon, and the **glory of the LORD filled the tabernacle**.
Num 14:21 But [as] truly [as] I live, all the earth shall be **filled with the glory of the LORD**.
Deu 26:12 When thou hast made an end of tithing all the tithes of thine increase the third year, [which is] the year of tithing, and hast given [it] unto the Levite, the stranger, the fatherless, and the widow, that they may eat within thy gates, and **be filled**;
Deu 31:20 For when I shall have brought them into the land which I sware unto their fathers, that floweth with milk and honey; and they shall have eaten and **filled themselves**, and waxen fat; then will they turn unto other gods, and serve them, and provoke me, and break my covenant.
1Ki 7:14 He [was] a widow's son of the tribe of Naphtali, and his father [was] a man of Tyre, a worker in brass: and he was **filled with wisdom, and understanding, and cunning** to work all works in brass. And he came to king Solomon, and wrought all his work.
1Ki 8:10 And it came to pass, when the priests were come out of the holy [place], that the **cloud filled the house of the LORD**, 1Ki 8:11 So that the priests could not stand to minister because of the cloud: for the **glory of the LORD had filled** the house of the LORD.
2Ki 3:17 For thus saith the LORD, Ye shall not see wind, neither shall ye see rain; yet that valley shall be filled with water, that ye may drink, both ye, and your cattle, and your beasts.
2Ki 3:20 And it came to pass in the morning, when the meat offering was offered, that, behold, there came water by the way of Edom, and the country was filled with water.
2Ki 21:16 Moreover Manasseh shed **innocent blood** very much, till he had **filled Jerusalem** from one end to another; beside his sin wherewith he made Judah to sin, in doing [that which was] evil in the sight of the LORD.

2Ki 23:14 And he brake in pieces the images, and cut down the groves, and filled their places with the bones of men.

2Ki 24:4 And also for the innocent blood that he shed: for he **filled Jerusalem with innocent blood**; which the LORD would not pardon.

2Ch 5:13 It came even to pass, as the trumpeters and singers [were] as one, to make one sound to be heard in praising and thanking the LORD; and when they lifted up [their] voice with the trumpets and cymbals and instruments of musick, and praised the LORD, [saying], For [he is] good; for his mercy [endureth] for ever: that [then] the house was **filled with a cloud,** [even] the house of the LORD; 2Ch 5:14 So that the priests could not stand to minister by reason of the cloud: for the **glory of the LORD had filled the house of God**.

2Ch 7:1 Now when Solomon had made an end of praying, the fire came down from heaven, and consumed the burnt offering and the sacrifices; and the **glory of the LORD filled the house**. 2Ch 7:2 And the priests could not enter into the house of the LORD, because the **glory of the LORD had filled the LORD'S house**.

Ezr 9:11 Which thou hast commanded by thy servants the prophets, saying, The land, unto which ye go to possess it, is an unclean land with the filthiness of the people of the lands, with their abominations, which have **filled it from one end to another with their uncleanness**.

Neh 9:25 And they took strong cities, and a fat land, and possessed houses full of all goods, wells digged, vineyards, and oliveyards, and fruit trees in abundance: so they did eat, and **were filled, and became fat**, and delighted themselves in thy great goodness.

Job 3:15 Or with princes that had gold, who filled their houses with silver:

Job 16:8 And thou hast **filled me with wrinkles**, [which] is a witness [against me]: and my leanness rising up in me beareth witness to my face.

Job 22:18 Yet he **filled their houses with good [things]**: but the counsel of the wicked is far from me.

Psa 38:7 For my loins are **filled with a loathsome [disease]**: and [there is] no soundness in my flesh.

Psa 71:8 Let my mouth be **filled [with] thy praise [and with] thy honour all the day**.

Psa 72:19 And blessed [be] his glorious name for ever: and let the whole earth be **filled [with] his glory**; Amen, and Amen.

Psa 104:28 [That] thou givest them they gather: thou openest thine hand, they are **filled with good**.

Psa 123:3 Have mercy upon us, O LORD, have mercy upon us: for we are **exceedingly filled with contempt**.

Psa 123:4 Our soul is **exceedingly filled with the scorning** of those that are at ease, [and] with the contempt of the proud.

Psa 126:2 Then was our mouth **filled with laughter**, and our tongue with singing: then said they among the heathen, The LORD hath done great things for them.

Pro 1:31 Therefore shall they eat of the fruit of their own way, and be **filled with their own devices**.

Pro 3:10 So shall thy barns be **filled with plenty**, and thy presses shall burst out with new wine.

Pro 5:10 Lest strangers be **filled with thy wealth**; and thy labours [be] in the house of a stranger;

Pro 12:21 There shall no evil happen to the just: but the wicked shall be **filled with mischief**.

Pro 14:14 The backslider in heart shall be **filled with his own ways**: and a good man [shall be satisfied] from himself.

Pro 18:20 A man's belly shall be satisfied with the fruit of his mouth; [and] with the **increase of his lips shall he be filled**.

Pro 20:17 Bread of deceit [is] sweet to a man; but afterwards his mouth shall be **filled with gravel**.

Pro 24:4 And by knowledge shall the chambers be **filled with all precious and pleasant riches**.

Ecc 1:8 All things [are] full of labour; man cannot utter [it]: the eye is not satisfied with seeing, nor the ear **filled with hearing**.

Ecc 6:3 If a man beget an hundred [children], and live many years, so that the days of his years be many, and his soul be **not filled with good**, and also [that] he have no burial; I say, [that] an untimely birth [is] better than he.

Ecc 6:7 All the labour of man [is] for his mouth, and yet the **appetite is not filled**.

Sgs 5:2 I sleep, but my heart waketh: [it is] the voice of my beloved that knocketh, [saying], Open to me, my sister, my love, my dove, my undefiled: for my head is **filled with dew**, [and] my locks with the drops of the night.

Isa 6:1 In the year that king Uzziah died I saw also the Lord sitting upon a throne, high and lifted up, and his **train filled the temple**.

Isa 6:4 And the posts of the door moved at the voice of him that cried, and the house was **filled with smoke**.

Isa 21:3 Therefore are my loins **filled with pain**: pangs have taken hold upon me, as the pangs of a woman that travaileth: I was bowed down at the hearing [of it]; I was dismayed at the seeing [of it].

Isa 33:5 The LORD is exalted; for he dwelleth on high: he hath **filled Zion with judgment and righteousness**.

Isa 34:6 The sword of the LORD is **filled with blood**, it is made fat with fatness, [and] with the blood of lambs and goats, with the fat of the kidneys of rams: for the LORD hath a sacrifice in Bozrah, and a great slaughter in the land of Idumea.

Isa 43:24 Thou hast bought me no sweet cane with money, neither hast thou **filled me with the fat of thy sacrifices**: but thou hast made me to serve with thy sins, thou hast wearied me with thine iniquities.

Isa 65:20 There shall be no more thence an infant of days, nor an old man that hath not **filled his days**: for the child shall die an hundred years old; but the sinner [being] an hundred years old shall be accursed.

Jer 13:12 Therefore thou shalt speak unto them this word; Thus saith the LORD God of Israel, Every bottle shall be **filled with wine**: and they shall say unto thee, Do we not certainly know that every bottle shall be filled with wine?

Jer 15:17 I sat not in the assembly of the mockers, nor rejoiced; I sat alone because of thy hand: for thou hast **filled me with indignation**.

Jer 16:18 And first I will recompense their iniquity and their sin double; because they have defiled my land, they have **filled mine inheritance with the carcases of their detestable and abominable things**.

Jer 19:4 Because they have forsaken me, and have estranged this place, and have burned incense in it unto other gods, whom neither they nor their fathers have known, nor the kings of Judah, and have **filled this place with the blood of innocents**;

Jer 46:12 The nations have heard of thy shame, and thy **cry hath filled the land**: for the mighty man hath stumbled against the mighty, [and] they are fallen both together.

Jer 51:5 For Israel [hath] not [been] forsaken, nor Judah of his God, of the LORD of hosts; though their land was **filled with sin against the Holy One of Israel**.

Jer 51:34 Nebuchadrezzar the king of Babylon hath devoured me, he hath crushed me, he hath made me an empty vessel, he hath **swallowed me up like a dragon**, he hath **filled his belly with my delicates**, he hath cast me out.

Lam 3:15 He hath **filled me with bitterness**, he hath made me drunken with wormwood.

Lam 3:30 He giveth [his] cheek to him that smiteth him: he is **filled full with reproach**.

Eze 8:17 Then he said unto me, Hast thou seen [this], O son of man? Is it a light thing to the house of Judah that they commit the abominations which they commit here? for they have **filled the land with violence**, and have returned to provoke me to anger: and, lo, they put the branch to their nose.

Eze 10:3 Now the cherubims stood on the right side of the house, when the man went in; and the cloud **filled the inner court**. Eze 10:4 Then the glory of the LORD went up from the cherub, [and stood] over the threshold of the house; and the house was filled with the cloud, and the court was **full of the brightness of the LORD'S glory**.

Eze 11:6 Ye have multiplied your slain in this city, and ye have **filled the streets thereof with the slain**.

Eze 23:33 Thou shalt be **filled with drunkenness and sorrow**, with the cup of astonishment and desolation, with the cup of thy sister Samaria.

Eze 28:16 By the multitude of thy merchandise they have **filled the midst of thee with violence**, and thou hast sinned: therefore I will cast thee as profane out of the mountain of God: and I will destroy thee, O covering cherub, from the midst of the stones of fire.

Eze 36:38 As the holy flock, as the flock of Jerusalem in her solemn feasts; so shall the waste cities be **filled with flocks of men**: and they shall know that I [am] the LORD.

Eze 39:20 Thus ye shall be filled at my table with horses and chariots, with mighty men, and with all men of war, saith the Lord GOD.

Eze 43:5 So the spirit took me up, and brought me into the inner court; and, behold, the **glory of the LORD filled the house**.

Eze 44:4 Then brought he me the way of the north gate before the house: and I looked, and, behold, the **glory of the LORD filled the house of the LORD**: and I fell upon my face.

Dan 2:35 Then was the iron, the clay, the brass, the silver, and the gold, broken to pieces together, and became like the chaff of the summer threshingfloors; and the wind carried them away, that no place was found for them: and the stone that smote the image became a great mountain, and **filled the whole earth**.

Hsa 13:6 According to their pasture, so were they filled; they were filled, and their heart was exalted; therefore have they forgotten me.

Hab 2:14 For the earth shall be **filled with the knowledge of the glory of the LORD**, as the waters cover the sea.

Hab 2:16 Thou art **filled with shame** for glory: drink thou also, and let thy foreskin be uncovered: the cup of the LORD'S right hand shall be turned unto thee, and shameful spewing [shall be] on thy glory.

Hag 1:6 Ye have sown much, and bring in little; ye eat, but ye have not enough; ye drink, but ye are **not filled** with drink; ye clothe you, but there is none warm; and he that earneth wages earneth wages [to put it] into a bag with holes.

Zec 9:13 When I have bent Judah for me, **filled the bow** with Ephraim, and raised up thy sons, O Zion, against thy sons, O Greece, and made thee as the sword of a mighty man.

Zec 9:15 The LORD of hosts shall defend them; and they shall devour, and subdue with sling stones; and they shall drink, [and] make a noise as through wine; and they shall be **filled like bowls, [and] as the corners of the altar.**

Mat 5:6 Blessed [are] they which do **hunger and thirst after righteousness: for they shall be filled**.

Mat 14:20 And they did all eat, and were filled: and they took up of the fragments that remained twelve baskets full.

Mat 15:37 And they did all eat, and were filled: and they took up of the broken [meat] that was left seven baskets full.

Mat 27:48 And straightway one of them ran, and took a spunge, and filled [it] with vinegar, and put [it] on a reed, and gave him to drink.

Mar 2:21 No man also seweth a piece of new cloth on an old garment: else the new piece that filled it up taketh away from the old, and the rent is made worse.

Mar 6:42 And they did all eat, and were filled.

Mar 7:27 But Jesus said unto her, **Let the children first be filled**: for it is not meet to take the children's bread, and to cast [it] unto the dogs.

Mar 8:8 So they did eat, and were filled: and they took up of the broken [meat] that was left seven baskets.
Mar 15:36 And one ran and filled a spunge full of vinegar, and put [it] on a reed, and gave him to drink, saying, Let alone; let us see whether Elias will come to take him down.
Luk 1:15 For he shall be great in the sight of the Lord, and shall drink neither wine nor strong drink; and he shall be **filled with the Holy Ghost**, even from his mother's womb.
Luk 1:41 And it came to pass, that, when Elisabeth heard the salutation of Mary, the babe leaped in her womb; and Elisabeth was **filled with the Holy Ghost**:
Luk 1:53 He hath **filled the hungry with good things**; and the rich he hath sent empty away.
Luk 1:67 And his father Zacharias was **filled with the Holy Ghost**, and prophesied, saying,
Luk 2:40 And the child grew, and waxed strong in spirit, **filled with wisdom: and the grace of God** was upon him.
Luk 3:5 Every valley shall be filled, and every mountain and hill shall be brought low; and the crooked shall be made straight, and the rough ways [shall be] made smooth;
Luk 4:28 And all they in the synagogue, when they heard these things, were **filled with wrath**,
Luk 5:26 And they were all amazed, and they glorified God, and were **filled with fear**, saying, We have seen strange things to day.
Luk 6:11 And they were **filled with madness**; and communed one with another what they might do to Jesus.
Luk 6:21 Blessed [are ye] that hunger now: for ye shall be filled. Blessed [are ye] that weep now: for ye shall laugh.
Luk 8:23 But as they sailed he fell asleep: and there came down a storm of wind on the lake; and they were filled [with water], and were in jeopardy.
Luk 9:17 And they did eat, and were all filled: and there was taken up of fragments that remained to them twelve baskets.
Luk 14:23 And the lord said unto the servant, Go out into the highways and hedges, and compel [them] to come in, that my **house may be filled**.
Luk 15:16 And he would fain have filled his belly with the husks that the swine did eat: and no man gave unto him.
Jhn 2:7 Jesus saith unto them, Fill the waterpots with water. And they filled them up to the brim.
Jhn 6:12 When they were filled, he said unto his disciples, Gather up the fragments that remain, that nothing be lost.
Jhn 6:13 Therefore they gathered [them] together, and filled twelve baskets with the fragments of the five barley loaves, which remained over and above unto them that had eaten.
Jhn 6:26 Jesus answered them and said, Verily, verily, I say unto you, Ye seek me, not because ye saw the miracles, but because ye did eat of the loaves, and were filled.
Jhn 12:3 Then took Mary a pound of ointment of spikenard, very costly, and anointed the feet of Jesus, and wiped his feet with her hair: and the house was filled with the odour of the ointment.
Jhn 16:6 But because I have said these things unto you, **sorrow hath filled your heart**.
Jhn 19:29 Now there was set a vessel full of vinegar: and they filled a spunge with vinegar, and put [it] upon hyssop, and put [it] to his mouth.
Act 2:2 And suddenly there came a sound from heaven as of a rushing mighty wind, and it **filled all the house** where they were sitting.
Act 2:4 And they were all **filled with the Holy Ghost**, and began to speak with other tongues, as the Spirit gave them utterance.
Act 3:10 And they knew that it was he which sat for alms at the Beautiful gate of the temple: and they were **filled with wonder and amazement** at that which had happened unto him.

Act 4:8 Then Peter, **filled with the Holy Ghost**, said unto them, Ye rulers of the people, and elders of Israel,

Act 4:31 And when they had prayed, the place was shaken where they were assembled together; and they were **all filled with the Holy Ghost**, and they spake the word of God with boldness.

Act 5:3 But Peter said, Ananias, why hath **Satan filled thine heart** to lie to the Holy Ghost, and to keep back [part] of the price of the land?

Act 5:17 Then the high priest rose up, and all they that were with him, (which is the sect of the Sadducees,) and were **filled with indignation**,

Act 5:28 Saying, Did not we straitly command you that ye should not teach in this name? and, behold, ye have filled Jerusalem with your doctrine, and intend to bring this man's blood upon us.

Act 9:17 And Ananias went his way, and entered into the house; and putting his hands on him said, Brother Saul, the Lord, [even] Jesus, that appeared unto thee in the way as thou camest, hath sent me, that thou mightest receive thy sight, and be **filled with the Holy Ghost**.

Act 13:9 Then Saul, (who also [is called] Paul,) **filled with the Holy Ghost**, set his eyes on him,

Act 13:45 But when the Jews saw the multitudes, they were **filled with envy**, and spake against those things which were spoken by Paul, contradicting and blaspheming.

Act 13:52 And the disciples were **filled with joy, and with the Holy Ghost**.

Act 19:29 And the whole city was **filled with confusion**: and having caught Gaius and Aristarchus, men of Macedonia, Paul's companions in travel, they rushed with one accord into the theatre.

Rom 1:29 Being **filled with all unrighteousness, fornication, wickedness, covetousness, maliciousness; full of envy, murder, debate, deceit, malignity; whisperers,**

Rom 15:14 And I myself also am persuaded of you, my brethren, that ye also are **full of goodness, filled with all knowledge**, able also to admonish one another.

Rom 15:24 Whensoever I take my journey into Spain, I will come to you: for I trust to see you in my journey, and to be brought on my way thitherward by you, if first I be somewhat filled with your [company].

2Cr 7:4 Great [is] my boldness of speech toward you, great [is] my glorying of you: I am **filled with comfort,** I am exceeding joyful in all our tribulation.

Eph 3:19 And to know the love of Christ, which passeth knowledge, that ye might be **filled with all the fulness of God**.

Eph 5:18 And be not drunk with wine, wherein is excess; but be **filled with the Spirit;**

Phl 1:11 Being **filled with the fruits of righteousness**, which are by Jesus Christ, unto the glory and praise of God.

Col 1:9 For this cause we also, since the day we heard [it], do not cease to pray for you, and to desire that ye might be **filled with the knowledge of his will in all wisdom and spiritual understanding**;

2Ti 1:4 Greatly desiring to see thee, being mindful of thy tears, that I may be **filled with joy**;

Rev 8:5 And the angel took the censer, and **filled it with fire of the altar**, and cast [it] into the earth: and there were voices, and thunderings, and lightnings, and an earthquake.

Rev 15:1 And I saw another sign in heaven, great and marvellous, seven angels having the seven last plagues; for in them is **filled up the wrath of God**.

Rev 15:8 And the temple was **filled with smoke from the glory of God, and from his power**; and no man was able to enter into the temple, till the seven plagues of the seven angels were fulfilled.

Rev 18:6 Reward her even as she rewarded you, and double unto her double according to her works: in the cup which she hath filled **fill to her double**.

Rev 19:21 And the remnant were slain with the sword of him that sat upon the horse, which [sword] proceeded out of his mouth: and all the fowls were **filled with their flesh**.

FILL

Lev 25:19 And the land shall yield her fruit, and ye shall eat your fill, and dwell therein in safety.

Deu 23:24 When thou comest into thy neighbour's vineyard, then thou mayest eat grapes thy fill at thine own pleasure; but thou shalt not put [any] in thy vessel.

1Sa 16:1 And the LORD said unto Samuel, How long wilt thou mourn for Saul, seeing I have rejected him from reigning over Israel? fill thine horn with oil, and go, I will send thee to Jesse the Bethlehemite: for I have provided me a king among his sons.

Job 8:21 Till he **fill thy mouth with laughing, and thy lips with rejoicing.**

Job 15:2 Should a wise man utter vain knowledge, and **fill his belly with the east wind**?

Job 20:23 [When] he is about to fill his belly, [God] shall cast the fury of his wrath upon him, and shall rain [it] upon him while he is eating.

Job 23:4 I would order [my] cause before him, and **fill my mouth with arguments**.

Job 38:39 Wilt thou hunt the prey for the lion? or **fill the appetite of the young lions**,

Job 41:7 Canst thou **fill his skin with barbed irons**? or his head with fish spears?

Psa 81:10 I [am] the LORD thy God, which brought thee out of the land of Egypt: open thy mouth wide, and **I will fill it**.

Psa 83:16 **Fill their faces with shame**; that they may seek thy name, O LORD.

Psa 110:6 He shall judge among the heathen, he shall **fill [the places] with the dead bodies**; he shall wound the heads over many countries.

Pro 1:13 We shall find all precious substance, we shall **fill our houses with spoil**:

Pro 7:18 Come, let us take our **fill of love** until the morning: let us solace ourselves with loves.

Pro 8:21 That I may cause those that love me to inherit substance; and I will **fill their treasures**.

Isa 8:8 And he shall pass through Judah; he shall overflow and go over, he shall reach [even] to the neck; and the stretching out of his wings shall fill the breadth of thy land, O Immanuel.

Isa 14:21 Prepare slaughter for his children for the iniquity of their fathers; that they do not rise, nor possess the land, nor fill the face of the world with cities.

Isa 27:6 He shall cause them that come of Jacob to take root: Israel shall blossom and bud, and fill the face of the world with fruit.

Isa 56:12 Come ye, [say they], I will fetch wine, and we will **fill ourselves with strong drink**; and to morrow shall be as this day, [and] much more abundant.

Jer 13:13 Then shalt thou say unto them, Thus saith the LORD, Behold, I will **fill all** the inhabitants of this land, even the kings that sit upon David's throne, and the priests, and the prophets, and all the inhabitants of Jerusalem, **with drunkenness.**

Jer 23:24 Can any hide himself in secret places that I shall not see him? saith the LORD. Do not I fill heaven and earth? saith the LORD.

Jer 33:5 They come to fight with the Chaldeans, but [it is] to **fill them with the dead bodies of men**, whom I have slain in mine anger and in my fury, and for all whose wickedness I have hid my face from this city.

Jer 51:14 The LORD of hosts hath sworn by himself, [saying], Surely I will fill thee with men, as with caterpillers; and they shall lift up a shout against thee.

Eze 3:3 And he said unto me, Son of man, cause thy belly to eat, and fill thy bowels with this roll that I give thee. Then did I eat [it]; and it was in my mouth as honey for sweetness.

Eze 7:19 They shall cast their silver in the streets, and their gold shall be removed: their silver and their gold shall not be able to deliver them in the day of the wrath of the LORD: they shall not satisfy their souls, neither fill their bowels: because it is the stumblingblock of their iniquity.

Eze 9:7 And he said unto them, Defile the house, and **fill the courts with the slain**: go ye forth. And they went forth, and slew in the city.
Eze 10:2 And he spake unto the man clothed with linen, and said, Go in between the wheels, [even] under the cherub, and **fill thine hand with coals of fire** from between the cherubims, and scatter [them] over the city. And he went in in my sight.
Eze 30:11 He and his people with him, the terrible of the nations, shall be brought to destroy the land: and they shall draw their swords against Egypt, and **fill the land with the slain.**
Eze 32:4 Then will I leave thee upon the land, I will cast thee forth upon the open field, and will cause all the fowls of the heaven to remain upon thee, and I will fill the beasts of the whole earth with thee.
Eze 32:5 And I will lay thy flesh upon the mountains, and fill the valleys with thy height.
Eze 35:8 And I will fill his mountains with his slain [men]: in thy hills, and in thy valleys, and in all thy rivers, shall they fall that are slain with the sword.
Zep 1:9 In the same day also will I punish all those that leap on the threshold, which **fill their masters' houses with violence and deceit.**
Hag 2:7 And I will shake all nations, and the desire of all nations shall come: and I will **fill this house with glory**, saith the LORD of hosts.
Mat 9:16 No man putteth a piece of new cloth unto an old garment, for that which is put in to fill it up taketh from the garment, and the rent is made worse.
Mat 15:33 And his disciples say unto him, Whence should we have so much bread in the wilderness, as to fill so great a multitude?
Mat 23:32 Fill ye up then the measure of your fathers.
Jhn 2:7 Jesus saith unto them, Fill the waterpots with water. And they filled them up to the brim.
Rom 15:13 Now the God of hope **fill you with all joy and peace in believing**, that ye may abound in hope, through the power of the Holy Ghost.
Eph 4:10 He that descended is the same also that ascended up far above all heavens, that he might **fill all things.**)
Col 1:24 Who now rejoice in my sufferings for you, and fill up that which is behind of the afflictions of Christ in my flesh for his body's sake, which is the church:
1Th 2:16 Forbidding us to speak to the Gentiles that they might be saved, to fill up their sins alway: for the wrath is come upon them to the uttermost.
Rev 18:6 Reward her even as she rewarded you, and double unto her double according to her works: in the cup which she hath filled **fill to her double**.

FILLETH

Job 9:18 He will not suffer me to take my breath, but **filleth me with bitterness**.
Psa 107:9 For he satisfieth the longing soul, and **filleth the hungry soul with goodness**.
Psa 129:7 Wherewith the mower filleth not his hand; nor he that bindeth sheaves his bosom.
Psa 147:14 He maketh peace [in] thy borders, [and] filleth thee with the finest of the wheat.
Eph 1:23 Which is his body, the fulness of him that filleth all in all.

FULL

Lev 19:29 Do not prostitute thy daughter, to cause her to be a whore; lest the land fall to whoredom, and the land become **full of wickedness**.
Deu 33:23 And of Naphtali he said, O Naphtali, satisfied with favour, and full with the blessing of the LORD: possess thou the west and the south.

Deu 34:9 And Joshua the son of Nun was **full of the spirit of wisdom**; for Moses had laid his hands upon him: and the children of Israel hearkened unto him, and did as the LORD commanded Moses.
2Ki 4:4 And when thou art come in, thou shalt shut the door upon thee and upon thy sons, and shalt pour out into all those vessels, and thou shalt set aside that which is full.
2Ki 4:6 And it came to pass, when the vessels were full, that she said unto her son, Bring me yet a vessel. And he said unto her, [There is] not a vessel more. And the oil stayed.
Est 3:5 And when Haman saw that Mordecai bowed not, nor did him reverence, then was Haman **full of wrath**.
Est 5:9 Then went Haman forth that day joyful and with a glad heart: but when Haman saw Mordecai in the king's gate, that he stood not up, nor moved for him, he was **full of indignation** against Mordecai.
Job 7:4 When I lie down, I say, When shall I arise, and the night be gone? and I am **full of tossings to and fro unto the dawning of the day**.
Job 10:15 If I be wicked, woe unto me; and [if] I be righteous, [yet] will I not lift up my head. [I am] **full of confusion**; therefore see thou mine affliction;
Job 14:1 Man [that is] born of a woman [is] of few days, and **full of trouble**.
Job 20:11 His bones are **full [of the sin] of his youth**, which shall lie down with him in the dust.
Job 21:24 His breasts are **full of milk**, and his bones are moistened with marrow.
Job 42:17 So Job died, [being] old and **full of days**.
Psa 10:7 His mouth is **full of cursing and deceit and fraud**: under his tongue [is] mischief and vanity.
Psa 26:10 In whose hands [is] mischief, and their right hand is **full of bribes**.
Psa 29:4 The voice of the LORD [is] powerful; the voice of the LORD [is] **full of majesty**.
Psa 33:5 He loveth righteousness and judgment: the earth is **full of the goodness of the LORD**.
Psa 48:10 According to thy name, O God, so [is] thy praise unto the ends of the earth: thy right hand is **full of righteousness**.
Psa 69:20 Reproach hath broken my heart; and I am **full of heaviness**: and I looked [for some] to take pity, but [there was] none; and for comforters, but I found none.
Psa 73:10 Therefore his people return hither: and **waters of a full [cup] are wrung out to them**.
Psa 74:20 Have respect unto the covenant: for the dark places of the earth are **full of the habitations of cruelty**.
Psa 75:8 For in the hand of the LORD [there is] a cup, and the wine is red; it is full of mixture; and he poureth out of the same: but the dregs thereof, all the wicked of the earth shall wring [them] out, [and] drink [them].
Psa 78:38 But he, [being] **full of compassion**, forgave [their] iniquity, and destroyed [them] not: yea, many a time turned he his anger away, and did not stir up all his wrath.
Psa 86:15 But thou, O Lord, [art] a God **full of compassion**, and gracious, longsuffering, and plenteous in mercy and truth.
Psa 88:3 For my soul is **full of troubles**: and my life draweth nigh unto the grave.
Psa 104:24 O LORD, how manifold are thy works! in wisdom hast thou made them all: the earth is **full of thy riches**.
Psa 111:4 He hath made his wonderful works to be remembered: the LORD [is] gracious and **full of compassion**.
Psa 112:4 Unto the upright there ariseth light in the darkness: [he is] gracious, and **full of compassion, and righteous**.
Psa 119:64 The earth, O LORD, is **full of thy mercy**: teach me thy statutes.
Psa 127:5 Happy [is] the man that hath his quiver full of them: they shall not be ashamed, but they shall speak with the enemies in the gate.
Psa 145:8 The LORD [is] gracious, and **full of compassion**; slow to anger, and of great mercy.

Pro 17:1 Better [is] a dry morsel, and quietness therewith, than an house **full of sacrifices [with] strife**.
Pro 27:7 The full soul loatheth an honeycomb; but to the hungry soul every bitter thing is sweet.
Pro 27:20 **Hell and destruction are never full**; so the eyes of man are never satisfied.
Pro 30:9 Lest I be full, and deny [thee], and say, Who [is] the LORD? or lest I be poor, and steal, and take the name of my God [in vain].
Ecc 1:7 All the rivers run into the sea; yet the sea [is] not full; unto the place from whence the rivers come, thither they return again.
Ecc 1:8 All things [are] **full of labour**; man cannot utter [it]: the eye is not satisfied with seeing, nor the ear filled with hearing.
Ecc 4:6 Better [is] an handful [with] quietness, than both the hands **full [with] travail and vexation of spirit.**
Ecc 9:3 This [is] an evil among all [things] that are done under the sun, that [there is] one event unto all: yea, also the heart of the sons of men is **full of evil**, and madness [is] in their heart while they live, and after that [they go] to the dead.
Ecc 10:14 A fool also is **full of words**: a man cannot tell what shall be; and what shall be after him, who can tell him?
Isa 1:11 To what purpose [is] the multitude of your sacrifices unto me? saith the LORD: I am **full of the burnt offerings of rams**, and the fat of fed beasts; and I delight not in the blood of bullocks, or of lambs, or of he goats.
Isa 1:15 And when ye spread forth your hands, I will hide mine eyes from you: yea, when ye make many prayers, I will not hear: your hands are **full of blood**.
Isa 1:21 How is the faithful city become an harlot! it was **full of judgment**; righteousness lodged in it; but now murderers.
Isa 2:7 Their land also is **full of silver and gold**, neither [is there any] end of their treasures; their land is also **full of horses**, neither [is there any] end of their chariots: Isa 2:8 Their land also is **full of idols**; they worship the work of their own hands, that which their own fingers have made:
Isa 6:3 And one cried unto another, and said, Holy, holy, holy, [is] the LORD of hosts: the whole earth [is] **full of his glory**.
Isa 11:9 They shall not hurt nor destroy in all my holy mountain: for the earth shall be **full of the knowledge of the LORD**, as the waters cover the sea.
Isa 30:27 Behold, the name of the LORD cometh from far, burning [with] his anger, and the burden [thereof is] heavy: his lips are **full of indignation**, and his tongue as a devouring fire:
Isa 51:20 Thy sons have fainted, they lie at the head of all the streets, as a wild bull in a net: they are **full of the fury of the LORD**, the rebuke of thy God.
Jer 5:27 As a cage is full of birds, so [are] their houses **full of deceit**: therefore they are become great, and waxen rich.
Jer 6:11 Therefore I am **full of the fury of the LORD**; I am weary with holding in: **I will pour it out** upon the children abroad, and upon the assembly of young men together: for even the husband with the wife shall be taken, the aged with [him that is] **full of days**.
Jer 23:10 For the land is **full of adulterers**; for because of swearing the land mourneth; the pleasant places of the wilderness are dried up, and their course is evil, and their force [is] not right.
Lam 3:30 He giveth [his] cheek to him that smiteth him: he is **filled full with reproach**.
Eze 7:23 Make a chain: for the land is **full of bloody crimes**, and the city is full of violence.
Eze 9:9 Then said he unto me, The iniquity of the house of Israel and Judah [is] exceeding great, and the land is **full of blood**, and the city **full of perverseness**: for they say, The LORD hath forsaken the earth, and the LORD seeth not.

Eze 28:12 Son of man, take up a lamentation upon the king of Tyrus, and say unto him, Thus saith the Lord GOD; Thou sealest up the sum, **full of wisdom**, and perfect in beauty.
Dan 3:19 Then was Nebuchadnezzar **full of fury**, and the form of his visage was changed against Shadrach, Meshach, and Abednego: [therefore] he spake, and commanded that they should heat the furnace one seven times more than it was wont to be heated.
Joe 3:13 Put ye in the sickle, for the harvest is ripe: come, get you down; for the press is **full, the fats overflow; for their wickedness [is] great**.
Mic 3:8 But truly I am **full of power by the spirit of the LORD, and of judgment, and of might,** to declare unto Jacob his transgression, and to Israel his sin.
Mic 6:12 For the rich men thereof are **full of violence**, and the inhabitants thereof have spoken lies, and their tongue [is] deceitful in their mouth.
Nah 3:1 Woe to the bloody city! it [is] all **full of lies** [and] robbery; the prey departeth not;
Hab 3:3 God came from Teman, and the Holy One from mount Paran. Selah. His glory covered the heavens, and the earth was **full of his praise.**
Mat 6:22 The light of the body is the eye: if therefore thine eye be single, thy whole body shall be **full of light**. Mat 6:23 But if thine eye be evil, thy whole body shall be **full of darkness**. If therefore the light that is in thee be darkness, how great [is] that darkness!
Mat 23:25 Woe unto you, scribes and Pharisees, hypocrites! for ye make clean the outside of the cup and of the platter, but within they are **full of extortion and excess**.
Mat 23:27 Woe unto you, scribes and Pharisees, hypocrites! for ye are like unto whited sepulchres, which indeed appear beautiful outward, but are within **full of dead [men's] bones, and of all uncleanness**.
Mat 23:28 Even so ye also outwardly appear righteous unto men, but within ye are **full of hypocrisy and iniquity**.
Luk 4:1 And Jesus being **full of the Holy Ghost** returned from Jordan, and was led by the Spirit into the wilderness,
Luk 6:25 Woe unto you that are full! for ye shall hunger. Woe unto you that laugh now! for ye shall mourn and weep.
Luk 11:34 The light of the body is the eye: therefore when thine eye is single, thy whole body also is **full of light**; but when [thine eye] is evil, thy body also [is] **full of darkness**.
Luk 11:36 If thy whole body therefore [be] **full of light**, having no part dark, the whole shall be **full of light**, as when the bright shining of a candle doth give thee light.
Luk 11:39 And the Lord said unto him, Now do ye Pharisees make clean the outside of the cup and the platter; but your inward part is **full of ravening and wickedness**.
Jhn 1:14 And the Word was made flesh, and dwelt among us, (and we beheld his glory, the glory as of the only begotten of the Father,) **full of grace and truth**.
Jhn 15:11 These things have I spoken unto you, that my joy might remain in you, and [that] your **joy might be full**.
Jhn 16:24 Hitherto have ye asked nothing in my name: ask, and ye shall receive, that your **joy may be full**.
Act 2:28 Thou hast made known to me the ways of life; thou shalt make me **full of joy** with thy countenance.
Act 6:3 Wherefore, brethren, look ye out among you seven men of honest report, **full of the Holy Ghost and wisdom**, whom we may appoint over this business.
Act 6:5 And the saying pleased the whole multitude: and they chose Stephen, a man **full of faith and of the Holy Ghost**, and Philip, and Prochorus, and Nicanor, and Timon, and Parmenas, and Nicolas a proselyte of Antioch:
Act 6:8 And Stephen, **full of faith and power**, did great wonders and miracles among the people.

Act 7:55 But he, being **full of the Holy Ghost**, looked up stedfastly into heaven, and saw the glory of God, and Jesus standing on the right hand of God,

Act 9:36 Now there was at Joppa a certain disciple named Tabitha, which by interpretation is called Dorcas: this woman was **full of good works and almsdeeds** which she did.

Act 11:24 For he was a good man, and **full of the Holy Ghost and of faith**: and much people was added unto the Lord.

Act 13:10 And said, O **full of all subtilty and all mischief**, [thou] child of the devil, [thou] enemy of all righteousness, wilt thou not cease to pervert the right ways of the Lord?

Act 19:28 And when they heard [these sayings], they were **full of wrath**, and cried out, saying, Great [is] Diana of the Ephesians.

Rom 1:29 Being **filled with all unrighteousness, fornication, wickedness, covetousness, maliciousness; full of envy, murder, debate, deceit, malignity; whisperers,**

Rom 3:14 Whose mouth [is] **full of cursing and bitterness**:

Rom 15:14 And I myself also am persuaded of you, my brethren, that ye also are **full of goodness**, filled with all knowledge, able also to admonish one another.

1Cr 4:8 Now ye are full, now ye are rich, ye have reigned as kings without us: and I would to God ye did reign, that we also might reign with you.

Phl 2:26 For he longed after you all, and was **full of heaviness**, because that ye had heard that he had been sick.

Jam 3:8 But the tongue can no man tame; [it is] an unruly evil, **full of deadly poison.**

Jam 3:17 But the wisdom that is from above is first pure, then peaceable, gentle, [and] easy to be intreated, **full of mercy** and good fruits, without partiality, and without hypocrisy.

1Pe 1:8 Whom having not seen, ye love; in whom, though now ye see [him] not, yet believing, ye rejoice with joy unspeakable and **full of glory**:

2Pe 2:14 Having eyes **full of adultery**, and that cannot cease from sin; beguiling unstable souls: an heart they have exercised with covetous practices; cursed children:

1Jo 1:4 And these things write we unto you, that your **joy may be full**.

2Jo 1:12 Having many things to write unto you, I would not [write] with paper and ink: but I trust to come unto you, and speak face to face, that our **joy may be full.**

Rev 15:7 And one of the four beasts gave unto the seven angels seven golden vials **full of the wrath of God**, who liveth for ever and ever.

Rev 16:10 And the fifth angel poured out his vial upon the seat of the beast; and his kingdom was **full of darkness**; and they gnawed their tongues for pain,

Rev 17:3 So he carried me away in the spirit into the wilderness: and I saw a woman sit upon a scarlet coloured beast, **full of names of blasphemy**, having seven heads and ten horns.

Rev 17:4 And the woman was arrayed in purple and scarlet colour, and decked with gold and precious stones and pearls, having a golden cup in her hand **full of abominations and filthiness of her fornication:**

Rev 21:9 And there came unto me one of the seven angels which had the seven vials **full of the seven last plagues**, and talked with me, saying, Come hither, I will shew thee the bride, the Lamb's wife.

FOUNTAIN / SPRING / WELL

Lev 11:36 Nevertheless a fountain or pit, [wherein there is] plenty of water, shall be clean: but that which toucheth their carcase shall be unclean.

Lev 20:18 And if a man shall lie with a woman having her sickness, and shall uncover her nakedness; he hath discovered her fountain, and she hath uncovered the fountain of her blood: and both of them shall be cut off from among their people.

Deu 33:28 Israel then shall dwell in safety alone: the fountain of Jacob [shall be] upon a land of corn and wine; also his heavens shall drop down dew.
Psa 36:9 For with thee [is] the **fountain of life**: in thy light shall we see light.
Psa 68:26 Bless ye God in the congregations, [even] the Lord, from the **fountain of Israel**.
Psa 74:15 Thou didst cleave the fountain and the flood: thou driedst up mighty rivers.
Psa 114:8 Which turned the rock [into] a standing water, the flint into a fountain of waters.
Pro 5:18 Let thy fountain be blessed: and rejoice with the wife of thy youth.
Pro 13:14 The law of the wise [is] a **fountain of life**, to depart from the snares of death.
Pro 14:27 The fear of the LORD [is] a **fountain of life**, to depart from the snares of death.
Pro 25:26 A righteous man falling down before the wicked [is as] a **troubled fountain, and a corrupt spring.**
Ecc 12:6 Or ever the silver cord be loosed, or the golden bowl be broken, or the pitcher be broken at the fountain, or the wheel broken at the cistern.
Sgs 4:12 A garden inclosed [is] my sister, [my] spouse; a spring shut up, a **fountain sealed**.
Sgs 4:15 A fountain of gardens, a well of **living waters**, and streams from Lebanon.
Jer 2:13 For my people have committed two evils; they have forsaken me the **fountain of living waters**, [and] hewed them out cisterns, broken cisterns, that can hold no water.
Jer 6:7 As a fountain casteth out her waters, so she casteth out her wickedness: violence and spoil is heard in her; before me continually [is] grief and wounds.
Jer 9:1 Oh that my head were waters, and mine eyes a **fountain of tears**, that I might weep day and night for the slain of the daughter of my people!
Jer 17:13 O LORD, the hope of Israel, all that forsake thee shall be ashamed, [and] they that depart from me shall be written in the earth, because they have forsaken the LORD, the **fountain of living waters**.
Hsa 13:15 Though he be fruitful among [his] brethren, an east wind shall come, the wind of the LORD shall come up from the wilderness, and his spring shall become dry, and his **fountain shall be dried up**: he shall spoil the treasure of all pleasant vessels.
Joe 3:18 And it shall come to pass in that day, [that] the mountains shall drop down new wine, and the hills shall flow with milk, and all the rivers of Judah shall flow with waters, and a fountain shall come forth of the house of the LORD, and shall water the valley of Shittim.
Zec 13:1 In that day there shall be a fountain opened to the house of David and to the inhabitants of Jerusalem for sin and for uncleanness.
Mar 5:29 And straightway the fountain of her blood was dried up; and she felt in [her] body that she was healed of that plague.
Jam 3:11 Doth a fountain send forth at the same place sweet [water] and bitter?
Jam 3:12 Can the fig tree, my brethren, bear olive berries? either a vine, figs? so [can] no fountain both yield salt water and fresh.
Rev 21:6 And he said unto me, It is done. I am Alpha and Omega, the beginning and the end. **I will give unto him that is athirst of the fountain of the water of life freely.**

FOUNTAINS / SPRINGS / WELLS

Gen 7:11 In the six hundredth year of Noah's life, in the second month, the seventeenth day of the month, the same day were all the fountains of the great deep broken up, and the windows of heaven were opened.
Gen 8:2 The fountains also of the deep and the windows of heaven were stopped, and the rain from heaven was restrained;

Deu 8:7 For the LORD thy God bringeth thee into a good land, a land of brooks of water, of fountains and depths that spring out of valleys and hills;

1Ki 18:5 And Ahab said unto Obadiah, Go into the land, unto all fountains of water, and unto all brooks: peradventure we may find grass to save the horses and mules alive, that we lose not all the beasts.

2Ch 32:3 He took counsel with his princes and his mighty men to stop the waters of the fountains which [were] without the city: and they did help him.

2Ch 32:4 So there was gathered much people together, who stopped all the fountains, and the brook that ran through the midst of the land, saying, Why should the kings of Assyria come, and find much water?

Pro 5:16 Let thy fountains be dispersed abroad, [and] rivers of waters in the streets.

Pro 8:24 When [there were] no depths, I was brought forth; when [there were] no fountains abounding with water.

Pro 8:28 When he established the clouds above: when he strengthened the fountains of the deep:

Isa 41:18 I will open rivers in high places, and fountains in the midst of the valleys: I will make the wilderness a pool of water, and the dry land springs of water.

Rev 7:17 For the Lamb which is in the midst of the throne shall feed them, and shall lead them unto **living fountains of waters**: and God shall wipe away all tears from their eyes.

Rev 8:10 And the third angel sounded, and there fell a great star from heaven, burning as it were a lamp, and it fell upon the third part of the rivers, and upon the fountains of waters;

Rev 14:7 Saying with a loud voice, Fear God, and give glory to him; for the hour of his judgment is come: and worship him that made heaven, and earth, and the sea, and the fountains of waters.

Rev 16:4 And the third angel poured out his vial upon the rivers and fountains of waters; and they became blood.

CUP

Psa 11:6 Upon the wicked he shall rain snares, fire and brimstone, and an horrible tempest: [this shall be] the **portion of their cup**.

Psa 16:5 The LORD [is] the portion of mine inheritance and of my cup: thou maintainest my lot.

Psa 23:5 Thou preparest a table before me in the presence of mine enemies: thou anointest my head with oil; **my cup runneth over**.

Psa 73:10 Therefore his people return hither: and waters of a full [cup] are wrung out to them.

Psa 75:8 For in the hand of the LORD [there is] a cup, and the wine is red; it is full of mixture; and he poureth out of the same: but the dregs thereof, all the wicked of the earth shall wring [them] out, [and] drink [them]. *{Bad stuff is RED.}*

Psa 116:13 I will take the **cup of salvation**, and call upon the name of the LORD.

Isa 51:17 Awake, awake, stand up, O Jerusalem, which hast drunk at the hand of the LORD the **cup of his fury**; thou hast drunken the dregs of the cup of trembling, [and] wrung [them] out.

Isa 51:22 Thus saith thy Lord the LORD, and thy God [that] pleadeth the cause of his people, Behold, I have taken out of thine hand the cup of trembling, [even] the dregs of the **cup of my fury**; thou shalt no more drink it again:

Jer 16:7 Neither shall [men] tear [themselves] for them in mourning, to comfort them for the dead; neither shall [men] give them the cup of consolation to drink for their father or for their mother.

Jer 25:15 For thus saith the LORD God of Israel unto me; Take the wine **cup of this fury** at my hand, and cause all the nations, to whom I send thee, to drink it.

Jer 25:17 Then took I the cup at the LORD'S hand, and made all the nations to drink, unto whom the LORD had sent me:

Jer 25:28 And it shall be, if they refuse to take the cup at thine hand to drink, then shalt thou say unto them, Thus saith the LORD of hosts; Ye shall certainly drink.
Jer 49:12 For thus saith the LORD; Behold, they whose judgment [was] not to drink of the cup have assuredly drunken; and [art] thou he [that] shall altogether go unpunished? thou shalt not go unpunished, but thou shalt surely drink [of it].
Jer 51:7 Babylon [hath been] a golden cup in the LORD'S hand, that made all the earth drunken: the nations have drunken of her wine; therefore the nations are mad.
Lam 4:21 Rejoice and be glad, O daughter of Edom, that dwellest in the land of Uz; the cup also shall pass through unto thee: thou shalt be drunken, and shalt make thyself naked.
Eze 23:31 Thou hast walked in the way of thy sister; therefore will I give her cup into thine hand. Eze 23:32 Thus saith the Lord GOD; Thou shalt drink of thy sister's cup deep and large: thou shalt be laughed to scorn and had in derision; it containeth much. Eze 23:33 Thou shalt be **filled with drunkenness and sorrow, with the cup of astonishment and desolation**, with the cup of thy sister Samaria.
Hab 2:16 Thou art filled with shame for glory: drink thou also, and let thy foreskin be uncovered: the **cup of the LORD'S right hand shall be turned unto thee**, and shameful spewing [shall be] on thy glory.
Zec 12:2 Behold, I will make Jerusalem a **cup of trembling** unto all the people round about, when they shall be in the siege both against Judah [and] against Jerusalem.
Mat 10:42 And whosoever shall give to drink unto one of these little ones a cup of cold [water] only in the name of a disciple, verily I say unto you, he shall in no wise lose his reward.
Mat 20:22 But Jesus answered and said, Ye know not what ye ask. Are ye able to drink of the cup that I shall drink of, and to be baptized with the baptism that I am baptized with? They say unto him, We are able. Mat 20:23 And he saith unto them, Ye shall drink indeed of my cup, and be baptized with the baptism that I am baptized with: but to sit on my right hand, and on my left, is not mine to give, but [it shall be given to them] for whom it is prepared of my Father.
Mat 23:25 Woe unto you, scribes and Pharisees, hypocrites! for ye make clean the outside of the cup and of the platter, but within they are **full of extortion and excess**. Mat 23:26 [Thou] blind Pharisee, cleanse first that [which is] within the cup and platter, that the outside of them may be clean also.
Mat 26:27 And he took the cup, and gave thanks, and gave [it] to them, saying, Drink ye all of it;
Mat 26:39 And he went a little further, and fell on his face, and prayed, saying, O my Father, if it be possible, let this cup pass from me: nevertheless not as I will, but as thou [wilt].
Mat 26:42 He went away again the second time, and prayed, saying, O my Father, if this cup may not pass away from me, except I drink it, thy will be done.
Mar 9:41 For whosoever shall give you a cup of water to drink in my name, because ye belong to Christ, verily I say unto you, he shall not lose his reward.
Mar 10:38 But Jesus said unto them, Ye know not what ye ask: can ye drink of the cup that I drink of? and be baptized with the baptism that I am baptized with? Mar 10:39 And they said unto him, We can. And Jesus said unto them, Ye shall indeed drink of the cup that I drink of; and with the baptism that I am baptized withal shall ye be baptized:
Mar 14:23 And he took the cup, and when he had given thanks, he gave [it] to them: and they all drank of it.
Mar 14:36 And he said, Abba, Father, all things [are] possible unto thee; take away this cup from me: nevertheless not what I will, but what thou wilt.
Luk 11:39 And the Lord said unto him, Now do ye Pharisees make clean the outside of the cup and the platter; but your inward part is full of ravening and wickedness.
Luk 22:17 And he took the cup, and gave thanks, and said, Take this, and divide [it] among yourselves:
Luk 22:20 Likewise also the cup after supper, saying, This **cup [is] the new testament in my blood**, which is shed for you.

Luk 22:42 Saying, Father, if thou be willing, remove this cup from me: nevertheless not my will, but thine, be done.
Jhn 18:11 Then said Jesus unto Peter, Put up thy sword into the sheath: the cup which my Father hath given me, shall I not drink it?
1Cr 10:16 The **cup of blessing** which we bless, is it not the communion of the blood of Christ? The bread which we break, is it not the communion of the body of Christ?
1Cr 10:21 Ye cannot drink the **cup of the Lord, and the cup of devils**: ye cannot be partakers of the Lord's table, and of the table of devils.
1Cr 11:25 After the same manner also [he took] the cup, when he had supped, saying, This **cup is the new testament in my blood**: this do ye, as oft as ye drink [it], in remembrance of me. 1Cr 11:26 For as often as ye eat this bread, and drink this cup, ye do shew the Lord's death till he come. 1Cr 11:27 Wherefore whosoever shall eat this bread, and drink [this] cup of the Lord, unworthily, shall be guilty of the body and blood of the Lord. 1Cr 11:28 But let a man examine himself, and so let him eat of [that] bread, and drink of [that] cup.
Rev 14:10 The same shall drink of the wine of the wrath of God, which is poured out without mixture into the **cup of his indignation**; and he shall be tormented with fire and brimstone in the presence of the holy angels, and in the presence of the Lamb:
Rev 16:19 And the great city was divided into three parts, and the cities of the nations fell: and great Babylon came in remembrance before God, to give unto her the **cup of the wine of the fierceness of his wrath**.
Rev 17:4 And the woman was arrayed in purple and scarlet colour, and decked with gold and precious stones and pearls, having a golden **cup in her hand full of abominations and filthiness of her fornication**:
Rev 18:6 Reward her even as she rewarded you, and double unto her double according to her works: in the **cup which she hath filled fill to her double**.

CUPS
Isa 22:24 And they shall hang upon him all the glory of his father's house, the offspring and the issue, all **vessels of small quantity, from the vessels of cups, even to all the vessels of flagons.** {different sizes}
Jer 35:5 And I set before the sons of the house of the Rechabites pots full of wine, and cups, and I said unto them, Drink ye wine.
Mar 7:8 For laying aside the commandment of God, ye hold the tradition of men, [as] the washing of pots and cups: and many other such like things ye do.

VESSEL
Psa 2:9 Thou shalt break them with a rod of iron; thou shalt dash them in pieces like a potter's vessel.
Psa 31:12 I am forgotten as a dead man out of mind: I am like a broken vessel.
Pro 25:4 Take away the dross from the silver, and there shall come forth a vessel for the finer. {holiness}
Isa 30:14 And he shall break it as the breaking of the potters' vessel that is broken in pieces; he shall not spare: so that there shall not be found in the bursting of it a sherd to take fire from the hearth, or to take water [withal] out of the pit.
Jer 18:4 And the vessel that he made of clay was marred in the hand of the potter: so he made it again another vessel, as seemed good to the potter to make [it].

Jer 19:11 And shalt say unto them, Thus saith the LORD of hosts; Even so will I break this people and this city, as [one] breaketh a potter's vessel, that cannot be made whole again: and they shall bury [them] in Tophet, till [there be] no place to bury.

Jer 48:11 Moab hath been at ease from his youth, and he hath settled on his lees, and hath **not been emptied from vessel to vessel**, neither hath he gone into captivity: therefore his taste remained in him, and his scent is not changed.

Jer 48:38 [There shall be] lamentation generally upon all the housetops of Moab, and in the streets thereof: for I have broken Moab like a **vessel wherein [is] no pleasure**, saith the LORD.

Jer 51:34 Nebuchadrezzar the king of Babylon hath devoured me, he hath crushed me, he hath made me an empty vessel, he hath swallowed me up like a dragon, he hath filled his belly with my delicates, he hath cast me out.

Hsa 8:8 Israel is swallowed up: now shall they be among the Gentiles as a **vessel wherein [is] no pleasure**.

Act 9:15 But the Lord said unto him, Go thy way: for he is a **chosen vessel** unto me, to bear my name before the Gentiles, and kings, and the children of Israel:

Rom 9:21 Hath not the potter power over the clay, of the same lump to make one **vessel unto honour, and another unto dishonour**? {different levels or uses or values}

1Th 4:4 That every one of you should know how to possess his **vessel in sanctification and honour**;

2Ti 2:21 If a man therefore purge himself from these, he shall be a **vessel unto honour**, sanctified, and meet for the master's use, [and] prepared unto every good work.

1Pe 3:7 Likewise, ye husbands, dwell with [them] according to knowledge, giving honour unto the wife, as unto **the weaker vessel**, and as being heirs together of the grace of life; that your prayers be not hindered.

VESSELS

Exd 40:9 And thou shalt take the anointing oil, and anoint the tabernacle, and all that [is] therein, and shalt hallow it, and all the vessels thereof: and it shall be holy. Exd 40:9 And thou shalt take the anointing oil, and anoint the tabernacle, and all that [is] therein, and shalt hallow it, and all the vessels thereof: and it shall be holy.

2Ch 36:18 And all the vessels of the house of God, great and small, and the treasures of the house of the LORD, and the treasures of the king, and of his princes; all [these] he brought to Babylon.

2Ch 36:19 And they burnt the house of God, and brake down the wall of Jerusalem, and burnt all the palaces thereof with fire, and destroyed all the goodly vessels thereof.

Ezr 5:14 And the vessels also of gold and silver of the house of God, which Nebuchadnezzar took out of the temple that [was] in Jerusalem, and brought them into the temple of Babylon, those did Cyrus the king take out of the temple of Babylon, and they were delivered unto [one], whose name [was] Sheshbazzar, whom he had made governor; Ezr 5:15 And said unto him, Take these vessels, go, carry them into the temple that [is] in Jerusalem, and let the house of God be builded in his place.

Ezr 7:19 The vessels also that are given thee for the service of the house of thy God, [those] deliver thou before the God of Jerusalem.

Isa 22:24 And they shall hang upon him all the glory of his father's house, the offspring and the issue, all **vessels of small quantity, from the vessels of cups, even to all the vessels of flagons**.

Isa 52:11 Depart ye, depart ye, go ye out from thence, touch no unclean [thing]; go ye out of the midst of her; be ye clean, that bear the vessels of the LORD.

Isa 65:4 Which remain among the graves, and lodge in the monuments, which eat swine's flesh, and broth of **abominable [things is in] their vessels**;

Jer 28:3 Within two full years will I bring again into this place all the vessels of the LORD'S house, that Nebuchadnezzar king of Babylon took away from this place, and carried them to Babylon:

Jer 28:6 Even the prophet Jeremiah said, Amen: the LORD do so: the LORD perform thy words which thou hast prophesied, to bring again the vessels of the LORD'S house, and all that is carried away captive, from Babylon into this place.

Jer 48:12 Therefore, behold, the days come, saith the LORD, that I will send unto him wanderers, that shall cause him to wander, and shall empty his vessels, and break their bottles.

Mat 13:48 Which, when it was full, they drew to shore, and sat down, and gathered the good into vessels, but cast the bad away.

Mat 25:4 But the wise took oil in their vessels with their lamps.

Rom 9:22 [What] if God, willing to shew [his] wrath, and to make his power known, endured with much longsuffering the **vessels of wrath** fitted to destruction: Rom 9:23 And that he might make known the riches of his glory on the vessels of mercy, which he had afore prepared unto glory,

2Cr 4:7 But we have this treasure in **earthen vessels**, that the excellency of the power may be of God, and not of us.

2Ti 2:20 But in a great house there are not only vessels of gold and of silver, but also of wood and of earth; and some to honour, and some to dishonour. *{noble and ignoble}*

Rev 2:27 And he shall rule them with a rod of iron; as the vessels of a potter shall they be broken to shivers: even as I received of my Father.

BOTTLE / BOTTLES (WINESKIN/S)

Psa 119:83 For I am become like a bottle in the smoke; [yet] do I not forget thy statutes.

Jer 13:12 Therefore thou shalt speak unto them this word; Thus saith the LORD God of Israel, Every bottle shall be filled with wine: and they shall say unto thee, Do we not certainly know that every bottle shall be filled with wine? 13 Then shalt thou say unto them, Thus saith the LORD, Behold, I will fill all the inhabitants of this land, even the kings that sit upon David's throne, and the priests, and the prophets, and all the inhabitants of Jerusalem, with drunkenness.

Job 38:37 Who can number the clouds in wisdom? or who can stay the **bottles of heaven**,

Jer 48:12 Therefore, behold, the days come, saith the LORD, that I will send unto him wanderers, that shall cause him to wander, and shall **empty his vessels, and break their bottles**.

Mat 9:17 Neither do men put new wine into old bottles: else the bottles break, and the wine runneth out, and the bottles perish: but they put new wine into new bottles, and both are preserved.

Mar 2:22 And no man putteth new wine into old bottles: else the new wine doth burst the bottles, and the wine is spilled, and the bottles will be marred: but new wine must be put into new bottles.

Luk 5:37 And no man putteth new wine into old bottles; else the new wine will burst the bottles, and be spilled, and the bottles shall perish. Luk 5:38 But new wine must be put into new bottles; and both are preserved.

CISTERN(S)

2Ki 18:31 Hearken not to Hezekiah: for thus saith the king of Assyria, Make [an agreement] with me by a present, and come out to me, and [then] eat ye every man of his own vine, and every one of his fig tree, and drink ye every one the waters of his cistern:

Pro 5:15 Drink waters out of thine own cistern, and running waters out of thine own well.

Ecc 12:6 Or ever the silver cord be loosed, or the golden bowl be broken, or the pitcher be broken at the fountain, or the wheel broken at the cistern.

Jer 2:13 For my people have committed two evils; they have forsaken me the fountain of living waters, [and] hewed them out cisterns, broken cisterns, that can hold no water. *{tried to fill their own cups from their own reservoirs}*

BOWL
Ecc 12:6 Or ever the silver cord be loosed, or the golden bowl be broken, or the pitcher be broken at the fountain, or the wheel broken at the cistern.
Zec 4:2 And said unto me, What seest thou? And I said, I have looked, and behold a candlestick all [of] gold, with a bowl upon the top of it, and his seven lamps thereon, and seven pipes to the seven lamps, which [are] upon the top thereof:
Zec 4:3 And two olive trees by it, one upon the right [side] of the bowl, and the other upon the left [side] thereof.

BOWLS
Num 7:84 This [was] the dedication of the altar, in the day when it was anointed, by the princes of Israel: twelve chargers of silver, twelve silver bowls, twelve spoons of gold:
Zec 9:15 The LORD of hosts shall defend them; and they shall devour, and subdue with sling stones; and they shall drink, [and] make a noise as through wine; and they shall be filled like bowls, [and] as the corners of the altar.
Zec 14:20 In that day shall there be upon the bells of the horses, HOLINESS UNTO THE LORD; and the pots in the LORD'S house shall be like the bowls before the altar.

OVERFLOW
Isa 10:22 For though thy people Israel be as the sand of the sea, [yet] a remnant of them shall return: the consumption decreed shall overflow with righteousness.
Joe 2:24 And the floors shall be full of wheat, and the fats shall overflow with wine and oil.
Joe 3:13 Put ye in the sickle, for the harvest is ripe: come, get you down; for the press is full, the **fats overflow; for their wickedness [is] great**. {that would be vats in regular English}

POT
2Ki 4:2 And Elisha said unto her, What shall I do for thee? tell me, what hast thou in the house? And she said, Thine handmaid hath not any thing in the house, save a pot of oil.
Job 41:31 He maketh the deep to boil like a pot: he maketh the sea like a pot of ointment
Pro 17:3 The fining pot [is] for silver, and the furnace for gold: but the LORD trieth the hearts.
Pro 27:21 [As] the fining pot for silver, and the furnace for gold; so [is] a man to his praise.
Ecc 7:6 For as the crackling of thorns under a pot, so [is] the laughter of the fool: this also [is] vanity.
Jer 1:13 And the word of the LORD came unto me the second time, saying, What seest thou? And I said, I see a seething pot; and the face thereof [is] toward the north.
Eze 24:3 And utter a parable unto the rebellious house, and say unto them, Thus saith the Lord GOD; Set on a pot, set [it] on, and also pour water into it: {pot used as parable}
Eze 24:6 Wherefore thus saith the Lord GOD; Woe to the bloody city, to the **pot whose scum [is] therein**, and whose scum is not gone out of it! bring it out piece by piece; let no lot fall upon it.
Mic 3:3 Who also eat the flesh of my people, and flay their skin from off them; and they break their bones, and chop them in pieces, as for the pot, and as flesh within the caldron.
Zec 14:21 Yea, **every pot in Jerusalem and in Judah shall be holiness** unto the LORD of hosts: and all they that sacrifice shall come and take of them, and seethe therein: and in that day there shall be no more the Canaanite in the house of the LORD of hosts.
Hbr 9:4 Which had the golden censer, and the ark of the covenant overlaid round about with gold, wherein [was] the golden pot that had manna, and Aaron's rod that budded, and the tables of the covenant;

POTS

Lev 11:35 And every [thing] whereupon [any part] of their carcase falleth shall be unclean; [whether it be] oven, or ranges for pots, they shall be broken down: [for] they [are] unclean, and shall be unclean unto you.
Psa 58:9 Before your pots can feel the thorns, he shall take them away as with a whirlwind, both living, and in [his] wrath.
Psa 68:13 Though ye have lien among the pots, [yet shall ye be as] the wings of a dove covered with silver, and her feathers with yellow gold.
Psa 81:6 I removed his shoulder from the burden: his hands were delivered from the pots.
Jer 35:5 And I set before the sons of the house of the Rechabites pots full of wine, and cups, and I said unto them, Drink ye wine.
Zec 14:20 In that day shall there be upon the bells of the horses, HOLINESS UNTO THE LORD; and the pots in the LORD'S house shall be like the bowls before the altar.
Mar 7:8 For laying aside the commandment of God, ye hold the tradition of men, [as] the washing of pots and cups: and many other such like things ye do.

DWELLETH

Jhn 6:56 He that eateth my flesh, and drinketh my blood, **dwelleth in me, and I in him**.   {blue stuff}
Jhn 14:17 [Even] the Spirit of truth; whom the world cannot receive, because it seeth him not, neither knoweth him: but ye know him; for he **dwelleth with you, and shall be in you**.
Act 7:48 Howbeit the most High dwelleth not in temples made with hands; as saith the prophet,
Act 17:24 God that made the world and all things therein, seeing that he is Lord of heaven and earth, dwelleth not in temples made with hands;
Rom 7:17 Now then it is no more I that do it, but **sin that dwelleth in me**. {red stuff}
Rom 7:18 For I know that in me (that is, in my flesh,) dwelleth no good thing: for to will is present with me; but [how] to perform that which is good I find not. {yellow stuff}
Rom 7:20 Now if I do that I would not, it is no more I that do it, but sin that dwelleth in me.
1Cr 3:16 Know ye not that ye are the temple of God, and [that] the **Spirit of God dwelleth in you**?
Col 2:9 For in him dwelleth all the fulness of the Godhead bodily.
2Ti 1:14 That good thing which was committed unto thee keep by the **Holy Ghost which dwelleth in us**.
Jam 4:5 Do ye think that the scripture saith in vain, The **spirit that dwelleth in us** lusteth to envy?
1Jo 3:24 And he that keepeth his commandments **dwelleth in him, and he in him**. And hereby we know that he abideth in us, by the Spirit which he hath given us.
1Jo 4:12 No man hath seen God at any time. If we love one another, **God dwelleth in us**, and his love is perfected in us.
1Jo 4:15 Whosoever shall confess that Jesus is the Son of God, **God dwelleth in him, and he in God**.
1Jo 4:16 And we have known and believed the love that God hath to us. God is love; and he that **dwelleth in love dwelleth in God, and God in him**.
2Jo 1:2 For the truth's sake, which **dwelleth in us**, and shall be with us for ever.

APPENDIX C:
PIECES THAT WERE LEFT OVER AFTER WE PUT THE BICYCLE TOGETHER

Col 1:27 To whom God would make known what [is] the riches of the glory of this mystery among the Gentiles; which is **Christ in you**, the hope of glory:

2Cr 13:5 Examine yourselves, whether ye be in the faith; prove your own selves. Know ye not your own selves, how that **Jesus Christ is in you**, except ye be reprobates?

Gal 4:19 My little children, of whom I travail in birth again until Christ be formed in you,

Phm 1:6 That the communication of thy faith may become effectual by the acknowledging of every good thing which is in you in Christ Jesus.

VATS
Joel 2:24 – The threshing floors will be filled with grain; the vats will overflow with new wine and oil.
Joe 3:13 Put ye in the sickle, for the harvest is ripe: come, get you down; for the press is full, the vats overflow; for their wickedness [is] great.

Foolish Rich Man – Built barns and stored wealth, got stagnant and God killed him. State of the Church.

Prov. 10:11 – The mouth of a righteous [man is] a **well of life**: but violence covereth the mouth of the wicked.

Prov. 25:26 – A righteous man falling down before the wicked [is as] a **troubled fountain, and a corrupt spring**.

Song of Solomon 4
9 You have stolen my heart, my sister, my bride; you have stolen my heart with one glance of your eyes, with one jewel of your necklace. 10 How delightful is your love, my sister, my bride! How much more pleasing is your love than wine, and the fragrance of your perfume than any spice! 11 Your lips drop sweetness as the honeycomb, my bride; milk and honey are under your tongue. The fragrance of your garments is like that of Lebanon. 12 You are a **garden locked up**, my sister, my bride; you are a **spring enclosed, a sealed fountain.** 13 Your plants are an orchard of pomegranates with choice fruits, with henna and nard, 14 nard and saffron, calamus and cinnamon, with every kind of incense tree, with myrrh and aloes and all the finest spices. 15 You are a garden fountain, a well of flowing water streaming down from Lebanon.

Isaiah 12:1-6 – 1 In that day you will say: "I will praise you, O LORD. Although you were angry with me, your anger has turned away and you have comforted me. 2 Surely God is my salvation; I will trust and not be afraid. The LORD, the LORD, is my strength and my song; he has become my salvation." 3 With joy you will **draw water from the wells of salvation**. 4 In that day you will say: "Give thanks to the LORD, call on his name; make known among the nations what he has done, and proclaim that his name is exalted. 5 Sing to the LORD, for he has done glorious things; let this be known to all the world. 6 Shout aloud and sing for joy, people of Zion, for great is the Holy One of Israel among you."

Hsa 13:15 – Though he be fruitful among [his] brethren, an east wind shall come, the wind of the LORD shall come up from the wilderness, and **his spring shall become dry, and his fountain shall be dried up:** he shall spoil the treasure of all pleasant vessels

Isa 41:17 – [When] the poor and needy seek water, and [there is] none, [and] their tongue faileth for **thirst, I the LORD will hear them, I the God of Israel will not forsake them**.
Isa 41:18 – I will open rivers in high places, and fountains in the midst of the valleys: I will make the wilderness a pool of water, and the dry land springs of water.
Isa 41:19 – I will plant in the wilderness the cedar, the shittah tree, and the myrtle, and the oil tree; I will set in the desert the fir tree, [and] the pine, and the box tree together:
Isa 41:20 – That they may see, and know, and consider, and understand together, that the hand of the LORD hath done this, and the Holy One of Israel hath created it.

{People will flourish in places where there should be no water. They will be out in the wilderness and yet they will thrive. Trees that should NOT grow in the desert will flourish. People will be outside of "church" and yet they will have great big cups full of Jesus. }

Rom 8:9 But ye are not in the flesh, but in the Spirit, if so be that the Spirit of God dwell in you. Now if any man have not the Spirit of Christ, he is none of his.
Rom 8:10 And if Christ [be] in you, the body [is] dead because of sin; but the Spirit [is] life because of righteousness.
Rom 8:11 But if the Spirit of him that raised up Jesus from the dead dwell in you, he that raised up Christ from the dead shall also quicken your mortal bodies by his Spirit that dwelleth in you.

Hosea 13:15 – Though he be fruitful among [his] brethren, an east wind shall come, the wind of the LORD shall come up from the wilderness, and his spring shall become dry, and his fountain shall be dried up: he shall spoil the treasure of all pleasant vessels.

Hosea 13:15 (NIV) – even though he thrives among his brothers. An east wind from the LORD will come, blowing in from the desert; his spring will fail and his well dry up. His storehouse will be plundered of all its treasures.

{If the Lord wants to, He will suck all the good stuff out of your cup and you will be dry. Then your jar of clay will crack and spoil, no matter how pleasant you think it is. }

John 4:14 But whosoever drinketh of the water that I shall give him shall never thirst; but the water that I shall give him shall be in him a well of water springing up into everlasting life.

John 4:23:24 But the hour cometh, and now is, when the true worshipers shall worship the Father in spirit and in truth: for the Father seeketh such to worship him. God [is] a Spirit: and they that worship him must worship [him] in spirit and in truth.

Not in mind and body. IN SPIRIT which is the only place true TRUTH can come from.

Rain Right NOW, Lord!

2 Pe 2:9 The Lord knoweth how to deliver the godly out of temptations, and to reserve the unjust unto the day of judgment to be punished:
2 Pe 2:10 But chiefly them that walk after the flesh in the lust of uncleanness, and despise government. Presumptuous [are they], selfwilled, they are not afraid to speak evil of dignities.
2 Pe 2:11 Whereas angels, which are greater in power and might, bring not railing accusation against them before the Lord.
2 Pe 2:12 But these, as natural brute beasts, made to be taken and destroyed, speak evil of the things that they understand not; and shall utterly perish in their own corruption;
2 Pe 2:13 And shall receive the reward of unrighteousness, [as] they that count it pleasure to riot in the day time. Spots [they are] and blemishes, sporting themselves with their own deceivings while they feast with you;
2 Pe 2:14 Having eyes full of adultery, and that cannot cease from sin; beguiling unstable souls: an heart they have exercised with covetous practices; cursed children:
2 Pe 2:15 Which have forsaken the right way, and are gone astray, following the way of Balaam [the son] of Bosor, who loved the wages of unrighteousness;
2 Pe 2:16 But was rebuked for his iniquity: the dumb ass speaking with man's voice forbad the madness of the prophet.
2 Pe 2:17 These are wells without water, clouds that are carried with a tempest; to whom the mist of darkness is reserved for ever.
2 Pe 2:18 For when they speak great swelling [words] of vanity, they allure through the lusts of the flesh, [through much] wantonness, those that were clean escaped from them who live in error.
2 Pe 2:19 While they promise them liberty, they themselves are the servants of corruption: for of whom a man is overcome, of the same is he brought in bondage.
2 Pe 2:20 For if after they have escaped the pollutions of the world through the knowledge of the Lord and Saviour Jesus Christ, they are again entangled therein, and overcome, the latter end is worse with them than the beginning.
2 Pe 2:21 For it had been better for them not to have known the way of righteousness, than, after they have known [it], to turn from the holy commandment delivered unto them.
2 Pe 2:22 But it is happened unto them according to the true proverb, The dog [is] turned to his own vomit again; and the sow that was washed to her wallowing in the mire.

Revelation 7:17 – For the Lamb which is in the midst of the throne shall feed them, and shall lead them unto living fountains of waters: and God shall wipe away all tears from their eyes.

There is also something really cool in Mark 12 about the parable of the tenants. The Landowner buys a piece of land - as God purchased all of us through Christ - even the unsaved are His, the enemy had to give up all his territory. Then the Landowner builds a wall around it - as God puts a hedge around us against the enemy. Then he dug a vat for the winepress - as God give us all a "cup". Then he built a watchtower - as God gives us conscience to keep guard. THEN he rents it all back to some tenants, on the condition that he get the first fruits and they respond appropriately to the commitment they made with Him. It's HIS land and they need to acknowledge it and act like it. When he comes to collect, they beat and kill his messengers. If they refuse to receive His Son, then He will come in and kill them and give all they possessed to another. If the Son stands at the door and knocks and they refuse to respond, then they will die. If they had Kingdom responsibilities and potential Kingdom treasure, it will be given to another to fulfill and benefit from. The bad tenants filled their vat with the wrong stuff.

do it yourself City Church Restoration

from doug perry
fellowship of the martyrs

www.FellowshipOfTheMartyrs.com
fotm@fellowshipofthemartyrs.com
Copyright © 2006 Doug Perry, Fellowship Of The Martyrs

All rights reserved.

ISBN: 1463798709
ISBN-13: 978-1463798703

The Bride gets her jewelry, but it's going to hurt to get it on, and once you're used to it, you're never going to want to rip it back off again. Heaven is free. HOLINESS is hard! If not us, who? If not here, where? If not now, when?

CONTENTS

Aren't Things Just Fine?	369
Scary Stats and Facts	370
Thus Saith The Lord	377
The Locusts Have Eaten Everything	378
The If/Then Axioms	380
The Body of Christ?	382
John 15 – If/Then Statements	384
Thus Saith The Lord	391
Declaration of War Against the Forces of Darkness	393
What Is The Solution?	394
What is a City Church?	400
What the City Church is NOT	405
Who is Part of the City Church?	409
Who is Not?	414
Why Restore the City Churches?	415
Lampstand Spirals	421
Warning Label	426
How Many People Are Required?	427
But Can You Pray The BIG Prayer?	429
An Autocratic Network Led By Super Apostles?	432
Declare a Holy Fast – Isaiah 58	434
Romans 12	438
Thus Saith The Lord	441
Call a Solemn Assembly and Sanctify the People	442
Repent and Weep and Mourn Before the Altar	444
Thus Saith The Lord	450
And THEN He Will Turn	454
Light the Lampstand	458
Thus Saith The Lord	463
Rebuild on the Ancient Foundations	465
Restore Streets with Dwellings	477
FOTM One Page Battle Plan	480
Church Hierarchy Diagram	481
How To "Do Church" in a Lampstand City	482
Thirteen Ways To Grieve The Holy Spirit	483
Be a M*A*S*H	484
Personal Attention For All	485
Who Has The Biggest Cup of Jesus?	487
Raise up elders.	489
Take the war to the enemy	490
Send Missionaries Out To Light Other Lampstands	490
Stay Out Of His Way	492
10 Great Ways To Be Absolutely Sure That You'll Die Spiritually and You Won't Even Notice	494
Refuse To Hear God's Voice? Bad Idea.	497
Final Prayer and Blessing	505
Appendix A – Cup Model Diagram	507

*"Your growth in Christ
is directly proportional
to your willingness
to RUSH HEADLONG
into the refining fire
and give it a wet, sloppy kiss."*

– Doug Perry

AREN'T THINGS JUST FINE?

There is only one prayer that I can find in the Bible that Jesus prayed and God didn't answer. This is the perfect, sinless, Son of God made flesh. Everyone He tried to heal got healed. Every demon He cursed jumped out of people. The Father gave Him all authority and loved Him and repeatedly confirmed this was His Son and He was proud of Him. So how come there is a prayer He prayed that hasn't been answered? Do you even know what it was?

> **John 17:20-23** (KJV) – *20 Neither pray I for these alone, but for them also which shall believe on me through their word; 21 **That they all may be one**; as thou, Father, art in me, and I in thee, that they also may be one in us: that the world may believe that thou hast sent me. 22 And the glory which thou gavest me I have given them; **that they may be one, even as we are one**: 23 I in them, and thou in me, that they may be made perfect in one; and that the world may know that thou hast sent me, and hast loved them, as thou hast loved me.*

The VERY last prayer Jesus Christ prayed before going to the Cross was for us. That we would be one as He and the Father are one. And we're about as far from ONE as you can get! We're the most divided, factious, competitive, selfish religion on the planet right now. Why didn't God answer that prayer?! Maybe because we're not praying it in agreement with Jesus. The Bible says that where two or more are gathered, He'll be there and whatever you ask in His Name, He will do. Maybe Jesus is praying all by Himself on this one!

If you say you love Jesus and He is your Lord and Christ, then maybe you ought to devote yourself entirely to seeing to it that this final wish of Jesus before the Cross is fulfilled no matter what. Maybe we should all stop praying for ANYTHING other than that God would do whatever it takes to answer this one, last, unanswered prayer of Jesus.

Now, I know, there will be those among you that say that the "Universal Church," the spiritual Bride is "one" and we all share the Holy Spirit so we're already One and God answered this prayer. But I'm not buying it. Sorry, you can show me your faith without works and I'll show you my faith with works. Faith without works is dead. (James 2) You can assert your pie-in-the-sky idealism that we're all One as much as you like, but the manifestation of His Body on earth is horribly fractured and divided and nobody is really acting out that Oneness. I don't want your cheap talk – if you're supposed to be known by your love, then get to loving each other!! And not just your friends or the folks who agree with you either. Love your enemies and turn the other cheek and forgive seventy times seven and stop doing the acts of the sinful nature (Gal. 5:19-21) or stop saying you love and obey Jesus! You're NOT going to inherit the Kingdom of God if you don't knock it off.

> **1 John 2:9-11** (KJV) – *9 He that saith he is in the light, and hateth his brother, is in darkness even until now. 10 He that loveth his brother abideth in the light, and there is none occasion of stumbling in him. 11 But he that hateth his brother is in darkness, and walketh in darkness, and knoweth not whither he goeth, because that darkness hath blinded his eyes.*

Exactly how broken are things? Is it measurable? Can we statistically show we're off track or is this just for effect so we'll repent? How bad could things really be?

Oh, yeah. It's measurable and verifiable. I'm not making this up. Things are FAR worse than you know.

Hold on to your hat. This gets really ugly.

We're not just NOT being One Body, we're doing everything pretty much exactly the opposite of the way Jesus wanted it. This has to be the worst warfare model in history! That's probably why we're getting creamed by the forces of darkness.

(I know that I'm probably preaching to the choir, because if you're reading this at all, you're probably already REALLY dissatisfied with the status quo and are desperate for change. But maybe this will give you some ammunition to empirically explain to other people why we have to try something different.)

SCARY STATS AND FACTS

This is a compilation of the scariest, most embarrassing, most shocking statistics and information about the Church and it's affairs. Somebody is going to have to stand before Jesus one day and explain their role in this. We don't want it to be US - or you. We don't quote anything haphazardly without having good documentation and sources. If you have stats you think we need to hear, find the source material and email us. fotm@fellowshipofthemartyrs.com

(Statistics from David Barrett & Todd Johnson, "World Christian Trends AD 30 – AD 2200 - The summary and analysis of the annual Christian mega-census." William Carey Library, 1991. Unless otherwise noted.)

Web Links
Status of global mission, AD 2006, in context of 20th and 21st centuries.
http://www.gordonconwell.edu/ockenga/globalchristianity/IBMR2006.pdf

Are there really 30,000+ denominations?!
http://www.bringyou.to/apologetics/a120.htm

Looking Forward: An Overview of World Evangelization, 2005-2025
http://www.lausanne.org/lcwe/assets/Looking_Forward.pdf#search=%22%22todd%20Johnson%22%20christianity%22

Assets of the Church
- USA Christians control TRILLIONS in assets while at any given time 200,000,000 brothers and sisters starve.
- 78 countries each have Great Commission Christians (evangelical) whose personal incomes cumulatively exceed US$1 billion a year.

Financial Fraud in the Church
- Annual church embezzlements by top custodians exceed the entire cost of all foreign missions worldwide. Emboldened by lax procedures, trusted church treasurers are embezzling from the Church $5,500,000 PER DAY. That's $16,000,000,000 per YEAR! That's Billion - with a "B"! *{For reference: TOTAL Christian spending on foreign missions - $15 Billion. God forgive us!}* **America's share of that crime is $5,693,060,314 per year.**
- Criminal penalties against clergy in sexual abuse cases now exceed $1 billion, causing a number of churches, dioceses, and even denominations to be forced into bankruptcy.

- Each year 600,000 full-time ordained workers (clergy, ministers, missionaries) reach retiring age; 150,000 then discover their employers provide no old-age pensions.

Wasteful Spending by the Church

- Most Christian bodies insist on full accountability to the last cent in finance *{But not very well. See above.}*, but ignore or even decry the collection of statistics about Christian workers/ministries and their effectiveness.
- More than 91% of all church budgets in the US are spent on people that are already church members. Less than 1% is spent on evangelism to the most unreached third of the world.
- 40% of the church's entire global foreign mission resources are being deployed to just 10 oversaturated countries already possessing strong citizen-run home ministries.
- All costs of ministry divided by number of baptisms per year: Cost per baptism in India - $9803 per person. Cost per baptism in the United States - $1,550,000 per person.
- Every year the churches hold a megacensus costing $1.1 billion, sending out 10 million questionnaires in 3,000 languages, which covers 180 major religious subjects.
- Christians spend more on the annual audits of their churches and agencies ($810 million) than on all their workers in the non-Christian world.
- The total cost of Christian outreach averages $330,000 for each and every newly baptized person. (USA $1.55 Million, India $9,800)
- Non-Christian countries have been found to have 227 million Bibles in place in their midst, more than needed to serve all Christians, but poorly distributed.
- 91% of all Christian outreach/evangelism does not target non-Christians but targets other Christians in World C* *{>95 Evangelized, >60% Christian}* countries, cities, peoples, populations, or situations. (* See key on pg 11.)
- Each year, 180 million Bibles and New Testaments are wasted - lost, destroyed, or disintegrated - due to incompetence, hostility, bad planning, or inadequate manufacture.
- Books primarily about Jesus in today's libraries number 175,000 different titles in 500 languages, increasing by 4 newly published every day. As in all scientific research, 70% of all new Christian books and published articles will never be quoted in print by their peers, ever.

Missions and the Church

- Some 250 of the 300 largest international Christian organizations regularly mislead the Christian public by publishing demonstrably incorrect or falsified progress statistics.
- Christian triumphalism - not as pride in huge numbers, but as publicized self-congratulation - is rampant in most churches, agencies, and ministries.
- All costs of ministry divided by number of baptisms per year. Cost per baptism in India - $9,803 per person. Cost per baptism in the United States - $1,550,000 per person.
- It costs Christians 700 times more money to baptize converts in rich World C countries (Switzerland) than in poor World A countries (Nepal). *{For descriptions of World A, B and C, see page 11}*

- Percent of Christian resources in countries that are already more than 60% evangelized - 99.7%. Percent spent in countries where less than half the people have EVER heard of Jesus - 0.3%.

- It is estimated that Christians worldwide spend around $8 BILLION dollars PER YEAR going to the more than 500 conferences to TALK about missions. That's more than HALF the total spent actually DOING missions.

- Everywhere on Earth can now easily be targeted with at least 3 of the 45 varieties of effective evangelism.

- 818 unevangelized ethnolinguistic peoples have never been targeted by any Christian agencies ever.

- Over 20 centuries Christians have announced 1,500 global plans to evangelize the world; most failed; 250 plans focused on AD 2000 fell massively short of stated goals.

- Because of the failure of the West, China's Christians have raised up tens of thousands of trained workers who began evangelizing the world de novo (all over again) soon after AD 2000. www.BackToJerusalem.com

- Regular listeners to Christian programs over secular or religious radio/TV stations rose from 22% of the world in 1980 to 30% in 2000.

- Out of 648 million Great Commission Christians, 70% have never been told about the world's 1.6 billion unevangelized individuals.

- The 3 least cost-effective countries over 1 million in population for Christian outreach are: Japan, Switzerland, Denmark.

- The 3 most cost-effective countries over 1 million in population for Christian outreach are: Mozambique, Ethiopia, Tanzania.

- Per hour of ministry, the 5 megapeoples most responsive to Christianity, Christ, and the gospel are: Khandeshi, Awadhi, Magadhi, Bai, Berar Marathi .

- Per hour of ministry, the 5 megapeoples least responsive to Christianity, Christ, and the gospel are: Swedish, Russian, Lithuanian, Polish, Georgian .

Denominations of the Church

- Currently there are over 41,000 Christian denominations in the United States. We add a new one every other day.

- A huge new Christian nonconfessional megabloc, the Independents/Postdenominationalists, is growing rapidly and numbers 19% of all Christians. These 386 million Independents in 220 countries have no interest in and no use for historic denominationalist Christianity.

- From only one million in AD 1900, Pentecostals/ Charismatics/Neocharismatics have mushroomed to 524 million affiliated (with unaffiliated believers, 602 million).

Growth of the Church

- From only 3 million in AD 1500, evangelicals have grown to 648 million worldwide, 54% being Non-Whites.

- The country with the fastest Christian expansion ever is China, now at 10,000 new converts every day.

Persecution of the Church

- More than 70% of all Christians now live in countries where they are experiencing persecution. In some cases EXTREME persecution.
- 14 million converted Hindus, Buddhists, and Muslims have opted to remain within those religions in order to witness for Christ as active believers in Jesus as Lord.

Global Population Issues

- Despite BILLIONS of dollars spent by dozens of denominations toward over a hundred major programs to fulfill the Great Commission by the year 2000, we didn't even keep up with population growth, much less reach the 2 billion unreached. Evidently no apologies are forthcoming for the giant waste of assets and broken promises.
- 124 million new souls begin life on Earth each year, but Christianity's 4,000 foreign mission agencies baptize only 4 million new persons a year.
- Since AD 1900, Christian urbanites have exploded from 100 million in 500 cities to 1,160 million in 5,000 cities.

Unreached Peoples

- Out of 648 million Great Commission Christians, 70% have never been told about the world's 1.6 billion unevangelized individuals.
- There are still thousands of language groups who do not have a SINGLE page of the Bible in their language. 98.7% of people have access to scripture in 6,700 languages leaving 78 million in 6,800 languages with no access at all.
- The majority of the unreached people groups are in restricted access countries. Western missionaries may not even be able to get to them.
- Despite Christ's command to evangelize, 67% of all humans from AD 30 to the present day have never even heard His name.
- 648 million Christians today (called Great Commission Christians) are active in Christ's world mission; 1,352 million Christians ignore this mission.
- Organized Christianity has total contact with 3,590 religions but no contact at all with 353 other religions and their over 500 million adherents.

Micro-Lending Stats

- We can help a Brother or Sister start a business in India with a loan of as little as $25.

Martyrdom

- Over the last 20 centuries, and in all 238 countries, more than 70 million Christians have been martyred - killed, executed, murdered - for Christ.
- More Christians have been martyred in the last 100 years than all others years since AD 30 combined.

Fellowship Of The Martyrs

Had Enough Yet? It gets worse.
We're stuffing the Fattest and starving the Hungriest!

KEY:

World A are the 38 countries that are primarily unevangelized. <50% (1.6 Billion souls)

World B are the 59 countries evangelized by not converted. >50% evangelized, but <60% Christian (2.9 Billion souls)

World C are the 141 countries primarily or predominantly Christian already. >95% evangelized and >60% Christian (2 Billion souls)

Broadcasting (radio/TV) per year - total spend $5.8 Billion World A - $6 Million (0.01%) World B - $226 Million (3.9%) World C - $5,568 Million (96.0%)	**Foreign Missions Money** per year - total spend $15 Billion World A - $250 Million (1.7%) World B - $1,750 Million (11.7%) World C - $13,000 Million (86.6%)
Finance (church/agency) per year - total spend $270 Billion World A - $188 Million (0.01%) World B - $1,370 Million (5.1%) World C - $256,100 Million (94.8%)	**Scripture distribution** per year - total 4,600 Million pieces World A - 20 Million (0.4%) World B - 680 Million (14.5%) World C - 3,900 Million (84.8%)
Christian Books (copies) per year - total 3.5 Billion pieces World A - 4 Million (0.1%) World B - 346 Million (9.9%) World C - 3,150 Million (90.0%)	**Foreign Mission Money** per year – total spend $15 Billion World A – 1.7% World B – 11.7% World C – 86.6%

(Plus 10 other scales that all look about the same. Tracts, Scripture languages, Literature, Periodicals, Computers, Full-time workers, Computer users, Foreign Missionaries, Home Missionaries, Lay leadership. Barrett, Page 55.)

Still not had enough?

Page 80 - "Where should foreign missionaries work?"

	As Currently Deployed	If Deployed where UNEVANGELIZED are located
World A Countries (<50% evangelized)	18,000	177,000
World B Countries (>50% evangelized)	68,000	242,000
World C Countries (>60% Christian)	335,000	1,000
Total	**420,000**	**420,000**

Statistics by Country

Canada (total population 31,147,000)
Unevangelized - 2.2%
Evangelized but non-Christian - 18.3%
Christian (of one sort or another) - 79.5%
  (self-described, includes Catholics)
Evangelization percent - 97.8%
Offers per person per year - 331
Cost effectiveness (Cost per baptism) - $1,189,000

France (total population 59,080,000)
Unevangelized - 3.7%
Evangelized but non-Christian - 21.8%
Christian (of one sort or another) - 75.8%
Evangelization percent - 95%
Offers per person per year - 360
Cost effectiveness (Cost per baptism) - $2,030,000

USA (total population 278,357,000)
Unevangelized - 1.5%
Evangelized but non-Christian - 13.8%
Christian (of one sort or another) - 84.7%
Evangelization percent - 98.5%
Offers per person per year - 368
Cost effectiveness (Cost per baptism) - $1,551,000

Britain (total population 58,830,000)
Unevangelized - 1.9%
Evangelized but non-Christian - 15.5%
Christian (of one sort or another) - 82.6%
Evangelization percent - 97%
Offers per person per year - 349
Cost effectiveness (Cost per baptism) - $1,816,000

Australia (total population 18,880,000)
Unevangelized - 1.6%
Evangelized but non-Christian - 19.1%
Christian (of one sort or another) - 92.9%
Evangelization percent - 98%
Offers per person per year - 336
Cost effectiveness (Cost per baptism) - $1,104,000

Japan (total population 126,714,000)
Unevangelized - 33.1%
Evangelized but non-Christian - 63.3%
Christian (of one sort or another) - 3.6%
Evangelization percent - 60%
Offers per person per year - 6
Cost effectiveness (Cost per baptism) - $2,721,000

Germany (total population 82,220,000)
Unevangelized - 2.4%
Evangelized but non-Christian - 21.8%
Christian (of one sort or another) - 75.8%
Evangelization percent - 95%
Offers per person per year - 381
Cost effectiveness (Cost per baptism) - $2,119,000

That's over ONE MILLION DOLLARS per baptism in the "West." Really? I mean, REALLY?!

So what is our cost effectiveness like in the "poor" countries?

Mozambique (total population 19,680,000) Unevangelized - 23.0% Evangelized but non-Christian - 38.6% Christian (of one sort or another) - 38.4% Evangelization percent - 80% Offers per person per year - 100 Cost effectiveness (Cost per baptism) - $1,400	**Cambodia (total population 11,168,000)** Unevangelized - 50.9% Evangelized but non-Christian - 48.0% Christian (of one sort or another) - 1.1% Evangelization percent - 49.1% Offers per person per year - 1 Cost effectiveness (Cost per baptism) - $4,300
India (total population 1,013,662,000) Unevangelized - 40.7% Evangelized but non-Christian - 53.1% Christian (of one sort or another) - 6.2% Evangelization percent - 59.3% Offers per person per year - 13 Cost effectiveness (Cost per baptism) - $9,800	**China (total population 1,262,557,000)** Unevangelized - 35.2% Evangelized but non-Christian - 57.7% Christian (of one sort or another) - 7.1% Evangelization percent - 64.8% Offers per person per year - 16 Cost effectiveness (Cost per baptism) - $15,800
Indonesia (total population 212,107,000) Unevangelized - 37.2% Evangelized but non-Christian - 49.7% Christian (of one sort or another) - 13.1% Evangelization percent - 62.8% Offers per person per year - 29 Cost effectiveness (Cost per baptism) - $40,800	**Bangladesh (total population 129,155,000)** Unevangelized - 42.8% Evangelized but non-Christian - 56.5% Christian (of one sort or another) - 0.7% Evangelization percent - 57.2% Offers per person per year - 1 Cost effectiveness (Cost per baptism) - $7,200
Afghanistan (total population 22,720,000) Unevangelized - 70.4% Evangelized but non-Christian - 29.6% Christian (of one sort or another) - 0.1% Evangelization percent - 29.7% Offers per person per year - < 1 Cost effectiveness (Cost per baptism) - $30,400	Do you think it makes more sense to spend $1.55 million on ONE soul in the USA or invest that in Mozambique and see 111 people saved?

An AD 2001 reality check: 50 new facts and figures about trends and issues concerning empirical global Christianity today. (from Table 1-1 and elsewhere in World Christian Trends, William Carey Library, David Barrett & Todd Johnson.) Country stats from p. 520 and following and p. 407 and following.

THUS SAITH THE LORD

Isaiah 1:2-31 (ESV)

2 Hear, O heavens, and give ear, O earth; for the Lord has spoken: "Children have I reared and brought up, but they have rebelled against me.
3 The ox knows its owner, and the donkey its master's crib, but Israel does not know, my people do not understand."
4 Ah, sinful nation, a people laden with iniquity, offspring of evildoers, children who deal corruptly! They have forsaken the Lord, they have despised the Holy One of Israel, they are utterly estranged.
5 Why will you still be struck down? Why will you continue to rebel? The whole head is sick, and the whole heart faint.
6 From the sole of the foot even to the head, there is no soundness in it, but bruises and sores and raw wounds; they are not pressed out or bound up or softened with oil.
7 Your country lies desolate; your cities are burned with fire; in your very presence foreigners devour your land; it is desolate, as overthrown by foreigners.
8 And the daughter of Zion is left like a booth in a vineyard, like a lodge in a cucumber field, like a besieged city.
9 If the Lord of hosts had not left us a few survivors, we should have been like Sodom, and become like Gomorrah.
10 Hear the word of the Lord, you rulers of Sodom! Give ear to the teaching of our God, you people of Gomorrah!
11 "What to me is the multitude of your sacrifices? says the Lord; I have had enough of burnt offerings of rams and the fat of well-fed beasts; I do not delight in the blood of bulls, or of lambs, or of goats.
12 "When you come to appear before me, who has required of you this trampling of my courts?
13 Bring no more vain offerings; incense is an abomination to me. New moon and Sabbath and the calling of convocations— I cannot endure iniquity and solemn assembly.
14 Your new moons and your appointed feasts my soul hates; they have become a burden to me; I am weary of bearing them.
15 When you spread out your hands, I will hide my eyes from you; even though you make many prayers, I will not listen; your hands are full of blood.
16 Wash yourselves; make yourselves clean; remove the evil of your deeds from before my eyes; cease to do evil,
17 learn to do good; seek justice, correct oppression; bring justice to the fatherless, plead the widow's cause.
18 "Come now, let us reason together, says the Lord: though your sins are like scarlet, they shall be as white as snow; though they are red like crimson, they shall become like wool.
19 If you are willing and obedient, you shall eat the good of the land;
20 but if you refuse and rebel, you shall be eaten by the sword; for the mouth of the Lord has spoken."
21 How the faithful city has become a whore, she who was full of justice! Righteousness lodged in her, but now murderers.
22 Your silver has become dross, your best wine mixed with water.
23 Your princes are rebels and companions of thieves. Everyone loves a bribe and runs after gifts. They do not bring justice to the fatherless, and the widow's cause does not come to them.
24 Therefore the Lord declares, the Lord of hosts, the Mighty One of Israel: "Ah, I will get relief from my enemies and avenge myself on my foes.

25 I will turn my hand against you and will smelt away your dross as with lye and remove all your alloy.
26 And I will restore your judges as at the first, and your counselors as at the beginning. Afterward you shall be called the city of righteousness, the faithful city."
27 Zion shall be redeemed by justice, and those in her who repent, by righteousness.
28 But rebels and sinners shall be broken together, and those who forsake the Lord shall be consumed.
29 For they shall be ashamed of the oaks that you desired; and you shall blush for the gardens that you have chosen.
30 For you shall be like an oak whose leaf withers, and like a garden without water.
31 And the strong shall become tinder, and his work a spark, and both of them shall burn together, with none to quench them.

THE LOCUSTS HAVE EATEN EVERYTHING

Because of the deception that has fallen on the "church," most folks are just as sure as they can be that they are rich and have acquired wealth and don't need a thing. They believe they already have all the treasure in heaven they need because they said the "Sinner's Prayer" once. But they don't realize they are lukewarm, wretched, pitiful, poor, blind and naked. (Revelation 3:17)

And do you know how they got so blind? Because <u>God</u> did it to them. He turned them over to their own reprobate minds because they insisted on going their own way. It's all in Deuteronomy 28. THIS is the true sign and wonder at the end of the age! Not peace and safety and prosperity. <u>Those</u> are the lying signs and wonders. The <u>true</u> sign to you and your descendants forever is that God did this to you because you did not joyfully and gladly obey the Lord your God in the time of prosperity, therefore in hunger and thirst, in nakedness and dire poverty you will serve the enemies the Lord sends against you! (Deuteronomy 28:45-48) Not teaching THAT in Sunday School, are we?

How about this? "You who were as numerous as the stars in the sky will be left but few in number, because you did not obey the Lord your God. Just as it pleased the Lord to make you prosper and increase in number, so it will please him to ruin and destroy you." (Deuteronomy 28:62-63) Did you get that?! He will prune you right off the vine and you won't even know He did it! You'll be eating moldy dirt and be convinced it's fillet mignon. Because our standards have been lowered so much, we'll pretty much buy anything nowadays. It's been so long since anybody came bringing pure, undiluted Truth that it freaks us out when somebody says something that radical! We perk up to see if they'll do it again, but we also start dissecting everything to find ANY error so that we can justify marginalizing and ignoring them.

In the end, we are searching, but we're not finding anything good to eat. There's milk out there – and a tidbit of meat mixed in with a bunch of other moldy, poisonous stuff – but mostly we're all starving to death, or eating things that aren't food at all. Surely you must see that locusts have come and sucked all the good stuff out of the "church"? If you could see inside the people, if you could see through the eyes of Jesus, you would see they're pretty much all shackled and oppressed and their cups are full of all kinds of nasty stuff – and there is no sign on the horizon that the "system" even cares or knows what to do to set them free. And I'm talking really, completely, all the way, holiness-walking, sanctified, big cup of Jesus, keep it full all the time, glow in the dark, peace, joy and victory – FREE. Do you even <u>know</u> anybody like that? Isn't that what we need? Aren't we all desperate for it, but don't want to admit we're not finding it? If we admit how truly, deeply unhappy we are – yet we've tried every available option with no success – then what will we do with ourselves except doubt that our faith is even real at all?

Surely the Lord knew this was coming. This passage in Joel is as good a description of the "church" in America as I can find:

Joel 1:16-18 (NIV)
16 Has not the food been cut off before our very eyes – joy and gladness from the house of our God? 17 The seeds are shriveled beneath the clods. The storehouses are in ruins, the granaries have been broken down, for the grain has dried up. 18 How the cattle moan! The herds mill about because they have no pasture; even the flocks of sheep are suffering.

The sheep and cattle mill around looking for green pasture, but can't find any. We have no real growth in "church" attendance in this country. It's all transfer growth. They're just milling around. Mostly going from dying small congregations to mega-churches with fancier shows and better childcare. But they're still just as hungry and oppressed.

Please hear me! I know it sounds crazy, but I see people's "cup". I can tell what's in there. I can see the spirits messing with them. (That's the gift of discernment of spirits. - I Corinthians 12:10) I can tell what's chewing on them and whispering to them. And I've been to 100+ "institutional churches" in the last two years and they are ALL full of shackled, oppressed, dying people who are trying desperately to find Truth – or convince themselves they're not really starving to death! And pastors just as oppressed! Please hear me! This isn't working! You only think it is because you don't know the difference. You don't know what it COULD be like. But I do. The Lord has shown me true community. Fellowship with believers who are fully cleaned out and walking in holiness and free of all systems and structures of Man. People who will take a bullet for you, that will love you even when you poke them in the eye – on purpose! People who will lay anything down for you, that will offer up their own marriage if only God would fix yours. People who can pray sincerely that God would send them to Hell if only He would bring revival to this town. (Exodus 32:32) People who have REAL, TRUE, FULL-ON joy and peace and victory. People that who been broken free of every yoke and God directs their EVERY step. Is that who you're hanging out with? Is that what your "church" is doing for you? Cause it should be.

Please! Please! Stop eating moldy stuff. Demand better. It's out there. It's within reach. It's your birthright! Don't settle for the status quo. Let's do it the way Jesus intended and get out of His way and see how different it could be. Please?

THE IF/THEN AXIOMS OF GOD'S WRATH

IF you are a child of God, **THEN** the requirements are higher on you than on the "world". (John 1:12, Luke 12:48)

IF you are a child of God, **THEN** you are supposed to obey God and God alone and lean not on your own understanding. (Acts 5:29, Proverbs 3:5)

IF you are a child of God and you are following a Man instead (including yourself), **THEN** you are in disobedience to God. (Matthew 9:9; I Peter 2:21; John 12:25-26)

IF you are a child of God in disobedience, **THEN** the Lord would like to draw you back to Himself – by whatever means necessary. (Luke 15)

IF you repeatedly refuse correction, **THEN** God will turn you over to increasingly bad stuff until you break. (Daniel 4:28-37; Romans 1:18-32)

IF you are really, really stubborn and rebellious, **THEN** God will harden your heart and send strong delusion on you until you are utterly destroyed – or you repent, whichever comes first. (Rom 1:18-32; Rom 9:18; John 12:40; 2 Thess 2:11-12)

IF you are a group of people, **THEN** God may collectively turn you over to satan to teach you not to blaspheme or send oppressions upon you. (I Timothy 1:20; I Timothy 6:1, Exodus, Judges, I and II Kings, etc.)

IF you persist in your rebellion, **THEN** expect MASSIVE negative consequences both spiritually and physically. (Isaiah 31:1, Deuteronomy 28, Lamentations; the bulk of the Bible is warnings of negative consequences for disobedience!)

IF there is a war between Good and Evil and we seem to be losing, **THEN** we are going our own way and God has blinded us and sent a strong delusion against us because we are being disobedient and rebellious. (Deuteronomy 28, Revelation 3:14-22)

THE IF/THEN AXIOMS OF GOD'S CRUSES

IF you are a child of God in disobedience, **THEN** God WILL send down curses on you until you turn. (2 Thessalonians 2:11-12; Acts 9:1-9; John 9:35-41, 12:40)

IF God sends down curses on you, **THEN** one of them is probably "strong delusion" or "blindness." (2 Thessalonians 2:11-12; Acts 9:1-9; John 9:35-41, 12:40)

IF God sends blindness or strong delusion on you, **THEN** you probably won't even know you're blind and deceived. (Revelation 3:15-17)

IF you are a prophet of God and you're in disobedience, **THEN** you will probably be VERY sure that you're hearing God really well, even though it's a lying spirit that is twisting everything up. (1 Kings 22:1-40; Matthew 15:14, 24:24; 2 Thessalonians 2:9-12; Revelation 3:15-17)

IF repentance is the only thing that can break the curse, **THEN** you really, really need to repent right now. (James 4:7-10; Mark 1:4; 2 Corinthians 7:9-11; Romans 2:4-5; Matthew 3:1-2; Luke 13:1-5; Acts 2:36-41; Acts 17:29-31; 2 Peter 3:9; Revelation 2:5, 2:16, 2:22, 3:3; 3:19)

But, **IF** you're under a delusion and are blind or asleep, **THEN** you can't repent or don't know what to repent for. (Matthew 15:14; Revelation 3:17; John 9:40; Matthew 13:13-14)

IF you don't repent, **THEN** you are toast. (And repentance is a gift that can ONLY come from God – and He is cursing you for being disobedient and may not pour out on you the Gift of Repentance.) (Romans 2:4; 2 Timothy 2:25-26; Acts 17:30; James 4:7-10, Acts 5:31)

IF you can't or won't repent and repentance is the only hope, **THEN** you're caught in a hopeless paradox loop.

IF there is going to be any hope for you, **THEN** either God Himself or someone who already HAS a gift of repentance has to come and pour it out on you so that you can get released. And then you have to turn and **stay** turned. If you go back like a dog to its vomit, it's going to go VERY badly for you. (2 Peter 2:20-22; 2 Timothy 2:25-26; 2 Corinthians 7:10)

THE IF/THEN AXIOMS OF CURRENT CHURCH CONDITIONS

IF God is for us, **THEN** nothing can stand against us. (Romans 8:31; Joshua 1:9; 1 John 4:13-18; 2 Chronicles 32:7-8; 2 Kings 6:15-17)

IF God says that if you obey, nothing can stand against you, and currently things are standing against us, **THEN** we must not be obeying God.

IF there is a war between good and evil and we seem to be losing, **THEN** we must be under the curses of Deuteronomy 28, not the blessings. (Deuteronomy 28)

IF there is hatred among brethren and adultery and envy and lust and dissension and factions and selfish ambition inside the Church and its leadership, **THEN** it CANNOT inherit the Kingdom of Heaven in its current state. (Galatians 5)

IF there is a love of money present and persistent in the Church, **THEN** the root of all evil is well entrenched in our structures and we're in big trouble. (I Timothy 6:10)

IF we are to be known as Christians by our love and we hate each other, **THEN** we might not actually be Christians. (I John 2:9,11; 3:14-24; 4:19-21; John 15:23)

IF we are not being good stewards of that which the Lord entrusted to us and we've buried our coin in the dirt, **THEN** we will be cast into outer darkness where there will be much crying and gnashing of teeth. (Luke 12:35-48; Matt. 25:25-46)

IF we can definitely show that the Church is basically doing everything exactly BACKWARDS of the way the Bible suggests we do it – and nobody seems to mind, **THEN** we have to come to the conclusion that there is a supernatural stupidity imposed on the system because nobody could intentionally design something this broken.

http://www.fellowshipofthemartyrs.com/scary_stats.htm
http://www.fellowshipofthemartyrs.com/pharisees.htm
http://www.fellowshipofthemartyrs.com/humansacrifice.htm
http://www.fellowshipofthemartyrs.com/business.htm

I don't have room or time to go into it in full detail here, but if you want to bring restoration to your town, you need to be fully Red Dragon-free. This is critically important!! You may already be, but you need to be sure. Repentance is the key.

Please take the time and read the Red Dragon book.

Fellowship Of The Martyrs

THE BODY OF CHRIST? YOU BETTER HOPE NOT!

As I've been looking intently at the state of the Church, I've grown more and more frustrated that hardly anybody seems to be really aware of the problems and the need for repentance. I struggle with what to make of that. Perhaps people think the 41,000+ denominations we have now are a good thing. Perhaps the fraud and waste and division and selfish ambition are just part of the human condition and can't be helped (although he says he's coming for a Bride without wrinkle or blemish and I think those are blemishes.) Perhaps no one ever told them how much this is hurting Jesus. I hope this helps with that. In fact, I hope it sears an indelible burn mark on your conscience that makes you cry in pain every day. That's probably what it's going to take to get this turned around.

The Romans and the Pharisees conspired together to crucify Jesus. They didn't just crucify him, they spit on him and beat him and whipped him until his bones showed. And then the Lamb of God bled all the way through Jerusalem and they nailed him to a cross naked and hung him up in front of everyone. The Bible says he was unrecognizable as a man – much less recognizable as Jesus. They put a sign over his bloodied, broken, humiliated body sarcastically declaring him King of the Jews. They fought over who would get his clothes. They stabbed him in the side to be sure he was dead, then buried him in a cave.

We have all heard of the pain and suffering he endured, not just physically, but the sin he carried must have been an unbelievable burden. The spiritual warfare and temptation to get him to back down and call up ten thousand angels to avenge him must have been horrific. None of us can even imagine what he went through in those last twenty-four hours.

How could the Pharisees and the Romans be so cruel? How could anybody inflict that kind of blood-thirsty, heartless damage on another human being – much less the Son of God?! What kind of monsters must they have been to so torture and degrade a person? What kind of evil spirits must have possessed them in that hour that they could do such a vile thing to an innocent man?

Everything that happens in our "natural" world has a spiritual counterpart. The human body of Christ was raised from the dead and abides with the Father. But I Corinthians 12:27 and Ephesians 4:12 and other places say that the Church is the Body of Christ. Do you know what that means? It means WE are the spiritual Body of Christ and that's <u>just</u> as real to Jesus as was his physical body. And it means we are meaner and more heartless and more possessed by evil than the Romans or the Pharisees could ever be.

You see, we have been hitting the Body of Christ with a cat-of-nine-tails daily for about eighteen hundred years (give or take). We have been hacking and slicing and shredding his flesh for generations. We have been fighting over his clothes and spitting on him since the first Christians started dying off. We have left a trail of his blood all over the world. And not in a good way.

To slice the Body of Christ up into 41,000+ denominations, we've basically had to run his flesh through a food processor. We've hacked off toes and then cloned them so we'd have a whole barn full of toes who refuse to reconnect with the rest of his body. We've ripped and shredded his flesh and stolen it from each other like a pack of hungry hyenas eating a fresh kill. Because he is Christ and he is SO much better than we could ever be, he has mostly taken it quietly like a sheep led to the slaughter. He has resisted the constant urge to call up 10,000 angels and avenge what we've done to his body. And it's a good thing too, because we should be FLATTENED by now for how much pain we've caused him. We've ignored those in need and focused on our own agendas. We've introduced malignant cancers and poisons and all kinds of disgusting stuff into his body.

When he came in the flesh, Jesus endured a few people beating him and a few people spitting on him. But it was pretty much all over in 24 hours. But in the spirit, we have been beating him mercilessly for hundreds of years. Under our own power, there is no sign on the horizon that the "church" system we've built is going to stop doing it either.

We refuse to connect up to the central nervous system and get commands from the brain. We refuse to coordinate our efforts with all the other body parts, so the whole Body just lays there and twitches in pain. Some parts look like they're getting somewhere, but it's more like the illusion of rigor mortise, than actual progress. Without ALL the pieces taking commands from the Head, we're just spinning our wheels and he bleeds more and more every day and the people we were supposed to reach out to are dying.

If you think this is just figurative and it isn't causing Jesus pain, then you surely don't really understand the nature of his love for us and his desire for his body to be whole. He prayed in John 17 that we would be one body because, if not, THIS is the result. In essence, he prayed that the cup of suffering on his physical body would be taken away if possible AND he prayed that the cup of suffering on his spiritual body would be taken away if possible. Neither was. He is crying every day and has been for centuries. And the Father is fuming.

He has been enduring daily torture of a scale none of us can imagine. We have inflicted far more pain than the Pharisees and Romans could have ever even imagined. The physical body has limits of what it can endure, but Christ's spiritual body evidently has no limits on how much it can be tortured. Worse yet, the Pharisees and Romans hated him and didn't believe in him – but we claim to know he is the Son of God and we say we love him, and yet, we're the ones doing the real damage. And we continue getting together in our little boxes every week and singing song of praise and taking communion with a straight face while we're collectively desecrating and defiling his body.

I can tell you this, if I were the Father and I loved my only son Jesus with all that I am, at some point I'm going to FORCE the torture of his body to stop. If they won't start being one body, I'm going to get their attention by whatever means necessary. If I have to, I'll send earthquakes, tsunamis, wars, plagues, famines ... whatever. If they keep on singing and dancing and being completely oblivious and asleep, I'll even kill two-thirds of the planet if that's what it takes for them to knock it off and start being one body. That's pretty much what the book of Revelation predicts is coming – and we deserve it.

And if I were you I wouldn't count on a "rapture" getting you out before the suffering starts. Since the Church was supposed to take the light to the world and it's REALLY dark out there, I'm pretty sure the sad state of things is our fault. We're the ones who knew better, we're the ones who have been butchering the body of Christ for centuries. I don't see any reason why we should get out of the consequences of what we've done. He's going to spank us really hard and we have it coming. Don't think you're going to avoid suffering, you're not.

Our only hope is to weep and repent and mourn before the altar. We need to apologize and mean it – and then we need to turn from our wicked ways and get under HIS headship. No more structures and systems and traditions of Man. If we don't start acting like One Body on our own, then the Father is going to kill off all the body parts who won't play nice together. Then He'll graft in bits who will appreciate it. Like prostitutes and drug dealers and homeless and the lost and kids with purple hair and hurting people who will defend his body to the death and refuse to listen to anyone but HIM.

Burn it into your brain. We ran the Body of Christ through a meat grinder. We sent people to seminary to learn how to slice the Body of Christ up into smaller and smaller pieces. We paid them to do it. We self-righteously took pleasure in splitting off from other people who had the Holy Spirit in them. We fought over his clothes. We placed a sign over his head that proclaimed proudly to the world that THIS beaten, bloody mess was an accurate representation of the King of Kings. We are thieves and liars and murders of the first order.

There's just one simple standard. If the Holy Spirit is in me and the Holy Spirit is in you, then we're just One Body and we're going to have to figure out how to get along without killing each other. We've got to knock it off before it's too late.

Please? If you love Jesus, could you please stop torturing his body? Could you tell him you're willing to share in his sufferings and help bear this burden until this is over? Could you acknowledge your part in it, however small, and stop? Could you insist on harmony from now on? Could you ask the Father to let you feel the pain Jesus feels? Could you ask the Father to let you see through His eyes? I know He wants to.

Please make it stop.

JOHN 15 – IF/THEN STATEMENTS

God does **not** change. What irritated Him then, still irritates Him now. What pleased and honored Him then, still pleases and honors Him now. These If/Then statements are <u>guarantees</u>! IF you do these things, then He <u>WILL</u> do what He said He would do – sooner or later, one way or the other. He reserves the right to manifest it in whatever way He wants, but He <u>WILL</u> do it.

It's equational. Like math. Just insert the quantity.

IF you do Behavior X **THEN** Consequence Y will result.   Quantity N is the only variable.

$$BX(N) = CY(N)$$

Positive Behavior = Positive Consequence   **OR**   Negative Behavior = Negative Consequence

Get it? Doesn't even require faith. It's just a guarantee from God. Now, it may not manifest like you expect or when you expect, but it WILL happen because God's promises are good. He is faithful and just.

So here we go. Let's look at the guarantees. *(Scripture quoted from Amplified Version.)*

John 15

1 I AM the True Vine, and My Father is the Vinedresser.

Just so we're clear who is whom. God is the one doing the pruning, with whatever tools He wants to use.

2 Any branch in Me that does not bear fruit [that stops bearing] He cuts away (trims off, takes away); and He cleanses and repeatedly prunes every branch that continues to bear fruit, to make it bear more and richer and more excellent fruit.

If you are stagnant my Father will spew you out. He repeatedly prunes EVERY branch. Don't think you're exempt and don't think the pruning you just went through is the last of it! And know that the ONLY reason He is doing it is so that you and the Vine will bear more fruit.

3 You are cleansed and pruned already, because of the word which I have given you [the teachings I have discussed with you].

The disciples to whom I was speaking were currently in pretty good shape. That wasn't always the case. Peter, in particular, required additional pruning later on. And then there was Judas.

4 Dwell in Me, and I will dwell in you. [Live in Me, and I will live in you.] Just as no branch can bear fruit of itself without abiding in (being vitally united to) the vine, neither can you bear fruit unless you abide in Me.

Here you should begin to see the recipe book of conditional statements that follow. It's very important to note that "abiding" is not at all the same as "believing in". It's not a one time acceptance of a truth, it's a constant relationship. Abiding infers constant and deep symbiotic relationship with Me, not just an acknowledgment.

"IF you remain in ME, THEN I will remain in you."

5 I am the Vine; you are the branches. Whoever lives in Me and I in him bears much (abundant) fruit. However, apart from Me [cut off from vital union with Me] you can do nothing.

Just so we're clear on who is whom. I'm the Source. You're the twig. You're the fruit bearers, but you CANNOT do it without a constant relationship with Me. If ANYTHING interrupts the flow or nourishment from me, you will NOT be able to bear good fruit. Just so we're clear.

"IF a man remains in Me AND I in him, THEN he will bear much fruit."
"IF you are cut off from Me, THEN you can do nothing."

6 If a person does not dwell in Me, he is thrown out like a [broken-off] branch, and withers; such branches are gathered up and thrown into the fire, and they are burned.

{Editors note: It's possible to be a fruit-bearing branch, stop bearing fruit and be thrown into the fire. This ought to scare the pants off of all of us!! Why else do you need to work out our salvation with fear and trembling?! If our acceptance of Jesus resulted in permanent, unchangeable salvation, how is this possible? These aren't branches that stay attached to the Vine and are refined by fire and then made useful again. The clear implication is that these are trimmed off, hauled off and burned. There is nothing here that indicates that it is for medicinal value and they eventually return to the Vine. I know this disrupts a lot of people's theology. I'd sure like somebody to tell me how else to interpret this! Note these are not some other kind of branch that is pruned off. These are <u>not</u> non-Christians. These are people that WERE connected to the Vine and stopped bearing fruit.}

"IF you stop dwelling in Me, THEN you will be cut off, hauled off and burned in the fire."

7 If you live in Me [abide vitally united to Me] and My words remain in you and continue to live in your hearts, ask whatever you will, and it shall be done for you.

As long as we're in relationship and you are producing good fruit, I'll listen to you and answer you.

"IF you abide in Me <u>AND</u> My words in you <u>AND</u> they continue to live in your heart (active and operating, not passive), THEN ask whatever you like and I'll do it for you."

8 When you bear (produce) much fruit, My Father is honored and glorified, and you show and prove yourselves to be true followers of Mine.

The Vinedresser is pleased with you when you effectively accomplish that for which you were designed. You are like the Vine when you take what the Vine feeds you and produce that which defines the Vine. If you produce nothing OR make olives on a grape vine, you're not pleasing to the Vinedresser. You must do as you were designed and as the Vine and the Vinedresser desire. You must obey THEIR design for you, not your own plans and goals.

9 I have loved you, [just] as the Father has loved Me; abide in My love [continue in His love with Me].

The Vinedresser lovingly cares for Me and I will lovingly care for You. Please don't do anything to screw it up. Please make good fruit so nothing bad will happen.

10 If you keep My commandments [if you continue to obey My instructions], you will abide in My love and live on in it, just as I have obeyed My Father's commandments and live on in His love.

The Vinedresser is pleased with Me, so He will be pleased with you if you are like Me and do as I instruct. Make the fruit in the time and in the way and in the proportions that I tell you to, or else.

"IF you keep My commandments, THEN you will abide in My love and live on."

11 I have told you these things, that My joy and delight may be in you, and that your joy and gladness may be of full measure and complete and overflowing.

I want everybody clear on the expectations and requirements. I don't want you to have to guess about what I'm expecting of you. This should be pretty clear. If you mangle it all up later, don't say I didn't warn you. You will not have joy and gladness in full measure, complete and overflowing, unless you operate within My guidelines. You and I both have to do it the way the Vinedresser designed it.

12 This is My commandment: that you love one another [just] as I have loved you.

Just so we're clear. If you don't keep My commandments, I'm not going to abide in you and you're in danger of being pruned, cast out and burned. So please obey Me on this. Love one another, just as I love you. What the Vine feeds you should flow THROUGH you and on to all the other members without interruption. Don't clog up the flow and don't add your own spin or flavor or virus to it. Just let what I do for you flow on through you to others. If not, then you're a wart and a cancer and you're keeping others from bearing fruit and the Vinedresser is NOT going to be happy. Nothing personal. I love you. I'm just saying so you're clear and there won't be any surprises. If you try to prune parts off yourself, you're going to be in big trouble. That's not your job. You need to love and feed all your members and let the Vinedresser take care of the rest.

13 No one has greater love [no one has shown stronger affection] than to lay down (give up) his own life for his friends.

This is what I'm doing for you. I'm serving and upholding and feeding and sacrificing so YOU can bear fruit. For a little while I was the Vine AND the Branches, but it was only a one-man show for a tiny sliver of time as it was growing. Now I'm the support mechanism so you can grow and prosper. And I love doing it! It would sure be great if you would be willing to do it, too. Lay down your own desires and just feed and love your members as they grow. And if they produce more fruit than you, that's OK, that was the plan. What you don't get is that even though I'm the Vine, when a branch gets pruned, that's part of Me too – and I'm willing to let that part of Me die for the sake of the whole. Be willing to lay down whatever is necessary for the sake of Me or for those around you. If you do, the Vinedresser will be REALLY happy with you.

14 You are My friends if you keep on doing the things which I command you to do.

A reminder of verse 10. Not just producers, not just branches, but FRIENDS if you KEEP ON doing what you are commanded. This is active and ongoing. Constant acknowledgment, listening and obedience results in friendship. I want you to be My friends. Please be My friends.

"IF you want to be My friends, THEN keep constantly doing what I command you to do."

15 I do not call you servants (slaves) any longer, for the servant does not know what his master is doing (working out). But I have called you My friends, because I have made known to you everything that I have heard from My Father. [I have revealed to you everything that I have learned from Him.]

You're not flying blind here – I've given you plenty of information about what the plan is. You are partners and team members, so long as you don't deny Me by going your own way.

16 You have not chosen Me, but I have chosen you and I have appointed you [I have planted you], that you might go and bear fruit and keep on bearing, and that your fruit may be lasting [that it may remain, abide], so that whatever you ask the Father in My Name [as presenting all that I AM], He may give it to you.

I picked you, I grafted you, I grew you, I feed you, I instruct you, all with one goal – that you will constantly bear good fruit that is lasting AND so that whatever you ask the Vinedresser, He will give you. We have an open heaven over us when we don't make it about us – we abide, we obey and we bear much lasting fruit.

17 This is what I command you: that you love one another.

Remember verse 12? I wasn't kidding. Do this or else. You CANNOT abide in me without this. You will surely be pruned sooner or later if you don't do this. And I'm not defining who "one another" is, but it's a lot wider sphere than you think. For sure it includes EVERYONE connected to the Vine. I'm talking to the whole lot of you. If ANY of you are not loving ALL the others, you're going to be in big trouble and you need to wonder if I'm really abiding in you. The Vinedresser might prune you off at any moment.

18 If the world hates you, know that it hated Me before it hated you.

You're not alone. The more you get to be like Me, the more you need to expect this stuff.

"IF the world hates you, THEN be comforted in knowing that it hated me first."

19 If you belonged to the world, the world would treat you with affection and would love you as its own. But because you are not of the world [no longer one with it], but I have chosen (selected) you out of the world, the world hates (detests) you.

This is pretty clear, isn't it? If the world is in love with you, you need to wonder how much you are like me. If you fit right in with them, you are a lot more like them than you are like Me. The world cannot produce the fruit My vine bears, so you might be in danger of pruning at any moment. Better turn.

"IF you belonged to the world, THEN the world would love you as is own."
"IF you are no longer of the world because I have chosen you, THEN the world hates you."

20 Remember that I told you, A servant is not greater than his master [is not superior to him]. If they persecuted Me, they will also persecute you; if they kept My word and obeyed My teachings, they will also keep and obey yours.

You will endure what I endured if you seek to be like me. You will not surpass me, but you should expect the same treatment. That may just be one of the most depressing sentences in the Bible. Since they

DIDN'T keep My word and obey Me, you really shouldn't expect anybody will listen to you either! Be surprised and thankful if they listen at all.

> "IF they persecuted Me, THEN they will also persecute you (assuming you're like me)."
> "IF they obeyed Me, THEN they will also obey you."

21 But they will do all this to you [inflict all this suffering on you] because of [your bearing] My name and on My account, for they do not know or understand the One Who sent Me.

Don't be ashamed, they're doing it because you are like Me! That's great! They would love you if you looked like them. They don't understand the Vinedresser and how He works – or they do and they hate the whole idea – it's not your fault they're mad at you.

22 If I had not come and spoken to them, they would not be guilty of sin [would be blameless]; but now they have no excuse for their sin.

Without my voice and my commands, they could not really be expected to produce fruit at all or they would not produce the correct kind. But now they have no excuse. If they expect to abide, then they need to obey.

> "IF I hadn't explained sin to them, THEN they would not be guilty."

23 Whoever hates Me also hates My Father.

> "IF you hate me, THEN you hate My Father as well."

24 If I had not done (accomplished) among them the works which no one else ever did, they would not be guilty of sin. But [the fact is] now they have both seen [these works] and have hated both Me and My Father.

They saw miracles. They saw undeniable proof that I am who I say I am. They have no more excuse to deny they need to obey Me. I am greater than you and that's just all there is to it. But instead they saw and hated both the Vine and the Vinedresser.

> "IF I had not done miracles, THEN they would have an excuse to disobey"
> "– but they do anyway – and by it show their hatred of Me and the Father."

25 But [this is so] that the word written in their Law might be fulfilled, They hated Me without a cause.

I saw it coming. They saw it coming. There's no avoiding it. Had to happen.

26 But when the Comforter (Counselor, Helper, Advocate, Intercessor, Strengthener, Standby) comes, Whom I will send to you from the Father, the Spirit of Truth Who comes (proceeds) from the Father, He [Himself] will testify regarding Me.

The Holy Spirit will explain it all later and help you hear My voice so you can produce good, abundant, lasting fruit forever. Hang loose, it's on the way. He will be your teacher, not Man.

27 But you also will testify and be My witnesses, because you have been with Me from the beginning.

You will tell the world. You will be witnesses (martureo from martus – meaning martyrs) because you can hear Me, are abiding in Me and are obeying Me. Big fruit comes when you are witnesses, no matter how much persecution comes, no matter how much the world hates you, even unto death.

SUMMARY

Below is a list of the If/Then's in this amazing chapter. These are straight from the mouth of Jesus. These are conditional statements and promises. It is a recipe for success and fruit bearing and a road map to know what to expect. It is also a condemnation of those who are not doing these things and should not expect ANY blessing! The thing you need to see is the equational nature of these. They aren't just On/Off switches, they are <u>Dials</u>. It should be obvious that some people bear more fruit than others. Why? Because they did these to a greater degree, they poured out more of themselves, they dialed it up higher. They've learned how to let Jesus flow through them without getting in the way. They have a bigger cup of Jesus. However you want to think about it. It's all math, just plug in the quantities.

IF you remain in ME, THEN I will remain in you.
IF you remain in 20%, THEN I will remain in you 20%.
If you remain in me ALL, THEN I will remain in you ALL.

IF a man remains in Me AND I in him, THEN he will bear much fruit.

IF you are cut off from Me, THEN you can do nothing.
IF you stop receiving from Me, THEN you WILL stop growing.
IF you turn the valve down to 50% of capacity, THEN you will grow 50% of capacity.
IF you try to grow on your own power, THEN nothing that looks like MY fruit will result.

IF you stop dwelling in Me, THEN you will be cut off, hauled off and burned in the fire.
IF you shut the valve all the way off and walk away, THEN you are in big trouble.

IF you abide in Me AND My words in you AND they continue to live in your heart (active and operating, not passive), THEN ask whatever you like and I'll do it for you.
IF you do this stuff a little bit, THEN you can ask for help with your headache.
IF you do this stuff all the way, THEN you can ask to raise the dead.

IF you keep My commandments, THEN you will abide in My love and live on.
If you keep some of my commandments, THEN you are abiding SOME.

IF you want to be My friends, THEN keep constantly doing what I command you to do.
IF you don't want to be my friends, THEN just do some of them sometimes.

IF the world hates you, THEN be comforted in knowing that it hated me first.
IF the world hates you once in a while, THEN you're probably like me a little bit.
IF the world boils you in oil and kills you, THEN you're probably like me all the time.

IF you belonged to the world, THEN the world would love you as is own.
IF the world loves you 40%, THEN there's probably 40% of you that's not obeying Me.
IF the world can't tell you apart from it's own people, THEN you're probably not much like Me.

IF you are no longer of the world because I have chosen you, THEN the world hates you.
IF I chose you <u>AND</u> you choose to let me, THEN I will make you someone the world despises.

IF they persecuted Me, THEN they will also persecute you (assuming you're like me).

IF they obeyed Me, THEN they will also obey you.
IF the vast majority ignored me, THEN don't expect any different.

IF I hadn't explained sin to them, THEN they would not be guilty.
IF you understand the equational nature of this chapter, THEN you need to give ALL.
IF you abide and obey 50%, THEN the other 50% is sin and you are guilty.

IF you hate me, THEN you hate My Father as well.
IF the world hates me and won't receive from me, THEN they won't receive from the Father either.
IF you abide in me 70%, THEN you hate me 30% - and the Father too.

IF I had not done miracles, THEN they would have an excuse to disobey – but they do anyway – and by it show their hatred of Me and the Father
IF you have EVER seen Me work, ever heal or transform or redeem,
THEN you have no excuse – and any disobedience is hatred toward Me and the Father.

Sing it like you mean it this time.

I Surrender All
by Judson W. Van DeVenter, 1896:

ALL to Jesus, I surrender; **ALL** to Him I freely give;
I will **EVER** love and trust Him, In His presence **DAILY** live.

I surrender **ALL**, I surrender **ALL**, **ALL** to Thee, my blessed Savior, I surrender **ALL**.

ALL to Jesus I surrender; Humbly at His feet I bow,
Worldly pleasures **ALL** forsaken; Take me, Jesus, take me now.

I surrender **ALL**, I surrender **ALL**, **ALL** to Thee, my blessed Savior, I surrender **ALL**.

ALL to Jesus, I surrender; Make me, Savior, **WHOLLY** Thine;
Let me feel the Holy Spirit, Truly know that Thou art mine.

I surrender **ALL**, I surrender **ALL**, **ALL** to Thee, my blessed Savior, I surrender **ALL**.

ALL to Jesus, I surrender; Lord, I give myself to Thee;
FILL me with Thy love and power; Let Thy blessing fall on me.

I surrender **ALL**, I surrender **ALL**, **ALL** to Thee, my blessed Savior, I surrender **ALL**.

ALL to Jesus I surrender; **NOW** I feel the sacred flame.
O the joy of **FULL** salvation! Glory, glory, to His Name!

I surrender **ALL,** I surrender **ALL, ALL** to Thee, my blessed Savior, I surrender **ALL**.

So what's it gonna be? How far are you willing to go? What still needs to be laid down? Could you do it now? Maybe pray this prayer, if you have the guts for it -

Lord, I really WANT to surrender ALL. I really do, but I don't know how. I know I'm not there and I'm sorry I ever held anything back. Please help me. Please? If there is anything that stands between me and You, anything I love more than You, whether I realize it or not, whether I like it or not, no matter where it came from or how long it's been there, would You just rip it, shred it, burn it, crush it, kill it, tear it out of my grip – even if I like it. Whatever You do, DO NOT stop breaking me until You are finished, no matter how much I whine. Do not dial down Your refining fire. YOU have your way with me. Give me Your Spirit right now in as big a measure as I can handle. I trust You. Please don't leave me like this, I stink. I'm sorry I didn't pray this sooner. I love You, Jesus. Do it now! Amen.

THUS SAITH THE LORD

Ezekiel 34:1-31 (ESV)

1 The word of the Lord came to me:
2 "Son of man, prophesy against the shepherds of Israel; prophesy, and say to them, even to the shepherds, **Thus says the Lord God:** Ah, shepherds of Israel who have been feeding yourselves! Should not shepherds feed the sheep?
3 You eat the fat, you clothe yourselves with the wool, you slaughter the fat ones, but you do not feed the sheep.
4 The weak you have not strengthened, the sick you have not healed, the injured you have not bound up, the strayed you have not brought back, the lost you have not sought, and with force and harshness you have ruled them.
5 So they were scattered, because there was no shepherd, and they became food for all the wild beasts.
6 My sheep were scattered; they wandered over all the mountains and on every high hill. My sheep were scattered over all the face of the earth, with none to search or seek for them.
7 **"Therefore, you shepherds, hear the word of the Lord:**
8 As I live, declares the Lord God, surely because my sheep have become a prey, and my sheep have become food for all the wild beasts, since there was no shepherd, and because my shepherds have not searched for my sheep, but the shepherds have fed themselves, and have not fed my sheep,
9 **therefore, you shepherds, hear the word of the Lord:**
10 Thus says the Lord God, Behold, I am against the shepherds, and I will require my sheep at their hand and put a stop to their feeding the sheep. No longer shall the shepherds feed themselves. I will rescue my sheep from their mouths, that they may not be food for them.
11 **"For thus says the Lord God:** Behold, I, I myself will search for my sheep and will seek them out.
12 As a shepherd seeks out his flock when he is among his sheep that have been scattered, so will I seek out my sheep, and I will rescue them from all places where they have been scattered on a day of clouds and thick darkness.
13 And I will bring them out from the peoples and gather them from the countries, and will bring them into their own land. And I will feed them on the mountains of Israel, by the ravines, and in all the inhabited places of the country.

14 I will feed them with good pasture, and on the mountain heights of Israel shall be their grazing land. There they shall lie down in good grazing land, and on rich pasture they shall feed on the mountains of Israel.
15 I myself will be the shepherd of my sheep, and I myself will make them lie down, declares the Lord God.
16 I will seek the lost, and I will bring back the strayed, and I will bind up the injured, and I will strengthen the weak, and the fat and the strong I will destroy. I will feed them in justice.
17 "As for you, my flock, **thus says the Lord God:** Behold, I judge between sheep and sheep, between rams and male goats.
18 Is it not enough for you to feed on the good pasture, that you must tread down with your feet the rest of your pasture; and to drink of clear water, that you must muddy the rest of the water with your feet?
19 And must my sheep eat what you have trodden with your feet, and drink what you have muddied with your feet?
20 "Therefore, **thus says the Lord God to them**: Behold, I, I myself will judge between the fat sheep and the lean sheep.
21 Because you push with side and shoulder, and thrust at all the weak with your horns, till you have scattered them abroad,
22 I will rescue my flock; they shall no longer be a prey. And I will judge between sheep and sheep.
23 And I will set up over them one shepherd, my servant David, and he shall feed them: he shall feed them and be their shepherd.
24 And I, the Lord, will be their God, and my servant David shall be prince among them. **I am the Lord; I have spoken.**
25 "I will make with them a covenant of peace and banish wild beasts from the land, so that they may dwell securely in the wilderness and sleep in the woods.
26 And I will make them and the places all around my hill a blessing, and I will send down the showers in their season; they shall be showers of blessing.
27 And the trees of the field shall yield their fruit, and the earth shall yield its increase, and they shall be secure in their land. **And they shall know that I am the Lord, when I break the bars of their yoke, and deliver them from the hand of those who enslaved them.**
28 They shall no more be a prey to the nations, nor shall the beasts of the land devour them. They shall dwell securely, and none shall make them afraid.
29 And I will provide for them renowned plantations so that they shall no more be consumed with hunger in the land, and no longer suffer the reproach of the nations.
30 **And they shall know that I am the Lord their God with them, and that they, the house of Israel, are my people, declares the Lord God.**
31 **And you are my sheep, human sheep of my pasture, and I am your God, declares the Lord God.**"

DECLARATION OF WAR AGAINST THE FORCES OF DARKNESS

Now, before you start thinking we're talking about YOU, this is about EVIL - not people. Sure, some people are stinkers, but we're to love people and we're to hate evil. The darkness from our sinful nature is in all of us. We're not any better, it's just Christ in us that helps us be redeemed. Anyway, this is about the BIG picture, not any specific person, organization, leader, etc.

No more. It ends now.

For too long we've ignored what was going on in the church. For too long we've sat out or even denied there was a war. We've been infiltrated. We've been co-opted. We've been dumbed down. We've had our greatest weapons ridiculed and demeaned until nobody wants them anymore. This is no kind of way to fight a war.

We've allowed ourselves to be fattened up and we've planted roots. We've been herded together in big groups like cattle and we bump around against each other making useless noises. Wolves have come in and we've welcomed them. We've accepted aid from the enemies of God. We've taken the enemy's advice about how to make war. We've hired consultants to show us how to be more like the world.

We've ignored our own King's plan. We've sent a pitiful few skirmishing parties out to do the work of missions for us and patronized them when they come home wounded and hungry. We've given all the ammunition to the supply clerks back home and deprived the infantry of what they needed to push back the darkness. Everything about what we're doing is upside down.

No more will we take on the names and philosophies of men to define and identify us. No more will we allow factions over secondary issues to divide us. We are to be OF Jesus and Him alone. Only He gets to put His brand on us. Only He gets to direct us. Only He is truth. This is war! Nothing else can be trusted. His is the unbreakable cypher. Pure, full, uncut Truth cannot be spoken by the enemy. Truth and Love are our uniform, our code, our defining characteristic. Only Truth and Love will suffice for battle against principalities and forces of darkness.

No more will we waste time on our own vain pleasures and indulgences. No more will we allow the egos and prides and traditions and philosophies of Man to divide us. We will love Truth and settle for nothing less. We will learn to sniff out and purge compromise and half-truths. We will force out of us every bad dark thing by being completely filled with the Bread of Life. We will be nourished by Truth. We will be armored by Truth. We will swing the Sword of Truth in big wide circles and pierce the hearts of anyone near. We will fight and not grow weary. We will charge forward and never retreat. Should one slip, others will lift him up. Should one fall, others will take his place.

No more. It ends now. There are those who are already equipped to fight and we will enlist them, organize them and send them back out to recruit more. We'll fight with love to awaken our brethren who are asleep and get them in fighting form. We will push back the darkness by speaking nothing but TRUTH. It is rare and precious - and only Jesus is the source. Every man-made thing will burn off in the fire. Only Jesus can be trusted.

As Gideon, we will lovingly restore our own altars first while the people are sleeping. Then we can rally a restored, awakened people to fight the forces of darkness. Those on the front lines who have proven themselves good and faithful servants and stewards of their talents will be provisioned with a hundred times their own needs so they can feed the hungry and give drink to the thirsty as they see any need. We will pray and encourage and support them and recruit more. We will always strive to continue growing up into Jesus, who is the Head.

In view of the great mercy shown us by Jesus Christ, we will offer our bodies as living sacrifices, holy and pleasing to God. We will stop conforming to the pattern of this world. We will be transformed by the renewing of our minds so that we will be able to test and approve what is God's good, pleasing and perfect will. Then we'll go and do it.

I Corinthians 14:8 "Again, if the trumpet make an uncertain sound, who will prepare for battle?"

No more. It ends now. As clear as we can say it, this is war.

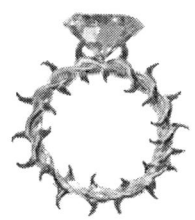

WHAT IS THE SOLUTION?

We need New Wineskins. We need to be corporately transformed by the renewing of our minds. (Romans 12:1-2) We don't need to invent some new system. A true New Wineskin isn't a mega-church with really excellent childcare and fancy shows. That's not resulting in radical transformation of economies and ecologies and taking back the culture. Transfer growth and massive budgets spent on discretionary things aren't going to get this done.

We have to be rebooted. We have to be re-NEW-ed. Set back to the defaults. Back to our first love. Things have to be put back into divine order, the way they were intended from the beginning. And that means the City Churches. That is the New Wineskin. That is the greatest challenge for us to face, will require the most Holy Spirit, is the most dangerous thing to the enemy and will prove our love for each other to the world in ways we can't even comprehend right now. THAT kind of community and sharing with each as they have a need is a true witness of what Christianity can and should be. Our endless divisions and factions are not.

Again, a City Church is NOT a matter of creating some new organization. If there are Christians in your town, then there is a "Church of YourTown" and there always has been. Odds are that the Body in your town is filled with all kinds of things that grieve God and will keep you corporately from inheriting the kingdom right now. (Galatians 5:19-21, Deut. 28) It's just a matter of following the Biblical prescriptions and getting it washed clean and then getting it filled with Jesus instead. It's a matter of confessing your sins and the sins of your fathers and forefathers and asking Him to do whatever it takes to show up and direct the affairs of this stiff-necked people. You have to ask Him to restore the Lampstand because you've almost surely lost it generations ago. America has been dark for a LONG time.

Revelation 2:1-7 (KJV)
1 Unto the angel of the church of Ephesus write; These things saith he that holdeth the seven stars in his right hand, who walketh in the midst of the seven golden candlesticks; 2 I know thy works, and thy labour, and thy patience, and how thou canst not bear them which are evil: and thou hast tried them which say they are apostles, and are not, and hast found them liars: 3 And hast borne, and hast patience, and for my name's sake hast laboured, and hast not fainted. 4 Nevertheless I have *somewhat* against thee, because thou hast left thy first love. 5 Remember therefore from whence thou art fallen, and repent, and do the first works; or else I will come unto thee quickly, and will remove thy candlestick out of his place, except thou repent. 6 But this thou hast, that thou hatest the deeds of the Nicolaitans, which I also hate. 7 He that hath an ear, let him hear what the Spirit saith unto the churches; To him that overcometh will I give to eat of the tree of life, which is in the midst of the paradise of God.

The "love" mentioned there is "agape". Their former agape was cold. Surely that was affecting their own bonds of harmony. Surely some of them were going their own way. They were commended because they were patient and had not fainted and hated the deeds of the Nicolaitans. But still they had lost their first love. Perhaps their focus had gotten diverted to all the things coming against them and not on the love for their Lord and for each other. But at least they hated the deeds of the Nicolatians (NOT the people themselves, their deeds). (See Psalm 141:5-6)

But who were the Nicolaitans? Some say they were a cult formed around a leader Nicolaus – whether that is the deacon Nicholas or not, no one really knows. It may be that it's not a name but a description of the main theology of the group – that it was transliterated instead of translated. The word itself is from the Greek *nikao*, which means "to conquer or overcome," and *laos*, which means "people" and from which the word "laity" comes. Together they mean destruction of the people and refers to the earliest form of a priest class or clergy that "lorded it" over the people. This divided the people and set up some who had the "deep mysteries" as more holy or more powerful or responsible to direct the affairs of others. That is decidedly against the truth that we are all priests and kings and none is greater than any other. We are to lean not on our own understanding – or that of any other man. (Proverbs 3:5-6) Only Jesus gets to direct all of our paths!

A good translation of Nicolaitan would be "those who prevail over the people." This clergy system would later turn into the papal hierarchy of the Catholic church. The Council of Trent stated, "If anyone shall say that there is not in the Catholic Church a hierarchy established by the divine ordination, consisting of bishops, presbyters and ministers, let him be anathema." (That means cursed and excommunicated.) The "Reformers" may have changed some things about the Catholic church, but they were very careful not to disrupt the hierarchy that empowered them, as well as the Catholics! It was a "reformation" that addressed all the inconsequential issues and left alone the things that would have really done some damage to the forces of darkness. It brought more division, didn't restore the City Churches and didn't eliminate the priest class. (But there were always those out in the woods who remained true – and were actively hunted by the Catholic church and her daughters. Do you know how many people Luther and Calvin had burned at the stake? Look it up.)

Those who are appointed by God to serve (apostles, prophets, evangelists, pastors/teachers) are NOT to "lord it over" the people!! They are GIFTS to the church to serve. To lead by the examples of their holy and broken and submitted lives – not to boss people around and legislate behavior. That is just stepping into the role set for God and God alone. No man should be directing our paths. Only God, through His Spirit, gets to direct us! Until the Church learns this and the pyramidal, hierarchical system comes crashing down and gets inverted to it's proper form, we cannot march shoulder to shoulder without jostling each other. (See page 243.)

Here is what the Matthew Henry Concise commentary says about this passage:

> These churches were in such different states as to purity of doctrine and the power of godliness, that the words of Christ to them will always suit the cases of other churches, and professors. Christ knows and observes their state; though in heaven, yet he walks in the midst of his churches on earth, observing what is wrong in them, and what they want. The church of Ephesus is commended for diligence in duty. Christ keeps an account of every hour's work his servants do for him, and their labour shall not be in vain in the Lord. But it is not enough that we are diligent; there must be bearing patience, and there must be waiting patience. And though we must show all meekness to all men, yet we must show just zeal against their sins. The sin Christ charged this church with, is, not the having left and forsaken the object of love, but having lost the fervent degree of it that at first appeared. Christ is displeased with his people, when he sees them grow remiss and cold toward him. Surely this mention in Scripture, of Christians forsaking their first love, reproves those who speak of it with carelessness, and thus try to excuse indifference and sloth in themselves and others; our Saviour considers this indifference as sinful. They must repent: they must be grieved and ashamed for their sinful declining, and humbly confess it in the sight of God. They must endeavour to recover their first zeal, tenderness, and seriousness, and must pray as earnestly, and watch as diligently, as when they first set out in the ways of God. If the presence of Christ's grace and Spirit is slighted, we may expect the presence of his displeasure. Encouraging mention is made of what was good among them. Indifference as to truth and error, good and evil, may be called charity and meekness, but it is not so; and it is displeasing to Christ. The Christian life is a warfare against sin, Satan, the world, and the flesh. We must never yield to our spiritual enemies, and then we shall have a glorious triumph and reward. All who persevere, shall derive from Christ, as the Tree of life, perfection and confirmation in holiness and happiness, not in the earthly paradise, but in the heavenly. This is a figurative expression, taken from the account of the garden of Eden, denoting the pure, satisfactory, and eternal joys of heaven; and the looking forward to them in this world, by faith, communion with Christ, and the consolations of the Holy Spirit. Believers, take your wrestling life here, and expect and look for a quiet life hereafter; but not till then: the word of God never promises quietness and complete freedom from conflict here. —Matthew Henry Concise

The enemy of our souls convinces us that when there is conflict we need to subdivide up into chunks that will have peace. Churches and denominations split because of conflict. And yet, there is no way to build spiritual muscles – to practice patience, kindness, long-suffering, brotherly love, godliness, etc. – without conflict! If the first time God takes sandpaper to our rough edges (at the hand of another Christian) we run for somewhere without sandpaper, the end result is thousands of denominations full of fat, soft, milk-fed, couch-potato, shackled, self-deluded, immature people who are sure they're going to heaven, even though they have no real Fruit. And that's pretty much what we have now. And the enemy is winning. (And God Himself turned us over to this and blinded us to our own state because we've gone our own way.)

God wants us to be One Body and to be known by our extravagant, unstoppable, unchanging, sacrificial love for Him and for each other. By our ability to forgive any wrong, to love despite any insult, to endure through any trial, to love unconditionally despite anything that comes. But that's not what the Church of

America is known for at all right now. We're known for our political involvement, for our massive buildings, for our endless divisions, for our dress codes, for our fancy shows, for our legalistic attitudes. But surely not for our fierce, absolute love for ALL the Brethren and willingness to sell all that we have and share with each as they have a need. We're not known for our desperate, unfailing love for community and harmony and respect for the final, last wishes prayer of Jesus in John 17.

I believe it can change, but not until your town gets a Lampstand back. Not until a fire is lit. That's what happened in Ephesus in the first place. That's how they first got a Lampstand. Paul was sent by Antioch (which got lit by Jerusalem - which got lit by God Himself in the upper room at Pentecost), and he went into Ephesus and found some Christians there. They had been baptized by John and repented, but hadn't received the Holy Spirit. So Paul explained it to them, laid hands on them and lit them up with the fire of God. That was the first "spiral". First, individuals have to be lit up.

> **Acts 19:1-7** (KJV) – *1 And it came to pass, that, while Apollos was at Corinth, Paul having passed through the upper coasts came to Ephesus: and finding certain disciples, 2 He said unto them, Have ye received the Holy Ghost since ye believed? And they said unto him, We have not so much as heard whether there be any Holy Ghost. 3 And he said unto them, Unto what then were ye baptized? And they said, Unto John's baptism. 4 Then said Paul, John verily baptized with the baptism of repentance, saying unto the people, that they should believe on him which should come after him, that is, on Christ Jesus. 5 When they heard this, they were baptized in the name of the Lord Jesus. 6 And when Paul had laid his hands upon them, the Holy Ghost came on them; and they spake with tongues, and prophesied. 7 And all the men were about twelve.*

Then Paul went into the synagogues for three months, speaking boldly and <u>proving</u> through the Scriptures (that's the Old Testament, by the way) that Jesus was the Christ.

> **Acts 19:1-20** (KJV) – *8 And he went into the synagogue, and spake boldly for the space of three months, disputing and persuading the things concerning the kingdom of God. 9 But when divers were hardened, and believed not, but spake evil of that way before the multitude, he departed from them, and separated the disciples, disputing daily in the school of one Tyrannus. 10 And this continued by the space of two years; so that all they which dwelt in Asia heard the word of the Lord Jesus, both Jews and Greeks. 11 And God wrought special miracles by the hands of Paul: 12 So that from his body were brought unto the sick handkerchiefs or aprons, and the diseases departed from them, and the evil spirits went out of them.*

So He left the "institutional churches" and went out into public space and disputed and taught daily in the school of Tyrannus. He labored for two years, so that ALL who dwelt in Asia heard the word of the Lord. And God confirmed it with miracles by the hands of Paul. Even handkerchiefs that touched his body were healing people and delivering them of demons! But <u>still</u> the town won't light up. Until …

> **Acts 19:13-20** (KJV) - *13 Then certain of the vagabond Jews, exorcists, took upon them to call over them which had evil spirits the name of the Lord Jesus, saying, We adjure you by Jesus whom Paul preacheth. 14 And there were seven sons of one Sceva, a Jew, and chief of the priests, which did so. 15 And the evil spirit answered and said, Jesus I know, and Paul I know; but who are ye? 16 And the man in whom the evil spirit was leaped on them, and overcame them, and prevailed against them, so that they fled out of that house naked and wounded. 17 **And this was known to all the Jews and Greeks also dwelling at Ephesus; and fear fell on them all, and the name of the Lord Jesus***

was magnified. 18 And many that believed came, and confessed, and shewed their deeds. *19 Many of them also which used curious arts brought their books together, and burned them before all men: and they counted the price of them, and found it fifty thousand pieces of silver. 20* ***So mightily grew the word of God and prevailed.***

Do you see what was required? The difference between the counterfeits and the real thing had to be illustrated. The people had to understand that posers and fakers will get their rear ends kicked by the forces of satan! It's not just using The Name, it's having the authority behind it to handle whatever comes – and that requires holiness. The people didn't really turn until the false got stripped naked and sent screaming into the night – and then the people realized how truly desperate their state was. THEN fear fell on them – and Fear of the Lord is the <u>beginning</u> of wisdom, you can't get anywhere without that. They held the name of Jesus in high regard. And <u>many</u> who were believers came and confessed and showed their deeds. There were LOTS more Christians than probably even Paul realized – FAR more! But they were hiding. They were lukewarm. They were unrepentant of their witchcraft and idolatry. But now they get a little fear and they come together and light a big bonfire in the middle of town.

Paul brought a fire from Antioch (which was a Lampstand city) to light Ephesus. He started immediately down by the river, but it doesn't manifest in a big way until two years later. Something is percolating and the stage is being set and the spiritual weapons of war are being turned against the town – and God is confirming it with miracles – but it doesn't really, <u>really</u> light up until this moment. Then, in the "natural" the Body of Christ comes together, repents and lights a fire – burning all the objects of their idolatry! And the witchcraft and spells and other things thrown into that fire amounted to fifty thousand pieces of silver! That is approximately 150 years worth of personal income at the average wage at the time! That is FAR more than those twelve guys down by the river! This is a BIG DEAL! In American terms, that would be like a $4,000,000 bonfire! ($27K x 150)

What do you think might happen if the Body of Christ in a town in America came together and burned all their Harry Potter and New Age books and porn and all the other things that had become idols in their lives and grieved God – maybe even their TV's and Playstations and their fishing poles and their Precious Moments collection? Do you think a $4,000,000 bonfire would make the news? Do you think it would get God's attention? Do you think He might pour out His Spirit on a town that came together like that and repented for all the things they had put ahead of Him and His will? I wonder what God might do to bless a place like that?!

Well, in Ephesus, the economy starts to change pretty much instantly. It is a pagan capital and has temples to many gods, foremost among them Diana (Artemis). The temple of Diana was one of the seven wonders of the ancient world, the largest building on the planet at the time and a MAJOR tourist attraction. The silversmiths (and their demonic rulers) in Ephesus realized how much this confession and repentance was going to hurt their livelihood and so they start a riot. They charge Paul with how many people he has converted – which is a compliment and a confirmation in a round-about way. The resulting riot and the people chanting for two hours would surely have made the news today!! And why are they rioting? Because they don't like change and because their WEALTH is at risk.

Acts 19:21-41 (KJV) – *23 And the same time there arose no small stir about that way. 24 For a certain man named Demetrius, a silversmith, which made silver shrines for Diana, brought no small gain unto the craftsmen; 25 Whom he called together with the workmen of like occupation, and said, Sirs, ye know that by this craft we have* ***our wealth.*** *26 Moreover ye see and hear, that not alone at*

*Ephesus, but almost throughout all Asia, this **Paul hath persuaded and turned away much people, saying that they be no gods, which are made with hands:** 27 So that not only this our craft is in danger to be set at nought; but also that the temple of the great goddess Diana should be despised, and her magnificence should be destroyed, whom all Asia and the world worshippeth. 28 And when they heard these sayings, they were full of wrath, and cried out, saying, Great is Diana of the Ephesians. 29 And the whole city was filled with confusion: and having caught Gaius and Aristarchus, men of Macedonia, Paul's companions in travel, they rushed with one accord into the theatre. 30 And when Paul would have entered in unto the people, the disciples suffered him not. 31 And certain of the chief of Asia, which were his friends, sent unto him, desiring him that he would not adventure himself into the theatre. 32 Some therefore cried one thing, and some another: for the assembly was confused; and the more part knew not wherefore they were come together. 33 And they drew Alexander out of the multitude, the Jews putting him forward. And Alexander beckoned with the hand, and would have made his defence unto the people. 34 But when they knew that he was a Jew, all with one voice about the space of **two hours** cried out, Great is Diana of the Ephesians. 35 And when the townclerk had appeased the people, he said, Ye men of Ephesus, what man is there that knoweth not how that the city of the Ephesians is a worshipper of the great goddess Diana, and of the image which fell down from Jupiter? 36 Seeing then that these things cannot be spoken against, ye ought to be quiet, and to do nothing rashly. 37 For ye have brought hither these men, which are neither robbers of churches, nor yet blasphemers of your goddess. 38 Wherefore if Demetrius, and the craftsmen which are with him, have a matter against any man, the law is open, and there are deputies: let them implead one another. 39 But if ye enquire any thing concerning other matters, it shall be determined in a lawful assembly. 40 For we are in danger to be called in question for this day's uproar, there being no cause whereby we may give an account of this concourse. 41 And when he had thus spoken, he dismissed the assembly.*

Finally the city clerk has to calm it down and dismiss them for fear that the Romans will call it an unlawful assembly and punish the town for revolting. Most of them don't even know why they are there, but remember, this is a SPIRITUAL battle and the forces of darkness whisper to the minds of the weak and defenseless and get them to obey. Without Jesus helping us take captive every thought and bring it into obedience with Christ, the rulers of darkness whisper to us and we often obey. The enemy really, REALLY didn't like what God was doing in Ephesus. I bet for a long time he thought he was winning and Paul wasn't getting anywhere, but then all in one burst God uses the sons of Sceva to glorify His own Name and turn the tide. The result is that Ephesus becomes a Christianized city and eventually the Temple of Diana is sacked repeatedly and mostly sinks into a swamp!

http://en.wikipedia.org/wiki/Ephesus
http://en.wikipedia.org/wiki/Temple_of_Artemis

But by the time John receives the Letter to the Church of Ephesus from Jesus around A.D. 100, the Body of Christ in Ephesus had lost most of its fire. It remained a watchful group, being in the midst of a town full of idolatry – and it hated the "priest class" that tried to elevate itself above the people. Surely those in this city would see the dangers of that. Surely many ran TO Christianity because of the abuses of the priest class in their former religion. But they had lost their agape love – for Jesus and for each other. You can't lose just one or the other, as our first love leads the way and empowers our agape love for all other people.

Fellowship Of The Martyrs

WHAT IS A CITY CHURCH?

I know this might get a little detailed and you might be tempted to skim over some of these without paying too much attention, but if you're really seeking TRUTH, please stay with me here. I want to lead with the Bible, so you can see it for yourself, as He explained it to me.

Biblically, the "church" or "ekklesia" is only one of three choices.

1) Either it is the Body of Christ universal – that consists of <u>all</u> of those who have "been called out":

<u>1 Corinthians 15:9</u> *For I am the least of the apostles, that am not meet to be called an apostle, because I persecuted **the church** {ekklesia} **of God**.*

<u>Ephesians 5:27</u> *That he might present it to himself a glorious **church**, not having spot, or wrinkle, or any such thing; but that it should be holy and without blemish.*

LOTS more example of this one. I'm not going to spend time on that. That one should be obvious.

These below are the only two instances of the word "ekklesia" in the Gospels:

<u>Matthew 16:18</u> *And I say also unto thee, That thou art Peter, and upon this rock I will build **my church** {ekklesia}; and the gates of hell shall not prevail against it.*

<u>Matthew 18:17</u> *And if he shall neglect to hear them, tell [it] unto **the church** {ekklesia}: but if he neglect to hear **the church** {ekklesia}, let him be unto thee as an heathen man and a publican.*

Those in Matthew are both from the mouth of Jesus – one referring to the universal church – His Body – and the other to the local assembly (you surely can't tell anything to the whole universal assembly). All the other "ekklesia" uses are in Acts and the epistles (and again from the mouth of Jesus in Revelation).

2) Or it consists of those who are called out that live in a particular municipality:

<u>Acts 8:1</u> *And Saul was consenting unto his death. And at that time there was a great persecution against **the church which was at Jerusalem**; and they were all scattered abroad throughout the regions of Judaea and Samaria, except the apostles.*

<u>Acts 11:22</u> *Then tidings of these things came unto the ears of **the church which was in Jerusalem**: and they sent forth Barnabas, that he should go as far as Antioch.*

<u>Acts 13:1</u> *Now there were in **the church that was at Antioch** certain prophets and teachers; as Barnabas, and Simeon that was called Niger, and Lucius of Cyrene, and Manaen, which had been brought up with Herod the tetrarch, and Saul.*

<u>Acts 15:4</u> *And when they were come to Jerusalem, they were received of **the church**, and [of] the apostles and elders, and they declared all things that God had done with them.* **{This is Jerusalem.}**

<u>Acts 15:22</u> *Then pleased it the apostles and elders, with **the whole church**, to send chosen men of their own company to Antioch with Paul and Barnabas; [namely], Judas surnamed Barsabas, and Silas, chief men among the brethren:* **{This is Jerusalem.}**

<u>Acts 20:17</u> *And from Miletus he sent to Ephesus, and called the elders of **the church**.* **{of Ephesus.}**

<u>Romans 16:1</u> *I commend unto you Phebe our sister, which is a servant of **the church which is at Cenchrea**: {a suburb city of Corinth}*

1 Corinthians 11:18 For first of all, when ye come together in **the church**, I hear that there be divisions among you; and I partly believe it. **{Corinth}**

1 Corinthians 1:2 Unto **the church of God which is at Corinth**, to them that are sanctified in Christ Jesus, called [to be] saints, with all that in every place call upon the name of Jesus Christ our Lord, both theirs and ours:

2 Corinthians 1:1 Paul, an apostle of Jesus Christ by the will of God, and Timothy [our] brother, unto **the church of God which is at Corinth**, with all the saints which are in all Achaia: **{Achaia is a region, not a city.}**

Colossians 4:16 And when this epistle is read among you, cause that it be read also in **the church of the Laodiceans**; and that ye likewise read the [epistle] from Laodicea.

2 Thessalonians 1:1 Paul, and Silvanus, and Timotheus, unto **the church of the Thessalonians** in God our Father and the Lord Jesus Christ:

Revelation 2:1 Unto the angel of **the church of Ephesus** write; These things saith he that holdeth the seven stars in his right hand, who walketh in the midst of the seven golden candlesticks; **{Note: these in Revelation are all Jesus talking.}**

Revelation 2:8 And unto the angel of **the church in Smyrna** write; These things saith the first and the last, which was dead, and is alive;

Revelation 2:12 And to the angel of **the church in Pergamos** write; These things saith he which hath the sharp sword with two edges;

Revelation 3:1 And unto the angel of **the church in Sardis** write; These things saith he that hath the seven Spirits of God, and the seven stars; I know thy works, that thou hast a name that thou livest, and art dead.

Revelation 3:7 And to the angel of **the church in Philadelphia** write; These things saith he that is holy, he that is true, he that hath the key of David, he that openeth, and no man shutteth; and shutteth, and no man openeth;

Revelation 3:14 And unto the angel of **the church of the Laodiceans** write; These things saith the Amen, the faithful and true witness, the beginning of the creation of God;

3) The third option is the segment of the local church that might be meeting in a particular place:

Romans 16:5 Likewise [greet] the **church** {assembly} that is in {Greek: kata} their house. Salute my wellbeloved Epaenetus, who is the firstfruits of Achaia unto Christ. **{Remember, Achaia is a region.}**

1 Corinthians 16:19 The churches of Asia salute you. Aquila and Priscilla salute you much in the Lord, with the **church** {assembly} that is in {kata} their house.

Colossians 4:15 Salute the brethren which are in Laodicea, and Nymphas, and the **church** {assembly} which is in {kata} his house.

Philemon 1:2 And to [our] beloved Apphia, and Archippus our fellowsoldier, and to the **church** in {kata} thy house:

(The literal translations translate "church" in these contexts as "assembly" – as even the King James does in Acts 19:12 when it refers to a riotous mob – which wants nothing to do with Jesus, but at least they're in one accord!)

The word "kata" is Strong's Concordance Greek number 2596 and you can read more about how it is translated here (or go to www.BlueLetterBible.com) The short of it is that that word – kata – is not as simple as just "which is in." It's translated dozens of different ways throughout the Bible and has a sense of increasing or starting, not just sitting there. So these passages may mean that the City Church sprang from the assembly that started in their house. I'm not a Greek scholar, but I know that this particular word is not as clear-cut as to make the translation absolutely sure. Work it out yourself.

Even if it is translated correctly and means that the ekklesia was meeting in their house, that doesn't infer that it was ALL of the ekklesia in that town or that it's OK to divide up into unconnected home groups – and the clear words of Jesus are to either the Universal Church or the City Church.

These four listed above are all the references that I can find to anything smaller than a city and in these there is no implication that this assembly is a self-contained unit, but only that SOME of the ekklesia of that town are meeting in these particular houses. It's clear that there are far more references to the church universal and to the city church.

These handful of verses are often used to justify the "house church" movement that wants to return to the apostolic roots of the church – but they miss that these aren't the ONLY places that the ekklesia was meeting – they also met in Solomon's Porch and in rented spaces and in the School of Tyrannus. (Acts 5:12, Acts 28:30, Acts 19:9) God is a lot more creative than just to use homes. If you make meeting in homes an idol, then all you've got is the programmatized system we already have, but with much smaller buildings. Jesus often met in the open air and by the wells and in the streets and even in the synagogues – AND in homes. And He preached repentance to whole cities.

> Luke 4:43 And he said unto them, I must preach the kingdom of God to other **cities** also: for therefore am I sent.

> Matthew 10:23 But when they persecute you in this city, flee ye into another: for verily I say unto you, Ye shall not have gone over the **cities** of Israel, till the Son of man be come.

He wants whole CITIES to repent!

> Matthew 11:20 Then began he to upbraid the **cities** wherein most of his mighty works were done, because they repented not:

> Luke 10:13 Woe unto thee, Chorazin! woe unto thee, Bethsaida! for if the mighty works had been done in Tyre and Sidon, which have been done in you, they had a great while ago repented, sitting in sackcloth and ashes.

What I'm trying to show is that we need to disconnect the word "church" from all of the baggage that we have attached to it by our systems and structures. You're going to have to set aside for a moment what you think "church" looks like or always has been and focus on what it SHOULD be in God's economy.

Here is further evidence that the City Church is the thing. There is no regional church in the Bible. There is no structure or leader that has oversight or control beyond one city. There are no denominations or national headquarters. Here are verses where the Bible refers to multiples of churches {ekklesias}:

> 2 Corinthians 1:1 Paul, an apostle of Jesus Christ by the will of God, and Timothy [our] brother, unto the church of God which is at Corinth, with **all the saints which are in all Achaia**: {Achaia is a region, not a city. Thus ALL the saints there are greeted, not the singular "church" of Achaia.}

> 1 Corinthians 16:19 The **churches of Asia** salute you. Aquila and Priscilla salute you much in the Lord, with the church that is in their house. {Asia is a region with multiple city churches.}

> Acts 15:41 And he went through Syria and Cilicia, confirming the **churches**. {Both are regions with multiple city churches}

Act 9:31 Then had **the churches** rest throughout all **Judaea and Galilee and Samaria**, and were edified; and walking in the fear of the Lord, and in the comfort of the Holy Ghost, were multiplied. *{Judaea, Galilee and Samaria are regions with multiple city churches}*

Acts 16:4 And as they went through **the cities**, they delivered them the decrees for to keep, that were ordained of the apostles and elders which were at Jerusalem. *Act 16:5* And so were the **churches** established in the faith, and increased in number daily. *{They went through the CITIES delivering the message and thus the CHURCHES grew.}*

Romans 16:4 Who have for my life laid down their own necks: unto whom not only I give thanks, but also all **the churches of the Gentiles**. *{This is a reference to the cities outside of Israel that are primarily populated by Gentiles. There were no ekklesias that were JUST for Gentiles and excluded Jewish Christians – that would have been against everything they were teaching! (I Corin 12:12-14, etc.) This is a reference to the cities of the Gentiles in which there were assemblies.}*

1 Corinthians 14:33 For God is not [the author] of confusion, but of peace, as in all **churches** of the saints.

1 Corinthians 16:1 Now concerning the collection for the saints, as I have given order to **the churches of Galatia**, even so do ye. *{Galatia is a region with multiple city churches.}*

1 Corinthians 16:19 The **churches of Asia** salute you. Aquila and Priscilla salute you much in the Lord, with the church that is in their house. *{Asia is a region with multiple city churches.}*

2 Corinthians 8:1 Moreover, brethren, we do you to wit of the grace of God bestowed on the **churches of Macedonia**; *{Macedonia is a region with multiple city churches.}*

2 Corinthians 8:18 And we have sent with him the brother, whose praise [is] in the gospel throughout all the **churches**;

2 Corinthians 8:19 And not [that] only, but who was also chosen of the **churches** to travel with us with this grace, which is administered by us to the glory of the same Lord, and [declaration of] your ready mind:

2 Corinthians 8:23 Whether [any do enquire] of Titus, [he is] my partner and fellowhelper concerning you: or our brethren [be enquired of, they are] the messengers of the **churches**, [and] the glory of Christ.

2 Corinthians 8:24 Wherefore shew ye to them, and before the **churches**, the proof of your love, and of our boasting on your behalf.

2 Corin 11:28 Beside those things that are without, that which cometh upon me daily, the care of all the **churches**.

2 Corinthians 12:13 For what is it wherein ye were inferior to other **churches**, except [it be] that I myself was not burdensome to you? forgive me this wrong. *{Message to the church of Corinth.}*

Galatians 1:2 And all the brethren which are with me, unto the **churches of Galatia**: *{Galatia is a region.}*

Galatians 1:22 And was unknown by face unto the **churches of Judaea** which were in Christ: *{Judaea is a region.}*

1 Thessalonians 2:14 For ye, brethren, became followers of **the churches of God which in Judaea** are in Christ Jesus: for ye also have suffered like things of your own countrymen, even as they [have] of the Jews: *{Judaea is a region.}*

*2 Thessalonians 1:4 So that we ourselves glory in you in **the churches of God** for your patience and faith in all your persecutions and tribulations that ye endure:*

*Revelation 1:4 John to **the seven churches which are in Asia**: Grace [be] unto you, and peace, from him which is, and which was, and which is to come; and from the seven Spirits which are before his throne; {Asia is a region.}*

There are those that that say the Church is one and is purely spiritual and is already one body and doesn't need to be restored. Fine, in the spiritual realms, the Body is one. True enough. But in the "natural" - in this world – they are plural – churches. You can't just say the "Church" is one body and then explain away all of those verses where the Bible refers to them as being more than one. It is both. In the spirit we are one, but in the natural, we are one body per city. That is the smallest division the Lord allows. That is the only thing I can find in the Bible. The problems we have are not with the ethereal, spiritual, universal Body. All the problems that we have are a result of disobedience and rebellion in the Body of Christ that manifests in the "natural." If we can touch it, we can mess it up!

Considered differently, in ALL of these verses that refer to "churches" – not ONCE, not a single time in the Bible is there a reference to the "church_es_ in Jerusalem" or the "church_es_ in Rome" or the "church_es_ in Corinth". It's just not in there. Not ever. One town, one ekklesia. Period.

The Lord had already explained all of this to me before we ever found Watchman Nee, but I'm quoting him here because many recognize that he was a great pillar of the Church and already did so much work on this nearly 90 years ago. Here is a quote from Chapter 4 of Watchman Nee's book "The Normal Christian Church Life." (I would strongly encourage you to read his entire book. It's available free on the FOTM website.)

Watchman Nee, Chapter 4 {**Bold** emphases are mine.}
"The seven churches in Asia, referred to in the book of Revelation, comprised the church in Ephesus, the church in Smyrna, the church in Pergamos, the church in Thyatira, the church in Sardis, the church in Philadelphia, and the church in Laodicea. They were seven churches, not one. Each was distinct from the others on the ground of the difference of locality. It was only because the believers did not reside in one place that they did not belong to one church. There were seven different churches simply because the believers lived in seven different places. Ephesus, Smyrna, Pergamos, Thyatira, Sardis, Philadelphia, and Laodicea are clearly all the names of places. Not only were the seven churches in Asia founded on the basis of locality, but all the churches mentioned in Scripture were founded on the same basis. Throughout the Word of God we can find no name attached to a church save the name of a place, for example, the church in Jerusalem, the church in Lystra, the church in Derbe, the church in Colosse, the church in Troas, the church in Thessalonica, the church in Antioch. **This fact cannot be overemphasized, that in Scripture no other name but the name of a locality is ever connected with a church, and division of the church into churches is solely on the ground of difference of locality.**"

Can't you see that if there were ever supposed to be multiple churches in one town, somebody at some point in the Bible would have mentioned it? Paul would have greeted the church_es_ in Rome or some other city. But he didn't – not once.

That's because the assembly of those that live in one town are supposed to be One Body. That doesn't mean they all meet in one place, but that they are all under Christ's headship and working together. So, Biblically speaking, in God's eyes, for as long as there have been Christians in your town, there has been a "Church of Your Town."

WHAT THE CITY CHURCH IS NOT.

It's ultimately about Pride, isn't it? Surely that's how we got to 41,000+ denominations. That just CAN'T have been God's desire for us, can it? Is THIS mess what Jesus prayed for in the Garden of Gethsemane? (John 17) No. His plan is for one body in one town. His plan does not include giant autocratic networks managed by some regional or national leadership – whether by a board or by a "pope" or even by a democratic vote.

Watchman Nee, Chapter 4

"We have just seen that the boundary of a church cannot be narrower than the locality to which it belongs. **On the other hand, its boundary cannot be wider than the locality.** In the Word of God we never read of the church in Macedonia, or the church in Galatia, or the church in Judea, or the church in Galilee. Why? Because Macedonia and Galilee are provinces, and Judea and Galatia are districts. A province is not a scriptural unit of locality; neither is a district. Both include a number of units; therefore, they include a number of separate churches and do not constitute one church. **A provincial church or a district church is not according to Scripture, since it does not divide on the ground of locality, but combines a number of localities.** It is because all scriptural churches are local churches that there is no mention of state churches, provincial churches, or district churches in the Word of God.

It was not God's plan to unite the churches of different places into one church, but to have a separate church in each place. There were as many churches as there were places.

"He passed through Syria and Cilicia, confirming the churches" (Acts 15:41). Again the reference is not to one single church, because Syria and Cilicia were vast districts, each comprising a number of different places. It is permissible in political circles to unite many different places into a district and call it Syria or Cilicia, but God does not unite the believers in a number of different places and call them the church in Syria, or the church in Cilicia. There may be unions or mergers in the commercial or political world, **but God sanctions no combinations among the churches.** Each separate place must have a separate church.

God sanctions no division of the church within any one locality, and He sanctions no denominational combination of the churches in a number of localities. In Scripture there is always one church in one place, never several churches in one place, nor one church in several places. God does not recognize any fellowship of His children on a basis narrower, or wider, than that of a locality.

Nanking and Soochow are as truly separate units as Nanking and Glasgow are. In the division of churches the question of country or province does not arise; it is all a question of cities. Two cities of the same country, or the same province, have no closer relationship than two cities of different countries or different provinces. God's intention is that a church in any one locality should be a unit, and in their relationship one to the other the different churches must preserve their local character.

When God's people throughout the earth really see the local character of the churches, then they will appreciate their oneness in Christ as never before. The churches of God are local, intensely local. If any factor enters in to destroy their local character, then they cease to be scriptural churches."

Do you understand the damage that is done when men come together to build larger and larger systems? Do you see that the power plays and the money and the politics increase exponentially as a system of Man incorporates ten or a hundred or ten thousand congregations? Whether you acknowledge it or not, whether you name it that or not, you eventually end up with a pope and a board of cardinals. You end up with aristocracy that controls and manages and passes it down to those they deem worthy. You end up at the Tower of Babel again – building something that isn't of God – and the Lord has to split you up again. Isn't that what He's done with all of our denominations? Are there any that haven't split? Can dissension, division, faction, selfish ambition, envy, lust, pride, greed be anything other than the acts of the sinful nature that keep us from inheriting the Kingdom of God? (Galatians 5:19-21) How do you split a denomination or a congregation without at least SOME of those being in play?

The point is that the system we have built is built on the wrong foundation all the way down the line. There was never supposed to be a separate priest class that dominated all the sheep. We are all priests and kings and each is the temple of God. The Holy Spirit is to be our teacher – not any dogma or doctrine of Man. Those men who insist the most that it is THEIR responsibility to guide us into all truth are probably the ones that hear God's voice the least. (John 16:13-15, Eze. 34)

Hear me, there is NO hierarchical, autocratic, administrative, or other structure in the Bible that extends beyond a single city. Except the universal Body of Christ as a totality that is under His headship, there is no conglomeration of churches. If there had been a "Bishop of Asia Minor" then the letters given to the Apostle John in the book of Revelation could have been addressed to him. But there wasn't and there's not supposed to be. Yes, those things did come into place later, but there is no scriptural justification for any such thing and it should be obvious by the fruit of them over the last 1900 or so years that they are NOT from God!

Can't you see the wisdom of God in all this? If the City Church is the biggest AND smallest allowable unit of the church, then heresy is limited, global or regional control by one person is eliminated, love of money is minimized, the massive inertia of a giant organization is eliminated, they can respond to local needs and crises much better, wholesale persecution and elimination of Christians is much harder – and many more. We'll cover that more later.

The City Church is also not about a "ministerial association" where all the denominational pastors get together. By it's very nature, that is just an effort at politeness, but not a representative governing body for the Body in that town. There are too many Christians that are no longer in the institutional churches. There are too many pastors that will not even socialize with other pastors. If we had to call up all the troops for war and we put an announcement in all the "institutional church" bulletins, who many of the true warriors would we reach? Half?

Restoring the City Church doesn't mean having a city-wide Christmas concert or a pastors prayer breakfast every couple of months. It means repenting for going your own way, repenting for not having been one body all along. It means getting under Christ's headship and no other. And it will require something different and it will manifest differently in every city. More on that under the "How" section.

One of the errors that has done great damage to the reputation and desirability of the City Church is a certain current group that is intent on "restoring" the role of the Apostles and Prophets, but they describe it in terms of a tiny handful of men sitting in authority OVER all the local city churches and directing their actions. That's just TOO close to a One World Government and Church for comfort! It's likely that any strategy about autocratic control under any headship other than Jesus' is dangerously likely to be coopted. Since a one world government and church is predicted in Revelation - and the leaders aren't on our team - this should be strongly resisted.

Clearly, the city churches MUST remain independent and should fight at ALL costs the imposition of outside autocratic authority models. This is another great defense against a (coming) One-World Church, since the towns are autonomous bodies with no outside dependencies for programs or processes or funds or leadership. They can't be co-opted and they can't have their resources siphoned off to some central command and control structure with leaders that aren't truly accountable to anyone. The error of C. Peter Wagner and others is not that they want to unite the body of Christ, it's that they misunderstand the nature of authority and hierarchy and servanthood within the Church of God. (And that they think they can have that much authority without it wrecking their heads.)

The true prophets and apostles called by God don't need restoring. They are out there doing as they're told without drawing too much attention to themselves. They are known by their deeds, not by their titles or their bank accounts or their big ministry budgets. And they know enough to not want autocratic control over anything. The real ones are servants at heart and know that absolute power corrupts absolutely. They don't even trust themselves, only Jesus.

Just so we're very clear, in case you missed it or I was being too subtle. I'm convinced that according to the Bible, taking the names of Men and dividing up into factions is a heresy. Promoting factions and dissensions and teaching people that it's OK to marginalize or ignore other parts of the Body is one of the acts of the sinful nature that will keep you (and your sheep) from inheriting the kingdom of heaven. Sugarcoat it and all it a "denomination" if you like, but you're a sect and, ultimately, a cult. You cannot walk in His power while you're doing stuff like that. The Bible says that if you have something against your brother, you should leave your sacrifice at the altar and go settle it first. (Matt. 5:23-24) It says that if you take Communion unworthily and have unforgiveness in your heart and aren't rightly discerning the Lord's body you will get sick and die. (I Corin. 11:27-30) We have people in the congregations all over America that are sick and dying and no sign of the Lord healing them on any large scale. Maybe it's because we're taking Communion unworthily. How do you split a congregation or a denomination and not be still holding something against a brother? Can that be rightly discerning the Lord's body? Could that be it? Is that why people are getting supernaturally healed in Africa and India, but not here? Because Deuteronomy 28 says that if we don't carefully obey the Lord our God in our time of prosperity all the diseases of Egypt will stick to us and nobody will heal us. Wasting diseases and boils and blindness and confusion of mind – and it even says that the Lord will INVENT new diseases to torture us for having gone our own way. (Like AIDS and Ebola and Smallpox and bird flu and mad cow and ...) Go read it! He even says that just as it pleased Him to see us prosper it will please Him to see us destroyed!! I don't think we're teaching that in Sunday School!

If you don't think God is irritated about what we've done to the Body of Christ, then you must think that God changes and what used to irritate Him doesn't irritate Him anymore. Because when His children were being rebellious in Hosea and Jeremiah and Ezekiel and other places, He had no problem at all whacking them with a big stick and turning them over to their own depraved minds. I'm pretty sure that's what He's done with us. We wanted to go our own way, so He let us. We wanted to set a king over us, so He let us. And we deserve everything we've gotten and more. But there is one chance to turn this around. He gave us a simple, one-step recipe to restore it all – REPENT. To all the city churches in Revelation 2 and 3 that were criticized, the solution is the same – repent. And you better mean it. And the more of you that do it, the better.

But even one man is enough to get Him to turn. (Ezekiel 22)

And I need to mention this, just because it affects our own backyard here. About 20 years ago there was a man here in Kansas City that had a big calling on him to bring revival and to restore the Body – by means of the city church. I don't doubt that his call was genuine, there are too many confirmations of it. I don't doubt his heart. I don't doubt that God told him to restore the true church outside of the denominational walls. (In fact, I can find evidence of God raising up men to do just that in Kansas City going back nearly 200 years!)

But I do question how well he was hearing God and interpreting what he was hearing. This particular man's vision of the city church was to get a bunch of "Spirit-filled" congregations reporting to HIM and that would be the restored "Church of Kansas City." That defies the clear indication of scripture that the city church already IS and consists of ALL who have Jesus. There is no need to BUILD one, just to tune up the one that's been there all along!

His model was autocratic and top-down in nature with him as the head. Which defies the clear indication of scripture that the elders are to be servants of all, not popes. And, when pastors of particular congregations didn't want to knuckle under and join the big move of God, the "prophets" from this ministry would go and publicly preach disaster on them and their congregations. Which is just manipulation and control – and ultimately witchcraft.

I grew up in the Baptist church in Kansas City during that time and never even heard of the guy until the Fall of 2004. Evidently, nobody bothered to consider that maybe the Baptists in the Northland were also part of the Body of Christ and they should maybe include us in the big move of God. The short of the story is that this particular city church movement (and ministry) fizzled rather dramatically and publicly and hurt a lot of people in the process. There are still pastors in town that were SUBSTANTIALLY injured and have a knee-jerk reaction now to any discussion of a city church. If God gives you a really big job to do that will potentially affect MILLIONS of people – and you make it about YOU and your conferences and DVD's and your prophets – the Lord is going to turn you over to your own depraved mind and you won't even know He did it. Now all that remains is a very large prayer network, which is just ONE of the four things the angel supposedly told him to do. And, you can pretty much trace all of the excesses and goofy "Charismania" manifestations that have afflicted the church in the last twenty years back to that time in Kansas City when it all imploded.

I'm familiar with several people that were raised up _after_ that to do the same job in Kansas City. Some wouldn't give up their money or their job or their "self". The eye of the Lord ranges to and fro seeking those who will obey. And if His eye lands on you, then He'll test you – and if you fail, He'll move on to the next guy. I suspect that there have been hundreds and hundreds of people just in Kansas City that God has tried to call to do this over the years.

But even if you _can_ keep it together under all the trials and tests and spiritual warfare, if the timing isn't right, it's never going to work anyway. So we need to show a lot of mercy, because if it wasn't God's time, there was no way they were going to be able to do it right anyway. God Himself will make it fail if He's not ready for it yet. But I think _now_ is the time.

Just because someone has tried before and failed, doesn't mean it can't be done. Just because someone that was a heretic on other things spoke about a city church, doesn't mean it's not the right thing to do. Just because Benny Hinn wears a suit to preach and takes up an offering, doesn't mean those things are automatically wrong. Does it?

And, in case you haven't, let me suggest again that you read the "Red Dragon" book. If God gives you a big job to do, like restore the City Church and get the bleeding in Jesus' Body to stop – and you make it about YOU – you're going to get one big, nasty, snarly Red Dragon spirit of delusion and not even know it. The closer you got to getting it right before you messed it up, the more of God you heard and saw before you stepped off the path, the worse it's going to go for you.

That guy twenty years ago didn't get the worst Red Dragon I've seen. Joseph Smith (the founder of the Mormons) was also sent to the Kansas City area (in fact, was right here in LIBERTY!) and told to restore the Body and the City Church. He made it about him and temples, started hearing from false angels – and it all grew into a really big cult (or denomination, same difference) with a NASTY Red Dragon!

WHO IS PART OF THE CITY CHURCH?

Everybody that has the Holy Spirit in them and lives in that town is part of the Body. Period. You don't have to "join" something or be a "member" or take some class. You're either part of the Body of Christ or you're not. Any effort to divide or eliminate people or refuse fellowship to those who are His is divisive and outside of the bounds of scripture.

Watchman Nee, Chapter 4
"What then is right? **All exclusiveness is wrong. All inclusiveness (of true children of God) is right.** Denominations are not scriptural, and we ought to have no part in them, but if we adopt an attitude of criticism and think, "They are denominational; I am undenominational. They belong to sects; I belong to Christ alone"—such differentiating is definitely sectarian.

Yes, praise God I am of Christ, but my fellowship is not merely with those who **say**, "I am of Christ," but with all who **are** of Christ. What is of vital importance is not the confession, but the fact. Although these other believers say they are of Paul, of Cephas, and of Apollos, yet in fact they are of Christ. I do not so much mind what they say, but I very much mind what they are. I do not inquire whether they are denominational or undenominational, sectarian or unsectarian; I only inquire, "Are they of Christ?" **If they are of Christ, then they are my brethren.**

To say, "I am of Paul," or "I am of Cephas," is obviously sectarian; but to say, "I am of Christ," is sectarian too, though less obviously so. The confession, "I am of Christ," is good as a confession, but it is not an adequate basis for forming a separate church, since it excludes some of the children of God in a given locality by including only a certain section who say, "I am of Christ." **That every believer belongs to Christ is a fact, whether that fact be declared or not; and to differentiate between those who proclaim it and those who do not, is condemned by God as carnal.** It is the **fact** that matters, not the **declaration** of it. The sphere of a church in any place does not merely include those in that place who say, "I am of Christ," but all in that place who **are** of Christ. It extends over the entire area of the locality, and includes the **entire** number of the Christians in the locality.

To take one's stand as belonging to Christ alone is perfectly right, but to divide between Christians who take that stand and Christians who do not, is altogether wrong. To brand as sectarian those who say, "I am of Paul," or "I am of Cephas," and feel spiritually superior as we separate ourselves from them and have fellowship only with those who say, "I am of Christ," makes us guilty of the very sin we condemn in others. If we make non-sectarianism the basis of our fellowship, then we are dividing the church on a ground other than the one ordained of God, and thereby we form another sect. The scriptural ground for a church is a locality and not non-sectarianism. Any fellowship that is not as wide as the locality is sectarian. **All Christians who live in the same place as I do, are in the same church as I am, and I dare exclude none. I acknowledge as my brother, and as a fellow member of my church, every child of God who lives in my locality.** "

We should all be absolutely committed to this! I'm not calling people to leave their denominations in order to be a part of the Body of Christ. That's just goofy! Either you are or you aren't <u>already</u> a part of the Body of Christ. What building you happen to visit on Sunday morning is irrelevant. We CANNOT continue to divide the Body of Christ, even by an insistence that only those who agree with us about <u>THAT</u> can be a part of what we're doing! Some of the people that tried to restore the City Churches in the past fell into this trap – "we're the true church and you're not." It just denies the reality of the situation. **I'll keep saying it – if the Holy Spirit is in you and the Holy Spirit is in me, then we're just <u>ONE</u> and that's all there is to it!** Now we need to figure out how to act like it.

But how do we know if the Holy Spirit is in someone? How do we know if we're supposed to be one with them?

Watchman Nee, Chapter 5

"The Spirit who dwells in the heart of every believer is one Spirit; therefore, He makes all those in whom He dwells to be one, even as He Himself is one. **Christians may differ from one another in innumerable ways, but all Christians of all ages, with their countless differences, have this one fundamental likeness—the Spirit of God dwells in every one of them.** This is the secret of the oneness of believers, and this is the secret of their separation from the world. The reason for Christian unity and for Christian separation is one.

It is this inherent unity that makes all believers one, and it is this inherent unity that accounts for the impossibility of division between believers, except for geographical reasons. **Those who do not have this are outsiders; those who have it are our brethren. If you have the Spirit of Christ and I have the Spirit of Christ, then we both belong to the same Church.** Paul besought all believers to endeavor "to **keep** the oneness of the Spirit" (Eph. 4:3); he did not exhort us to **have** the oneness, but merely to **keep** it. We have it already, for obviously we cannot keep what we do not have. God has never told us to become one with other believers; we already are one. Therefore, **we do not need to create oneness; we only need to maintain it.**

We cannot **make** this oneness, since by the Spirit we **are** one in Christ, and we cannot break it, because it is an eternal fact in Christ; but we can destroy the **effects** of it, so that its expression in the Church is lost. **Alas! that we have not only failed to preserve this precious oneness, but have actually so destroyed the fruits of it, that there is little outward trace of oneness among the children of God.** "

Did you get that? We were supposed to KEEP the Oneness. What are you doing in your current situation or congregation that actively works to assure the KEEPING of the Oneness of the Spirit amongst the believers in your city? How much are you reaching out? How much are you forgiving and overlooking so that peace can reign?

Are we not the most hypersensitive, error-seekers on the planet? Even the slightest hint of a difference of opinion, and we call it heresy, throw up our hands and split off. We might even split a church because we didn't like the way a business meeting went. Or take sides in a personnel dispute and allow it to split the Body.

If it weren't so devastatingly painful to millions and insulting to God, it would almost be funny how we think so much of ourselves that we can just do our own thing and tell the rest of the Body to go take a flying leap.

Watchman Nee, Chapter 5

"How are we going to determine who are our brothers and our fellow members in the Church of God? Not by inquiring if they hold the same doctrinal views that we hold, or have had the same spiritual experiences; nor by seeing if their customs, manner of living, interests, and preferences tally with ours. We merely inquire, Are they indwelt by the Spirit of God or not? **We cannot insist on oneness of opinions, or oneness of experience, or any other oneness among believers, except the oneness of the Spirit.** That oneness there can be, and always must be, among the children of God. All who have this oneness are in the Church.

In your travels has it not sometimes happened that on a boat or train you have met a stranger, and after only a few moments of conversation you have found a pure love for him welling up in your heart? That spontaneous outgoing of love was because of the one Spirit dwelling in both hearts. Such inner spiritual oneness transcends all social, racial, and national differences.

How can we know whether or not a person has this oneness of the Spirit? In the verse immediately following Paul's exhortation to keep the oneness of the Spirit, he explains what those have in common who possess this oneness. **We cannot expect believers to be alike in everything, but there are seven things which all true believers share, and by the existence or absence of these we can know whether or not a person has the oneness of the Spirit.** Many other things are of great importance, but these seven are vital. They are indispensable to spiritual fellowship, and they are at once the minimum and the maximum requirements that can be made of any person who professes to be a fellow believer.

SEVEN FACTORS IN SPIRITUAL ONENESS

"One Body and one Spirit, even as also you were called in one hope of your calling; one Lord, one faith, one baptism; one God and Father of all, who is over all and through all and in all" (Eph. 4:4-6). A person is constituted a member of the Church on the ground that he possesses the oneness of the Spirit, and that will result in his being one with all believers on the above seven points. They are the seven elements in the oneness of the Spirit, which is the common heritage of all the children of God. In drawing a line of demarcation between those who belong to the Church and those who do not, we must require **nothing** beyond these seven lest we exclude any who belong to the family of God; and we dare not require anything **less**, lest we include any who do not belong to the divine family. **All in whom these seven are found belong to the Church; all who lack any of them do not belong to the Church.**

(1) ONE BODY. The question of oneness begins with the question of membership of the Body of Christ. The sphere of our fellowship is the sphere of the Body. Those who are outside that sphere have no spiritual relationship with us, but those who are inside that sphere are **all** in fellowship with us. We cannot make any choice of fellowship in the Body, accepting some members and rejecting others. We are all part of the one Body, and nothing can possibly separate us from it, or from one another. Anyone who has received Christ belongs to the Body, and he and we are one. **If we do not wish to extend fellowship to anyone, we must first make sure that he does not belong to the Body; if he does, we have no reason to reject him** (unless for such disciplinary reasons as are clearly laid down in the Bible).

(2) ONE SPIRIT. If anyone seeks fellowship with us, however he may differ from us in experience or outlook, provided he has the same Spirit as we have, he is entitled to be received as a brother. **If he has received the Spirit of Christ, and we have received the Spirit of Christ, then we are one in the Lord, and nothing must divide us.**

(3) ONE HOPE. This hope, which is common to all the children of God, is not a general hope, but the hope of our calling, that is, the hope of our calling as Christians. What is our hope as Christians? We hope to be with the Lord forever in glory. There is not a single soul who is truly the Lord's in whose heart there is not this hope, for to have Christ in us is to have "the hope of glory" in us (Col. 1:27). If anyone claims to be the Lord's, but has no hope of heaven or glory, his is a mere empty profession. **All who share this one hope are one, and since we have the hope of being together in glory for all eternity, how can we be divided in time? If we are going to share the same future, shall we not gladly share the same present?**

(4) ONE LORD. There is only one Lord, the Lord Jesus, and all who recognize that God has made Jesus of Nazareth to be both Lord and Christ are one in Him. **If anyone confesses Jesus to be**

Lord, then his Lord is our Lord, and since we serve the same Lord, nothing whatever can separate us.

(5) ONE FAITH. The faith here spoken of is the faith—not our beliefs in regard to the interpretation of Scripture, but the faith through which we have been saved, which is the common possession of all believers; that is, the faith that Jesus is the Son of God (who died for the salvation of sinners and lives again to give life to the dead). Anyone who lacks this vital faith does not belong to the Lord, but all who possess it are the Lord's. **The children of God may follow many different lines of scriptural interpretation, but in regard to this fundamental faith they are one.** Those who lack this faith have no part in the family of God, but all who possess it we recognize as our brothers in the Lord.

(6) ONE BAPTISM. Is it by immersion or by sprinkling? Is it single or triune? There are various forms of baptism accepted by the children of God, so if we make the form of baptism the dividing line between those who belong to the church and those who do not, we shall exclude many true believers from our fellowship. There are children of God who even believe that a material baptism is not necessary, but since they are the children of God, we dare not on that account exclude them from our fellowship. What then is the significance of the one baptism mentioned in this passage? Paul throws light on the subject in his first letter to the Corinthians. "Is Christ divided? Was Paul crucified for you? Or were you baptized into the name of Paul?" (1:13). **The emphasis is not on the form of baptism, but on the name into which we are baptized.** The first question is not whether you are sprinkled or immersed, dipped once or three times, baptized literally or spiritually; the important point is this: Into whose name have you been baptized? If you are baptized into the name of the Lord, that is your qualification for church membership. **If anyone is baptized into the name of the Lord, I welcome him as my brother, whatever the manner of his baptism.** By this we do not imply that it is of no consequence whether we are sprinkled or immersed, or whether our baptism is spiritual or literal. The Bible teaches that baptism is literal, and is by immersion, but the point here is that the **manner** of baptism is not the ground of our fellowship, but the **name** into which we are baptized. All who are baptized into the name of the Lord are one in Him.

(7) ONE GOD. Do we believe in the same personal, supernatural God as our Father? If so, then we belong to one family, and there is no adequate reason for our being divided.

The above seven points are the seven factors in that divine oneness which is the possession of all the members of the divine family, and **they constitute the only test of Christian profession.** They are the possession of every true Christian, no matter to what place or period he belongs. Like a sevenfold cord the oneness of the Spirit binds all the believers throughout the world; and however diverse their character or circumstances, provided they have these seven expressions of an inner oneness, then nothing can possibly separate them.

If we impose any conditions of fellowship beyond these seven—which are but the outcome of the one spiritual life, then we are guilty of sectarianism, for we are making a division between those who are manifestly children of God. If we apply any test but these seven, such as baptism by immersion, or certain interpretations of prophecy, or a special line of holiness teaching, or a so-called Pentecostal experience, or the resigning from any denominational church—then we are imposing conditions other than those stipulated in the Bible. All who have these seven points in common with us are our brothers, whatever their spiritual experience, or doctrinal views, or so-called church relationships. Our oneness is not based on our appreciation of the truth of our oneness, nor on our coming out from all that would contradict our oneness, but upon the actual fact of our oneness, which is made real in our experience by the indwelling Spirit of Christ. "

So, there you have it. Can you tell me where that's not scriptural? Can you show me where the Bible says it's okay to disfellowship people over differences on secondary issues? In fact, didn't the Bible say to not get caught up in useless quarrels and senseless disputes? (See references below.) I'm pretty sure.

So if the church consists of those who are called out – the ekklesia – in the local city or town, and all who have the Holy Spirit in them are a part of it, then how well are we manifesting that oneness in our cities? Is there ANY city in America where truly, the Lord is in charge and the Body in that town is under His headship? Surely the enemy has worked hard to make sure that even in the smallest towns in America there are usually two or three or more congregations of different denominations that refuse to talk to each other.

If there is a war between Good and Evil, who benefits most if the Christians refuse to work together? If there is a war between Good and Evil, whose strategy to divide and conquer is working the best? Ours or theirs?

I Timothy 6:20-21 *O Timothy, keep that which is committed to thy trust, avoiding profane and vain babblings, and oppositions of science falsely so called: which some professing have erred concerning the faith. Grace be with thee. Amen.*

2 Timothy 2:14 *Of these things put them in rememberance, charging them before the Lord that they strive not about words to no profit, but to the subverting of the hearers.*

Titus 1:10-11 *For there are many unruly and vain talkers and deceivers, especially they of the circumcision: whose mouth must be stopped, who subvert whole houses, teaching things which they aught not, for filthy lucre's sake.*

Titus 3:9-11 *But avoid foolish questions, and genealogies, and contentions and strivings about the law; for they are unprofitable and vain. A man that is a heretic after the first and second admonition reject; knowing that he that is such is subverted, and sinneth, being condemned of himself.*

James 1:26-27 *If any man among you seem to be religious, and bridleth not his tongue, but deceiveth his own heart, this man's religion is vain. Pure religion and undefiled before God and the Father is this, to visit the fatherless and widows in their affliction, and to keep himself unspotted from the world.*

Colossians 2:8 *Beware lest any man spoil you through philosophy and vain deceit, after the tradition of men, after the rudiments of the world and not after Christ.*

I Timothy 1:3-5 *As i besought thee to abide still at Ephesus, when I went into Macedonia, that thou mightest charge some that they teach no other doctrine, neither give heed to fables and endless genealogies, which minister questions, rather than godly edifying which is in the faith: so do. Now the end of the commandment is charity out of a pure heart, and of good conscience, and of faith unfeigned: from which some have swerved have turned aside unto vain jangling; desiring to be teachers of the law; understanding neither what they say, nor whereof they affirm.*

Mark 7:6-8 *He answered and said unto them, Well hath Isaiah prophesied of you hypocrites, as it is written, this people honoreth me with their lips, but their heart is far from me. Howbeit in vain do they worship me, teaching for doctrines the commandments of men. For laying aside the commandment of God, ye hold the tradition of men, as the washing of pots and cups: and many other such like things ye do.*

WHO IT'S NOT A PART?

This isn't about the real estate. It's not about the actual city itself. And it's not about the members of the "world" in that city. This is about those who are a part of the Body of Christ and live in a particular city or town.

But what about the people that live outside of city limits? Well, in Jesus' day there pretty much wasn't anybody that didn't assign their allegiance to a particular city. They might have been farmers outside the city, but when an enemy approached, they all went inside the walls and defended the town. In America in our day, it's not so clean-cut.

What we learned as we began to apply these things in Liberty, Missouri is that the Lord assigns His forces across the battle lines from those of the enemy. At one point, the Lord asked us to drive around the town seven times on seven Sunday mornings. We got out a map and began to figure the best way to drive around city limits, but the Lord stopped us and had us drive the circumference of the school district instead. In our case, that included a couple other little towns like Missouri City and Mosby and Roosterville. (Yeah, really, that's a real town.)

I asked the Lord about why the school district instead of just city limits. Didn't those towns have their own city church? Weren't they autonomous? The answer was clear. If you put a spiritual hedge of protection (or sphere) around Liberty and then go out Monday morning and bus in drug dealers and witches and all kinds of other problems from the neighboring towns into your schools, your shield is going to be useless. The Lord wanted us to line up our forces across from the system of Man (satan) that could do the most damage. And, think about it, which has more impact on the lives of a city in the long run – the city government or the school district? So in Liberty, it means that we are sister cities with those other towns because we share a system of Man that impacts our children. That doesn't mean the elders of Missouri City have to obey the elders of Liberty because their kids go to Liberty schools. It means we have to work together on that particular issue because we share a common interest there. But Missouri City is autonomous and self-directing and may choose not to be a part of anything that Liberty does. That's just fine, but Liberty still has primary responsibility for the spiritual protection and warfare over the school district.

Liberty is also the county seat and may need to coordinate with all the other city churches on county-wide prayer initiatives and other things. There may also be a time when all the city churches in the metropolitan Kansas City area or all of Missouri come together to conference or pray or repent for a wider area or coordinate resources on some other issue. But that doesn't mean that the elders from any one city get to tell the elders from any other city what to do. God will raise up the leaders in each city and appoint and anoint them himself. They don't need to be called or recruited or transferred from some other city. If God sees there is a need in a particular city that's under His headship – He will meet it. He will send or raise up all the pastors and teachers and evangelists and prophets and apostles that are needed to serve the Body in that town. And it will probably sometimes be someone really unlikely – because God always uses the foolish things to confound the wise.

I've met lots of the true elders in cities all over the country. And they are rarely (if ever) the pastors of the denominational congregations in town. But they're the most humble, and the best servants and most amazing lovers of people that you've ever met. That's what God looks for in an elder, not the number of degrees on the wall in their office. Whoever has the biggest cup of Jesus with the least "self" left in it are probably the ones that are the most dangerous to satan.

Don't let titles get you all puffed up. To be an "elder," all you have to be is a four year old in a room full of three year olds. Paul went into a town and found those who were slightly more mature than the others, set them in place as servants to all and came back in a couple years to see if they were still standing. I'm just sure that it wasn't about degrees, but about spiritual maturity, faithfulness, holiness, sacrifice and a humble, servant's heart.

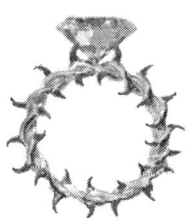

WHY RESTORE THE CITY CHURCHES?

So, Biblically speaking, in God's eyes, as long as there have been Christians in your town, there has been a "Church of YourTown."

So how is it doing?

That's the question the Lord asked me and I took a long, hard look around my town – Liberty, Missouri – and had to come to the conclusion that as one body we really, really stunk. We have a town with about 28,000 people and 40+ congregations – not including house churches or any other groupings that are hard to find. We have pastors that hate each other. We have some groups that refuse to fellowship with any other group – under ANY circumstances. We have people going hungry and homeless. We have heresies running rampant. We have a ministerial association that doesn't even represent everybody and is basically useless. (I'm sorry, if you're on it and you're reading this. You just are. People are lost and hungry and naked and you're doing pretty much diddly compared to the resources at your disposal and the expectations of our Lord. I love ya, but you're just not trying hard enough.)

Have you read Galatians 5:19-21?

> *Galatians 5:19-21* – *19 Now the works of the flesh are manifest, which are [these]; Adultery, fornication, uncleanness, lasciviousness, 20 idolatry, witchcraft, hatred, variance, emulations, wrath, strife, seditions, heresies, 21 envyings, murders, drunkenness, revellings, and such like: of the which I tell you before, as I have also told [you] in time past, that they which do such things shall not inherit the kingdom of God.* (KJV)

Some of those words are outside of our normal vocabulary, so let me give you that in the Amplified Version:

> *Galatians 5:19-21* – *19 Now the doings (practices) of the flesh are clear (obvious): they are immorality, impurity, indecency, 20 Idolatry, sorcery, enmity, strife, jealousy, anger (ill temper), selfishness, divisions (dissensions), party spirit (factions, sects with peculiar opinions, heresies), 21 Envy, drunkenness, carousing, and the like. I warn you beforehand, just as I did previously, that those who do such things shall not inherit the kingdom of God.*

Got any of those inside the body of Christ in your town? Yep. Us, too. That can't be good, can it? How can we expect to inherit all that God has for us, how can we expect to walk in the power of God, when we're full of THAT kind of stuff?! You can't. You're in direct disobedience to God and the curses of

Deuteronomy 28 will cling to you – and they are. Our people aren't getting healed, our children are being given over to foreign nations (and demons) and we are sowing much and reaping very little.

Hmmm... I thought that if we were His and we were obeying nothing could stand against us? I thought He would lift us up above all nations and we'd be the head and not the tail? So, how come we look like the tail? Must be because we're not really obeying. I can't come to any other conclusion.

How about these:

> *Proverbs 6:16-19* – *These six things doth the Lord hate: yea, seven are an abomination unto him: A proud look, a lying tongue, and hands that shed innocent blood, a heart that deviseth wicked imaginations, feet that be swift in running to mischief, a false witness that speaketh lies, and he that soweth discord among brethren.*

Let's try those one at a time:

1) **A proud look** – to raise or increase or extol self, to presumptuously promote or set up. Yep. We're sure doing that in the congregations of America.
2) **A lying tongue** – speaking vain, false or deceitful things. Yep. Lots of vanity. And if we're telling people that we don't have to be one with all the rest of the body, then we're lying to them all. Probably so that we don't have to share our stuff or be uncomfortable in any way.
3) **Hands that shed innocent blood** – taking those who have no fault and forcing error and sin upon them. Just like the Pharisees in Matt. 23, we travel to the world to make a single convert and then make them twice the denominational son of hell that we are. Read Matt. 23 and see if we're not doing every single thing in there. Jesus spoke seven woes on them. And I think we deserve every one.
4) **A heart that deviseth wicked imaginations** – this speaks to the emotions of the heart and the soulish nature and how we use our feelings to generate programs and systems and processes that feel good and vainly accomplish our own purposes. If God is to direct all of our paths, but we are directing our own, then anything we do devise are wicked imaginations and schemes of our own.
5) **Feet that are swift in running to mischief** – Are we not the most error-sensitive, heresy hunters on the planet? Are we not constantly searching for some reason to excommunicate or eliminate someone from our fellowship? The Hebrew meaning of that word "mischief" means calamity. That we are always jumping from the frying pan into the fire. Is not the "system" that we have built in America on fire?
6) **A false witness that speaketh lies** – this seems like a duplicate of the lying tongue, but God not only hates the tongue, he hates the person who allows themselves to speak lies. He puts it here twice for emphasis and to show the premium that He places on Truth. And the truth is that we are way outside of the model of harmony that He set for us.
7) **One who sows discord amongst the brethren** – How can we have gotten to 41,000+ denominations without being experts at that one?! Can there be any doubt about our guilt? Can there be any question about how God feels about what we've done?

Why the City Church? Because it's the only thing you can find in the Bible. Because it's the only thing Jesus established. Because it's the only thing that will work. Because it pleases God.

Still not buying it?

You're kidding!? After all of this, you're still holding out on me? Well, I'll keep trying.

How about this? The city church is the only thing that has a chance to withstand widespread persecution. I certainly see some really deep wisdom here as it applies to the possibility of persecution in a given locality. Since local leaders, local funds, and local assets are used, it is much harder to eliminate Christianity widely in one blow. This kind of "compartmentalization" not only limits the chances of accumulation of assets and control by one individual, but it makes it very hard for any enemy to actively stamp out the work of the Church. When wide-spread persecution of Christians comes to America (which it WILL as soon as enough Christians are acting like Jesus), the local city church model will provide lots of redundant systems and leadership and people that can take the reigns at a moments notice and even shift between localities if necessary. A state-run church can be co-opted. A few mega denomational leaders can be assassinated or bribed or threatened. Giant infrastructures can be destroyed or incorporated into a One World Church. But local assets, controlled by local leaders, led by God are VERY hard to stamp out.

If there is a war, which is harder to target? One Pentagon where all leadership and command and control is centralized – or thousands of self-contained, self-directed, self-supporting cell groups spread all over the world? And even in your particular town, which will the enemies of God have an easier time eliminating? The institutional churches with their big buildings and the pastor's name on the sign out front? Or the small groups that meet in homes and businesses and underground if necessary? It would NEVER even occur to the house church Christians in China to make a pictorial directory or report to the government how much money they've giving to a church!! If persecution comes to America, we're really going to regret that we made it so easy for them to round us all up! A local church model could effectively avoid many of these.

There is also a Biblical imperative to go to Jerusalem, Judea, Samaria and unto the ends of the earth. But if you're ignoring Jerusalem, why do you think you're qualified to go to the ends of the earth? Take care of your own home first! Are there hungry and naked and oppressed in your own town? Are there even people inside the local Body that are bleeding all over and we're ignoring them? How much budget are we spending on ourselves or sending overseas while we show the "world" in our own towns that we don't care about them? A local City Church model would bring the focus back to healing the local area first and bringing repentance and unity and harmony to the Body and to the local community, THEN we can go out and accomplish His purposes in the power of His might. Until then, we cannot inherit the Kingdom of God as He would like it to manifest on the earth right now.

This model also is ideal for general emergency management. If a natural disaster comes to a city, if the Body of Christ in that town is really talking to each other well and communicating about needs and available resources, there is probably nothing they can't do. Very high on God's priority list is the creation and application of an internet portal that connects the Body of Christ in each town to itself and to all the other local churches. (I'm aware of several redundant people that have been commissioned by God to do this and are racing to get it built.) If there is a war between good and evil, shouldn't we have some kind of central communication network that's accessible to all? Yep. God designed it and it's in the process of being built right now.

Watchman Nee, Chapter 4
"There is a beautiful balance in the teaching of God's Word regarding the relationship between the various churches. On the one hand, they are totally independent of one another in matters relating to responsibility, government, and organization. On the other hand, they are to learn from one another and to keep pace with one another. But in everything it is essential to have both the guidance of the Holy Spirit and the pattern in God's Holy Word."

Imagine if there had been a communication network across the whole of the Body of Christ in place before the hurricane hit Mississippi. The Church in New Orleans (and every other town in the Gulf) could have sent out an alert across the internet to every other town and made requests for shelter and supplies and volunteers and there could have been national and global coordination and communication with no loss or duplication of resources. If we were not divided, then each local church could inventory their assets and pray and seek God on how they were to help. Those with much could share with each as they had a need.

The life of the first century Christians described in Acts 2:42-47 is to be the same kind of relationship as that of the local churches with each other. Ultimately it's a one-on-one relationship with Christ, but we are known by our love and self-sacrifice for each other. Each town with true community. Each connected to every other community, but each reporting directly to God. Full participation and efficient delivery of resources and skills. The world would be transformed in a matter of months if the Christians actually started working together seamlessly! That's the goal. Not about authority or control, all about love and being under His headship. And He is NOT a God of confusion – we made this mess ourselves!

The local city church model also minimized the spread of heresy inside the larger Body. If a city or town goes their own way and error is rampant (as it was in Corinth), then the other cities can stem the flow of it into their own cities. We are to test and approve, after all. As with Corinth or Sardis or Laodecia, they can be in big trouble with God and it not effect Philadelphia or Smyrna or Jerusalem. But in our current model, if (for example) the Southern Baptist Convention in Nashville goes rogue, it will affect the ministry and effectiveness of tens of thousands of congregations all over the country (and the world). We are seeing it with Rome and the Episcopalians and the Lutherans and all other monoliths of man. Administrative decisions are handed down from a handful of "Cardinals" that have massive repercussions across a huge public. The media eats that up and it embarrasses the Body of Christ. But who cares if this or that little town decides something dopey that only affects a few people? That's not likely to make the news.

Additionally, if a pillar of fire descends on a denominational "church" it will likely take about 12 seconds for that denomination to send out press releases gloating about how this proves that they were the right ones all along. If a pillar of fire descends on a whole town, no one will be able to claim it and bottle it and try to sell it. God is just NOT going to allow anyone to individually promote and package what's coming. The Body of Christ in a whole town working together will make it very difficult for any single congregation, leader or denomination to take the credit for any miracles, signs, wonders or other blessings.

I can't find any other model that will work. I can't find any other model that fits with the Bible. I can't find any other model that shows as much divine wisdom and would have minimized all the problems that we're now seeing. In fact, it should be clear that pretty much as soon as the Roman empire could, they outlawed house churches, established temples, set up a priest class and began demanding sacrifices. As quickly as they could, they took the Bible away from the people so no one could even double check what they were doing against the Bible. Even now, many in the priest class will tell the laity that question them that they shouldn't be reading their Bibles because it's "over their head" or they couldn't understand it anyway without a seminary degree.

The Reformation worked in reforming some of the errors that the Roman church had established as doctrine and tradition, but it didn't actually change the fundamental structure. There remained a firmly entrenched priest class with temple worship and a willingness to kill anyone that disagreed with the leadership. We don't really talk much about how many people Martin Luther burned at the stake because they were against infant baptism (or some other thing). (Did you know that about him?) The system didn't really get rebooted back to the defaults, they just put a patch on it.

Why do it? Because it's the only thing that has EVER worked. All the Great Awakenings were about whole cities. Whether Finney or Etter or Wesley or the Salvation Army, the great moves of God involved whole towns. Not just the congregation at the intersection of Main and Broadway. The places in the world where major revivals are breaking out and cities are being changed (and economies and even ecologies!) are all about a move across the whole of the Body in that place, not just this or that denomination. Cali, Columbia changed when the Body repented. Fiji is changing because the Body repented.

Want to see how pretty it might be if the Body came together and repented and God swooped into action? Read about what happened in Manchester, Kentucky when the Body came together on the drug issue (and I wonder what might happen if they came together on ALL the issues, not just this!) - www.FellowshipOfTheMartyrs.com/manchester.htm

Yet another major benefit is that it forces us to not just BE One Body, but also to STAY One Body. There is no escape. If you don't like what is happening in the Body in your town, then either fix it or move out to another town. You don't get to split off and start your own thing just because you didn't get your way on the color of the new carpet. God hates divorce and that's what we do when we divide one body.

How else will we be able to practice those things in 2 Peter 1:5-8 (faith, goodness, knowledge, self-control, perseverance, godliness, brotherly kindness, love) and have them in increasing measure if we don't have difficult situations and people to deal with? How are we going to practice peace and forebearance and longsuffering (Romans 2:4, Ephesians 4:2, 2 Timothy 3:10-12) if we are never in situations that require longsuffering? If we keep looking for calm, peaceful congregations with no conflict and no "rubbing" on each other, then we're going to continue to be spiritual weaklings that never have any resistance training to build our Jesus muscles.

How else are we going to show the fruits of the Spirit if we don't have difficult situations to endure?

> *Galatians 5:22-26 – But the fruit of the Spirit is love, joy, peace, longsuffering, gentleness, goodness, faith, meekness, temperance: against such there is no law. And they that are Christ's have crucified the flesh with the affections and lusts. If we live in the Spirit, let us also walk in the Spirit. Let us not be desirous of vain glory, provoking one another, envying one another.*

Did you get that? How many verses do you need to read to see that if we are provoking each other and desirous of vain glory then maybe we are NOT walking in the Spirit. That can't be good!

> *Colossians 3:12-15 Put on therefore, as the elect of God, holy and beloved, bowels of mercies, kindness, humbleness of mind, meekness, longsuffering; forbearing one another, and forgiving one another, if any man have a quarrel against any: even as Christ forgave you, so also do ye. And above all these things put on charity, which is the bond of perfectness. And let the peace of God rule in your hearts, to the which also ye are called in one body; and be ye thankful.*

Exactly how many is seventy times seven? Is that how many times we forgave each other before we decided to split the church? Why do we need to be one body? Because we should have been one body all along, but we went our own way. Because we're grieving God and torturing the Body of Christ. His physical body was tortured for twenty-four hours. But His spiritual body has been undergoing endless torture for nearly 1800 years. We've been hacking His body up into smaller and smaller bits and watching it bleed – and putting a sign over this blood mess that proudly proclaims, "Behold the King of the Jews." The "world" knows this is whacked. We might as well just admit it. This can't possibly be about Jesus and what HE wants. It must be about us and what WE want.

Why do we need to do this? Because it's the right thing and it's long overdue. Because it's what the Lord wants. And, frankly, because it's coming whether you like it or not and if you fight against it, you'll just find yourself fighting against God.

MUSICAL INTERLUDE

**Sing along if you know it.
Ask a kid to sing it for you if you don't.**

This is my commandment

that you love one another

that your joy may be full.

That your joy may be full.

That your joy may be full.

This is my commandment

that you love one another

that your joy may be full.

LAMPSTAND SPIRALS

The Bible doesn't just come right out and say to do this, but there are lots of spirals. That is, repeating, increasing echoes of this and the needfulness of it. I look for the patterns of scripture, not just the direct instructions.

For example, we normally think Passover was first visible when the Children of Israel put the blood over their doorposts and the death angel killed the first born of the Egyptians. When Noah and his family closed the door behind them and were saved from the flood, that's a Passover. (Genesis 7) When Abraham offered to sacrifice Isaac and he was saved and the ram given instead, that was a type of Passover. (Genesis 22) When the Assyrians are about to destroy Jerusalem and Hezekiah repents and they leave, that's a kind of Passover (I Kings 19). When the Jews were faced with imminent destruction under Haman, but Esther turned the tide, that was a Passover. (Esther 8) When Jesus as a child avoided being killed by Herod, that was a kind of Passover. The Jewish tradition instituted by God to celebrate the Pessach (Passover) was a reminder of all the times that God had covered them and they had escaped sure death. But the big fulfillment of that was Jesus, the Lamb of the World that was slain and His Blood spread on the doorposts of our hearts so that we might not die. All those other mini-spirals were pointing to Him. And we still don't fully understand what He did for us because it's not complete. There is yet a restoration of all things and a new heaven and new earth to come.

In the same way, there are lots of examples of water baptism spirals and ritual cleansing and the need to be washed clean so that the Lord can use you. The Children of Israel had to put the blood over the doorposts in order to be saved, but then they also had to obey and leave all behind and go, and they had to go through the waters of the Red Sea and come out the other side. This is a type of baptism that cleansed them – and their Egyptian pursuers were trapped below the water. They arose from the water as free men (and women). The annointing on King Saul that made him a new man was a kind of baptism. (I Samuel 10:1) The ritual cleansing of the priests before they could be useful to God is another example (Exod. 29:4).

You getting this? Spirals. Like ripples in a pond when you throw in a rock. These repeating patterns help explain and understand what God is doing and will do. Consistency with the spirals is VERY important to Him. If something used to annoy Him, it still annoys Him. If something used to please Him, it still pleases Him. It's just a matter of the quantity involved. If America does something that is just like what Israel did and it brought massive judgement down on their heads, then we shouldn't expect it to be any different with us. You just have to insert the quantity to get an idea of the expected severity. Because we are three part beings – Body, Soul and Spirit – these spirals can have application across multiple levels all at once. Some can be physical manifestations, some spiritual – sometimes both at the same time.

Read this for more - www.fellowshipofthemartyrs.com/big_picture_one.htm

Anyway, I want to illustrate just a few of the spirals about lighting a fire that I think have application to the Lampstand understanding. Hopefully they will show you there is a consistent pattern of this in the Bible. I'm not expecting you to take my word for this – and there are surely spirals I haven't seen.

The fire of sacrifice that Abraham was willing to light, even if it cost his own son is an early example. That fire transformed the world. Without his willingness to light that fire, who knows what would have happened. (Gen. 22)

The Lord also lit the fire on the burning bush that didn't consume the bush. That is what got Moses' attention so that he would come to God and get drafted into service. It wasn't as big and flashy as the pillar of fire, but it was just for a personal application, not nationwide. Still, it's a spiral.

The Lord also lit the fire that led the Children of Israel out of Egypt and protected them from the Egyptians. The Lord Himself provided a cloud by day and a pillar of fire by night. This directional beacon guarded them, was a witness to their enemies of the power of God, lit their way and generally reminded them of the constant presence of God. (Exod. 13)

At the bottom of Sinai, the people watch as Moses goes up to meet God. The Lord doesn't need to light the fire, He IS the fire!

> **Ex 19:18** (KJV) – *And mount Sinai was altogether on a smoke, because the LORD descended upon it in fire: and the smoke thereof ascended as the smoke of a furnace, and the whole mount quaked greatly.*

The seven pronged golden lampstand in the Tabernacle and the Temple are foreshadows and spirals of the seven independent golden lampstands in Revelation. (Exod. 25; Rev. 2-3) They were one lampstand when it was one people worshipping God in one place, but now WE are the "church" and we are independent one from another because of locality. And yet, Christ walks among us and amongst all the Lampstands. In Leviticus, the priests were to tend the lamps all the time and make sure they never stopped burning.

The Ark of the Covenant itself is a type of spiral because it is a symbol of the power and presence of God in a place. When the Ark went before them, no enemy could stand against them. And it was untouchable, lest someone die. (2 Sam. 6:6-7) God's fire is real, but the power of it is too much for any man to try to harness – much less make DVD's and books and try to profit from it. It WILL reach out and kill you – and you might not even know you're dead. Be warned.

When the Children of Israel first go into the Promised Land, the VERY first thing the Lord has them do is light a fire all together. He sent them against a pagan capital, Jericho, told them how to crush it, then had them light it up like a giant sacrifice. (Judges 6) This is very much like the bonfire the Ephesians have in Acts 19 where they burn all their pagan idols. There was lots of good stuff in there they could have used, but it was a kind of First Fruits offering to God, so all of it was off-limits and to be sacrificed. This is a communal, nationwide, Lamplighting ceremony to go ahead of the Children of Israel into their Promised Land. And it worked, it scared the pants off of all the people who lived in the land!

Another good example is Gideon in Judges 6. The Lord had sent the Midianites to oppress Israel because they all had altars of Baal in their backyard. But He hears their cry and decides to free them (after sending an unnamed prophet to tell them to repent), and raises up Gideon to do it. But before Gideon can go, he has to get the altar of Baal out of his <u>own</u> backyard. God will not send him out to conquer 150,000 men while he still has an altar to a foreign God on his own land! So God doesn't require Gideon to go and preach to all of Israel and get rid of ALL the altars, just that he light ONE fire. Get one altar to God doing what it's supposed to do and then the MASSIVE weapons of war you get access to when God is your defender will kick into gear. So Gideon and ten servants go under cover of darkness and knock the altar down, use their own resources against them and burn the Asherah poles (big pointy, male fertility symbols that God hates – much like the steeples on churches) and then use his dad's second best bull as the sacrifice.

> **Judges 6:25-31** (KJV) – *25 And it came to pass the same night, that the LORD said unto him, Take thy father's young bullock, even the second bullock of seven years old, and throw down the altar of Baal that thy father hath, and cut down the grove that is by it: 26 And build an altar unto the LORD thy God upon the top of this rock, in the ordered place, and take the second bullock, and offer a burnt sacrifice with the wood of the grove which thou shalt cut down. 27 Then Gideon took ten men of his servants, and did as the LORD had said unto him: and so it was, because he feared his father's household, and the men of the city, that he could not do it by day, that he did it by night. 28 And when the men of the city arose early in the morning, behold, the altar of Baal was cast down, and the grove was cut down that was by it, and the second bullock was offered upon the altar that was built. 29 And they said one to another, Who hath done this thing? And when they enquired and asked, they said, Gideon the son of Joash hath done this thing. 30 Then the men of the city said unto Joash, Bring out thy son, that he may die: because he hath cast down the altar of Baal, and because he hath cut down the grove that was by it. 31 And Joash said unto all that stood against him, Will ye plead for Baal? will ye save him? he that will plead for him, let him be put to death whilst it is yet morning: if he be a god, let him plead for himself, because one hath cast down his altar.*

Immediately after this, Gideon blows the trumpet for war and the whole tribe shows up to help. Now, get this, they wanted to kill him, but why didn't they? Why didn't they convert the altar back? All Joash said was "Aw, c'mon guys, let Baal fight his own battles." And they left. And THEN they answer Gideon's trumpet for war a verse later! The answer is, they HATE change. Their instant reaction was to kill whoever disrupted the altar they were so used to. But something inside of them knows that the kid has a point. Yahweh is their God and this altar is better anyway. So they leave him alone. They don't go home and knock their own altars down, but they wait and watch. When God gives Gideon victory with 300 guys and the craziest warfare plan in history, then ALL the altars to Baal in all of Israel get knocked down and the people live at peace with God – until Gideon dies.

The Lord began speaking to me two years ago, "Give me ONE altar. Light ONE fire and I'll give you victory over the world. Fix the altar in your own backyard and then see what happens." My backyard is Liberty. That one fire needed to be lit. And it was lit – Praise God – on October 31, 2005.

Other examples include times when the Lord lit the fires of repentance and restoration Himself. Like the showdown between Elijah and the prophets of Baal. (I Kings 18) The whole nation got to watch God light the fire and they repented substantially and killed all the prophets of Baal.

When Solomon builds and dedicates the Temple, the Lord lights it up Himself.

> **2 Chron 7:1-3** (KJV) – *1 Now when Solomon had made an end of praying, the fire came down from heaven, and consumed the burnt offering and the sacrifices; and the glory of the LORD filled the house. 2 And the priests could not enter into the house of the LORD, because the glory of the LORD had filled the LORD'S house. 3 And when all the children of Israel saw how the fire came down, and the glory of the LORD upon the house, they bowed themselves with their faces to the ground upon the pavement, and worshipped, and praised the LORD, saying, For he is good; for his mercy endureth for ever.*

There's also practically no end to the number of times in the Bible when God is REALLY mad about all the times we light fires to foreign gods. Even when we have high places to the Lord that aren't where He intended them to be or aren't doing it right! If you complain and grumble too much, He might even send His consuming fire after YOU! (Numbers 11,16)

But God is faithful and He says He will never let it go too far. And yet, even embedded in this verse is a symbolism that references the spirals we're talking about – baptism with water and with fire.

Isaiah 43:2 (KJV) – *2 When thou passest through the waters, I will be with thee; and through the rivers, they shall not overflow thee: when thou walkest through the fire, thou shalt not be burned; neither shall the flame kindle upon thee.*

Here it is specifically laid out. Can't deny it – it's right there in the Bible. (Did you already get the "fire" part? Still waiting?)

Luke 3:16 (KJV) – *16 John answered, saying unto them all, I indeed baptize you with water; but one mightier than I cometh, the latchet of whose shoes I am not worthy to unloose: he shall baptize you with the Holy Ghost and with fire:*

The Lord Himself lit the first City Church Lampstand when He sent down tongues of fire on the people.

Acts 2:1-4 (KJV) – *1 And when the day of Pentecost was fully come, they were all with one accord in one place. 2 And suddenly there came a sound from heaven as of a rushing mighty wind, and it filled all the house where they were sitting. 3 And there appeared unto them cloven tongues like as of fire, and it sat upon each of them. 4 And they were all filled with the Holy Ghost, and began to speak with other tongues, as the Spirit gave them utterance.*

That was a change in the spiral from lighting fires on sacrifices and inanimate objects to putting the fire directly into all people. Now that WE are the temple, the fire itself doesn't change, but the vehicle changed. He didn't change. The Holy Spirit didn't change. But because we were ready, the fire could manifest inside of us. There's no reason to believe that this fire in us stopped being necessary when the Bible was completed. These are increasing spirals with increasing applications across broader and broader groups and in more powerful ways. See?

Matt 5:13-16 (KJV) – *13 Ye are the salt of the earth: but if the salt have lost his savour, wherewith shall it be salted? it is thenceforth good for nothing, but to be cast out, and to be trodden under foot of men. 14 Ye are the light of the world. A city that is set on an hill cannot be hid. 15 Neither do men light a candle, and put it under a bushel, but on a candlestick; and it giveth light unto all that are in the house. 16 Let your light so shine before men, that they may see your good works, and glorify your Father which is in heaven.*

In Acts 19, God uses an encounter with a demon to motivate the Body of Christ in Ephesus to come together, get cleaned out and light a fire that changes the town forever.

Acts 19:16-20 (KJV) – *16 And the man in whom the evil spirit was leaped on them, and overcame them, and prevailed against them, so that they fled out of that house naked and wounded. 17 And this was known to all the Jews and Greeks also dwelling at Ephesus; and fear fell on them all, and the name of the Lord Jesus was magnified. 18 And many that believed came, and confessed, and shewed their deeds. 19 Many of them also which used curious arts brought their books together, and burned them before all men: and they counted the price of them, and found it fifty thousand pieces of silver. 20 So mightily grew the word of God and prevailed.*

The final application of this spiral is when we are all in One City with One Lampstand – and it's the Lord Himself.

Rev 21:23 (KJV) – *23 And the city had no need of the sun, neither of the moon, to shine in it: for the glory of God did lighten it, and the Lamb is the light thereof.*

Won't that be great! All together in one New Jerusalem with one Lampstand – and it's HIM!! All we need to do in order to see what He wants from us is to go out to the final spiral – the biggest possible application of the City Church and the Lampstands - and then backtrack through the spirals and see how it applies to us now. What we need to do is get everything that we have now to act as much like it will in heaven as possible. Sounds reasonable, right?

If you pray the Lord's prayer, "Thy will be done in earth as it is in heaven." - then shouldn't you want us to be One Body under His headship with His fire burning right now, just like we will be later? Are we going to have denominations in heaven? Are we going to have strife and dissension and division and sects? Are we going to try to hide HIS light under a bushel?! So why is it OK to do that stuff now?

If you can't pray it and really mean it, it's probably better if you just stop praying the Lord's Prayer at all.

Helpful Visual Aid

Music Anyone?

When conditions are right a certain note is played - whether it's string tension or key positioning or wind volume. Certain conditions always result in certain notes, the only difference is octave (frequency).

People don't get the complexity of God!! His ability to say ONE thing and have DOZENS of applications!

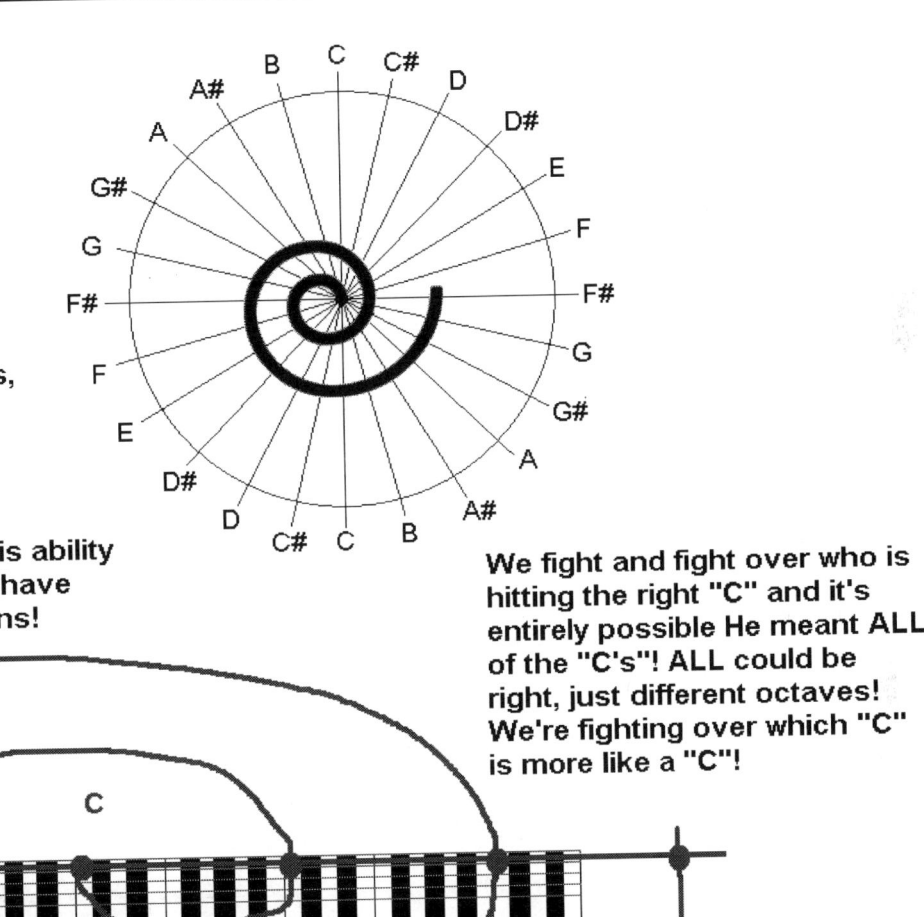

We fight and fight over who is hitting the right "C" and it's entirely possible He meant ALL of the "C's"! ALL could be right, just different octaves! We're fighting over which "C" is more like a "C"!

Different Octave, Same Note
Unison, but not identical.

Before we go any further, now might be a good time for the WARNING label.

WARNING! WARNING! DANGER! DANGER!

Proceed at your own risk!

We will NOT be responsible for ANYTHING that happens from here forward. You have been warned.

We want you to be ABSOLUTELY clear that this is <u>FOR</u> <u>SURE</u>, <u>NO DOUBT ABOUT</u> <u>IT</u> going to hurt <u>A LOT</u>.

You can drive 20 miles an hour and you probably won't get hurt too bad in an accident. If you drive 200 miles an hour and you make a mistake, it's going to get really ugly.

This IS <u>NOT</u> for sissies!

If you have ANY desire in you to slow down, DO IT NOW!
DO NOT GO THIS WAY!! DO NOT take our advice on this stuff!!
It will totally transform your life and things you love will be ripped from you.
Nothing – <u>NOTHING</u> – that you have will be your own any more.
So He can rebuild you His way, God will IMMEDIATELY start yanking chunks out of you. Probably stuff you really liked.
The fire will get VERY hot!

If you even so much as TRY to do this in your own power, you're gonna be toast!
<u>ONLY Jesus in you can get you through this.</u>

Last chance. Get out now! ALL the darkness WILL come for you!

We've seen it over and over. We <u>ARE</u> <u>NOT</u> kidding around!

If you miss a step you could end up on crack or beating your wife or drinking like a fish or in jail. We've seen it happen to good, Jesus-loving people who weren't <u>all</u> <u>the</u> <u>way</u> sold out. God will get you through, but it will hurt even more if you bail out. You BETTER mean it! We're serious.

We love you very much. We want to see you refined and purified and REALLY dangerous <u>to the enemy, but we want you to be FULLY READY before you pull into the Fast Lane!</u>

HOW MANY PEOPLE ARE REQUIRED?

This may be a shocker to you, but the Lord doesn't require some big repentance meeting in a football stadium. If it happens, great, but that's not the minimum necessary. If you're waiting until you can get 1,000 people to pray with you because you don't think it will count with just a handful – or just ONE man – then get over it and start praying.

> **Ezek 22:23-31** (KJV) – *23 And the word of the LORD came unto me, saying, 24 Son of man, say unto her, Thou art the land that is not cleansed, nor rained upon in the day of indignation. 25 There is a conspiracy of her prophets in the midst thereof, like a roaring lion ravening the prey; they have devoured souls; they have taken the treasure and precious things; they have made her many widows in the midst thereof. 26 Her priests have violated my law, and have profaned mine holy things: they have put no difference between the holy and profane, neither have they shewed difference between the unclean and the clean, and have hid their eyes from my sabbaths, and I am profaned among them. 27 Her princes in the midst thereof are like wolves ravening the prey, to shed blood, and to destroy souls, to get dishonest gain. 28 And her prophets have daubed them with untempered morter, seeing vanity, and divining lies unto them, saying, Thus saith the Lord GOD, when the LORD hath not spoken. 29 The people of the land have used oppression, and exercised robbery, and have vexed the poor and needy: yea, they have oppressed the stranger wrongfully. 30* **And I sought for a man among them, that should make up the hedge, and stand in the gap before me for the land, that I should not destroy it: but I found none.** *31 Therefore have I poured out mine indignation upon them; I have consumed them with the fire of my wrath: their own way have I recompensed upon their heads, saith the Lord GOD.*

Do you see? He was searching for **A** man, even a single solitary man, who would stand in the gap and make a hedge (a wall, a defense, a shield, a sphere). He's actively looking for one. And this wasn't just about Jerusalem. It's the same now in every city. He's actively seeking someone who will stand in the place of the original bonfire the Lord started, someone who will beg for a Lampstand and then hold it up over their head defiantly and refuse to be moved. Like Shadrach, Meshach and Abednego – someone who will take on whatever comes, knowing God will protect them. And even if He doesn't they're still not going to bow down to idols.

> **Daniel 3:17-18** (God's Word) – *17 If our God, whom we honor, can save us from a blazing furnace and from your power, he will, Your Majesty. 18 But if he doesn't, you should know, Your Majesty, we'll never honor your gods or worship the gold statue that you set up."*

We need some Davids who are fearlessly willing to go out against the Goliaths in the Land – <u>alone</u> if necessary. He has always had a soft spot for crazy, radical adventurers who have faith like a child and just KNOW that He will back them up even against 10,000 Philistines or 1,000,000 screaming demons. He wants men like Elisha who will see the defenders He has set around us – not wimps like Elisha's servant who only focus on the natural.

> **2 Kings 6:13-17** (KJV) – *13 And he said, Go and spy where he is, that I may send and fetch him. And it was told him, saying, Behold, he is in Dothan. 14 Therefore sent he thither horses, and chariots, and a great host: and they came by night, and compassed the city about. 15 And when the servant of the man of God was risen early, and gone forth, behold, an host compassed the city both with horses and chariots. And his servant said unto him, Alas, my master! how shall we do? 16 And he answered, Fear not: for they that be with us are more than they that be with them. 17 And Elisha prayed, and said, LORD, I pray thee, open his eyes, that he may see. And the LORD opened the*

eyes of the young man; and he saw: and, behold, the mountain was full of horses and chariots of fire round about Elisha.

Elisha went out and took care of this whole army alone. He walked out to meet them and by his prayers captured the whole Syrian force without any bloodshed when God made them blind. Elisha marched them inside the walls of Samaria where they were surrounded and THEN their eyes were opened – and they stopped attacking Israel when they saw the power of God and the hopelessness of trying to attack Elisha.

Now how much faith in God does it take to KNOW your prayer was already answered and go outside the walls to meet this force intent on killing you personally? Don't you think God would back up somebody who trusts Him that much? One man *is* sufficient. It will be REALLY hard and it will be a long uphill battle and you better be fully cleaned out and willing to lose anything – but one man can turn a town. In fact, for good or ill, every big thing in history is because ONE man sets his face like flint and won't be moved no matter the cost. Pick one; Martin Luther, Tyndale, Gutenberg, George Whitefield, Charles Finney, John Wesley, Alexander the Great, Napoleon, Adolf Hitler, Carl Marx, King Solomon, Elvis. One person CAN have a huge impact. (OK, Elvis is a stretch. Just seeing if you were listening.)

BUT CAN YOU PRAY THE BIG PRAYER?

The point is, when we act like Jesus, God honors it. And Jesus had MASSIVE backup. His army included enough angels to FLATTEN the planet in an instant! But He never called them. He stood alone, knowing God would back Him up. He stood in the gap for all people for all time against ALL of Hell and the weight of ALL sin. He just knew that He knew that He knew that God would back Him up. He just knew HIS Dad was bigger than THEIR Dad. That's why God loved David – and the others throughout history who have gone up against impossible odds alone (but with God at their back) and willing to lay down anything for others. That's why He loved Moses and Paul. Can you pray the BIG Prayer?

> **Exodus 32:30-32** (KJV) – *30 And it came to pass on the morrow, that Moses said unto the people, Ye have sinned a great sin: and now I will go up unto the LORD; peradventure I shall make an atonement for your sin. 31 And Moses returned unto the LORD, and said, Oh, this people have sinned a great sin, and have made them gods of gold. 32 Yet now, if thou wilt forgive their sin--; and if not, blot me, I pray thee, out of thy book which thou hast written.*

> **Romans 9:1-5** (KJV) – *1 I say the truth in Christ, I lie not, my conscience also bearing me witness in the Holy Ghost, 2 That I have great heaviness and continual sorrow in my heart. 3 For I could wish that myself were accursed from Christ for my brethren, my kinsmen according to the flesh: 4 Who are Israelites; to whom pertaineth the adoption, and the glory, and the covenants, and the giving of the law, and the service of God, and the promises; 5 Whose are the fathers, and of whom as concerning the flesh Christ came, who is over all, God blessed for ever. Amen.*

Clearly, as the ultimate Apostle, this is the model Jesus set forth for us when He offered Himself as the scapegoat for all the sins of everyone for all time. He had to have known He could never go before the Father again with all that sin on Him! Can you get your head around the kind of sacrifice that was? Not just about His physical body being beaten, but what it was like for the Son of God to be fully separated from the Father by the weight of ALL sin?

Are you willing to pray that God would blot YOU out of the Book of Life if only He would send the people into the Promised Land? What is the Promised Land for us now, but a true community under God's headship, in oneness and harmony and sharing with each as they have a need? What is the Promised Land but "church" outside the walls, all day, every day, being One Body? Doesn't that sound great?! What's it worth to you for Christ's Body to be restored and for Jesus' final prayer in the Garden of Gethsemane (John 17:21) to be answered? How much have you been begging and weeping and groaning for it to come? Can you pray the prayer of Moses? What HAVE you prayed?

> **John 15:12-13** (KJV) – *12 This is my commandment, That ye love one another, as I have loved you. 13 Greater love hath no man than this, that a man lay down his life for his friends.*

I'm not going to mince any words. (Why try to be subtle now all of a sudden?) Which is more valuable? Your physical life or your eternal life? You are a blade of grass that withers. (Job 14:1-2) But your eternal life is where your treasure is.

> **John 10:27-28** (KJV) – *27 My sheep hear my voice, and I know them, and they follow me: 28 And I give unto them eternal life; and they shall never perish, neither shall any man pluck them out of my hand.*

If you are one of His, no one can take it from you – but you CAN lay it down. I just gave you three examples of people who did (Moses, Paul and Jesus). It's your birthright, but you can offer it in exchange for another. If you have too much of YOU in your cup, there's no way you can pray that prayer. But if there is hardly any of YOU left and you're so crammed packed full of Jesus that nothing else can fit, it's no problem – because He prays that prayer really well.

I'm not going to make any excuses about this. My goal is to raise up or gather together (or whatever) the people who understand this and get them to pray together the biggest prayers they can pray and see what breaks. I know lots of them. I've helped grow some of them. NOTHING is more loving than to be willing to lay EVERYTHING down. It's nice that people give 10% to the "church". It's better that some people will offer up their car or sell their boat or invite strangers into their home. It's amazing when someone sacrifices their life for the Gospel. But ALL the forces of Hell quake in fear before those who are broken enough and sincere enough and fearless enough and so full of Jesus that they can offer up their eternal salvation if only their kinsman could enter into the Promised Land – whatever that "land" might be.

These are people who love God so much and trust Him so much that if it brings Him glory and furthers His kingdom – or heals one little old lady or restores one marriage – they will be willing to go to Hell for eternity. And this isn't a reckless self-deception or bravado or empty offer. These are not people who don't know what they are doing. These are people who may have even seen Hell. These are people who have their eyes fully open and are STILL willing to go.

Hear me, DO NOT pray that prayer unless you mean it!! You may THINK you mean it, but God will correct you REAL FAST if you're holding something back! I've seen it happen and it hurts!

My goal is to raise up the kind of people who love the brethren enough to lay down anything – including praying the Big Prayer – if only the Gospel will be preached in power and things will change. Those kind of people don't really want to argue about dogma or doctrine or any man-made thing. They do not hold tightly to their cash or their stuff or have other idols. They will lay down their family, their marriage, their hobbies, their job – anything if God tells them to. They hear His voice and they won't settle for anything less than Him directing ALL of their paths ALL of the time. They will NOT listen to man anymore. They know Jesus' voice – even when it's coming out of another person – and they won't settle for less.

Never mind teleporting through walls or being bullet proof or fire coming out of your mouth or whatever other stuff some folks have been preaching. Those people I just described are the "Manifest Sons of God" that the earth is crying out for! (Romans 8) Those who are dead to self, have a giant cup of Jesus, are walking in holiness and are unshackled from this world. Those whose love for each other is so big, so sacrificial, so totally not like the world that no one can figure them out. They are led by the Spirit and hear Him – and go and do as He says. The "glorious liberty of sonship" is absolute submission! The "Manifest Sons of God" are those who understand the meaning of the word "ALL".

> **Prov 3:5-6** (KJV) – *Trust in the LORD with **ALL** thine heart; and lean **not** unto thine own understanding. In **ALL** thy ways acknowledge him, and **he** shall direct thy paths.*

ALL thy ways and ALL thy paths. Period. All means everything – what to eat, what to wear, what to say, where to go, how to spend every dollar, what to pray – everything at every moment. Unless you think "ALL" means something else? How much freewill does a Bondservant really get? I think you had freewill just long enough to decide to be a Bondservant. Now you're not your own anymore. Bondservants don't need forty days to decide what their "personal purpose" is. They don't get to decide what they think they would like to do for the Master and King. They trust and obey – ALL the time. (Here's a tip: There's no other way to be happy in Jesus, but to trust and obey.)

These are the people who can walk shoulder to shoulder without jostling each other because they're not looking at each other for cues, they're watching the Commander in Chief – and He is their Head. (Joel 2) They keep their eyes straight ahead and keep marching. And if one falls, they don't stop and pick him up, they just keep marching and another takes his place. And yet, they are true community and have true love for each other. It is a great mystery how both can happen – and God's wisdom will be revealed in them. When they come together, the world has never seen anything like them before. But they are just the first-fruits of what's to come.

Said another way, it's entirely possible that you have made your going to heaven an idol. Ever consider that?! Are we worshiping salvation more than we're worshiping the Saver? Are we giving people a "short-cut" method to get saved and escape Hell, but allowing them to make THAT the end-all-be-all of their spiritual walk? That would make heaven an idol. And it's just as deadly to do that as to make an idol of wood or stone and bow down to it every day in your living room. We are not to worship ANY created thing – and heaven and our own eternal soul are created things – we're to worship the Creator and Him only. If you hold onto something too tightly, it's an idol. We have to hold everything in an open hand. It's all His anyway, and if He wants it, He can have it.

Extended to the extreme, that applies even to our own salvation. If He wants to send me to Hell, I totally deserve it. A thousand thousand times over I deserve it. It's only by His grace and mercy that I'm not already there. And He is really big and I'm really not, so if He wants to change His mind or cash my soul in to save someone else, who am I to argue with Him? Whatever brings Him the most glory is fine with me.

If you hear God, ask Him if I'm bluffing - or if this is bravado or blind stupidity. I'm deadly serious about this. As the Lord is my witness. *"I lie not, my conscience also bearing me witness in the Holy Ghost."*

This is the big league. If you're going to try to restore the Body of Christ, you better be ALL THE WAY willing to lay down anything He asks for. He will allow the enemy to test you – like Job. Or like Abraham's willingness to sacrifice Isaac, the son of promise. Those are the kind of people who change things. (And if you make it about YOU, He'll crush you.)

Zechariah 2:5 (KJV) – *5 For I, saith the LORD, will be unto her {the city} a wall of fire round about, and will be the glory in the midst of her.*

AN AUTOCRATIC NETWORK LED BY SUPER APOSTLES?

The City Church is NOT a massive network of apostles and prophets organized from some national headquarters to do spiritual warfare over a region larger than ONE CITY. It is NOT a hierarchical pyramid controlled by a handful of self-appointed Super Apostles who tell everyone else what to do. That is the model of C. Peter Wagner and is HUGELY dangerous and misses the whole point of the role of an apostle. I cannot stress enough the distance between what I'm talking about and what he is talking about. Just because two people are both talking about the City Church and restoration and even "transformation" does NOT mean that they are in agreement! This IS the right thing to do, but MANY have come in the past and done it the wrong way. Just because someone has tried and failed, doesn't mean it can't be done (or shouldn't). C. Peter Wagner is one of the ones who has substantially done it the wrong way. Mike Bickle did it wrong too, and admitted as much. Witness Lee did it wrong. Even Joseph Smith tried and did it wrong! I pray that C. Peter Wagner will repent and that the structures and contacts he has built will be redeemed and used for God's glory and not his own. I've never met the man, never read anything of his and I'm sure he won't like me saying this. But I expect God will back me up if I'm right. What he is building is the road to ecumenical footsies and a one world religion, not the City Church.

This is about the LOCAL city church and it's need to repent and be restored. It will have all the local leaders and elders it needs. It will have all the training and education it needs. The Holy Spirit will be their teacher and if they have a need they can't meet internally, the Holy Spirit will send the resources they need. God will make sure that the Star of the city has all the resources necessary to accomplish God's purposes. There can be NO autocratic, controlling system that is wider – or smaller – than the city itself. We must resist at all costs the imposition of legislative controls from some outside religious structure. Laodecia does not get to tell Philadelphia what to do. Jerusalem can give advice because they are the eldest, but ultimately it is only advice, not dictatorial control over any other city. Paul never went into a new city to set himself up as their new pope and tell them what to do – or force them to knuckle under the national headquarters. He went in with a team to train and teach and to raise up the elders of the city. Then he left and let them stand on their own, if they could. Sometimes he would check back and make course corrections – and he would implore or reason or cajole or beg, but he didn't have any autocratic control over any of the City Churches he planted. He was their spiritual father, but it didn't mean he got to boss them around. Ultimately Corinth or Sardis or Smyrna or Laodecia or Antioch stands or falls on their own. The Lord judges them independently of each other. (See Rev. 2-3)

The City Church model shows God's divine wisdom and is the only thing He will pour His Spirit into. It is the New Wineskin – that is, it is what we need to be renewed into. It was the first wineskin, and it was working and transforming the world, until we got into bed with the state, they outlawed house churches and we went back to the same old pagan/synagogue temple worship with a priest class. That's what satan wanted all along; to get the spread of the Gospel out of the hands of the many and put it into the hands of an elite few – who can be indoctrinated, propagandized, bribed, controlled and/or institutionalized. I don't trust any Man. Least of all some super apostles with autocratic control over hundreds of thousands or millions of people (and their dollars). The greatest among you should be the best servants.

The City Church model is the most persecution proof. It will be much harder to stamp out Christianity when it has 30,000 independent groups of elders in each locality in America who are fully self-sufficient and meeting local needs. The spread of heresy is limited if they are compartmentalized like that. If

Pittsburgh goes rogue, then all the other cities can just choose not to receive messengers from Pittsburgh and exhort and encourage them to straighten up. If the denominational walls come down, then all the members of the Body in that locality can work together and eliminate the duplication of resources and effectively meet local needs. The City Church model empowers the little guy to go be creative, to hear God and to have a huge impact. We don't even know what all the missed opportunity costs have been by stiffling the little guys through our massive networks that just hand them materials and programs and siphon off funds for global missions agencies with massive overheads and minimum impact. Dollar for dollar, there are MANY one or two person ministries having a much larger impact – and don't have a love of money ruling them. Local City Churches would have the freedom to identify and support those ministries God leads them to where they would get maximum return in heavenly treasure per dollar. If there is a widespread economic or natural disaster, the local City Church fully functioning together and meeting the needs of each without divisions or walls is the most capable of surviving. There are all kinds of other reasons why the wisdom of God will be clear in this. The point is, nothing will work better and there's nothing else (no other model) that I can find in the Bible.

REMINDER:

The City Church is NOT about getting all the Christians in town to meet in one building or under one "pastor."

The City Church is NOT about getting all the denominations together on some project – while they still remain denominational the rest of the time.

The City Church is NOT about a group prayer meeting for all the pastors.

The City Church is NOT about getting all the Christians to vote the same way so they can take over the government.

The City Church is NOT about getting agreement out of everybody on secondary theological issues.

The City Church IS simply trying to get all the Christians in town to ACT like Jesus, get under His headship and start ACTING like One Body.

If your name is in the Book of Life and my name is in the Book of Life then we're just brothers and that's all there is to it. Now we have to figure out how to get along without devouring each other.

It WILL be the hardest things you've ever tried to do.

DECLARE A HOLY FAST – ISAIAH 58

God does not change. What irritated Him then, still irritates Him now. What pleased and honored Him then, still pleases and honors Him now. These If/Then statements are guarantees! IF you do these things, then He WILL do what He said He would do – sooner or later, one way or the other. He reserves the right to manifest it in whatever way He wants, but He WILL do it.

It's equational. Like math. Just insert the quantity.

IF you do Behavior X **THEN** Consequence Y will result. Quantity N is the only variable.

$$BX(N) = CY(N)$$

Positive Behavior = Positive Consequence **OR** Negative Behavior = Negative Consequence

Get it? Doesn't even require faith. It's just a guarantee from God. Now, it may not manifest like you expect or when you expect, but it WILL happen because God's promises are good. He is faithful and just.

So here we go. Let's look at the guarantees.

Isaiah 58 (NIV)

1 "Shout it aloud, do not hold back. Raise your voice like a trumpet. Declare to my people their rebellion and to the house of Jacob their sins.

I think He's serious about this. I guess we're supposed to point out the problem as loudly as possible. This is my personal attempt to fulfill this command.

2 For day after day they seek me out; they seem eager to know my ways, as if they were a nation that does what is right and has not forsaken the commands of its God. They ask me for just decisions and seem eager for God to come near them.

So, it's not for lack of praying or evidently a desire to know what God wants. They are a whole nation who is praying and seems eager. Is it possible our churches in America seem eager, but they're off track? Could it be? That they are just pretending they are actually obeying and doing what is right?

3 'Why have we fasted,' they say, 'and you have not seen it? Why have we humbled ourselves, and you have not noticed?'

They don't seem to be getting through. God doesn't seem to be answering them very much or at all. They are praying every day, they are even fasting – and yet it doesn't seem like they are satisfied with God's response to them.

"Yet on the day of your fasting, you do as you please and exploit all your workers.

4 Your fasting ends in quarreling and strife, and in striking each other with wicked fists. You cannot fast as you do today and expect your voice to be heard on high.

Here we get God's response to them. They are fasting, but they're also exploiting people – like volunteers in the churches? Or illegal alien workers? Or sweatshop workers and child and prison labor in other countries so we can buy stuff cheap at Walmart? Could be. Oh, yeah, and we're fasting, but it always ends in quarreling and strife and striking each other. Could that be like church splits and power struggles and denominational divisions? Could that be like dividing the Body of Christ up into tiny little pieces because we don't want to play nice with others? Yeah, that could be it. Maybe we're ignoring the starving Brethren in other countries so we can have our fancy new building? That would do it. Evidently fasting and praying like we've been doing and still being selfish stinkers just isn't getting our prayers through to God. Evidently He's not paying too much attention to our petitions when we aren't acting like Jesus.

5 Is this the kind of fast I have chosen, only a day for a man to humble himself? Is it only for bowing one's head like a reed and for lying on sackcloth and ashes? Is that what you call a fast, a day acceptable to the Lord?

I think it would be quite a shocker if you actually saw someone in a "church" in sackcloth nowadays! We can't even humble ourselves and pray in public without looking like freaks! But, thankfully, here we get to hear Him tell us what He wanted all along. Now all we have to do is implement it and we'll be fine. He didn't want a show. He didn't want sackcloth and ashes when our hearts were really unrepentant and it was just for effect. If we're quarreling and striking each other, how much fear of the Lord do we really have? How much are we being like Jesus? How much do we really love each other? He says if we love Him, we'll obey Him – and He commanded us to put HIM first and each other second. (Matt. 22:37-40) How seriously should He take our fast when we're doing neither?

6 "Is not this the kind of fasting I have chosen: to loose the chains of injustice and untie the cords of the yoke, to set the oppressed free and break every yoke?

OK, we need to loose the chains of injustice, untie the yokes, set the oppressed free and break every yoke. What's that mean? Well, there are three dimensions – Body, Soul and Spirit. We need to settle issues of physical injustice and fight for those who are oppressed (like the child and prison laborers and sweat shops) and we need to set them free and then we need to break the yokes so they can't be applied to anyone else. For the Soul we need to break the chains binding people to legalism and dogma and the doctrinal laws of Man. We need to untie them from the Tree of the Knowledge of Good and Evil so they can go eat from the Tree of Life. Then we need to break the yoke permanently, so they won't get trapped again. This is primarily in the area of the mind – of teaching and training and discipleship. For the Spirit, we need to identify spiritual oppressions that have trespassed into the lives of Christians, and we need to release them from those yokes, set them free, teach them to walk it out and keep the yoke broken. This means deliverance from demonic strongholds, generational curses, addictions, lusts, fears, abuses and others. The more we do this, **on all three levels**, the more we fulfill this instruction of the Lord. NOTE: If we leave out one of the three, we are <u>not</u> in full compliance.

7 Is it not to share your food with the hungry and to provide the poor wanderer with shelter— when you see the naked, to clothe him, and not to turn away from your own flesh and blood?

Again, three levels. We need to feed and shelter and clothe and care for our own. For the Soul, we need to share the true meat of the Gospel of Life, give it to them to eat and to drink. We need to cover them and clothe them in protective armor and the white robes that are their birthright. We need to especially minister to the brethren in need. (Romans 12) In the Spirit, we need to feed them from what we have. We need to pour ourselves out and sacrificially offer anything we have in the Spirit from the abounding riches of our inheritance to meet the needs of those who are poor in spirit. We especially need to make sure we have bandaged, healed and empowered the saints in need. He promises that if you sacrifice for His Kingdom, He will replace it abundantly in this life and in the next. If you give sacrificially, that's so much like Jesus, He will always give you more. So long as you pour yourself out, He'll keep filling you and giving you a bigger cup of Jesus.

8 THEN your light will break forth like the dawn, and your healing will quickly appear; THEN your righteousness will go before you, and the glory of the Lord will be your rear guard.

9 THEN you will call, and the Lord will answer; you will cry for help, and he will say: Here am I.

So here we see the first of the consequences. <u>IF</u> you do those behaviors in verses 6 and 7, <u>THEN</u> your light will break forth like the dawn and YOUR OWN healing will quickly appear, your righteousness will go before you (because you're obeying God) and the glory of the Lord will be your rear guard AND when you call He will answer and say, "Here am I." Now that's cool! At the beginning of the chapter, they are complaining because they don't seem to be getting through to the throne. Now He says if you'll just do <u>this</u> stuff, He will ALWAYS answer you and be present. How about that?! And all we had to do was stop making it about ourselves and care for other people. Who knew?

"IF you do away with the yoke of oppression, with the pointing finger and malicious talk,

Yeah, boy, that'd be nice, wouldn't it? So, we have to lift the yokes of oppression (Body, Soul, and Spirit). Presumably we have to do it to ourselves as well, because there's no way to stop the pointing finger and malicious talk as long we still have things oppressing us. (And we wouldn't be pointing fingers and talking maliciously UNLESS we had things oppressing us, so don't think you don't. Things like jealousy, control, envy, pride, fear, bitterness – they're all strongholds of the enemy.) You can be sure our light WILL NOT arise so long as we're pointing fingers and talking maliciously about each other! Why don't more miracles happen in America? Maybe because we're the most finger-pointing, malicious-talking branch of the church on the planet. Could be. Why should God show up and be our rear guard and answer our call and bring healing quickly given what stinkers we're being? If your six year old bashed his brother over the head with a toy truck, you'd put him in a time out to think about what he's done until he's ready to say he's sorry. "But I'm hungry." Forget it. "But I want to watch TV." Forget it! You're not getting out of the time out until you say you're SORRY for bashing your brother over the head – and mean it – and then I expect you to stop doing it from now on! What kind of parent lets them keep bashing their brother over the head without consequences?

10 and IF you spend yourselves in behalf of the hungry and satisfy the needs of the oppressed, THEN your light will rise in the darkness, and THEN your night will become like the noonday.

What do you think "spend yourselves" means? That seems like it means "all the way spent." The King James says if you "draw out thy <u>soul</u> to the hungry." Seems practically sacrificial! Probably substantially more than the 2% Americans average in giving to church and charity. Not to mention that less than 5% of the income of the churches themselves is actually spent on the hungry and needy. (That's 5% of the 2% feeding the hungry. Hmmm. That's 0.1%!) The vast majority of the money is spent on ourselves, our own programs and buildings and staffs. Anyway, so IF we spend ourselves – really spend ourselves – on the hungry (Body, Soul and Spirit) and meet the needs of the oppressed (Body, Soul and Spirit), THEN our light will rise in the darkness and our night will be like noonday. That's how bright we will be! Even in the middle of the night it will be like noonday. Even in the midst of gross darkness (like America), the shadows will flee from the glory of God shining through us and reflecting off of us. And all we had to do was stop making it about ourselves. Wow. It's all so simple – how did we squirrel it up this badly?

Actually this is a compound formula – "IF and IF/THEN and THEN" but the formula works the same.

11 The Lord will guide you always; he will satisfy your needs in a sun-scorched land and will strengthen your frame. You will be like a well-watered garden, like a spring whose waters never fail.

This is a continuation of the THEN/THEN. He promises to guide your steps (Prov. 3:5-6). He promises to satisfy your needs and to make you strong. He promises to bring fruit to your garden. That means water and light will come to grow our harvests. He says rivers of living water will flow up from inside us and will never be quenched – even though we're in a dry, sun-scorched land.

12 Your people will rebuild the ancient ruins and will raise up the age-old foundations; you will be called Repairer of Broken Walls, Restorer of Streets with Dwellings.

More positive consequences from careful devotion and obedience. We get to rebuild on the ancient foundations – which is Jesus. We get to stand in the gap and rebuild the ancient walls – the defenses and protections to the people inside (which are currently clearly not working). And we get to restore streets with dwellings. People will come home and be safe. People will flourish inside the walls and be protected again. Note that this is about a city. He wants us rebuilding and restoring the walls of protection around our cities. That means Body, Soul and Spirit. That we become a true community again and meet local needs for physical and spiritual protection. What is a true community? Do we even remember what it was like? Was Andy Griffith's Mayberry the last one in America? Is it possible to have that again in this post-modern world? God says it is. At least within the Body of Christ on the local level.

13 "IF you keep your feet from breaking the Sabbath and from doing as you please on my holy day, IF you call the Sabbath a delight and the Lord's holy day honorable, and IF you honor it by not going your own way and not doing as you please or speaking idle words,

That means resting when He tells us to rest. It also means that we honor the Sabbath (and Jesus, who is our Sabbath Rest) by NOT going our own way and by obeying Him implicitly. (Heb. 4:9-10) We bring all these blessings on us by NOT doing as we please and speaking idle words. What are idle words? For sure that malicious talk stuff from v.9, but also ANYTHING that comes out of our mouth that JESUS didn't put there. All the useless quarrels and arguments about doctrines of demons and endless genealogies and all the stuff that doesn't upbuild the kingdom or break yokes, lift chains, free captives – but makes us look smart to people that are impressed by that kind of stuff. Not just on Sunday (or Saturday), it means EVERY day you stop the idle, useless words and stop going your own. EVERY day is His. All means all.

14 THEN you will find your joy in the Lord, and I WILL cause you to ride on the heights of the land and to feast on the inheritance of your father Jacob."

The mouth of the Lord has spoken.

Amen!

Do you see how the inverses of all of this work the same? Why would He bless us when we are actually PLACING heavier and heavier yokes on the people? Why would He cause us to ride on the heights of the land when America is the main producers and exporters of idle talk and pointing fingers on this whole planet? Why would He have us rebuild on the ancient foundations if we're just going to make it all about US?!

These blessings come when you do these things. Your fire, your Lampstand, WILL NOT light until you repent and start doing it the right way. How many of you? The more the better, but even ONE MAN will do. (Ezek. 22) But if it's just one guy, it's probably going to really, really be a long, hard, uphill fight! The more the better.

ROMANS 12

Romans 12 (KJV) – *1 I beseech you therefore, brethren, by the mercies of God, that ye present your bodies a living sacrifice, holy, acceptable unto God, which is your reasonable service. 2 And be not conformed to this world: but be ye transformed by the renewing of your mind, that ye may prove what is that good, and acceptable, and perfect, will of God.*

There's the simple three step plan: **1)** Get all cleaned off (holy) and offer your bodies as a living sacrifice. What body? Your own body? Yes. Your family? Yes. The Body of Christ in your city? Yes. All have to be holy so they will be an acceptable sacrifice to God. This is your reasonable – and bare minimum – service in thanks for His mercy and patience with you. **2)** climb up on the altar and lay there naked – which is definitely not conforming to the "world". **3)** When He is good and ready, He'll take a big sword and hack your head off and graft His head on. THEN you will know what is the good, acceptable, perfect will of God.

Until you get cleaned off and offer up everything you have as a sacrifice, stop conforming to the world, and grow up into Him who is the head (Eph. 4:15), then you won't really know what He wants. You'll just have to guess – or lean on your own understanding (Prov. 3:5-6), which is a bad thing, right? Maybe you could hire consultants and do demographic studies. Maybe you could see what seems to be working in the business world and apply it to the "church". Whatever you do, you're on your own power until you know what is His pleasing, perfect will. And you CANNOT know that until your mind is renewed and it won't get renewed until you STOP CONFORMING TO THE WORLD! Do I need to say this again? Please hear me. It's all very simple. If you love the world and look just like them and the way they do things, then you're a whore and you're an enemy of God. Period.

Does that seem too harsh? Cause I didn't make it up. It's right there in the Bible.

James 4:4 (KJV) – *Ye adulterers and adulteresses, know ye not that the friendship of the world is enmity with God? whosoever therefore will be a friend of the world is the enemy of God.*

We're supposed to be strangers in a strange land. (I Peter 2:11) This is NOT our home. The natural man can never understand the things of the spirit. We're not supposed to fit in. We're not supposed to be like them. (John 15)

3 For I say, through the grace given unto me, to every man that is among you, not to think of himself more highly than he ought to think; but to think soberly, according as God hath dealt to every man the measure of faith.

Humility is an accurate assessment of who you are in Christ and what your role is in the big picture. It is understanding that the greatest among you will be the one who is the best servant. The one who seeks to gain – and enjoys glory and power and public notice – is living in his reward already and shouldn't expect any more in heaven. The one who washes feet, the one who sits at the end of the table, the one who lifts everyone else up to God instead of drawing men unto himself – <u>that</u> is the one Jesus loves. If we see ourselves through the eyes of Jesus, we will be intensely encouraged by the inheritance of our position as adopted sons, but we will also be hugely humbled to see how we really fit into HIS economy. Do not make this about YOU! It's all about Jesus.

4 For as we have many members in one body, and all members have not the same office: 5 So we, being many, are one body in Christ, and every one members one of another.

We need to accurately understand who each is in Christ and what they bring. Not to serve the pastor or the institution, but to serve the Body. Every town will have all that it needs. All the giftings will be present when the Body in that town is under Christ's headship and going where He directs. He will make sure every need is met and all the right people are in place to accomplish His purposes. When we start actually loving and respecting all the different and unique Body Parts, there is no telling what will happen!

6 Having then gifts differing according to the grace that is given to us, whether prophecy, let us prophesy according to the proportion of faith; 7 Or ministry, let us wait on our ministering: or he that teacheth, on teaching; 8 Or he that exhorteth, on exhortation: he that giveth, let him do it with simplicity; he that ruleth, with diligence; he that sheweth mercy, with cheerfulness.

These are all Gifts of the Spirit that are still active and necessary today. You can't pick and choose which ones ended when the Bible was completed! We still need mercy and exhortation and teaching – and we still need prophecy as well. Not to add to the Bible, but to help the people be built up and complete in Christ. All of them need to be operating decently and in order and so that we will grow up.

9 Let love be without dissimulation. Abhor that which is evil; cleave to that which is good. 10 Be kindly affectioned one to another with brotherly love; in honour preferring one another;

That word, "dissimulation" is sort of obscure. What it means is "unfeigned" or truthfully without any fakeness. We need to love all the way and not just be polite with a veneer of putting up with each other. Like the Pharisees and Sadducees put up with each other – until Paul said something about the resurrection of the dead, then the fight was on! (Acts 23:6-10) I wonder what would happen at a Ministerial Association breakfast if someone stood up and said, "The Gifts of the Spirit are real and alive and God speaks to people and anybody who says otherwise is a heretic and a liar!" I bet that would peel away the veneer of politeness! What the Lord wants is for us to REALLY love each other, not just tolerate. We're to have brotherly love for each other, setting the other person's needs first. Is that what we have out there in the Body of Christ in America? Is that how we got 41,000+ denominations?

11 Not slothful in business; fervent in spirit; serving the Lord; 12 Rejoicing in hope; patient in tribulation; continuing instant in prayer; 13 Distributing to the necessity of saints; given to hospitality. 14 Bless them which persecute you: bless, and curse not. 15 Rejoice with them that do rejoice, and weep with them that weep.

You have to understand that all of this is about a holy fast. This is about giving up stuff we like. We put ourselves on the altar as a sacrifice. We love others when we want to wring their neck. We give up our time to prayer. We share our stuff with the saints. We open our home to strangers. We weep with those who are weeping, even if we don't feel like it. This is all about the same kind of holy fast Isaiah 58 talks about. It's about what the Lord wants us to give up – not just food – but everything we have and are, so <u>others</u> can be built up and God can be glorified by the harmony and cooperation of His Body.

16 Be of the same mind one toward another. Mind not high things, but condescend to men of low estate. Be not wise in your own conceits.

We're not going to all agree on everything. But maybe we could agree on this one thing – we all see through a glass darkly. NONE of us have all the answers. If you think you do, then you are "wise in your own conceits." On some things, maybe I see less darkly than you do. On others, I see more clearly. Regardless, we're all sinners and heretics and have something we're probably holding on to that is grieving God. Why argue about whose theology is more messed up? Why throw rocks at who we think is the bigger heretic? If you are a part of a sect of Christianity, then you've made up your own religion and cut and pasted out of the Bible all the parts about not doing that. Can't we just all agree we're ALL whacked? Maybe we could just all hit your knees in agreement and repent for SOMETHING. Let's stop fighting about who is the <u>most</u> whacked. What's the point? If you think you have all the answers than you're wise in your own conceits.

17 Recompense to no man evil for evil. Provide things honest in the sight of all men.

We're supposed to turn the other cheek and forgive seventy times seven. That's a hard fast. Giving up what we want to say or fighting back is a hard one. Far easier to not eat for a day or two than to have a friend stab you in the back and smile about it. But the Lord has very high expectations of His children who say they want to be like Jesus.

18 If it be possible, as much as lieth in you, live peaceably with all men.

Are we doing that? Or are we just living at peace with the people that are like us? We're supposed to live at peace with even the most difficult, disagreeable, hair-pulling, back-stabbing folks. We're not supposed to divide the Body up into pieces so we can avoid them. We're supposed to feed them and clothe them and pray for them and let Christ in us be shown by our love for each other – especially the MOST difficult people to love.

19 Dearly beloved, avenge not yourselves, but rather give place unto wrath: for it is written, Vengeance is mine; I will repay, saith the Lord.

Couldn't we just wait and trust that He will sort it out? Unbelief is as the sin of witchcraft and He REALLY hates witchcraft. Why is unbelief like witchcraft? Because we don't think He will get things the way we want them, so we try to help Him by forcing movement ourselves. We don't believe that if we needed something to be different, He would have changed it already. We don't wait on Him to do His work, we try to do it ourselves according to our own understanding. And that's witchcraft and manipulation – and He hates that. He'll take care of it. Just rest.

20 Therefore if thine enemy hunger, feed him; if he thirst, give him drink: for in so doing thou shalt heap coals of fire on his head.

Here's God's backwards strategy for warfare. If they want to get the burning coals off their head, then they need to be a friend and stop being an enemy. This has natural and spiritual applications. We feed them physically and spiritually, as He directs. We share with each as they have a need, from the abundance of what He's given us. And see what happens.

21 Be not overcome of evil, but overcome evil with good.

How are we doing on that one? Who is winning? Maybe we're not doing it right.

THUS SAITH THE LORD

Ephesians 4:1-32 (ASV)
1 I therefore, the prisoner in the Lord, beseech you to walk worthily of the calling wherewith ye were called,
2 with all lowliness and meekness, with longsuffering, forbearing one another in love; 3 giving diligence to keep the unity of the Spirit in the bond of peace.
4 There is one body, and one Spirit, even as also ye were called in one hope of your calling; 5 one Lord, one faith, one baptism, 6 one God and Father of all, who is over all, and through all, and in all.
7 But unto each one of us was the grace given according to the measure of the gift of Christ. 8 Wherefore he saith, When he ascended on high, he led captivity captive, And gave gifts unto men. 9 (Now this, He ascended, what is it but that he also descended into the lower parts of the earth? 10 He that descended is the same also that ascended far above all the heavens, that he might fill all things.)
11 And he gave some to be apostles; and some, prophets; and some, evangelists; and some, pastors and teachers; 12 for the perfecting of the saints, unto the work of ministering, unto the building up of the body of Christ: 13 till we all attain unto the unity of the faith, and of the knowledge of the Son of God, unto a fullgrown man, unto the measure of the stature of the fulness of Christ: 14 that we may be no longer children, tossed to and fro and carried about with every wind of doctrine, by the sleight of men, in craftiness, after the wiles of error; 15 but speaking truth in love, we may grow up in all things into him, who is the head, even Christ; 16 from whom all the body fitly framed and knit together through that which every joint supplieth, according to the working in due measure of each several part, maketh the increase of the body unto the building up of itself in love.
17 This I say therefore, and testify in the Lord, that ye no longer walk as the Gentiles also walk, in the vanity of their mind, 18 being darkened in their understanding, alienated from the life of God, because of the ignorance that is in them, because of the hardening of their heart; 19 who being past feeling gave themselves up to lasciviousness, to work all uncleanness with greediness.
20 But ye did not so learn Christ; 21 if so be that ye heard him, and were taught in him, even as truth is in Jesus: 22 that ye put away, as concerning your former manner of life, the old man, that waxeth corrupt after the lusts of deceit; 23 and that ye be renewed in the spirit of your mind, 24 and put on the new man, that after God hath been created in righteousness and holiness of truth.
25 Wherefore, putting away falsehood, speak ye truth each one with his neighbor: for we are members one of another.
26 Be ye angry, and sin not: let not the sun go down upon your wrath: 27 neither give place to the devil.
28 Let him that stole steal no more: but rather let him labor, working with his hands the thing that is good, that he may have whereof to give to him that hath need.
29 Let no corrupt speech proceed out of your mouth, but such as is good for edifying as the need may be, that it may give grace to them that hear.
30 And grieve not the Holy Spirit of God, in whom ye were sealed unto the day of redemption.
31 Let all bitterness, and wrath, and anger, and clamor, and railing, be put away from you, with all malice: 32 and be ye kind one to another, tenderhearted, forgiving each other, even as God also in Christ forgave you.

CALL A SOLEMN ASSEMBLY AND SANCTIFY THE PEOPLE

When the locusts have eaten everything and you've declared a holy fast, the next step is to gather the people and have a solemn assembly with those who are consecrated/sanctified.

> **Joel 1:14** (KJV) – *14 Sanctify ye a fast, call a solemn assembly, gather the elders and all the inhabitants of the land into the house of the LORD your God, and cry unto the LORD,*

> **Joel 2:12-17** (ASV) – *12 Yet even now, saith Jehovah, turn ye unto me with all your heart, and with fasting, and with weeping, and with mourning: 13 and rend your heart, and not your garments, and turn unto Jehovah your God; for he is gracious and merciful, slow to anger, and abundant in lovingkindness, and repenteth him of the evil. 14 Who knoweth whether he will not turn and repent, and leave a blessing behind him, even a meal-offering and a drink-offering unto Jehovah your God? 15 Blow the trumpet in Zion, sanctify a fast, call a solemn assembly; 16 gather the people, sanctify the assembly, assemble the old men, gather the children, and those that suck the breasts; let the bridegroom go forth from his chamber, and the bride out of her closet. 17 Let the priests, the ministers of Jehovah, weep between the porch and the altar, and let them say, Spare thy people, O Jehovah, and give not thy heritage to reproach, that the nations should rule over them: wherefore should they say among the peoples, Where is their God?*

But what does it mean? Who qualifies as "elders" or "priests"? How do you "sanctify the assembly"? If you just get the whole town together in a football stadium, does that do it?

Surely, the best thing is to get everybody on board. This verse indicates that even those on their honeymoon need to stop everything. Even breastfeeding babies need to be there! The community needs to show a level of dedication to this that shows their understanding of the priority that needs to be placed on repentance. But it doesn't mean they are all in a place to pray with authority. While they all gather, it's the "priests, the ministers of Jehovah" who are to weep publicly and cry out to God. They're the ones with authority and legal ground.

Whoever gathers, they need to be sanctified. How do you do that? Well, first you make sure they are personally cleaned out, that they are circumcised of heart and have fully repented for themselves. You need people who have the inside of their cup clean – and not just the outside. (Matt. 23:25-26) You make it clear that the first order of business is to sweep clean any personal sins for which they are unrepentant. That means they need to be covered and washed in the Blood of Jesus. Which you can't do if you're not one of His. So the first thing is that this isn't about the "world" coming to pray with us, this is about the Jesus lovers.

And who are the "elders" and "ministers of Jehovah"? Well, don't get a big head. All you have to do to be "elder" is be a four year old in a room full of three year olds! The point is, these CANNOT be the denominational leaders who refuse to lay down their man-made divisions and dogmas. They are not sanctified and cannot pray for unity and harmony with any credibility until they lay down their own baggage. More likely these are the people in town with the biggest cup of Jesus who are outside of the boxes. These are the people God Himself has set in place to minister to Him and to the people. They're probably already feeding the hungry and clothing the naked and being like Jesus. They have a gift of repentance and can repent in spirit and in truth when they ask Him to make the people One Body. They could be little old ladies in wheelchairs, they could be kids, they could be the apostles and prophets and pastors the Lord Himself has raised up and nobody even knows are there. There is absolutely NO indication that this means the members of the Ministerial Association. They may or may not even be part of the Body of Christ. I'm not saying that some of them may not be the "elders" and "priests" over the town – I've met some who are – but it is rare that seminarians can lay down everything and really be one body.

They must be people that who legal ground to repent for the city. They have to be residents of the city or have been sent by God to the city for this purpose. Paul had legal ground to repent for Ephesus because God sent him there as an apostle. But people from the next town over aren't going to be helpful in getting these prayers through. They need to go pray for the Body of Christ in their own town. Identificational confession is important here. Moses could confess on Sinai for the people, because they were his people. I can confess for sins of the Body of Christ in my town, including the African-Americans and other groups who live here. But I can't just confess and repent for the sins of the African-American community as a whole, because I'm not a member and don't have legal ground there. God has raised up someone else for that. I can't repent for all the women who have let the spirit of Jezebel rule and taken spiritual headship away from their husbands. But I can repent for the Body of Christ in Liberty not having taught them right sooner. God is VERY technical about authority lines and legal authority. If we are going to march shoulder to shoulder without jostling each other, then we need to be very clear about the importance of not trying to do someone else's job for them – or overstepping our boundaries of authority. We need to understand very clearly from the Lord what is our sphere of authority. It may just be your own home – or your business.

The hypocrites need to stay home. Those who are unwilling to repent, those who think everything is just fine, those who think we need to have denominations and they are a good thing. They need to all just stay home. All they're going to do is quench the Spirit and clog up the pipeline. Their hearts are hard and the Lord is evidently not ready to release them from their Red Dragons. So a gift of repentance cannot be poured out on them and they're no good for this kind of praying. Those who can will need to pray for them – and pray around them – but it's better if they stay home.

If you get the whole Body of Christ in the town to come together in a football stadium or a big tent to pray, you're surely going to also gather up witches and warlocks and others trying desperately to stop this. You're going to pick up denominational leadership who thinks this is nuts and unnecessary and would like to stop it. So in addition to the massive spiritual resistance from the enemy who doesn't want to see a town light up, you're going to have people (who are listening to the enemy) resisting at every step. Maybe even legally or illegally trying to stop it. I have no idea how ugly this could get. The Salvation Army officers in the height of their revival days were regularly assaulted, beaten, threatened and even killed. Most of the great revivalists had constant warfare spiritually and physically. Many died young.

I'm not telling you not to do it that way. I'm not telling you to do it any particular way. You need to get everything out of the way, hear God really well and do whatever He tells you. What I am telling you is that those who are actually weeping and mourning between the temple porch and the altar need to really mean it and have authority. Nobody should be there for show or because everybody else is doing it or for any reason other than the true brokenness of their heart and desire for God to restore the land. If there is any selfish motive in it, the Holy Spirit will know that it's not pure. Ananias and Sapphira tried to lie to the Holy Spirit and He killed them on the spot. (Acts 5:1-11) Don't mess with God!

When the Lord asked us to do this in Liberty in August of 2005, we invited everybody we could think of who might be an elder (over 60 people, including the pastors of all 40+ congregations in town) and left it to the Lord to get the right people there. Three business men showed up. But they were outside of the "boxes" and had legal ground and were repented up personally and in divine order. The Lord made sure He had the right people there to repent on behalf of the town.

Whoever and however many gather, the first order of business should be a complete personal repentance, then for our families and our homes, THEN for our city. You have to work your way up through the progression. Like spirals or ripples in a puddle. Taking each bit of ground and making sure it's clean. Before the high priest would go into the temple to offer sacrifices for the people each year, he had to offer sacrifices for himself and his own house, then wash his hands, put on the consecrated garments and THEN he could go into the holy of holies and offer sacrifices for the people of Israel. They would tie a rope around his waist just in case he wasn't all the way clean when he went in – and God killed him. That way they could drag his dead body out and decide who was going to go in next!

God is really motivated to get this done, so He'll help a lot. Just seek Him and do whatever He tells you. He'll make sure all the right folks are there. Just make sure you keep your focus on confession and repentance, not on worship and praise while you're all still knee-deep in your unrepented sins and man-made idolatry. He hates that.

> **Psalms 106:1-48** (KJV) – 34 They did not destroy the nations, concerning whom the LORD commanded them: 35 But were mingled among the heathen, and learned their works. 36 And they served their idols: which were a snare unto them. 37 Yea, they sacrificed their sons and their daughters unto devils, 38 And shed innocent blood, *even* the blood of their sons and of their daughters, whom they sacrificed unto the idols of Canaan: and the land was polluted with blood. 39 Thus were they defiled with their own works, and went a whoring with their own inventions. 40 Therefore was the wrath of the LORD kindled against his people, insomuch that he abhorred his own inheritance. 41 And he gave them into the hand of the heathen; and they that hated them ruled over them. 42 Their enemies also oppressed them, and they were brought into subjection under their hand. 43 Many times did he deliver them; but they provoked him with their counsel, and were brought low for their iniquity. 44 Nevertheless he regarded their affliction, when he heard their cry: 45 And he remembered for them his covenant, and repented according to the multitude of his mercies. 46 He made them also to be pitied of all those that carried them captives. 47 Save us, O LORD our God, and gather us from among the heathen, to give thanks unto thy holy name, *and* to triumph in thy praise. 48 Blessed *be* the LORD God of Israel from everlasting to everlasting: and let all the people say, Amen. Praise ye the LORD.

REPENT AND WEEP AND MOURN BEFORE THE ALTAR

The translations of the Bible sort of use the word "repent" and "confess" interchangeably at times, but it's very important that we be specific here about what we're talking about. I have had pastors (never laity) complain that we can't repent on behalf of someone else. That public repentance for a city is wrong and unbiblical. OK, here's the thing, the word "repent" means to turn away from your sin. It's an action and I can't take that action on behalf of someone else. I can't stop sinning for my wife or my kids or my ekklesia. But I certainly <u>can</u> confess my sins and the sins of my house. There are lots of Biblical examples – and even commands – about that. You need to understand that forgiveness of sins doesn't come in the <u>repenting</u>, it comes in the <u>confessing</u>. First you wash it clean by confessing it and offering a sacrifice (in our case the Blood of the Lamb of God), then you stop doing it (turn away). You don't get forgiven when you don't do it again. You get forgiven when you confess it and say you're sorry. Need Biblical proof?

> **1 John 1:8-10** (KJV) – 8 *If we say that we have no sin, we deceive ourselves, and the truth is not in us. 9 If we **confess** our sins, he is faithful and just to forgive us our sins, and to cleanse us from all unrighteousness.*

Num 5:6-7 (KJV) – *6 Speak unto the children of Israel, When a man or woman shall commit any sin that men commit, to do a trespass against the LORD, and that person be guilty; 7 Then they shall **confess** their sin which they have done: and he shall recompense his trespass with the principal thereof, and add unto it the fifth part thereof, and give it unto him against whom he hath trespassed.*

Psalms 32:5-6 (KJV) – *5 I acknowledged my sin unto thee, and mine iniquity have I not hid. I said, I will **confess** my transgressions unto the LORD; and thou forgavest the iniquity of my sin. Selah. 6 For this shall every one that is godly pray unto thee in a time when thou mayest be found: surely in the floods of great waters they shall not come nigh unto him.*

Psalms 38:18 (KJV) – *18 For I will declare mine iniquity; I will be sorry for my sin.*

See? We need to admit we have a problem and then we need to say we're sorry. And He'll forgive us. But THEN He expects us to show fruit in keeping with repentance. (Matt. 3:8) We need to stop going back to our sin like a dog to its vomit. (2 Peter 2:22) We need to make recompense or be willing to accept our just punishment.

Are you with me? I'm NOT saying you can repent on behalf of someone else. But you CAN confess on behalf of someone else IF you have authority. If you're an elder, you're the spiritual leader, or you are set in place and anointed by God for that purpose. You CAN also transfer the sins of the people – or take them on yourself if you're willing.

Lev 16:21-22 (KJV) – *21 And Aaron shall lay both his hands upon the head of the live goat, and **confess** over him all the iniquities of the children of Israel, and all their transgressions in all their sins, putting them upon the head of the goat, and shall send him away by the hand of a fit man into the wilderness: 22 And the goat shall bear upon him all their iniquities unto a land not inhabited: and he shall let go the goat in the wilderness.*

Ex 32:30-32 (KJV) – *30 And it came to pass on the morrow, that Moses said unto the people, Ye have sinned a great sin: and now I will go up unto the LORD; peradventure I shall make an atonement for your sin. 31 And Moses returned unto the LORD, and said, Oh, this people have sinned a great sin, and have made them gods of gold. 32 Yet now, if thou wilt forgive their sin--; and if not, blot me, I pray thee, out of thy book which thou hast written.*

Here we see two examples of Old Testament transferral of the sins. The high priest Aaron, would go into the temple every year, after making atonement for his own sins, and would confess all the sins of Israel and place them on the head of the "scape goat" that would then be led off into the wilderness to never be seen again. This is a "spiral," a foreshadowing of the Lamb of God who would take away the sins of the whole world. Jesus Christ was the scape goat for all of us. The Father transferred onto Him all the sins of all men for all time.

John 1:29 (KJV) – *29 The next day John seeth Jesus coming unto him, and saith, Behold the Lamb of God, which taketh away the sin of the world.*

1 John 2:1-2 (KJV) – *1 My little children, these things write I unto you, that ye sin not. And if any man sin, we have an advocate with the Father, Jesus Christ the righteous: 2 And he is the propitiation for our sins: and not for ours only, but also for the sins of the whole world.*

We no longer have to offer sacrifices of animals, because the Blood of Jesus is good for all time. But we DO still need to avail ourselves of the Blood. Sometimes we need to specifically confess our sins and ask the Father to cover them in the Blood and wash them away – to send them out into the wilderness of His forgetfulness. And sometimes He calls us to confess for our people or for our land. I'm not making this up. It's entirely Biblical.

Lev 26:40-42 (KJV) – *40 **If** they shall confess their iniquity, and the iniquity of their fathers, with their trespass which they trespassed against me, and that also they have walked contrary unto me; 41 And that I also have walked contrary unto them, and have brought them into the land of their enemies; **if** then their uncircumcised hearts be humbled, and they then accept of the punishment of their iniquity: 42 **Then** will I remember my covenant with Jacob, and also my covenant with Isaac, and also my covenant with Abraham will I remember; and I **will** remember the land.*

(It's another IF/THEN guarantee. See it? IF you confess for you and your fathers, THEN I will remember you.)

2 Chron 7:12-14 (KJV) – *12 And the LORD appeared to Solomon by night, and said unto him, I have heard thy prayer, and have chosen this place to myself for an house of sacrifice. 13 **If** I shut up heaven that there be no rain, or **if** I command the locusts to devour the land, or **if** I send pestilence among my people; 14 **If** my people, which are called by my name, shall humble themselves, and pray, and seek my face, and turn from their wicked ways; **then** will I hear from heaven, and will forgive their sin, and **will** heal their land.*

James 5:15-16 (KJV) – *15 And the prayer of faith shall save the sick, and the Lord shall raise him up; and if he have committed sins, they shall be forgiven him. 16 Confess your faults one to another, and pray one for another, that ye may be healed. The effectual fervent prayer of a righteous man availeth much.*

Besides Moses (listed above praying the BIG Prayer), here are some specific examples of people doing this very thing.

Nehemah 1:5-9 (KJV) (Nehemiah praying for his people.)

5 And said, I beseech thee, O LORD God of heaven, the great and terrible God, that keepeth covenant and mercy for them that love him and observe his commandments: 6 Let thine ear now be attentive, and thine eyes open, that thou mayest hear the prayer of thy servant, which I pray before thee now, day and night, for the children of Israel thy servants, and confess the sins of the children of Israel, which we have sinned against thee: both I and my father's house have sinned. 7 We have dealt very corruptly against thee, and have not kept the commandments, nor the statutes, nor the judgments, which thou commandedst thy servant Moses. 8 Remember, I beseech thee, the word that thou commandedst thy servant Moses, saying, If ye transgress, I will scatter you abroad among the nations: 9 But if ye turn unto me, and keep my commandments, and do them; though there were of you cast out unto the uttermost part of the heaven, yet will I gather them from thence, and will bring them unto the place that I have chosen to set my name there.

Daniel 9:1-19 (KJV) (Daniel praying for his people.)

*3 **And I set my face unto the Lord God, to seek by prayer and supplications, with fasting, and sackcloth, and ashes:** 4 And I prayed unto the LORD my God, and made my confession, and said, O Lord, the great and dreadful God, keeping the covenant and mercy to them that love him, and to them that keep his commandments; 5 We have sinned, and have committed iniquity, and have done wickedly, and have rebelled, even by departing from thy precepts and from thy judgments: 6 Neither have we hearkened unto thy servants the prophets, which spake in thy name to our kings, our princes, and our fathers, and to all the people of the land. 7 O Lord, righteousness belongeth unto thee, but unto us confusion of faces, as at this day; to the men of Judah, and to the inhabitants of Jerusalem, and unto all Israel, that are near, and that are far off, through all the countries whither thou hast driven them, because of their trespass that they have trespassed against thee. 8 O Lord, to us belongeth confusion of face, to our kings, to our princes, and to our fathers, because we have sinned* *against thee. 9 To the Lord our God belong mercies and forgivenesses, though we have rebelled against him; 10 Neither have we obeyed the voice of the LORD our God, to walk in his laws, which he set before us by his servants the prophets. 11 Yea, all Israel have transgressed thy law, even by departing, that they might not obey thy voice; therefore the curse is poured upon us, and the oath that is written in the law of Moses the servant of God, because we have sinned against him. 12 And he hath confirmed his words, which he spake against us, and against our judges that judged us, by bringing upon us a great evil: for under the whole heaven hath not been done as hath been done upon Jerusalem. 13 As it is written in the law of Moses, all this evil is come upon us: yet made we not our prayer before the LORD our God, that we might turn from our iniquities, and understand thy truth. 14 Therefore hath the LORD watched upon the evil, and brought it upon us: for the LORD our God is righteous in all his works which he doeth: for we obeyed not his voice. 15 And now, O Lord our God, that hast brought thy people forth out of the land of Egypt with a mighty hand, and hast gotten thee renown, as at this day; we have sinned, we have done wickedly. 16 O Lord, according to all thy righteousness, I beseech thee, let thine anger and thy fury be turned away from thy city Jerusalem, thy holy mountain: because for our sins, and for the iniquities of our fathers, Jerusalem and thy people are become a reproach to all that are about us. 17 Now therefore, O our God, hear the prayer of thy servant, and his supplications, and cause thy face to shine upon thy sanctuary that is desolate, for the Lord's sake. 18 O my God, incline thine ear, and hear; open thine eyes, and behold our desolations, and the city which is called by thy name: for we do not present our supplications before thee for our righteousnesses, but for thy great mercies. 19 O Lord, hear; O Lord, forgive; O Lord, hearken and do; defer not, for thine own sake, O my God: for thy city and thy people are called by thy name.*

Lamentations 2:10-19 (KJV) (These are the elders of Jerusalem praying for their people.)
10 The elders of the daughter of Zion sit upon the ground, and keep silence: they have cast up dust upon their heads; they have girded themselves with sackcloth: the virgins of Jerusalem hang down their heads to the ground. 11 Mine eyes do fail with tears, my bowels are troubled, my liver is poured upon the earth, for the destruction of the daughter of my people; because the children and the sucklings swoon in the streets of the city. 12 They say to their mothers, Where is corn and wine? when they swooned as the wounded in the streets of the city, when their soul was poured out into their mothers' bosom. 13 What thing shall I take to witness for thee? what thing shall I liken to thee, O daughter of Jerusalem? what shall I equal to thee, that I may comfort thee, O virgin daughter of Zion? for thy breach is great like the sea: who can heal thee? 14 Thy prophets have seen vain and foolish things for thee: and they have not discovered thine iniquity, to turn away thy captivity; but have seen for thee false burdens and causes of banishment. 15 All that pass by clap their hands at thee; they hiss and wag their head at the daughter of Jerusalem, saying, Is this the city that men call The perfection of beauty, The joy of the whole earth? 16 All thine enemies have opened their mouth against thee: they hiss and gnash the teeth: they say, We have swallowed her up: certainly this is the day that we looked for; we have found, we have seen it. 17 The LORD hath done that which he had devised; he hath fulfilled his word that he had commanded in the days of old: he hath thrown down, and hath not pitied: and he hath caused thine enemy to rejoice over thee, he hath set up the horn of thine adversaries. 18 Their heart cried unto the Lord, O wall of the daughter of Zion, let tears run down like a river day and night: give thyself no rest; let not the apple of thine eye cease. 19 Arise, cry out in the night: in the beginning of the watches pour out thine heart like water before the face of the Lord: lift up thy hands toward him for the life of thy young children, that faint for hunger in the top of every street.

Will He really forgive us and our people if we pray and mean it?

> **Micah 7:18-19** (KJV) – *18 Who is a God like unto thee, that pardoneth iniquity, and passeth by the transgression of the remnant of his heritage? he retaineth not his anger for ever, because he delighteth in mercy. 19 He will turn again, he will have compassion upon us; he will subdue our iniquities; and thou wilt cast all their sins into the depths of the sea.*

He'll even forgive the worst of the worst if they humble themselves!

> **1 Kings 21:25-29** (KJV) (This is Ahab, the worst king Israel ever had!)
>
> *25 But there was none like unto Ahab, which did sell himself to work wickedness in the sight of the LORD, whom Jezebel his wife stirred up. 26 And he did very abominably in following idols, according to all things as did the Amorites, whom the LORD cast out before the children of Israel. 27 And it came to pass, when Ahab heard those words, that he rent his clothes, and put sackcloth upon his flesh, and fasted, and lay in sackcloth, and went softly. 28 And the word of the LORD came to Elijah the Tishbite, saying, 29 Seest thou how Ahab humbleth himself before me? because he humbleth himself before me, I will not bring the evil in his days: but in his son's days will I bring the evil upon his house.*

> **Jonah 3:5-10** (KJV) (This is Ninevah, the most evil city of the day!)
>
> *5 So the people of Nineveh believed God, and proclaimed a fast, and put on sackcloth, from the greatest of them even to the least of them. 6 For word came unto the king of Nineveh, and he arose from his throne, and he laid his robe from him, and covered him with sackcloth, and sat in ashes. 7 And he caused it to be proclaimed and published through Nineveh by the decree of the king and his nobles, saying, Let neither man nor beast, herd nor flock, taste any thing: let them not feed, nor drink water: 8 But let man and beast be covered with sackcloth, and cry mightily unto God: yea, let them turn every one from his evil way, and from the violence that is in their hands. 9 Who can tell if God will turn and repent, and turn away from his fierce anger, that we perish not? 10 And God saw their works, that they turned from their evil way; and God repented of the evil, that he had said that he would do unto them; and he did it not.*

Other examples also of God having mercy on Saul, on David, on Samson, on Nebuchadnezzar, and many others.

But what happens if we are <u>supposed</u> to repent and weep and mourn for the sad state of things but we <u>refuse</u>?

Oh, you just had to go and ask that, didn't you. Well, it gets <u>really</u> ugly.

> **Isaiah 22:12-14** (KJV) – *12 And in that day did the Lord GOD of hosts call to weeping, and to mourning, and to baldness, and to girding with sackcloth: 13 And behold joy and gladness, slaying oxen, and killing sheep, eating flesh, and drinking wine: let us eat and drink; for to morrow we shall die. 14 And it was revealed in mine ears by the LORD of hosts, Surely this iniquity shall not be purged from you till ye die, saith the Lord GOD of hosts.*

Here the Lord calls for repenting, but they're going on with their party. In fact, they're partying even more because they're going to die anyway. But He would have turned if they had heard His voice and obeyed. Instead, He's going to flatten them. Go read Lamentations to see what results from this kind of stuff. Women are cooking and eating their own babies. Just like Deuteronomy 28 said would happen if you didn't obey.

> **Isaiah 1:18-20** (God's Word) – *18 "Come on now, let's discuss this!" says the* L*ORD*. *"Though your sins are bright red, they will become as white as snow. Though they are dark red, they will become as*

white as wool. 19 If you are willing and obedient, you will eat the best from the land. 20 But if you refuse and rebel, you will be destroyed by swords." The Lord has spoken.

OUCH! You think that's bad? Try this one!

Ezek 9:1-11 (KJV) – *1 He cried also in mine ears with a loud voice, saying, Cause them that have charge over the city to draw near, even every man with his destroying weapon in his hand. 2 And, behold, six men came from the way of the higher gate, which lieth toward the north, and every man a slaughter weapon in his hand; and one man among them was clothed with linen, with a writer's inkhorn by his side: and they went in, and stood beside the brasen altar. 3 And the glory of the God of Israel was gone up from the cherub, whereupon he was, to the threshold of the house. And he called to the man clothed with linen, which had the writer's inkhorn by his side; 4 And the LORD said unto him, Go through the midst of the city, through the midst of Jerusalem, and* **set a mark upon the foreheads of the men that sigh and that cry for all the abominations that be done in the midst thereof**.

5 And to the others he said in mine hearing, Go ye after him through the city, and smite: let not your eye spare, neither have ye pity: 6 Slay utterly old and young, both maids, and little children, and women: but come not near any man upon whom is the mark; and begin at my sanctuary. Then they began at the ancient men which were before the house. 7 And he said unto them, Defile the house, and fill the courts with the slain: go ye forth. And they went forth, and slew in the city. 8 And it came to pass, while they were slaying them, and I was left, that I fell upon my face, and cried, and said, Ah Lord GOD! wilt thou destroy all the residue of Israel in thy pouring out of thy fury upon Jerusalem? 9 Then said he unto me, The iniquity of the house of Israel and Judah is exceeding great, and the land is full of blood, and the city full of perverseness: for they say, The LORD hath forsaken the earth, and the LORD seeth not. 10 And as for me also, mine eye shall not spare, neither will I have pity, but I will recompense their way upon their head. 11 And, behold, the man clothed with linen, which had the inkhorn by his side, reported the matter, saying, I have done as thou hast commanded me.

Here we see the remnant that is weeping and mourning for the sins of Jerusalem getting a mark. The glory of the Lord leaves the Temple and everybody who <u>doesn't</u> have the mark gets mercilessly slaughtered! And all their dead bodies get piled in the Temple. I think we're WAY overdue for weeping and mourning. I think God has been sending prophets to preach the urgency of this to the people for a long time. But nobody will listen.

One day the Lord led me back to this passage again. After I read it, out of the blue, the Lord quietly said, "You know, I already did that. Your temples are all full of dead bodies." OUCH!! He's totally right! I've been to dozens of them and I have to admit that mostly the people there are spiritually dead, but think they're just fine! I think we're WAY overdue. If we don't start weeping and mourning in a big way soon, there may not be anybody left.

THUS SAITH THE LORD

Jeremiah 3:12-25 (KJV)
12 Go and proclaim these words toward the north, and say, Return, thou backsliding Israel, saith the LORD; *and* I will not cause mine anger to fall upon you: for I *am* merciful, saith the LORD, *and* I will not keep *anger* for ever. 13 **Only acknowledge thine iniquity**, that thou hast transgressed against the LORD thy God, and hast scattered thy ways to the strangers under every green tree, and ye **have not obeyed my voice**, saith the LORD. 14 Turn, O backsliding children, saith the LORD; for I am married unto you: and I will take you one of a city, and two of a family, and I will bring you to Zion: 15 And I will give you pastors according to **mine** heart, which shall feed you with knowledge and understanding. 16 And it shall come to pass, when ye be multiplied and increased in the land, in those days, saith the LORD, they shall say no more, The ark of the covenant of the LORD: neither shall it come to mind: neither shall they remember it; neither shall they visit *it*; neither shall *that* be done any more. 17 At that time they shall call Jerusalem the throne of the LORD; and all the nations shall be gathered unto it, to the name of the LORD, to Jerusalem: neither shall they walk any more after the imagination of their evil heart. 18 In those days the house of Judah shall walk with the house of Israel, and they shall come together out of the land of the north to the land that I have given for an inheritance unto your fathers. 19 But I said, How shall I put thee among the children, and give thee a pleasant land, a goodly heritage of the hosts of nations? and I said, **Thou shalt call me, My father; and shalt not turn away from me.**
20 Surely *as* a wife treacherously departeth from her husband, so have ye dealt treacherously with me, O house of Israel, saith the LORD. 21 A voice was heard upon the high places, weeping *and* supplications of the children of Israel: for they have perverted their way, *and* they have forgotten the LORD their God. 22 **Return, ye backsliding children, *and* I will heal your backslidings.**
Behold, we come unto thee; for thou art the LORD our God. 23 Truly in vain is salvation hoped for from the hills, and from the multitude of mountains: truly in the LORD our God is the salvation of Israel. 24 For shame hath devoured the labour of our fathers from our youth; their flocks and their herds, their sons and their daughters. 25 We lie down in our shame, and our confusion covereth us: for we have sinned against the LORD our God, we and our fathers, from our youth even unto this day, and have not obeyed the voice of the LORD our God.

Hosea 4:1-10 (KJV)
1 Hear the word of the LORD, ye children of Israel: for the LORD hath a controversy with the inhabitants of the land, because *there is* no truth, nor mercy, nor knowledge of God in the land. 2 By swearing, and lying, and killing, and stealing, and committing adultery, they break out, and blood toucheth blood. 3 **Therefore** shall the land mourn, and every one that dwelleth therein shall languish, with the beasts of the field, and with the fowls of heaven; yea, the fishes of the sea also shall be taken away. 4 Yet let no man strive, nor reprove another: for thy people *are* as they that strive with the priest. 5 Therefore shalt thou fall in the day, and the prophet also shall fall with thee in the night, and I will destroy thy mother.
6 **My people are destroyed for lack of knowledge: because thou hast rejected knowledge, I will also reject thee, that thou shalt be no priest to me: seeing thou hast forgotten the law of thy God, I will also forget thy children.** 7 As they were increased {*the priests*}, so they sinned against me: *therefore* will I change their glory into shame. 8 They eat up the sin of my people, and they set their heart on their iniquity. 9 And there shall be, like people, like priest: and I will punish them for their ways, and reward them their doings. 10 For they shall eat, and not have enough: they shall commit whoredom, and shall not increase: because they have left off to take heed to the LORD.

Isaiah 58:1-5 (God's Word)

1 Cry aloud! Don't hold back! Raise your voice like a ram's horn. Tell my people about their rebellion and the descendants of Jacob about their sins. 2 They look for me every day and want to know my ways. **They act as if they were a nation that has done what is right and as if they haven't disregarded God's judgment {on them}.** They ask me for just decrees. They want God to be near them.

3 Why have we fasted if you are not aware of it? Why have we inflicted pain on ourselves if you don't pay attention?

Don't you see that on the days you fast, you do what you want to do? You mistreat all your workers. 4 Don't you see that when you fast, you quarrel and fight and beat your workers? The way you fast today keeps you from being heard in heaven. 5 Is this the kind of fasting I have chosen? Should people humble themselves for {only} a day? Is fasting just bowing your head like a cattail and making your bed from sackcloth and ashes? Is this what you call fasting? Is this an acceptable day to the LORD?

Ezekiel 7:3-27 (KJV)

3 Now *is* the end *come* upon thee, and I will send mine anger upon thee, and will judge thee according to thy ways, and will recompense upon thee all thine abominations. 4 And mine eye shall not spare thee, neither will I have pity: but I will recompense thy ways upon thee, and thine abominations shall be in the midst of thee: and ye shall know that I *am* the LORD. 5 Thus saith the Lord GOD; An evil, an only evil, behold, is come. 6 An end is come, the end is come: it watcheth for thee; behold, it is come. 7 The morning is come unto thee, O thou that dwellest in the land: the time is come, the day of trouble *is* near, and not the sounding again of the mountains. 8 Now will I shortly pour out my fury upon thee, and accomplish mine anger upon thee: and I will judge thee according to thy ways, and will recompense thee for all thine abominations. 9 And mine eye shall not spare, neither will I have pity: I will recompense thee according to thy ways and thine abominations *that* are in the midst of thee; and ye shall know that I *am* the LORD that smiteth. 10 Behold the day, behold, it is come: the morning is gone forth; the rod hath blossomed, pride hath budded. 11 Violence is risen up into a rod of wickedness: none of them *shall remain*, nor of their multitude, nor of any of theirs: neither *shall there be* wailing for them. 12 The time is come, the day draweth near: let not the buyer rejoice, nor the seller mourn: for wrath *is* upon all the multitude thereof. 13 For the seller shall not return to that which is sold, although they were yet alive: for the vision *is* touching the whole multitude thereof, *which* shall not return; neither shall any strengthen himself in the iniquity of his life. 14 They have blown the trumpet, even to make all ready; but none goeth to the battle: for my wrath *is* upon all the multitude thereof. 15 The sword *is* without, and the pestilence and the famine within: he that *is* in the field shall die with the sword; and he that *is* in the city, famine and pestilence shall devour him. 16 But they that escape of them shall escape, and shall be on the mountains like doves of the valleys, all of them mourning, every one for his iniquity. 17 All hands shall be feeble, and all knees shall be weak *as* water. 18 They shall also gird *themselves* with sackcloth, and horror shall cover them; and shame *shall be* upon all faces, and baldness upon all their heads. 19 They shall cast their silver in the streets, and their gold shall be removed: their silver and their gold shall not be able to deliver them in the day of the wrath of the LORD: they shall not satisfy their souls, neither fill their bowels: because it is the stumblingblock of their iniquity. 20 As for the beauty of his ornament, he set it in majesty: but they made the images of their abominations *and* of their detestable things therein: therefore have I set it far from them. 21 And I will give it into the hands of the strangers for a prey, and to the wicked of the earth for a spoil; and they shall pollute it. 22 My face will I turn also from them, and they shall pollute my secret *place*: for the robbers shall enter into it, and defile it. 23 Make a chain: for the land is full of bloody crimes, and the city is full of violence. 24 Wherefore I will bring the worst of the heathen, and they shall possess their houses: I will also make the pomp of the strong to cease; and their holy places shall be

defiled. 25 Destruction cometh; and they shall seek peace, and *there shall be* none. 26 Mischief shall come upon mischief, and rumour shall be upon rumour; then shall they seek a vision of the prophet; but the law shall perish from the priest, and counsel from the ancients. 27 The king shall mourn, and the prince shall be clothed with desolation, and the hands of the people of the land shall be troubled: I will do unto them after their way, and according to their deserts will I judge them; and they shall know that I *am* the LORD.

Ezekiel 16:3-63 (God's Word)

3 Tell them, 'This is what the Almighty LORD says to the people of Jerusalem: Your birthplace and your ancestors were in the land of the Canaanites. Your father was an Amorite, and your mother was a Hittite. 4 When you were born, your umbilical cord wasn't cut. You weren't washed with water to make you clean. You weren't rubbed with salt or wrapped in cloth. 5 No one who saw you felt sorry enough for you to do any of these things. But you were thrown into an open field. You were rejected when you were born. 6 "'Then I went by you and saw you kicking around in your own blood. I said to you, "Live." 7 I made you grow like a plant in the field. You grew up, matured, and became a young woman. Your breasts developed, and your hair grew. Yet, you were naked and bare. 8 "'I went by you again and looked at you. You were old enough to make love to. So I spread my robe over you, and covered your naked body. I promised to love you, and I exchanged marriage vows with you. You became mine, declares the Almighty LORD. 9 "'Then I bathed you with water, and I washed off your blood. I poured olive oil over you. 10 I put an embroidered dress on you and fine leather sandals on your feet. I dressed you in fine linen and covered you with silk. 11 I gave you jewelry. I put bracelets on your wrists and a necklace around your neck. 12 I put a ring in your nose, earrings on your ears, and a beautiful crown on your head. 13 So you wore gold and silver jewelry. You were dressed in fine linen, silk, and embroidered clothes. Your food was flour, honey, and olive oil. You were very beautiful, and eventually you became a queen. 14 **You became famous in every nation because of your beauty.** Your beauty was perfect because I gave you **my** glory, declares the Almighty LORD.

15 "'**But you trusted your beauty, and you used your fame to become a prostitute. You had sex with everyone who walked by. 16 You took some of your clothes and made your worship sites colorful. This is where you acted like a prostitute.** Such things shouldn't happen. They shouldn't occur. 17 You took your beautiful gold and silver jewelry that I had given you and made **male idols** for yourself. **Then you committed adultery with them.** 18 You took off your embroidered clothes and covered the idols with them. You offered my olive oil and incense in their presence. 19 You also offered them sweet and fragrant sacrifices. You gave flour, olive oil, and honey—all the food that I gave you to eat. This is what happened, declares the Almighty LORD. 20 "'You took your sons and daughters, who belonged to me, and you sacrificed them as food to idols. **Wasn't your prostitution enough? 21 You slaughtered my children and presented them as burnt offerings to idols.** 22 With all the disgusting things that you did and all your acts of prostitution, you didn't remember the time when you were young. You didn't remember when you were naked and bare, kicking around in your own blood.

23 "'**How horrible! How horrible it will be for you!** declares the Almighty LORD. After all your wickedness, 24 you built yourself platforms and **illegal worship sites in every city square**. 25 **You also built worship sites at the head of every street.** You used your beauty to seduce people there. You offered your body to everyone who passed by. You increased your acts of prostitution. 26 You had sex with your lustful neighbors, the Egyptians. You used your prostitution to make me angry. 27 "'**So I used my power against you.** I took away some of your land, and I handed you over to your greedy enemies, the Philistines, who were ashamed of what you had done. 28 "'You had sex with the Assyrians because you weren't satisfied. You still weren't satisfied. 29 **So you increased your acts of prostitution to**

include the land of the merchants, the Babylonians. Even after that, you weren't satisfied. 30 "'**You have no will power! declares the Almighty Lord. You do everything a shameless prostitute does.** 31 You build your platforms at the head of every street and place your illegal worship sites in every square. **Yet, you aren't like other prostitutes, because you don't want to be paid.** 32 You are an adulterous wife who prefers strangers to her husband. 33 All prostitutes get paid. **But you give gifts to all your lovers and bribe them to come to you from all directions to have sex with you.** 34 You are a different kind of prostitute. No one goes after you for favors. You are the opposite. **You pay them, and you don't accept payment.**

35 "'Listen to the word of the Lord, you prostitute. 36 This is what the Almighty Lord says: You exposed yourself and uncovered your naked body when you gave yourself to your lovers and to all your disgusting idols. You also killed your children and sacrificed their blood to these idols. 37 **That is why I will gather all your lovers with whom you found pleasure. I will have all those who love you and hate you gather around. I will uncover your body for them, and they will see you naked.** 38 I will punish you the same way that those who are guilty of prostitution and murder are punished. **I will give you the death penalty in my fury and burning anger.** 39 I will hand you over to your lovers. They will destroy your platforms and tear down your illegal worship sites. **They will tear off your clothes, take away your beautiful jewelry, and leave you naked and bare. 40 They will also bring a mob against you. They will stone you and cut you into pieces with their swords. 41 They will burn your houses and punish you in the presence of many women. I will put an end to your prostitution, and you will no longer pay others.**

42 Then I will rest from my fury against you, and I will stop being angry. I will be at peace. I will no longer be angry. 43 "'You didn't remember the time when you were young, and you made me very angry with all these things. So I will pay you back for what you have done, declares the Almighty Lord. **Didn't you make wicked plans in addition to all your disgusting practices?** 44 "'Everyone who uses proverbs will speak the following saying against you: Like mother, like daughter. 45 You are your mother's daughter. She rejected her husband and her children. You are exactly like your sisters. They rejected their husbands and their children. Your mother was a Hittite, and your father was an Amorite. 46 "'Your older sister was Samaria. She and her daughters lived north of you. Your younger sister is Sodom. She lives south of you with her daughters. 47 You didn't follow their ways. You didn't do the same disgusting things that they did. **It only took you a little time to be more corrupt than they ever were.** 48 As I live, declares the Almighty Lord, your sister Sodom and her daughters never did what you and your daughters have done. 49 This is what your sister Sodom has done wrong. **She and her daughters were proud that they had plenty of food and had peace and security. They didn't help the poor and the needy. 50 They were arrogant and did disgusting things in front of me. So I did away with them when I saw this.** 51 "'Samaria didn't commit half the sins you did. You have done **many more** disgusting things than they ever did. Because of all the disgusting things that you have done, you make your sisters look innocent. 52 You will have to suffer disgrace because you accused your sisters. **Yet, your sins are more disgusting than theirs. They look like they are innocent compared to you.** Be ashamed of yourself and suffer disgrace, because you have made your sisters look like they are innocent. 53 "'I will restore the fortunes of Sodom and her daughters, and Samaria and her daughters. I will also restore your fortune along with theirs. 54 You will have to suffer disgrace and be ashamed of everything you have done, including comforting them. 55 When Sodom and her daughters and Samaria and her daughters return to what they once were, you and your daughters will return to what you once were. 56 You didn't mention your sister Sodom when you were arrogant. 57 You didn't mention her before your wickedness was revealed. Now the daughters of Aram and their neighbors despise you. The daughters of the Philistines also despise you. Those around you hate you. 58 **You must suffer because of all the crude and disgusting things you have done, declares the Lord.** 59 "'This is what the Almighty Lord says: **I will**

give you what you deserve. You despised your marriage vows and rejected my promise. 60 I will remember the promise that I made with you when you were young, and I will make it a promise that will last forever. 61 Then you will remember what you have done. You will be ashamed when I return your older and younger sisters to you. I will give them to you as daughters, but not because of my promise with you. 62 Then I will make my promise with you, and you will know that I am the Lord. 63 **You will remember and be ashamed. You will never again open your mouth because of your disgrace when I forgive you for everything you did, declares the Almighty Lord.'"**

AND THEN HE WILL TURN

I get the penalty if we don't, but what's the payoff if we do this?

Well, first of all, you do it because He told you to, not because of the payoff. He might turn and He might not. But you do it anyway because it's the right thing to do. But if He does decide to turn, He reserves the right to manifest that however He wants to, but odds are good that it will be GLORIOUS!

Joel 2:18-29 (God's Word) – 18 Then the Lord became concerned about his land, and he had pity on his people. 19 The Lord said to his people, "I am going to send grain, new wine, and olive oil to you. You will be satisfied with them. I will no longer make you a disgrace among the nations. 20 "I will keep the northern {army} far from you, and I will force it into a dry and barren land. The soldiers in front will be forced into the eastern sea. The soldiers in back will be forced into the western sea. A foul odor will rise from the dead bodies. They will stink." He has done great things! 21 Land, do not be afraid. Be glad and rejoice. The Lord has done great things! 22 Wild animals, do not be afraid. The pastures in the wilderness have turned green. The trees have produced their fruit. There are plenty of figs and grapes. 23 People of Zion, be glad and find joy in the Lord your God. The Lord has given you the Teacher of Righteousness. He has sent the autumn rain and the spring rain as before. 24 The threshing floors will be filled with grain. The vats will overflow with new wine and olive oil. 25 "Then I will repay you for the years that the mature locusts, the adult locusts, the grasshoppers, and the young locusts ate your crops. (They are the large army that I sent against you.) 26 You will have plenty to eat, and you will be full. You will praise the name of the Lord your God, who has performed miracles for you. My people will never be ashamed again. 27 You will know that I am in Israel. I am the Lord your God, and there is no other. My people will never be ashamed again. 28 "After this, I will pour my Spirit on everyone. Your sons and daughters will prophesy. Your old men will dream dreams. Your young men will see visions. 29 In those days I will pour my Spirit on servants, on both men and women.

Isaiah 1:18-20 (God's Word) – 18 "Come on now, let's discuss this!" says the Lord. "Though your sins are bright red, they will become as white as snow. Though they are dark red, they will become as white as wool. 19 If you are willing and obedient, you will eat the best from the land.

Zechariah 10:3-9 (God's Word) – 3 "My burning anger is directed against the shepherds. I will punish the male goats. The Lord of Armies takes care of his flock, the people of Judah. He makes them like his splendid war horse." 4 From them will come a cornerstone, from them a tent peg, from them a battle bow, from them every leader. 5 Together they will be like warriors who trample the enemy in the mud on the streets. They will fight because the Lord is with them. They will put to shame those who ride on horses. 6 "I will strengthen the people of Judah. I will rescue Joseph's people. I will bring them back, because I have compassion for them. It will be as though I had never rejected them, because I am the Lord their God, and I will answer them. 7 The people of Ephraim will be like mighty warriors. Their hearts will be glad as if they had some wine {to drink}. Their sons will see it and be glad. Their hearts will find joy in the Lord. 8 I will signal them with a whistle and gather them because I have reclaimed them. They will be as numerous as they have ever been. 9 Although I have scattered them among the nations, they will remember me even in faraway places. They will live with their children and then return.

Deuteronomy 28:1-14 (God's Word) – 1 Carefully obey the Lord your God, and faithfully follow all his commands that I'm giving you today. If you do, the Lord your God will place you high above all the other nations in the world. 2 These are all the blessings that will come to you and stay close to you because you obey the Lord your God: 3 You will be blessed in the city and blessed in the country. 4 You will be blessed. You will have children. Your land will have crops. Your animals will have offspring. Your cattle will have calves, and your flocks will have lambs and kids. 5 The grain you harvest and the bread you bake will be blessed. 6 You will be blessed when you come and blessed when you go. 7 The Lord will defeat your enemies when they attack you. They will attack you from one direction but run away from you in seven directions. 8 The Lord will bless your barns and everything you do. The Lord your God will bless you in the land that he is giving you. 9 You will be the Lord's holy people, as he promised you with an oath. He will do this if you obey the commands of the Lord your God and follow his directions. 10 Then all the people in the world will see that you are the Lord's people, and they will be afraid of you. 11 The Lord will give you plenty of blessings: You will have many children. Your animals will have many offspring. Your soil will produce many crops in the land the Lord will give you, as he swore to your ancestors. 12 The Lord will open the heavens, his rich storehouse, for you. He will send rain on your land at the right time and bless everything you do. You will be able to make loans to many nations but won't need to borrow from any. 13 The Lord will make you the head, not the tail. You will always be at the top, never at the bottom, if you faithfully obey the commands of the Lord your God that I am giving you today. 14 Do everything I'm commanding you today. Never worship other gods or serve them.

Isaiah 57:1-21 (God's Word) – 1 Righteous people die, and no one cares. Loyal people are taken away, and no one understands. Righteous people are spared when evil comes. 2 When peace comes, everyone who has lived honestly will rest on his own bed. 3 But you—come here, you children of witches, you descendants of adulterers and prostitutes! 4 Whom are you making fun of? Whom are you making a face at? Whom are you sticking out your tongue at? Aren't you rebellious children, descendants of liars? 5 You burn with lust under oak trees and under every large tree. You slaughter children in the valleys and under the cracks in the rocks. 6 Your idols are among the smooth stones in the ravine. They are your destiny. You have given them wine offerings and sacrificed grain offerings to them. Do you think I am pleased with all this? 7 You've made your bed on a high and lofty mountain. You've gone to offer sacrifices there. 8 You've set up your idols beside doors and doorposts. You've uncovered yourself to the idols. You've distanced yourself from me. You've made your bed with them. You've made a deal with those you have pleasure with in bed. You've seen them naked. 9 You've journeyed to the king with perfumed oils and put on plenty of perfume. You've sent your ambassadors far away and sent them down to Sheol. 10 You've tired yourself out with many journeys. You didn't think that it was hopeless. You've found renewed strength, so you didn't faint. 11 Whom did you dread and fear so much that you lied to me? You haven't remembered me or cared about me. I've been silent for a long time. Is that why you don't fear me? 12 I'll tell you about your righteous ways and what you have done, but they won't help you. 13 When you cry for help, let your collection of idols save you. A wind will carry them all away. A breath will take them away. But whoever trusts me will possess the land and inherit my holy mountain. 14 It will be said: "Build a road! Build a road! Prepare the way! Remove every obstacle in the way of my people!" 15 The High and Lofty One lives forever, and his name is holy. This is what he says: I live in a high and holy place. But I am with those who are crushed and humble. I will renew the spirit of those who are humble and the courage of those who are crushed. 16 I will not accuse you forever. I will not be angry with you forever. Otherwise, the spirits, the lives of those I've made, would grow faint in my presence. 17 I was angry because of their sinful greed, so I punished them, hid {from them}, and remained angry. But they continued to be sinful. 18 I've seen their {sinful} ways, but I'll heal them. I'll guide them and give them rest. I'll comfort them and their mourners. 19 I'll create praise on their lips: "Perfect peace to those both far and near." "I'll heal them," says the LORD. 20 But the wicked are like the churning sea. It isn't quiet, and its water throws up mud and slime. 21 "There is no peace for the wicked," says my God.

Jeremiah 30:1-24 (KJV) – 10 Therefore fear thou not, O my servant Jacob, saith the LORD; neither be dismayed, O Israel: for, lo, I will save thee from afar, and thy seed from the land of their captivity; and Jacob shall return, and shall be in rest, and be quiet, and none shall make him afraid. 11 For I am with thee, saith the LORD, to save thee: though I make a full end of all nations whither I have scattered thee, yet will I not make a full end of thee: but I will correct thee in measure, and will not leave thee altogether unpunished. 12 For thus saith the LORD, Thy bruise is incurable, and thy wound is grievous. 13 There is none to plead thy cause, that thou mayest be bound up: thou hast no healing medicines. 14 All thy lovers have forgotten thee; they seek thee not; for I have wounded thee with the wound of an enemy, with the chastisement of a cruel one, for the multitude of thine iniquity; because thy sins were increased. 15 Why criest thou for thine affliction? thy sorrow is incurable for the multitude of thine iniquity: because thy sins were increased, I have done these things unto thee. 16 Therefore all they that devour thee shall be devoured; and all thine adversaries, every one of them, shall go into captivity; and they that spoil thee shall be a spoil, and all that prey upon thee will I give for a prey. 17 For I will restore health unto thee, and I will heal thee of thy wounds, saith the LORD; because they called thee an Outcast, saying, This is Zion, whom no man seeketh after. 18 Thus saith the LORD; Behold, I will bring again the captivity of Jacob's tents, and have mercy on his dwellingplaces; and the city shall be builded upon her own heap, and the palace shall remain after the manner thereof. 19 And out of them shall proceed thanksgiving and the voice of them that make merry: and I will multiply them, and they shall not be few; I will also glorify them, and they shall not be small. 20 Their children also shall be as aforetime, and their congregation shall be established before me, and I will punish all that oppress them. 21 And their nobles shall be of themselves, and their governor shall proceed from the midst of them; and I will cause him to draw near, and he shall approach unto me: for who is this that engaged his heart to approach unto me? saith the LORD. 22 And ye shall be my people, and I will be your God. 23 Behold, the whirlwind of the LORD goeth forth with fury, a continuing whirlwind: it shall fall with pain upon the head of the wicked. 24 The fierce anger of the LORD shall not return, until he have done it, and until he have performed the intents of his heart: in the latter days ye shall consider it.

Want some New Testament references? *(You're not one of those "the Old Testament doesn't count anymore" people, are you?)*

James 4:7-10 (KJV) – 7 Submit yourselves therefore to God. Resist the devil, and he will flee from you. 8 Draw nigh to God, and he will draw nigh to you. Cleanse your hands, ye sinners; and purify your hearts, ye double minded. 9 Be afflicted, and mourn, and weep: let your laughter be turned to mourning, and your joy to heaviness. 10 Humble yourselves in the sight of the Lord, **and he shall lift you up**.

Eph 5:25-27 (KJV) – *25 Husbands, love your wives, even as Christ also loved the church, and gave himself for it; 26 That he might sanctify and cleanse it with the washing of water by the word, 27* ***That he might present it to himself a glorious church, not having spot, or wrinkle, or any such thing; but that it should be holy and without blemish.***

Rev 2:5,7 (KJV) – *5 Remember therefore from whence thou art fallen, and* ***repent****, and do the first works; or else I will come unto thee quickly, and will remove thy candlestick out of his place, except thou repent. 7 He that hath an ear, let him hear what the Spirit saith unto the churches;* ***To him that overcometh will I give to eat of the tree of life, which is in the midst of the paradise of God.***

Rev 2:11 (KJV) – *11 He that hath an ear, let him hear what the Spirit saith unto the churches;* ***He that overcometh shall not be hurt of the second death.***

Rev 2:16-17 (KJV) – *16* ***Repent****; or else I will come unto thee quickly, and will fight against them with the sword of my mouth. 17 He that hath an ear, let him hear what the Spirit saith unto the churches;* ***To him that overcometh will I give to eat of the hidden manna, and will give him a white stone, and in the stone a new name written, which no man knoweth saving he that receiveth it.***

Rev 2:22-23,26-28 (KJV) – *22 Behold, I will cast her into a bed, and them that commit adultery with her into great tribulation, except they* ***repent*** *of their deeds. 23 And I will kill her children with death; and all the churches shall know that I am he which searcheth the reins and hearts: and I will give unto every one of you according to your works. 26* ***And he that overcometh, and keepeth my works unto the end, to him will I give power over the nations: 27 And he shall rule them with a rod of iron; as the vessels of a potter shall they be broken to shivers: even as I received of my Father. 28 And I will give him the morning star.***

Rev 3:3,5 (KJV) – *3 Remember therefore how thou hast received and heard, and hold fast, and* ***repent****. If therefore thou shalt not watch, I will come on thee as a thief, and thou shalt not know what hour I will come upon thee. 5* ***He that overcometh, the same shall be clothed in white raiment; and I will not blot out his name out of the book of life, but I will confess his name before my Father, and before his angels.***

Rev 3:11-12 (KJV) – *11 Behold, I come quickly: hold that fast which thou hast, that no man take thy crown. 12* ***Him that overcometh will I make a pillar in the temple of my God, and he shall go no more out: and I will write upon him the name of my God, and the name of the city of my God, which is new Jerusalem, which cometh down out of heaven from my God: and I will write upon him my new name.***

Rev 3:15-22 (KJV) – *15 I know thy works, that thou art neither cold nor hot: I would thou wert cold or hot. 16 So then because thou art lukewarm, and neither cold nor hot, I will spue thee out of my mouth. 17 Because thou sayest, I am rich, and increased with goods, and have need of nothing; and knowest not that thou art wretched, and miserable, and poor, and blind, and naked: 18 I counsel thee to buy of me gold tried in the fire, that thou mayest be rich; and white raiment, that thou mayest be clothed, and that the shame of thy nakedness do not appear; and anoint thine eyes with eyesalve, that thou mayest see. 19 As many as I love, I rebuke and chasten: be zealous therefore, and* ***repent****. 20 Behold, I stand at the door, and knock: if any man hear my voice, and open the door, I will come in to him, and will sup with him, and he with me. 21* ***To him that overcometh will I grant to sit with me in my throne, even as I also overcame, and am set down with my Father in his throne.*** *22 He that hath an ear, let him hear what the Spirit saith unto the churches.*

LIGHT THE LAMPSTAND

Lighting or restoring the Lampstand is not so much an action in and of itself, as it is a byproduct of doing the things above to prepare the ground for it to be restored and lit. I do believe that someone from a city with a Lampstand needs to help you light yours, but that may just be a matter of reading this book. It's certainly not about ME personally and I don't know that it requires someone present. It may just be a matter of someone telling you to ask for it. Don't focus so much on getting the Lampstand lit as on preparing the ground. Isaiah 58 says that it WILL happen when you do those things that please Him – including not turning away from your own flesh and blood and stopping the malicious talk and the pointing finger. Keep asking for Him to light it – but to show you what it's going to take to do it. And whatever He tells you, DO IT!

What is it going to take to make this work?

Watchman Nee, "The Normal Christian Church Life" - Chapter 5
"It was **never** God's purpose that a number of churches in different places should be combined under any denomination or organization, but rather that each one should be independent of the other. Their responsibilities were to be independent and their government likewise. When our Lord sent messages to His children in Asia, He did not address them as "the church in Asia," but "the seven churches which are in Asia." His rebuke of Ephesus could not be applied to Smyrna, because Smyrna was independent of Ephesus. The confusion in Pergamos could not be laid to the charge of Philadelphia, because Philadelphia was independent of Pergamos. And the pride of Laodicea could not be attributed to Sardis, because Sardis was independent of Laodicea. Each church stood on its own merits and bore its own responsibility. Since God's children lived in seven different cities, they consequently belonged to seven different churches. And since each was independent of the other, each had its own special commendation, or exhortation, or rebuke.

And not only were there these seven churches on earth; there were seven lampstands representing them in heaven. In the Old Testament there was only one lampstand with seven different branches, but in the New Testament there were seven distinct lampstands. Had the New Testament representation been the same as the Old, then believers in the seven Asiatic churches might have united to form one church; but there are now seven separate lampstands, each upon its own base, so that the Lord is able to walk "in the midst of the seven golden lampstands" (Rev. 2:1). Therefore, though all churches stand under the authority of the one Head and express the life of the one Body (for they are all made of gold), still they are not united by any outward organization, but each stands on its own base, bearing its own responsibility, maintaining its local independence."

That leads right into the Lampstands and the need for one. In November of 2004, the Lord showed me a vision of complete blackness over America, with little, black tendrils of nastiness spreading out all over the world. I could FEEL the wrath of God at what we were doing to His children and it changed me forever. Later He began to talk to me about the City Church and what it was and how it should be.

He led me to Revelation 2 and 3 and the messages from Jesus to the seven City Churches in Asia Minor. In the very first one – the message to the Church in Ephesus – the Lord tells them they've lost their first love and threatens to take away their Lampstand if they don't get back to it. Their first love has to be Jesus – and He says they will know us by our love, for each other. So He's telling them to get back to Him and stop going their own way and get back to being One Body under His headship, or else.

Do It Yourself City Church Restoration

Please note there are not JUST seven golden lampstands. There are clearly other city churches in existence at the time of the writing of the book of Revelation. For example, the church in Jerusalem, the church in Antioch, the church in Corinth and others are not listed. Certainly the Lord had His reasons for choosing these seven, but it should be clear that there were others at the time and each local city church in divine order has a Lampstand. Those could not have been the ONLY seven, they were just the ones chosen for the Lord's purposes for this book of Revelation.

But what IS a Lampstand? In Rev. 2, the Lord threatens the church in Ephesus that they are at risk of losing their Lampstand if they don't repent and change their ways. So what would happen if a city church lost it's Lampstand? Does that mean the Holy Spirit leaves the town? Surely not, He is omnipresent. Does it mean there are no more Christians there? Surely not. Does it mean they stop gathering and fellowshipping? No. It means the Body of Christ in that town is not really under Christ's headship anymore. They're on their own power. They lose the "Seal of Approval" and their access to the really big lights that push back the darkness in a huge way. What's the fastest way to lose your Lampstand? Allowing division inside the Body and grieving God. Even though Laodecia is asleep and Sardis is dead, the Lord doesn't threaten to take away their Lampstand. They may be in error, they may be useless, they may be allowing heresy, but at least they're all in it together! The Lord simply urges the overcomers there to stand firm. At least they're still being One Body! He hates <u>division</u> MORE than He hates bad behavior or incorrect secondary doctrinal issues. How desperately we need to learn that lesson! You can be wrong, you can be dead, you can be lukewarm – but don't lose your first love!

Consider it this way, "the prayer of a righteous man availeth much." (James 5:16) But the prayer of a slightly-righteous man probably availeth practically nothing. It's hard to tell whose team a <u>semi</u>-obedient man is even on!

Likewise, the prayer of a righteous city or town availeth a WHOLE LOT. In fact, if you look at the big revivals in history, the Great Awakenings (which were always focused on towns) and other examples, when a town comes together, repents and seeks God, it doesn't just change lives, it can change economies and crime rates, affect the course of wars and can even alter ecologies! But the prayer of a slightly-righteous, divided Body of Christ in a town availeth practically nothing. In fact, it might even be hard to tell whose side they are on.

The Lord gave me a little word picture that might help explain it.

> Imagine that the Lord started a bonfire in the middle of each town. In the beginning of that town, there was just one church. They were one body and they were seeking Him only. The fire is refining and purifying and powerful. Nothing can stand against it. It blazes brightly and pushes back all the darkness. The angel of the city (the Star in Revelation) blows on the fire and helps keep it burning.

> But one day, one of the little flames in the fire decided that he wanted to see what was out there beyond the communal bonfire, so he wandered off on his own. Maybe he even talked some others into going with him. Eventually some others started to drift off too, to investigate what was beyond. Maybe some of them got in a fight with some of the other little flames and decided they didn't want to be around them anymore. They all took their own little candles and went their own way. Eventually everyone leaves the bonfire and there is nothing left but a pile of ash in the spot where God's bonfire used to be. The little flames may collect into little fires of their own – sometimes 20 or 100 or maybe even 10,000 all in one place. But the Star of the city is not going to help – he is assigned to <u>God's bonfire</u> and no other. None of their little flames can compare to the raw power of what used to be when <u>all</u> the little flames were together in harmony. They have their own little candles, and they

might get enough of them together to create quite a little flame, but it's NOTHING like what it used to be or what it could be. Some of them are extinguished by the darkness, some die out alone, some die in large groups, some turn into strange fire. It's a LOT easier for the darkness to pick them off when they're not all together. In fact, it's the siren song of the darkness that lured them away from the bonfire in the first place – specifically so that this would happen!

The Star waits in the original ash pile, whispering to the little flames to come back. The Lord seeks even ONE man who will stand in the gap for the city. If even ONE of the little flames goes back to the original ash pile and repents and stands there defiantly burning as brightly as he can, insisting he will not be moved – then the Star will blow on his flame and start calling others back. The Star will send help from any source possible. The Star is HIGHLY motivated to make this work, so all kinds of resources will be available to those who commit to stand in the place of unity where God originally planted them. Nothing can stand against them when they are where God planted them. Only when they step outside the fire ring and go their own way can the enemy pick them off.

Whether all of them come back or just a few, when ANYONE comes back and repents and sets their face like flint and refuses to be moved ever again, the city will start to turn. The original bonfire will start to burn brightly and the Lampstand will be lit again. They will have access to the nuclear powerplants in the sky instead of just their own little candles. When the Body of Christ goes in repentance and unity and brokenness to accomplish a task the Lord directed, nothing can stand against them. They will inherit His promises as soon as they stop going their own way and they repent.

Why do we hear stories about some little missionary girl who went to some Pacific island where the Gospel had never been preached and astounding miracles follow her all over? But nothing like that happens when she's back in England? Why are headhunters and cannibals being healed and raised from the dead and miraculous financial provision for every need shows up, but she can never do it elsewhere? Because on that little island she is the ENTIRETY of the Body of Christ and she is there at His direction and under His headship and the Body is One. Just like Paul when he went into an unreached city, she IS the Lampstand. But as soon as another ministry shows up, or her converts split off and start their own brand of "church" and they refuse fellowship with each other and it becomes divisive, revivals stops dead in it's tracks and the power leaves the building. Every single time. (How many historical examples do you want?)

If the relit Lampstands mean access to the really BIG weapons of war, then it is VERY much is the enemy's best interest to keep us from having access to those weapons – from seeing the problem and doing something about it. That's why the Body of Christ in EVERY town in America has been methodically and systematically divided up into little pieces. And we fell for it. If we're going to keep praying "Thy will be done on earth as it is in heaven" then maybe we ought to start being One Body – you know, like we will be in heaven.

So it seems to me that the entire focus of EVERY town should be, "What is it going to take to get our Lampstand back?" We believe God has shown us the formula for that. We believe that the Church of Liberty, Missouri, has a Lampstand and others around the country are being lit now. More on that below.

Let me try this from a different direction. The Apostles received the Holy Spirit in John 20:22 when Jesus breathed on them and said, "Receive the Holy Spirit." They had already been out in pairs healing people and casting out demons. Nobody can convince me that you can do that without the Holy Spirit in you! Then, just before Jesus' ascension to the Father, He charged them with the Great Commission to go take the Gospel into Jerusalem, Judea, Samaria and unto the ends of the world. But He also told them NOT to go do it until the Holy Spirit came to them. Huh? They already had the Holy Spirit. But this isn't the redemptive aspects of the Holy Spirit, this is the empowering of the Holy Spirit. They had some in there, but they weren't fully baptized, submerged, dunked, swamped, lit up by the Holy Spirit yet. Even though they had been with Him, even though they had been commissioned to go, they were NOT allowed to go until the tongues of fire descended upon them.

The Bible always speaks in spirals, multiple applications of the same process on increasing populations or situations. Hosea applies to the Israel at the time, Israel in the future, America, me, the Church, etc. The Sermon on the Mount applies to me, my family, my city, my country, the Bride, etc. It's a Living Word and it's mysteries are endless (and require the Holy Spirit to unlock them). And I want you to see that this instruction to stay in Jerusalem until the fire came has application to the City Church as well. The model we have is that the disciples stayed and were all together praying and seeking God until Pentecost when the tongues of fire fell on them and lit them up. Peter goes from being a guy who denied Christ three times just fifty days before, to being a determined, fearless leader and public speaker whose first (fully extemporaneous) sermon brings 3,000 people to repentance. He's interrogated and whipped and praises Jesus – and gets filled with the Holy Spirit again (Acts 4:31)! Before this, even a little servant girl made him deny Christ three times! Now he's making so much sense that none of the religious leaders can argue with him!

Here's the point. If the Body of Christ in your town doesn't have a Lampstand, then **stay in your Jerusalem** and pray together and seek His face until the tongues of fire light it up. DO NOT go into Judea, Samaria and the ends of the earth when your own fire isn't lit. I would highly recommend that EVERY local body that doesn't have a lit Lampstand stop immediately doing or sending or funding anything elsewhere until you have cried out to the Lord sufficiently that His fire has fallen and you can then go in His authority according to His ways. Whatever you do without a Lampstand is going to be in your own power and not fully in His. It might have positive effects, but NOTHING like it will when you're fully inside His will and under His headship and operating as One Body!

It's like a bullseye. Don't go trying to fix someplace else when your own home is out of order. Start in the center and work your way out. In my case, He didn't let me leave Liberty for over a year and half until the Lampstand was lit. I know others who have been alone on their face weeping for their city for DECADES without leaving. We pulled back all support of native missionaries in India, all outside focus and kept all of our attention on the local Body. When it had achieved a "critical mass" and it lit up, the Lord released me to go out wider and help others.

Nothing is more important – or more empowering – than having a Lampstand behind you that certifies that you are His and have His firepower behind you. Without it, you are just going to have your own little candles to light your way and push back the darkness. Please hear me. Look at the Biblical model before us. Don't go trying to fulfill the Great Commission until you've fulfilled Isaiah 58 at home. Only THEN will your light rise in the darkness and He'll be your rear guard and when you call He will answer.

Every Temple needs to have a Lampstand burning in it. Every application – every leg of the spiral – needs to have a fire burning. Not burned out, not out of oil, not under a bushel, not under the bed – but a fire set on a lampstand for all men to see and burning brightly to push back the darkness and expose all that is hidden. We are to resist the enemy so he will flee. How? By the brightness and boldness and obviousness of our Light. By keeping our Lamps full of oil of His Spirit all the time. The foolish virgins are the ones who aren't full when the Bridegroom comes.

Every Temple needs a Lamp burning brightly. We need our assemblies cleansed and purified and spotless and white – so that the Light of Jesus reflects off every wall and every person and everything that we do and say. If we're to be useful vessels then we need to be silver and gold, not clay and wood – useful for noble purposes, not ignoble. We need our homes well lit with the Gospel and the Spirit of God. The Temples ALL need cleansing. On every spiral, on every level, on every dimension – Body, Soul and Spirit.

What Temples are we talking about? ALL of them. (I don't have to go back and explain "all" to you again, do I?)

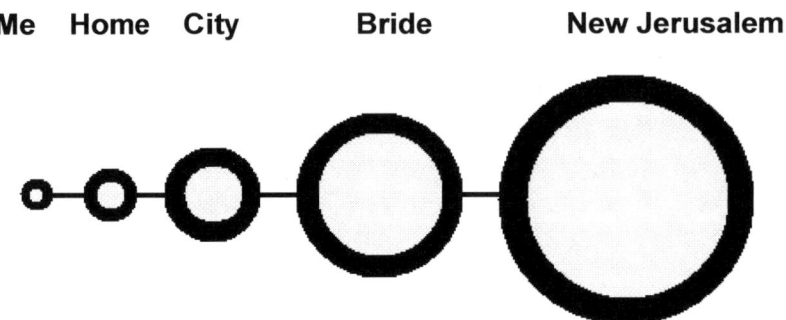

- My own heart lit by my own little candle of the Spirit
- My own home lit by the combined fire of the "one flesh" living there
- My City Church – lit by the Lampstand of the combined fire of the Body living there
- The Bride, the entirety of the Body of Christ – lit by His Spirit in all of us
- The New Jerusalem lit by the Light of the World

It applies to all of them. All of them should be a city on a hill. None of them should be hidden under a bushel or under the bed. All of them need to be burning brightly. (Matthew 5:13-16)

And any of them whose lamp runs out of oil will be considered foolish and cast out into outer darkness. Spirals. See?

Matthew 25:1-13 (KJV)
1 Then shall the kingdom of heaven be likened unto ten virgins, which took their lamps, and went forth to meet the bridegroom. 2 And five of them were wise, and five were foolish. 3 They that were foolish took their lamps, and took no oil with them: 4 But the wise took oil in their vessels with their lamps. 5 While the bridegroom tarried, they all slumbered and slept. 6 And at midnight there was a cry made, Behold, the bridegroom cometh; go ye out to meet him. 7 Then all those virgins arose, and trimmed their lamps. 8 And the foolish said unto the wise, Give us of your oil; for our lamps are gone out. 9 But the wise answered, saying, Not so; lest there be not enough for us and you: but go ye rather to them that sell, and buy for yourselves. 10 And while they went to buy, the bridegroom came; and they that were ready went in with him to the marriage: and the door was shut. 11 Afterward came also the other virgins, saying, Lord, Lord, open to us. 12 But he answered and said, Verily I say unto you, I know you not. 13 Watch therefore, for ye know neither the day nor the hour wherein the Son of man cometh.

THUS SAITH THE LORD

Ezekiel 36:1-38 (God's Word)
1 {The LORD said,} "Son of man, prophesy to the mountains of Israel. Tell them, 'Mountains of Israel, listen to the word of the LORD. 2 This is what the Almighty LORD says: **Your enemies said this about you, "Aha! The ancient worship sites now belong to us."'** 3 "So prophesy. Say, 'This is what the Almighty LORD says: Your enemies turned you into ruins and crushed you from every side. You became the possession of the rest of the nations, and people began to talk and gossip about you. 4 "'Mountains of Israel, listen to the word of the Almighty LORD. This is what the Almighty LORD says to the mountains and hills, to the ravines and valleys, and to the **empty ruins** and **abandoned cities** that have become prey and are mocked by the rest of the surrounding nations: 5 In my fiery anger I have spoken against the rest of the nations and against all of Edom. **The Edomites have taken possession of my land with wholehearted joy and with complete scorn.** They forced out the people and took their land.' 6 "So prophesy about Israel. Tell the mountains and hills and the ravines and valleys, 'This is what the Almighty LORD says: **I am speaking in my anger and fury because you have been insulted by the nations.** 7 So this is what the Almighty LORD says: I raise my hand and swear that the nations which surround you will be insulted. 8 "'But you, mountains of Israel, will grow branches and bear fruit for my people Israel. My people will come home soon. 9 **I am for you.** I will turn to you, and you will be plowed and planted. 10 **I will increase the number of people who live on you.** All the people of Israel, all of them, will live on you. **The cities will be inhabited, and the ruins will be rebuilt.** 11 I will increase the number of people and animals that live on you. They will grow and become many. I will let people live on you as in the past, and **I will make you better off than ever before**. Then you will **know** that I am the LORD. 12 I will bring people, my people Israel, to you. They will take possession of you, and you will be their inheritance. You will no longer take their children away from them. 13 "'This is what the Almighty LORD says: **People say that you devour your people and take the children away from your nation.** 14 So you will no longer devour your people or take the children away from your nation, declares the Almighty LORD. 15 I will no longer let you hear the insults from the nations. **You will no longer suffer the disgrace of the people.** You will never again take the children away from your own nation, declares the Almighty LORD.'"

16 The LORD spoke his word to me. He said, 17 "Son of man, **when the people of Israel lived in their land, they dishonored it by the way they lived and by everything they did. Their ways were as unclean as a woman's menstrual period.** 18 So **I poured out my fury** on them because they poured out blood on the land and they dishonored the land with their idols. 19 I forced them into other nations, and they became scattered among the nations. **I judged them based on the way that they lived and based on everything that they had done.**

20 But wherever they went among the nations, they dishonored my holy name. People said about them, '**These are the LORD's people, yet they had to leave his land.**' 21 I became concerned about my holy name because my people dishonored it among the nations wherever they went. 22 "So tell the people of Israel, '**This is what the Almighty LORD says: I am about to do something, people of Israel. I will not do this for your sake but for the sake of my holy name, which you have dishonored among the nations wherever you have gone.** 23 I will reveal the holiness of my great name, which has been dishonored by the nations, {the name} that you have dishonored among them. **Then the nations will know that I am the LORD, because I will reveal my holiness among you as they watch, declares the Almighty LORD.** 24 "'I will take you from the nations and gather you from every country. I will bring you back to your own land. 25 **I will sprinkle clean water on you and make you clean instead of unclean.** Then I will cleanse you from all your idols. 26 **I will give you a new heart and put a new spirit in you.** I

will remove your stubborn hearts and give you obedient hearts. 27 I will put my Spirit in you. I will enable you to live by my laws, and you will obey my rules. 28 Then you will live in the land that I gave your ancestors. You will be my people, and I will be your God. 29 **I will rescue you from all your uncleanness.** I will make the grain grow so that you will never again have famines. 30 I will make fruit grow on the trees and crops grow in the fields so that you will no longer suffer disgrace among the nations because of famines. 31 **Then you will remember your evil ways and the bad things that you did, and you will hate yourselves for all these wicked and disgusting things.**

32 I want you to know that I'm **not** doing this for **your** sake, declares the Almighty Lord. **Be ashamed and disgraced because of your ways**, people of Israel. 33 "'This is what the Almighty Lord says: On the day that I cleanse you from all your wickedness, **I will cause your cities to be lived in again, and your ruins will be rebuilt.** 34 The wasteland will be plowed. It will no longer remain empty for everyone passing by to see. 35 People will say, "This wasteland has become like the garden of Eden. **The cities were destroyed. They were empty and ruined, but now they are fortified and have people living in them."** 36 The surrounding nations that are left will know that I, the Lord, have rebuilt the ruined places and planted crops in the land that was empty. I, the Lord, have spoken, and I will do it.' 37 "This is what the Almighty Lord says: I will also **let** the people of Israel **ask me** to **make them** as numerous as sheep. 38 They will be like the sheep for sacrifices, like the sheep in Jerusalem during the appointed festivals. **Their ruined cities will be filled with flocks of people. Then they will know that I am the Lord."**

REBUILD ON THE ANCIENT FOUNDATIONS

The ancient foundation has to be Christ and Him crucified. That is the foundation the Apostles laid and no other can be laid. No improvement can be made on the truth of the Cross and the Resurrection. Without that, we have nothing. Whatever we build has to be founded on that one thing. Without His sacrifice for us and the reality of Jesus Christ's Lordship and His death and resurrection, we have nothing at all and we should all just go home and get drunk.

> **1 Corinthians 15:1-19** (KJV) – *1 Moreover, brethren, I declare unto you the gospel which I preached unto you, which also ye have received, and wherein ye stand; 2 By which also ye are saved, if ye keep in memory what I preached unto you, unless ye have believed in vain. 3 For I delivered unto you first of all that which I also received, how that Christ died for our sins according to the scriptures; 4 And that he was buried, and that he rose again the third day according to the scriptures: 5 And that he was seen of Cephas, then of the twelve: 6 After that, he was seen of above five hundred brethren at once; of whom the greater part remain unto this present, but some are fallen asleep. 7 After that, he was seen of James; then of all the apostles. 8 And last of all he was seen of me also, as of one born out of due time. 9 For I am the least of the apostles, that am not meet to be called an apostle, because I persecuted the church of God. 10 But by the grace of God I am what I am: and his grace which was bestowed upon me was not in vain; but I laboured more abundantly than they all: yet not I, but the grace of God which was with me. 11 Therefore whether it were I or they, so we preach, and so ye believed. 12 Now if Christ be preached that he rose from the dead, how say some among you that there is no resurrection of the dead? 13 But if there be no resurrection of the dead, then is Christ not risen: 14 And if Christ be not risen, then is our preaching vain, and your faith is also vain. 15 Yea, and we are found false witnesses of God; because we have testified of God that he raised up Christ: whom he raised not up, if so be that the dead rise not. 16 For if the dead rise not, then is not Christ raised: 17 And if Christ be not raised, your faith is vain; ye are yet in your sins. 18 Then they also which are fallen asleep in Christ are perished. 19 If in this life only we have hope in Christ, we are of all men most miserable.*

If we can't agree on that, there's nothing left to say. We can't back down and we can't compromise.

> **1 Corinthians 3:10-23** (KJV) – *10 According to the grace of God which is given unto me, as a wise masterbuilder, I have laid the foundation, and another buildeth thereon. But let every man take heed how he buildeth thereupon. 11 For other foundation can no man lay than that is laid, which is Jesus Christ. 12 Now if any man build upon this foundation gold, silver, precious stones, wood, hay, stubble; 13 Every man's work shall be made manifest: for the day shall declare it, because it shall be revealed by fire; and the fire shall try every man's work of what sort it is. 14 If any man's work abide which he hath built thereupon, he shall receive a reward. 15 If any man's work shall be burned, he shall suffer loss: but he himself shall be saved; yet so as by fire. Every man is the temple of God and the dwelling place of His Spirit 16 Know ye not that ye are the temple of God, and that the Spirit of God dwelleth in you? 17 If any man defile the temple of God, him shall God destroy; for the temple of God is holy, which temple ye are. 18 Let no man deceive himself. If any man among you seemeth to be wise in this world, let him become a fool, that he may be wise. 19 For the wisdom of this world is foolishness with God. For it is written, He taketh the wise in their own craftiness. 20 And again, The Lord knoweth the thoughts of the wise, that they are vain. 21 Therefore let no man glory in men. For all things are yours; 22 Whether Paul, or Apollos, or Cephas, or the world, or life, or death, or things present, or things to come; all are yours; 23 And ye are Christ's; and Christ is God's.*

2 Timothy 2:19-21 (KJV) – *19 Nevertheless the foundation of God standeth sure, having this seal, The Lord knoweth them that are his. And, Let every one that nameth the name of Christ depart from iniquity. 20 But in a great house there are not only vessels of gold and of silver, but also of wood and of earth; and some to honour, and some to dishonour. 21 If a man therefore purge himself from these, he shall be a vessel unto honour, sanctified, and meet for the master's use, and prepared unto every good work.*

In the end, it's all very simple. If the Holy Spirit is in me and the Holy Spirit is in you, then we're just One Body and that's all there is to it. Now we need to figure out how to get along without killing each other or breaking into pieces. Period.

Below are excerpts from Chapter 5 of Watchman Nee's book, "*The Normal Christian Church Life.*" I quote him here because he was someone who sacrificed <u>everything</u> for God. He spent the last decades of his life in a Communist prison because he refused to back down. He understood love and he laid the foundation for and played a part in much of what has happened in the Chinese church in the last fifty years. We have never seen ANY growth in the church like we have seen in China in the last few years. Not even during the Book of Acts period has the Gospel spread so fast – and in horrifyingly bad conditions. I would encourage you to read all of his book. It's available in its entirety online for free here - http://www.ministrybooks.org/watchman-nee-books.cfm . I'm not following Nee, the Lord had already started me down this path before I ever found him, but he makes so much sense and says it so well, it's just easier to quote him directly.

SEVEN FACTORS IN SPIRITUAL ONENESS

"One Body and one Spirit, even as also you were called in one hope of your calling; one Lord, one faith, one baptism; one God and Father of all, who is over all and through all and in all" (Eph. 4:4-6). A person is constituted a member of the Church on the ground that he possesses the oneness of the Spirit, and that will result in his being one with all believers on the above seven points. They are the seven elements in the oneness of the Spirit, which is the common heritage of all the children of God. In drawing a line of demarcation between those who belong to the Church and those who do not, we must require nothing beyond these seven lest we exclude any who belong to the family of God; and we dare not require anything less, lest we include any who do not belong to the divine family. All in whom these seven are found belong to the Church; all who lack any of them do not belong to the Church.

(1) ONE BODY. The question of oneness begins with the question of membership of the Body of Christ. The sphere of our fellowship is the sphere of the Body. Those who are outside that sphere have no spiritual relationship with us, but those who are inside that sphere are all in fellowship with us. We cannot make any choice of fellowship in the Body, accepting some members and rejecting others. We are all part of the one Body, and nothing can possibly separate us from it, or from one another. Anyone who has received Christ belongs to the Body, and he and we are one. If we do not wish to extend fellowship to anyone, we must first make sure that he does not belong to the Body; if he does, we have no reason to reject him (unless for such disciplinary reasons as are clearly laid down in the Bible).

(2) ONE SPIRIT. If anyone seeks fellowship with us, however he may differ from us in experience or outlook, provided he has the same Spirit as we have, he is entitled to be received as a brother. If he has received the Spirit of Christ, and we have received the Spirit of Christ, then we are one in the Lord, and nothing must divide us.

(3) ONE HOPE. This hope, which is common to all the children of God, is not a general hope, but the hope of our calling, that is, the hope of our calling as Christians. What is our hope as Christians? We hope to be with the Lord forever in glory. There is not a single soul who is truly the Lord's in whose heart there is not this hope, for to have Christ in us is to have "the hope of glory" in us (Col. 1:27). If anyone claims to be the Lord's, but has no hope of heaven or glory, his is a mere empty profession. All who share this one hope are one, and since we have the hope of being together in glory for all eternity, how can we be divided in time? If we are going to share the same future, shall we not gladly share the same present?

(4) ONE LORD. There is only one Lord, the Lord Jesus, and all who recognize that God has made Jesus of Nazareth to be both Lord and Christ are one in Him. If anyone confesses Jesus to be Lord, then his Lord is our Lord, and since we serve the same Lord, nothing whatever can separate us.

(5) ONE FAITH. The faith here spoken of is the faith—not our beliefs in regard to the interpretation of Scripture, but the faith through which we have been saved, which is the common possession of all believers; that is, the faith that Jesus is the Son of God (who died for the salvation of sinners and lives again to give life to the dead). Anyone who lacks this vital faith does not belong to the Lord, but all who possess it are the Lord's. The children of God may follow many different lines of scriptural interpretation, but in regard to this fundamental faith they are one. Those who lack this faith have no part in the family of God, but all who possess it we recognize as our brothers in the Lord.

(6) ONE BAPTISM. Is it by immersion or by sprinkling? Is it single or triune? There are various forms of baptism accepted by the children of God, so if we make the form of baptism the dividing line between those who belong to the church and those who do not, we shall exclude many true believers from our fellowship. There are children of God who even believe that a material baptism is not necessary, but since they are the children of God, we dare not on that account exclude them from our fellowship. What then is the significance of the one baptism mentioned in this passage? Paul throws light on the subject in his first letter to the Corinthians. "Is Christ divided? Was Paul crucified for you? Or were you baptized into the name of Paul?" (1:13). The emphasis is not on the form of baptism, but on the name into which we are baptized. The first question is not whether you are sprinkled or immersed, dipped once or three times, baptized literally or spiritually; the important point is this: Into whose name have you been baptized? If you are baptized into the name of the Lord, that is your qualification for church membership. If anyone is baptized into the name of the Lord, I welcome him as my brother, whatever the manner of his baptism. By this we do not imply that it is of no consequence whether we are sprinkled or immersed, or whether our baptism is spiritual or literal. The Bible teaches that baptism is literal, and is by immersion, but the point here is that the manner of baptism is not the ground of our fellowship, but the name into which we are baptized. All who are baptized into the name of the Lord are one in Him.

(7) ONE GOD. Do we believe in the same personal, supernatural God as our Father? If so, then we belong to one family, and there is no adequate reason for our being divided.

The above seven points are the seven factors in that divine oneness which is the possession of all the members of the divine family, and they constitute the only test of Christian profession. They are the possession of every true Christian, no matter to what place or period he belongs. Like a sevenfold cord the oneness of the Spirit binds all the believers throughout the world; and however diverse their character or circumstances, provided they have these seven expressions of an inner oneness, then nothing can possibly separate them.

If we impose any conditions of fellowship beyond these seven—which are but the outcome of the one spiritual life, then we are guilty of sectarianism, for we are making a division between those who are manifestly children of God. If we apply any test but these seven, such as baptism by immersion, or certain interpretations of prophecy, or a special line of holiness teaching, or a so-called Pentecostal experience, or the resigning from any denominational church—then we are imposing conditions other than those stipulated in the Word of God. All who have these seven points in common with us are our brothers, whatever their spiritual experience, or doctrinal views, or so-called church relationships. Our oneness is not based on our appreciation of the truth of our oneness, nor on our coming out from all that would contradict our oneness, but upon the actual fact of our oneness, which is made real in our experience by the indwelling Spirit of Christ.

LOCAL CHURCHES

Now what is true of the universal Church is also true of a local church. The universal Church comprises all those who have the oneness of the Spirit. The local church comprises all those who, in a given locality, have the oneness of the Spirit. The Church of God and the churches of God do not differ in nature, but only in extent. The former consists of all throughout the universe who are indwelt by the Spirit of God; the latter consists of all in one locality who are indwelt by the Spirit.

Anyone wishing to belong to a church in a given locality must answer two requirements—he must be a child of God, and he must live in that particular locality. Membership in the Church of God is conditioned only by being a child of God, but membership in a church of God is conditioned, firstly, by being a child of God and, secondly, by living in a given locality.

In nature the Church is indivisible as God Himself is indivisible. Therefore, the division of the Church into churches is not a division in nature, life, or essence, but only in government, organization, and management. Because the earthly church is composed of a vast number of individuals, a measure of organization is indispensable. It is a physical impossibility for all the people of God, scattered throughout the world, to live and meet in one place; and it is for that reason alone that the Church of God has been divided into churches.

We must realize clearly that the nature of all the local churches is the same throughout the whole earth. It is not that the constituents of one local church are of one kind, and the constituents of another local church are of another kind. In nature there is no difference whatever. The only difference is in the localities that determine their respective boundaries. The Church is indivisible; therefore, in nature the churches are indivisible too. It is only in outward sphere that there is any possibility of dividing them. Physical limitations make geographical divisions inevitable, but the spiritual oneness of believers overcomes all barriers of space.

Locality is the divinely-appointed ground for the division of the Church, because it is the only inevitable division. Every barrier between all believers in the world is avoidable, except this one. As long as believers remain in the flesh they cannot exist apart from their dwelling places; therefore, the churches which consist of such believers cannot but be restricted by their dwellings. Geographical distinctions are natural, not arbitrary, and it is simply because the physical limitations of the children of God make geographical divisions inevitable, that God has ordained that His Church be divided into churches on the ground of locality. Such division is scriptural, and all other divisions are carnal. Any division of the children of God other than geographical implies not merely a division of sphere, but a division of nature. Local division is the only division which does not touch the life of the Church.

Most believers of today are so utterly blind to the scriptural basis of a church that if one asks another, "To what church do you belong?" The first thought of the one questioned is of the specific line of teaching he approves of, or the group of people with whom he has special fellowship, or how his group of Christians is different from others, or perhaps the name that particular group bears, or the form of organization they have adopted—in short, anything but the place in which he lives. Few would answer that question with, "I belong to the church in Ephesus," or "I belong to the church in Shanghai," or "I belong to the church in Los Angeles." It is our being in Christ that separates us from the world, and it is our being in a given locality that separates us from other believers. It is only because we reside in a different place from them that we belong to a different church. The only reason I do not belong to the same church as other believers is that I do not live in the same place as they do. If I wish to be in the same church, then I must change my residence to the same place. If, on the other hand, I wish to be in a different church from others in my locality, then the only solution to my problem is to move to a different locality. Difference of locality is the only justification for division among believers.

SEVEN FORBIDDEN GROUNDS OF DIVISION

On the positive side we have just seen the ground on which God has ordained that His Church be divided. Now, on the negative side, we shall see on what ground the Church ought not to be divided.

(1) SPIRITUAL LEADERS. "Now I mean this, that each of you says, I am of Paul, and I of Apollos, and I of Cephas, and I of Christ" (1 Cor. 1:12). Here Paul points out the carnality of the Corinthian believers in attempting to divide the church of God in Corinth, which, by the divine ordering, was indivisible, being already the smallest scriptural unit upon which any church could be established. They sought to divide the church on the ground of a few leaders who had been specially used of God in their midst. Cephas was a zealous minister of the gospel, Paul was a man who had suffered much for his Lord's sake, and Apollos was one whom God certainly used in His service, but though all three had been indisputably owned of God in Corinth, God could never permit the church there to make them a ground of division. He ordained that His Church be divided on the basis of localities, not of persons. It was all right to have a church in Corinth and a church in Ephesus, and quite all right to have several churches in Galatia and a number in Macedonia, for difference of locality justified division into these various churches. It was also all right for the believers to esteem those leaders whom God had used among them, but it would have been quite wrong to divide the churches according to the respective leaders by whom they had been helped.

Paul, Cephas, and Apollos were true-hearted servants of God who allowed no party-spirit to separate them; it was their followers who were responsible for the separation. Hero worship is a tendency of human nature, which delights to show preference for those who appeal to its tastes. Because so many of God's children know little or nothing of the power of the cross to deal with the flesh, this tendency to worship a man has expressed itself frequently in the Church of God, and much havoc has been wrought in consequence. It is in keeping with God's will that we should learn from spiritual men and profit by their leadership, but it is altogether contrary to His will that we should divide the Church according to the men we admire. The only scriptural basis for the forming of a church is difference of locality, not difference of leaders.

(2) INSTRUMENTS OF SALVATION. Spiritual leaders are no adequate reason for dividing the Church; neither are the instruments used of God in our salvation. Some of the Corinthian believers proclaimed themselves to be "of Cephas," others "of Paul," others "of Apollos." They traced the beginning of their spiritual history to these men, and so thought they belonged to them. It is both natural and common for persons saved through the instrumentality of a worker, or a society, to consider themselves as belonging to such a worker or society. It is likewise both natural and common for an individual, or a mission, through whose means people have been saved, to consider the saved ones as belonging to them. It is natural, but not spiritual. It is common, but nevertheless, contrary to God's will. Alas! that so many of God's servants have not yet realized that they are servants of the local church, not masters of a private "church." Churches are divided on the ground of geography, not on the ground of the instruments of our salvation.

(3) NON-SECTARIANISM. Some Christians think they know better than to say, "I am of Cephas," or "I am of Paul," or "I am of Apollos." They say, "I am of Christ." Such Christians despise the others as sectarian, and on that ground start another community. Their attitude is—"You are sectarian; I am non-sectarian. You are hero worshippers; we worship the Lord alone."

But God's Word condemns not only those who say, "I am of Cephas," "I am of Paul," or "I am of Apollos." It just as definitely and just as clearly denounces those who say, "I am of Christ." It is not wrong to consider oneself as belonging only to Christ; it is right and even essential. Nor is it wrong to repudiate all schism among the children of God; it is highly commendable. God does not condemn this class of Christians for either of these two things; He condemns them for the very sin they condemn in others—their sectarianism. As a protest against division among the children of God, many believers seek to divide those who do not divide from those who do, and never dream that they themselves are divisive! Their ground of division may be more plausible than that of others who divide on the ground of doctrinal differences, or personal preference for certain leaders, but the fact remains that they are dividing the children of God. Even while they repudiate schism elsewhere, they are schismatic themselves.

When you say, "I am of Christ," do you mean to say others are not? It is perfectly legitimate for you to say, "I am of Christ," if your remark merely implies to whom you belong; but if it implies, "I am not sectarian; I stand quite differently from you sectarians," then it is making a difference between you and other Christians. The very thought of distinguishing between the children of God has its springs in the carnal nature of man, and is sectarian. If we look on other believers as sectarian and consider ourselves to be non-sectarian, we are immediately differentiating between God's people and thereby manifesting a divisive spirit even in the very act of condemning division. No matter by what means we distinguish between the members of God's family—even if it be on the pretext of Christ Himself—we are guilty of schism in the Body.

What then is right? All exclusiveness is wrong. All inclusiveness (of true children of God) is right. Denominations are not scriptural, and we ought to have no part in them, but if we adopt an attitude of criticism and think, "They are denominational; I am undenominational. They belong to sects; I belong to Christ alone"—such differentiating is definitely sectarian.

Yes, praise God I am of Christ, but my fellowship is not merely with those who say, "I am of Christ," but with all who are of Christ. What is of vital importance is not the confession, but the fact. Although these other believers say they are of Paul, of Cephas, and of Apollos, yet in fact they are of Christ. I do not so much mind what they say, but I very much mind what they are. I do not inquire whether they are denominational or undenominational, sectarian or unsectarian; I only inquire, "Are they of Christ?" If they are of Christ, then they are my brethren.

Our personal standing should be undenominational, but the basis of our fellowship is not undenominationalism. We ourselves should be non-sectarian, but we dare not insist on non-sectarianism as a condition of fellowship. Our only ground of fellowship is Christ. Our fellowship must be with all the believers in a locality, not merely with all the unsectarian believers in that locality. They may make denominational differences, but we must not make undenominational requirements. We dare not differentiate between ourselves and them, because they differentiate between themselves and others. They are the children of God, and because they make distinctions between themselves and other children of God, they do not on that account cease to be the children of God. Their denominationalism or sectarianism will mean that severe limitations are imposed upon the Lord as to His purpose and mind for them, and this will mean that they will never go beyond a certain measure of spiritual growth and fullness. Blessing there may be, but fullness of divine purpose never.

All believers living in the same locality belong to the same church. This is an unchanging principle. We dare not alter "all the believers in a locality" to "all the undenominational believers in a locality." If we make undenominationalism or unsectarianism the boundary of our church, instead of locality, then we lose our local standing as a church and become a sect. It is not a denominational church, nor an interdenominational church, nor even an undenominational church we are after, but a local church. The difference between a local church and an undenominational church is as vast as the difference between heaven and earth. A local church is undenominational, but an undenominational church is denominational. "The church in Corinth" is scriptural, but "the church of all those who say, 'I am of Christ' in Corinth" is unscriptural. Our work is positive and constructive, not negative and destructive. We are out to establish churches, not to destroy denominations. Human nature is prone to go to extremes; it is so easy for us either to be undenominational ourselves and demand undenominationalism of others, or else to tolerate denominationalism in others and gradually become denominational ourselves. We ourselves must be undenominational, but we must not demand undenominationalism of other Christians as the basis of our fellowship.

Therefore, if we come to a place where Christ is not named, we must preach the gospel, win men to the Lord, and found a local church. If we come to a place where there are already Christians, but on various grounds these believers separate themselves into denominational "churches," our task is just the same as in the other place—we must preach the gospel, lead men to the Lord, and form them into a church on the scriptural ground of locality. All the while we must maintain an attitude of inclusiveness, not exclusiveness, towards those believers who are in different sects, for they, as we, are children of God, and they live in the same locality; therefore, they belong to the same church as we do. For ourselves, we cannot join any sect or remain in one, for our church connection can only be on local ground, but in regard to others we must not make leaving a sect the condition of fellowship with those believers who are in a sect. That will make undenominationalism our church ground, instead of locality. Let us be clear on this point, that an undenominational church is not a local church. There is a vast difference between the two. A local church is undenominational, and it is positive and inclusive; but an undenominational church is not a local church, and it is negative and exclusive.

Let us be clear as to our position. We are not out to establish undenominational churches, but local churches. We are seeking to do a positive work. If believers can be led to see what a local church is —the expression of the Body of Christ in a locality—they will certainly not remain in any sect. On the other hand, it is possible for them to see all the evils of sectarianism, and leave them, without knowing what a local church is. We must help those, to whom God has been pleased to use us, to understand clearly the truth regarding local churches, and not to lay emphasis on the question of denominations. They must realize that whenever they use the term "we" in relation to the children of God, they must include all the children of God, not merely those who are meeting with them. If when we say "our brethren," we do not include all the children of God, but only those who continually meet with us, then we are schismatic.

I do not condone sectarianism, and I do not believe we should belong to any sect, but it is not our business to get people to leave them. If we make it our chief concern to lead people to a real knowledge of the Lord and the power of His cross, then they will gladly abandon themselves to Him, and will learn to walk in the Spirit, repudiating the things of the flesh. We shall find there will be no need to stress the question of denominations, for the Spirit Himself will enlighten them. If a believer has not learned the way of the cross and the walk in the Spirit, what is gained by his coming out of a sect?

(4) DOCTRINAL DIFFERENCES. In the Greek the word rendered "heresies" in Galatians 5:20 [KJV] does not necessarily convey the thought of error, but rather of division on the ground of doctrine. The Interlinear New Testament translates it as "sects," while Darby in his New Translation renders it "schools of opinion." The whole thought here is not of the difference between truth and error, but of division based upon doctrine. My teaching may be right or it may be wrong, but if I make it a cause of division, then I am guilty of the "heresy" spoken of here.

God forbids any division on doctrinal grounds. Some believe that rapture is pre-tribulation; others, that it is post- tribulation. Some believe that all the saints will enter the kingdom; others believe that only a section will enter. Some believe that baptism is by immersion; others, that is by sprinkling. Some believe that supernatural manifestations are a necessary accompaniment to the baptism in the Holy Spirit, while others do not. None of these doctrinal views constitute a scriptural basis for separating the children of God. Though some may be right and others wrong, God does not sanction any division on account of difference as to such beliefs.1 If a group of believers split off from a local church in their zeal for certain teaching according to the Word of God, the new "church" they establish may have more scriptural teaching, but it could never be a scriptural church. To bring error into a church is carnal, but to divide a church on account of error may also be carnal. It is carnality that so often destroys the oneness of the church in any place.

If we wish to maintain a scriptural position, then we must see to it that the churches we found in various places only represent localities, not doctrines. If our "church" is not separated from other children of God on the ground of locality alone, but stands for the propagation of some particular doctrine, then we are decidedly a sect, however true to the Word of God our teaching may be. The purpose of God is that a church should represent the children of God in a locality, not represent some specific truth there. A church of God in any place comprises all the children of God in that place, not merely those who hold the same doctrinal views.

Should we arrive at a place where a church has already been established on clear local ground, and discover that its members hold views which we consider unscriptural, or that they consider the views we hold as unscriptural, if we then refuse to recognize them as the church of God in that locality and withdraw from fellowship, we are divisive. The question is not whether they agree with our presentation of truth, but whether they are standing on clear church ground.

If our hearts are set to preserve the local character of the churches of God, we cannot fail to come up against problems in our work. Unless the cross operates mightily, what endless possibilities of friction there will be if we include in one church all the believers in the locality with all their varying views. How the flesh would like just to include those holding the same views, and to exclude all whose views differ from ours. To have constant and close association with people whose interpretation of Scripture does not tally with ours, is hard for the flesh, but good for the spirit. God does not use division to solve the problem; He uses the cross. He would have us submit to the cross, so that through the very difficulties of the situation, the meekness and patience and love of Christ may be deeply wrought into our lives. Under the circumstances, if we do not know the cross, we shall probably argue, lose our temper, and finally go our own way. We may have right views, but God is giving us an opportunity to display a right attitude; we may believe aright, but God is testing us to see if we love aright. It is easy to have a mind well stored with scriptural teaching, and a heart devoid of true love. Those who differ from us will be a means in God's hand to test whether we have spiritual experience, or only scriptural knowledge, to test whether the truths we proclaim are a matter of life to us, or mere theory.

Romans 14 shows us how to deal with those whose views differ from ours. What would we do if in our church there were vegetarians and Sabbatarians? Why, we should consider it almost intolerable if in the same church some of the believers kept the Lord's Day and others the Sabbath, and some ate meat freely, while others were strict vegetarians. That was exactly the situation Paul was facing. Let us note his conclusions. "Now him who is weak in faith receive, but not for the purpose of passing judgment on his considerations" (v. 1). "Who are you who judge another's household servant? To his own master he stands or falls; and he will be made to stand, for the Lord is able to make him stand" (v. 4). "Therefore let us judge one another no longer, but rather judge this: not to put a stumbling block or cause of falling before your brother" (v. 13). Oh, for Christian tolerance! Oh, for largeness of heart! Alas! that many of God's children are so zealous for their pet doctrines that they immediately label as heretics, and treat accordingly, all whose interpretation of Scripture differs from theirs. God would have us walk in love toward all who hold views contrary to those views that are dear to us (v. 15).

This does not mean that all the members of a church can hold whatever views they please, but it does mean that the solution to the problem of doctrinal differences does not lie in forming separate parties according to the different views held, but in walking in love toward those whose outlook differs from ours. By patient teaching we may yet be able to help all to "the oneness of the faith" (Eph. 4:13). As we wait patiently on the Lord, He may grant grace to the others to change their views, or He may grant us grace to see that we are not such good teachers as we thought we were. Nothing so tests the spirituality of a teacher as opposition to his teaching.

The teachers must learn humility, but so must all the other believers. When they recognize their position in the Body, they will know that it is not given to everyone to determine matters of doctrine. They must learn to submit to those who have been equipped of God for the specific ministry of teaching His people. Spiritual gifts and spiritual experience are necessary for spiritual teaching; consequently not everyone can teach.

"Make my joy full, that you think the same thing, having the same love, joined in soul, thinking the one thing, doing nothing by way of selfish ambition nor by way of vainglory, but in lowliness of mind considering one another more excellent than yourselves; not regarding each his own virtues, but each the virtues of others also" (Phil. 2:2-4). When the churches have laid to heart what Paul wrote to the church in Philippi, then it will be perfectly possible to have only one church in one locality with no friction whatever among its many members.

(5) RACIAL DIFFERENCES. "For also in one Spirit we were all baptized into one body, whether Jews or Greeks, whether slaves or free, and were all given to drink one Spirit" (1 Cor. 12:13). Jews have always had the strongest racial prejudice of all peoples. They regarded other nations as unclean, and were forbidden even to eat with them; but Paul made it very clear, in writing to the Corinthians, that in the Church both Jew and Gentile are one. All distinctions in Adam have been done away with in Christ. A racial "church" has no recognition in the Word of God. Church membership is determined by place of residence, not by race.

Today in the large cosmopolitan cities of the world there are churches for the whites and churches for the blacks, churches for the Europeans and churches for the Asiatics. These have originated through failure to understand that the boundary of a church is a city. God does not permit any division of His children on the ground of difference of color, custom, or manner of living. No matter to what race they belong, if they belong to the same locality, they belong to the same church. God has placed believers of different races in one locality, so that, by transcending all external differences, they might in one church show forth the one life and the one Spirit of His Son. All that comes to us by nature is overcome by grace. All that was ours in Adam has been ruled out in Christ. The whole matter hinges here—are all carnal differences done away with in Christ, or is there still a place for the flesh in the Church? Are our resources in Christ sufficient to overcome all natural barriers? Let us remember that the church in any locality includes all the believers living there and excludes all who live elsewhere.

(6) NATIONAL DIFFERENCES. Jews and Gentiles represent national as well as racial distinctions, but in the Church of God there is neither Jew nor Greek. There is no racial distinction there, and there is no national distinction either. All believers living in one place, no matter what their nationality, belong to the one church. In the natural realm there is a difference between Chinese, French, British, and Americans, but in the spiritual realm there is none. If a Chinese believer lives in Nanking, he belongs to the church in Nanking. If a French believer lives in Nanking, he also belongs to the church in Nanking. The same holds good for Britishers, Americans, and all other nationalities, provided they are born again. The Word of God recognizes the church in Rome, the church in Ephesus, and the church in Thessalonica, but it does not recognize the Jewish church, or the Chinese church, or the Anglican church. The reason the names of cities appear in Scripture in connection with the churches of God is that the difference of dwelling place is the only difference recognized by God among His children. Their life is essentially one, and is therefore indivisible, but the place in which that life is lived cannot but vary as long as they remain in the flesh.

Since the churches are all local, if a believer—whatever his nationality—moves from one place to another, he immediately becomes a member of the church in the latter place, and has no church connection in the place of his former residence. You cannot live in one place and be a member of the church in another. There is no extraterritoriality in connection with the churches of God. As soon as you exceed the city limit, you exceed the church limit. If a Chinese brother moves from Nanking to Hankow, he becomes a member of the church in Hankow. In like manner, a British brother coming from London to Hankow immediately becomes a member of the church in Hankow. A change of residence necessarily involves a change of church, whereas naturalization has no effect on church membership.

Our fellow workers who have gone from China to the South Sea Islands must be careful not to form an Overseas Chinese church there. It is possible to have an Overseas Chinese Chamber of Commerce, or an Overseas Chinese College, or an Overseas Chinese Club. Anything you like can be Overseas Chinese, but not a church. A church is always local! If you go to any city in a foreign land, then it follows as a matter of course that you belong to the church in that city. There is nothing Chinese about the churches of God.

How glorious it would be if the saved in every city could overlook all natural differences and only consider their spiritual oneness. "We are the believers in Christ in such-and-such a place" is the finest confession a company of Christians can make. Whether Christ is in you or not, determines whether or not you belong to the Church; where you live determines the particular church to which you belong. The question put by God to the world is, "Do they belong to Christ?" The question put by God to believers is, "Where do they live?" Not nationality but locality is the question raised. The churches of God are built on city ground, not on national ground.

The usual conception of an indigenous church, while quite right in some respects, is fundamentally wrong at the most vital point. Since the divine method of dividing the Church is according to locality, not nationality, then all differentiation between Christian and heathen countries is contrary to God's thought. The Church of God knows neither Jew nor Greek; therefore, it knows neither native nor foreigner, neither heathen country nor Christian country. The Scriptures differentiate between cities, not between countries, heathen and Christian. So if we would be in full accord with the mind of God, we must make no difference whatever between the Chinese and foreign church, between Chinese and foreign workers, or between Chinese and foreign funds.

The thought of the indigenous church is that the natives of a country should be self-governing, self-supporting, and self-propagating, while the thought of God is that the believers in a city—whether native or foreign—should be self-governing, self-supporting, and self-propagating. Take, for instance, Peking. The theory of the indigenous church distinguishes between Chinese and foreigners in Peking, whereas the Word of God distinguishes between the believers in Peking—whether Chinese or foreign—and the believers in other cities. That is why in Scripture we read of the churches of the Gentiles, but never of the church of the Gentiles. The attempt to form all Chinese believers into one church shows a lack of understanding in regard to the divine basis of forming churches.

On the one hand, there is no church of the Gentiles in Scripture; on the other hand, we read of "the church of the Thessalonians." It is suggestive that this is the only expression of its kind used in the New Testament. The Word does not speak of the church of the Greeks (a race, or nation), but of the church of the Thessalonians (a city). There is no such thing in the thought of God as the church of the Chinese, but there is such a thing as the church of the Pekinese. Scripture knows nothing of the church of the French, but it does recognize the church of the Parisians. A clear apprehension of the divine basis of church formation—according to the difference of cities and not of countries—will save us from the misconception of the indigenous church. There should be no distinction whatever between Chinese and foreign Christians, between Chinese and foreign workers, or between Chinese and foreign money in any given locality.

(7) SOCIAL DISTINCTIONS. In Paul's day, from a social point of view, there was a great gulf fixed between a free man and a slave; yet they worshipped side by side in the same church. In our day, if a rickshaw coolie and the president of our republic both belong to Christ and live in the same place, then they belong to the same church. There may be a mission for rickshaw coolies, but there can never be a church for rickshaw coolies. Social distinctions are no adequate basis for forming a separate church. In the Church of God there "cannot be slave nor free man."

In Scripture we have at least seven definite things referred to which are forbidden by God as reasons for dividing His Church. As a matter of fact these seven points are only typical of all other reasons the human mind may devise for dividing the Church of God. The two millenniums of Church history are a sad record of human inventions to destroy the Church's oneness.

Well, that pretty much covers it, eh?

He's not very subtle either. That's why I like him. :-)

To Summarize:

- Preach Christ and Him crucified.
- Preach repentance and the need to not conform to the world.
- Get out of the Holy Spirit's way.
- Be non-sectarian, but don't demand it as a requirement of others.
- Listen really good and do whatever He tells you.
- Feed and clothe and care for the hurting.
- Take it outside the "boxes".
- Stay fully independent of extra-local control structures.
- Let the people walk in their gifting.
- Focus on individuals.
- Love without ceasing.
- Test everything.
- Stay REALLY flexible!

RESTORE STREETS WITH DWELLINGS

Spiritually, the cities in America are in ruins. They are dark. They are havens for wild animals and demons of every sort. The enemy has purposely spent generations bringing division into every city and town in America and making sure the Body of Christ couldn't get any traction and start working together. In November of 2004, the Lord showed me America as if from looking down on the globe from outer space – and it was covered in complete, inky, black darkness.

That doesn't mean there aren't any good Christians or there aren't good ministries doing the right thing. Just like if you were looking out the window of the Space Shuttle at night, you would not see Susie's TV on, or the lights left on at the high school. All you would see is the combined fires of whole cities. I'm not saying God isn't moving in America. I'm just saying what I believe He showed me in November of 2004 – that there were NO Lampstands in America, no cities where Christ was the Head and they were burning as one.

I think some lights are burning now and I'm really excited about how far we've come and what's about to happen. I'm also working urgently because I believe our time to do this is short. I believe persecution is coming to America and we don't have long to get this into place. It's just equational, the Lord said the more we were like Him (and His design for us), the more we would be persecuted. Every time we move toward doing it the right way, the enemy is going to fight back. There are already structures in place to hunt us down and kill us. Research the "Alliance of Civilizations" of the United Nations. Maybe that will get you to hurry.

What will it look like to restore streets with dwellings? Honestly, I don't really know how it will manifest. I know common components that are likely, but each city or town will be different. I can tell you from revival history, from the Great Awakenings and from study of the Bible what it will likely entail, but God has different plans for the Body in each town and city – plans for good and not for evil to give them a future and a hope. (Although some may include evacuation.)

Here are just a few of the things we will see. How they will manifest in your town or in what quantities, I have no idea.

- Massive increase in "house churches" and other worship "centers" - including businesses and outdoor venues.
- Stadiums and fields and parks full of people worshiping and praying, led entirely by the Holy Spirit.
- Training and equipping centers to get people full and walking in their giftings.
- Extravagant giving to the poor – meeting physical needs of hungry, naked, lonely, homeless and hurting.
- Emphasis on personal holiness and the need to walk clean before the Lord.
- Shockingly radical people who refuse to conform to the world and will not back down under any threat.
- Large groups coming together to burn their idols – or sell them and give to those in need.
- Transferal of ministry responsibility to the people instead of a priest class.
- Massive changes in financial, capitalistic structures. Some will be changed, some will be crushed.

- Effective local networks to share resources and meet local needs. Local sending of resources for missions.
- Massive movement of people moving away from denominational structures as they find Truth elsewhere.
- Secession of entire local congregations from their national or international governing bodies and traditions in favor of the city church.
- True community on a scale we don't even comprehend – real, true love for one another.
- Identification and equipping of local servant leaders.
- Movement of the Gifts of the Spirit on a scale we haven't seen. New music and art and other things.
- Increased relevance and impact of Christian businesses.
- Voluntary regional and international connectedness between sister cities.
- The regular exposing of more and more wolves within the ranks of the "institutional churches".
- Substantial changes in local economies, including closing of "vice" businesses and reductions in crime rates.
- Extravagant personal attention to every lost sheep.

We will likely also see:

- Massive increases in persecution against Christians from all sides.
- Desperate ploys by "institutional church" leadership to maintain the status quo at all costs.
- Increasing pressure toward a One World Church and ecumenical agreement with all religions.
- Increasing persecution of anyone who claims they have the sole source of religious truth. (Like us!)
- Increasing blame on those who are giving to the poor and are withdrawing from this consumer-driven society as being "economic terrorists".
- Bank foreclosures on "institutional churches" that can't pay their mortgages and other bills.

I don't think those things are particularly prophetic. Many of them are already visible now and I'm just asserting that the "spirals" will continue to escalate. Some of those are predictable given Scriptural instructions, some are historically just what happens when God moves on people and they start acting like Jesus. I don't feel like I'm stepping out on a limb too much on any of that stuff. (And I want to make it clear that I am NOT a "Kingdom Now" or "Apostolic Reformation" or "Dominionism" proponent. I don't think we're going to take over the world – or that if we don't, Jesus can't come back. I just believe that we're going to see a restoration of the Body – and the City Church is the thing. I don't believe it will affect EVERY town or sweep across all the world before Tribulation starts. I think it will be just enough to give us something to look forward to and equip people and establish the necessary structures and partnerships to get us through the Great Tribulation when we are heavily persecuted and marginalized by the forces of evil. And I think we don't have any time to waste.)

How do you do it in your town? I have no idea. I'm not your boss and I don't want you to lean on MY understanding. You're not even supposed to lean on YOUR understanding! The only way for any of us to do this is to get our own heads (and our wants) out of the way and listen to Him really well and do whatever He tells us – no matter how weird it sounds. As long as it lines up with the Bible, then you go and do it.

Just remember this, we are three part beings – Body, Soul and Spirit – and try to keep your eyes on the eternal one. Not the soulish nature, but the spirit. You need to do Isaiah 58 in as big a way as you can and across all three of those dimensions. He will help. He will provide all the help you need. He will open doors and light the way.

I'm sure that what He will want is for the Body to be the Body all the time, not just in one particular place or on a certain day of the week. We're to fellowship and minister daily and from house to house. But it may start with one event in one place. That's OK, it's all about the spirals. You have to light the fire somewhere and it may burn quietly in that one place until it breaks loose. But as it grows, expect it to jump like a wildfire into all kinds of unexpected venues and audiences. Watch for how to involve the "least of these". He likes using the foolish things to confound the wise, so ask yourself who or where or how is the most foolish thing the "institutional church" would ever think to use or do – and then pray about if you're supposed to do that. He's way more creative than you, so it might be better to just do whatever He tells you – but keep your eyes open for opportunities amongst all the people who have been marginalized and discarded previously.

The most important thing is to continue to do what got you here – that is, weep and pray in humility, listen to Him and do whatever He tells you and don't get in His way. Let the Spirit lead in ALL things. If money starts pouring in, put it into the hands of people who have already had the "love of money" beaten out of them. DO NOT entrust it to people who are used to handling lots of money – like business people and pastors, just because that's the way it was always done. (Do whatever God tells you. I'm not saying He's not going to use business people.)

The people who might be the most trustworthy may be those who were eating out of a dumpster a few days ago before God lit them up and delivered them. Doesn't it seem odd that the board of directors of a ministry helping homeless people is almost always full of business people and pastors? Shouldn't it be full of homeless people? Or at least people who have been homeless at some point?

Do not listen to people who are not walking free when they tell you how to structure things or provide ministry or meet needs. Remember that the Church of YourTown is fully autonomous in all things and has no Biblical requirement to answer to anyone other than God. Do not allow autocratic control from outside of your city under any circumstances. Receive the prophets and apostles that are sent to you, but test them all. Pray about what they bring and reject everything that isn't Truth.

Expect LOTS of warfare. Expect infiltrators and spies. This is a war! The enemy we're fighting is the KING of lies.

Whatever you do, DO NOT make it about YOU!! I'm not even sure it's possible if this is really a sovereign move of God, but just in case – don't do it!! He'll squash you like a bug!

Anti-Making-It-About-You Prescription
Say sincerely, loudly and publicly:

**"THINE is the Kingdom, THINE is the Power,
THINE is the Glory, FOREVER.
Not mine, not EVER, not even a LITTLE BIT. Amen."**

Repeat as needed.
(You might also read Daniel 4:28-37 as needed.)

FELLOWSHIP OF THE MARTYRS – ONE PAGE BATTLE PLAN
See extended version with scripture references –
www.FellowshipOfTheMartyrs.com/battle_plan_long.htm

Acknowledge your complete needfulness for God and inability to reach Heaven and escape the consequences of sin on your own power. Repent of every sin. Acknowledge Jesus as the risen Son of God and beg Him to wipe you clean. Commit to Him that He will be Lord and Master and that He alone will direct you. Without any reservation or evasion, you must mean that you intend to seek Him and do as He leads - even if it means discomfort, abuse, sacrifice, change, suffering, separation or even death. Ask for the indwelling of the Holy Spirit in as great a measure as He is willing to give you. Don't seek gifts for the sake of gifts, seek God - and He'll decide on the gifts for you. Be willing to chase holiness - to strive and urge forward for it everyday. Go and sin no more.

If you mean that Christ is Lord, then you must mean that His Word is the final authority. Spend most of your time in praise and worship of God because He is holy. This is the most pure expression of our love - for this we were made. Seek out anybody else that is absolutely committed to doing as God directs and is willing to speak only Truth, even if it's hard. Spend time together praising God and seeking His face. Each of you be prepared to minister. Don't rely on a paid staff person to do it.

The ultimate source of Truth is God's Word. Learn to love it, take it everywhere, read it and ask the Holy Spirit to explain and teach you what you need. Practice speaking pure Truth with no hint of Man inserted. Test everything against the Word of God.

Hold onto the good, run from evil. Learn to have no love for any created thing that exceeds your love for the Creator. Work hard. Whatever you do, do it as if you are doing it for God. Pray that God will help you have as large a positive impact as possible. More than anything else, God wants to first restore His people and convert all the altars back to the worship of God. Pray for the churches.

Take big arm loads of Truth and begin feeding the hungry. Go out as missionaries to speak into the hearts of the people where God leads you. Always speak in love and humility, pointing the way to Christ alone. Remember, you are trying to save eternal souls - never focus even for a moment on the immediate, always on the eternal.

Find those who can also commit themselves fully to Christ and involve them in your Fellowship. Praise God always for His use of you to save others. As your act of obedience, divert all available resources and assets only to those individuals and organizations most efficiently converting earthly treasure into heavenly treasure - that is, feeding the hungry, reaching the lost, caring for widows and orphans, supporting the Brethren in the hard places, equipping missionaries to push back the darkness - the same priorities that Christ has. Anyone that shows a "love of money" should be instantly suspect of being ensnared by the enemy and should be prayed for desperately - that is the root of much evil. God has already prepared many who are no longer susceptible to attack from that direction - find them and give them what they need.

Seek out other Fellowships and submit to each other in love. Seek to support the members of your own Fellowship as they go to serve or split off to start more Fellowships. Seek unity through harmony. Don't get distracted for a single moment by secondary issues or debates. We don't want everybody singing the melody, we want everyone in harmony and singing the part written for them by God. We need all the pieces. None can be wasted. But be willing to rebuke as God directs, and forgive if they repent. Expect wolves and spies and infiltrators. Expect the enemy to be sneaky. This is war.

As you stay inside of Truth, get to know the will of God and use all your gifts and talents within His will, amazing things are likely to happen. Expect miracles. Beg to be filled with the empowering of the Holy Spirit and use what gifts He's given you. Stay filled by a constant focus on holiness and purity and praise. Then pray that God will enlarge you so you can hold more. Pray for the greater gifts - those that can do the most damage to the enemy.

Obey God only. Time is short - so don't waste any. Go in love - and never give in.

HELPFUL VISUAL AIDS

The way the systems of man and satan work.

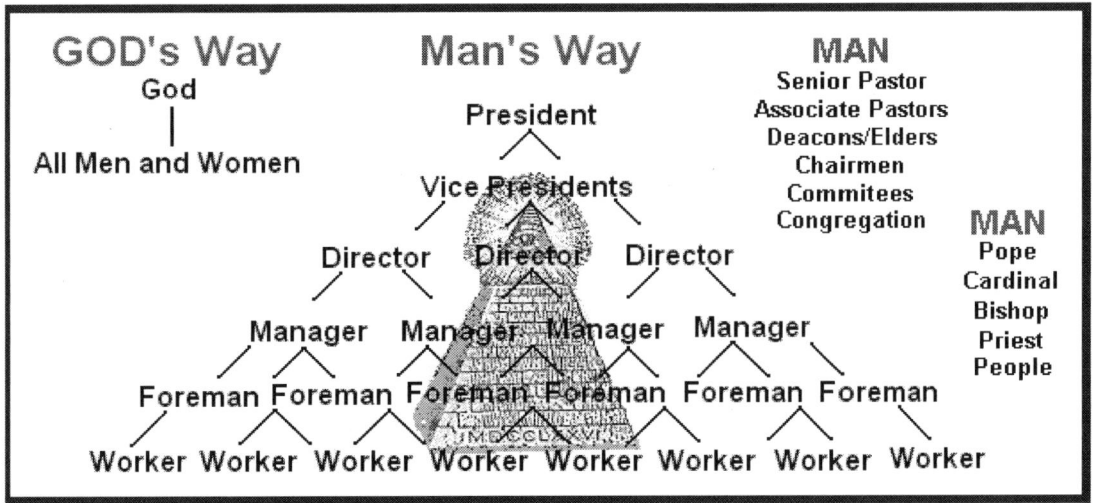

The Way the TRUE Church Works
Leaders always lift people toward God.
Not draw them unto themselves.

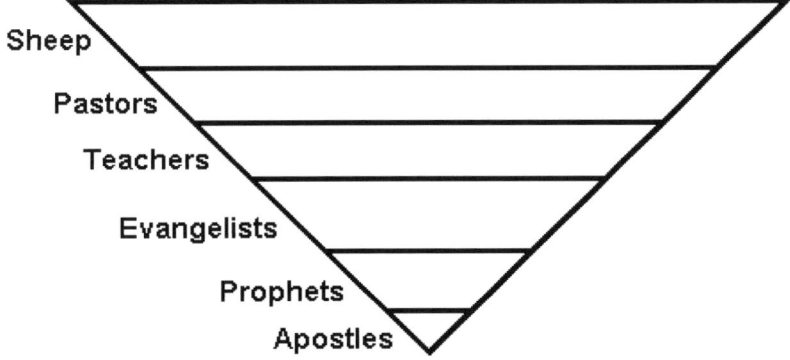

Shepherds care for the flock and support and feed.
All submit to one another out of love.
The Leaders lead because they're the best Servants.
The blood of a lost Sheep flows downhill on all leaders.

(If you were a sheep, which would you rather be a part of?)

HOW TO "DO CHURCH" IN A LAMPSTAND CITY

Rule #1 – DO <u>NOT</u> GRIEVE THE HOLY SPIRIT!

Rule #2 – See Rule #1

THIRTEEN EASY WAYS TO GRIEVE THE HOLY SPIRIT

You don't have to do them all, you can just pick ONE. That's sufficient.

- Tell Him when to show up and when to leave. Schedule His appearances and make sure everyone knows that you have control of His reins so He will be gone in time for everyone to get to Sunday lunch on time.

- Let somebody who isn't anointed and isn't supposed to be speaking run the show.

- Tell God how great He is and how much you love and adore Him and sing songs to Him while you completely ignore all the bleeding people around you. Tell them to call the office if they want to talk to someone, but don't disrupt the carefully planned presentation scheduled for this time period.

- Divide the Body of Christ up into smaller and smaller pieces and fill it with dissension, factions, division, selfish ambition, strife, quarreling, etc. That's a sure fire way to get the Gentle Dove to take off.

- Tell Him what He can and can't do. Be absolutely positive you know how He operates and make sure and tell everyone you have all the answers. Then program and plan and schedule everything in your own power and don't leave Him any room (or any invitation) to show up in any way other than what you've arranged.

- Give lip service to wanting Him to show up, but don't really mean it or get out of His way. If He does actually try to break through, squelch it as fast as you can. Pray fervently that the Lord would "shake things up" - but when He does, deny it was Him and go back to sleep.

- Cancel your prayer meetings because people are on their faces crying out to the Lord and it's "creepy". We need people to be HAPPY in church! It's just not "en vogue" to have people crying all the time.

- Convince the people that worshiping the Holy Spirit and getting HIM to come is the goal. Seek manifestations and displays of emotionality above all else. (We DO want Him to show up – but as a confirming side effect of the fact that the Truth is being spoken and the Bible is being spread and people are being transformed – not as the whole point of the meeting so that we can just all lay around and giggle.)

- Tell people that something glorious that He did wasn't actually Him – in fact, tell them satan did it. That'll do it.

- Take all of the spiritual assets the Lord has given you and hoard them and don't share with anybody – and make sure you let everyone know you are special.

- Make sure that only people with the proper degrees and certifications from approved structures and systems of Man are allowed to speak. Whatever you do, don't let the person with the biggest cup of Jesus say anything!

- Lie to the people in your congregation about spiritual gifts. Maybe even publicly deny that YOU speak in tongues or walk in one of the other Gifts – when you actually do and you know it. That'll make Him leave for sure – but it may keep you out of hot water with your denomination. (I've personally seen that one work really well. There is no telling what He will turn you over to, but it will NOT be pretty and you won't even see it coming. Be warned.)

- Make it all about YOU. Your Kingdom, Your Power, Your Glory, Forever. Amen.

WHAT DO WE DO FIRST? BE A M*A*S*H

Before we start trying to equip people or even worship in spirit and in truth, we better be sure we're all cleaned out – personally and collectively. You have to purify the Temple first. The most common thing I've seen in all my visiting different denominations is that almost universally there is a tendency toward putting on programs and ignoring the individual. The bigger the congregation, the greater the tendency. It always manifests in a statement about family and concern for the individual, but then it's offset and negated by the reality of a structure seemingly engineered to disregard individual needs. However unconscious this may be, the reality is clearly that millions of Christians are NOT walking in the fullness of Christ or worse, walking around with massive oppressions that continue to go untreated. We really shouldn't even try to go "dialing up" and people who have lots of open doorways. They are lame duck leaders.

TONS of people are leaving the institutional churches. Millions of them per year. Why? Because they don't feel like their individual needs are getting addressed. They may sit through a good sermon with some life application, but they don't see or feel the radical transformation that should come as a part of the normal Christian life. Or worse, they have a crisis or a need and nobody in the "church" responds appropriately.

We are NOT honoring God. We are singing and dancing and pretending everything is fine while people are bleeding to death in the pews (not to mention in the streets). Listen to me, God does NOT want you to praise and worship Him while you're ignoring the person sitting next to you who is having a crisis! It DOES NOT bring Him honor for you to raise your hands and tell Him how great He is while you FAIL to act like Him and heal those nearest to you. Heal them – or at least TREAT them – and THEN you can go praising and worshiping and telling Him how great He is. He just DOES NOT want to hear you singing while you're ignoring people who are crying inside! Your prayers are going to bounce off of the brass over your head until you act like Jesus. Just knock it off – or else. He's not going to ignore their cries much longer.

The church should be like the TV show "M*A*S*H". If they're having a party and someone shouts "Choppers!" then the music stops and everybody rushes into action to do *triage*. That means rapidly identifying and categorizing the wounded based on needs - the bleeding, sucking chest wounds go first, then the broken legs, then the scratches. AFTER everybody is treated and in Recovery – THEN you can go back to your party. But what kind of hospital would you be if you let them bleed to death in the compound because you refuse to stop singing and dancing because you had a schedule to keep?! You planned for this party to take an hour and a half and, by golly, you're going to stay on time no matter what! The sick people can just wait until the show is over.

Even when Jesus was right in the middle of a great sermon and had them all in the palm of His hand, if a paralyzed guy dropped down out of the roof, Jesus STOPPED TALKING and healed him. (Mark 2:1-12) THEN He could go on with his sermon - AND everybody was REALLY impressed because of the miracle that had just happened in front of them! I'm not sure which would be the bigger miracle in some churches, that a paralytic rose and walked away or that the pastor actually stopped in the middle of a sermon!

The people of God need to be trained up in how to rapidly identify the physical, emotional and spiritual warfare oppressing and killing their brethren and they need to be empowered to go and treat them on the spot. The music needs to stop until EVERYBODY in your camp is bandaged up. "Church" will not be **The**

Church until it stops being a show and starts being a hospital, first and foremost. The reason it's not that now is because we abdicated to paid leadership to do all the work for us and they can't possibly keep up. In fairness (to us), many of them got to liking it and now don't trust the Body to help them - so it's a vicious cycle. But it's got to stop. The Body has to learn to care for the Body, whether or not there is a paid staffer. We need the Gifts of Discernment of Spirits and Word of Knowledge and Wisdom operating in force and we need to get back to fulfilling the Great Commission - first by cleaning up the messes in our own assemblies, then by GOING. We can't wait for them to COME - cause when we do, they're mostly not staying, and it's because they're not getting healed (which is because we're too busy talking and we're not really acting like Jesus).

If any of this stuff convicted you and you realize you played a part in sustaining a system that hasn't been working or you ever ignored someone who was bleeding because you had your own agenda, now would be a good time to find a quiet place, hit your knees and say you're sorry. Crying helps God know you're serious. You might also want to admit it publicly to the people affected. How are they ever going to learn how to repent really good if somebody doesn't show them? Don't wait for somebody else to do it. It has to start with you.

If you kneel down and repent and cry in front of them, it might just start a revival. Some of them have never seen ANYBODY do that before! (If nothing else, it will give them something new to gossip about.) :-)

PERSONAL ATTENTION FOR ALL

If we were going to do things exactly backwards of the way things are currently being done, then we would start with radical, extravagant personal attention to each individual. That's the total opposite of the mega-church, herd-them-in, herd-them-out, take-a-number mentality. Personal attention and love is what the people are desperately hungry for. Somebody – ANYBODY – to show them some love and concern and hold them accountable and not let them drift off into the darkness. Kids will join just about any club or cult or gang or clique that will show them some personal concern and affirmation. Grown-ups aren't that different. So why are we losing over a million people a year out of the churches? Because we're speaking hard truth and people don't like it? No. It's because we're treating them like cattle.

We need to understand that the Good Shepherd will leave the 99 unattended and go find the ONE that is lost. (Matthew 15:4) That doesn't seem fair to the group, but that's His economy. We have incorporated more of a Henry Ford, assembly line, industrialized, economies of scale, kind of thinking about "church" – and it's clearly not working.

If we really commit to give every single person in a congregation (or a city) personal attention and discipleship (and deliverance) as they need it, even if that means individualized attention, how are we ever going to have enough staff time to minister to them all?! See? <u>There</u> is the fallacy right there. This isn't about "staff"! This is about raising up thousands of people that can minister to each other. This is about empowering the Body to minister to the Body as the Lord leads them. If we focus on training up their intellect and knowledge, then we need seminary trained, big brains to tell them stuff. But our battle is NOT against flesh and blood, it's a spiritual battle – and what have all these big brains really gotten us anyway – except 41,000+ denominations and another new one every other day? We can argue for days about who wrote the book of Hebrews or how to debunk the Davinci Code, but the people are dying in their sins and aren't free! They don't have their cups full and don't know how to get them full! But they know stuff. Unfortunately the "Sheep and Goats Final Exam" in Matthew 25 doesn't include their Bible trivia knowledge or the purity of their understanding of the Trinity or how well they line up with denominational dogma – it's about what you DID for the "least of these". (Matt. 25:31-46) You better read that and be really sure you know the right answers when you get to that final judgement. EVERYBODY goes through it, you don't get to skip it because you said a little prayer when you went down the aisle one day. (Right this minute are you a sheep or a goat? If you're the pastor, which are your people? It's on YOUR head!)

I have no idea how this is all going to work in every given situation, but I trust that the Lord will find a way. We need to equip people to break the chains, lift the yokes, feed the hungry, clothe the naked, take in the poor wanderer and teach them how to hear God's voice so HE can direct all of their paths. Then we need to trust that God has things under control and not try to micromanage what He's doing. VERY few people right now are wired to manage this. God has a remnant, and they're really beautiful, but the thing they have in common is a king-sized, faith like a child that resists all imposition of structure and just radically believes God has it all under control, no matter how wild the ride looks.

That doesn't mean they are going to accept infiltration of the enemy or acts of the flesh either. They are furiously loyal to God and won't tolerate disruptions to the flow of the Spirit from any source. We need to watch like a hawk and establish a "sphere" around our locations of ministry that is shielded with the Blood of Jesus and in which we repeatedly and constantly demand that nothing but Pure Truth be allowed to manifest. We need to try not to limit God, but still insist we want bread and not a stone, a fish and not a snake. (Matthew 7:7-11) The Lord will honor that and defend the gates. We have the authority to rebuke the works of the enemy – or of the flesh. The remnant are fierce and fiery in their absolute commitment to Truth. They will have very little tolerance for anything that smells of Man. How exactly you tell someone who is speaking to sit down and shut up, while still living at peace with all men, has yet to be seen. But we're going to have to learn how and submit to each other.

For me, nothing has worked better than the "Cup Model" at the back of this book. It transcends denominations and makes it clear we need to be walking in holiness and we don't need to repent once to come to Jesus – we need to confess and repent all the time when stuff sneaks in that shouldn't. We need to keep our cup all the way full ALL the time. Most folks don't even know how to do that and maybe never have been full their whole life! It's hard to explain, but there is a lot more detail in the "Rain Down NOW, Lord!" book online - FellowshipOfTheMartyrs.com/rain_down_now.htm. The short of it is that we need to be pouring out all we have and helping equip each other as quickly as possible. We're not waiting on the Lord to pour His Spirit out on all flesh – He's waiting on US to pour His Spirit out on all flesh!! The book explains how to do it, but it's critically important to understand so we can get people fully cleaned out and equipped in the quickest possible way. And I'm not sure there is a shortcut other than personal attention by someone who sees and hears really well and can help each individual.

We'll need to raise those folks up, but there are probably already lots of them in place. You have to learn how to identify the "shiny" ones real fast, see who has the biggest cup of Jesus, set them into their proper roles and let them work.

WHO HAS THE BIGGEST CUP OF JESUS?

This is kind of hard to explain, but if you have Discernment of Spirits, you just sort of know when someone is extra full of Jesus. Sometimes you meet someone and you just really hit it off and you like them and later you find out they are a Christian. Sometimes people are just sort of more "shiny" than other people. Do you know what I mean? It's like the Spirit in me is in love with the Spirit in them and can tell they're on our team – and a big gun, at that. The more in tune you are with the Holy Spirit, the more you can feel that attraction.

Please reference the graphic at the end of this book. The point is that the people with the great big, cleaned out cups are the ones who should be leading things. It's not always the pastor. Seminaries don't really teach you how to walk in holiness and have faith like a child. They mostly teach you how to have more of YOU in your cup. They put the emphasis on diplomas and degrees and how big your brain is. But God's economy says that if you don't accept the Kingdom of Heaven as a little child, you can't get in. That seems kind of counter to "seminary," doesn't it?

What we need is for the people with the great big cup of Jesus who are all cleaned out to stand up and lead the way. They are the ones who know how to walk in holiness and keep their cup full. They are probably the ones with the most spiritual gifts – or their "dials" up the highest. They are the ones who can give sacrificially and equip and fill other people. They are the ones who hear God the best and have the legal authority to do serious warfare against the enemy.

The guy that is _slightly_ righteous is also slightly sinful. You might as well stay home until you're ready to repent and get cleaned out and filled up. Don't pretend that your prayers are going to get answered. Why is God going to listen to you when you're not listening to Him? He's convicting you about stuff and showing you things that need to change, but you're unwilling. So don't expect any help from Him with the new job or your kid in the hospital. If He comes through, it's just grace and mercy, not because you deserve it.

But the guy with a big, cleaned out cup will benefit from all the If/Then promises of God for those who carefully obey His commands. If I'm desperately sick in the hospital and everyone has given up hope for me, I want the guy with the biggest cup of Jesus – and practically none of himself left – to come pray for me! If I'm being punished for something, maybe that guy loves me enough to tell me the truth and probably hears God well enough to tell me what it is that I've done and will pray with me to do something about it. If I've got something demonic messing with me and making me sick, that guy has the spiritual authority to rip it off and shred it. Maybe he's even in a place where he can pray for my healing and God will actually answer right on the spot. Either way, I don't want the lukewarm, half-full guy anywhere near me.

The problem is, are we really sure who is who? Haven't we been taught that the guy with the diploma on the wall has the biggest cup of Jesus? And wasn't it the guys with the diplomas who taught us that? But you and I both know that if everybody in a given congregation prays, it's probably that little old lady with the walker who sits in the back who is the one Jesus is REALLY going to listen to. She has the purest heart there. Maybe it's one of the kids in the youth group. Maybe it's somebody we would never suspect. That's the way God does things. He uses the foolish things to confound the wise. The guy up front who says he's the wisest one there might not actually be the one God uses best.

I happen to know a lot of prophets and apostles nobody knows are there. <u>They</u> may not even know that's what they are. They're "just" a janitor or a servant of some kind, but they are the pillar holding up that congregation and pastor. They are the heart and the conscience and the God-appointed intercessors for the place. My grandfather was a janitor in churches for decades. One of the pastors there once let me know he knew Bob was the guy to go to when he needed advice or prayer. He was a pastor to pastors. They knew they could trust him and get good advice and deep wisdom from him. He would just lean on a broom and speak Truth to them. He just quietly served and prayed and spoke hard truth with good humor and changed things – without anyone noticing or trying to draw any attention to himself. He just served and was the least of these – and was an apostle in every sense of what they are to be. He spent the last few days of his life, after being diagnosed with pancreatic cancer, in bed on the phone calling his oldest friends who had never received the Gospel and demanding they come over and give him one last chance to tell them about Jesus. Many, many people came to his funeral and were deeply affected by this quiet, unassuming farmer from a 200 person town in southern Missouri. And he was the quiet head of a family of teachers and preachers and missionaries who have devoted their lives to God. I don't remember him ever <u>telling</u> me what to do or be, he just <u>showed</u> me.

The key is learning to see who has the biggest cup and then letting them walk in their gifting and getting out of their way. If we're going to learn how to minister to each individual, then we're going to have to quickly learn how to identify those who are ready to help. You're going to have to ask the Lord to let you see through the eyes of Jesus and have Him show you who are the most equipped, most cleaned out, biggest cups in the room. We need to be able to identify their spiritual condition on the fly, identify areas needing attention, deal with them, dial them up and launch them.

RAISE UP ELDERS

Like I said before, to be an "Elder" all you have to be is a four-year-old in a room full of three-year-olds! Lots of people in your town think they should be Elders because they were a pastor or a deacon or a bishop in their denominational "church". But that doesn't qualify someone. You come into a new mix, you may have a whole different group of people. You might have been an Elder in a room full of three year olds, but if you go into the high school class, you're not an elder anymore. Ultimately, you'll know them by their fruit. The true elders are probably the ones who know they are elders, but are too humble to admit it or seek a position or title. They'll just show up and serve.

What Paul did was go into a town, preach the Gospel, pour himself out, teach by the example of his life – and then see who "got it" the best. He just watched to see who was standing head and shoulders above the crowd, then poured everything out into them, equipped and anointed them, set them into place as servants to the rest of the Body and then left town. In a couple years he would come back through and see who was still standing. He trusted that the Lord would sort the wheat from the chaff and the angel (the Star) assigned to the city would sort it all out one way or the other.

The Elders may not be people who agree with you on everything. We are not to be respecters of persons. And we're absolutely, positively not to show favoritism – especially because of wealth. (James 2)

James 2:1-10 (God's Word)
1 My brothers and sisters, practice your faith in our glorious Lord Jesus Christ by not favoring one person over another. 2 For example, two men come to your worship service. One man is wearing gold rings and fine clothes; the other man, who is poor, is wearing shabby clothes. 3 Suppose you give special attention to the man wearing fine clothes and say to him, "Please have a seat." But you say to the poor man, "Stand over there," or "Sit on the floor at my feet." 4 Aren't you discriminating against people and using a corrupt standard to make judgments? 5 Listen, my dear brothers and sisters! Didn't God choose poor people in the world to become rich in faith and to receive the kingdom that he promised to those who love him? 6 Yet, you show no respect to poor people. Don't rich people oppress you and drag you into court? 7 Don't they curse the good name {of Jesus}, the name that was used to bless you? 8 You are doing right if you obey this law from the highest authority: "Love your neighbor as you love yourself." 9 If you favor one person over another, you're sinning, and this law convicts you of being disobedient. 10 If someone obeys all of God's laws except one, that person is guilty of breaking all of them.

The bottom line is, again, listen to God and do whatever He tells you. He will raise up the Elders He wants and I'm sure He will find a way to make it clear to you who they are. Don't rebel against Him. And don't stop loving them, no matter how weird they are. And trust me, I know from experience, they'll probably be <u>very</u> weird. :-) But in a really pretty way.

TAKE THE WAR TO THE ENEMY

We've let the enemy twist us into pretzels for too long. It's time to take the war to the enemy. We don't have to go very far, the enemy is pretty well entrenched in just about everybody around us. The way to do the most damage is by radically transforming individuals by extravagant love and sacrifice.

My focus isn't on deliverance except to get someone unclogged so the Spirit can flow through them freely – and to defend the ground. Never mind what you'll been told, it does <u>NOT</u> bring glory to the enemy to acknowledge they are real! Nobody in the Pentagon worries for a second that by studying the enemy and his position and his troop movements and his weaknesses they might be accidentally worshiping him!! That's just goofy. This is a war! We're not going to honor them, but we're not going to ignore them either. We're going to acknowledge they're real, they are dangerous, they are trying to kill us – and the Blood of Jesus is WAY stronger. We deal with them and move on.

Demons are real and they do mess with us and they do oppress us – even Christians. When we give them room and listen to their whispers and do whatever they tell us, they might as well "possess" us for how well they have us trained. That's why they're called "rulers" - because if we let them rule over us, they displace Jesus and what He wants us to be doing. If someone has "rulers" then we need to identify them, they need to repent, and then we'll crush them.

The way to transform the world is by loosing the chains of wickedness, untying the straps of the yoke, letting the oppressed go free and breaking every yoke. (Isaiah 58:6) It's not enough to just untie the yokes, we need to BREAK them so they can't be used again. That yoke is the demonic burden set on the neck of someone and ruling them. We need to untie all the chains, lift the yoke off, shoo them out from under and then smash the yoke. <u>That</u> is LIBERTY!

SEND MISSIONARIES OUT TO LIGHT OTHER LAMPSTANDS

When your fire is burning and the Lord says it's time, He'll probably send you out – or send people to you – to light other Lampstands. He will make it clear who and when. It will probably be someone with an apostolic calling who can be sent to equip others and it will almost certainly need to be someone with a big Gift of Repentance who can weep and repent and mourn in front of people to show them how it's done and help them break the chains and yokes over their local Body.

I'm not sure I can tell you much more than that. I have no idea how He's going to do it with you or at what stage. He sent me out long before any more than a tiny handful of people could tell that Liberty had a Lampstand. There was no big evidence of it in the natural, no city-wide revival – but we knew it was burning and there were a tiny handful capable of guarding it and keeping it burning and standing in the gap so that I could go elsewhere. I thought it was premature, but God's ways are not our ways. What followed was a four and a half month long, country-wide van trip of over 17,500 miles to 32 states. I got to meet countless amazing ministries and divine appointments, trust God for every dollar and have to listen very carefully for direction for every next step. And I got to see five new Lampstands get lit and a whole bunch that are getting closer and closer. From that handful MANY more will be lit when it's time.

Remember the equation in the Great Commission; Jerusalem, Judaea, Samaria and unto the ends of the earth – in that order. (Acts 1:8) Like a bulls-eye or ripples in a pond or spirals. Get Jerusalem where it needs to be (according to God) before you head out to help Judaea.

I know I did this before, but it's important, so the Lord wants me to do it again. (Please note the spirals.)

The Apostles received the Holy Spirit in John 20:22 when Jesus breathed on them and said, "Receive the Holy Spirit." They had already been out in pairs healing people and casting out demons. Nobody can convince me that you can do that without the Holy Spirit in you! Then, just before Jesus' ascension to the Father, He charged them with the Great Commission to go take the Gospel into Jerusalem, Judea, Samaria and unto the ends of the world. But He also told them NOT to go do it until the Holy Spirit came to them. Huh? They already had the Holy Spirit. But this isn't the redemptive aspects of the Holy Spirit, this is the empowering of the Holy Spirit. They had some in there, but they weren't fully baptized, submerged, dunked, swamped, lit up by the Holy Spirit yet. Even though they had been with Him, even though they had been commissioned to go, they were NOT allowed to go until the tongues of fire descended upon them.

And I want you to see that this instruction to stay in Jerusalem until the fire came has application to the City Church as well. The model that we have is that the Apostles stayed and were all together praying and seeking God until Pentecost when the tongues of fire fell on them and lit them up. Peter goes from being a guy that denied Christ three times just fifty days before, to being a determined, fearless leader and public speaker whose first (fully extemporaneous) sermon brings 3,000 people to repentance. He's interrogated and whipped and praises Jesus – and gets filled with the Holy Spirit again (Acts 4:31)! Before this, even a little servant girl made him deny Christ three times! Now he's making so much sense that none of the religious leaders can argue with him!

Here's the point. If the Body of Christ in your town doesn't have a Lampstand, then **stay in your Jerusalem** and pray together and seek His face until the tongues of fire light it up. DO NOT go into Judea, Samaria and the ends of the earth when your own fire isn't lit. I would highly recommend that EVERY local body that doesn't have a lit Lampstand stop immediately doing or sending or funding anything elsewhere until you have cried out to the Lord sufficiently that His fire has fallen and you can then go in His authority according to His ways. Whatever you do without a Lampstand is going to be in your own power and not fully in His. It might have positive effects, but NOTHING like what it will when you're fully inside His will and under His headship and operating as One Body!

It's like a bullseye. Don't go trying to fix someplace else when your own home is out of order. Start in the center and work your way out. In my case, He didn't let me leave Liberty for over a year and half until the Lampstand was lit. I know others who have been alone on their face weeping for their city for DECADES without leaving. We pulled back all support of native missionaries in India, all outside focus and kept all of our attention on the local Body. When it achieved a "critical mass" and lit up, the Lord released me to go out wider and help others.

Nothing is more important – or more empowering – than having a Lampstand behind you that certifies you are His and have His firepower behind you. Without it, you are just going to have your own little candles to light your way and push back the darkness. Please hear me. Look at the Biblical model before us. Don't go trying to fulfill the Great Commission until you've fulfilled Isaiah 58 <u>at home</u>. Only THEN will your light rise in the darkness and He'll be your rear guard and when you call He will answer. You can't go help somebody else rebuild on the ancient foundations and restore streets with dwellings if you're not doing it at home yourself.

STAY OUT OF HIS WAY!

At the Azusa Street revival in 1906, the pastor, William Seymour, spent most of his time on his knees praying. He rarely spoke and didn't really "preach" much. And they ran 24/7 for over three years! There was a long walkway down the middle of this barn to a soap box "pulpit" - rows of benches faced each other across the center. Whoever had a word or a song or a prayer just stood up and gave it. The people who could feel the presence of God would weep and cry out if someone stood up to speak and wasn't supposed to be up there. They would feel the Holy Spirit begin to leave when someone thought it would be a "good idea" to say something, but the anointing wasn't on it. They learned how to stay in the "flow" of the Spirit without grieving God and making it about them. Thus they eliminated "idle words."

One older, black sister named Mother Brown developed a reputation for her awareness of the presence of the Spirit and she would fearlessly walk up to whoever was in the "pulpit" and gently say to them, "You know you're not supposed to be up here right now, don't you?" It got to where, if Mother Brown stood up from her seat, whoever was in the pulpit ducked for cover. She was like a barometer that helped them to stay in the flow. (Now whether or not you think Azusa was a move of God, something did happen there and it was a huge turning point for missions and for the church. Was it pure? No. Was some of it God? Surely. Do we want to do it just like they did? Surely not. But there are lessons to be learned.)

In our fellowship, we had asked God for "barometers". It can be awkward and seem rude, but it's more important to keep on God's agenda than to risk potentially hurting someone's feelings who is blabbering "self". One of the people who came to our meetings early on was a really sweet girl in her twenties who had a real, physiological response to the presence of the Holy Spirit. Some folks just get butterflies in their stomach or feel a peace, but this sister's hands would get hot. Really, really hot! You could hold your hand inches above hers and feel the heat radiating off of them. They didn't sweat or hurt, but they would get hotter and hotter the more we were in the flow and the Spirit was present. I'm not one for manifestations, but I know the Holy Spirit affects people in a variety of ways, some that are regular and predictable. We rebuked it and bound it and covered it in the Blood and all I know how to do to make sure it wasn't the enemy. It's a dangerous thing to trust someone's "feelings" - but she was very reliable and there was never a time when I felt she had called it wrong or tried to manipulate the meeting. Sometimes I would be speaking and she would just look at me and shake her head, "No" and hold up her hand. I would stop instantly and seek the Lord about what we had done wrong. Then we would repent, I would shut up and we'd do whatever we were supposed to be doing before I rambled on too long! And her hands would get hot again. In regular "church" her hands would get hot during the worship music, be instantly cold during the announcements and offering and might or might not get warm during the sermon, depending on if it was God's message or just the pastor's ideas. We had other barometers as well including chaos among the kids, people leaving, and other signs we learned to pay attention to indicating that the Holy Spirit was leaving the meeting and we were off-track. If everything was in divine order, there would be peace. If we drifted, then things started to unravel – if there were animals, they would misbehave, if there was something that could make noise, it would. Cell phones that had been quiet, started ringing and disruptions would abound. But if we were on His agenda, accomplishing His purposes and His Spirit was in charge, then He would clear out any conflicts or problems and make the way smooth and straight.

He gives grace to those who don't know better, but we were on a very short leash as we learned all of these things. Because we always prayed right up front that He would control everything in every way and because we meant it and made room for Him to do so, and expected He would – He did. If we stepped to the left or the right, He would let us know. The better we got at it, the more subtle the signs and the more we would have to listen and watch, but He will ALWAYS find a way to get your attention and let you know there is a problem.

I pray that God will raise up Mother Brown's who will fearlessly, and lovingly, insist that a meeting stay on course and in the flow. People who will not act out of self or control or desire to manipulate, but just to please God and keep His presence strong during the time together. Pray for barometers to help you, then test everything. But expect Him to be creative! For awhile He used a toothache in our group!

Which is more important to you? That you planned on speaking and, by golly, you're going to get up and speak – or that the Holy Spirit be fully present and people be transformed? If you come to one of our meetings, even if you're invited to speak or to sing or to minister, be ready to be flexible. It may not go the way you expect. We're not going to let you ramble if the Holy Spirit is leaving the building. There are sanctuaries all over town where you can go and do that all day long. We want the Spirit of God to hover among us and stay there – and that means we're going to do as He directs, even if it might risk hurting someone's feelings or upsetting the schedule. So be warned. We'll try to do it in love, but if you can't accept it, that's on you.

Which is more important to you? Haven't we grieved Him long enough by all of our idle words? Maybe it's time for something new – like getting out of His way. Maybe keeping our "self" to ourselves. That would be nice.

10 GREAT WAYS TO BE ABSOLUTELY SURE YOU WILL DIE SPIRITUALLY AND YOU PROBABLY WON'T EVEN NOTICE

1) Get Comfy

This kills ministries all the time. They are radical and living on faith and "praying in" every dollar, until things start to take off, then they get loose with the money, stop praying so hard, and their lifestyles upgrade. I've seen it happen to missionaries and others who move to the USA and settle right in, get nice and plump, and go to sleep. It's like the big Thanksgiving meal of turkey and all the fixings and then you take a nice long nap while the football games are on. If persecution stops, you stopped being dangerous!! Listen! Do NOT get comfy. I don't mean content or have joy or peace. You know the difference. Be ready to move at any moment and be ready to lay it all down if He asks.

2) Follow Man

Surefire way to kill a move of God. Stop listening to Him and start paying attention to the advisors and prophets and apostles and other people telling you what to do. There is a place where we submit to each other in love, but there is NEVER a place where a person gets to direct your paths and you should lean on THEIR understanding. God may speak through them and you should receive it, but test everything. If it's their own flesh – or worse their own pride or control or rulers or sinfulness or self – coming out, then you HAVE to take it to the Lord and have Him tell you what's what. Don't seek to be like John G. Lake or Smith Wigglesworth or Benny Hinn or Rick Warren or some other man. Don't seek someone else's anointing or "mantle." Seek to be so full of Jesus that nothing else can fit and HE will direct all of your paths and give you your own anointing – for whatever it is He made you to be and do. This includes preaching what someone else tells you to preach, even though God is telling you otherwise. Does God really want all evangelical pastors to preach four Sundays in a row on tithing every January? There aren't other, more urgent needs? God's not more creative than that? Maybe we're obeying Man.

3) Look Like The World

The more the world likes you, the less you're like Jesus. It's equational. They may respect you because of your good deeds, but that's different. If you adopt their models for marketing or growth or hiring or whatever, instead of doing what He tells you to do, you're in big trouble. If you make yourself a friend of the world, then you are an enemy of God. Just in case I'm being too subtle, if you build your ministry on the backs of demographic studies and consultant reports and marketing surveys, then you look like the world and you're in bed with them. And God hates adultery. His ways are NOT our ways and if you insist on doing it YOUR way, then you're going to be thoroughly unable to do it HIS way – which would have worked a lot better, but been thoroughly crazy and a test of faith and obedience. It's harder, but it sure works better and God gets all the glory instead of the MBAs you hired to help you build a "church".

4) Accept Some Sin

Decide certain things are acceptable with God and you don't have to stop doing them. Or listen to the voice in your head that says He loves you just the way you are and you don't need to sacrifice or change. If you're not walking in holiness, you're not there yet. Yeah, He'll use you, but not like He could if you were pure. And the enemy is going to use you, too. Until you shut all the doors and keep them shut, you're coopted and you can't be fully reliable in what you're hearing. You've got blind spots the enemy will use to sneak up and bite you at the worst possible moment. And you've cut and pasted the Bible and made up your own mystery religion that allows for certain things in your case - like overeating or sexual sin or pride or self. Everybody <u>else</u> has to crucify ALL of their flesh daily except you because you have a special "Exemption Anointing" from the Lord because He loves you so much. Guess again.

5) Hold On To Unforgiveness

If you are still angry with any person or unforgiving in any area, then you are taking Communion unworthily and you are probably sick and dying inside. He said to settle it before you bring your sacrifice. Why? Because you don't put a one-eyed lamb or a crippled ram up on the altar and think it's an acceptable sacrifice. You bring your <u>best</u> – holy, pleasing and acceptable – that is your reasonable act of service in thanks for His mercy. You can't say you want to be like Him and still hold on to old wrongs. He said that if you don't forgive others, He won't forgive you. If you have a cup full of nasty stuff, there's no room for Him to come and fill you. And why is He going to give you a bigger cup when you're not even keeping the one you have cleaned out? Again, you're making up your own religion if you think you can hold onto bitterness and unforgiveness and be OK with God. You're in more spiritual danger every second you refuse to lay it at the foot of the Cross and truly forgive as He forgives us. That means keeping no record of wrong. When He forgives us, He forgets that we plunged a knife into His chest. He just opens His arms again to us – and we stab Him again. Then we say we're sorry and He forgives us and opens His arms and then we do it again. Is that the way you're forgiving people? Or are your defenses up because you're never going to forget what they did to you? That's not the way Jesus forgives – thank God! He washes the slate fully clean.

6) Compromise The Faith

Love for all and trying to live at peace with all, as much as you may be able, does <u>NOT</u> mean ecumenism and bringing all faiths together in one pot and pretending to get along. Jesus and Paul and others did NOT accept the Gnostics and the Nicolaitans and the circumcision group and those who denied the resurrection and others promoting heresies that denied the reality of Christ. We cannot compromise on the raw, bottom line truths of the Gospel. There is only ONE way to heaven and it is through Christ Jesus our Lord. And the path is narrow and requires life-long obedience and self-sacrifice and love. It requires the Holy Spirit in full measure to walk the Narrow Path. The Broad Way is playing footsies with whatever "faith" wants to blend with ours. We are not to spiritually intermarry with the nations. On secondary issues, we offer grace – on the primary issue of Christ and Him crucified there can be no compromise. We are to test the spirits always, and the spirit of antichrist cannot acknowledge that Jesus is Lord. If we're in a group and some cannot acknowledge that Jesus is their Lord (Christ, Messiah, King) – then we have a salvation issue to talk about, but you can't praise and worship and expect unity and for the Holy Spirit to come and help you make decisions when some among you are not in The Book. I'm not talking about a large evangelistic meeting where people are coming to hear about Jesus, I'm talking about leadership or directional meetings where there has to be one spirit present – and it has to be HIS Spirit!

7) Water Down The Message

What this does is show a lack of stewardship for time and a disregard for the importance of the souls of the people. If you preach on pop psychology or self-help topics and someone dies that week without Jesus (but knowing how to budget effectively), their blood is on YOUR head. If they came to hear about Jesus and you fed them something else, even if it was for just part of the sermon, then whatever they missed is on you. If you pulled a sermon off of the internet and delivered it as your own, or recycled something because you didn't have time this week to hear what God was saying (or didn't believe He talks to people and you've been on your own power all along), then you're in big trouble if they needed something you weren't there to give them. You HAVE to see the opportunity costs of disobedience and self. Please?! I was speaking to a home group in Fort Worth once when my cell phone rang and a sister in Liberty called and said, "The Lord says you're talking about yourself too much and you need to shut up and listen to them." OK. Thanks, Lord. Yep, He was right (and she was obedient – and God DOES speak to people). And because I actively SEEK correction and expect that God <u>will</u> correct me, He will find a way to do so – even if through another person out of state. I don't think I'd crossed the line in that meeting, but I was about to and He made adjustments before it was too late. We hadn't yet covered the things that the Lord wanted covered in that meeting and He was GOING to have His way – because I always invite Him to and expect Him to, one way or the other.

8) Make Sure Other People Are Comfy Too

Closely related to the one previous (#7), this is where you tickle their ears and help them go back to sleep. This is mostly motivated by a desire to keep them around, usually because you don't want to alienate good, paying customers. It may be the theology you have adopted just wants them to be fat and satisfied and rich, because you think that's what God desires for them. Well, you made up your own Gospel, cause that ain't in there. We're to give up all that we have, we're dead and it's Christ in us that lives, we're to walk without sin and we're NOT to conform to the world (among others things it says). There is no rich, fat, lazy, comfy, American, acceptable walk in the Bible. You made up your own mystery religion and by preaching it to the people you have given way to a Fear of Man and probably a Love of Money that have become strongholds (rulers) in your life now. And you'll probably prosper because LOTS of people want to come hear your message and you'll think God is blessing you, but it's just a decoy to lull you into a false sense of security until you are destroyed. Read Deuteronomy 28 and Revelation 3:14-22 again. It's bad enough when YOU are comfy, but if you're <u>teaching</u> it, then ALL the blood of them AND those they might have reached – but aren't because they're unmotivated – is ALL on your head. Be afraid. God is <u>not</u> amused.

9) Try To Help God Along

We're supposed to wait on the Lord. I know it's hard. I know you're getting twitchy, but He can raise up stones to replace you. He doesn't need your diploma or your talents or your speaking ability. I've met little kids who were the best worship leaders I've ever met. God has a plan and you need to NOT try to get ahead of Him and help Him along. Just wait and do whatever He tells you. And if He says "Rest," then you rest. For however long it takes, including years. You do NOT try to help Him out with your own schemes and programs and plans. If it's not anointed, it's going to fail and it's going to take people down with it. Just wait, listen, and do whatever He tells you. Know His voice well enough to know the difference between His instructions and your desires (or the enemy's whisperings). If you go out from under His umbrella and do something on your own, don't expect Him to defend you and bless it. In fact, He may turn you over to it – and it will wreck you. He'll probably find a way to redeem it and use it to His glory somehow, but that's no excuse to go your own way. The collateral damage and personal cost may be great. Just wait on the Lord.

10) Refuse To Hear God's Voice

This is a big one. So big that He said to put it last and deal with it specifically on the following pages.

REFUSE TO HEAR GOD'S VOICE? BAD IDEA.

In essence, what the above (and others) will do is get you under a Red Dragon curse from God and He will send strong delusion on you that is meant for your destruction and you won't even know it. You have made up your own religion and you're going your own way. And He'll turn you over to it. Read www.FellowshipOfTheMartyrs.com/red_dragon.htm

Probably the worst deception of all, the most dangerous to your soul and the most beneficial to the enemy, is the lie that God doesn't talk to us anymore. It denies relationship, it neuters the Holy Spirit, and it keeps us from really being able to have Him write His law on our hearts so He can explain everything to us on the fly and show its personal application to our daily walk with Him. (And it's really impolite to talk AT Him all the time and never expect Him to say anything back – or ignore Him if He tries. That's no way to treat your Dad. What kind of relationship do you expect to have like that?)

There is no factual or observational reason I can discern that we needed to stop hearing from Him just because the Bible was completed. The fact that there are abuses and fakers and liars, doesn't mean the real thing isn't out there. God offered Man a whole bunch of chances to hear His voice, but we keep refusing to hear from Him and instead preferring to listen to Man – or satan. And every time we do listen to somebody else instead of Him, there are bad consequences. Here are some examples:

> **Genesis 3:13, 16** (KJV) – *13 And the LORD God said unto the woman, What is this that thou hast done? And the woman said, The serpent beguiled me, and I did eat. ... 16 Unto the woman he said, I will greatly multiply thy sorrow and thy conception; in sorrow thou shalt bring forth children; and thy desire shall be to thy husband, and he shall rule over thee.*

Eve listened to the snake instead of the voice of God. And she got cursed.

> **Genesis 3:17-19** (KJV) – *17 And unto Adam he said, Because thou hast hearkened unto the voice of thy wife, and hast eaten of the tree, of which I commanded thee, saying, Thou shalt not eat of it: cursed is the ground for thy sake; in sorrow shalt thou eat of it all the days of thy life; 18 Thorns also and thistles shall it bring forth to thee; and thou shalt eat the herb of the field; 19 In the sweat of thy face shalt thou eat bread, till thou return unto the ground; for out of it wast thou taken: for dust thou art, and unto dust shalt thou return.*

Adam listened to Eve instead of the voice of God. And he got cursed.

> **Genesis 16:2** (KJV) – *And Sarai said unto Abram, Behold now, the LORD hath restrained me from bearing: I pray thee, go in unto my maid; it may be that I may obtain children by her. And Abram hearkened to the voice of Sarai.*

God told Abram to wait and Sarai would have a child. But Abram listened to Sarai instead and got Hagar pregnant and had Ishmael. And Ishmael is the father of all the Arabs and has been no end of trouble for Israel ever since.

> **Hebrews 3:12-19** (KJV) – *Take heed, brethren, lest there be in any of you an evil heart of unbelief, in departing from the living God. 13 But exhort one another daily, while it is called To day; lest any of you be hardened through the deceitfulness of sin. 14 For we are made partakers of Christ, if we hold the beginning of our confidence stedfast unto the end; 15 While it is said,* **To day if ye will hear his voice, harden not your hearts**, *as in the provocation. 16 For some, when they had heard, did*

provoke: howbeit not all that came out of Egypt by Moses. 17 But with whom was he grieved forty years? was it not with them that had sinned, whose carcases fell in the wilderness? 18 And to whom sware he that they should not enter into his rest, but to them that believed not? **19 So we see that they could not enter in because of unbelief.**

Here they hardened their hearts, refused to listen to His voice and they all died in the desert.

Deuteronomy 21:18-21 (KJV) – *18 If a man have a stubborn and rebellious son, which will not obey the voice of his father, or the voice of his mother, and that, when they have chastened him, will not hearken unto them: 19 Then shall his father and his mother lay hold on him, and bring him out unto the elders of his city, and unto the gate of his place; 20 And they shall say unto the elders of his city, This our son is stubborn and rebellious, he will not obey our voice; he is a glutton, and a drunkard.* **21 And all the men of his city shall stone him with stones, that he die: so shalt thou put evil away from among you; and all Israel shall hear, and fear.**

God obeys His own rules. And His rule here says that if a son refuses to obey the voice of his father, then he's to be taken out and stoned. Better to have no son at all then a rebellious, drunkard, disgraceful, disobedient son. Jesus was the opposite of that. What are you? You may not get stoned in the "natural" - but if you refuse to listen to God, you'll get pelted with rocks spiritually until you repent or die. He'll do it Himself. Evidently fear is not such a bad thing. God talks about the need for us to fear Him a lot! It is supposed to make us VERY attentive and obedient! Unfortunately we have a really serious "Fear of the Lord" shortage in America. What are you doing to turn that around?

Jeremiah 7:21-28 (KJV) – *21 Thus saith the LORD of hosts, the God of Israel; Put your burnt offerings unto your sacrifices, and eat flesh. 22 For I spake not unto your fathers, nor commanded them in the day that I brought them out of the land of Egypt, concerning burnt offerings or sacrifices: 23 But this thing commanded I them, saying,* **Obey my voice, and I will be your God, and ye shall be my people: and walk ye in all the ways that I have commanded you, that it may be well unto you.** *24 But they hearkened not, nor inclined their ear, but walked in the counsels and in the imagination of their evil heart, and went backward, and not forward.* **25 Since the day that your fathers came forth out of the land of Egypt unto this day I have even sent unto you all my servants the prophets, daily rising up early and sending them:** *26 Yet they hearkened not unto me, nor inclined their ear, but hardened their neck: they did worse than their fathers.* **27 Therefore thou shalt speak all these words unto them; but they will not hearken to thee: thou shalt also call unto them; but they will not answer thee.** *28 But thou shalt say unto them,* **This is a nation that obeyeth not the voice of the LORD their God, nor receiveth correction: truth is perished, and is cut off from their mouth.**

That's a pretty depressing commissioning service for Jeremiah isn't it? "Go and speak this, but I can tell you ahead of time that they're going to completely ignore you." (And throw him in prison.) Fun. God's cool. Not only are they not going to listen to God, they're not going to listen to anybody He sends to try to get through to them either. They're not listening to the Commandments or the written Law – or to the prophets sent to speak Truth to them and call them back the Lord. And why exactly do we not need prophets to do that anymore? Are we not a thousand times more rebellious and selfish and murderous than Israel? Oh yeah! I forgot – "that which is perfect has come" and Bible is complete now so we don't need prophets. That's what Israel said. We have the Torah, go away and leave us alone. God would not send prophets to speak if the people were actually obeying the Bible! It's the same today. If we were obeying the Bible, we wouldn't need God to send prophets to tell us to repent. But since we're totally blaspheming the Holy Spirit and full of dissension, factions, selfish ambition, envy, lust, pride, greed and so many other things, how can it be said we're even obeying the Bible? (Gal. 5:19-21) Are we not quarreling? Are we not taking the names of men and dividing up into factions? Are we not divorcing? Are we not sold out to the world? Why would He give us meat when we are puking up the milk we already have?! We're not loving each other. We're not sacrificing. We're not being One Body. Of course, we still need prophets and apostles! We're not on the right foundation at all! We're worshiping another Jesus and have been for generations! Somebody has to speak Truth no matter the consequences because we're so stubborn and stiff-necked that we can explain away and justify even the written words in front of our own face!

We need prophets who will hear the voice of God and speak hard truth because we refuse to hear His voice ourselves or He might actually write His law on our hearts and keep us from sinning – and we desperately don't want that to happen because we like our sin too much. (And the enemy really, REALLY doesn't want that to happen!)

Here it is, right here. The people have been getting chances to hear His voice all the way back to the Garden, but we keep insisting we'd rather listen to ANYTHING but His voice. Eve listened to the snake, Adam listened to Eve. Here the children of Israel want to listen to Moses instead of God.

> **Exodus 20:18-21** (KJV) – *18 And all the people saw the thunderings, and the lightnings, and the noise of the trumpet, and the mountain smoking: and when the people saw it, they removed, and stood afar off. 19 And they said unto Moses,* **Speak thou with us, and we will hear: but let not God speak with us, lest we die.** *20 And Moses said unto the people,* **Fear not: for God is come to prove you, and that his fear may be before your faces, that ye sin not.** *21 And the people stood afar off, and Moses drew near unto the thick darkness where God was.*

> **Deuteronomy 5:22** (ASV) – *22 These words Jehovah spake unto* **all your assembly** *in the mount out of the midst of the fire, of the cloud, and of the thick darkness, with a great voice: and* **he added no more.** *And he wrote them upon two tables of stone, and gave them unto me.*

You see? He spoke to ALL of them. It wasn't just Moses alone up on the mountain like in the movies. They ALL heard His voice and heard the Ten Commandments. And it freaked them out!

> **Deuteronomy 5:23-25** (ASV) – *23 And it came to pass, when ye heard the voice out of the midst of the darkness, while the mountain was burning with fire, that ye came near unto me, even all the heads of your tribes, and your elders; 24 and ye said, Behold, Jehovah our God hath showed us his glory and his greatness, and* **we have heard his voice** *out of the midst of the fire: we have seen this day that* **God doth speak with man,** *and he liveth. 25 Now therefore* **why should we die?** *for this great fire* **will** *consume us:* **if we hear the voice of Jehovah our God any more, then we shall die.**

And they begged and pleaded not to have to hear Him anymore. This is satan logic here. They're definitely hearing other voices because this makes absolutely no sense at all. God wanted to talk to them all the time. He only gave them those Ten Commandments – and then His voice with them all individually all the time would keep them from sinning. The fear of the Lord would be in the people because His constant presence would write the laws on their heart and show them the application of all the Big Ten to the whole rest of their circumstances. But they acknowledge they just heard God and aren't dead. But they don't want to hear Him anymore or they will die. (Something in them will die, that's for sure – their rulers and the "self" that likes the sin!) They don't believe any man can hear God and live, but they admit they just did. See the logic problems here? It gets worse.

> **Deuteronomy 5:26** (ASV) – *26 For who is there of all flesh, that hath heard the voice of the living God speaking out of the midst of the fire, as we have, and lived?*

Well, that's a stupid question. THEY just heard Him and are still standing, but they're sure if you hear Him you'll die. Huh?

> **Deuteronomy 5:26** (ASV) – 27 Go thou near, and hear all that Jehovah our God shall say: and **speak thou unto us** all that Jehovah our God shall speak unto thee; and **we will hear it, and do it.**

So what do they do because they're so sure no flesh can hear God and live? They send Moses up to see what He wants! Isn't that a suicide mission? Is he not flesh? What kind of self-sacrifice and brotherly kindness and love is this?! They just shoved him up into the fire because they're too scared to get that close to God! They want Moses to go get instructions from God and they promise they'll obey Moses. They just exchanged the voice of God AGAIN for the voice of a man. And they never do really obey Moses! He can't individually and personally write it on their hearts and explain all the personal applications of those Ten Commandments to them on the fly as their day is going on. It's a whole lot easier to blow off the words of a man than when God is speaking to you directly and personally! (Believe me.) Satan knows that, and that's why he always wants us to NOT hear the voice of God for ourselves. And see what happens next?

> **Deuteronomy 5:26** (ASV) – 28 And Jehovah heard the voice of your words, when ye spake unto me; and Jehovah said unto me, I have heard the voice of the words of this people, which they have spoken unto thee: they have well said all that they have spoken. 29 **Oh that there were such a heart in them, that they would fear me, and keep all my commandments always, that it might be well with them, and with their children for ever!** 30 Go say to them, Return ye to your tents. 31 But as for thee, stand thou here by me, and I will speak unto thee **all the commandment, and the statutes, and the ordinances, which thou shalt teach them,** that they may do them in the land which I give them to possess it. 32 Ye shall observe to do therefore as Jehovah your God hath commanded you: ye shall not turn aside to the right hand or to the left. 33 Ye shall walk in **all** the way which Jehovah your God hath commanded you, that ye may live, and that it may be well with you, and that ye may prolong your days in the land which ye shall possess.

The Lord gives the people ten little rules and lets them know He will write them on their hearts and keep them from sinning. All other rules fit inside those ten. He would have walked beside them personally and individually and kept them in line with those ten commandments, but they refused to personally hear His voice. They preferred – as we still do today – to send someone else up the mountain so we don't have to hear Him for ourselves. But the man who tells us what God wants for us can never really keep us from sinning. Because they refused to hear His voice, instead of just the ten, Moses had to go up the mountain and get 609 more rules and statutes and procedural instructions and dietary laws. How to handle property, what happens if your bull gets loose, what to do if someone has leprosy, how to properly wash things. It goes on and on and on! If they're not going to listen to God, then God is going to have to give it all in one dump to Moses and leave it to him to communicate it to the people and make sure they obey – which they never really do.

Are you getting this? It could have been so much more simple!! We could have just had the ten and God explaining it to us on the fly, but we would have rather listened to a Man than the Living God because it was too scary and we might have to give up some stuff we like. So God suggests another solution to get this done.

> **Deuteronomy 18:15-19** (KJV) – 15 The LORD thy God will raise up unto thee a Prophet from the midst of thee, of thy brethren, like unto me; unto him ye shall hearken; 16 According to all that thou desiredst of the LORD thy God in Horeb in the day of the assembly, saying, **Let me not hear again the voice of the LORD my God**, neither let me see this great fire any more, that I die not. 17 And

> *the LORD said unto me, They have well spoken that which they have spoken. 18 **I will raise them up a Prophet from among their brethren, like unto thee, and will put my words in his mouth; and he shall speak unto them all that I shall command him. 19 And it shall come to pass, that whosoever will not hearken unto my words which he shall speak in my name, I will require it of him.***

God gets that maybe He's too big and scary for them to handle directly – but they're still not listening to Moses, so He agrees to raise up a prophet that maybe they will listen to. He agrees to send His Son to come in the flesh and talk to us personally. And when He did, we crucified Him. But God is still serious about you having to listen to Him, so even though Jesus isn't among us in the flesh anymore, He sent His Spirit back to talk to us and explain everything.

> **John 16:7-15** (KJV) – *7 Nevertheless I tell you the truth; It is expedient for you that I go away: for if I go not away, the Comforter will not come unto you; but if I depart, I will send him unto you. 8 And when he is come, he will reprove the world of sin, and of righteousness, and of judgment: 9 Of sin, because they believe not on me; 10 Of righteousness, because I go to my Father, and ye see me no more; 11 Of judgment, because the prince of this world is judged. 12 I have yet many things to say unto you, but ye cannot bear them now. 13 Howbeit when he, the Spirit of truth, is come, **he will guide you into all truth: for he shall not speak of himself; but whatsoever he shall hear, that shall he speak: and he will shew you things to come.** 14 He shall glorify me: for he shall receive of mine, and shall shew it unto you. 15 All things that the Father hath are mine: therefore said I, **that he shall take of mine, and shall shew it unto you.***

> **Hebrews 8:8-13** (KJV) – *8 For finding fault with them, he saith, Behold, the days come, saith the Lord, when I will make a new covenant with the house of Israel and with the house of Judah: 9 Not according to the covenant that I made with their fathers in the day when I took them by the hand to lead them out of the land of Egypt; because they continued not in my covenant, and I regarded them not, saith the Lord. 10 For this is the covenant that I will make with the house of Israel after those days, saith the Lord; **I will put my laws into their mind, and write them in their hearts: and I will be to them a God, and they shall be to me a people: 11 And they shall not teach every man his neighbour, and every man his brother, saying, Know the Lord: for all shall know me, from the least to the greatest.** 12 For I will be merciful to their unrighteousness, and their sins and their iniquities will I remember no more. 13 In that he saith, A new covenant, he hath made the first old. Now that which decayeth and waxeth old is ready to vanish away.* (Also Hebrews 10:15-18)

See? That's what He wanted to do all the way back in Exodus 20 at Sinai, but they refused. So He sent Jesus and we killed Him. Then He sent the Holy Spirit and we're still trying to deny that even He can talk to us – despite it being right there in writing in the Bible! Meanwhile we have great huge chunks of the Church who do NOT have His law written on their hearts and so He has not washed away their sin and iniquities. We're still denying Christ (and His Spirit) before men, so He's denying us before the Father. All because we refuse to listen to His voice. No matter what form it comes in. We're such stupid, stubborn sheep. We deserve whatever we get for this mess.

I don't want to argue about whether God talks to people today or not, it should just be obvious that if you do not have His laws written on your heart and mind enough to keep you from sinning, then you are probably refusing to listen to Him and/or have decided He can't talk to people and/or don't think He can actually keep you from sinning. We have pews full of sinners who are members of "churches" and think they are just fine. Somebody is lying to them – and it ain't God.

We have leaders who ferociously and fervently assert that God doesn't talk to people anymore. Why are they saying that? Well, partly because if nobody is going to have to teach their neighbor anymore because they "will all know God from the least to the greatest," then we don't really need those guys up on stage anymore, do we? That's a real job security problem. What were all those years in seminary for if anybody can hear God and He will tell them what to do? What exactly do we need expository sermons for? Can the pastor really write God's law on your heart? Is that working across the spectrum of Christianity? If so, then why are we so full of wickedness and look so much like the world? I think, despite God showing up and talking, Jesus showing up and talking, and the Holy Spirit showing up and talking – we're still absolutely committed to only listening to MEN tell us what to do. (Or satan – either way – anything but God.)

> **Deuteronomy 8:19-20** (KJV) – *19 And it shall be, if thou do at all forget the LORD thy God, and walk after other gods, and serve them, and worship them, I testify against you this day that ye shall surely perish. 20 As the nations which the LORD destroyeth before your face, so shall ye perish;* ***because ye would not be obedient unto the voice of the LORD your God.***

> **Deuteronomy 28:62** (KJV) - *And ye shall be left few in number, whereas ye were as the stars of heaven for multitude;* ***because thou wouldest not obey the voice of the LORD thy God.***

> **Psalms 81:8-16** (KJV) – *8 Hear, O my people, and I will testify unto thee: O Israel, if thou wilt hearken unto me; 9 There shall no strange god be in thee; neither shalt thou worship any strange god. 10 I am the LORD thy God, which brought thee out of the land of Egypt: open thy mouth wide, and I will fill it. 11* ***But my people would not hearken to my voice; and Israel would none of me.*** *12 So I gave them up unto* ***their own hearts' lust****: and they walked* ***in their own counsels.*** *13 Oh that my people had hearkened unto me, and Israel had walked in my ways! 14 I should soon have subdued their enemies, and turned my hand against their adversaries. 15 The haters of the LORD should have submitted themselves unto him: but their time should have endured for ever. 16 He should have fed them also with the finest of the wheat: and with honey out of the rock should I have satisfied thee.*

> **Psalms 106:21-27** (KJV) – *They forgat God their saviour, which had done great things in Egypt; 22 Wondrous works in the land of Ham, and terrible things by the Red sea. 23 Therefore he said that he would destroy them, had not Moses his chosen stood before him in the breach, to turn away his wrath, lest he should destroy them. 24* ***Yea, they despised the pleasant land, they believed not his word: 25 But murmured in their tents, and hearkened not unto the voice of the LORD.*** *26 Therefore he lifted up his hand against them, to overthrow them in the wilderness: 27 To overthrow their seed also among the nations, and to scatter them in the lands.*

Want some more. How about this? Kind of hard line here, isn't it? I'm <u>not</u> suggesting we do this literally, but I <u>do</u> believe God follows His own rules and He's already done it in the spirit to us. He has executed a bunch of people. We already have ruined and abandoned cities all over America. There wasn't a single city church – a single Lampstand – in America two years ago. Total darkness. Don't take my word for it, double check with God (if you can hear His voice).

> **Deuteronomy 13:1-18** (God's Word) – *1 One of your people, claiming to be a prophet or to have prophetic dreams, may predict a miraculous sign or an amazing thing. 2 What he predicts may even take place. But don't listen to that prophet or dreamer if he says, "Let's worship and serve other gods." (Those gods may be gods you've never heard of.) 3* ***The LORD your God is testing you to find out if you really love him with all your heart and with all your soul****. 4 Worship the LORD your God,* ***fear him, obey his commands, listen to what he says, serve him, and be loyal to him.***

*5 That prophet or dreamer must be put to death because he **preached rebellion** against the LORD your God, who brought you out of Egypt and freed you from slavery. He was trying to lead you **away from following the directions** the LORD your God gave you. You must get rid of this evil.*

*6 Your own brother, son, or daughter, the wife you love, or your best friend may secretly tempt you, saying, "Let's go worship other gods." (Those gods may be gods that you and your ancestors never knew. 7 **They may be the gods of the people around you, who live near or far, from one end of the land to the other.**) 8 Don't be influenced by any of these people or **listen** to them. Have no pity on them. Don't feel sorry for them or protect them. 9 You must put them to death. You must start the execution. Then all the other people will join you in putting them to death. 10 Stone them to death because they were trying to **lead you away** from the LORD your God, who brought you out of slavery in Egypt. 11 **All Israel will hear about it and be afraid. Then no one among you will ever do such a wicked thing again.***

*12 You may hear that the residents in one of the cities which the LORD your God is giving you to live in 13 have been led away from the LORD your God by worthless people. You may hear that these people have been saying, "Let's worship other gods." (Those gods may be gods you've never heard of.) 14 Then make a thorough investigation. If it is true, and you can prove that this disgusting thing has been done among you, 15 you must kill the residents of that city with swords and destroy that city and everyone in it, including the animals, because they are claimed by God. 16 Gather their goods into the middle of the city square. **Then burn their city and all their goods as a burnt offering to the LORD your God. It must remain a mound of ruins and never be rebuilt**. 17 Don't ever take any of the things claimed for destruction. Then the LORD will stop being angry and will show you mercy. In his mercy he will make your population increase, as he swore to your ancestors. 18 The LORD your God will do this if you listen to him, obey all the commands that I'm giving you today, and do what he considers right.*

Are we doing anything even closely resembling that? Are we even holding ANYBODY accountable for whatever stupid thing they feel like saying about God? What about this command?

1 Timothy 5:19-21 (KJV) – *19 Against an elder receive not an accusation, but before two or three witnesses. 20 Them that sin rebuke before all, that others also may fear. 21 I charge thee before God, and the Lord Jesus Christ, and the elect angels, that thou observe these things without preferring one before another, doing nothing by partiality.*

When was the last time you saw an elder rebuked publicly? More likely somebody said something stupid like, "Touch not God's anointed," to keep you from even thinking about doing it! The Bible clearly commands us to publicly rebuke elders who are sinning. And preaching another Jesus definitely qualifies! What kind of other Jesus? Well, there's Emergency-Only-Jesus, Not-Quite-As-Good-As-The-Virgin-Mary-Jesus, Once-Saved-Always-Saved-Lifeguard-Jesus, All-Nice-People-Go-To-Heaven-Jesus, Manifestation-Jesus, Can't-Talk-Or-Heal-People-Jesus, Prosperity-Jesus, Purpose-Driven-Jesus, Seeker-Friendly-Jesus and thousands of others. Some folks just skip Jesus and worship the Holy Spirit!

Jeremiah 2:28-29 (NIV) – *"Where then are the gods you made for yourselves? Let them come if they can save you when you are in trouble! **For you have as many gods as you have towns**, O Judah. Why do you bring charges against me? You have **all** rebelled against me," declares the Lord.*

The number of our gods has exceeded the number of our towns – and none of these gods are getting the job done because mostly we made them all up. We have about 33,000 municipal governments in America and we have 41,000+ denominations that call themselves "Christian". Most of them won't talk to the other ones. We're in big trouble. I hope you can see that. And how did it get this bad? Because we said stuff like this and totally didn't mean it at all.

> **Joshua 24:19-24** (God's Word) – *19 But Joshua answered the people, "Since the L*ORD *is a holy God, you can't possibly serve him. He is a God who does not tolerate rivals. He will not forgive your rebellious acts and sins. 20 If you abandon the L*ORD *and serve foreign gods, he will turn and bring disaster on you. He will destroy you, although he has been so good to you." 21 The people answered Joshua,* **"No! We will {only} serve the L**ORD**!"** *22 Joshua said to the people, "You have testified that you have chosen to serve the L*ORD*." They answered,* **"Yes, we have!"** *23 "Get rid of the foreign gods that are among you. Turn yourselves entirely over to the L*ORD *God of Israel." 24 The people replied to Joshua,* **"We will serve the L**ORD **our God and obey him."**

They lived at peace with God only until Joshua died and nobody was watching, then they all turned back to their idols. They said all the right things, but they didn't really mean it. They turned their children over to the world around them.

I'm tired. You're probably tired, too. I don't want to keep pounding this note. If you haven't gotten it by now, there's probably nothing else I can say to you. Here's the upside – there are those coming who WILL listen and obey and they will be fierce and mighty because they will not look like the world and they will be under His command ALL the time. And when they come, they'll be bringing a consuming fire to test all that has been built by Man.

> **Joel 2:11** (KJV) - *And the LORD shall utter his voice before his army: for his camp is very great: for he is strong that executeth his word: for the day of the LORD is great and very terrible; and who can abide it?*

You're supposed to be hearing Him. You're supposed to obey. Please ask Him what's clogging you up so that you can hear His voice better. Please? You're no good for this war if you can't hear commands from Headquarters.

> **Mark 9:7** (KJV) – *And there was a cloud that overshadowed them: and a voice came out of the cloud, saying, This is my beloved Son: hear him.*

> **Luke 9:35** (KJV) – *And there came a voice out of the cloud, saying, This is my beloved Son: hear him.*

> **John 10:27** (KJV) – *My sheep hear my voice, and I know them, and they follow me:*

> **Isaiah 6:8** (KJV) – *Also I heard the voice of the Lord, saying, Whom shall I send, and who will go for us? Then said I, Here am I; send me.*

CLOSING PRAYER AND BLESSING

Dear Lord, we love You. We don't get all of this, but we know something is desperately wrong. We can't possibly get our head around how wrong and how bad and how much we've disobeyed you, but we get that it's a really big deal. Please, Abba, please show us anything in us that is standing between us and You. Purge us and cleanse us and rip it out. If there is a doctrine or a filter or an unforgiveness or anything keeping us from walking in the fullness of all You have for us, please show us and we'll say we're sorry. Please show us what to do to fix our cities. We're sorry we made such a mess. We're sorry we didn't follow the instructions and tried to put it together ourselves and now there are pieces left over and we don't know where they go and it's not working right. We're sorry, Dad. Please fix it. Please reboot it and set it back to the defaults and get it working again. We'll try to stay out of Your way and not pester You. Just do whatever it is You're going to do. If we get in Your way, just roll right over us. Whatever it takes, just please get this ride turned around. We love You, Lord. We're sorry. Please pour out Your Spirit on us in as big a measure as we can hold. If we're ready, give us a bigger cup and fill it full, shaken, pressed down and overflowing. We need more of You and less of us. Whatever it takes, if there is something we love and can't lay down, just rip it out of our grip. Please raise up all the warriors and let them come together and march shoulder to shoulder. Please show us what true community and true love really is. And even if nobody else goes, we'll stand alone. Even if you don't come and fix it, we're not going to believe in You any less. Just please hold our hand and explain it all to us. We don't want to hear it from any Man anymore. We need You to explain all of this to us. Thanks for Your grace and mercy. We should be toast by now for how badly we've messed this all up. Please forgive us and cleanse our land and restore Your people. Not for us, but for Your Name's sake. It's Your kingdom, Your power and Your glory forever – not ours, not ever. In the mighty Name of Jesus, our Lord. Amen.

2 Corinthians 3:17-18 (KJV) – *17 Now the Lord is that Spirit: and where the Spirit of the Lord is, there is liberty. 18 But we all, with open face beholding as in a glass the glory of the Lord, are changed into the same image from glory to glory, even as by the Spirit of the Lord.*

Dear Brethren,
May the Lord Jesus Christ richly bless you in whatever way He thinks best. If there is any treasure in heaven that I have, if there is any resource or gift, any faith or peace or wisdom or discernment or authority, you're welcome to it. Even if I don't get it back. If the Lord says you can have it, then just reach out and take it in faith. He'll give me more. I love you. This isn't about me (or you). Just get everything out of the way, hear His voice really good and do whatever He tells you. And test everything.

I love you all and I'm not going to stop no matter what.

Doug Perry, servant of God

---

1 Corinthians 2:12-15 (God's Word) – *12 Now, we didn't receive the spirit that belongs to the world. Instead, we received the Spirit who comes from God so that we could know the things which God has freely given us. 13 We don't speak about these things using teachings that are based on intellectual arguments like people do. Instead, we use the Spirit's teachings. We explain spiritual things to those who have the Spirit. 14 A person who isn't spiritual doesn't accept the teachings of God's Spirit. He thinks they're nonsense. He can't understand them because a person must be spiritual to evaluate them.*

APPENDIX A

WHAT'S IN YOUR CUP?

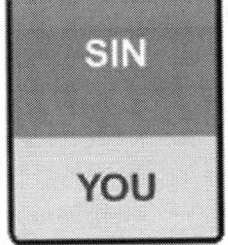 **Got No Jesus?** Then you had better get Him soon!

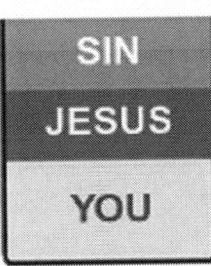 **Got Lots of Sin?** He really doesn't like being in there with it. Better turn.

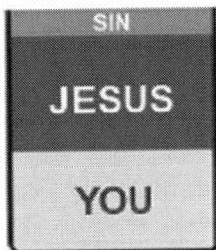 **Got A Little Sin?** That's still not victory, is it?

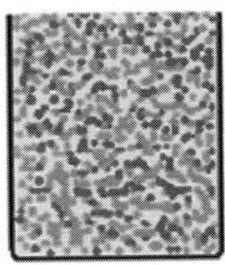 **Got No Rest?** Life can shake you up. Prayer can sort it out.

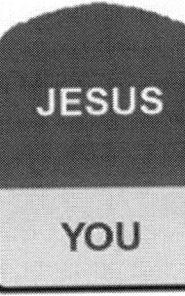 **Got Lots of Jesus?** Only walking in HOLINESS means peace and joy and victory!.

 **Got Less of You?** He must increase and YOU must decrease.

Got a BIG Cup of Jesus?

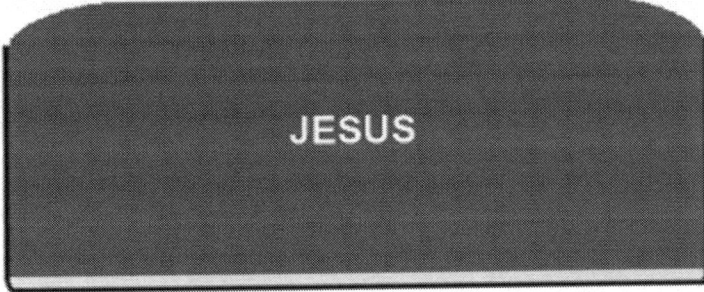

Better keep it full EVERY DAY or the red stuff will come crush you! It's a DAILY walk! Never forget that.

If you already are one of these, then what are you doing for the Kingdom and how can I help? The prayer of a righteous man is powerful and effective.

Which One ARE You Today?
Which One Do You WANT To Be?

(Which one's prayers do think God answers the best?)

www.FellowshipOfTheMartyrs.com

More about the "Cup Model" on the site or in the book, "Rain Right <u>NOW</u>, Lord!"

*"OK, so the whole thing is a mess.
What do we DO about it?"*

www.TheChurchOfLiberty.com

"The first PRE-Denominational Church in America."

The City Church is the only thing that will work.
It's the only thing in the Bible. And it's coming.

And

www.FellowshipOfTheMartyrs.com

Or in Greek: "Koinonia ton Marturon"

Witnesses to the world, even unto the death.
What the "Church" was always supposed to be:
those who have ALREADY given their lives and died to self –
long before anyone ever put a gun to their heads.

Much more on the website.

Post to: Fellowship Of The Martyrs
118 N. Conistor, #B251
Liberty, MO 64068

*Email to: fotm@fellowshipofthemartyrs.com
if we can help in any way.*

OTHER TITLES FROM FELLOWSHIP OF THE MARTYRS PUBLISHING

Rain Right NOW, Lord! - from Doug Perry
What is it going to take for God to pour His Spirit out on all flesh? Or is He waiting for us? Are spiritual gifts real and for today – and how do you get more of them?

The Apology to the World – from Doug Perry
The "Apology to the World" letter has influenced thousands and been all over the world. This book spawned from responses to that letter and collected writings about the need for change.

Left-Handed Warriors – from Linda Carriger
A suspenseful tale of the supernatural vs. the natural. What was it like for kids growing up in the book of Acts? Linda paints a picture of what it's like to be radically sold out to Christ – and still a kid.

Missionaries are Human, Too – from Nancy Perry
A sweet, candid look at what it's like to be a missionary family learning to trust God in a foreign country. Written in 1976.

Dialogues With God – from Doug Perry
Some discussions between Doug and the Almighty, along with a trouble-shooting guide to help you get unclogged, get your cup full and hear God better.

DEMONS?! You're kidding, right? - from Doug Perry
A very detailed guide to spiritual warfare – how the bad guys act, what they look like, where they hide and much more. For experts only. Not for sissies. Seriously. We're not kidding.

Do It Yourself City Church Restoration – from Doug Perry
What was 'church' supposed to be like all along? Are we doing it right? What's it going to take to fix it? If Jesus Christ wrote a letter to the Body of Christ in your city, could you bear to read it? What would happen if you were One Body in your town?

Who Neutered the Holy Spirit?! - from Doug Perry
Why do people say that the Holy Spirit stopped doing all the cool stuff that used to happen? This details the scriptural evidence of the work of the Spirit in the Old Testament, in the New Testament, after Pentecost, and in the church today. Along with help to get you unclogged so you can walk in the fullness of what God has for you.

The Red Dragon: the horrifying truth about why the 'church' cannot seem to change – Doug Perry
How bad are things? How did they get this bad? In fact, they're SO bad, they have to be considered supernaturally bad! In fact, it's a curse from God. A delusion sent on those that went their own way. Weep. No really, weep! That's your only hope.

Expelling Xavier – from Dorothy Haile
A love story between a girl possessed by something dark and a boy just learning who he is in Christ – and their Savior. A very different kind of Christian novel, gritty, rough and fiercely transparent about the realities of life under the control of the darkness.

The Dad Filter– from Doug Perry
How to have a right relationship with Father God after all you've learned about Dad's is that they're awful and won't come through for you.

And LOTS more titles coming soon!!   And in SPANISH!

Made in the USA
San Bernardino, CA
04 June 2017